D1565130

Engrafted into Christ

american
university
studies

Series VII
Theology and Religion

Vol. 233

PETER LANG
New York • Washington, D.C./Baltimore • Bern
Frankfurt am Main • Berlin • Brussels • Vienna • Oxford

Christopher J. Malloy

Engrafted into Christ

A Critique of the Joint Declaration

PETER LANG
New York • Washington, D.C./Baltimore • Bern
Frankfurt am Main • Berlin • Brussels • Vienna • Oxford

Library of Congress Cataloging-in-Publication Data

Malloy, Christopher J.
Engrafted into Christ: a critique of the Joint declaration /
Christopher J. Malloy.
p. cm. — (American university studies. Series VII,
Theology and religion; v. 233)
Includes bibliographical references and index.
1. Justification (Christian theology). 2. Lutheran World Federation.
Gemeinsame Erklärung zur Rechtfertigungslehre. 3. Catholic Church—
Relations—Lutheran Church. 4. Lutheran Church—Relations—
Catholic Church. I. Title. II. Series.
BT764.3.M35   234'.7—dc22   2004014121
ISBN 0-8204-7408-8
ISSN 0740-0446

Bibliographic information published by **Die Deutsche Bibliothek**.
Die Deutsche Bibliothek lists this publication in the "Deutsche
Nationalbibliografie"; detailed bibliographic data is available
on the Internet at http://dnb.ddb.de/.

The paper in this book meets the guidelines for permanence and durability
of the Committee on Production Guidelines for Book Longevity
of the Council of Library Resources.

Printed in the United States of America

Dedicated to the Immaculate Conception:

"Pray for us who have recourse to you."

TABLE OF CONTENTS

PREFACE

THIS BOOK has taken over five years to complete. I would like thank the many people who have helped me in various ways. First, I would like to thank my lovely wife, Flory, my delight on this sojourn, for her love, wit, and insights. Secondly, I would like to thank my parents, Timothy and Patricia Malloy, for their generous support, without which I would not now be teaching and writing. Thirdly, I am grateful to my wife's parents, Liviu and Cathy Tomutsa, for assisting in the production of this book. Fourthly, I would like to thank those who have generously responded to my queries with theological advice and constructive criticism, including Avery Cardinal Dulles, S.J., Nelson Minnich, Michael Root, Augustine DiNoia, O.P., Ansgar Santogrossi, O.S.B., Michael Waldstein, David Balás, O.Cist., Manfred Hauke, Werner Löser, S.J., Richard Schenk, O.P., Patrick Granfield, Aidan Nichols, O.P., Matthew Lamb, Christian Washburn, Michael Sirilla, Barry Jones, Gregory LaNave, Giuseppe Butera, Peter Kwasniewski, Matthew Levering, James Kruggel, Luigi Iacono, William Murphy, Scott Hahn, Andrew Moran, and Bill Brownsberger. I would not wish to burden any of these with responsibility for what is faulty in my opinions and argumentation, but I am grateful for their fruitful and charitable insights and criticism. I would like to make special mention of the resources and staff of the library of Catholic University of America, especially former employee Bruce Miller. The library at the Dominican House of Studies complemented the collection at CUA. I cannot forget to thank my beloved University of Dallas, which aided my research through a grant. My colleagues John Norris and Mark Lowery have been most helpful and encouraging. Administrative Assistant Wayne Crawford has not only helped but also expressed an interest in my work. Former graduate student Michael Fagge assisted me with bibliographical work. The resources and the staff of our university library, especially Alice Puro, were very helpful. The staff and resources of Bridwell Library at Southern Methodist University were invaluable. The outstanding staff at Newman Bookstore in Washington, D.C., especially former manager Andrew Ament, obtained numerous works not available in the "ordinary" theological bookstore. Finally, I wish to express thanks to *The Thomist*, which printed my first work on this subject (Christopher J. Malloy, "The Nature of Justifying Grace: A Lacuna in the *Joint Declaration*," *The Thomist* 65 [2001]: 93–120). May whatever is true and of use in my book not be obscured by what is false or vain.

LIST OF ABBREVIATIONS

CCC	*Catechism of the Catholic Church*
CDF	Congregation for the Doctrine of Faith
Cf	Confer by way of contrast (as per Chicago Manual of Style)
CRE	*The Condemnations of the Reformation Era: Do They Still Divide?* (German Dialogue)
CT	*Concilium Tridentinum*, vol. 5
DE	*Decrees of the Ecumenical Councils*
DS	*Enchiridion Symbolorum*, edited by Denzinger-Schönmetzer
DTC	*Dictionnaire de théologie catholique*
ELCA	Evangelical Lutheran Church in America
GE	Gemeinsame Erklärung zur Rechtfertigungslehre
GS	*Gaudium et spes*
GTP	"The Critical Response of German Theological Professors"
JD	Joint Declaration on the Doctrine of Justification
JF	*Justification by Faith: Do the Sixteenth-Century Condemnations Still Apply?* (German Dialogue)
LG	*Lumen gentium*
LW	*Luther's Works* (English)
LWF	Lutheran World Federation
NCCB	National Council of Catholic Bishops
OCS	Official Common Statement
OVR	Official Vatican Response
PCPCU	Pontifical Council for Promoting Christian Unity
SCG	*Summa contra gentiles*
ST	*Summa theologiae*
UR	*Unitatis redintegratio*
USA	*Justification by Faith*, vol. 7, *Lutherans and Catholics in Dialogue* (American Dialogue)
UUS	*Ut unum sint*
WA	*Luthers Werke* (German)

INTRODUCTION

CHRISTIANS HAVE recently witnessed a partial answer to the priestly prayer that Christ offered up moments before his final hour: "[I pray] that they may all be one; even as thou, Father, art in me, and I in thee, that they also may be in us, so that the world may believe that thou hast sent me" (Jn 17:21, RSV). Catholics and Lutherans signed an agreement on the doctrine of justification on October 31, 1999, laying to rest five centuries of failed communication. Dr. Ishmael Noko, General Secretary of the Lutheran World Federation (LWF), and Edward Cardinal Cassidy of the Catholic Church met in Augsburg, birthplace of the Reformation, and ratified a bilateral document on justification entitled *Joint Declaration on the Doctrine of Justification* (JD).[1] The occasion was hailed as the resolution of a bitter dispute over the answer to the following question: How shall the sinner be justified in the sight of God? Pastors, theologians, and lay persons of both communions rejoiced in renewed fellowship and rekindled hope for mutual Eucharistic fellowship.[2] A great breach had apparently been bridged.

The proximate history of the agreement commenced with the official inauguration of the Catholic Church's participation in ecumenical dialogue at the Second Vatican Council (1962–1965) and the publication of "Justification Today" by the Assembly of the LWF in Helsinki (1963).[3] Theologians from both communions in different nations began to meet in order to listen to each other and to the scriptural witness in hopes of achieving an agreement about the essential truths of justification. In 1972, a document entitled "The Gospel and the Church," now known as the "Malta Report," was issued by the Joint Study Commission of the Lutheran World Federation and the Vatican Secretariat for Promoting Christian Unity.[4] The report promised that an extensive consensus on once church-dividing issues was developing. In the United States, over five years of dialogue culminated in the 1983 common confession of faith, interpreted in accordance with distinct but compatible confessional emphases, published in a volume entitled *Justification by Faith* (USA).[5] In his 1980 visit to Germany, Pope John Paul II inspired a similar dialogue on the Continent. This dialogue focused on confirming the common conviction of theologians and pastors that the condemnations of the past no longer apply to the current partner in dialogue. The achievements of USA and the "Malta Report" made such focus possible.[6] The most significant results of this dialogue were summed up in *The Condemnations of the Reformation Era* (CRE), published in 1986.[7] Both USA and CRE enjoyed episcopal oversight and approval.[8] In 1994, officials from the Catholic Church and from the LWF appointed several theologians to gather together the fruits of the ecumenical dialogues in order to make possible a common, worldwide statement. These theologians drew up three successive drafts of the Joint Declaration: the Geneva text (1995), the Würzburg I text (1996), and the Würzburg II text (1997).[9] The final text (Würzburg II) enjoyed acceptance by the LWF in the summer of 1998 but met a different fate with the Pontifical Council for Promoting Christian Unity (PCPCU), the Catholic ecclesial office charged with advancing ecumenical relations.

In the summer of 1998, the PCPCU published the Official Vatican Response (OVR), which both affirmed the achievements of the JD and also raised questions to certain apparent difficulties in the text.[10] The OVR disheartened many a theologian, for it appeared to be the death knell of dialogue. The Vatican saw things otherwise, urging hope and vowing to sign the document provided that the difficulties articulated in the OVR were addressed.[11] In late 1998, Lutheran and Catholic officials began to discuss the OVR. Joseph Cardinal Ratzinger of the Congregation for the Doctrine of Faith (CDF), the Catholic ecclesial body charged with guarding the integrity of doctrine, helped draft a working paper. For a number of months, members of both communions labored to articulate a bilateral response to the questions posed in the OVR and to lingering concerns of certain members of the LWF. The Annex presented the fruits of this theological labor, which was guided by pastors of both communions; it was not a correction of the JD but a statement of assurance that further clarified what might have appeared ambiguous or problematic in the JD.[12] The introduction of the Annex into the official agreement necessitated another document, the Official Common Statement (OCS), that specified the nature of the agreement and the relationship between the JD and the Annex.[13]

Cardinal Cassidy (then President of the PCPCU), Walter Cardinal Kasper (then Secretary, now President, of the PCPCU), Dr. Noko, and Bishop Christian Krause (President of the LWF) signed the OCS and the JD.[14] By its reference to the Annex, the OCS claims that the concerns expressed in the OVR were adequately addressed and that no genuine obstacle to a joint signing remained.[15] The OCS points to the JD as the focal point of the agreement: "By this act of signing, the Catholic Church and the Lutheran World Federation confirm the Joint Declaration on the Doctrine of Justification in its entirety" (OCS, 3). Accordingly, the Annex does not qualify or correct the JD but "further substantiates the consensus reached" (OCS, 2).

The Joint Declaration does not purport to resolve all disputes between the two communions; it expressly leaves undecided, for example, ecclesiology, sacraments, and ministerial authority (JD, 43). The JD nonetheless does claim to reconcile both communions' teachings on the "basic truths" of the doctrine of justification. Some have been disgruntled with this approach. They contend that, in dismantling this chief article from the whole fabric of Christian doctrine, which provides necessary test cases, the current ecumenical endeavor risks foundering upon uncertain ground.[16] Notwithstanding a certain legitimacy in these reservations, I believe it is necessary to address disputed issues distinctly, though with a mind to the whole. Therefore, while the fruits of this dialogue are yet to be tested in some concrete applications, its approach in this regard is to be commended.

The JD's central claim is twofold. First, in ratifying the contents of the JD, both communions pledge agreement about the substance of the doctrine of justification and recognize that remaining differences are not church-dividing: "[The JD] does encompass a consensus on basic truths of the doctrine of justification and shows that the remaining differences in its explication are no longer the occasion for doctrinal condemnations" (JD, 5; see also JD, 14).[17] The consensus is "substantial" but differentiated. As "substantial," the consensus precludes all differences that entail ecclesial division on this issue. Remaining differences, considered to be compatible and/or complementary, do not manifest real disagreement about the substance of the deposit of faith and are, therefore, not hindrances to full communion.[18] In the matter of justification, the JD claims to settle all disputes belonging to the deposit of faith. In short, "Consensus and [remaining] condemnation are mutually exclusive."[19] In a recent article, American Catholic theologian Br. Jeffrey Gros articulates this minimum threshold of ecumenical dialogue lucidly:

> For authentic unity there must be agreement in the fundamental truths necessary as a basis for a common faith. Such a consensus does not require uniformity of formulation or emphasis, but the church-dividing issues must be resolved. The recent *Joint Declaration on the Doctrine of Justification* is an exemplary case in point. The text provides a common affirmation of Lutheran and Catholic faith that resolves the issue of the 16th century. The text also goes on to give seven affirmations of issues in which Catholics and Lutherans continue their different emphases. Within this internally differentiated consensus there is both unity and diversity.
>
> Consensus means that sufficient agreement has been reached so that a doctrinal issue, such as justification, is no longer church dividing.[20]

Even if one were to differentiate between a consensus "in basic truths" and a consensus "in *the* basic truths," one would not alter the logical implication of the JD's claim that the remaining differences are no longer church-dividing. The implication is that no truths about justification known to be held in the deposit of faith are any longer matters of dispute: "In light of this consensus, the corresponding doctrinal condemnations of the 16th century do not apply to today's partner" (JD, 13). This was a more forceful claim than that of the 1995 draft, which assessed the result as a "basic consensus [*Grundkonsens*]" that called for a *reexamination* of those condemnations.[21] The 1995 claim was more circumspect.

Second, the doctrine of justification presented in the JD conflicts with neither the Decree on Justification issued by the Council of Trent (1547) nor the teachings on justification in the Lutheran confessional documents (1530–1577): "The teaching of the Lutheran churches presented in this declaration does not fall under the condemnations from the Council of Trent. The condemnations in the Lutheran confessions do not apply to the teaching of the Roman Catholic Church presented in this declaration" (JD, 41). This second claim is inseparable from the first, "Since it would be self-contradictory to claim a consensus without also stating that the past condemnations of each other's teachings are no longer applicable."[22]

The JD's twofold claim logically entails two further claims. First, the theological developments that made the JD possible must not be seen as deviations from the original positions of either communion. Although both partners attest to developments that have taken place, these developments are held to be organically related to the confessional statements of the Reformation era (JD, 7). The JD's insistence that it does not conflict with either Trent or the Lutheran confessional documents necessarily implies that no repudiation of past doctrine has occurred. Neither communion has forgone its past.[23] Indeed, the JD itself states that the original condemnations remain valid as salutary warnings: "Nothing is thereby taken away from the seriousness of the condemnations related to the doctrine of justification" (JD, 42). The reason supplied is a bit understated: "Some were not simply pointless" (JD, 42).[24] Second, the original positions of both communions were never actually in conflict with one another.[25] If theologians from both sides interpreted the original positions as antithetical understandings of justification, the judgment of these theologians must be called into question.[26] This second claim is entailed as follows: If the JD presents the *substance* of the doctrine of justification and if the JD conflicts with neither Trent nor the confessional Lutheran teachings, then Trent and confessional Lutheran teaching must be intrinsically compatible, if the principle of noncontradiction is not to be jettisoned.[27] If they were not compatible, it would be impossible to create an ecumenical agreement that presents the *substance* of the doctrine of justification, leaving unresolved only non-church-dividing differences.[28]

It is understood that the JD is not an authoritatively binding document. Because Lutherans do not approach the LWF as Catholics approach their Magisterium, the abundance of Lutheran critics was not scandalous. The official endorsement of the JD by the PCPCU, however, makes many Catholics understandably reticent to undertake any critical inquiry. Nevertheless, a minority of Catholics have not withheld themselves from objections to certain portions of this cluster of documents. Of these, two are cardinals and well-respected theologians: American theologian Avery Dulles, S.J., and German theologian Leo Scheffczyk.[29] In the year of the signing, Dulles acknowledged it as a blessing, yet he cautioned, "The Joint Declaration, helpful though it is, has not overcome all difficulties. More theological work is needed." This work includes respectfully critical analysis: "The Roman Response [i.e., the OVR] indicates that theological misgivings can legitimately be expressed from the Catholic side, and the same will presumably be true among Lutherans."[30] More recently, Dulles wrote, "The *Joint Declaration* does not present itself as an authoritative magisterial statement, binding on the faithful of the respective communions."[31] Similarly, Scheffczyk, who has himself produced numerous articles opposing the claims of the ecumenical accord, frankly avowed, "Since with respect to the JD it is not a matter of a dogmatic decision or of a binding confession of faith, its significance is not to be ascertained independently of its reception."[32]

The canonical status and authority of the signing party is relevant in this regard. The document was signed by Cardinal Cassidy of the PCPCU. The signing received the public but merely informal and nonauthoritative approval of Pope John Paul II. Cardinal Ratzinger, charged with the leadership of the CDF, also informally consented to, but did not appear at, the official signing in Augsburg. Finally, the PCPCU is a Roman dicastery not charged with doctrinal responsibility and authority. Short of specific and formal approval by the Papal See, documents issuing from the PCPCU command no assent from the faithful.

Because the JD does not have doctrinal authority, Catholic theologians can freely consider it their responsibility to examine the viability of the claims made therein. Those who play a fruitfully critical role do not violate their ecclesial vocation.[33] Investigation of the agreement's viability is a necessary part of the ongoing ecumenical dialogue. It is evident that this task calls for great care, for the JD witnesses to nearly forty years' labor, overseen by pastors of both communions.

There are two lines of scrutiny that can be pursued in an effort to verify the merits of the Joint Declaration. On the one hand, its historical implication can be investigated: Did the original positions of each communion not, in fact, substantially conflict with one another? If there was no original conflict, the JD's explicit claim not to contradict the teachings of either communion may be valid. That is, it would not violate the principle of noncontradiction. On the other hand, the contents proper of the JD can be investigated: Does the JD adequately represent the teachings of both communions? If the JD neither distorts nor dilutes the substance of either communion's teachings on justification, its claim to leave unsettled only non-church-dividing differences is valid.

In order to determine the answers to these questions, the theologian must rigorously examine the official teachings of both communions.[34] These are to be found in two classic texts. Those of the Catholic Church are found in the tridentine Decree on Justification, conciliarly approved January 13, 1547, and promulgated in 1563. In virtue of their profession of faith, Catholics adhere to the teachings articulated in this decree. Their participation in the ecumenical movement, which is not optional, includes a basic conviction that the entire deposit of faith and the whole means of salvation entrusted by Christ to his Church are found in the Catholic Church.[35] Any theological development in the understanding of justification must be in harmony with that deposit, to which the teachings already promulgated give authentic and definitive witness.[36] The teachings and the very formulations employed at Trent retain perennial value in themselves. If, as clearly is the case, some teachings are expressed in a mode of thought subject to change, the very teachings themselves, in the same sense and according to the same signification of the original formulations, must never be compromised, even though they can be further refined.[37] While this conviction is in human terms an obstacle to the ecumenical movement, Catholics are invited to perceive it as a unique contribution to that movement, though they ought willingly admit the shortcomings and sins of both laity and hierarchy of this Church.[38]

The official teachings of the Lutheran communion are found in the collection entitled *The Book of Concord* (first published in 1580).[39] Although Lutherans do not share the Catholic notion of ecclesial teaching authority, they regard their confessional documents as authentic exegesis of the Gospel and, therefore, as doctrinally authoritative, that is, as normative for exegesis.[40] According to their self-understanding, therefore, the vast majority of Lutherans do not expect to reject or substantially alter the teachings in *The Book of Concord*.[41] Illustrating this point, the German dialogue states:

> Nor can the solemn obligation to accept the Confessions which apply in any given case be overlooked in Protestantism either, particularly in the Lutheran churches. The service of ordination includes an "injunction" based on particular Confessions, which are often listed by name. Even more modern orders for ordination have not abandoned this custom. What point would there be in binding oneself, not only to the whole body of confessional documents, but to the condemnatory judgments they include, and to do so in solemn form, while at the same time more or less ignoring these judgments? Common honesty toward the inheritance we have received and toward our own present conduct therefore enjoins us, in the context of our specific and binding commitment, to turn our attention to the condemnations also.[42]

I take it as a given, then, that the Lutheran confessional documents are functionally authoritative.[43] Notwithstanding this, it should be noted that different Lutheran communions evaluate the authoritative status of the documents within *The Book of Concord* differently. Most Lutherans hold that the Augsburg Confession (1530) is the hermeneutical key to the entire collection. Some Lutheran synods and national churches did not accept all of the ten documents collected in *The Book of Concord*. A number of contemporary Lutheran theologians distance themselves from noteworthy elements of the *Apology of the Augsburg Confession* (1531) and the *Formula of Concord* (1577), appealing to either Luther's own work or the Augsburg Confession, which is irenic in tone and somewhat protean in content. The *Formula* was drawn up, primarily, to settle internal disputes among Lutherans.[44] Still, the *Formula*, a collaborative effort developed over a number of years, was written well after the publication of the decrees of Trent, and its framers also desired to articulate Lutheran orthodoxy against both Catholic and radical Reformation teaching.[45] The collection of confessions of faith in *The Book of Concord* was intended "to govern public teaching and ecclesiastical life in German Lutheran lands as a *corpus doctrinae*," i.e., a body of doctrine.[46] American Lutheran theologian Conrad Bergendoff has summarized the uneven Lutheran reception of *The Book of Concord*. In light of this uneven reception, the JD acknowledges, "Some Lutheran churches include only the Augsburg Confession and Luther's Small Catechism among their binding confessions" (JD, note 3) Despite these exceptions, attested by differing ordination vows, the traditional rule among Lutherans is as follows: "Church fellowship is possible without the [*Formula of Concord*] but not against it."[47] Some have observed that the lack of clarity about the authority of these documents among Lutherans poses potential difficulties for the JD's claim to have reconciled the two communions on the issue of justification. Unfortunately, the JD neglects to acknowledge the intra-critical situation within the Lutheran communions.[48]

In my evaluation of the JD, I take the perspective of those Lutherans who embrace also the *Apology* and the *Formula*. Since the JD and its accompanying Annex cite these documents as authoritative sources, my method of proceeding is warranted in this context. Although I sympathize with those Lutherans who have difficulties with the latter documents and who thus wish to use the Augsburg Confession as the hermeneutical lens through which ecumenical rapprochement with Catholics can be furthered, I am undertaking to engage the JD as it presents itself. With this in mind, I would like to present the central topic of the present work.

Among the most critical issues in the dispute between Lutherans and Catholics is the identity of justifying grace, otherwise called the "formal cause" of justification or that by which the human person stands just before God.[49]

This issue surely counts as one of the "basic" truths of the doctrine of justification. The Council of Trent defined the essence of justifying grace as inhering righteousness.[50] For months, the council fathers debated the definition of the formal cause, carefully refining the definition so as to avoid any ambiguity. Despite the central importance of this issue, neither the JD nor the Annex nor the OCS nor the OVR even mentions the phrase "formal cause."[51] In itself, the omission of the phrase in these ecumenical documents is not *ipso facto* tantamount to failure to address the issue. Nevertheless, the omission of the phrase may betray a lingering ambiguity in the ecumenical situation.[52] It is therefore incumbent upon systematic theologians to investigate whether there is a deleterious ambiguity in the dialogue on this point. Since the notion of "justifying grace" serves as a focal point of reference for many other issues, such as the nature of remnant sin, obedience to the law, progress in grace, and merit, equivocal readings of "justifying grace" would have manifold consequences threatening to hinder ecumenical progress.

The present book proposes to inquire both about the historical implication of the JD (in Part One) and about the contents proper of the JD (in Part Three). An intervening investigation of three theological attempts at rapprochement (Part Two) will set the stage for the examination of the JD and its preparatory dialogues. Finally, the book concludes with a set of theological reflections on the significance of this issue with respect to issues from anthropology, eschatology, and Christology (Part Four).

NOTES

1   "Joint Declaration on the Doctrine of Justification," *Origins* 28:8 (1998): 120–27. For the official German text, see "Gemeinsame Erklärung zur Rechtfertigungslehre" [online; accessed July 16, 2004], available at www.theology.de/recht-fertigungslehre.html.

2   Throughout this work, I almost invariably refer to the various national churches and synods of Lutherans as one communion (singular). By this I do not mean to overlook local differences, even serious ones. Rather, I find this expression more felicitous and also more ecumenically friendly.

3   "'Justification Today,' Document 75—Assembly and Final Versions," *Lutheran World* 12.1, Supplement (1965): 1–11.

4   See Alister E. McGrath, *Iustitia Dei: A History of the Christian Doctrine of Justification*, 2nd ed. (Cambridge: Cambridge University Press, 1998), p. 389.

5   *Justification by Faith*, vol. 7, *Lutherans and Catholics in Dialogue*, ed. H. George Anderson, T. Austin Murphy, and Joseph A. Burgess (Minneapolis: Augsburg Publishing House, 1985). References to USA correspond either to paragraph numbers or to page numbers and are explicitly labeled.

6   See Paweł Holc, *Un ampio consenso sulla dottrina della giustificazione: Studio sul dialogo teologico cattolico-luterano* (Rome: Editrice Pontificia Università Gregoriana,

1999), p. 343.

7   *The Condemnations of the Reformation Era: Do They Still Divide?* ed. Karl Lehmann
     and Wolfhart Pannenberg, trans. Margaret Kohl (Minneapolis: Fortress Press, 1990).
     For the original, see *Lehrverurteilungen—Kirchentrennend?* Band 4, *Dialog der*
     Kirchen (Freiburg: Herder, 1986). A selection of the many papers that made this
     common German statement possible is published in English in *Justification by Faith:*
     Do the Sixteenth-Century Condemnations Still Apply? (hereafter, JF) ed. Karl
     Lehmann, trans. Michael Root and William G. Rusch (New York: The Continuum
     Publishing Company, 1997).

8   Holc discusses the NCCB's approval of USA (Holc, *Un ampio*, pp. 120–23) and also
     the Lutheran approval of the same (ibid., pp. 123–26). He presents both the German
     bishops' evaluation (ibid., pp. 203–07) and the PCPCU's evaluation of CRE (ibid., pp.
     201–03).

9   For an excellent article by one of the participants, which lays out each of these drafts
     side by side, see Dorothea Wendebourg, "Zur Entstehungsgeschichte der
     'Gemeinsamen Erklärung,'" *Zeitschrift für Theologie und Kirche*, Beiheft 10, *Zur*
     Rechtfertigungslehre, ed. Eberhard Jüngel, pp. 140–206 (Mohr Siebeck, 1999).

10   "Official Vatican Response," *Origins* 28:8 (1998): 130–32.

11   See Herbert Anderson, "The Agreed Statement on Justification: A Lutheran
     Perspective," *Ecumenical Trends* 28, no. 5 (1999): 1.

12   "Annex," *Origins* 29:6 (1999): 87–88. Spanish theologian José Villar rightly claims
     that the PCPCU considers that the Vatican's concerns have been adequately addressed
     in the Annex (José R. Villar, "La Declaración común Luterano-Católica sobre la
     doctrina de la justificación," *Scripta theologica* 32 [2000]: 128).

13   "Official Common Statement," *Origins* 29:6 (1999): 85–87.

14   On the reception of the JD, see Matthias Turk, "The Reception of the *Joint Declaration*
     on the Doctrine of Justification," *One in Christ* 37 (2002): 61–66.

15   Some theologians are perplexed by the sheer number of documents, wondering which
     is of central importance. Dutch theologian Peder Nørgaard-Højen decries the situation
     as making the JD "in its original shape useless for the intended purpose" (Peder
     Nørgaard-Højen, "A Point of No Return? The Joint Declaration and the Future of
     Lutheran-Catholic Dialogue," *The Ecumenical Review* 52 [2000]: 218). Granted, the
     situation may appear confusing, but it is clear that the Annex is not intended as an
     emendation of the JD, the heart of the agreement.

16   The German Lutheran theologians who protested the signing of the JD contend against
     the very "bracketing" of issues outside of justification. They maintain that because
     justification is the article upon which everything depends—because it is *the*
     criterion—to isolate it from other issues is not fruitful (see "The Critical Response of
     German Theological Professors to the *Joint Declaration on the Doctrine of*
     Justification," [hereafter, GTP], *In Dialogue* 38 [1999]: 71–72).

17   The German reads, "nicht länger Anlaß für Lehrverurteilungen sind" (GE, 5).

18   See Walter Kasper, "The *Joint Declaration on the Doctrine of Justification*: A Roman
     Catholic Perspective," in *Justification and the Future of the Ecumenical Movement:*
     The Joint Declaration on the Doctrine of Justification, ed. William G. Rusch
     (Collegeville: The Liturgical Press, 2003), pp. 17–18.

19   André Birmelé, Theodor Dieter, Michael Root, and Risto Saarinen, eds., *Joint*
     Declaration on the Doctrine of Justification: A Commentary by the Institute for
     Ecumenical Research, trans. staff team (Hong Kong: Clear-Cut Publishing & Printing
     Co., 1997), p. 47.

20   Br. Jeffrey Gros, "Toward Full Communion: Faith and Order and Catholic

Ecumenism," *Theological Studies* 65 (2004): 28. I believe Gros's articulation to be less ambiguous than that of Karl Cardinal Lehmann. Lehmann, in an article on the preparatory dialogues, suggests that a "basic consensus" does not constitute a full consensus, which would provide the necessary foundation for full communion. The difficulty with this way of framing the wider methodological issues in ecumenical dialogue is that it obscures Lehmann's simple point, that a "basic consensus" removes all that is church-dividing. How, one might ask, does a basic consensus, which removes all that is church-dividing, not also remove all obstacles to full communion *on the issue at hand*? Granted, disputes about other issues could still present obstacles, but appeal to such "other issues" does not play an explicit role in Lehmann's distinction between full consensus and "basic consensus." See Karl Lehmann, "Is the 'Step Backward' Ecumenical Progress?: Introduction to the Method and Hermeneutics of the Study," in JF, p. 47. Gros's point is clearer in that he uses the term "consensus" to refer to the specific issue in question.

21   See Wendebourg, "Zur Entstehungsgeschichte," p. 161.

22   Birmelé, *A Commentary*, p. 48.

23   "The confessional texts will not themselves be changed.... Nothing is being added to or removed from the confessions" (Birmelé, *A Commentary*, p. 19). Villar writes, "No se trata de renegar del propio pasado" (Villar, "La Declaración," p. 109). Lehmann finds the same intention in the German dialogue (Lehmann, "Step Backward," p. 51).

24   The German was slightly more emphatic: "Etliche waren nicht einfach gegenstandslos" (GE, 42).

25   The difference in wording between the initial draft and the 1997 draft is instructive. The 1995 draft reads, "We recognize that the Lutheran teaching no longer [*nicht mehr*] falls under the relevant condemnations from the Council of Trent, and that the corresponding condemnations in the Lutheran Confessions no longer [*nicht mehr*] apply to the Roman Catholic Church" (JD 1995, par. 43). One can read this to mean that "once" the teachings did fall under mutual condemnation. The final draft evades this problematic implication by simply stating that the teachings of each communion as presented in the JD do not conflict with the condemnations of the Reformation era of either side (JD, 41). There is a similar pattern between par. 12 (1995 draft) and par. 13 (1997 draft).

26   In his paper for the American dialogue, George Lindbeck focuses on "whether Trent and the Lutheran Confessions anathematize each other." If Catholics and Lutherans can come to see that their confessional documents, though diverse, do not contradict one another, then "a doctrinal reconciliation which was practically impossible in the sixteenth century may be possible today" (George Lindbeck, "A Question of Compatibility: A Lutheran Reflects on Trent," in USA, pp. 231 and 232). The burden of Lindbeck's paper is to ascertain whether or not one can demonstrate a contradiction between the two. There can be no contradiction, he maintains, unless one side affirms precisely that which the other denies in precisely the same sense.

27   George Lindbeck perfectly describes the onlooker's perplexity at the phenomenon of once-contradictory teachings coming to be aligned without violence to the organic nature of legitimate development (George Lindbeck, *The Nature of Doctrine: Religion and Theology in a Postliberal Age* [Louisville: Westminster John Knox Press, 1984], p. 15). Lindbeck, rather than questioning the developments of recent ecumenical accords that do not require change when substantive issues were certainly at stake (I am not thinking, e.g., of the *filioque* versus an intra-Trinitarian *per filium* here), takes occasion to search for a justification for these conclusions: "If one credits these testimonies, the problem is not with the reality but with the comprehensibility of this

strange combination of constancy and change, unity and diversity. The proper response in that case is not to deny the reality on the grounds that it seems impossible, but rather to seek to explain its possibility" (ibid.). Lindbeck implicitly puts these results of human discussions in the category of *credenda* (things to be believed). What is one to make of this? I am not loath to assent to the scriptures and to their interpretation by the Catholic Magisterium, but I think it premature to begin with an analogous attitude to ecumenical discussions. Lindbeck's own hypothesis is that fundamental theology needs to rearticulate the function of doctrine in Christian communities. The ancient model is propositionalist. According to this model, doctrine is stated in propositions with specific referents; the propositions are to be understood and intellectually accepted. The strength of this approach is intellectual rigor and the capacity to distinguish the claims of different religions. The second model, worked out especially by Schleiermacher, is the "experiential-expressive" model. According to this approach, doctrines are expressive of core values and religious experience; apparent conflicts of symbolic expressions do not necessarily (i.e., rarely, if ever) represent conflicts in core values or experiences. The strength of this model is that it can foster, without the fear of proselytization, inter-religious dialogue. The propositionalist model's weakness is that it cannot carry into new contexts the meaning it intends to carry; it is laborious and its achievements, misunderstood. Its very "tradition-minded" intention is undermined by the fact that, in new contexts, the ancient propositions carved in stone engender thoughts at odds with the original intention of the framers. One can think, for instance, of both Schleiermacher's and, following him, Barth's and Rahner's wariness about the term "person" when applied to the three divine hypostases. But Schleiermacher's expressivism is too nebulous; it veils the distinct identities of divergent religions too easily. What's more, it fails to allow for the fact that inner experience is formed and molded under the influence of the community's patterns of speech, worship, and behavior. Drawing on the work of Wittgenstein, Fei, and others, Lindbeck thus proposes a third model, which he sketches in his *Doctrine*. This is the "cultural-linguistic" approach, according to which doctrines are rules for speech, worship, and behavior. They set up the parameters and framework within which these activities can be conducted in fidelity to the heritage of the community. Doctrines, or at least *most* doctrines, ought not be thought of as first-order propositions with singular referents; rather, they are like "second-order guidelines for Christian discourse" (ibid., p. 94). As regulative, they help guide human experience of the divine; they have a cognitive edge but are not reducible to intellectually graspable propositions. My present work is not the place for a detailed discussion of Lindbeck's proposal and assessment of its shortcomings. Suffice it to say that, although Lindbeck is at pains *not* to rest the validity of his hypothesis, which he appears not to question, upon his "test cases," it is nonetheless instructive that his Christological test case is hardly acceptable. He argues that Athanasius—because he was wily enough to encourage the "semi-Arians" (i.e., those who, unlike the disingenuous Homoeans, acccepted the term *homoiousios*) not to let a term trip them up—understood Nicaea as a second-order discourse. The result? But three "rules" sufficiently guide Christian speech about Christ: First, that God is one; second, that there is a "historical specificity" to the man Jesus; and third, that Christians espouse a "Christological maximalism: every possible importance is to be ascribed to Jesus that is not inconsistent with the first rules" (ibid.). I gather that not a few Christians would find this maximalism minimalistic, not least because no human being would have dreamed that God would become incarnate. So, how does one move from this maximalism to the "only-begotten God" (Jn 1:18) who became flesh (Jn 1:14)? On "monogenes theos," see Bruce Metzger, *A Textual Commentary on the*

Greek New Testament, 2nd ed. (Stuttgart: United Bible Societies, 1994), pp. 169–70. Avery Dulles is warmly receptive of the alternative to a strictly propositionalist approach (Avery Dulles, *The Craft of Theology: From Symbol to System* [New York: Crossroad, 1992], pp. 17–21). He yet recognizes more acutely the cognitive charge and ontological depth of scriptural and ecclesial symbols. He rightly asks "what task remains for theology" in Lindbeck's approach (ibid., p. 82). Granted, Lindbeck rightly contends that the Bible ought to serve as a sort of cultural milieu within which ongoing Christian discourse is expressed. However, is there not *also* a greater role (greater than Lindbeck appears to espouse) for the cognitive dimension in symbolic discourse (i.e., both the symbols of propositions and the symbols of worship)? Dulles's criticism gets more pointed towards the end of his work. Proposals such as Lindbeck's, indebted in part to Wittgenstein's philosophy of language, perhaps reconcile conflicting schools of thought, but only at great cost: "Peace between religion and science is achieved in these systems, but only at the price of depriving religion or science of its capacity to say anything true about the world of ordinary experience" (ibid., p. 140). It is not surprising that in suggesting some of the shortcomings of the Joint Declaration Dulles quips, "Performative language cannot be unrelated to informative; the law of prayer must harmonize with the law of belief" (Avery Dulles, "Two Languages of Salvation: The Lutheran-Catholic Joint Declaration," *First Things* 98 [1999]: 29).

28 Jos E. Vercruysse correctly comes to this conclusion about the premise of the JD and of CRE: "Im Gutachten zur Studie 'Lehrverurteilungen—kirchentrennend?' des Einheitssekretariates kommt man zu dem Ergebnis, die Canones im Trienter Rechtfertigungsdekret beträfen eigentlich die lutherische Lehre, wie sie in den Bekenntnisschriften niedergelegt ist, nicht; dies sei 'durch neuere Untersuchungs- und Dialogergebnisse gestützt'" (Jos E. Vercruysse, "Luthers Reformation und ihre Bedeutung für die Katholische Kirche," *Zeitschrift für Katholische Theologie* 121 [1999]: 41–42). The Göttingen Theological Faculty came to the same conclusion about the preparatory dialogue in Germany (see Göttingen, "An Opinion on *The Condemnations of the Reformation Era. Part One: Justification*," *Lutheran Quarterly* 5 [1991]: 1–6). This faculty likewise critiqued the dialogue in part because of this implication. Catherine Clifford, on the contrary, offers a different perspective within which to consider the original "conflict" itself. She finds that theologians are now able to address the question of an original contradiction within a new horizon. Borrowing from twentieth-century Catholic theologian Bernard Lonergan, she suggests that, now, one's gathering of data about the Reformation-era teachings can benefit from the JD, which fosters a new horizon within which to address the mutual condemnations (see Catherine Clifford, "The Joint Declaration, Method, and the Hermeneutics of Ecumenical Consensus," *Journal of Ecumenical Studies* 38 [2001]: 82 and 86).

29 There are relatively few Catholic critiques of the 1997 JD. I would refer the reader to the following: Avery Cardinal Dulles, "Justification: The Joint Declaration," *Josephinum Journal of Theology* 9 (2002) [online; accessed July 16, 2004], available at www.pcj.edu/journal/Dulles9-1.htm; idem, "Two Languages"; Manfred Hauke, "Die Antwort des Konzil von Trient auf die Reformatoren," in *Der Mensch zwischen Sünde und Gnade: Theologische Sommerakademie Dießen 2000*, pp. 75–109, ed. Anton Ziegenaus (Buttenwiesen: Stella-Maris-Verlag, 2000); Werner Löser, "'Jetzt aber seid ihr Gottes Volk' (1 Petr 2,10): Rechtfertigung und sakramentale Kirche," *Theologie und Philosophie* 73 (1998): 321–33; Christopher J. Malloy, "The Nature of Justifying Grace: A Lacuna in the *Joint Declaration*," *The Thomist* 65 (2001): 93–120; Ansgar Santogrossi, "Un accord œcuménique en faux-semblant," *Catholica* 66 (1999): 51–68; Leo Cardinal Scheffczyk, "'Differenzierter Konsens' und 'Einheit in der Wahrheit':

Zum Ersten Jahrestag der Unterzeichnung der Gemeinsamen Offiziellen Feststellung zur Rechtfertigungslehre," *Theologisches: Katolische Monatsschrift* 30 (2000): 437–46; idem, "Einig im Uneins-Sein—Zu den Konsensdokumenten in der Rechtfertigungslehre," *Theologisches Katholische Monatsschrift* 29 (1999): 453–68; idem, "Die 'Gemeinsame Erklärung zur Rechtfertigungslehre' und die Norm des Glaubens (Teil I)," *Theologisches Katholische Monatsschrift* 28 (1998): 61–68; idem, "Die 'Gemeinsame Erklärung zur Rechtfertigungslehre' und die Norm des Glaubens (Teil II)," *Theologisches Katholische Monatsschrift* 28 (1998): 125–32; idem, "Kirche und Ökumene: Eine Momentaufnahme in kritischem Licht," *Theologisches Katholische Monatsschrift* 33 (2003): 74–86; idem, "Ökumene auf dem Weg: Gemeinsamkeit bei verbleibenden Verschiedenheiten in der Rechtfertigungslehre (Die 'Gemeinsame Erklärung' und die vatikanische 'Präzisierung')," *Forum Katholische Theologie* 14 (1998): 213–20; idem, "Der ökumenische Dialog und das bleibende Katholische," *Theologisches Katholische Monatsschrift* 30 (2000): 218–30; and idem, "'Ungeschaffene' und 'geschaffene' Gnade," *Forum Katholische Theologie* 15 (1999): 81–97. I would like to make one note at this point. Löser cites the enthusiastic Catholic exegete Michael Theobald, who in 1998 joined the Lutheran critique of the JD because of its *lack* of the explicit affirmation that it is *sola fide* that we are justified (Löser, "Rechtfertgung," pp. 323–24). One can hardly appreciate Theobald's intervention. In this connection, Löser astutely notes that the Catholic Church has always understood baptism to be but the beginning of a life in the Church, a life that must be lived in faith, hope, and love (ibid., pp. 332–33); Löser thus appears to be drawing attention to the conditions associated with living a justified life and remaining justified, conditions which, it will be shown in this book, are not tantamount to those associated with the doctrine of *sola fide*.

30 Dulles, "Two Languages," p. 29.

31 Dulles, "Justification: The Joint Declaration."

32 "Da es in der GE nicht um dogmatische Entscheidungen oder um glaubens verbindliche Bekenntnisse geht, ist ihre Bedeutung nicht unabhängig von ihrer Rezeption zu erheben" (Scheffczyk, "'Differenzierter Konsens,'" p. 441).

33 Even a member of the hierarchy, German bishop Hans Christian Knuth, noted in a general synod that not every statement of the JD was accepted by mutual agreement. Rather, only the OCS was signed. This comment acknowledges the possibility of criticism of the JD, but it is somewhat perplexing, since the OCS states that the JD is approved "in its entirety." Still, the bishop is right to note the nonbinding status of the JD itself. Moreover, the bishop's comments accurately point to the ongoing significance of the OVR. Without doubt, Catholics are not asked to consider themselves doctrinally bound by this document. Knuth's remarks are noted in Hauke, "Die Antwort," pp. 95–96.

34 For a fine example of a German Lutheran undertaking in this regard, see Reinhard Brandt, "Gemeinsame Erklärung—kritische Fragen: Die 'Gemeinsame Erklärung zur Rechtfertigungslehre' und Fragen zu ihrer Rezeption in den deutschen lutherischen Kirchen," *Zeitschrift für Theologie und Kirche* 95 (1998): 63–102. In addition, see Eberhard Jüngel's remarks on the declaration itself: Eberhard Jüngel, "Um Gottes willen—Klarheit!" *Zeitschrift für Theologie und Kirche* 94 (1997): 394–406.

35 See John Paul II, *Ut unum sint* (hereafter, UUS), Vatican translation (Boston: St. Paul Books & Media, 1995) arts. 11, 14, and 86–88; *Lumen gentium* (hereafter, LG), art. 8; and *Unitatis redintegratio* (hereafter, UR), art. 3.

36 See UUS, arts. 18 and 19, and also the teaching at Vatican I *Dei Filius*, chap. 4, and canon 3 of the same.

37   See Pope Paul VI, *The Credo of the People of God*; see also CDF, *Mysterium ecclesiae*, art. 5. For further treatment of *Mysterium ecclesiae*, see Chapter 6.

38   See UUS, art. 9, and LG, art. 14. "To uphold a vision of unity which takes into account all of the demands of revealed truth does not mean to put a break on the ecumenical movement. On the contrary, it means preventing it from settling for apparent solutions which would lead to no firm and solid results. The obligation to respect the truth is absolute" (UUS, art. 79).

39   See *The Book of Concord: The Confessions of the Evangelical Lutheran Church*, trans. and ed. Theodore G. Tappert (Philadelphia: Fortress Press, 1959). For the German, see *Die Bekenntnisschriften der evangelisch-lutherischen Kirche* (Göttingen: Vandenhoeck & Ruprecht, 1955).

40   See Robert Kolb, "Melanchthonian Method as a Guide to Reading Confessions of Faith: The Index of the Book of Concord and Late Reformation Learning," *Church History* 72 (2003): 523.

41   On the development of the *Formula of Concord* and of *The Book of Concord*, see Kolb, "Melanchthonian Method," pp. 505–08, and Conrad Bergendoff, *The Church of the Lutheran Reformation: A Historical Survey of Lutheranism* (St. Louis: Concordia Publishing House, 1967), pp. 114–22.

42   CRE, p. 6. Many Lutheran theologians uphold the authoritative nature or *content* of these documents. American theologian Carl E. Braaten writes, "Lutheran churches and pastors subscribe to the Ecumenical Creeds and the *Lutheran Confessional Writings*, starting with the *Augsburg Confession*, although quoting Luther has in fact functioned as an appeal to authority" (Carl E. Braaten, "Response to Simo Peura, 'Christ as Favor and Gift,'" chap. in *Union with Christ: The New Finnish Interpretation of Luther*, ed. Carl E. Braaten and Robert W. Jenson [Grand Rapids: Eerdman's, 1998], p. 72). American Lutheran theologian Robert Bertram attempts to strike a middle ground between critique of the Confessional documents and neglect of Luther's high estimation of faith's righteousness. He states clearly that the Confessional documents alone are normative: "Even though some Roman Catholic admirers of Luther prefer him to Melanchthon and use that as a reason for not acknowledging the Augsburg Confession, and though some Lutherans may share that preference, it is the Ausburg Confession and the other Lutheran Confessions, not Luther, which in fact are normative for Lutherans in interconfessional dialogue" (Robert Bertram, "'Faith Alone Justifies': Luther on *Iustitia Fidei*," in USA p. 172). Bertram adds that many of these documents themselves point to Luther's works. The *Formula*, e.g., points to his 1535 Galatians lectures. Bertram sees hope for ecumenical dialogue precisely through serious attention to the *Formula*'s recommendation to study the Galatians commentary as a more detailed explanation of justification by faith. Bertram then offers a reading of these documents with attention to Luther's lectures. George Lindbeck claims that although Luther's own theology is more important theologically, *The Book of Concord* presents the more authoritative ecclesial teaching of Lutherans (See Lindbeck, "Compatibility," p. 232).

43   See Lehmann, "'Step Backward,'" p. 49, and Friedrich Beisser, "The Doctrine of Justification in the Formula of Concord: How Far Do Its Condemnations Apply to the Roman Catholic Church?" in JF, pp. 149–60.

44   See Bergendoff, *The Church*, pp. 121–22.

45   See Kolb, "Melanchthonian Method," p. 520.

46   Kolb, "Melanchthonian Method," p. 505.

47   Gunther Wenz, "Damnamus?: The Condemnations in the Confessions of the Lutheran Church as a Problem in the Ecumenical Dialogue between the Lutheran and Roman

Catholic Churches," in JF, p. 101.

48　There is of course the related question of the nature of official exegesis among the Lutheran churches. Perhaps this is not so much an issue among Lutherans, since all alike look to the scriptures as the sole authoritative norm. When it comes to the matter of unity with Catholics, however, the issue of establishing what constitutes official Lutheran exegesis is of great importance. This question is also intimately tied with the question of ecclesial unity among Lutherans (see Nørgaard-Højen, "No Return?" p. 219).

49　A brief description of the meaning of the phrase "formal cause" is provided in Chapter 1.

50　I explain this term more thoroughly below but can briefly describe it here. Inhering, supernatural righteousness or justice is a gift from God poured into the sinner by which the sinner is made truly righteous. This gift includes the theological virtues, the infused moral virtues, and the fruits of the Holy Spirit; it is inseparable from the indwelling of the Trinity. Since, however, all of these gifts of the Spirit flow from the fundamental gift of sanctifying grace, inhering justice can also be named sanctifying grace. Sanctifying grace is the Catholic term referring to the "new nature" that God bestows upon a sinner in justification. A thing's nature makes it to be what it is and is the source from which all its acts flow. That is, a thing's nature is the source of unity of its various parts and the ultimate principle for the explanation of its various acts. Human nature underlies human acts of appetite and apprehension on the vegetative, sensitive, and rational levels. The "new nature" of sanctifying grace does not change the sinner into a new species: The sinner is not made "not human" from having been a human. The new nature changes the way in which this person is human, hence, the way in which he acts or can act. The new nature given to the sinner in justification heals the effects of original sin and orients his powers to God himself, so that he can know and love God as an intimate friend. The necessary correlate of sanctifying grace is the indwelling of the Trinity, since through grace God makes himself present to the justified. Again, this new nature is not a nature that determines what its bearer is substantially: man or beast or tree. Rather, the new nature is a healing and elevating qualification of what he is. The new nature is that by which the justified more truly enters into the divine calling. Finally, I would like to add that this "new nature" is not understood as an isolable element in the justified by which he merely relates to himself. This "new nature" is the power for relationship with Christ. The whole thrust of this teaching is that by this new nature, the formerly damnable sinner now enjoys the capacity to relate rightly to Christ—to be his friend. Through Christ, human beings come into contact with God the Father in his Holy Spirit. For this reason, the whole point of the infusion of this grace is the indwelling of God, enjoyed now in faith and to be revealed definitively in glory.

51　There is some discussion of the "formal cause," whether described as such or not, in the national and preparatory dialogues. See, e.g., CRE, pp. 47–49. See also JF, pp. 36–37, 56–59, 78–79, 115–18, 137–38. Finally, see the results of the American dialogue in USA, pars. 46–48 and 90–107.

52　A similar criticism has been leveled at the dialogue between Catholics and Anglicans. Richard White notes the criticisms of Alister McGrath, Richard Hooker, Christopher Fitzsimons Allison, and even the Congregation for the Doctrine of Faith. See Richard White, "Justification in Ecumenical Dialogue: An Assessment of the Catholic Contribution," Ph.D. diss., Marquette University, 1995, pp. 74–76.

PART ONE

The Teachings of the Reformation Era

CHAPTER 1

An Original Divide

THE CRUX of the incompatibility between Catholicism and Lutheranism is, in the end, not difficult to grasp. Nevertheless, one must take care to attend to the relevant qualifications and subtleties not as readily perceived. The work demanded in this attention is not slight and its relevance to daily life might easily, yet only with danger, be overlooked. As stated in the introduction, the crux of the matter is the formal cause of justification. Now, it might seem that something as recondite as a "formal cause of justification" ought no longer prolong the realization of Christ's prayer for unity. For pedagogical reasons, then, the simplicity of the issue is something with which this work must both begin and end. The present chapter serves to trace out the general contours of the traditional dispute in a readily discernible form, while introducing the significant qualifications to be expounded in subsequent chapters. Chapter 2 refines this outline by consideration of the Acta of Trent, which witness the tridentine rejection of a proposed compromise between Catholicism and Lutheranism. The present chapter examines the tensions between Catholic and Lutheran conceptions of the following four points: the formal cause of justification, the character of remnant sin, the relationship between justification and sanctification, and the possibility of merit.

Catholic Doctrine

First, for Catholicism, the formal cause of justification is intrinsic; it is the "justice" infused by God that inheres in the justified. Second, no damnable sin remains in the justified, since the divine infusion of this justice, together with a volitional renunciation of past sins, expunges all mortal sin from the justified. Third, through cooperation with God's help, the justified person can perform works in grace and grow in sanctification, which is *eo ipso* a growth in justification. Fourth, by works performed in grace, the justified person not only satisfies the demands of the law but also merits eternal life.

The Formal Cause of Justification

According to the Catholic faith, the formal cause of justification is a grace given by God that inheres in the justified person. Inhering grace, the grace by which one stands just before God, is the believer's share in God's own justice. This share in divine justice comes to the sinner, as do all good gifts, from the Father of lights (Jas 1:17) through the mediation of his incarnate Son, Jesus Christ, in the sanctifying power of the Holy Spirit. This share in divine justice is traditionally called sanctifying grace.

Facile criticisms of this belief are frequently rooted in caricatures or misunderstandings of Catholic teaching. The belief that the formal cause of justification is inhering grace does not entail the belief that the sinner is justified by works of law (*erga nomou*).[1] Who will challenge the Apostle when he declares, "We hold that a man is justified by faith apart from works of law [*choris ergôn nomou*]" (Rom 3:28)? Nor does this belief preclude Christ as the foundation of God's saving act, for Catholics confess that "while we were yet helpless, at the right time Christ died for the ungodly" (Rom 5:6). Again, this belief does not downplay the sole operative causality of God as the first mover in justification: "By grace you have been saved through faith; and this is not your own doing, it is the gift of God—not because of works, lest any man should boast" (Eph 2:8–9). Finally, this belief does not sever the human person from Christ (Gal 5:4), as though the justified could boast of a righteousness not from God (Phil 3:8–9); instead, justified persons enjoy the gift that wells up "to eternal life" (Jn 4:14), for by the grace of the Spirit they have become members of Christ (1 Cor 12:12–27), living branches of the true vine (Jn 15:1–8). Catholic and Lutheran teachings agree on all these points, yet they do not agree on the very nature of the event of justification, its formal cause.[2]

In summary, Catholics confess that the triune God is the efficient cause of justification, that Christ in his death and resurrection is the meritorious cause of justification, and that inhering grace is the formal cause of justification. What is meant by these terms, especially by the phrase "formal cause"? It will be fruitful to digress a bit about the meaning of the phrase "formal cause" before returning to the basic point about the believer's share in God's own justice as constitutive of the formal cause of justification.

The phrase "formal cause," as used at Trent, is an adaptation of the scholastic distinctions among causes, which distinctions can be traced back to Aristotle.[3] By "cause," the scholastics did not mean simply "that which makes" something to be, in the sense of the way in which an agent brings about an effect, e.g., the way in which a carpenter makes a house to be. The carpenter is a cause, though only one of several, for he helps answer the question, "What brings this house about?" For the scholastics, a "cause" is something that helps to explain or determine the identity of some entity. A "cause" is an explanation, partial or total, for some thing or event. Since things and events frequently have many explanations (depending upon the inquiry at hand), they can have many causes. One can explain the being of an entity or event by referring to its maker, its parts, its purpose, or its very identity or structure—the "what it is." In scholastic terminology, each of these explanations is assigned a term, for each answers a specific question, and the contours of specificity are traced by appropriate naming. The maker is the "efficient cause"; the parts are in an extended sense the "material cause"; the purpose is the "final cause"; and the principle of identity or intelligibility—in an extended sense, the "identity" of the thing in question—is the "formal cause."

Perhaps additional explanations would be desirable in order to articulate a given entity or event more fully, but at least these four notes are necessary to articulate precisely what one understands about any reality. Because the present issue is justification, it is useful to add one further cause, the meritorious cause, which is that on account of which (*propter*) an event happens or a thing comes about. Now, how does each of these scholastic categories apply to something tangible, such as a house? A typical family house has many causes. The efficient cause of a house is the builder and his laborers. The meritorious cause of the house is the person who pays the builder (or who pays the previous owner). The final cause of the house is the security, comfort, and pleasure of the owner's family. The material cause of the house is the many items of which the structure is constructed. Finally, the "formal cause," to speak in an extended sense, is the structure of the parts fitted together that makes these parts to be parts "of this house." Bricks and boards do not provide shelter unless they are arranged in a suitable fashion. By themselves, they remain potential to (merely capable of) some form or arrangement. The design or arrangement of the house's material elements can be likened to its "formal cause."[4] A dispute about the formal cause of anything is a dispute about the very reality in question. Two may well agree about the agent, the parts, the purchaser, and the purpose, but if they cannot reconcile their views of that which the agent brings about, they cannot be said to agree; indeed, one may well ask whether they can be said to agree on the very agency of the agent.

Before returning to an exposition of the Catholic position, I wish to offer an intellectual defense, however cursory, of the very idea of "formal causality," since the very notion is esteemed so little today among philosophers and theologians. Postmoderns are wary of the very notion of formal causality: It appears to be an imposition upon the manifold of experience. Granted, one should be quite cautious in determining the nature of the formal cause when it comes to specifics, but to reject the concept of formal causality a priori is more deleterious than is naïve realism. There are several reasons for this. First, short of having recourse to formal causality, one cannot account for diversity, the difference between this and that *kind* of thing. "This" cannot be distinguished from "that" *kind* of thing unless the differences between "this" and "that" are noted. To what do we refer when we take note of differences between this and that *kind* of thing? Such differences are constituted through formal divergences, and it is these of which we take note. The only other explanation of such differences, which claims to have no recourse to formal causality, is reductive atomism.[5] Still, reductive atomism must conclude *either* to fundamentally divergent "atoms" *or* to a fundamental identity underlying apparently different "kinds" of atoms. In the former case, formal causality is implicitly in place; in the latter case, things in this world cannot differ except according to number, arrangement, and degree. This would include any purported differences between living and nonliving matter. If one were willing to swallow this implication, then perhaps one could dismiss formal causality, and therewith any genuine friendship, for what heap of atoms can be a thou?[6]

Second, being a bit less poetic, one can appeal to the scientific discipline itself. If one were to insist that reality can be explained only with reference to the simplest parts or elements of things, then one would fail to recognize (to call to mind) that those very parts—taken to be elemental—are themselves composed of parts, or at least *might be composed of parts*. Thus, what one takes to be fundamental is further analyzable. And yet on its own level, that which was taken as fundamental is itself intelligible in some respect.[7] That is, it has an intelligible structure, for one is thinking of it in some respect. Or is one thinking of anything at all? Now, this intelligible structure touches upon its formal cause. Whatever can be known must have formal constitution, for it must be "this" and not "that." This constitution can be a proper form or an improper form. Fabricated entities such as the house are not unities in such a way that their parts have no autonomous existence; fabricated entities *are* heaps. The question is, are all entities that we experience heaps? Are there not occasions when what is before the observer is not a heap of the tiniest particles accidentally conjoined but a reality determined by form in such a way that its "parts" no longer retain their being and characteristics as autonomous elements? Schrödinger implied an affirmative answer, warning against a popularized reception of quantum theory as warrant for relativism. He held that whereas classical physics is imaginable by analogy with the "stuff" of human experience, quantum physics is not.[8] Physicists do not now analyze the elements of atoms the way a builder analyzes a house into bricks and wood, parts that can stand on their own. As they peer into the smallest "elements" of the universe, they discover greater indeterminacy, a characteristic of Aristotle's prime matter. It was for this reason that the renowned physicist Werner Heisenberg recognized in Aristotle's hylomorphism something compatible with the findings of contemporary physics. Energy provides the indeterminacy, the potency to being, and form provides the actualization of energy as this or that being.[9] At this point, the chemist can weigh in with the following simple observation: The independent properties of hydrogen and oxygen are *not* present in water, for water is not merely the accidental aggregate of hydrogen and water. It is a new reality, and analysis of its elements into autonomous parts destroys the reality of water.[10] How can this be explained without recourse to formal causality?

Third, perhaps more can be said against the Heraclitan contention, adopted by much of postmodern thought, that "all is flux" and that being is simply becoming and that no constant form whatsoever carries things through any flux. The postmodern contention that "all is flux" is not the simple judgment "Everything observable is in motion." Yes, everything observable is in motion. But the "all is flux" opinion with which I am contending entails a refusal to assign any identity to any "thing" and rejects the idea that, relative to a specific change under consideration, something relatively constant must underlie the change. To this it must be asked, can one who contends that "all is flux" account for *any* motion? Does not motion *per se* involve the "passing by" of things? Clearly, things cannot pass by unless something remains somewhat stable or continuous—relative to the passing.[11] A river's water cannot flow past me unless I stand still in the river. Indeed, my standing in the river is the condition for the possibility of the river's water being in motion with respect to me. Thus, the motion of what moves is "measured" against what remains still. One could add, moreover, that the self-identity of the water molecules themselves must be preserved if they are to "be in motion" and if one is to predicate "motion" of them. If all things were truly in motion according to the "all is flux" opinion, then nothing would be stable relative to anything. But then, paradoxically, all would be still, for there would be no chafing of divergent elements against one another. There's the rub that, as I take it, ought to serve as a point of departure for addressing the difficult yet refreshing challenges posed by postmodern thinkers.[12]

Finally, the experience and behavior of all persons attest to the universally operative "belief" in formal causality. All persons perceive the several items of their environment as distinct things having identities and cohering together, each one distinctly, as functional wholes. And yet it is clear to all that these same items are constituted of parts. All of us alike treat living beings, most especially, as wholes, with more or less circumscribed behavioral patterns. Human relationships depend on this outlook. Or has the groom taken a lump? All of us alike anticipate certain ranges of behavior coming from what we take to be certain types of things. This universal phenomenon of human perception—and may the one who disagrees not hit a wall—is wedded to a universal phenomenon of behavior, for all alike behave in accordance with a valuation of things presently experienced. This valuation is based in large part upon anticipations rooted in past experience. All of us act as though all things have definite, or at least not "indeterminate," identities. By "at least not indeterminate," I mean to bow to our evidently frequent failure to know precisely what things are. There is a "blurring" of our thought, no doubt, as Socrates showed centuries ago and as the clanging of postmodern thinkers reminds us in our day. Notwithstanding this blurring, the very fact that we can *notice* the slippage or "difference" of things and of words, together with the fact that we can be amused by such slippage (for Derrida is humorous), indicates all the more that we observe things as being, in general, determinate. Intelligence must recognize the determinacy first, in order then to be amused at the indeterminacy. What fool would be brought to laughter by Derrida?

In short, things are only *relatively* indeterminate; they are more fundamentally determinate and defined. Words, too, are only *relatively* indeterminate. But definition and determination are not possible unless something like formal causality is operative in these complex, or composite, beings. Therefore, to proceed dialectically, I submit that either all of us radically misconstrue reality or experienced things have formal causes. None of the forgoing need be qualified as applying merely to a "realistic epistemology." Even if one were to limit the forgoing to experience within the categories of human perception, one would admit no alternative explanation to things experienced. Now, since formal causality cannot be impugned as unreasonable, except rashly and with disastrous consequences, I take it that the tridentine appeal to this category offers a teaching on doctrine intelligible over the centuries.

The Council of Trent, by employing the terms "efficient," "meritorious," and "formal causality," articulates the complex of factors that converge in the mysterious event of justification. Who produces or brings about this event? The triune God, the efficient cause. On whose account is this event brought about, or because of whom does this event happen? The Word made flesh, Jesus Christ, who gained merit for all by his passion and cross; he is the meritorious cause. Why does the triune God bring about this event? To show forth his glory and to save sinners from ruin—the final cause(s). But what happens in justification? What does God do? What *is* this event? What is its formal cause?

According to Catholic faith, justification itself has several elements that are linked through a single formal cause. Justification includes the following elements: the gratuitous remission of eternal punishment due to sin, the infusion of new life into the one being justified, and the rectification of the sinner's disordered intellect and will. The formal note that links these elements is the God-infused gift of sanctifying grace (formal cause), by which the remission of sins occurs and by which the person's mind and heart are purified and elevated. To summarize, on account of the Word made flesh (meritorious cause), the triune God freely infuses (efficient cause) sanctifying grace (formal cause) into the sinner, which grace makes him just and inheres in his being. Trent reads, "[Justification] is not only the remission of sins, but also the sanctification and renewal of the inner man through the voluntary acceptance of grace and gifts. Thus, a man is made just from having been unjust and is made a friend from having been an enemy."[13] This process of justification is constituted by the introduction of supernatural justice into the repentant person seeking justification. That by which the justified stands just before God, that which is lacking in unjustified persons, is the "formal cause" of justification, which Trent defines as follows:

> Finally, the only formal cause is the justice of God, not that by which he himself is just, but that by which he makes us just. Given by him, it is that by which we are renewed in the spirit of our minds. We are not merely considered to be just, but we are truly named and are just, each one of us receiving justice in ourselves according to the measure which the Holy Spirit imparts to each as he wills and according to the proper disposition and cooperation of each.[14]

The one formal cause is the "justice of God." However, lest the reader interpret "justice of God" to be the very justice of God himself, who is his own justice and who does not participate in justice, the authors employ Augustine's terminology, "not that by which he himself is just, but that by which he makes us just."[15]

Augustine employed this terminology to affirm, on the one hand, that in light of Adam's fall, no human person can be just or wise or holy without God's mercy. He also employed this terminology, on the other hand, in order to distinguish God's own justice, wisdom, and holiness from human participation in that justice, wisdom, and holiness.[16] The twofold purpose for this pattern of expression appears clearly in his commentary on John. In Tractate 26, Augustine linked the "bread of heaven" to the "righteousness" for which the blessed (in the beatitudes) hunger. This "righteousness" does not arise from human powers; that is, it is not according to human works. It is, nonetheless, given to the human person by God (Rom 10:3): "The justice of God is here said not of the justice by which God is just but of that which God gives to man so that man might be just through God."[17] Augustine's concern, here, is with the agent that establishes this justice. He contends, against the Pelagians, that the agent is God. The sinner is miserable in himself apart from God; he can do nothing to help himself. However, the sinner can be changed so as to know and love God if God turns him to himself. So, Augustine distinguished the justice of God from the justice of man not in order to explain the former forensically but in order to show that the former is "given freely."[18] When the "love of God" is poured forth into the human heart, the justified person can fulfill the law.[19] God changes the creature but remains the same, since God, who is his own being and justice, cannot change. The human creature, in contrast, exists and is just only by participation.[20] This participation in God's justice truly makes the human person just, even though only the saints enjoy perfect justice, since all earthly pilgrims sin at least venially. McGrath contrasts Augustine's understanding of the communication of God's justice with the Protestant understanding: "Man's righteousness, effected in justification, is regarded by Augustine as *inherent* rather than *imputed*, to use the vocabulary of the sixteenth century."[21]

In connection with the theme of participation, Augustine drew a parallel between the expression "justice of God" and the expression "salvation of the Lord." The latter expression refers to the salvation God gives to those he saves; so too "The justice of God is said to be not that by which the Lord is just but that by which he justifies those whom he makes just from being sinners."[22] Similarly, in reflecting on the participatory relation between the gift of justice given to human persons and the very justice of God, Augustine considered the difference between the singular "righteousness" and the plural "righteousnesses" in Psalm 11:7 (10:7) significant: "Like as when one face looks upon many mirrors, what in it is one only, is by those many mirrors reflected manifoldly." This distinction is of great import, for it pertains to the final judgment: God "doth not allow Himself to be known by the evil, but by the good; and this is equity."[23] Augustine's circumlocution "the justice of God, not that by which he himself is just," by distinguishing between God's own justice and the rational being's participation in that justice, inchoately anticipates Aquinas's contention that the formal cause of justification is a created justice. Augustine himself even employed the language of creation in articulating Rom 5:5. He wrote, "Our affectionate love by which we abide in God, God created. And he saw that it was good, for indeed he made that which he loved. Now, he would not have wrought in us that we love God, except that he loved us before he wrought it."[24] Trent employs Augustine's language to the effect of distinguishing God's own justice from man's share in it.

Granted, Augustine did not draw the precise distinctions found in scholasticism, those between sanctifying grace and actual grace and those between operative and cooperative grace. He was yet cognizant of the diverse ways in which God acts upon the human person. God operates on an evil person so as to bring about a good will from a bad will, and God helps strengthen those whose wills he has already made good. The defining difference between a person with a good will and a person with an evil will is the presence or absence of charity, a gift by which the Holy Spirit makes the human person a lover of God. It would appear that the trajectory of Augustine's thought is to identify the justice introduced into the human person by God as the participation itself in divine justice. This participation is certainly not a work of human hands (*erga nomou*) but the gift of God. Augustine's dexterous use of words—"not that by which he himself is just"—helps him employ the Platonic notion of participation in a way that does justice both to the real fruit of God's effective power and to God's transcendent simplicity.

Trent follows out the inchoate trajectory of Augustine's thought, building on the advances made in the high middle ages, and thus distinguishes the formal cause of justification from God's own justice and from the personal righteousness of the Word made flesh (Christ's righteousness). Although the believer's own righteousness, given by God, is not identified with Christ's own righteousness, it is utterly dependent upon that righteousness and contributes nothing to the virtual intensity of that righteousness.[25] In short, for Catholics, Christ's righteousness is not simply the "onetime" meritorious cause of justification.[26] It also has an exemplar relation to the justified's personal share in it. Exemplar causes are extrinsic formal causes, just as the blueprints of a house can be considered to be the extrinsic formal cause of a house. By "exemplar," I mean that model to which some entity is made to be similar but which is itself extrinsic to the entity formed on the basis of this model. Now the form of a house is *in* the house; otherwise, the boards and bricks would remain disordered. An exemplar cause, in contrast, is more like a model of something, that upon which the artisan bases his design, but not the formal constitution of the new artifact. The exemplar does not enter into formal constitution with the parts to render "these" parts to be "this thing." The exemplar is never part of the "whole thing" that is established on its basis. An intrinsic form, on the other hand, renders these very parts to be this very thing. For instance, clay might be sculpted to the likeness of some person (exemplar), but the actual shape of the resultant statue is (loosely speaking) the "formal cause" of the statue.

Given these distinctions, I can now explain a tradition in Catholicism which holds that Christ's righteousness can in a sense be described as the extrinsic "exemplar" of inhering righteousness in justification. Christ's righteousness is not to be confused with the intrinsic formal cause. That which makes a person "to be just" is the justice of God poured forth into his heart. Christ's righteousness is both the meritorious cause and the exemplar cause of that justice. And yet Catholics can press the bond between Christ's righteousness and justifying righteousness even further. Christ is not simply "extrinsic," as though inhering righteousness existed separately from his own. Christ is much more intimately involved in human justification. There is a notion of Christ as having "capital grace," which constitutes the sum of all grace dispersed throughout the Church and, through the Church, throughout the world, the grace of the Spirit, of which Christ was full. The "capital grace" of Christ links the sanctifying grace bestowed upon a believer to the personal grace of Jesus Christ, mediated through his humanity. Jesus Christ is author of grace because he is divine; yet, because he has united to himself a perfect human nature, he is also subject of grace or participant in uncreated grace. Whereas other human beings, including Mary the Mother of God, are blessed with grace as something on which they *qua* creatures have no claim, the human nature of Jesus Christ is endowed with the fulness of grace as something to which he has a strict right, since he is a divine person. Nevertheless, although in his human nature Jesus has a strict title to grace, although he is not an *adopted* son, still, in his human nature he participates in uncreated grace; that is, he participates in the divine nature. All human persons redeemed by him partake of the grace of the Word made flesh, which is mediated through his human nature.[27]

The justifying grace infused into every living member of Christ therefore flows from the very font thereof, Jesus Christ. A biblical inspiration for this tradition comes from John 1:16, "And from his fulness have we all received, grace upon grace," read in conjunction with the extended metaphor of the vine and the branches (Jn 15:1–8). Now, from this perspective, would it not seem that Christ's grace or righteousness *is* the formal cause of righteousness? Not according to Trent. The grace of justification bestowed upon the believer truly inheres in him as his own. Granted, this grace is not something coming from the human realm or springing from natural powers. This grace is always received from above (Jn 3:5–6) and accepted through faith. St. Paul expresses this beautifully, praying that he "be found in [Christ], not having a righteousness of my own, based on law, but that which is through faith in Christ, the righteousness from God that depends on faith" (Phil 3:8–9). However, this grace is bestowed so as to become that which inheres within the justified. Twentieth-century Catholic exegete Fernand Prat comments, "Here 'the justice [i.e., righteousness] of God,' which replaces man's own justice, being made the property of man, is therefore inherent in man."[28] This righteousness is not identical to Christ's righteousness, which is superabundant, but it flows from this very righteousness and takes root in the believer. Whereas the branches draw life only from the vine, the branches truly live by the life drawn from the vine (Jn 15:1–12). The human person is justified by being engrafted into Christ in order to draw life from the very heart of the loving Savior so as to live by that life as the branch of a vine draws upon the superabundance of the vine in order to bear fruit. The branch never supports itself; it never becomes an independent vine. Nonetheless, the branch is good in itself and bears fruit that lasts inasmuch as it draws from the vine.[29] What Jesus says of the "good tree" can, in turn, be applied to his metaphor of the vine and the branches: No good branch bears bad fruit (Mt 7:17). Furthermore, this metaphor of the vine and the branches is paralleled by Paul's insistence that baptism configures the Christian to Christ, so that the Christian can die to sin and rise to life with Christ.[30] Indeed, those who are "born from above" or "born of God" cannot sin (1 Jn 3:9); that is, no such persons can continue as God's children if they commit grave sin, for even the children of God sin venially (1 Jn 1:10). In short, justified persons do not bear sin in a way that can be called "damnable," though they can sin mortally and thus cease to be justified.[31]

Trent employs the biblical metaphors of the vine and the branches and of the body of Christ in order to underscore the inseparability between Christ and the justified. But, defining doctrine more precisely in a situation of ambiguity, Trent also employs the technical terms rooted in Aristotelian causality, declaring a person to be formally "just" by the "justice of God" that is neither God's own justice nor Christ's own justice. These two teachings are not contradictory. They can be intelligibly linked by recourse to the notion of participation. The justified participates in the righteousness of Christ, into whom he is engrafted and on whom he constantly depends. There is both a distinction between Christ's righteousness and that of the believer and also a polyvalent dependence of the latter upon the former. Since each living member participates in the same head, the justified is severed neither from Christ nor from other persons. The notion of Christ as having capital grace—a participation of uncreated grace inhering in his human nature that is sufficient for the salvation of the entire world—is the door to a more ecclesial articulation of justification. From the heart of the risen Anointed One flow forth grace and truth upon all who lovingly believe in him. Through this lens, Catholics can articulate a vision of justification that is social or ecclesial. Such a topic would be worthwhile to pursue, especially in dialogue with the East, but exigencies demand another focus.[32] Furthermore, the metaphor of the vine and the branches, which allows of a more Christocentric reading of justification, is of paramount importance in addressing the ecumenical situation in the West with greater acumen. This metaphor also parallels the Pauline and Johannine teachings on adoptive filiation of human persons, conformed by the Holy Spirit to the Incarnate Son of God so that they may be children of the Heavenly Father. Catholics have begun to work on this topic, but too few have done so with an adequate attentiveness to the tridentine teaching on the formal cause of justification.[33] Finally, it is most important to understand that the infused justice by which the Christian is justified is not that to which the justified person relates. Rather, the person endowed with this gift is thereby enabled to relate to the triune God, the second person of whom is "humanated." Jesus Christ, the Holy Spirit, and God the Father are the one "object of justifying grace," that is, the ultimate end of the justified person, who is inserted into the divine life with distinct relations to the three persons.[34]

Justifying righteousness or the formal cause of justification, then, is the justified person's share in the justice of God, a share communicated through the Holy Spirit, who makes him a living member of Christ and an adopted child of God. The human person's participation in the justice of God remains formally distinct even though absolutely dependent upon Christ's righteousness. There is some analogy to this distinction in dependence in the relation of creatures to God: God is not the being of creatures (contra pantheism) although they are absolutely dependent upon his being (contra deism).[35] In his paper on Trent delivered for the ecumenical discussion in America, Catholic theologian Carl Peter writes, "What is it that is within a justified person and that makes him or her just in his or her own distinctive way? This is, in the council's terms, to ask about formal causality; to this question Trent answered: 'A created justice distinct from that of God and Christ!'"[36] Infused grace, which Trent calls inhering justice inasmuch as it abides in the justified as a stable disposition ever-flowing to the justified person by the power of God through Jesus Christ, is the formal cause of justification because it is by this grace that the human person becomes truly pleasing to God. The first moment of the infusion of this grace is the justification of the ungodly (first justification), an infusion by which God changes the sinner from a servant of sin to a son or daughter, who cries out with the Holy Spirit, "Abba" (Rom 8:15). By becoming pleasing to God, justified persons are all the more dependent upon God; they are "slaves of righteousness" (Rom 6:18). It would be only a caricature to describe the tridentine teaching as leading the justified to a presumptuous independence. Through grace, the justified are turned towards God—we could specify this as being turned towards the Father in the manner in which the eternal Son is towards the Father (Jn 1:1), *pros ton theon* being taken to resemble *pros ton patera*, especially in light of the fact that the New Testament authors almost always signify God the Father by the term *ho theos*. Christians are turned toward the Father in the core of their being and in their rational faculties, thus becoming children in the Son. By grace, they are united with the Father, who loves them through Jesus Christ. These children of God neither "relate" to nor trust in justifying grace insofar as it is created.[37] Rather, by grace they leave behind the ways of the flesh, depart this world, and journey towards the Father (Jn 13:1) that they might be alive in the Life that is towards the Father (1 Jn 1:2).[38] Precisely in the sense that it orients them in a life-giving way toward God, makes them dependent upon him as his children, sanctifying grace is sufficient for the justified to appear before God and inherit eternal life. This grace and the indwelling of the Spirit always go together, purging away all that is damnable and qualifying the human creature as worthy of beatitude. Carl Peter continues, "What is more, this created justice, received in baptism, will suffice, if preserved without mortal sin, for one to enter into eternal life. But the sufficiency in question presupposes that the justified are anointed with the Holy Spirit and engrafted into Christ."[39]

Trent's teaching on the formal cause of justification is not absent, although it is expressed in somewhat different terminology, from the recent *Catechism of the Catholic Church* (CCC). In its treatment of justification in art. 1992, the CCC establishes the inseparable link between discussion of justification and discussion of baptism, referring the reader to art. 1266, on baptism. In the latter article, the CCC declares, "[In baptism] the Most Holy Trinity gives the baptized sanctifying grace, the grace of *justification*."[40] But sanctifying grace is defined, in art. 2000, as "an habitual gift, a stable and supernatural disposition that perfects the soul itself to enable it to live with God, to act by his love." Furthermore, in art. 1999, sanctifying grace is described as infused *by* the Holy Spirit. Thus, the reader is not to identify sanctifying grace with the Holy Spirit himself. Finally, there can be an increase of sanctifying grace through God's help and meritorious human cooperation (CCC, art. 2010). The CCC, while not employing scholastic terminology, conveys the sense of Trent's definition. This is the first distinctive element of Catholic doctrine: Sanctifying grace is the formal cause of justification.

Forgiveness and Remnant Sin

The initial infusion of sanctifying grace is the moment of justification, traditionally called "first justification." There are two elements of first justification: the remission of sins and interior sanctification. Neither of these aspects is formally forensic. They are both caused formally by the infusion of sanctifying grace. The elements of first justification can be described as two "*termini*" or poles of the instantaneous process whereby "There is a transition from that state in which a man is born a son of the first Adam to the state of grace and of adoption of the sons of God, through the second Adam, Jesus Christ our Savior."[41] This initial description of justification as a "transition" or "translation" (in the sense of "carrying over") sets up the intellectual framework for Trent's decree. Justification consists in the transformation of the sinner into a friend of God. A transformation is a change. Therefore, Trent teaches that justification is a change, and Trent further refines the elements of this change by drawing upon the scholastic categories of causality. When read in light of this opening description of justification as a change, the decree's teaching on forgiveness becomes intelligible.[42]

The council's expression "Justification is not only the remission of sins, but also the sanctification and renewal" ought not to be understood as bifurcating the formal aspect of the process of justification into forensic and intrinsic elements.[43] Trent does not merely use the single term "justification" to signify two distinct formal causes of the process of justification—forgiveness through extrinsic, justifying grace and interior transformation through inhering, sanctifying grace.[44] The expression "not only forgiveness but also renewal" is directed against those who assert justification to be "only" forgiveness, thus portraying forgiveness itself as declarative or forensic.[45] In contrast to this, the council describes the very nature of justification as a "translation" or "carrying over" from an evil state to a holy state. This translation is accomplished by God's efficient causality but not without the sinner's non-meritorious cooperation. Inspiring the sinner to repent through his constant help or "actual grace," God pours into the repentant sinner's heart a share in his own justice. This inhering share in God's justice is the single formal cause of justification, of both forgiveness and renewal.

The tridentine approach to justification is grounded in the perception that the human person, in order really "to be" in a right relationship with God, must love God as his ultimate end and friend, subordinating all other loves to that of God. Sin thwarts this subordination, for mortal sin—sin in the most proper sense—replaces God with some other good as the human person's last end. Sin is a disorder of the will. Therefore, no sinner can be in a "right relationship" with God without a rectification of the will. So, when God forgives, he makes the sinner "right" with himself. But if "being right" with God involves adoptive sonship and a "right will" to which God concretely calls all human beings, then forgiveness requires such gifts. By "requires" I refer not to prerequisites but to "*con*requisites" or rather "constituents" of forgiveness.[46] Therefore, the formal nature of forgiveness includes a creaturely change wrought by God.

Trent's teaching on the sacraments also contrasts with the notion of a formally forensic forgiveness. In baptism, saving grace is first infused into the sinner and the whole guilt of original and personal sin is *erased*. Sin is not "taken away" by a merely extrinsic remission; rather, sin is blotted out: "In those reborn, God hates nothing because *there is nothing damnable* in those who have truly been buried with Christ by baptism into death, *who walk not according to the flesh,* but putting off the old man and putting on the new man who is created in accord with God, they are made innocent, spotless, pure, blameless and beloved sons of God."[47] Forgiveness occurs through this "making clean." More recently, the CCC conveys the point clearly in describing the two elements of baptismal justification as "purification from sins and new birth in the Holy Spirit" (CCC, art. 1262). The two elements are not "extrinsic remission and new birth" but "*purification* and new birth." Sins are forgiven, according to Catholic belief, not by imputation but by being removed through the purification of the sinner, so that nothing of the true essence of sin remains in the baptized (CCC, arts. 1263 and 1264). Forgiveness thus conceived is the first element of justification, and the second element is the infusion of new life.

Perhaps the point can be made even clearer by reference to the sacrament of reconciliation and to temporal punishment. The sacrament of reconciliation reestablishes the sinner in a *living* sonship but does not necessarily eliminate all temporal punishment.[48] Thus, a *sine qua non* element of forgiveness is the profound rectification of the sinner's own person, wrought by God. Once again, Carl Peter captures the Catholic sensibility: "It is a human being who is justified. One who starts out as a sinner ends up as a friend and intimate of God because of and through Jesus Christ.... To be justified is to be turned freely by God's grace from sin to divine friendship."[49] As Matthias Scheeben said in the 19th century, "[As long as] the sinner himself clings to his sinful will or does not retract his sinful will, God's all-seeing eye cannot look upon him as guiltless." The non-imputability of still-present sin is "an utter absurdity [*schlechterdings ein Unding*]."[50] In sum, forgiveness does not occur without the infusion of sanctifying grace. This very grace of forgiveness can grow in the justified.

Relationship between Justification and Sanctification

One can be more and more justified through sanctification, which was traditionally called second justification. There can be such increase *because* justification and sanctification share the same formal cause, an inhering grace distinct from the justice by which God is just. Trent proclaims:

> By mortifying the members of their flesh and by offering them as weapons of justice towards sanctification by observance of the commandments of God and of the Church, they increase in the very justice received through the grace of Christ, cooperating by faith and good works, and they are more justified.[51]

The council envisions the grace of justification as increasing through human cooperation with the Holy Spirit. Many Lutherans find it difficult to accept this affirmation. Their reluctance shows greater appreciation of the content of the message than do the exaggerated exegetical efforts of some Catholics. George Tavard says of the council: "Had the Council also emphasized that one is always at the beginning, that the greatest saint is also the greatest sinner, and that the fruits of justification are implicitly given in justification itself, then the difference with Luther would have remained minimal."[52] But one is not always at the beginning, for justification is a "translation" from an evil state to a state of friendship, in which one may ever grow on earth.

Merit and Eternal Life

The sanctity bestowed in justification, that in which the living member of Christ can grow, further enables the just person truly to merit eternal life and an increase in his share in eternal life.[53] Because merit rests on the gift of grace, eternal life is both a "grace mercifully promised through Jesus Christ to the sons of God and also a reward to be faithfully rendered from the promise of God himself for the good works and merits of the just."[54] The clarity of Trent's affirmation that the justified person "truly merits" the attainment of eternal life must be understood against the rejection of the novel theory of double justice (to be discussed in detail in Chapter 2), according to which even justified persons who enjoy sanctifying grace require a final imputation of Christ's righteousness in order to be saved. Double justice denies that by good works the child of God can merit eternal life. Trent holds that justified persons can satisfy the demands of God's law by perseverance in divine grace. Because those who die faithfully have satisfactorily obeyed the ten commandments, they are rightly said to merit eternal life.[55]

The tridentine teaching further links sanctification with degrees of glory. The glory of the saints is both one and many. It is one, since God is one, and God is the ultimate object of eternal life, for it is by union with God that the saints are glorified. The human person's union with God, however, can vary in degree, for one can be more united to God than another insofar as one is more suffused with the divine grace and more capable of receiving the divine glory. Since union with God involves created grace and proper disposition, union admits of different degrees, for no creature can so attain to God that it could not attain God in a greater degree. Just persons "merit" eternal life in different degrees, depending upon their cooperation and the will of the Holy Spirit. Consequently, when viewed from the perspective of creaturely union with God, eternal life admits of degrees. Just as every relationship, provided it is established, admits of degrees of excellence, so does the human relationship with God. Eternal life is not primarily a remission of punishment, although in view of sin it includes that. Much more, eternal life is an unending union with the triune God. God is the ultimate object of human thirst, and he who thirsts for God strives for union with him and "purifies himself as he is pure" (1 Jn 3:3). Sanctification is thus a *sine qua non* condition of beatitude, as our Lord himself teaches: "Blessed are the pure in heart, for they shall see God" (Mt 5:8).

From the Catholic perspective, therefore, it does not obscure God's glory to insist that God makes the sinner to be truly righteous and enables the righteous person to merit eternal life. Rather, this insistence proclaims God's power. Moreover, this perspective makes more intelligible the relationship between earthly life and eschatological fulfillment. Through grace and works, the human person adopted as God's child is called to grow in divine friendship until at last he receives the promised inheritance.[56] Now I turn to the Lutheran perspective.

Lutheran Doctrine

Traditional Lutheran thought finds fault with Catholic teaching on each of these four points. Before turning to the correlative Lutheran view of each of these four points, I wish to present in brief the overall Lutheran approach to the matter of justification. The overarching Lutheran concern is "to find God to be gracious." The Lutheran asks, "How can I find a gracious God?" The question arises from the acute realization of the demands of the law, which issue—in the face of sin—in accusation and condemnation. In hearing the law, the human person stands under the demands of God's righteous will. These demands find their superlative expression in the twofold commandment of love: Love God with all your strength and love your neighbor as yourself. The love that God demands is absolute. No other love can take precedence, for one cannot serve two masters. Therefore, any infraction against the law of loving of God above all things and for his own sake constitutes a violation of God's demands. But the law is one, so any violation is a violation of the entire law—it is an offense against God. The person who hears the rigorous demands announced in the law fears for his salvation: All sinners are to be punished by eternal death. The law condemns everyone, for all have sinned and fallen short of the glory of God (Rom 3:23).

But God is gracious. He does not hold sins against the sinner. Rather, he wishes to have mercy on sinners. Out of his love, he sent his only Son as an expiation to die for those who were yet his enemies (Rom 3:24–26 and 5:6–8). The law manifests to the sinner the vanity of confidence "in the flesh," that is, in self-righteousness. The law silences all persons, for before God (*coram deo*) no one can stand. Before God, all righteous deeds are but filthy rags (Is 64:6). The law serves to eviscerate the presumption that one can hold something against God so as to make God a debtor. Once the law accomplishes its purpose (although it must be ever-active), the sinner is ripe to be surprised by the Good News that God has manifested his righteousness apart from the law. God acquits the sinner in Jesus Christ, who paid the price for sin by his expiatory death. Nonetheless, although the price has been paid, yet no one benefits from Christ's redemption except by accepting him as mediator through faith. Laid low by the law, the sinner is left with one fruitful option: to believe. To believe means to entrust oneself entirely to God's gracious mercy through Jesus Christ.

To believe, then, is to trust in only one mediator—Christ alone—and thus to accept justification through God's beneficence alone (grace alone). Hence, by faith alone through grace alone is one justified. Yet the doctrine of "faith alone" is not license to sin (Rom 6:1). By faith, the sinner begins to live outside of himself, no longer for himself, but for Christ. By this faith, the sinner receives the promise of mercy without putting forth his own righteous works as a contribution to justification. By this faith, the believer acknowledges sin, past and present and future, and gratefully accepts God's promise not to reckon sins against his account (corollary of Rom 4:5). Through this faith, and through it alone, the believer receives forgiveness of sins and the promise of eternal salvation. Faith, then, is to live in Jesus Christ and to accept him as mediator, not merely for one moment but forever.[57] If Christ is mediator throughout life, then the believer need not deny the existence of remnant sin so as to become a liar (1 Jn 1:10). Sin remains, and this is truly sin (Rom 7); yet remnant sin is not reckoned against one's account so long as one believes from the heart that God has mercy on account of Christ. Notwithstanding the persistence of sin, one must not yield oneself to sin as its slave, for whoever does this loses the faith that alone justifies (Rom 6:16). Once justified, the sinner is set free for a fruitful life in the Spirit (Rom 8).

Freed from all self-preoccupation by God's word of promise, the believer now lives in gratitude for divine mercy. Moved by the Holy Spirit, who begins to renew his being, the believer confidently shares his joy with others in the form of self-giving love. He has been exalted through faith in Christ—a faith that is never presumptuous but is aware of its stance as freedom from the ever valid accusation of the law—and now humbles himself before his neighbor in love. God continues to work within his being, warring against the remnant, damnable sin through sanctifying gifts. The believer is gradually transformed into Christ as a first fruits of the promise of eternal life, wherein all the justified will be made totally righteous and love God with an undivided heart. But at no point in this transformative process, called sanctification and not to be confused with justification, is the believer to trust in himself. If the believer were to do so, he would immediately be set back in his relationship with Christ. No, he would forego that relationship, which consists precisely in faith, since by faith the believer acknowledges both himself as sinner and Christ as savior and mediator. Throughout life, the believer is called to attend only to the promise of mercy in Christ and to make no provision for his own flesh (Gal 6:13–14), i.e., to make no consideration of his own accomplishments. This faith sets the sinner free. And within the freedom and shelter of this faith, the believer can be renewed and grow from grace to grace until, at last, he is totally cleansed from his sins and welcomed into the heavenly kingdom by Jesus Christ.

The above account is, I hope, an accurate reflection of the basic Lutheran approach to the doctrine of justification. I have attempted to render this account according to a Lutheran structure of thought. In order to begin an examination of the compatibility of this thought with Catholic thought, I will now transpose key elements of this thought into the Catholic framework. There will doubtless be some rancor about this approach. Daphne Hampson has challenged Catholics to understand Luther for the first time, instead of shackling his thought within the framework of the Augustinian model of transformation.[58] Within the Catholic framework, a single subject undergoes a change or transformation by which the property of sinfulness is expelled by the property of righteousness. Insofar as one is "righteous," according to the Augustinian model, one must not be "sinful." Because of this structure of thought, Catholics insist upon an inverse proportion between sin and righteousness. Catholics cannot therefore brook the Lutheran axiom "simultaneously a just person and a sinner."

Hampson's challenge has legitimacy. I hope that my work can withstand the scrutiny of her line of thought for three reasons. First and foremost, since it is not a priori a matter of two neutral structures of thought, I critique the very structure of Lutheran thought in my theological reflections in chapter 10. Second, Luther, Melanchthon, Eck, Bellarmine, De Soto, Emser, De Sales, and others—all minds of no mean stature—communicated with theologians of the "other side." Their prowess enabled genuine communication. Perhaps one might consider them to have been utterly mistaken, but they themselves saw fit to communicate with one another and to recognize real contradictions in substance. We in this third millennium will not do a disservice if we begin by taking these thinkers at their word, without denying that at times certain formulations from each party failed to target the actual teaching of the other party. Our recognition of caricatures or misunderstandings, however, ought not tempt us into becoming belated tutors to these observant thinkers. Third, Luther at times assessed the importance of his exegesis of Paul on the basis of the Catholic Augustinian model of transformation, both early in his career and at the height of his career. The arguments that follow throughout the course of this work should make this point abundantly clear. Nor is Luther anomalous in this endeavor. German Lutheran theologian Eberhard Jüngel admits that the Catholic intellectual framework of Aristotelian causes, which serves an analysis of change à la the Augustinian model of transformation, could have been employed to express the core Lutheran belief. "This Aristotelian-Scholastic scheme of causes can be interpreted to say that the justification of sinners is founded on Jesus alone and that there is no question of other mediators."[59] In short, the adoption of the Lutheran conception of justification has not prevented all use of the "single subject" framework. If, then, my contention is correct, I am not misguided in moving forward with my analysis of Lutheran doctrine.

The Lutheran notion of justification is at odds with the Catholic faith on each of the four points noted in the previous section. First, the formal cause of salvific righteousness is not inhering grace but rather Christ's own righteousness attributed to faith. Forgiveness is, in itself, forensic. Second, the formal cause of salvific righteousness *must not* be what Catholics call inhering grace, since in the forgiven believer there remains sin that is of its nature damnable. While making his pilgrim way here below, even the forgiven believer is burdened by daily sins and by that pervasive reality of sin called concupiscence, which is, like all sin, of its nature damnable opposition to God. Third, justification, unlike sanctification, remains perfect and as such cannot be increased through good works. What can increase is imperfect, but justification is perfect, although it can be lost. Fourth, heavenly beatitude remains a pure gift ever dependent upon the constant forgiving love of God and not due in any way to the gifts bestowed upon the believer, much less to his cooperation with grace, but simply to God's forgiving love. Each of these points will now be examined at length.

The Essence of Justifying Righteousness

Lutherans confess that the essence of justification, what Catholics call the formal cause of justification, is the righteousness of Christ insofar as it is attributed to the human person on account of faith. This teaching is found in starkest manner in the *Formula of Concord*:

> Neither renewal, sanctification, virtues, nor other good works are our righteousness before God, nor are they to be made and posited to be a [form or a] part or a cause of our justification, nor under any kind of pretense, title, or name are they to be mingled with the article of justification as pertinent or necessary to it. The righteousness of faith consists solely in the forgiveness of sins by sheer grace, entirely for the sake of Christ's merit, which treasures are offered to us in the promise of the Gospel and received, accepted, applied to us, and made our own solely through faith.[60]

Here, we do not find a rejection *merely* of a caricature of Catholic faith; nor do we find a rejection merely of some aberrant school of Catholic thought, such as that of Gabriel Biel (d. 1495).

Indeed, in the Lutheran confessions we do encounter rejections of aberrant presentations of Catholic theology, but this is not all that we find. Biel's thought, rooted especially in that of Ockham (which will be discussed below), provided both a lasting framework for the Reformers and also an object worthy of scorn. As for the lasting framework, Biel so distinguished the "absolute power of God," what God can do given his freedom, and the "ordained power of God," what God has committed himself to by his free will, that he denied any *de iure* or *per se* connection between grace and glory. That is, for Biel, God could, by his absolute power, damn a person who dies in grace and glorify a person who dies in sin.[61] This framework underlay the thought of the Reformers, who wished also to uphold the freedom of God. In this respect, both the nominalists and the Reformers shared a voluntaristic conception of God. Beyond this commonality, however, the Reformers were zealous not to detract in any way from the glory of Christ.[62] Indeed, on this point there emerged a significant contradiction between the nominalists and the Reformers. Biel's analysis of the concrete human condition does not square with the Reformation insight. He emphasized good works to the point that he believed that a human person could merit the grace of justification by an effort rooted in natural powers (*erga nomou*). Biel thus joined the nominalist chant, "*Facienti quod in se est, Deus non denegat gratiam,*" that is, "If you do what is within your (natural) power to do, God will not deny you grace."[63] Although pastors may find this advice useful on occasion, the underlying conceptual approach is semi-Pelagian: The beginning of a life of faith is put in the hands of the human, and God's operative grace is obscured from view. Few if any would question that the Lutherans were reacting, in part, against the likes of Biel; moreover, no Catholic today would want to eschew the Lutheran attack on Biel, since Trent rightly joined Luther in rejecting any form of Pelagianism. This rejection marks the beginning of the canons of the Decree on Justification.

Notwithstanding this shared conviction, the *Formula* goes beyond Catholic limits: It denies that anything in man, whether a product of work (*erga nomou*) or a divinely infused gift, constitutes one's righteousness before God, either in whole or in part. It proposes instead the "forensic" notion of justification as a forgiving "non-imputation" of sins.[64] Forgiveness involves the non-imputation of sins and the imputation of the righteousness of Christ. To justify "means to declare righteous and free from sins and from the eternal punishment of these sins on account of the righteousness of Christ which God reckons to faith."[65] To "reckon" is to declare the unrighteous to be righteous, not, as in Catholic thought, to make interiorly righteous.

It may well be objected that this radically extrinsic portrayal of justifying grace is found predominantly in the *Formula* and that earlier documents of the Lutheran confessions do not admit of such a stark distinction between intrinsic and extrinsic righteousness. To the contrary, this description of *justification* as exclusively extrinsic or forensic is not limited to the *Formula*. The exclusivity appears also in Melanchthon's 1531 *Apology*. In defending his thesis against Catholics who draw on the Epistle of James for support that faith alone does not justify, Melanchthon maintains that good works must always accompany true faith. However, true faith does not justify because of works. Rather, good works follow true faith. He concludes, "'To be justified' here does not mean that a wicked man is made righteous but that he is pronounced righteous in a forensic way."[66] This statement helps clarify the ambiguity in the Augsburg Confession, an ambiguity in service of its conciliatory aim: "For God wishes to consider and reckon this faith as righteousness before him, as Saint Paul says in Romans 3 and 4."[67]

Now, just as the authors of the *Formula* were, Melanchthon was in part reacting against a certain Pelagian element in nominalism; he was, in part, denying that any human labor can count as righteousness before God.[68] For this reason, one finds him contrasting his own position against a kind of purely philosophical notion of justice. Justification means "to be regarded as righteous. However, God does not regard a person as righteous in the way that a court or philosophy does (that is, because of the righteousness of one's own works, which is rightly placed in the will). Instead, he regards a person as righteous through mercy because of Christ, when anyone clings to him by faith."[69] The Pelagian notion would appear to interpret God's justifying act as one of recognition, not of reckoning: God recognizes a human person to be just. Such a Pelagian conception has been described as an "analytic" judgment, whereby God perceives the predicate "righteousness" to belong *already* to the subject "human person." McGrath explains:

> If justification involves an *analytic* judgement on the part of God, God is understood to 'analyse' the righteousness which is already present in the *objectum iustificationis*, and on the basis of this analysis, to pronounce the sentence of justification. This pronouncement is thus based upon a quality already present within man, prior to his justification, which God recognizes and proclaims in the subsequent verdict of justification.[70]

A conception of God's justifying act as an analytic judgment is clearly loathsome to Paul both because it obfuscates the priority of divine action in redemption (Rom 5:10; 2 Cor 5:18–21; Col 1:19–20) and, consequently, because it neglects the source of righteousness—not human works but God's promise (Gal 2:15–16; Rom 10:3; Eph 2:8–9).[71]

Notwithstanding the observation that Melanchthon and Luther were in part reacting against an aberrant (it can surely be called heretical) Catholic theology, still, Melanchthon was not merely condemning this aberrant position. We can, pace Karl Adam, draw a similar conclusion with Luther, who rejected even the more Thomistic school, which conceived of justifying grace as an infused habit.[72] The reader can gather Melanchthon's rejection of even the authentic Catholic tradition from Melanchthon's evaluation of faith's properties and role. For Melanchthon, Christ's redemptive work has no value (*unnütz ist*) unless it is grasped (*ergreift*) by faith. Faith is a gift, given to the sinner, which has a purifying effect. God's extrinsic grace, then, and his infused gift, though distinguished, are not to be separated.[73] Faith purifies in two ways. Foremostly, faith frees the sinner from self-trust and replaces self-righteousness with gratitude. From this gratitude springs the second purifying effect of faith: good works.

Because faith brings the human person into this proper relationship with Jesus Christ, whereby the believer grasps Jesus as mediator even "after" baptism, faith is also "saving 'assurance.'"[74] Melanchthon himself even called faith the grace that makes pleasing (*gratia gratum faciens*).[75] This attribution has led some Catholics, notably Vinzenz Pfnür, to misunderstand Melanchthon to be proposing something similar to Catholic teaching on "faith formed by love [*fides caritate formata*]" or, in other words, "justification through (sanctifying) grace."[76] For Pfnür, Melanchthon's notion of faith is identifiable with the Catholic notion of "created grace" by which humans are formally just. I will critique Pfnür's interpretation in my discussion of remnant sin. In fact, Melanchthon's position is that faith does not make the believer actually to be pleasing to God. For Melanchthon, faith is righteousness "not because it is a work worthy in itself, but because it receives God's promise."[77] The righteousness by which the human person stands just is Christ's own righteousness, which God attributes to the believing sinner.[78] Even after justification and regeneration, by which there is an incipient renewal, the justified person is still "not worthy of eternal life, but just as the forgiveness of sins and justification are reckoned through mercy on account of Christ and not on account of the law, so also the eternal life associated with justification is offered not on account of the law or the perfection of our works but through mercy on account of Christ."[79] Because the implications of Melanchthon's thought were not always clear, Lutherans have frequently relied on the *Formula*'s greater precision. The *Formula* makes explicit what is entailed in Melanchthon's thought on remnant sin:

> We unanimously reject and condemn [the following error: that] when the prophets and the apostles speak of the righteousness of faith, the words "to justify" and "to be justified" do not mean "to absolve from sins" and "to receive forgiveness of sins," but to be made really and truly righteous on account of the love and virtues which are poured into them by the Holy Spirit and the consequent good works.[80]

This confessional statement contests not merely the Pelagian anomaly found in nominalism but also the Catholic teaching that one is justified by the gifts that God pours into the heart so that sins may be washed away. In case one is misled by the *Apology*, the *Epitome* defines justification in terms of "absolution," a *pronouncing* free from sin.[81] This pronouncement is the inverse aspect of the attribution of Christ's righteousness to the sinner. Through this attribution,

Christ himself is the righteousness whereby the human person is considered righteous before God.[82] Justifying righteousness, then, is extrinsic to the human person, even though it is never without concomitant effects. The Lutheran refusal to describe justifying righteousness as the inhering justice poured forth by God is the pivotal point of disagreement with Catholicism.

Even Lutherans who argue, in a more Catholic manner, for the *effective* character of justification, in contrast with the forensic and extrinsic language of the *Apology* and the *Formula*, still do not accept the tridentine teaching. Rather, they hold that Christ himself is the righteousness by which Christians are righteous. In anticipation of a more detailed examination of Lutheran attempts to modify the *Formula*'s extremism, we can witness American Lutheran theologian Bruce Marshall, who emphasizes the sanctifying effects of God's grace. Despite all his considerable effort to link Lutheran and Catholic thought, his thought is yet counter to the tridentine teaching:

> These gifts, in fact, turn out to be nothing other than Christ's own person. He himself is our righteousness and life, in that we receive nothing less than his own divine qualities just because we are united with him and possess him dwelling within us by faith.... [In] faith we are righteous by Christ's own righteousness and we live his own eternal life.[83]

This Lutheran equation of Christ's righteousness with justifying grace is integrally linked with the Lutheran conception of remnant sin.

Forgiveness and Remnant Sin

Although the human person is justified and therefore "considered righteous," the justified person remains simultaneously sinner. Now, before proceeding I must add a significant point frequently missed by Catholic readings of Lutheran thought. Lutherans have *always* upheld a "real sanctification" inseparably connected with forensic justification. Unfortunately, Catholic polemics have failed to admit this.[84] Luther himself distinguished between "grace" or God's favor, an external good which wars against the external evil of wrath, and "gift" or the internal good (from God) that wars against the internal evil of sin (from man). The distinction between grace and gift has served as the basis for increasingly "Catholic" readings of Luther in the ecumenical movement, two of which will be treated in Chapters 4 and 5.

Still, Lutherans do not evaluate sanctification as Catholics do. Perhaps the chief reason for the difference is that Lutherans wish to preserve trust in God alone and to guard against trust in sanctification. Accordingly, although God indeed bestows gifts concurrent with his acceptance of sinners through forgiving love, faith is trust in God, not in self. Melanchthon summed this up pithily in the Confession, saying, "It is also taught that such faith should bring forth good fruit and good works and that good works must be done. These kinds of things must be done for God's sake, as he has commanded, and not so that one would put confidence in such works so as to merit grace before God."[85]

Christ must be not merely the meritorious cause of a grace given in baptism (à la Catholic thought) but the ever active mediator before God. Insistent on Christ's permanent role as mediator, Lutherans fear that the Catholic notion tends almost inexorably to lead to trust in self. Catholics are exhorted to examine their consciences before every Eucharist in order to "verify" whether or not they have persevered in *sanctifying* grace. This amounts to self-contemplation, whereas God would have the sinner turn to his divine promise.[86] For Lutherans, the assurance of faith is not "vain confidence" but rather the very content of faith, which is *neither* a self-examination *nor* presumption but rather trust in the *favor* of God, who in his mercy seeks to console sinners. Created things offer no genuine consolation. Consolation lies in the love of God, the love by which God loves sinners (Rom 5:5 and 8:38–39). Therefore, Lutherans conclude, absolutely nothing in the believer's being constitutes or contributes to his righteousness before God.[87] What this conception allows, or perhaps what causes it, is the Lutheran confession of ever present damnable sin, even in the justified.

The believer is never fully cleansed of sins in this life. Sin ever clings to the sinner. Although sanctification follows justification, the sanctifying gifts poured forth by God do not obliterate the reality of damnable sin. The *Formula* puts it well: "For because this inchoate righteousness or renewal in us is imperfect and impure in this life on account of the flesh, no one can therewith and thereby stand before the tribunal of God."[88] Because sins are never actually blotted out and because the believer experiences this, consolation must not lie in *sanctifying grace*. On the contrary, it would terrify the conscience to clam both that infused grace justifies the believer and that infused grace and sin are incompatible. Not merely the *Formula* but Luther and Melanchthon strove to console just such a conscience. Melanchthon stated,

> If faith receives the forgiveness of sins on account of love, the forgiveness of sins will always be uncertain because we never love as much as we should. In fact, we do not love at all unless our hearts are sure that the forgiveness of sins has been granted to us. If our opponents require us to trust in our own love for the forgiveness of sins and justification, they completely abolish the Gospel of the free forgiveness of sins. For men can neither render nor understand this love unless they believe that the forgiveness of sins is received freely.[89]

Throughout life, humans remain unable to fulfill the demands of the law.[90] The *Formula* echoes Melanchthon:

> Because the inchoate renewal remains imperfect in this life and because sin still dwells in the flesh even in the case of the regenerated, the righteousness of faith before God consists solely in the gracious reckoning of Christ's righteousness to us, without the addition of our works, so that our sins are forgiven and covered up and are not reckoned to our account (Rom. 4:6–8).[91]

The justifying act whereby God wills not to "reckon" sins but rather to "reckon" the believer as righteous is not merely a past event. Humans are in constant need of forgiveness precisely because damnable sin remains. So, Luther urges all to beseech God for constant forgiveness because no one, even a justified person, deserves anything: "We sin daily and deserve nothing but punishment."[92] The sanctifying gifts bestowed together with justification do not expel all damnable sin, but this sin is no longer harmful for those who have faith and who make an effort to fight against sin.

It is at this point that I wish to critique Vinzenz Pfnür's attempt to read Melanchthon in a Catholic manner. Although Melanchthon sometimes referred to faith as the "grace that makes pleasing," he clearly did not conceive of faith as tantamount to that "justice of God" by which (according to Trent) God makes the human person truly just. Pfnür believes that Melanchthon's notion of imputed righteousness was not simply a matter of denying the existence of justifying righteousness *in* the human person. He reads Melanchthon's forensic language as basically an insistence that what is at issue is the dichotomy between human works and Christ's obedience.[93] If not human works, then Christ's obedience is that which justifies, that by which one is justified. Melanchthon (not to mention Paul) was clear: It is not by human works; therefore, it is by Christ's obedience. Justification itself, according to Pfnür, is simply the *synthetic* pronouncement of forgiveness. A synthetic pronouncement, unlike an analytic pronouncement, actively links the predicate with the subject although the predicate does not belong to the subject: God attributes righteousness to the ungodly synthetically. The sanctification that follows is called human righteousness analytically but is not that by which the human person stands right before God. The burdensome fact of remnant sin demands such a notion of justification, if any human person is to be considered just before God. Pfnür understands Melanchthon aright on remnant sin. So grave is the sin that remains, Pfnür avows, that "All works are necessarily of such a kind that they could be reckoned as sins."[94] These works that could be reckoned as sin are not merely works performed before faith, nor only certain works that follow faith, but "each work [*jene Werke*]." One year after his

Apology, Melanchthon commented on Rom 4, underscoring the importance of a perpetual (*dauernden*) forgiveness by God. Forgiveness must be perpetual because "We are unworthy and impure" even after our justification.[95] Despite this, Pfnür remarks, sin and the failure to fulfill the law are not reckoned against the believer.[96] Every good work has this element of failure in it; therefore, every good work is somewhat sinful. Despite the qualifier "somewhat," every sin is worthy of damnation; therefore, every work is also *damnable*. Pfnür's accurate reading of Melanchthon ought to have given him pause in his attempt to discern compatibility between Catholic teaching and the *Apology*.

Relationship between Justification and Sanctification

The first two points of disagreement can be articulated compositely with the following observation: Lutheran thought entails a formal distinction between justification and sanctification. No doubt, the presence of sanctifying gifts in the justified is not only admitted but upheld. In many ecumenical circles (e.g., among Finnish Lutherans and in the thought of W. Pannenberg) it is increasingly emphasized. As just noted, though, Lutherans are agreed that the sanctifying effects of God's love do not expel all that is damnable in the believer. This position correlates logically with a distinction between the notes of justification and sanctification.

Lutherans draw a clear distinction, albeit not a separation, between justification and sanctification. Only the latter can grow, while the former remains perfect and is preserved through faith alone. In his recent book on the subject, Evangelical theologian Anthony Lane describes the twofold dimension of the basic Protestant position. His description is faithful to both Lutheran and Reformed thought:

> Justification is about God's attitude to me changing; sanctification is about God changing me. Justification is about how God looks on me; sanctification is about what he does in me. Justification is about Christ dying for my sins on the cross; sanctification is about Christ at work in me by the Holy Spirit changing my life.[97]

Lane's words adequately convey the distinction between justification and sanctification, the distinction required if one is to maintain the presence of damnable sin (*et peccator*) in the justified (*simul iustus*).

In contrast to Pfnür's reading of him, Melanchthon depicted faith as "making one pleasing" to God precisely in its function as *forensically* justifying, not in its function as sanctifying: "And since this faith alone receives the forgiveness of sins, renders us acceptable to God, and brings the Holy Spirit, it should be called 'grace that makes us acceptable to God' rather than love, which is the effect resulting from it."[98] Melanchthon consistently maintained his careful distinction between the gifts associated with justification and the forensic character of justification itself. In his 1559 *Loci praecipui theologici*, he argued that although God gives as gifts both the Holy Spirit and newly infused virtues, these gifts play no part whatsoever in the essence of forgiveness, which is simply forensic.[99] In this, Melanchthon was faithful to his teacher Martin Luther.

In his 1535 *Commentary on Galatians*, Luther attacked the Catholic reading of Gal 5:6—justifying faith is "faith formed by love"—insisting instead that the active engine is faith, not love, for the Apostle says "faith working [*energoumene*] through love." Luther's remarks, cited in the *Formula*, read, "We are justified alone through faith in Christ, and not through the works of the law or through love—[but] not in such a way as if we thereby utterly rejected works and love."[100]

Because justification and sanctification are formally distinct, good works performed in grace do not increase justification. Articulating the Lutheran position even more starkly, the *Formula* cannot brook the Catholic teaching on sanctification:

> We rightly reject the decree of the Council of Trent and anything else that tends toward the same opinion, namely, that our good works preserve salvation, or that our works either entirely or in part sustain and preserve either the righteousness of faith that we have received or even faith itself.[101]

Again, one must admit that this and other Lutheran texts appear to delimit sanctification to "good works." In these texts, it is contended that works alone do not make someone righteous. Since the Catholic position is *not* that "works" make righteous but rather that infused grace makes righteous and enables righteous works to follow, the following question naturally arises: Has the *Formula* overshot the Catholic position mistakenly? In a certain respect, the answer is yes. Understandably, the Reformers perceived the need to dislodge the nominalist aberration from Christian doctrine and practice. Can one, however, further argue that the Lutheran rejection of "works righteousness" does *not* also include a rejection of the Catholic position? Can one, in short, conclude that Lutheranism and Catholicism are at one in condemning works righteousness and that there is no substantive difference between the two doctrines?[102] To the contrary, as shown above, the double insistence that justification is forensic and that damnable sin remains in the justified logically entails the rejection of the Catholic teaching on the essence of justifying righteousness.[103] To put it another way, the insistence that the imputation of Christ's righteousness is the believer's righteousness leaves room for the insistence that remnant sin, present in every work, "could be reckoned as sin" unto damnation. Neither of these tenets is reconcilable with Catholic teaching, and neither is the ultimate consequent, the Lutheran position on merit.

Eternal Life and Merit

The formal distinction between justification and sanctification has eschatological ramifications. Because salvation is that which is granted in justification alone, the degrees of sanctity associated with sanctification and good works do not determine one's degree of eternal glory. Good works—though they are held to be necessary, though they are encouraged, and though they are held to be integral to Christian life—are excluded from the article of salvation. Justification by "faith alone" remains the only way of salvation, for the believer is to cling to Christ as mediator by faith not only at the first moment of justification but throughout life. Those who believe that once one is justified, one can subsequently merit eternal life ignore the fact that "Christ remains the mediator at all times."[104] All merit is thereby categorically excluded; salvation is nothing but a gift given to those who grasp Christ in faith. Consequently, as Christ is one, so salvation is one; there are no degrees of the gift of eternal life.

Melanchthon did not demur to Paul's talk of reward (again, *misthos* in relation to *ergon*, 1 Cor 3:8, 14). For him, rewards can be due even to works performed by natural human power![105] Still, such rewards are merely temporal. Human experience shows there to be some connection, though not a strict one, between work and reward in this life, for many who work hard get ahead. Melanchthon also spoke of rewards due to works performed in faith, the good works of the justified. In the Latin edition of the *Apology*, he wrote, "We teach that good works are meritorious, not for the remission of sins, nor for grace and justification (for we obtain this by faith alone), but for other bodily and spiritual rewards, both in this life and after this life, as Paul says."[106]

Eternal life itself could never be the due for any good work or for all good works, since no human person obeys the law in such a way that God could not condemn him. Since God can condemn everyone, no one merits eternal life. Christ is mediator yesterday, today, and forever:

> When this keeping of the law and obedience to the law is perfect, it is indeed righteousness; but in us it is weak and impure. Therefore it does not please God for its own sake, and it is not acceptable for its own sake. From what we have said it is clear

that justification does not mean merely the beginning of our renewal, but the reconciliation by which we are later accepted.[107]

Melanchthon offered an alternative: Eternal life is either due to grace or due to works. If due to works, eternal life is no more of grace. Melanchthon does not appear to have allowed for the possibility that eternal life is due to good works performed in grace. This possibility could not occur to him, because of his understanding of *how* Christ serves as perpetual mediator: extrinsically and forensically. Whereas in the Catholic conception Christ is head of the mystical body and, through his Holy Spirit, causes human persons as secondary efficient causes to merit eternal life for Melanchthon, Christ is ever the mediator who intercedes for believing sinners whose every good work is in need of mercy.[108] What Paul meant by eternal life as a reward, Melanchthon contended, is not that works are proportionate thereto but rather that the son has a title to an inheritance, even if he be without any works. If the son has performed good works or suffered patiently, then the joy of eternal life can be considered as compensation, but not truly a reward. Melanchthon consistently maintained his position that good works merit, not eternal life, but "other" bodily and spiritual goods.[109]

Characteristically, the *Formula* clarifies any lingering ambiguity in the *Apology*:

> For this reason Paul uses and urges exclusive terms (that is, terms that wholly exclude works and our own merit, such as "by grace" and "without works") just as emphatically in the article of salvation as he does in the article of justification.[110]

There is simply no bridging the tridentine affirmation that the justified fulfill God's law and thus "truly merit" eternal life with the Lutheran insistence that no one satisfies the law and that therefore no one merits eternal life itself.

Like Catholics, Lutherans believe that justification itself cannot be merited, but unlike Catholics, they also believe that eternal life itself cannot be merited. In conclusion, there are several significant contradictions between Lutheran and Catholic doctrine. The focal point of these contradictions is the divergence between Lutheran and Catholic conceptions of what has been called "the formal cause of justification." For Lutherans, the "formal cause" is not sanctifying grace and is always perfect; for Catholics, it inheres in the just person and, by God's power, can be increased through good works, enabling the just to merit eternal life. The vast difference between these two doctrines is set in relief by their equal and opposite rejections of a theory once developed in an attempt to reconcile these doctrines: double justice, or *duplex iustitia*. I now turn to this theory as it was developed, discussed, and rejected before and during the sixth session of the Council of Trent.

NOTES

1   The interpretation of the Pauline phrase "works of law" is of course a matter of dispute. Many scholars interpret it in a manner in which I use it in the text. British biblical scholar James Dunn has offered a well-known alternative to this interpretation: the so-called "New Perspective" on Paul. He notes that in both Romans and Galatians, Paul has an eye especially to the sociological function of the law as demarcating Jew from Gentile. Therefore, Dunn claims, Paul is warning the Jewish Christians, whom he addresses in these two epistles, not to claim special status before God because of the law. Paul's contention is that what marks out the true member of the new covenant is not being Jewish—i.e., rooting one's identity in the law—but rather faith—i.e., rooting one's identity in the blood of Jesus. Dunn concludes that it is rash to presume that Paul has contradicted himself in his various treatments of the law (Romans 2 and 10, for instance). Rather, "When Paul speaks of the 'letter' killing he is not thinking of the law as such, or even of the law understood literally, but of the law as defining the covenant people with the physical visible rite of circumcision (as in Rom. 2.29)" (James D.G. Dunn, *Jesus, Paul and the Law: Studies in Mark and Galatians* [Louisville, KY: Westminster/John Knox Press, 1991], p. 224).

2   One can claim at the start that both sides agree on "all these points." Still, one ought to be aware that a closer examination of "all these points" demands attention to their configuration in the schema of each communion's teaching. When one looks at the justification event itself, its effects, and its implications, one can discern that the communions may well have difficulty agreeing even on God's efficient causality, for that causality cannot be understood without reference to what it effects. If the parties dispute about this effect, can they coherently be said to agree even on the divine causality? For pedagogical reasons, however, I leave this troublesome implication aside for the moment.

3   "Scholastic" refers to the methodology used by medieval scholars, both theologians and philosophers. The method consisted most notably in a set of interrelated questions, each composed of arguments against some thesis, a general response, and specific answers to the contrary arguments.

4   I say "can be likened" in order to convey this as a quite extended sense of "formal causality." Indeed, the formal causality involved in this instance is posited in virtue of the function that this product of human labor serves.

5   By "atoms" I do not mean elements in the periodic table; I mean ultimate units of explanation with reference to which "higher" phenomena are accounted for.

6   It is no accident that, frequently enough, an ideological agenda underlies the (in)human effort to expunge formal causality from academic discourse. Bernard Lonergan, one theologian who cannot be accused of ignorance of the physical sciences, makes an excellent case to scientists on behalf of the principle of unity and intelligibility, what I call the formal cause. See Bernard Lonergan, *Insight*, vol. 3, *Collected Works of Bernard Lonergan* (Buffalo: University of Toronto Press, 1992), pp. 287–95.

7   We could enter into this point in greater detail in terms of the different properties manifest by different orders of being. Whereas the physicist studies the schemes of recurrence at level X (if we may be generic, to get the point across), the chemist observes sets of characteristics inexplicable on the basis of the physicist's approach,

and these sets of characteristics form a legitimate object of thought. They form a legitimate object of thought because they are not merely a coincidental set of characteristics of the physicist's object (as though a chemist were a lunatic searching for meaning in the realm of coincidence). Indeed, there is displayed in the objects of the physicist's research a coincidence of "aggregates." Examination of the coincidence of aggregates can yield an insight into a pattern manifest by what appeared on one level to be merely coincidence. This pattern calls for a higher insight (See Lonergan, *Insight*, pp. 287–88). The justification for the chemist's insight is in the end somewhat Aristotelian: what happens for the most part is not intelligently explained by appeal to "chance."

8   See Robert Augros and George Stanciu, *The New Biology: Discovering the Wisdom in Nature* (Boston: Shambhala, 1988), p. 33. I am grateful to John Finley, graduate student at The University of Dallas, for informing me about this book.

9   See Augros, *New Biology*, p. 34.

10 See Augros, *New Biology*, pp. 34–35.

11 See Lonergan, *Insight*, pp. 460–63.

12 See, for instance, John Caputo, *Radical Hermeneutics: Repetition, Deconstruction, and the Hermeneutical Project* (Bloomington, IN: Indiana University Press, 1987).

13 Non est sola peccatorum remissio, sed et sanctificatio et renovatio interioris hominis per voluntariam susceptionem gratiae et donorum, unde homo ex iniusto fit iustus et ex inimico amicus (chap. 7, Decree on Justification, p. 673: 15–17 of *Trent to Vatican II*, vol. 2, *Decrees of the Ecumenical Councils*, ed. Norman P. Tanner, S.J. [Washington: Georgetown University Press, 1990]). Unless otherwise noted, all translations are mine. Hereafter, references to the Decree on Justification will note the chapter, common to all texts, and the pagination and line numbers specific to this collection (e.g., chap. 7, DE, 673: 15–17).

14 Demum unica formalis causa est iustitia Dei, non qua ipse iustus est, sed qua nos iustos facit, qua videlicet ab eo donati renovamur spiritu mentis nostrae, et non modo reputamur, sed vere iusti nominamur et sumus, iustitiam in nobis recipientes unusquisque suam, secundum mensuram, quam Spiritus sanctus partitur singulis prout vult, et secundum propriam cuiusque dispositionem et cooperationem (chap. 7, DE, 673: 26–32).

15 This formulation appears in several places. Augustine used the formula to distinguish the justice by which God is just—his own justice which he is—from the justice he gives (*dat*) man in justification (see St. Augustine, *De Trinitate*, XIV, chap. 12 [15], in *Corpus Christianorum*, La, vol. 50a, pp. 442–43). A person receives this justice so that he can merit to receive beatitude (see ibid., chap. 14 [21], pp. 449–51). In his interpretation of the Johannine statement "God is love," Augustine argued that God is charity not in the sense that he is the substance of a human person's charity but in the sense that he gives the gift of charity (see ibid., XV, chap. 17 [21], pp. 501–02). Augustine used this distinction in his anti-Pelagian writings as well. In *On the Spirit and the Letter*, For instance, he used this distinction to interpret the following statement in 2 Cor 5:21: "So that in [Christ] we might become the righteousness of God." Augustine read this statement not to mean that we might be righteous by the righteousness whereby God is righteous but that by God we might be made righteous. Augustine's chief preoccupation, a preoccupation which most Lutheran scholars do not deny, was with the identity of the agent that works the change in man (the efficient cause), not with whether or not a genuine change takes place precisely through justification (see St. Augustine, *De Spiritu et littera*, chaps. 18–19 [31–32], in PL 44, col. 220). Augustine rejected Pelagius's reading of Abel as a sinless man, but

Augustine also considered Abel a righteous man. Augustine declared Abel to be both righteous and a sinner: righteous because he was truly made righteous by the gift of God and sinner because in non-major matters Abel fell short of perfect moral action. Augustine means that Abel was a sinner insofar as he was a venial sinner (see St. Augustine, *De natura et gratia*, chap. 38 [45], in PL 44, col. 269).

16 See Augustine, *De Trinitate*, XIV, chaps. 12–15 [15–21], pp. 442–51.

17 Iustitia Dei hic dicitur, non qua iustus est Deus, sed quam dat homini Deus, ut justus sit homo per Deum (Augustine, *In Iohannis evangelium*, tractatus 26.1, in *Corpus Christianorum*, La, vol. 36, p. 260).

18 Augustine, Enarrationes in psalmos, XXX, 6 (PL 36, col. 233–34).

19 Augustine, *Epistle CXL: De gratia novi testamenti liber*, chap. 4, par. 11 (PL 33, col. 542). Hence, faith alone cannot justify, according to Augustine, who conceived of faith as an assent to revealed truth. Rather, only faith that is accompanied by love can justify (see McGrath, *Iustitia Dei*, p. 30).

20 See *Epistle CXL*, pars. 10 and 12 (PL 33, col. 541–42).

21 McGrath, *Iustitia Dei*, p. 31.

22 Justitia Dei dicitur, non qua justus est Dominus, sed qua justificat eos quos ex ipiis justos facit (Augustine, *Sermo CXXXI*, chap. 9; PL 38, col. 733).

23 St. Augustine, "Commentary on Psalm 11," verse 7, par. 11, in St. Augustine of Hippo, *Expositions on the Book of Psalms*, ed. and trans. A. Cleveland Coxe, vol. 8, *Nicene and Post-Nicene Fathers*, first series, ed. Philip Schaff (Peabody, MA: Hendrickson Publishers, Inc.). For the Latin, see PL 36, col. 137.

24 Amorem itaque nostrum pium quo colimus Deum, fecit Deus, et uidit quia bonum est; ideo quippe amauit ipse quod fecit. Sed in nobis non faceret quod amaret, nisi antequam id faceret, nos amaret (Augustine, *In Iohannis*, tractate 102.5, in *Corpus Christianorum*, La, vol. 36, p. 597).

25 Infused justice, though a real perfection of the human person bestowed by God, adds nothing to the intensive plenitude of Christ's grace. One must assert, however, that the extensive reach of that same grace to a greater number of subjects does, by virtue of its causal efficacy, increase. Moreover, one must assert that the hold of Christ's grace on one and the same subject can increase. One can be "more" justified by being in Christ to a greater degree than one was previously. Because of its inexhaustible plenitude, however, Christ's grace never ceases to have the power to reach more subjects or to increase in any given subject.

26 This is a complaint, understandable in light of less than sophisticated catechesis, of Protestants against Catholic teaching.

27 For a superb exposition of this dependence in distinction, see Hubert Jedin, *The First Sessions at Trent (1545–47)* vol. 2, *A History of the Council of Trent*, trans. Ernest Graf (St. Louis: B. Herder Book Co., 1961), pp. 255–56.

28 Fernand Prat, *The Theology of St. Paul*, 2 vols., trans. John Stoddard (Westminster, MD: Newman Bookshop, 1956) II, p. 244.

29 I appeal to the notion of engrafting or incorporation into Christ because it is ecumenically viable. It tells against the erroneous reading of infused righteousness as something alien to Christ's own righteousness. Still, the Catholic understanding of engrafting is much more "ontologically realistic" than that of Evangelicals and Lutherans. For the debate among Evangelicals, see Michael F. Bird, "Incorporated Righteousness: A Response to Recent Evangelical Discussion Concerning the Imputation of Christ's Righteousness in Justification," *Journal of the Evangelical Theological Society* 47 (2004): 253–75.

30 See Fernand Prat, *Theology of St. Paul*, esp. I, pp. 221–24. Prat writes, "To be baptized

into Christ . . . is not simply to be made subject to him, like a slave to his master, or like a liegeman to his lord, nor is it merely to be bound to him by an oath like a soldier to his general, nor even to be consecrated to him as a temple to a divinity; it is still more and above all to be incorporated with him, to be immersed in him, as if in a new element, to become a part of him as another self. . . . Ineffable union, compared by Paul to the grafting, which intimately mingles two lives even to the point of blending them, and absorbs into the life of the trunk the life of the grafted branch; a marvelous operation, which makes both Christ and ourselves [*sumphutoi*] (animated by the same vital principle), [*summorphoi*] (subject to the same active principle), or, as Paul says elsewhere, clothes us with Christ and makes us live of his life" (ibid., I, pp. 222–23). Joseph Fitzmeyer's analysis of Rom 6:5 echoes the insight Prat articulates. He translates the opening clause as follows: "If we have grown into union with him" (Joseph Fitzmeyer, *Romans: A New Translation with Introduction and Commentary* [New York: Doubleday, 1993], p. 435).

31   For a sound assessment of the placement of justification within the distinction between created and uncreated grace, see Irene Willig, *Geschaffene und Ungeschaffene Gnade: Bibeltheologische Fundierung und Systematische Erörterung* (Münster Westfallen: Aschendorffsche Verlagsbuchhandlung, 1964), pp. 259–83. Willig brilliantly treats the manifold riches of grace, by which humans are made God's children, freed from sins, sanctified, and introduced into the Trinitarian processions. Willig argues that Trent's teaching on the "unica causa formalis" is not sufficiently understood if (à la the trajectory of Rahner's thought) one simply retorts to the traditional interpretation (the formal cause as created grace), "Is that all? Created grace alone?" Instead, one must attend to the biblical metaphors allusive of participation in Christ and to the crowning chapter 16, which explicitly affirms the dependence of *iustitia inhaerens* upon the *iustitia Christi*. If one attends to these matters, one can safely conclude that the single formal cause, the grace by which one is formally just before God, is nothing other than created grace, by which the human person also enjoys the divine indwelling (ibid., pp. 260–62).

32   See Susan Wood, "Lutherans and Roman Catholics: Two Perspectives on Faith," *One in Christ* 37 (2002): 46–60. Wood notes that the Catholic emphasis on the communal dimension of faith appears to be lacking in the JD (ibid., pp. 57–58). Although I have a different view of the accomplishments of the JD, I concur with her that a more ecclesial approach to justification is urgently needed and is as yet not sufficiently addressed in the dialogue. This void would be filled, without excessive focus on the hierarchical nature of the Church, by closer attention to the capital grace of Christ and to the mystery of the Church as "communion." Valerie Karras makes a point similar to Wood's in an excellent article (Valerie Karras, "Beyond Justification: An Orthodox Perspective," in *Justification and the Future of the Ecumenical Movement*, ed. William Rusch [Collegeville: Liturgical Press, 2003], pp. 99–131).

33   The work of Scheeben, which is dependent in part upon Petavius's recovery of the Greeks, as well as the more recent work of Karl Rahner, offer a crucial contribution. The difficulty, I believe, is that Scheeben's and Rahner's "*nicht nur, sed auch* [not only created grace, but also uncreated grace]" has been much abused by those who now chant, "*nicht auch, sed nur* [not also created grace, but only uncreated grace]." If Rahner himself ambled in this direction, his earlier work, in vols. 1 and 4 of his *Investigations*, is not susceptible of this exclusive dichotomy. For a fruitful proposal on this topic, and an exception to the contemporary neglect of the formal cause, see Richard White, "Justification in Ecumenical Dialogue," pp. 149–208. He rightly underscores (on pp. 197–201) the "filial motif" of the tridentine teaching.

34 See Josef Hefner's excellent summary of Lainez's speech at the council in Josef Hefner, *Die Entstehungsgeschichte des Trienter Rechtfertigungsdekretes: Ein Beitrag zur Dogmengeschichte des Reformationszeitalters* (Paderborn: Druck und Verlag von Ferdinand Schöningh, 1909), pp. 233–34.

35 This analogy breaks down at some point, because the human nature of Christ makes the distinction between Christ's righteousness and man's righteousness all the more subtle.

36 Carl J. Peter, "The Decree on Justification in the Council of Trent," in USA, p. 226.

37 I will discuss below the theories of those who hold the grace of filiation to include the uncreated grace as well.

38 For a treatment relating the prologue and 1 Jn, see Rudolph Schnackenburg, *The Gospel According to St. John*, vol. 1, trans. Kevin Smyth (New York: Herder and Herder, 1968), pp. 232–35.

39 Carl J. Peter, " Decree," p. 226. The potential ecumenical import of the theme "being engrafted into Christ" cannot be underestimated. I concur with Peter and also with Luis Ladaria, who writes, "Me interesa ahora subrayar que la realidad de la justificación se define expresamente como inserción en Cristo" (Luis F. Ladaria, *Antropologia teologica*, no. 24, Analecta Gregoriana [Rome: Università Gregoriana Editrice, 1983], p. 345).

40 *Catechism of the Catholic Church*, trans. United States Catholic Conference (Vatican City: Libreria Editrice Vaticana, 1994).

41 Ut sit translatio ab eo statu, in quo homo nascitur filius primi Adae, in statum gratiae et adoptionis filiorum Dei, per secundum Adam Iesum Christum salvatorem nostrum (chap. 4, DE, 672: 14–16).

42 Tavard's assertion that as of chapter 4 of the decree "there is no difference between the Catholic and Reformation teaching" is simply untenable (George H. Tavard, *Justification: An Ecumenical Study* [New York: Paulist Press, 1983], p. 72). The very structure of justification is that of a change or transformation. Daphne Hampson, following McGrath, has it right (see Daphne Hampson, *Christian Contradictions: The Structures of Lutheran and Catholic Thought* [New York: Cambridge University Press, 2001], p. 83, and McGrath, *Iustitia Dei*, p. 269).

43 When I examine the Acta of the Council of Trent, I will also examine this misleading interpretation of the conciliar decree. At this point, I would only make note of the following study by Paul O'Callaghan: *Fides Christi: The Justification Debate* (Portland, OR: Four Courts Press, 1997). O'Callaghan concludes his examination of the tridentine decree with two statements the harmony of which is difficult to discern (ibid., p. 94). The two statements reflect his reading of the council. On the one hand, he affirms the inhering, infused, and created nature of the charity by which the believer "loves" God. On the other hand, he cites Tavard,'s judgment that Trent "differs somewhat in words, but not truly in substance, from Luther's understanding of justification as making the sinner just," (Tavard, *Justification*, p. 76 [cited in O'Callaghan, *Fides Christi*, p. 83, note 67]). I find it difficult to determine O'Callaghan's reading of the council, but it seems that he would read the phrase "not only remission but also renewal" as a basic insistence on both the gratuity of grace and also the effective character of grace, without conceiving these two as linked in the single formal cause. He simply sees these as two juxtaposed elements the unity of which was left undecided. O'Callaghan closes his account with the following two sentences, the first of which leans towards a loose reading of Trent and the second of which leans closer to my reading: "The principal point rejected was the purely *forensic or exterior view of justification* which the Council saw as amounting to a denial of the reality and efficacy of saving grace, and by implication, a toning down of the solid

realism of human response to God's gifts. Against this, [Trent] clearly and unequivocally stated the inherent or infused nature of justification, the realism of incarnate redemption and the meaningfulness of human 'cooperation'. Other issues in the decree are either directly related to this one, or of lesser importance" (ibid., p. 94). O'Callaghan appears to be dependent upon Gérard Philips's study of created grace (see Gérard Philips, *L'Union personnelle avec le Dieu vivant: Essai sur l'origine et le sens de la grâce créée* [Leuven: Leuven University Press, 1989]). I believe that there are some weaknesses in Philips's study. I note these in Chapter 2.

44   Tavard, for example, proffers a misleading alternative: "On whether impiety and piety, injustice and justice, sin and holiness, co-exist in the saints, the one coming from the human person, the other from divine grace, the Council of Trent remains ambiguous where Luther is clear. Two readings are in fact possible. One may see the two extreme moments in the conciliar formulation, sin and justice, as separated by a time lag so that one would be made just only *after* forgiveness has taken away sin. Yet the texts may also be read as describing a permanent tension in the Christian heart, caught between the human sinfulness which is its own and the divine righteousness which comes by grace. In this second reading the Council does not outline a history; it depicts a state" (Tavard, *Justification*, p. 76). Pace Tavard, *neither* of these readings is tenable. The second reading is less tenable, for it neglects the very framework of the council's analysis, that of transformation, and the council's insistence that the justified person is not a damnable sinner. The first reading begs the question, "What does it mean to 'take sins away'?" Jedin observes that by mid-November 1546 the president of the council and the majority of the fathers would not admit the thesis that faith cannot exist without charity. Thus, the Abbot Luciano was persuaded to admit the distinction between faith formed by charity and genuine albeit unformed faith; the distinction is critical in affirming that mortal sin is not compatible with the former although it is compatible with the latter (see Jedin, *Council*, pp. 290–91). Karl Rahner critiqued Küng on a similar point decades before Tavard's book was published. Rahner insisted that forgiveness and sanctification are two sides of the same reality, not two phases in God's action. See Karl Rahner, "Controversial Theology on Justification," *More Recent Writings*, trans. Kevin Smyth, vol. 4, *Theological Investigations* (Baltimore: Helicon Press, 1966), p. 199. See also Hampson, *Christian Contradictions*, pp. 133–35.

45   The Reformers strictly identified justification and forgiveness: "Forgiveness of sins is the same as justification. . . . We obtain the forgiveness of sins only by faith in Christ, not through love, or because of love or works, though love does follow faith" (*Apology*, IV: 76–77, in *Book of Concord*). For the *Apology*, cited from the Tappert edition, which includes those sections of the quarto edition not included in the more recent edition (*The Book of Concord: The Confessions of the Evangelical Lutheran Church*, ed. Robert Kolb and Timothy Wengert, trans., Charles Arand, Eric Gritsch, Robert Kolb, William Russell, James Schaaf, Jane Strohl, and Timothy Wengert [Minneapolis: Fortress Press, 2000]). In passages not included in the octavo edition, I either cite Kolb's edition or explicitly note that the citation is taken from the quarto edition. Ladaria notes the very framework of "change" by which the council defined justification: "La justificación 'del impío' es definida como el paso del estado en que el hombre nace como hijo de Adán (por lo tanto el estado de pecado) al estado de gracia y de la filiación adoptiva" (Ladaria, Antropologia, p. 339). He continues, "Se ve claramente a dónde apunta el Concilio; se trata de excluir una simple 'no imputación' de los pecados que no comporte una radical transformación del hombre; esta transformación es definida como sanctificación y renovación del hombre interior" (ibid., p. 342). He regards Trent as conceiving the formal cause as that to which

Catholics have referred as "habit" or "created grace," though without using the terminology of the schools.

46 The CCC describes justification as "cleansing" from sin (art. 1987). This cleansing involves our God-enabled "detachment" from sin (art. 1990), for in justification, God grants us the power to obey his will (art. 1991). The context of this cleansing from sin and empowerment for obedience is our being "engrafted" into Christ by the Holy Spirit, who grants to us a share in Christ's grace (arts. 1988 and 1997). It is instructive that the *Catechism* cites Rom 6 at considerable length in the introduction to its discussion of justification.

47 In renatis enim nihil odit Deus, quia *nihil est damnationis* iis, qui vere consepulti sunt cum Christo per baptisma in mortem, *qui non secundum carnem ambulant,* sed veterem hominem exuentes et novum, qui secundum Deum creatus est, induentes, innocentes, immaculati, puri, innoxii ac Deo dilecti filii effecti sunt (Decree on Original Sin, par. 5, in DE, 667: 6–7, first emphasis mine).

48 See Chap. 14, DE, 677: 1–17, and canon 30, DE, 681: 12–16.

49 Peter, "Decree," pp. 222–23.

50 Matthias Joseph Scheeben, *The Mysteries of Christianity,* trans. Cyril Vollert, S .J. (St. Louis: B. Herder Book Co., 1947), p. 618. For the German, see *Die Mysterien des Christenthums,* 2nd ed. (Freiburg im Breisgau: Herder, 1898), p. 548.

51 Mortificando membra carnis suae et exhibendo ea arma iustitiae in sanctificationem per observationem mandatorum Dei et ecclesiae: in ipsa iustitia per Christi gratiam accepta, cooperante fide bonis operibus, crescunt atque magis iustificantur (chap. 10, DE, 675: 2–7). See again DE, 673: 26–27.

52 Tavard, *Justification,* p. 79.

53 Chap. 16, DE, 678: 13–14 and canon 32, DE, 681: 19–24.

54 Tamquam gratia filiis Dei per Christum Iesum misericorditer promissa, et tamquam merces ex ipsius Dei promissione bonis ipsorum operibus et meritis fideliter reddenda (chap. 16, DE, 678: 1–4).

55 See Jedin, *Council,* pp. 255–56 and 308.

56 Fitzmeyer notes that, in Rom 8:17, the Greek *kleronomoi* translates the Hebrew *yores,* meaning "to give title to a possession." As God's adopted child, the justified person is made an heir of the estate, and heirs have a right to the inheritance: "By reason of the same gratuitous adoption [he] receives the right to become master of his Father's estate" (Fitzmeyer, *Romans,* pp. 501–02). Fitzmeyer observes that Paul links this eventual inheritance with the sufferings of this life; somehow, these sufferings are instrumental in the inheritance to come. Although Paul does not explicate his thought further, it is still apparent that Melanchthon's notion of the inheritance to which sons are entitled minimizes the full scope of Paul's thought. See also Gal 3:25–4:7. Cf. *Apology,* IV: 358 (Kolb, octavo edition, pp. 170–73).

57 Vinzenz Pfnür describes Melanchthon's thought on the stable character of justification with the word *Zustande,* meaning state or condition. In this way, one avoids erroneously attributing to Melanchthon the notion widely held in some contemporary evangelical circles (at least in America), "Once saved always saved," as though justification were an event in the past alone. See Vinzenz Pfnür, *Einig in der Rechtfertigungslehre?: Die Rechtfertigungslehre der Confessio Augustana (1530) und die Stellungnahme der katholischen Kontroverstheologie zwischen 1530 und 1535,* Abteilung abendländische Religionsgeschichte, ed. Joseph Lortz, no. 60 (Wiesbaden: Franz Steiner Verlag, 1970), pp. 172 and 174.

58 She makes this argument throughout her book (Hampson, *Christian Contradictions*).

59 Eberhard Jüngel, *Justification: The Heart of the Christian Faith,* trans. Jeffrey Cayzer

(New York: T&T Clark), p. 170.

60 *Formula of Concord (Solid Declaration)* III: 39 in *The Book of Concord*. For explicit recognition of Trent as the target here, see Kolb, *The Book of Concord*, p. 569, note 118.

61 See Pfnür, *Einig*, p. 170 and note 225.

62 Gerrish does not hesitate to attribute to Ockham (via Biel) considerable influence upon Luther himself, despite the latter's tremendous creativity. Luther was "thoroughly grounded in the philosophy and theology of Nominalism," and called Ockham his "beloved Master" (B. A. Gerrish, *Grace and Reason: A Study in the Theology of Luther* [Oxford: Clarendon Press, 1962], pp. 44–47).

63 Roger Haight, *The Experience and Language of Grace* (New York: Paulist Press, 1979), p. 81.

64 It appears to be the consensus that the forensic reading of Rom 4:5 (*logizetai*) as "imputatum est" instead of the Vulgate's "reputatum est" came to the Lutheran communion by way of Melanchthon's acceptance of Erasmus's 1516 translation of the New Testament. On this see Pfnür, *Einig*, p. 171 and note 230; see also Fitzmeyer, *Romans*, p. 374; McGrath, *Iustitia Dei*, p. 281; and O'Callaghan, *Fides Christi*, p. 49, note 38. The Vulgate's use of "imputatum" with reference to sin, however, was common well before Erasmus (e.g., Ps 31:2, Vulgate). It appears that it was the thematically forensic reading of Rom 4:5 that arose in the sixteenth century.

65 *Solid Declaration*, III: 17. The Latin text reads "imputare," not "reputare," and the German, similarly, "zugerechnet" (*Die Bekenntnisschriften*, p. 919).

66 *Apology*, IV: 252.

67 Dann diesen Glauben will Gott fur Gerechtigkeit vor ihme halten und zurechnen, wie Sant Paul sagt zun Romern am 3. und 4 (Augsburg Confession IV: 3, my translation). The Latin has "Hanc fidem imputat Deus pro iustitia coram ipso."

68 See Augsburg Confession, XVIII: 8, *editio princeps*.

69 *Apology*, IV: 283 (Kolb, octavo edition, p. 165). The paragraph numbers between Kolb's edition and Tappert's edition do not match. Kolb gives no number for those passages in the octavo edition not found in the quarto edition. He does not give numbers for those passages in the octavo edition that replace passages in the quarto edition. Tappert, translating the quarto edition, renders this: "Our righteousness is the imputation of someone else's righteousness [which is] different ... from the philosophical or judicial investigation of a man's own righteousness, which certainly resides in the will.... Therefore faith is righteousness in us by imputation" (*Apology*, IV: 306–07).

70 McGrath, *Iustitia Dei*, pp. 351–52.

71 See Pfnür, *Einig*, pp. 168–73.

72 Karl Adam's reading of Luther is unsustainable. He contends that Luther's "sola fide" was "directly aimed only against the Ockhamist supposition that a man, once he is called to salvation by God's grace, can and must work out his own salvation by his own power and his own self-mastery." He continues, "We can affirm absolutely that Luther's battle, fundamentally and essentially, was only with the Ockhamist perversion of the Catholic doctrine of justification, with an abuse within the Church, as Melanchthon rightly saw, an abuse which was never accepted by the Church" (Karl Adam, *One and Holy* [New York: Greenwood Press Publishers, 1951], pp. 58 and 60). For an opinion similar to Adam's, see Peter Manns, "Absolute and Incarnate Faith—Luther on Justification in the Galatian's Commentary of 1531–1535," in *Catholic Scholars Dialogue with Luther*, ed. Jared Wicks (Chicago: Loyola University Press, 1970), pp. 124–25.

73 See Pfnür, *Einig*, pp. 156–57.

74 See Göttingen, "An Opinion," p. 17.

75 See *Apology*, IV: 116.

76 See Pfnür, *Einig*, pp. 152–53.

77 *Apology*, IV: 86.

78 See, e.g., *Apology*, IV: 116 in *The Book of Concord*.

79 *Apology*, IV: 283 (Kolb, octavo edition, p. 166). A similar passage in Tappert reads, "'to absolve a guilty man and pronounce him righteous,' and to do so on account of someone else's righteousness, namely Christ's, which is communicated to us through faith" (*Apology*, IV: 305).

80 *Solid Declaration*, III: 59 and 62. See also *Formula of Concord* (*Epitome*) III: 15 in *The Book of Concord*.

81 *Epitome*, III: 7.

82 See *Epitome*, III: 4.

83 Bruce Marshall, "Justification as Declaration and Deification," *International Journal of Systematic Theology* 4 (2002): 9 and 11.

84 In this regard, Martin Chemnitz's complaint about Trent is understandable: there are many expressions in Trent that condemn extreme positions that entirely exclude sanctification. These positions cannot rightly be interpreted as touching upon Lutheran doctrine. See *Examination of the Council of Trent, Part I*, trans. Fred Kramer (St. Louis: Concordia Publishing House, 1971), pp. 465–66. It should be noted, however, that ecumenical councils normally condemn errors without naming specific persons or groups. The fact that there were at the time other groups holding various positions on forensic justification, some of whom the Lutheran communions themselves condemned, may explain some of the "phantom heresies" condemned at Trent.

85 Auch wird gelehrt, daß solcher Glaube gute Frucht und gute Werk bringen soll, und daß man musse gute Werk tun, allerlei, so Gott geboten hat, um Gottes willen, doch nicht auf solche Werk zu vertrauen, dadurch Gnad für Gott zu verdienen (Augsburg Confession, VI: 1, my translation).

86 See Melanchthon's treatment of this in the Augsburg Confession, XX.

87 See Göttingen, "An Opinion," p. 18.

88 *Solid Declaration*, III: 32. See also ibid., 33–36.

89 *Apology*, IV: 110.

90 Lutherans are keenly and soberly aware of human sinfulness. Perhaps Lutherans and Catholics are quite close on this point. Lutherans look around and notice that sin is everywhere. Catholics say that "if sin is forgiven, it is removed," but Catholics have not said where sin has actually been forgiven. Catholic doctrine claims to state *what is the case* but not which persons are justified. Perhaps, though, this qualification only makes matters worse. The Lutheran concern about the terrors of conscience becomes all the more pressing! Lutherans, aware of the predicament of sinners anxious to please God, insist that forgiveness must be formally distinct from infused, sanctifying grace.

91 *Solid Declaration*, III: 23.

92 *The Small Catechism*, III: 16, in *The Book of Concord*.

93 See Pfnür, *Einig*, pp. 169–70.

94 Alle Werke notwendigerweise von der Art sind, daß sie als Sünden angerechnet werden könnten (Pfnür, *Einig*, p. 171).

95 "Sie enim sentit nos *pronuntiari iustos*, quia Deus per misericordiam *acceptat* nos, etsi simus indigni et immundi. Et haec *acceptatio* est *perpetua quaedam remissio peccati*, h. e. immunditiae praesentis" (Philip Melanchthon, *Römerbrief - Kommentar 1532*, ed. Rolf Schäfer, vol. 5, *Melanchthon's Werke*, ed. Robert Stupperich [Gütersloh:

Gütersloher Verlagshaus Gerd Mohn, 1965], p. 134, 7–11, cited in Pfnür, *Einig*, p. 172, note 237).

96   See Pfnür, *Einig*, p. 173.

97   Anthony Lane, *Justification by Faith in Catholic-Protestant Dialogue: An Evangelical Assessment* (New York: T&T Clark, 2002), p. 18.

98   *Apology*, IV: 116.

99   See Philip Melanchthon, *Loci praecipui theologici von 1559 (2. Teil) und Definitiones*, ed. Hans Engelland, vol. 2, *Melanchthons Werke in Auswahl*, ed. Robert Stupperich (C. Bertelsmann Verlag, 1953), pp. 358–60 (on grace and justification); pp. 420–21 (response to the fifth argument of the adversaries); and pp. 422–23 (response to the eighth argument).

100   LW 26: 127; WA 40.1: 240, cited in *Solid Declaration*, III: 29. I cite Luther's commentary on a number of occasions throughout this book. Although some would dispute the reliability of the text, since it was composed of student notes, Gerrish makes a convincing argument for its trustworthy character. The chief stenographer was the highly reputed George Rörer (Gerrish, *Grace and Reason*, pp. 61–63).

101   *Solid Declaration*, IV: 35.

102   At this point, I am simply presenting the stark outlines of each communion's thought. I take up these suggestions in detail in my analysis of the JD.

103   This rejection of infused grace as the "formal cause" of sanctification is common to both Lutherans and Reformed, as Lane attests: "For the Reformers the cause of our justification is the external or 'alien' righteousness of Christ reckoned or imputed to us. In other words, we remain sinful in ourselves but the righteousness of Christ is reckoned to our account" (Lane, *Justification*, p. 25).

104   Christus allzeit der Mittler bleibt (*Apology* IV: 357, my translation).

105   See *Apology*, IV: 24.

106   Docemus bona opera meritoria esse, non remissionis peccatorum, gratiae aut iustificationis, (haec enim tantum fide consequimur), sed aliorum praemiorum corporalium et spiritualium in hac vita et post hanc vitam, quia Paulus inquit (*Apology*, IV: 194, my translation). Not all of this text appears in the second (1532) octavo edition. Nevertheless, the key point that these works are worthy not of eternal life but rather of "other bodily and spiritual rewards" does appear in the octavo edition. That Melanchthon removed some of these passages from the octavo edition may be due to the apparent confusion they can occasion.

107   *Apology*, IV: 160–61. Melanchthon rephrases this paragraph in the octavo edition, retaining the sense and expanding his critique (see Kolb, octavo edition, p. 145).

108   See *Apology*, IV: 358 (Kolb, octavo edition, pp. 170–71).

109   See his *Loci praecipui theologici*, pp. 408–12 (on rewards).

110   *Solid Declaration*, III: 53.

CHAPTER 2

Trent and Double Justice

The Colloquy of Regensburg

BEFORE THE General Council, which would eventually be held at Trent, Catholics and the Reformers attempted on several occasions to heal the growing rifts between their communions.[1] The most notable of these attempts was a meeting convened in Germany in 1541, under the impetus of Emperor Charles V. The Emperor was interested in the reunion of Christians, chiefly in order to solidify European military defenses against the imminent threats from the Ottoman Turks. For the pope, this attempt at ecumenism meant forestalling the general council he had called.[2] The pope sent a theologian whom the Reformers could trust: Gasparo Contarini (1483–1542). The colloquy for reunion was held at the Regensburg Diet in the spring of 1541 and came to be called the Colloquy of Regensburg (or "Ratisbon"). Contemporary efforts at ecumenical dialogue often locate a tangible reason for hope in the dialogue at Regensburg. Among the Protestants in attendance were Bucer, Melanchthon, and Pistorius. Among the Catholics were (besides Contarini) Pflug, Gropper, and Eck.[3] After quickly agreeing on issues regarding original sin and free choice, both sides discussed the issue of justification for about a week. After numerous drafts were produced, a final version was accepted on May 2, 1541; it was entitled "On the Justification of Man."[4] This text formed Article V of the Regensburg agreement. I here present Anthony Lane's translation of paragraphs 4 and 5 of the text:

4. So it is a reliable and sound doctrine that the sinner is justified by living and efficacious faith, for through it we are pleasing and acceptable to God on account of Christ. And living faith is what we call the movement of the Holy Spirit, by which those who truly repent of their old life are lifted up to God and truly appropriate the mercy promised in Christ so that they now truly recognize that they have received the remission of sins and reconciliation on account of the merits of Christ, through the free [*gratuita*] goodness of God, and cry out to God: "Abba Father." But this happens to no one unless also at the same time love is infused [*infundatur*] which heals the will so that the healed will may begin to fulfil the law, just as Saint Augustine said. So living faith is that which both appropriates mercy in Christ, believing that the righteousness which is in Christ is freely imputed to it, and at the same time receives the promise of

the Holy Spirit and love. Therefore the faith that truly justifies is that faith which is effectual through love. Nevertheless it remains true, that it is by this faith that we are justified (i.e. accepted and reconciled to God) inasmuch as it appropriates the mercy and righteousness which is imputed to us on account of Christ and his merit, not on account of the worthiness or perfection of the righteousness imparted [*communicatae*] to us in Christ.

5. Although the one who is justified receives righteousness and through Christ also has inherent [righteousness], as the apostle says [1 Cor 6:11]: 'you are washed, you are sanctified, you are justified, etc.' (Which is why the holy fathers made use of [the term] 'to be justified' even to mean 'to receive inherent righteousness'), nevertheless, the faithful soul depends not on this, but only on the righteousness of Christ given to us as a gift, without which there is and can be no righteousness at all. And so by faith in Christ we are justified or reckoned to be righteous, that is we are accepted through his merits and not on account of our own worthiness or works. And on account of the righteousness inherent in us we are said to be righteous, because the works we perform are righteous, according to the saying of John [1 John 3:7]: 'whoever does what is right is righteous'.[5]

The reader will appreciate the noble attempt at balance that is manifest in the agreement. Article V maintains that justification is by faith but that such justification does not take effect except together with a concomitant gift of infused love from which good works can follow. The term inhering (*inhaerens*) righteousness can refer to this love and the works that follow therefrom.[6] Justification itself is by imputation on account of faith in Christ, even though this imputation is accompanied by the gift of infused love. Sinners are justified "by faith" but not "on account of" the gift infused into them nor on account of works. The text represents an attempt to balance the traditional Lutheran and scholastic views: 1) the basic Reformation position that justification is through faith on account of Christ's merits alone, a position that avoids attributing any formally justifying role to the gift infused into the justified; and 2) the basic traditional insight that God changes the sinner and seeks a manifest attitude of repentance. Lane sums up the achievement: "The key contribution of Regensburg was to insist that with conversion we receive *both* of these: inherent *and* imputed righteousness."[7] The text implies two distinct but related righteousnesses: the righteousness of Christ attributed to the justified and the righteousness inhering within the justified. The text tethers the two together but does not articulate how or why they are to be so tethered. The formulation was certainly influenced by Gropper and Bucer, the figures who first inspired the doctrine of double justice.[8]

To the frustration of the men of goodwill who attended the Colloquy, the agreement was short-lived. The immediate historical reason for the failure was not the conflict on justification, which many of the delegates believed to be in large part settled, but rather disputes about the sacraments and ecclesiastical authority.[9] This immediate reason, however, only made manifest the depths of the rift even on justification, giving evidence of the need for that general council that the pope had, in concession to Charles's request, postponed.[10] Moreover, neither Luther nor the Roman Curia received the text warmly. In several letters, Luther denounced the article on justification as being a less than careful mix of two incompatible views of justification. He compared it to an old patch sewn on a new garment.[11] Calvin, on the other hand, received it warmly and noted the considerable concessions that the Catholic party made in the statement.[12] Although the pope apparently never rejected it, neither did he approve the agreement; at length, a formal consistory rejected it.[13]

It is not certain that the agreement constituted any genuine theological achievement. British theologian Alister E. McGrath contends that the text solved nothing because it failed to grapple with the crux of the dispute. "It is clear," he says, "that Article V *de iustificatione* represented a mere juxtaposition of the Catholic and Protestant positions, with a purely superficial engagement with the serious theological issues at stake."[14] Elizabeth Gleason suggests that the very project itself was futile.[15] British theologian Dermot Fenlon ascribes a distinctly Protestant character to the document. Lane tacitly concurs with this, for he contends that "Protestant concerns are effectively met by the clear and unambiguous insistence that acceptance is on the basis of imputed and not inherent righteousness."[16] It is not denied that good deeds flow from inherent righteousness; it is denied only that acceptance is based either on these deeds or on inherent righteousness. Here we discover the reason for the lack of theological contribution in Regensburg.

The implication of a twofold righteousness detracts from the excellence of inherent righteousness, "edging" out human cooperation. Contarini did not avert to this problematic implication directly. Nevertheless, although he was sympathetic to Luther's *sola fide*, he did not integrate the *sola fide* doctrine into his understanding of the hierarchy and sacraments. He upheld the papal power and the efficacy of the sacraments, yet both of these imply that human cooperation has a salvific significance.[17] This implication could not go unnoticed; thus, it is not surprising that the dialogue broke down over discussion of the sacraments. Moreover, this breakdown only unearthed the lack of agreement about the *meaning* of Article V. Catholics and Protestants could not in fact agree about justification.[18] The Catholic belief in the efficacious communication of grace through sacraments, which involve human cooperation, betrayed a greater appreciation of the transformation of man through grace than was articulated in Article V at Regensburg. Fenlon's judgment is correct: "Apart from its concession to an (ineffectual) inherent justice, the orientation of the formula was Protestant.... The Regensburg agreement was designed to legitimate the proclamation of salvation 'de sola fide': the 'addition' of good works in reality conceded the Protestant case."[19]

The *implicit* teaching of a twofold righteousness, discernible in the Regensburg agreement, would eventually find *explicit* expression, albeit within a theologically different position, in a draft at the Council of Trent.[20] The influence of Regensburg on that draft was mediated, in part, through Contarini's defense of the Regensburg agreement. Against those who shortly after Regensburg accused him of error, Contarini contended that justified persons enjoy a double justice (*duplex iustitia*), an inward justice that remained imperfect and the perfect justice of Christ. Contarini argued, on this basis, that sinners are justified both by faith and by works, since through works the justified can increase in sanctification. Contarini perceived the differences between the Catholic and Reformation parties to be matters of "emphasis" and not matters of doctrinal contradiction.[21] Despite his valiant attempt to be as conciliatory as he thought was legitimate, he unwittingly fell prey to a compromising logic that doomed the Regensburg Colloquy. Since inherent justice always remains imperfect, it cannot truly be that by which the justified are saved.[22] Mirroring the defects of Regensburg, Contarini simply failed to draw the logical conclusion that only Luther had the courage to draw: "Man remained inherently unjust, and was, rather *accounted* just, by the righteousness of Christ, imputed to him."[23]

Another Catholic sympathetic to Luther's basic insight was Reginald Pole (1500–1558), a cardinal deacon and papal legate at the Council of Trent. He wrote a work entitled *De Concilio* (if we may trust most of it to be his work from 1545). In this work, he took up Contarini's task of "recuperating" the losses of Regensburg.[24] *De Concilio*, too, exhibits the doctrine of *sola fide* with a qualification of practical exhortation: Works, too, ought to be preached. The very qualification only confirmed Pole's basically Lutheran leanings.[25]

The stage had been set for Catholics sympathetic with Lutheran concerns to introduce a more explicit form of "double justice" (*duplex iustitia*).[26] The mature form of the theory did not merely state that in the justified there are "two justices." Rather, it appeared to "combine" the strictly Lutheran and strictly Catholic notions of justifying grace itself, appealing to two formal causes. The "first" cause, as it was often labeled, was the incipient renewal called inhering righteousness (a kind of good works or inhering grace, depending upon the version of the theory). The "second" cause was the justice of Christ imputed to the sinner (forensic declaration). Proponents of double justice taught that the second formal cause is needed because the first cause cannot render one truly just before God.

Just as the Regensburg agreement found no lasting home among either Lutherans or Catholics, the explicitly formulated theory of double justice drew disfavor from both communions, since each communion zealously guarded only one of the two formal causes of justification. The Catholic Church came to reject the doctrine of double justice because it implied the formal insufficiency of sanctifying grace to justify the human person before God. In the post-tridentine *Formula of Concord*, Lutherans rejected the logic of double justice by excluding all inhering justice from justification.[27] These mutual but opposed rejections of double justice underscored the contrast between Catholic and Lutheran doctrines. Against the incessant murmuring of those who failed to appreciate the radical character of the difference between the parties, Luther, his followers, and Catholic theologians emphatically denied the truth of the following assumption: "You may say that we seem to be tormented by a merely verbal disagreement over a matter on which we essentially agree."[28] In what follows, I intend to investigate the proceedings of the Council of Trent, which with meticulous care proscribed the compromise theory of double justice from the domain of acceptable Catholic opinion.

The Initial Drafts of the Decree

Girolamo Seripando (1492–1563), papal legate and superior general of the Augustinians, was to be the chief proponent of an explicit theory of "double justice" at the Sixth Session of the Council of Trent, which commenced in June 1546.[29] Seripando was also to be the chief architect of several drafts of the tridentine decree. He displayed eminent character throughout the proceedings, for he was willing to submit his personal opinions to the judgment of the majority, yet he fought in defense of those same opinions with erudition, eloquence, and conviction. He deserves to be sung as a quiet hero whose views, although understandable insofar as they were reflective of an acute sense of human infirmity, were not in the end acceptable. Whereas he was hesitant to distinguish his own piety from theology, the council wished to demarcate the objective limits of Catholic faith.

Already, before the start of the Sixth Session, Seripando suffered a defeat during the drafting of the Decree on Original Sin at the Fifth Session. A draft read, "God hates nothing in those reborn." Seripando, defending a proposal by Pole, suggested emending the draft to read, "No wickedness, which God hates, remains in those reborn, but there remains a great sickness through all of life." Seripando's request was denied; the final draft of the Decree on Original Sin maintained that God hates nothing in the baptized.[30] The defeat was not minimal, for the edifice of "double justice" rested upon an evaluation of concupiscence. Rather than being simply the "tinder" of sin, both flowing from and leading to what alone is properly called sin, concupiscence, for Seripando, hinders "perfect fulfillment of the law of God." For this reason, no one can properly be said to merit heaven, even though, Seripando maintained, concupiscence does not merit damnation *in* those whose sins are remitted.[31] Seripando's suggestion was not heeded; the council maintained the strong wording, "God hates nothing in those reborn." Seripando appeared to maintain privately his own opinion—which, of course, he had a certain license to do, for the council was not promulgated until 1563—as the debates on justification commenced; he would wait until he could more fully articulate his theory of justification before renouncing what he held as indubitable, namely, that concupiscence is sinful.[32]

The first draft of the Decree on Justification was presented on July 24, 1546.[33] The text, traditionally but erroneously ascribed to the Scotist Andreas de Vega, O.F.M., consisted in roughly twenty-one condemnations—called canons—of various positions concerning justification Each condemnation was followed by a brief explanation of the acceptable way of understanding the pertinent issue.[34] Of this draft, the fourth through seventh canons are of primary interest for my purposes.[35]

Canon 4 condemned descriptions of the justified person as still evil and worthy of judgment. Canon 5 rejected the restriction of justification to the remission of sins alone. These canons did not necessarily exclude the idea of a twofold formal cause of justification. Canon 6, however, offered a more precise account of the various aspects of justification, without explicit mention of the scholastic categories of causality (formal, meritorious, etc.), although with mention of other scholastic categories, namely, quality and habit. It reads:

> If anyone says that the justice which is given in this justification is only that justice of Christ...let him be anathema. For Christ Jesus alone by that great justice of his merited (*promeruit*) that a man be made just by him. But that justice which is in the justified man himself is not in Christ. The act (*actus*) of that justice of Christ is in him but not in us. The justice by which we are just is a habit of divine grace, which is in us, although it is not through (*per*) us but through him—through him and by God. This justice is by God as by the one who effects it; it is through Christ as through him who merited.[36]

The canon was accepted by all of the theologians at the council. All but five wished the scholastic term "habit" (*habitus*) to remain.[37] The discussion of the decision not to include the term "habit" in the final decree will be presented below. The July 24 draft drew a distinction between the justice of the believer and the justice of Christ. Christ's own justice is that which inheres in his very person, whereas the justice by which the Christian stands just before God is interior: It is an ontological habit or virtue bestowed by God through the merits of Christ. The draft made use of the scholastic term "habit." Scholastics, borrowing from Aristotle, employed the term "habit" to acknowledge three aspects of the mystery of grace: that grace is a stable qualification of the justified person rendering him holy; that grace is a gift from God, not a human deed and not an acquired virtue; and that the person blessed with grace is the very subject who was once wretched without grace, for a "habit" is a "qualification," not the very essence, of its subject.[38]

The above citation gives evidence, albeit inchoately, of a threefold distinction of justice: as coming from the triune God, as merited by Christ, and as inhering in the human person. These distinctions were ultimately made more precise through the employment of the scholastic categories of causality, but such precision took time. The first draft gave several causes for complaint, not the least of which was its homiletic quality; it lacked definition.[39] Moreover, although the July 24 draft certainly condemned the exclusively forensic conception of justification, it did not appear to be decisive enough.[40] A new draft was needed.[41]

Another papal legate, and perhaps the most influential with respect to the final decree, Marcello Cervini (1501–1555), charged Seripando with drafting a new decree.[42] To Seripando's credit, neither this draft (which he presented to Cervini on August 11) nor the subsequent draft reflects his personal opinion about concupiscence and merit. Seripando's views contradicted those of the vast majority of fathers, who held that a properly meritorious character could be ascribed to the works of the just, Scotists appealing to the concrete conditions of the divine pact and Thomists appealing to the very character of grace.[43] Seripando personally believed that even justified persons could not truly merit beatitude; he nonetheless submitted himself, as author, to the manifest intention of the fathers on these issues. The August 11 draft remedied a noteworthy omission of the July draft. It defined justification as being "nothing other than the translation of a man, through a certain new and spiritual nativity, from that state in which he was born according to the flesh (i.e., of the first Adam) under the wrath and enmity of God, to the state of adoption of sons of God through the second Adam, Jesus Christ."[44] This description formed the basis for the brief description of justification, in chapter 4 of the final decree, as a translation or change from the state of enmity to the state of friendship with God. Seripando's August 11 draft also affirmed the necessity of an infusion of charity into the justified person, an infusion uniting him to Christ.[45] This claim, too, found its home in chapter 7 of the final decree. Fenlon notes that even this draft, which was far from the precision of the final decree, "was quite inimical to Pole's" view of justification.[46] If this draft contradicted Pole's view, all the more did it contradict the Lutheran view.[47] The August 11 draft served mostly as the basis for Seripando's revised draft, submitted two weeks later.[48]

Seripando and Double Justice at Trent

On August 29, Seripando presented a markedly new form of the decree.[49] He inverted the order of condemnations and positive descriptions, increasing the size of the latter and placing them before the former. These innovations enhanced the presentation of the Catholic teaching; they were retained from that point forward.[50] Surprisingly, though Seripando did not allow himself to express his own views on merit and concupiscence, he included in the August 29 draft the technical phrase "double justice" in the title of a chapter. Pas remarks that in light of Seripando's willingness to forgo his other positions, his inclusion of this term and the conceptualization of justification it entailed attested to his conviction of the veracity of his opinion.[51] Although he did not explicitly mention two "formal causes," observant readers recognized this as the implication, and Seripando's subsequent oral defense of two formal causes confirmed that observation.[52] A key passage in this chapter described the justice "by which the justified are called just" as having two elements:

[That justice is,] in addition to the most pure and perfect justice of Christ our savior and head which is poured into his whole body, i.e., the whole Church, communicated and applied to all his members through faith and the sacrament, [also,] by the merit of our same Redeemer, the grace and charity poured into the hearts of those who are justified through the Holy Spirit who is given to them.[53]

Seripando carefully shaped the canon related to this teaching so that it would not exclude the theory of double justice from the ambit of free opinion. The canon anathematized those who say, "By faith alone a man is justified, or solely by the imputation of Christ's justice, to the exclusion of all justice poured into our hearts."[54] It is to be observed that in both the canon and the chapter, Seripando juxtaposed the pure justice of Christ and an infused grace (alternatively called charity or justice). The draft did not juxtapose the justice of Christ and *merely* human works performed in grace. The draft juxtaposed the justice of Christ and the sanctifying gifts bestowed by God.[55] This is made clear by the double use of the phrase "poured into the heart." Whereas contemporary scholars frequently impugn the logic of double justice for its, albeit unintended, Pelagian character (works righteousness *plus* the justice of Christ), this draft cannot be so described. Furthermore, Seripando's own statements at the council frequently bear the mark of greater sophistication than recent scholars are wont to admit.

Seripando's introduction of this theory aroused discontent among the council fathers for widely divergent reasons. Among those regarded as conciliatory, there was a "mixture of dismay and indignation" because the assertion that inhering justice forms "part" of the justice by which one is just militates against *sola fide*. Even in this draft the Lutheran position stood condemned. Further, the draft brought doctrinal issues to the fore whereas those who were conciliatory wished to keep the decree "pragmatic."[56] Others, forming the majority, were discontent for the opposite reason, namely, that the (imputed) justice of Christ was juxtaposed with infused or inhering justice, the latter thus being rendered insufficient for salvation. The council fathers were perplexed by this theory, which they considered "novel." Slowly, they attempted a response.

Before narrating the discussion that led to the condemnation of double justice, I should clarify the theory of double justice, in particular, Seripando's articulation of it. Seripando's fundamental point of departure was the perpetually sinful character of concupiscence. He asked the fathers to think "not merely speculatively" but practically, that is, with a pastoral view to the final judgment.[57] Because of concupiscence, the works of even the greatest saints could scarcely avail to acquit them before God's judgment. Good works performed in grace always stand in need of supplementation by the mercy of God. Although the August 29 draft juxtaposed *infused* grace and the justice of Christ, Seripando personally conceived of "inhering justice" as the sum total of good works performed in grace.[58] He argued that since inhering righteousness cannot satisfy God's demands, even one who dies as "regenerate" needs a final imputation of Christ's alien righteousness in order to escape hell. To respond to Seripando's view-under-construction, the council formulated a question on October 15: Do the justified merit eternal life by good works done in a state of grace, or do the justified require an additional application of the mercy and justice of Christ?[59] This question corralled the few proponents of double justice into a limited way of responding: If they were to cling to their view, they would have to defend a "final" application of the justice of Christ—a *second* justice—to supplement an already inhering justice (good works or grace, depending upon the proponent)—a first justice.

The description of this imputation as "final" has frequently been cause for confusion. Since the formal cause was described as twofold, it has been tempting for many to think that according to the double justice theory regeneration and works precede the imputation of Christ's righteousness.[60] Such interpretations do not, in my opinion, accurately reflect the scope of Seripando's position taken as a whole. The phrase "final imputation" does not exclude a prior imputation; it only accentuates the *perpetual* inadequacy of inhering grace. The ultimate reason for this perpetual inadequacy, of course, is the persistence of concupiscence. Seripando, being a good Augustinian, did not believe (as some Scotists might have believed) that good works precede grace. He did not believe that the sinner has first to "do what is within him" (*facere quod in se est*) so that God consequently might grant justification and salvation by a final imputation of Christ's righteousness. Seripando was far from saying anything of the sort. He in fact emphasized, in Augustinian fashion, that every movement towards God depends upon a prior grace from God:

> For no other reason do we desire the first mercy of God (or prevenient grace) except that we, who are turned away from God through sins committed by our free and wicked will, are freely prepared and disposed, by God's awakening and assisting grace, towards our conversion, i.e., towards our justification through a good will.[61]

For Seripando, God's grace goes before (prevenes [the older translation being "prevents"]) the human response. He distinguished two meanings of the word "justification." There is St. Paul's "by faith without works," which emphasizes prevenient grace. There is St. James's "faith without works is dead," which emphasizes the subsequent human response. The scholarship on double justice frequently labels the "second justice" as the fresh application of divine mercy on account of Christ, and labels the "first justice" human works and sanctification. Seripando is not to be read so simply. He accepted St. Paul's use of "justification" as the primary sense of the word and St. James as the secondary sense of the word.[62] Paul spoke of the initial reception of justification, through faith apart from works, and James contended that the faith that avails must operate through charity. Seripando clearly held that God's grace precedes good human action. Moreover, he was not the only proponent of the theory of double justice, taken broadly, to uphold prevenient grace. The Catholics involved in the Regensburg accord—the thrust of which Seripando refined in his speeches at Trent—insisted that God first works in the sinner so that the sinner can subsequently cooperate. Regensburg and Seripando alike held the imputation to precede sanctification and works.[63]

As stated above, Seripando conceived of the justified as always encumbered by weakness and sin, so much so that good works—what he often understood by the phrase "inhering grace"—are insufficient to gain eternal life. Most of the council fathers conceived of "inhering grace" not as the sum of works but as a habit or stable disposition infused by God. For the fathers, the works that flow from inhering grace might be estimable in some cases and less than noteworthy in other cases, but in the end, the habit of grace itself qualifies the justified person as a child of God, and hence, as an heir entitled to reward. The fact that Seripando estimated works as insufficient does not imply that he evaluated the state of sanctifying grace itself as sufficient. Quite the opposite. Seripando considered the state of grace itself to be even less sufficient than sanctifying grace and good works combined.[64] Because many of the fathers conceived of inhering grace as a habit, and described that habit as sufficient, their rejection of double justice—which they read in light of their (mis)understanding—stands *a fortiori* as a condemnation of the view of double justice actually espoused by Seripando.[65]

The September Draft: "The One Justice of God"

Seripando—guided strictly by Cervini, who consulted the secretary Massarelli and several theologians—worked the August 29 draft into the September draft. The fine results of the collaboration and of the intense scrutiny of the text under construction were not to be denied. The archbishop of Palermo, representative of the majority, pronounced it "masterly and scholarly."[66] Chapter 7 of the September 23 draft reads:

> Therefore, the justice which is in us is called the justice of God because we receive it freely from God himself alone. It can also be called the justice of Christ because Christ himself alone merited that it be given us.... So there are not two justices which are given to us, that of God and that of Christ. There is one justice of God through Jesus Christ. (This justice is charity itself or grace). By this justice, we are not merely considered, but are named and are truly just.[67]

The draft was intended to delineate further the differences between Lutheran and Catholic thought.[68] In service of this end, the draft denies that there are two justices by which humans are justified. The teaching of double justice "was expressly rejected."[69]

Unfortunately, this effort to mitigate or exclude double justice was not without ambiguity. First, the "reduction" of the number of justices by which sinners are justified to the "one justice of God through Jesus Christ" could lend itself to a gross misinterpretation.[70] Whereas the intention was to exclude the need for a second justice in addition to inhering justice, the reader might mistakenly exclude inhering justice in favor of the imputed justice of Christ. Moreover, as Jedin notes, another sentence, describing Christ's grace as attributed or imputed to the sinner, could be taken in a Lutheran sense.[71] Pole, however, appeared wary that the decree (after he received it from a distance in October) sounded the rejection of his own position, as his hesitant criticisms betray.[72] He noted the incongruity between the sentence on "imputation" and the declaration "not two justices" but feared the latter proposed inhering justice as the essential factor in justification.[73] In any case, the condemnation of the statement "sinners are justified solely by the imputation of justice" did not exclude double justification.[74]

Pole was savvy to the intention behind the draft, which was evident from the context of the trajectory of the debates. The text itself adverts to reasons for the different expressions used with reference to justification, the "justice of God" and the "justice of Christ." It is called the "justice of God" because God gives it freely. It is called the "justice of Christ" because it is given on account of Christ's merits. The expression "justice of Christ" could be read as signifying Christ's own righteousness by which he gained merit for the world. In this respect, it is not identified with the justice by which the sinner is justified. Read in this light, the draft's insistence on "not two justices...[but] one" allows for only one formal cause of justification: inhering justice. Those who maintained two formal causes likely understood the draft to exclude their position, for they did not take kindly to this phrase.[75] Nonetheless, for the aforesaid reasons, it was clear that precision was needed; the debates intensified.

The October Debates

Seripando would renounce the September 23 draft in his famous October 8 vote, but most of the fathers concurred with the draft's intended aim: to reject double justice. One of the more important points made against double justice was a critique of the novel notion of an "imputation" of Christ's justice as something *distinct from*, albeit not separate from, an actual communication of that justice. Seripando's August 29 draft included the expression that the most pure justice of Christ, head of his body, "is communicated through faith and the sacraments." Yet, this "communication" through faith was simply juxtaposed to the "grace or charity" actually infused into human hearts. The draft clearly distinguished the "communication and application" of Christ's justice from the infusion of grace.[76] One of the only remaining traces of Seripando's theory of double justice in the September 23 draft read, "For [Christ's] justice is in like manner communicated and imputed to us, when we are justified...."[77] This anomalous sentence, not unfavorable to double justice, was criticized. The archbishop of Aix, Antoine Filheul, argued for an assertion of the identity of the "communication and application" of Christ's justice with the infusion of grace, so that the former could not be seen as implying that the human person is righteous by a righteousness distinct from that which is infused into him.[78] Philos Roverella, bishop of Ascoli, echoed Filheul; the argument won favor.[79] The suggestion was retained in the final decree, which specifies that the merits of Christ are communicated through the infusion of the love of God: "For though no one can be just unless the merits of the passion of our lord Jesus Christ are communicated to him; nevertheless, in the justification of a sinner this in fact takes place when, by the merit of the same most holy passion, the love of God is poured out by the agency of the holy Spirit in the hearts of those who are being justified, and abides in them."[80]

Presentations were then made by two men whom Cervini consulted for the September draft: the bishop of Bitonto, Cornelio Musso; and Bonaventura Costacciaro, superior general of the Conventuals. Costacciaro offered a lengthy speech on October 7, clearly delineating the proper and improper ways of attributing justification to the divine imputation. He argued that God actively establishes a covenant with us and that in this sense we are justified actively by "imputed justice"; God shares Christ's merits out to us and in this sense we are justified passively by "imputed justice."[81] Still, in neither sense are we formally justified by an "imputed justice." Just as Christ is named just and is just by only one justice, the sanctifying grace that inheres in him, so we are justified by only one justice, the sanctifying grace that inheres in us.[82]

In response to these and like suggestions, Seripando resolutely drew attention to the seriousness of the question for the human person confronted with sin and anticipating judgment.[83] Echoing the anomalous line in the September draft, he argued that Christ's justice becomes that of the justified person not by informing him but by being communicated through the sacraments.[84] Further, he referred in his defense to the work of such "eminent writers" as Cervini, Cajetan, and Gropper.[85] "Should these be lumped together with the heretics?" he asked. Certainly, Cervini and Gropper had espoused a view of justification like his own. Rightly cautious, Seripando never attributed double justice to Cajetan's thought, but he did look for support from Cajetan's work on the mystical body of Christ and on justifying faith.[86] Seripando appears to have understood Cajetan to teach something proximate to double justice, but his reading of Cajetan leaves much to be desired.[87] Cajetan (Thomas de Vio) accepted Thomas Aquinas's opinion that the formal cause of justification was sanctifying grace, without which there could be no forgiveness.[88] Faith is "justifying," for Cajetan, only insofar as it is informed by charity.[89] Consequently, Seripando's understanding of the mystical body as constituted through a "communication" of Christ's merits that is distinct from the infusion of grace did not match Cajetan's Thomistic conception, according to which the "communication" of Christ's merits through baptism is the very infusion of sanctifying grace.

Perhaps Seripando's greatest complaint was that some of the fathers were misreading Paul. According to Seripando, Paul's proclamation of the gift of divine love through the Holy Spirit (Rom 5:5) signifies not an inhering form, sanctifying grace, but the Holy Spirit himself as loving the sinner.[90] Hence, he wished the phrase "and inheres in them" be removed. The September draft appeared to Seripando to take everything away from the imputation of Christ's justice, without any warrant from the patristic witness.[91] On this point, however, Seripando did not follow the genuine Augustinian doctrine. Augustine fought Pelagius on the source of grace and the beginning of all work. With these, Seripando rightly agreed. But, as we have seen in chapter 1, the Doctor of Grace did not conclude to a notion of "imputed justice" understood as distinct from the divine transformation of the sinner into a righteous son. Nor did he identify the Holy Spirit as the very "charity" by which humans love God and by which they are just.[92]

Seripando was clearly disappointed by the September draft. Pole, who wrote to Seripando to express his complaints about the draft, was dejected. Pole held that Christ's own justice was the "essential" part of justification and that no justified person could fulfill the whole law.[93]

In appealing to a supplementary imputation, Seripando implied a formally forensic notion of forgiveness whereby sins are "not reckoned" to one's account. Bishop Gregorio Castagnola took issue with such a notion:

> We say that peace [with God] consists in the love of God by which he loves us. On the part of the act of God this love is eternal and immutable. But on the part of its effect which is worked in us, it is at times disrupted as happens when through sin we are alienated from God and through grace are led back to him again. Now the effect of divine [love] in us, which is destroyed by sin, is nothing other than the grace by which man is made worthy of eternal life. Since mortal sins exclude one from this life, it follows that for the remission of sins, the infusion of grace is required.[94]

Bishop Castagnola held that a sinner is not admissible to eternal life until his fallen nature is healed. Such change can occur only through the infusion of grace. Thus, transformation through grace is not, as per double justice, simply a gift concomitant with forensic forgiveness.

For the majority, to uphold infused grace does not take anything away from Christ's own justice. Christ's own justice is the meritorious basis for infusion in the first place. Moreover, Christ's own justice is the font from which humans receive their share of justice. A proper conception of the mystical body appears to have been of decisive importance. A number of speakers wished to express the inseparable connection between the justice of Christ, which inheres in Christ himself, and that which is truly communicated to the human person in justification, that which inheres in the justified. Vicente de Leone, a Sicilian Carmelite theologian, stated:

> Therefore, since inhering justice is not alien to the justice of Christ from which it flows and on which it depends, though it is proper to the justified, it follows that those who, having retained inhering justice, present themselves before the judgment seat of Christ have no need of a new and special application of Christ's justice.[95]

This articulation helped deflect any charge that to ascribe sufficiency to infused grace necessarily detracts from Christ's proper role.

This effort to draw an inseparable connection between Christ and the justified was effective. The archbishop of Toledo, Bartolomeo Carranza de Miranda, O.P., connected the notion of the mystical body of Christ to the formal cause.[96] Miranda was one of several who focused on the mystical body. He compared the relationship between inhering justice and Christ's justice to that between branches and a vine, small brooks and a spring, or illuminated air and the sun:

> The air is illuminated by the sun, yet it is not formally lit by the light of the sun, but by the light existing in itself which is caused by the light from the sun. So thus, we are justified by Christ effectively and meritoriously, but we are not just formally by the justice which is in Christ, but by that which is in us, in which we have partaken from Christ and which depends on Christ constantly.[97]

Miranda's speech was theologically exquisite. He affirmed only one justice by which the justified are "formally just," and yet recognized that this is caused by the justice of Christ, so that one can say Christ's justice justifies sinners "effectively and meritoriously."[98] The importance of emphasizing the distinction between the "formal" and "meritorious and effective" justices is not slight. To make the distinction allowed Miranda properly to predicate degrees of sanctity and corresponding degrees of glory to the saints.[99] Miranda showed delicate touch, though, in continually calling to mind the close association of the justified with Christ: As living members of Christ and only as his members, the justified can "truly satisfy" the divine demands.[100] Finally, in light of the importance of these distinctions and of the singularity of the formal cause of justice, Miranda proposed his opinion that the souls of the just in purgatory do not receive a supplemental application of Christ's justice. Rather, their defects of body and soul are really changed so as to make these just persons fit for heaven; their venial sins are destroyed by charity, which is opposed to sin; and their outstanding punishment is satisfied through the pains of purgatory.[101] Though later accused of (but not condemned for) heresy, Miranda clung to these important elements in his *Commentary on the Christian Catechism*. He underscored the justified person's bridal union with Christ.[102]

The final decree does reflect to a certain extent the primary importance of the justified person's integration into Christ's body through faith, hope, and charity. This comes to expression through the metaphor of the vine and the branches and in the language of (living) membership in the body of Christ. Still, one can regret, with French theologian Paul Pas, that more doctrinal attention was not placed on the mystical body of Christ until Pius XII.[103] Jedin contrasts the Protestant theory of imputation with the Catholic tradition, expressed in the final decree, that sanctifying grace, or inhering justice, "precisely brings about that ontological union with Christ—that communion between Head and members—which makes it possible for us to be acknowledged as God's children and renders works done in a state of grace meritorious, in spite of their imperfection."[104] To assert the need for something besides this inhering grace is to threaten, in the end, the proper sense of merit and the really cleansing character of baptismal grace, already defined in the Fifth Session.[105]

The importance of this unity in distinction, so deep in Catholic thought, cannot be overestimated. The October debates were heated because of the subtlety of the issue. In a sense, one could say that the human person is justified both by inhering justice and by the righteousness of Christ. But it seemed to most that the meanings of each prepositional phrase (by X and by Y) had to differ. For most of the fathers, that which is the gratuitous reason for justification—the meritorious cause—is the righteousness of Christ: "By his stripes we were healed" (Is 53:5). But that which constitutes justification—that by which the sinner is *made just*—is inhering justice. The key issue at stake, in the fathers' eyes, was not the sinner's absolute need for Christ's merits but the identity of the reality by which one stands just before God. The key issue in dispute was the formal cause, not the meritorious cause.

The Emergent Doctrine: "The Only Formal Cause"

The draft of October 31 introduced more precise terminology, drawing upon the scholastic distinctions of "causes" that together can explain more thoroughly the mystery of justification.[106] The draft noted that there are three elements simultaneously constitutive of justification: absolution from sins, sanctification, and infusion of gifts. The draft then proceeded to identify and distinguish the various "causes" of justification. Most importantly, the draft attempted to define the formal cause, the very nature of justification. The draft reads, "The formal cause is the one justice of God by which we are renewed in the spirit of our mind and are not merely reckoned but are named and are truly just."[107] This statement was intended to define Catholic orthodoxy against the novel theory of double justice. The formal cause was specified as the one justice of God poured into the hearts of those whom God justifies. But no explicit affirmation of the singularity of the formal cause appeared in this draft. As McGrath remarks, "Seripando's position could still be accommodated without difficulty if it were conceded that there was more than one formal cause of justification."[108] The fathers continued to push for greater clarity.

On November 23, Claude Le Jay suggested that the "one" in "the one justice of God" should rather modify "formal cause," clearly limiting the latter to one.[109] The council fathers followed Le Jay's suggestion. Moreover, a new version of the chapter on the "causes" of justification was proposed for examination on December 11, replacing "una" (one) with "unica" (only).[110] The draft reads:

> Finally, the only formal cause is that justice of God, not by which he himself is just, but by which he makes us just in his sight. This justice is given by God, and, by it, we are renewed in the spirit of our minds. We are not merely considered but are truly named and are just, each one of us receiving his own justice according to the measure that the Holy Spirit wills to impart to each and according to the distinct dispositions and cooperation of each.[111]

One of the fathers noted that the change from "una" to "unica" was made "that it might be shown that the justice by which we are formally justified is one."[112] This draft made it absolutely clear that there is only one formal cause of justification: This is not the justice of God himself but rather the justice imparted to the sinner, making him to be truly just.[113] In other words, the formal cause was defined as inhering grace, freely and divinely infused through the merits of Christ, provided the human person freely accepts God's mercy with the help of prevenient grace. The above formulation was retained practically word for word in chapter 7 of the final, binding decree. Not the justice of the Incarnate Son, not the justice of the triune God, but that which is infused into and inheres in the human person is the only formal cause of justification.

In one of the most significant studies on this issue at Trent, attentive to the Acta, Anton Prumbs showed that, on the one hand, the fathers did not decide the legitimate differences held in dispute between the schools of Catholic theologians (Thomists and Scotists, etc.), and that, on the other hand, the bishops "with one voice [*einhellig*]" excluded the notion that Christ or the indwelling Holy Spirit constitutes the formal cause of justification. He wrote, "[The formal cause] cannot be the 'uncreated grace,' but rather the habit of grace or justice, that is created by God and infused into the human soul through the Holy Spirit, the grace inhering in the soul."[114] Whereas the Reformers held justification to obtain equally among all of the justified, the bishops at Trent held justifying grace to be distributed in different degrees and to be capable of increase. What was not decided at Trent was *not* whether or not the Reformers were condemned but rather whether or not the formal cause could be strictly identified with charity itself (as with the Scotists) or with grace conceived of as a principle of charity that is really distinct, albeit inseparable, from charity (as with the Thomists).[115] Hefner's study, as can be seen in citations above and in those to follow, supports this reading.[116] Michael Schmaus, uncommonly ecumenical for his time, wrote, "The justice found in man, created by God and mirroring the divine justice, is the formal cause, not the efficient cause, of man's justification. This is so because the relation between the justice of God and that of man is one of analogy, not of identity."[117] More recently, Carl Peter stated unequivocally in the American dialogue that the formal cause of justification is the created grace given by God.[118] German theologian Leo Cardinal Scheffczyk is in agreement with this reading:

> Without needing to use the terms "quality" or "habit" to signify sanctifying grace, the council indeed clearly conveys this by its conviction that man is justified "through grace and love," which "are infused through the Holy Spirit" (DS 1561). By these expressions the Person of the Holy Spirit is clearly distinguished from the gift of grace, which inheres in man.[119]

This justifying grace, Scheffczyk contends, is simply created grace. German theologian Manfred Hauke agrees:

> Here [i.e., in this teaching on the formal cause] we find in a straightforward way a passage about that which the theology of grace calls *gratia creata*, "created grace," which renews man inwardly and which can increase and decrease in him. Created grace is to be distinguished from the *gratia increata*, "uncreated grace," which is the triune God himself, who dwells in the blessed as the giver of all grace.[120]

It is indeed an ecclesiastically sound position to hold that justifying grace, the single formal cause of justification, is created.[121] The language of Trent implies it, and the overwhelming evidence of tradition affirms it. It is erroneous for Catholics to deny that justifying grace involves created grace. It has appeared speculatively admissible to some respected theologians, however, to include uncreated grace, namely, the indwelling of the Spirit, in the overall, concrete state of adoptive filiation by which the human person is not only justified but also inducted into participation of the eternal relations of God's triune life. Of these, Matthias Joseph Scheeben (1835–1888) is especially worthy of note.[122] He did not exclude created grace from the state of grace; nor did he intend to think of created grace as inadequate for the expulsion of sins, requiring supplementation by a forensic acquittal, a là double justice. He recognized that the tridentine teaching on the formal cause excluded that opinion as well as the more extreme opinion that justification is purely forensic.[123] Indeed, he acknowledged that created grace *is* the single formal cause of justification itself, if justification is conceived strictly as the process of making man righteous in his being.[124] Notwithstanding this, he further argued that God has ordained the human person not simply to be just in a supernatural sense but also to be an adopted child of the Father. Accordingly he rightly recognized that the tridentine teaching, as well as the ongoing mind of the Church, did not exclude speculation on the role of the Spirit as integral to the *filial state* of the justified persons.[125] Against his interlocutor Granderath, Scheeben perceived himself not as downplaying the significance of created grace but as upholding it, for, he held, created grace forms the necessary disposition for the human person to be made a temple of the Spirit and child of God.[126] Scheeben took special care not to allow his affirmation of uncreated grace to be taken as promotion of the notion that the created gift infused into the human soul does not truly please God unless its defects are supplemented by the reckoning of God's mercy.[127]

As far as its authority goes, the definition in chapter 7 on the one formal cause is to be considered a permanent patrimony of the Catholic Church.[128] It would be erroneous to limit the binding elements of the tridentine decree to the canons.[129] Twice, the decree presents its positive teachings as binding on the faithful. At the beginning, the decree proclaims:

> Its intention is to set out for all the christian faithful the true and sound doctrine on justification which the sun of justice, Jesus Christ, pioneer and perfecter of our faith, taught, the apostles handed down, and the catholic church under the prompting of the holy Spirit has always retained. This it does by imposing a strict check on anyone who dares to believe, preach or teach otherwise than is defined and declared in the present decree.[130]

At the end of the positive teachings, the decree describes the chapters that present the Catholic teaching as something that must be firmly held; the canons add what must be rejected: "After this Catholic teaching on justification, which, unless one faithfully and firmly receives it, he cannot be justified, it pleased the holy synod to attach these canons, so that all may know not only what they must hold and follow but also what they must shun and flee."[131] This is not to say that every definitive teaching in Trent is expressly held to be revealed truth, i.e., to be "of divine and catholic faith." It is to say, however, that Trent used not merely canons, but also chapters, as vehicles of definitive or infallible teachings.[132]

Attesting to the Church's acceptance of these teachings as definitive, the profession of faith imposed upon all the participants of the First Vatican Council demanded fidelity to Trent's teachings on original sin and justification. This fidelity was demanded not simply for those teachings expressed in canons but to "each and every declared and defined" teaching.[133] The more recent 1989 Profession of Faith also demands of the theologian adherence to "each and every [*omnia et singula*]" definitive teaching of the Church. The Holy Father has recently added canonical penalties for those who refuse obedience to those matters that do not belong (or are not yet recognized to belong) to the deposit of faith but simply "relate" to it (*pertinens ad fidem*).[134] These are the definitive teachings of the Church which must be held firmly and definitively.

I find instructive the examples of definitive teaching the CDF offers in its "Commentary on the Profession of Faith's Concluding Paragraphs."[135] The

CDF refers to the Christological dogma of Chalcedon (DS 301–02), Trent's teaching on the real presence of Christ in the Eucharist (DS 1636), Trent's teaching on the sacrificial character of Mass (DS 1740 and 1743), Vatican I's reaffirmation that Christ founded the Church (DS 3050), and Benedict XII's definition of the immortality of the soul and the bestowal of the divine vision upon saints immediately after death (DS 1000–02). The CDF refers the reader, in the examples I have listed, to chapters, not to canons. These references bespeak the following: The Church can define a matter of faith without explicitly condemning "the" opposite heresy. After all, the errors opposed to truth are legion, yet faith has its positive content. Granted, some of the teachings I have listed from the CDF's document are also accompanied by canons, to which the CDF does not refer. However, not all are accompanied by explicit condemnations.[136] Theologians are to recognize that the doctrinal decisions of the Council of Trent, prompted by the Holy Spirit, remain binding for Catholics for the ages to come. In light of the positive teachings of Trent, the theologian can conclude that double justice and, *a fortiori*, traditional Lutheran teaching are proscribed by implication. In furtherance of this conclusion, a close examination of two critical canons reveals even more clearly the incompatibility between Catholic faith and the theory of double justice as well as key elements of traditional Lutheran teachings.

Correlative Condemnations

Two key canons act in concert as a pair of "shears." Together, they specify the identity of the grace by which the justified stands just before God. Canon 11 maintains the reality of inhering grace, a gift infused through the Holy Spirit, as a necessary component of justification: Men are not justified solely by the favor of God. Canon 10 maintains both that sinners cannot be justified except on account of the merits of Jesus Christ and also that sinners are not justified formally by Christ's own justice. Together, these two canons exclude from Catholic faith opinions that do not identify the formal cause of justification as the sanctifying gift of grace and/or charity, bestowed by God, that inheres in the human person.

Canon 11

The doctrinal affirmation in chapter 7 proscribes double justice by implication but is not framed as a condemnation.[137] As late as December 11, there was no canon even implicitly against double justice itself. The closest candidate was that which became canon 11 of the final decree, a canon that Seripando himself helped formulate. Canon 11 reads:

> If anyone says that men are justified either by the imputation of the justice of Christ alone or by the remission of sins alone, to the exclusion of grace and charity which are poured forth through the Holy Spirit into their hearts and which inhere in them, or even that the grace by which we are justified is only the favor of God, let him be anathema.[138]

Taken in isolation from chapter 7 of the final decree, canon 11 can be seen as allowing for Seripando's theory of a twofold formal cause. Perhaps for this reason, McGrath opines that the canon also allows for the Reformers' doctrines: "The canon does not censure any magisterial Protestant account of *justificatio hominis* [the justification of man]."[139] McGrath argues that since Lutherans do not deny renewal in the overall redemptive process (in the "*esse* of Christian existence"), they are not touched by canon 11. The astute Chemnitz, similarly, complained that canon 11 appeared to be a "sidelong thrust" against Lutheranism, mischievously caricaturing the position as utterly denying any sanctification in the process of redemption. Notwithstanding this observation, Chemnitz rightly recognized that canon 11 did strike at Lutheran doctrine since the gifts of sanctification do not, according to him, form any part whatsoever of the justice by which Christians are saved.[140]

Contrary to McGrath's contention, canon 11 refers not to redemption as a whole but to justification proper. Lutherans exclude works and inhering grace from justification proper, though they acknowledge the reality of a logically subsequent sanctification.[141] Double justice, on the other hand, includes inhering justice as one of the formal causes of justification and salvation, however slight its contribution might be. Seripando's canon condemns the Lutheran exclusion of inhering righteousness from justification proper. Why else was Pole so averse to Seripando's formulation, which was otherwise so conciliatory? Pole could not accept the implication of the condemnation: that justification involves at least an inhering righteousness. Both Pole (at the time) and the Lutheran confessional documents rejected formulations resembling Seripando's. The *Epitome* rejected two propositions resembling double justice, thus condemning even canon 11. One statement reads:

> We reject and condemn all the following errors.... That believers are justified before God and saved both by the righteousness of Christ reckoned to them and by the incipient new obedience, or in part by the reckoning to them of Christ's righteousness and in part by our incipient new obedience.[142]

The conclusion that canon 11 does not "touch" the traditional Lutheran position is not tenable. The real thrust of canon 11 is to affirm that justifying righteousness itself is constituted, at least in part, by the gift of grace infused through the Holy Spirit on account of the merits of Christ. Lutherans do not deny the presence of such a gift in the human person, though they formulate their understanding of it in a much different way than Catholics do. Still, the Lutheran confessional documents exclude any opinion that would "include" in justifying righteousness the gifts that God infuses into the forgiven sinner. Canon 11 excludes not Seripando's position but the Lutheran position; more importantly, it expresses something vitally important for Catholic faith: the inhering nature of justifying righteousness. Working in concert with this condemnation, canon 10 explicitly proscribes the notion that Christ's righteousness formally justifies the sinner. The inhering righteousness affirmed in canon 11, therefore, constitutes the sole formal cause of justification.

Canon 10

The fathers were asked, on December 6, if they were satisfied with the condemnation of justification solely by an imputation of Christ's righteousness. Correlatively, they were asked if it was sufficiently clear that faith is not the justice by which the believer is justified.[143] Fourteen out of twenty-four fathers, evidently not content to rest simply with Seripando's formulation in what became canon 11, voted in favor of a stronger and clearer condemnation.[144]

The newly proposed condemnation took time to develop.[145] Jedin relates that the discussions in this period were limited to bishops with extensive theological training; they were to hammer out certain intricacies carefully before returning a draft to the plenary session.[146] Early in the discussion, Pedro Cardinal Pacheco, bishop of Jaen, specified that, although justification solely by imputation had been sufficiently condemned already, the theory of double justice had not been sufficiently proscribed.[147] The fathers turned their attention to related issues before returning to a condemnation of imputed justice. It was within this context, several days after the aforesaid vote and after Pacheco's statement, that there occurred the change from "the one formal cause [*una causa formalis*]" to "the only formal cause [*unica formalis causa*]."[148]

Discussion of the change from *una* to *unica* was then quickly followed by reactions to a significant addition to chapter 16, first proposed on December 14.[149] The December 14 draft affirmed, "For the justice of God and our justice through Jesus Christ, by which (justice) we are justified, is one: (it is called) 'God's' because it is by God; 'ours' because it is in us; 'Christ's' because it is through Christ."[150] In the discussion of the newly proposed chapter, Philos Roverella, bishop of Ascoli, expressed his desire for a condemnation of the necessity of a "new" or "second" imputation of justice for those who would gain heaven.[151] The suggestion was relevant because chapter 16 centered around the issue of merit; the bishops were debating whether or not the justifying grace and good works of the faithful departed sufficed for admittance into the kingdom of God. Interestingly, Tommaso Campeggio, bishop of Feltre, wanted to *remove* the following statement from chapter 16: "One is the justice of God and our justice." He wanted to do so, not in order to protect double justice, but in order to preserve the *distinctions* between these God's own justice and that which is in the justified person.[152] The intent behind this suggestion was perhaps better served by the suggestion of Coriolano Martirano, bishop of San Marco. Martirano noted that the phrase "[it is called] ours because it is in us" alludes—by way of opposition—to the theory of imputed justice. He desired that this allusion be made more explicit by the addition of the term "inhering justice."[153] Luigi Lippomani, coadjutor of Verona, desired to specify that the reason the justice is "through Christ" is that the justice is given to humans in virtue of Christ's merits.[154] Francesco Romeo da Castiglione, superior general of the Dominicans, wanted the phrase "by which we are justified [*qua iustificamur*]" moved closer to the words "the justice of God is one [*una est iustitia Dei*]."[155] According to the Acta, the final formulation of canon 10 appeared one day after this congregation on chapter 16, but, as the editor observantly notes, subsequent debate shows that it is unlikely that the final formulation appeared this early.[156] In any case, there is little doubt that some attempt at a new condemnation of imputed justice appeared in this context. The discussion of canon 10 witnesses to the connection between the new condemnation, the issues in chapter 16, and the theory of "double justice."

Bracccio Martelli, bishop of Fiesole, suggested a more rigorous condemnation of imputed justice, either in canon 32—a canon defending the power of works done in grace to "truly merit" everlasting life—or in the newly proposed canon. In either case it should be made clear, he contended, that the faithful departed have no need for a further imputation of Christ's justice.[157] Dispute again broke out about the number of justices by which a person is formally justified. Although indeed only one justice inheres in the human person, still, this justice flows from that of Christ. This fact of faith raised the following question: Is a person justified formally by one or by two justices?[158] The Dominican Thomas Casellus, bishop of Bertinoro, argued that only inhering justice formally justifies but that both the justice of Christ and inhering justice are "essentially" involved, in order that sinners be justified.[159] Inhering justice, he held, is given on account of (*propter*) the justice of Christ. The basic line of thought among the fathers was clear: Both the justice of Christ and inhering justice are necessary in the process. The emerging opinion linked the justice of Christ with merit and linked inhering justice with the formal cause.[160] The debates manifested, in addition, the desire of some to express the "organic" relation between inhering justice (the formal cause of justification) and the justice of Christ from which it flows.[161] This relation is expressed in the final decree by the twin metaphors of "body and member" and "vine and branches," found in chapter 7, chapter 16, and canon 32.

The council fathers then proceeded to address the issue of the Pauline phrase "justification by faith." They arrived at a basic agreement that Paul cannot be understood as saying that sinners are justified by faith alone but ought rather be understood as saying that faith is the beginning of the process. After intervening discussions on issues such as the certitude of grace and the final cause of justification, the fathers returned to the proposed addition to chapter 16 in early January. On January 5, Cardinal Cervini proposed the following in its place: "[This justice] *is called ours because we are justified by it inhering in us; it is that same justice of God because it is infused into us by God through the merit of Christ.*"[162] Robert Wauchop, archbishop of Armagh, concurred but suggested including the word "formaliter."[163] Cervini's formulation was more favorable to the fathers. He hit the matter squarely: "It is called ours because we are justified by it inhering in us." Given Cervini's unambiguous formulation, the technical term *formaliter* in this location would have been redundant. Cervini's emendation of this sentence in chapter 16 evoked the very teaching on the "only formal cause" already in place in chapter 7. The final formulation, taken almost verbatim from Cervini's intervention, expresses the Catholic belief that saving justice is described as "ours" because it justifies us by inhering in us.[164] Saving justice is "God's" because he infuses it, efficiently causing justification. It is "Christ's" because it is bestowed on account of Christ's merits. These formulations made precise the distinctions between the various "causes" of justification, articulated in chapter 7.

After the change to chapter 16 was seen to be acceptable, attention turned to the canons. At this point, there emerged a suggested reformulation of canon 10. The day's discussion concluded with this suggestion. On the next day, January 6, the discussion of canon 10 resumed, and the fathers quickly finalized the wording.[165] It becomes clear that the clarifications added to chapter 16 were intimately related with the revised formulation of canon 10. Cardinal Cervini desired greater precision in the new canon, because the proposal "could be taken as [allowing for] double justice."[166] Cervini's concern mirrored that of Francesco Romeo da Castiglione, who wrote to him that the canon could even be taken in a Lutheran sense. The General suggested that the canon ought explicitly to distinguish the justice of Christ from the justice formally existing in the justified.[167] Canon 10 appeared in its final form on that same day. Canon 10 reads, "If anyone says that men are justified without the justice of Christ, by which he merited [justification] for us, *or that they are formally just by that very justice: let him be anathema.*"[168]

The canon is divided into two parts, each of which refers to Christ's justice. The first part condemns those who deny that Christ's justice is the meritorious cause of justification. The second part condemns those who hold Christ's *own* (*eam ipsam*) justice to be that by which one is formally just.[169] The second part proscribes the various errors contrary to the affirmation in chapter 7 on the "only formal cause." This canon complements the condemnation, in canon 11, of a purely forensic conception of justifying righteousness—Christ's righteousness as the "sole" formal cause. Canon 11 is not rendered redundant by canon 10 since canon 11 also affirms the necessity of upholding the *infused* nature of justifying righteousness. Canon 10 does not mention inhering righteousness but excludes the idea that Christ's own righteousness constitutes the believer's justifying righteousness, either in whole or in part. One cannot hold, therefore, that Christ's righteousness is even one of two formal causes of justification. The only formal cause is thereby delimited to the justice of God, distinct from but dependent upon God's own justice, infused into the believer on account of Christ's merits. Canons 10 and 11 together form "shears" by which justifying righteous is held both to include inhering righteous and also not to include Christ's own righteousness.[170] In conclusion, chapters 7 and 16, as well as canons 10 and 11, define that Christ's own justice is neither the sole formal cause nor one of two formal causes of justification.

Despite the importance of canon 10, many scholarly and ecumenical works inexplicably neglect it.[171] Very few see this canon for what it is.[172] Instead, most scholars turn to the *prima facie* weaker canon 11, only to deny that it condemns the Lutheran position. Certainly, the council often rejected related teachings of varying degrees of error. For example, canons 1, 2, and 3 are rejections of both Pelagianism and semi-Pelagianism. Canon 1 is aimed at those who exclude any need for the grace of Christ whatsoever, except in the sense that Christ gives the law. Perhaps this canon condemns Pelagius's doctrine, but it does not condemn that of semi-Pelagians, who admit the need for the help of Christ's grace to obey the commandments. Canon 2 condemns those who claim that Christ's grace only assists the sinner to convert and obey the commandments. Canon 3 strikes more rigorously and maintains that even the first movements of a sinner towards God depend upon the prevenient grace of the Holy Spirit. The "less rigorous" condemnations (i.e., those in canons 1 and 2) are not intended to "excuse" the errors that are condemned only by the more rigorous one (i.e., canon 3). If one were to read only canon 1 and then laud those who maintain that all sinners somehow need the grace of Christ, one would miss the precision of canon 3. The contemporary scholarly scene neglects the precision of canon 10, which is the bottom half of the shears by which both double justice and Lutheran doctrine are neatly excluded from the legitimate diversity to which Catholic faith is open.[173]

The Omission of the Term "Habit"

Some contemporary scholars also consider it doctrinally significant that the traditional scholastic term "habit" or "quality" (*habitus*) does not appear in the final decree as a description of justifying grace. These scholars then conclude that the "reality" to which the term "habit of grace" refers is not a matter of Catholic doctrine. Scholastic theologians used the term "habit" to refer to the stable and inhering character of the supernatural life, or justifying grace, continually bestowed on the justified by God, yet distinct from the essence of the justified. The fathers at Trent avoided, when possible, imposing scholastic terminology. In this case, they ultimately elected not to include the term "habit."

Gérard Philips

Gérard Philips, among others, argues that the omission of the terms "habit," "quality," and "created grace" shows definitively that Trent did not define justifying righteousness as something created that inheres in the human soul.[174] Philips appears to bypass the key phrase in chapter 7, "not that by which he himself is just," and focuses instead on the omission of the technical terms. He cites the following, poor translation of the important statement in chapter 16: "That which we call our *justice*—because by its inhering in us we are justified—is the same as the *justice of God* because it is infused into us through the merit of Christ."[175] He notes that "merit" attaches to Christ and that the terms "habit" and "accident" do not appear; he concludes that the council is here speaking of the uncreated grace of God. Pace Philips, I maintain that the omission of this term does not signify Trent's refusal to define justifying righteousness as that which scholastics refer to as an infused habit of grace.

It should be noted, first of all, that Philips's translation is inaccurate; it should read, "The justice of God...[is] called ours because we are justified by it inhering in us; it is the same justice of God because it is infused into us *by God* through the merit of Christ" (emphasis mine).[176] This is the justice of God because it is infused "by God." Philips's translation merely employs the passive voice, "it is infused," obscuring the reason for calling this justice the "justice of God," namely, that God infuses it. His conclusion, that this is the very justice by which God is just, does not accurately reflect the mind of the council, as I have shown from my study of the Acta. There was no need, in chapter 16, to repeat the technical terms for cause that appeared in chapter 7; as the Acta show, Cervini clarified the three ways in which the same justice could be called by different names: "God's" because it is infused by Him, "Christ's" because it given on account of his merit; "ours" because we are justified by it inhering in us. Had Philips paid greater attention to the Latin and to the Acta, he would have little reason for his conclusion. Moreover, his conclusion is difficult to maintain theologically, given the set of characteristics attributed to justifying righteousness in the decree. It is clear that Christ's grace cannot increase, nor can the uncreated grace increase. However, the very grace received in justification is said to be given unequally and is said to "increase." Philips even notes these characteristics of justifying grace. Do these characteristics not require an appeal to created grace as constitutive of the state of grace, even if in that state is included, as necessary correlate, the indwelling of the Holy Spirit? Still, he draws the tenuous conclusion that chapter 16 speaks simply of the uncreated justice. Paul O'Callaghan, regretfully, follows Philips's assessment.

Otto Hermann Pesch

Otto Hermann Pesch offers some inconclusive reflections on canons 10 and 11.[177] His reflections on canon 11 largely echo those of McGrath, so I refer the reader to my comments on McGrath's reading of that canon. Methodologically, he appears to limit the reach of these canons to the works of those thinkers that came to the explicit attention of the council fathers. Although Luther appears to be the target of canons 10 and 11, Trent missed the mark:

> *Formaliter*, as understood by the fathers of Trent, blocks in any case an understanding of that which Luther thought. The fathers, in case they knew Luther's statements at least by hearsay, considered them in terms of the conceptuality of scholasticism. As a comparison with chapter 7 (Dz 1529; ND 1932) shows, the cited formula then becomes nonsense.[178]

He defends this conclusion by appeal to Luther's doctrines of the "joyous exchange" and of the distinction in union between "grace and gift."[179] As shall be made clear in the course of chapter 10, Luther's notion of the "joyous exchange" was a soteriological articulation of his theory of the communication of idioms. His theory of the communication of idioms was not in harmony with Chalcedonian doctrine. Moreover, his distinction between gift and grace, most evident in his 1521 work against Latomus, clearly attests to a substantive conflict with Trent, as will be shown in chapter 7. On what basis can Pesch conclude that *"substantively* Luther is not struck"? He contends that what was of chief concern for Trent was not missing in Luther: "Neither the newly creative power of justifying grace, nor the ethical effect, and most definitively not the decisive and strict connection between the event of justification and the saving action of God in Christ."[180] Why, we may wonder, was Cardinal Pole so worried? Why was Seripando distraught by the Decree on Original Sin? Why did both wish to avoid the definition of the formal cause as a singular, infused justice? The reader is more perplexed when Pesch writes, only one page later, "In short: we have here for the first time a genuine occasion to ask the fourth question," i.e., we here encounter a real contradiction, which makes us ask whether it still applies.[181] In a significant explanatory note, Pesch leans on the scholarship of Pfnür, insisting that Luther reacted merely against the nominalist Pelagianism of late scholasticism. He hints that Seripando's attempt to caution the fathers against excessive optimism about God's sanctifying work would have sufficed, had it been heeded, to win back open-minded Lutherans.[182] But the reader will remember that Pole took even Seripando's canon 11 as an assault upon his own opinion and that Seripando felt the pinch when he humbly acquiesced not only to chapter 7 but also to canon 10. Neither Pfnür's scholarship, owing to its manifest weaknesses, nor Pesch's argument, burdened with its ambiguities, are convincing. Granted, Pesch rightly holds that the proper way to adjudicate divergent claims stemming from divergent systems of thought is to appeal to the reality under dispute.[183] Although he does not seem to follow this principle out, we can conclude from the principle that the partners in dialogue ought to let the characteristics organically associated with each doctrinal position tell the story. Chapter 9 of my work undertakes this task.

Alister McGrath

The Claim. McGrath, more venturous than Philips and clearer than Pesch, argues that by the omission of the term "habit" as a description of justifying grace Trent has left open the question of "whether the formal cause of justification was an intrinsic created habit of grace or the extrinsic denomination of the divine acceptation."[184] He links this claim to the observation, in itself legitimate, that the intra-scholastic debates between Thomists and Scotists about this matter were not decided by the conciliar decree. McGrath's claims about Trent's indecision can be criticized on at least four counts: the nature of the intra-scholastic disputes, the trajectory of the conciliar debates, the overall thrust of the final decree, and the post-tridentine interpretations of this decree.

Criticism: Intra-Scholastic Disputes. First, the intra-scholastic debates about justifying grace, to which McGrath alludes,[185] do not warrant the conclusion that the Protestant account of justification is not proscribed at Trent. William of Ockham (1285–1347) and John Duns Scotus (1265–1308), both scholastics, held that absolutely speaking God is not bound to justify any person through the infusion of an intrinsic habit. Rather, God can justify simply through an extrinsic acquittal. Both Ockham and Scotus disagreed with Aquinas and Bonaventure about the *per se* power of charity or grace to justify the human person formally before God. Aquinas and Bonaventure taught that charity, of its very nature (*ex rei natura*), formally justifies the human person before God: God cannot condemn anyone who enjoys the habit of infused grace. Scotus and Ockham, on the contrary, argued that absolutely speaking God is not constrained to "save" anyone who has the habit of charity. Nor, they contended, is he constrained to damn anyone who dies without that habit.[186] Had God not ordained that man be obligated to have the habit of original justice, then original sin could have been "deleted" by God's power without the infusion of grace.[187]

Notwithstanding this serious dispute, God's "absolute power" was not the end of the story for Scotus and Ockham. According to both, God has actually committed himself in a divine pact or covenant.[188] God has freely chosen to judge people precisely on the basis of their possession or non-possession of the habit of charity that he graciously infuses. For Scotus and Ockham, therefore, according to God's freely chosen covenantal plan, justification—the divine acceptance of a sinner into favor with God—actually requires the created habit of charity, for the sons of the kingdom and the sons of perdition are divided precisely by the possession or non-possession of this habit.[189] Further, the decision against Pelagius, they contended, was a decision merely against the *de facto* state of affairs! Hypothetically, God could have freely instituted an order within which even Pelagius's understanding of merit would have been operative, based upon a different divine covenant with the world. Gabriel Biel, with whose works Luther and Melanchthon were familiar and by which they were considerably influenced, shared Ockham's analysis of justification. In his monumental study of Biel, Obermann decidedly chastises Biel and Ockham for failing to guard effectively against Pelagianism. Even though both spoke of the gratuity of the divine pact, their appeal to this pact did not hinder them from affirming what they thought he "decided" to do, namely, to reward those who "do what is within them to do [*facere quod in se est*]." The ambiguity of this dictum smacked, in practice, of semi-Pelagianism, even though the believer was also encouraged to have recourse to God's prevenient grace. Hence, while the outer structure of the nominalist framework may have been in agreement with Luther's and Melanchthon's thought, the inner content of the nominalist school was quasi-Pelagian: "*sola gratia* [and] *sola operibus*," chides Obermann.[190]

Because the scholastic dispute to which McGrath refers deals with the realm of God's absolute power, not with the realm of his concretely chosen path of action, that particular scholastic dispute does not alter my reading of the council.[191] Whether or not the majority of fathers of Trent *personally* sided with Aquinas or with Scotus on the point of the *absolute possibilities* of God's power is irrelevant to the definition of the formal cause as the infused justice inhering in the justified person. The scholastic dispute is, therefore, not relevant to a reading of Trent as definitively proscribing Lutheran doctrine. Trent's Decree on Justification deals simply with the concrete order that God has established. Scotus and Ockham agreed that, within this order, the formal cause of justification is inhering grace. Oddly, even according to *McGrath's* account, it would seem that *only* Gregory of Rimini, Hugolino of Orvieto, and their disciples actually affirmed that, in the concrete order, God forgives sins through an extrinsic remission (or, less emphatically, through a remission that does not *per se* involve a created formal cause).[192] Josef Hefner, who makes every effort to praise Seripando's contributions and who holds that the academic question between Scotists and Thomists about the absolute possibilities for God was not decided, asserts, "De facto, sins are not forgiven without grace."[193] He contends that the council made clear the distinctions between the justice of God, the justice of Christ, and the justice of man, excluding any erroneous interpretation. He sums up the conciliar teaching on the formal cause as follows: "Inhering justice, which is a habit of grace, remains dependent both upon God as its efficient cause and also upon Christ as its meritorious cause."[194] It ought to be noted, moreover, that many contemporary Catholics, whether more or less progressive, shrink from the voluntarism implicit in Ockham and Scotus. Voluntarism led to a heteronomous conception of God's authority, which in turn provoked the more recent overreaction to this heteronomy in the form of radical human autonomy.[195]

Criticism: Conciliar Debates. Second, the debates make it clear that the omission of the term "habit" was not intended to leave open the question of the inhering nature of justifying grace. Canon 6 of the first (July 24) draft of the decree asserts, "The justice by which we are just is a habit of divine grace."[196] All the theologians who discussed this draft accepted the canon; only five were displeased with the word "habit."[197] One of the early complaints from the bishops about the inclusion of the technical terms "habit" and "sanctifying grace" came from a Thomist! It was Johannes de Salazar, bishop of Lanciano. Salazar did not doubt the referent of these terms but cautioned against use of the scholastic terminology itself: "Where it is said that the justice by which we are just is a habit, there ought to be, in place of the word 'habit,' the word 'gift' or some other expression. This should be so that the adversaries [i.e., the Reformers] would not accuse us of being unable to speak except in figments, as they have said of the scholastics."[198] The reason he asked for a change in expression was not that the terms were inaccurate or inadequate. Rather, the simple reason was the ecumenical necessity not to burden the Reformers with any unnecessary scholastic terminology.

The October 31 draft did not return to the description of justifying grace as a "habit." The stated reason for this silence is noteworthy:

> Beyond the word "inhering" there has been desire for another phrase, namely, "a certain infused habit." But this would seem to be superfluous, since by the word "inheres" is understood [that to which we refer] as habit. It is also the case, according to all the fathers, that the charity referred to is poured forth through the Holy Spirit and is not acquired by us.[199]

Seripando, who appears to have been the author of this draft, though under the strict guidance of Cervini, judged that the term "habit" was superfluous since justifying grace was amply described as "inhering," necessarily implying that this grace was that to which scholastics referred by the term "habit." The reader will recall Seripando's previous opposition to the very description of the love of God as "inhering" in the justified. Once again, he willingly surrendered personal preference in order to manifest the mind of the majority. Constructively, Seripando added that the omission of "habit" might even help avoid the charge of Pelagianism, for someone might mistakenly read "habit" as standing for an acquired virtue.[200]

In summary of my second argument, examination of the debates removes reasonable doubt about whether Trent left undecided the identity of the formal cause of justification as inhering righteousness. The omission of the term "habit" was not tantamount to indecision about, let alone denial of, the inhering nature of justifying grace.

Criticism: Final Decree. Third, the final decree itself teems with affirmations of the inhering nature of the justice received by us. The fathers of the council understood these descriptions as sufficient to convey the Church's judgment that justifying grace was that to which scholastics referred as a habit of grace or charity. The justice by which one is justified is understood to be "that grace, given by God, by which we are renewed in the spirit of our mind and are not merely considered but are truly called and are just." Each of us "receives his own justice according to the measure which the Holy Spirit distributes to each person as he wishes, and according to the proper disposition and cooperation of each person." The significance of "degrees" of participation in the grace by which Christians are just cannot be understated. An assertion of degrees of participation in justifying grace corresponds to an understanding of that grace as a habit and not as an extrinsic denomination or imputation.[201]

Moreover, the council maintains that no one is able to be just unless the merits of Jesus' passion are communicated to the sinner. This communication takes place when "through the Holy Spirit, the love (charity) of God is poured forth into the hearts of those who are justified and inheres within them." Justifying grace is "received" and yet can be lost and restored.[202] By this grace, the justified person is renewed interiorly. Each person receives this grace in a certain measure, according as the Spirit wills and according to each person's cooperation. The communication of Christ's merits takes place precisely when the love of God is poured forth into the human heart and inheres in it. "Therefore, in justification itself, together with the remission of sins, man receives all of these infused at once, through Jesus Christ into whom he is inserted: faith, hope, and charity."[203] The true and Christian justice received in justification "is given to them through Jesus Christ."[204] The *"per Iesum Christum"* and *"per Spiritum"* and *"ab Deo"* in the above citations highlight the distinctions between the formal cause of justification and the following: the Holy Spirit Himself, the justice of Christ, and God's eternal justice. These distinctions become pronounced in light of the attribution of possible "increase" to justifying grace, an increase not attributable either to the Spirit or to God's justice or to Christ's justice. The council teaches that, by cooperating in faith and good works through the observance of the commandments, "[the just] increase in that justice received through the grace of Christ...and are more justified."[205] Again, the key sentence in chapter 16, echoing the teaching on the formal cause in chapter 7, articulates the reasons for the distinctions between various terms for the reality of justifying grace: it "is called our justice because we are justified by it inhering in us; it is the same justice of God because it is infused into us by God through the merits of Christ."[206] Definitively teaching a position proposed as "more probable" at the Council of Vienne (see below), the council declares that justification does not take place solely by an attribution of forgiveness, but must include "the grace and charity which are poured forth into their hearts by the Holy Spirit and inhere in them."[207] This canon, together with the affirmations of the inhering character of the justice by which a person is justified, shows that the fathers intended the *"iustitia Dei, non qua ipse iustus est"* to mean the supernatural justice inhering in a man, not an extrinsic denomination of the divine acceptation.

Criticism: Post-tridentine Interpretations. Fourth, the post-tridentine interpretations of the decree witness that, according to the sense of the faithful, justifying righteousness was *defined* as something infused into and inhering in the human soul. The sixteenth and seventeenth century interpreters situated Trent within the historical context of dogmatic development. Many of them read Trent as definitively affirming what the Council of Vienne in 1312 decided was a "more probable" opinion. The specific issue at Vienne was whether or not infants who are baptized receive the forgiveness of sins alone or whether they receive a grace "informing [*informans*]" the soul.[208] Whether adults receive this informing grace was not in question. At Vienne, the Church saw the "more probable" opinion to be that the gift of informing grace is conferred upon infants as well as upon adults. Interpreters of Trent, some of whom were present at the council itself, contended that chapter 7 and canon 11 settled the issue definitively. Hefner relates, moreover, that Seripando, Pflug, Gropper and others recanted and submitted to the council's decision.[209] I wish to consider several noteworthy interpreters of the Tridentine decree.

St. Robert Bellarmine (1542–1621), doctor of the Church, argued that the phrase in chapter 7 "Justification is…not only remission of sins but also the sanctification and renewal…" was not intended to bifurcate the formal cause. The formal cause is not composed of the extrinsic grace of forgiveness and the intrinsic grace of renewal. The formal cause is singular. The conciliar phrase signifies, instead, the two terms of the act of justification: the state of sin and the state of justice, each of which is contrary to the other. He rightly maintained that the "only formal cause" is neither the indwelling justice of God, nor the imputed justice of Christ, but the infused quality of supernatural charity.[210] He also called to his support the following pronouncement in the *Roman Catechism*, a sure guide for the authentic sense of the council:

> Grace, as the Synod of Trent decreed as proposed for all to believe under pain of anathema, is not only that by which the remission of sins is accomplished, but the divine quality inhering in the soul. This grace is like a certain splendor and light, that destroys all the sins of our souls, and renders souls more beautiful and resplendent.[211]

Pope Pius V approved the *Roman Catechism* in 1566, only three years after approving the entire council and only one year before condemning Baius (see below).

Ruard Tapper (1487–1559), an ardent opponent of Baius's apparent Pelagianism, maintained that justifying grace consists in an infused quality. Like Bellarmine, he interpreted chapter 7 in light of the affirmation in chapter

4 that justification consists in a "translation" or change of the human person from one state to another state.[212] The justice by which we are justified is "the quality from which we are said to be truly just by intrinsic denomination, because this quality is true justice."[213] In no other way can we truly be just than by actually having the quality of justice in us, just as no one can be wise or brave, except if they have those virtues.[214] This quality of justice is derived from that in which it participates: the capital grace of Christ.[215] Created grace is thus not independent of Christ. Still, the formal cause of justification is not extrinsic. The formal cause has to be understood as intrinsic, just as the disobedience of Adam did not result merely in an extrinsic denomination of sin for his descendants.[216] Tapper took it as a definitively taught doctrine that justifying grace is an intrinsic and inhering reality in the soul, and he perceived this teaching as a dogmatic development of the proposal of the Council of Vienne. He saw canon 11 as the specific locus in which Trent made definitive what Vienne taught as "more probable."[217]

The eminent theologian Dominic de Soto (1494–1560), present at the council during the sixth session and writing on the decree only two years after its conciliar acceptance, took to task those who denied the nature of the formal cause of justification as an intrinsic habit.[218] Like others, he made reference to the Council of Vienne as establishing the precedent for Trent.[219] He acknowledged that the term "habit" was not used.[220] He even conceded that, according to God's absolute power, forgiveness could be given without an infusion of grace, but he argued that such a situation would necessarily correspond to a world in which God created man in the state of pure nature, without grace.[221] Moreover, he considered it vain to dispute about the absolute power of God. In the concrete order, God chooses not to justify human persons without infusing grace, just as he chose from the beginning to communicate his grace to our first parents. Against the Reformers, whom he cited in a reliable manner and with whose works he appears to have been familiar, de Soto contended that the "remission of sins" consists in the destruction of sins.[222] Forgiven sins are no longer present in the human soul. He recognized that grace is present according to the different degrees to which the justified participate therein. He contrasted the Catholic insistence on degrees of grace with the Protestant insistence that justifying grace cannot be made more perfectly present in a Christian through sanctification.[223] Nor did he agree with Protestants that the fact that no one is "perfectly justified" entails that no one can satisfy the divine law. He understood the perfectibility of justice to mean that everyone can be made more just.[224] He observed that the different degrees of justice in human persons and the eradication of sins were clearly expressed in the council. These teachings all rest upon an understanding of the formal cause as that to which the scholastic terms "quality" and "habit" refer.[225] In other words, the formal justice of the justified is neither the justice of Christ nor the justice of God but a participation in the justice of God through Jesus Christ. Trent avoided the term "habit," although the term is most apt, in order not to alienate those who, misunderstanding the term, would malign it.[226] The formal cause of justification that inheres in the human person requires no supplemental "imputation," for this inhering grace is the effect of Christ, the very influx of the superabundant justice of Jesus.[227]

The Franciscan theologian Andreas de Vega (d. 1560) played a major role at the Council of Trent, fiercely debating Soto. McGrath cites him in support of his contention that the council left undecided the nature of the formal cause: "Vega defined justification in a noticeably extrinsicist manner in terms of three elements.... It is evident that Vega's conception of justification parallels that of the later Franciscan school...and is reflected in the statements of other Franciscan theologians in these congregations."[228] Especially considering his opposition to certain elements of Thomism, Vega would be just the sort of theologian who might lend plausibility to McGrath's contention (let us repeat it here): "The entire medieval debate over whether the formal cause of justification was an intrinsic created habit of grace or the extrinsic denomination of the divine acceptation...was circumvented by a reversion to the Augustinian concept of *iustitia Dei.*"[229] As a matter of fact, however, Vega interpreted the council's decision as definitively teaching the formal cause to be a created habit of grace, even though the terms themselves were not employed. It is not possible, Vega held, to denominate us absolutely by a predicate unless the perfection to which that predicate refers exists in us.[230] He interpreted Paul's statement in 1 Cor. 1:30, "God made Christ our wisdom, justice, sanctification, and redemption," as affirming Christ to be not the formal cause but the efficient and meritorious cause of Christian righteousness.[231] "Our justice," he maintained, "is by its nature something intrinsic in us and truly inhering in us. Therefore, only figuratively can one say that God or Christ or any act of God or Christ is our formal justice. All expressions of this sort must be interpreted causally."[232] By "causally," Vega was alluding to efficient and meritorious causality. Vega recognized that the great master, Peter Lombard, taught something different in his own time. Lombard identified charity not as infused habit but as the Holy Spirit himself, present to the believer and effecting in the believer an act of love. Vega saw the Council of Vienne as providing magisterial guidance away from Lombard's opinion. Due to lingering doubts and the Reformation movement, Trent solemnly defined that the formal cause of justification is a created gift, infused into the soul, "even though [the council did not do so] under the name of 'habit.'" The terms employed by the council to describe the justice of God that constitutes the formal cause make it absolutely clear; the words of the council "*cannot be understood* if our justice is not something created.... We must not deny that charity is a certain created accident" (emphasis mine).[233] Vega taught the very contrary of McGrath's thesis.

Another Franciscan, the Capuchin friar St. Laurence of Brindisi (1559–1619), declared doctor of the Church in 1959 by Bl. Pope John XXIII, held the formal cause to be distinct from but dependent upon the Holy Spirit, just as the light in the air is formally light by the light diffused in it from the sun and not by the very sun itself.[234] The "favor of God" is not to be taken as the formal cause but as the efficient cause of justification.[235] Because we enjoy a living relationship with God by faith informed by charity, and not by faith alone, and because the charity by which we love God is not identical with the charity by which God loves us, it is possible for us to be separated from God; that is, we can separate ourselves from him by sin.[236]

Bishop of Geneva and doctor of the Church, St. Francis de Sales (1567–1622) castigated the Reformers for their notion of justification through imputation, since it implied weakness in the power and efficacity of Christ's justice. We are justified, he held, through the actual communication of Christ's justice: From Christ's own justice there is infused into our hearts the justice by which we are formally just.[237] He argued that those who sin are made just not by a fresh imputation but by a new granting of that justice derived from Christ. Those who follow the lamb are "white" not by the whiteness of the Lamb of God but by their own robes, washed in the blood of the Lamb.[238] St. Francis juxtaposed Paul's magnificent hymn on love to Luther's disparaging remarks on love, recorded in his Galatians commentary.[239]

Two authoritative witnesses to interpretation of the council, nearly contemporaneous with the council, are the *Roman Catechism* and the condemnations of some of Baius's positions (1567). As has been stated in the treatment of Bellarmine, the Catechism taught that grace is a divine quality of radiant beauty in the soul. The condemnations of Baius, which appeared only several years later, continue to reveal the ongoing mind of the papal office. It is instructive, moreover, that these condemnations were issued against a danger to the faith quite different from that posed by the Reformers. Baius was condemned for teaching that obedience itself without grace—that is, merely good works and obedience to the law of God—constitutes the formal justice of justified persons. This teaching contradicts Paul's incessant claims that justification is not through human effort and works (*erga*) but by God's grace, which is received through faith. Most relevant to the present discussion, the following proposition was condemned:

> The justice by which the sinner is justified through faith consists formally in obedience to the commandments, which is the justice of works; it does not consist in any infused

grace of the soul, by which man is adopted as a son of God and is renewed according to the inner man and is made a sharer in the divine nature, that, thus renewed through [*per*] the Holy Spirit, he is consequently able to live well and to obey the commandments of God.[240]

This proposition gives witness to the Church's understanding that the grace by which humans are justified is, on the one hand, not works done by natural human powers but that, on the other hand, justifying grace is rather a grace infused into the soul, making the human person an adopted child of God and a participant in the divine nature.[241]

The forgoing arguments show that the Council of Trent defined the formal cause to be the justice of God that inheres in the human soul as a participation in the divine justice, diffused through the Holy Spirit, and taken from the side of Jesus Christ into whom the justified are engrafted. I wish to conclude this chapter with a sketch demonstrating that the tridentine teaching is firmly rooted in Christian tradition.

Brief History of Grace as "Habit" or "Accident"

French theologian Fr. Jean-Miguel Garrigues has recently argued, against the prevailing presumption of contemporary theologians, that the notion of grace as a supernatural "habit" inhering in the human person is not merely of scholastic provenance. Garrigues argues in the spirit of one who, like Pope. Bl. John XXIII, can distinguish intelligently between form and content. This distinction does not merely work to promote a multiplicity of expressions; it also serves to account for the possibility that similar insights can underlie divergent expressions. Further, Garrigues shows that, although the term "*habitus*" does not emerge immediately, it is nonetheless accurately expressive of the scriptural and patristic data. Although scripture scholars may well not be convinced by Garrigues' article, his observations on the use of "*hexis* [Greek for 'habit']" among the patristics, especially in St. Maximus the Confessor (580–662), effectively demolishes Gérard Philips's thesis that the term emerged only in the 12th century, a thesis Philips marshals to support his reading of Trent as noncommital on the subject.[242] Maximus not only used the term "*hexis* [habit]" to describe the love that enlivens the human person but also traced the root of this "habit of love" to the fulness of grace that Jesus Christ enjoys in his humanity and which he pours forth through the Spirit into the hearts of the members of his body. Maximus thus inchoately anticipated the elements of the "scholastic" doctrine of capital grace.[243] Garrigues has studied this element of tradition in Maximus and his predecessors. I wish to offer a complementary sketch, tracing a line of thought in Origen, Athanasius, Basil of Caesarea, Gregory of Nyssa, and Cyril of Alexandria.

As early as the third century, there appeared an explicit use of the term "accident" to describe holiness or sanctification in the creature. Origen (185–254) stated, "To be stainless is a quality which belongs essentially to none except the Father, Son and Holy Spirit; for holiness is in every created being an accidental quality, and what is accidental may also be lost."[244] Patristic scholars will recognize that many of the Greek Fathers expressed similar understandings of holiness in creatures through their contrast between holiness by essence and holiness by participation.[245] God alone is holy by his essence, for he is his own holiness; in him, holiness and being are one and the same. All creatures are holy by participation, for in them essence is other than holiness. Fr. David Balás, American theologian and native of Hungary, sums up Origen's thought: "As in Middle-Platonism and in the beginning of Neo-Platonism, which constitute his philosophical background, so in Origen too 'participation' serves to distinguish and to connect the different levels of reality."[246]

One century later, Athanasius (296–373) expressly employed not only the term "accident" but also the term "habit" to describe grace in creatures. In his *Discourses against the Arians* (356–360), he contrasted the divinity of Christ with the status of believers as participants in the divine nature. Whereas Christ is divine, creatures merely participate in divinity. Whereas Christ is Uncreated Wisdom, righteous creatures participate in wisdom. If Christ were not divine, Athanasius contended, he would be but a partaker in the divine nature. He would be one thing, while grace in him would be another. In other words, Christ, according to his pre-existent nature, would "have" grace as a virtue or habit in his essence. Athanasius's refutation of Arius's conception of the Son as a creature is worth noting, since he found it expedient to describe grace in creatures in terms foreshadowing scholastic usage:

> How is He longer the Word, if He be alterable? Or can that be Wisdom which is changeable? Unless perhaps, as accident in essence, so they would have it, viz. as in any particular essence, a certain grace and habit of virtue exists accidentally, which is called Word and Son and Wisdom, and admits of being taken from it and added to it.[247]

Nor is this anomalous in the works of Athanasius. Written at about the same time as the *Four Discourses* was completed, the *De Synodis* (359–361) contains similar expressions. Athanasius attempted to win over the semi-Arians who claimed that, while the Son is not of the same substance as the Father, he is "of like substance [*homoiousios*]." Athanasius retorted:

> Like is not predicated of essence, but of habits, and qualities; for in the case of essences we speak, not of likeness, but of identity. Man, for instance, is said to be like man, not

in essence, but according to habit and character; for in essence men are of one nature. And again, man is not said to be unlike dog, but to be of different nature. Accordingly, while the former are of one nature and coessential, the latter are different in both. Therefore, in speaking of Like according to essence, we mean like by participation; (for Likeness is a quality, which may attach to essence), and this would be proper to creatures, for they, by partaking, are made like to God. For "when He shall appear," says Scripture, "we shall be like Him" (1 John iii. 2), like, that is, not in essence but in sonship, which we shall partake from Him. If then ye [i.e., the undecided of the homoiousios party] speak of the Son as being by participation, then indeed call Him Like-in-essence; but thus spoken of, He is not Truth, nor Light at all, nor nature in God.... And this, again, is proper to creatures and works.[248]

These descriptions of participation in God imply a distinction between the participant and the participated perfection. But since participation truly "qualifies" the participant, one can assert a composition in the participant: subject and participated perfection. Moreover, the characteristics attributed to the participated perfection—namely, greater and less—imply a differentiation between the infinite perfection itself—sometimes called the unparticipated—and the participated perfection. It was somewhat fitting that terms favored by unfavored Aristotle would be used, albeit sparsely, to articulate holiness by participation in Christian discourse.

For his part, St. Basil of Caesarea emphasized human transformation as the heart of Christ's redeeming work and the Spirit's sanctifying mission:

So, too, is the Spirit to every one who receives It, as though given to him alone, and yet It sends forth grace sufficient and full for all mankind, and is enjoyed by all who share It, according to the capacity, not of Its power, but of their nature.... Shining upon those that are cleansed from every spot, He makes them spiritual by fellowship with Himself. Just as when a sunbeam falls on bright and transparent bodies, they themselves become brilliant too, and shed forth a fresh brightness from themselves, so souls wherein the Spirit dwells, illuminated by the Spirit, themselves become spiritual, and send forth their grace to others.[249]

God's indwelling presence purifies the soul, drawing her to participate in the radiant holiness of the Spirit. Faithful to his appreciation of the creaturely conditions for union with God, Basil spoke of degrees of grace and of degrees of heavenly glory.[250] Basil observed that the Spirit comes anew to dwell in human persons and yet that the Spirit does not change. Grace, then, is the sanctifying effect of God's eternal love in the creature: It is the participation of the creature in God. Christians receive a share in the Holy Spirit through the humanated Word of God. Basil's insights resonate with the scholastic distinctions between created and uncreated grace, between efficient and formal causality.

Gregory of Nyssa does not explicitly describe grace or holiness as an accident, but his theological analysis of participation implies as much. David Balás has presented what remains the most authoritative study of participation in the thought of Gregory of Nyssa. The category of participation played a central role in Gregory's theological anthropology. The terms expressive of this category, "when used in a technical manner to express the relation between the (intellectual) creatures and God, indicate first of all a derived, secondary possession of a quality or perfection, i.e., the fact that the subject does not own that perfection in virtue of its nature, *is* not that perfection itself, but has received it from a higher source."[251] What follows logically is that the participating subject is composed of subject and the participated quality.[252] God, in contrast to every being that participates in perfection, is utterly simple.[253] With respect to creatures, however, Gregory's texts "clearly affirm a distinction between the subject which participates and the perfection participated."[254] Now, Gregory understood the participated perfection to be, on the one hand, God's own perfection and, on the other hand, the perfection that truly qualifies the intellectual creature. Indeed, the primary composition implied in participation is that "between the subject and its own (participated) perfection."[255] Thus the participated perfection is not identical with God, as would be the case in a pantheistic system of thought. Nor for Gregory is the participated perfection an "uncreated divine energy," as in Gregory Palamas.[256] The clearest manifestation of this composition is in the fact that whereas a creature's sharing in a possession can be more and less, the divine possession of a perfection is infinite.[257] A creature that responds more openly to God's grace will enjoy a greater participation in divine perfection. Thus, as did Athanasius, Gregory links degrees of participation with "excellence in virtue."[258] Gregory knew that the "more and less" is not predicated of the essence or substance. The "greater and lesser" are predicated of, among other categories, qualities.[259]

Similarly, the notion of holiness as "virtue [*arete*]" was not foreign to Cyril of Alexandria (d. 444), who upheld both the ontological reality of man's "likeness" to God established by the Holy Spirit and also the dynamic thrust of that likeness towards its archetype. Walter Burghardt finds the scholastic category of created grace capable of describing the substance of Cyril's thought: "The sanctified soul, therefore, is graced with a created quality, a [morphosis], whose function is to form Christ in us." Burghardt does not shy away from this conclusion, even though he recognizes—as do contemporary scholars, who so insist on this legitimate point that they mistakenly deny that Cyril also upheld the participatory nature of man's enjoyment of the Spirit—Cyril's insistence that this "quality of grace" is never separate from the Holy Spirit but ever dependent upon him.[260]

Origen and Athanasius explicitly employed terminology that the scholastics eventually made mainstream. Their purpose was to describe creaturely participation in the divine perfections. The chorus of Greek theologians joined in this celebration of creaturely participation. Though the terms "quality" and "accident" were less frequently employed, phrases such as "according to virtue" were abundant, as is clear in Gregory of Nyssa. Cyril's emphasis on the indwelling of the Holy Spirit did not preclude his appreciation of the creaturely effects of that sanctifying presence. Similarly, the scholastics who disagreed with Lombard about charity, affirming it to be not simply the uncreated love of the Holy Spirit but also the created participation in that very love, did not deny the Lombardian insight: the Holy Spirit dwells within those whom he makes just.[261]

It must, finally, be asked whether there are sufficient theological grounds to repudiate the conception of grace as a *"habitus,"* even if one prefers not to use the term. The thrust of Karl Rahner's early insistence upon the ontological priority of uncreated grace, i.e., the divine indwelling, cannot be gainsaid.[262] There is a long history behind this contention, including Petavius's speculations rooted in a rereading of the Greeks and perhaps culminating in the disputes between Granderath and Scheeben.[263] The whole point of insisting upon the infusion of a quality of grace, according to the Catholic teaching, is to account for the necessary conditions for God's indwelling.[264] The justified person is set in relation not with this grace, but, rather, with the Holy Trinity, the second person of whom is incarnate. There is legitimate Catholic dispute about the way in which the divine indwelling and the infusion of grace are related.[265] That both are inseparable is indisputable. That every trace of damnable sin is expelled by infused grace, which is inseparably linked with the indwelling of the most Holy Trinity, is also indisputable. Finally, the indwelling presence of the divine Trinity cannot be conceived as touching the human person without the latter's attunement to God. Such attunement involves change. Thomas and Bonaventure offered the following intellectual contribution to balance what they perceived as Lombard's reductive tendencies. They insisted that, for the attuning change to mark a permanent disposition of the creature in a profound way, bringing about a connatural inclination to beatitude in the justified, there is need of an infused, habitual grace. This grace renders the supernatural elements of Christian life sweet, so that the indwelling Spirit can call and direct the Christian to greater holiness in ways that resonate with the very being of the justified. Created grace serves as the counterpart to the Spirit's call of and indwelling presence within the Christian.

In our age which is tempted by a similar reductionism, the father of the *Nouvelle Theologie*, Henri Cardinal de Lubac warned Catholics, in one of his last works, against neglecting the category of "created grace":

Call it an accident, or call it a *habitus*, or "created grace": these are all different ways of saying (even if one thinks they need various correctives or precisions) that man becomes in truth a sharer in the divine nature.... We do not need to conceive of it as a sort of entity separated from its Source, something like cooled lava—which man would appropriate to himself. On the contrary, we wish to affirm by these words that the influx of God's Spirit does not remain external to man; that without any commingling of natures it really leaves its mark *on* our nature and becomes in us a principle of life. This Scholastic notion of created grace, so often belittled today, does express the incontrovertible fact that "it is we, ourselves, and our creaturely being, which the active presence in us of the Spirit makes divine, without for that reason absorbing us and annihilating us in God."[266]

De Lubac goes on to defend the patristic and Scriptural roots of this putatively "merely scholastic" doctrine: "Let us admit that this doctrine elaborated by Thomas Aquinas was in fact a revival of the tradition of the first centuries, which without a doubt had its source in the Gospel and in St. Paul."[267] The subtle contours of both de Lubac's and (the early) Rahner's theologies have been trampled flat in the contemporary endeavor to displace created grace (and nature?) with uncreated grace.

Perhaps it is no surprise that de Lubac issued such a warning so late in his career, for the rejection of the intrinsic necessity of created grace in justification at times coincides with the assertion of the possibility of a creation of man in the state of "pure nature." Those scholastics who before Trent upheld the possibility that God could absolve sinners without infusing a quality of grace appealed to the possibility that God could have created humans in the state of pure nature. God could have created the first pair without grace and could have "imputed" the disobedience of Adam to his descendants by way of an extrinsic denomination of judgment. Similarly, given such a hypothetically possible state of affairs, God could have remitted such "extrinsically imputed" sin by an extrinsic denomination of his forgiving acceptance. But the edifice of this hypothetical possibility—which, as I have stated, Trent did not accept as the concrete way in which God has chosen to order the world—rests upon the premise of "pure nature." De Lubac devoted much of his life's work to battling against the late scholastic development of this category.

I will close this brief sketch with the thought of John Paul II. According to the Holy Father, the anointing of the Christian is the gift of the Holy Spirit, source of all gifts.[268] This gift is given to man, made in the image and likeness of God, so that he may be restored to the likeness, which had been obliterated by sin. Man, remaining in the image of God despite sin, remains a being capable of divine friendship with God.[269] The realization of this capacity, however, requires the gift of grace by which the Holy Spirit inspires and enables the sinner freely yet non-meritoriously to turn towards his own conversion through a tender sorrow for sin and a love of God.[270] The end of this conversion is the remission of sins through the grace of the Holy Spirit, who dwells within those he sanctifies.[271] Echoing Basil's work, Pope John Paul II not only emphasizes the continuity of the sinner to be forgiven and transformed but also draws attention to the inseparable unity in distinction between the Holy Spirit, uncreated gift, and the sanctifying grace through which he dwells within the justified:

> Thus there is a supernatural "adoption", of which the source is the Holy Spirit, love and gift. *As such he is given to man*. And in the *superabundance of the uncreated gift there begins* in the heart of all human beings that particular *created gift* whereby they "become partakers of the divine nature". Thus human life becomes permeated, through participation, by the divine life, and itself acquires a divine, supernatural dimension.[272]

To accept McGrath's reading of Trent, and even that of Philips, is to misread a defined teaching of faith that has its roots in the scriptures as they have been interpreted in the Christian tradition. Theologically, neglect of this tridentine teaching threatens to jeopardize the progress made in Catholic thought in the 20th century on nature and grace. Granted, those not familiar with the scholastic categories might mistakenly take the "habitus" doctrine for a Catholic affirmation of man's ability to "wield" something against God or to "possess" grace as something rooted in his own being—and not to receive it as an abiding gift. Such misunderstandings can be corrected at the level of a sophisticated catechesis. One must underscore the gift character of this "habit" and note that, although grace informs the human person so that he truly becomes just and holy by this abiding gift, the human person never becomes the source of that grace. In the spirit of Bonaventure, who insisted that it is not man who possesses God but God who possesses man, Schmaus and Rahner offer helpful correctives in this regard.[273] Even Hans Urs von Balthasar, who once described himself as Samson in the Temple of neo-scholasticism, accepted the category of "habit" as a description of the grace that makes holy, against the late 20th century repudiation of the term as an inaccurate reading of Rom 5:5.[274]

Concluding Assessment

To understand Catholic faith aright, one should not read the teachings of Trent with a hermeneutic that attempts to balance God's efficient causality with the formal effect of that causality, offsetting these against one another. Neither should Christ's perfect merit be weighed against the gift given on account of that merit. Finally, the exemplary plenitude of the grace of triune God should not be set in competition with the ontological richness of the gift he freely gives. The gift of integration into Christ is the fruit of the Father's loving mercy, of Christ's death and resurrection, and of the Spirit's in-breathing grace. In proclaiming the one formal cause as an inhering grace, Trent does not simply "emphasize" human sanctification in the face of a perceived threat to that sanctification. According to Trent, justification *is* God's merciful transformation of the inner being of the human person. Trent places this transformation within the context of God's merciful and redeeming power. While defining the doctrine of the one formal cause, Trent does not downplay the gratuity and the finality of grace.

The opening chapter of the Decree on Justification draws attention to the utter powerlessness of the sinner to save himself, a teaching already established in the Decree on Original Sin. In his paper for the American dialogue, Carl Peter suggests, "There may in fact be even more stress placed on the human inability to merit the grace of forgiveness."[275] The very last chapter, thanks to Seripando, exhorts the Christian to boast not in himself but in the grace of Christ because "Our own justice is [not] something springing from ourselves."[276] God's grace is gratuitous, but gratuity involves the freedom of the Giver, not the absence or poverty of the gift. In the genuine spirit of Vatican II, the American dialogue rightly claims, "To minimize God's gifts...is not a way of magnifying the giver."[277] Similarly, Carl Peter writes, "Trent spoke guardedly but did endorse human cooperation with God's grace in the process leading to justification. It did not thereby intend to exalt the sinful creature at the expense of the God of mercy or to give sinners unwarranted confidence to the detriment of Christ's grace."[278] Trent likewise describes a man as dependent upon God for both special help (actual grace) and the continual infusion of this gift.[279] Lastly, Trent proclaims the glory of God as the final end of justification. The saints are to fix their gaze not on themselves but on God. Indeed, *without* sanctifying grace their love can be for themselves alone.[280]

The Council of Trent upholds both God's mercy and the inhering character of justifying grace, both Christ's merits and sanctification, both God's primacy and human cooperation, both human sinfulness and the power of baptismal grace. Although one may certainly wish for a development of Catholic doctrine and a deeper understanding of the faith, a Catholic cannot conclude that the definitions and condemnations of Trent, when read aright, obscure the mystery of salvation or detract from God's glory:

> If anyone says that by this catholic doctrine concerning justification, set out in this present decree by the holy council, anything is taken away from the glory of God or the merits of Jesus Christ our Lord, and that the truth of our faith and the glory of both God and of Jesus Christ is not better illustrated by it: let him be anathema.[281]

In the effort to achieve full communion, neither side must shrink from the rigorous demands of intellectual honesty and confessional fidelity. This honesty should bring each communion, first, to acknowledge the antithetical positions on justification in the tridentine and Lutheran confessional statements. This would be a salutary starting point for dialogue: In proper humility, not applying condemnations to persons of the other communion but honestly admitting the substance of one's own heritage and the consequent need, should ecclesial union ever be achieved, for one or both parties to alter its doctrine(s). From the Catholic perspective, *alteration* of the teachings of Trent is not possible; Catholics who recognize the original conflict of doctrines will thus hope that developments outside of such alteration can pave the way towards reconciliation. Many Lutherans, while critical of Trent, already stress the need for corrections of the confessional teachings of their heritage. The same do not shy from calling Catholics to alter some of their teachings. If such requisite honesty was better integrated into the contemporary dialogue, theologians would not find themselves party to intellectual compromise. A broad and deep theological hope (Rom 4:18) is necessary to endure such honesty in a fruitful way.[282]

NOTES

1 See Anthony Lane, "Twofold Righteousness: A Key to the Doctrine of Justification?" in *Justification: What's at Stake in the Current Debates*, ed. Mark Husbands and Daniel Treier (Downers Grove, IL: InterVarsity Press, 2004), pp. 206–07.

2 See Dermot Fenlon, *Heresy and Obedience in Tridentine Italy: Cardinal Pole and the Counter Reformation* (Cambridge: Cambridge University Press, 1972), p. 47.

3 See Lane, *Justification*, p. 51.

4 See Lane, "Twofold Righteousness," p. 208.

5 Translation by Anthony Lane; cited in Anthony Lane, *Justification*, pp. 234–35.

6 "Inhering" conveys the activity of "inhering in" but does not have the problematic implication of being something "native" or "intrinsic" to the human person. The typical translation "intrinsic" might be seen as smacking of Pelagianism.

7 Lane, "Twofold Righteousness," p. 212.

8 See Jedin, *Council*, pp. 257–58, and Lane, "Twofold Righteousness," p. 217. Contarini, Pighius, and Seripando were influenced by Gropper in their adherence to double justice.

9 See Fenlon, *Heresy*, p. 48, and Lane, "Twofold Righteousness," p. 208.

10 See Fenlon, *Heresy*, p. 49.

11 See Lane, *Justification*, pp. 53–54, and idem, "Twofold Righteousness," p. 209, and note 21.

12 See Lane, "Twofold Righteousness," p. 209.

13 See Lane, *Justification*, p. 53.

14 McGrath, *Iustitia Dei*, p. 248.

15 "The modern reader will search in vain for logical consistency, since the essence of the

agreed upon text was a compromise between two basically incompatible positions"
(Elizabeth G. Gleason, *Gasparo Contarini: Venice, Rome, and Reform* [Berkeley:
University of California Press, 1993], p. 228).

16   Lane, "Twofold Righteousness," p. 212; see also p. 215.

17   See Fenlon, *Heresy*, p. 105.

18   For one of the most thorough and recent studies, which concludes that substantive
differences divided the communions on the doctrine of justification and that ecumenical
progress depends upon admission of that fact, see Athina Lexutt, *Rechtfertigung im
Gespräch: Das Rechtfertigungsverständnis in den Religionsgeshprächen von Hagenau,
Worms und Regensburg 1540/41* (Göttingen: Vandenhoeck & Ruprecht, 1996).

19   Fenlon, *Heresy*, p. 55.

20   At Regensburg, both Gasparo Contarini and Johannes Gropper spoke of two justices,
one inhering (communicated or infused) and one in Christ (imputed). Most scholars
suggest that the Regensburg agreement did not espouse double justice strictly speaking
(see McGrath, *Iustitia Dei*, pp. 244–47). Gropper was reaching back to the medieval
concept of infused grace (habitual grace), by which persons are justified and from
which a just life of concrete action can follow. Thus, although he expressed
justification as forgiveness by imputation and also renewal, McGrath argues, he meant
by imputation what Thomas meant by divine acceptance through infusion (such, at
least, is the implication of McGrath's thesis). Contarini, in addition, thought it possible
for a very saintly man to grow in inhering righteousness until he had no need of an
additional, final imputation of Christ's own righteousness. Contarini, then, believed
that a "second justice" or second imputation of Christ's own righteousness might not
be necessary in all cases. The Regensburg agreement strives to place all merit with
Christ. Logically, however, the agreement tends to confuse the meritorious cause and
the formal cause of forgiveness, linking them both on the same plane: what is attributed
to one cannot be attributed to the other. According to the Regensburg agreement, it
seems, an increase in one justice, inhering righteousness, entails a corresponding
decrease in the need for a second righteousness, Christ's righteousness as imputed.
Granted, both parties at Regensburg held that the believer's ultimate trust had to be not
in inhering righteousness but in Christ's saving work and person. Still, the suggestion
that imputed righteousness is necessary *because* of remnant sin and the continued
imperfection of communicated righteousness logically entails an inverse relationship
between the two kinds of righteousness. This inverse relationship appears to obscure
the participatory dependence of inhering righteousness on Christ. In reality, inhering
righteousness depends upon Christ's own righteousness precisely in the order of formal
causality: the latter is an exemplar cause of the former. With Thomas, it can be added
that inhering righteousness receives its reality precisely from the fullness of the
righteousness of Christ, the capital grace of all the just. See also Jill Raitt, "From
Augsburg to Trent," in USA, pp. 209–13. Is it possible, however, to see real
anticipations of "double justice" at Regensburg? Contarini came close to espousing
double justice proper. He asserted that most people do not die in the state of perfection.
He asserted that "extant" imperfections are supplemented by the imputation of Christ's
perfect righteousness. Thus, Contarini implicitly asserted two formal causes by which
one stands just before God: charity and extrinsically imputed righteousness. Contarini's
suggestion that inhering righteousness can reach perfection in isolated cases is not
contradictory to double justice. The chief proponent of double justice, Girolamo
Seripando, at times seemed to admit that some great saints do not need a final
imputation.

21   See Fenlon, *Heresy*, p. 59.

22   Fenlon's phrasing is not precise on this point. He describes inhering justice as an "agent of salvation." I take him to mean not an agent that performs but a reality "by which" one is just, a formal cause of salvation.

23   Fenlon, *Heresy*, p. 58.

24   Thomas Mayer, *Reginald Pole: Prince & Prophet* (Cambridge: Cambridge University Press, 2000), pp. 143–44, and 146.

25   See Fenlon, *Heresy*, pp. 109–14.

26   For a thorough treatment and bibliography on the tridentine teaching on justification, including the conciliar debates on double justice, see McGrath, *Iustitia Dei*, pp. 250–73. See also Paul Pas, "La doctrine de la double justice au Concile de Trente," *Ephemerides theologicae Lovaniensis* 30 (1954): 5–53; Vittorino Grossi, "La giustificazione secondo Girolamo Seripando nel contesto dei dibattiti Tridentini," *Analecta Augustiniana* 41, ed. V. Grossi, Q. Fernández et al., pp. 5–24; Carl E. Maxcey, "Double Justice, Diego Laynez, and the Council of Trent," *Church History* 48 (1979): 269–78; Stephan Ehses, "Johannes Groppers Rechtfertigungslehre auf dem Konzil von Trient," *Römische Quartalschrift für christliche Altertumskunde und für Kirchengeschichte* 20 (1906): 175–88. For more background on Trent, see Jedin, *Council*, pp. 166–96 and 239–316; in German, *Die erste Trienter Tagungsperiode (1545–47)*, vol. 2, *Geschichte des Konzils von Trient* (Freiburg: Herder, 1957), pp. 139–268.

27   See *Solid Declaration*, III: 23 and *Epitome*, III: 20–21.

28   Martin Luther, *Confutation of Latomus*, in *Career of the Reformer II*, ed. George W. Forell, pp. 137–264, vol. 32, *Luther's Works*, ed. Helmut T. Lehmann (Philadelphia: Fortress Press, 1958) p. 236 (emphasis mine). See also Melanchthon's *Apology*, IV: 362 (358 in the quarto edition). As for Catholic theologians, to name a few of quite diverse perspectives, Bellarmine, Brindisi, Petavius, Möhler, Scheeben, etc. all agreed that Catholicism and Lutheranism diverge in a real and substantial way. Martin Chemnitz showed sufficient appreciation of the issues to thwart the murmuring as well: "For the dissension and strife in the article of justification is not only about words but chiefly about matters themselves" (Chemnitz, *Examination*, pp. 467–68). Later in the same work he specified, "But they [i.e., Catholics] say that this is the whole merit of Christ, that on account of it the mercy of God pours into us the new quality of inherent righteousness, which is love, that we may be justified by it. This means that we are absolved before the judgment of God, adopted as sons, and received into life eternal not because of the obedience of Christ but on account of our love so that the mercy of God is only the efficient cause, and the obedience of Christ only the meritorious cause, that from these we may have in ourselves some inherent thing which we can plead against the judgment of God, in which we must trust, that on account of it, and not on account of Christ, we are absolved, adopted as children of God, and receive the inheritance of life eternal" (ibid., pp. 517–18. Chemnitz was correct in stating that the difference is not merely verbal. Nevertheless, I would qualify two of his points. First, Catholic doctrine does not call Christians to trust *in* sanctifying grace. Rather, it calls them to trust *in* God *for* true healing. Second, Chemnitz failed to distinguish the formal cause from "that on account of which" (*propter quod*) God receives the sinner. The formal cause is, rather, that by which (*quo*). It is, in a sense, one's very "being received" by God. For a superb analysis of Chemnitz's misreading, see the treatment by Robert Bellarmine, *De justificatione impii*, II, chap. 2, vol. 6, *Opera omnia* (Paris: Minerva, 1873), pp. 210–11. See a similar mistake in JF, 159. Despite these mistakes, Chemnitz understood Catholic doctrine well enough to reject it, not out of ignorance but rather out of allegiance to a different doctrine. He recognized that Catholics affirm

God as the efficient cause and Christ as the meritorious cause: that God infuses this inhering quality of righteousness into an undeserving sinner. He disagreed that one's inhering righteousness is the reason why, before God, one is just and worthy of heaven. Catholics believe Christ to be the "propter quod" of first justification. That is, Christ is the meritorious basis for God's decision to justify someone. But Catholics are forbidden to believe that the righteousness of Christ is the formal cause of justification (canon 10). However, justifying righteousness is the formal ground for admittance into eternal life; therefore, Catholics are forbidden to believe that the righteousness of Christ is the formal ground for admittance into eternal life. Chemnitz, in contrast, could not affirm that *inhering righteousness* itself formally acquits a man, makes him pleasing to God, disposes him towards beatitude, and enables him to merit it. Chemnitz believed, rather, that "the judgment of God does not find in us in this life, not even in the regenerate, so perfect and so pure an inherent righteousness that we can stand before God in this way, that we may on account of it be justified to life eternal" (Chemnitz, ibid., p. 493).

29   For Seripando's early formulation at the council, see *Concilii Tridentini actorum: Pars altera*, ed. Stephen Ehses, vol. 5, *Concilium Tridentinum: Diariorum, actorum, epistularum, tractatuum* (hereafter, CT) ed. Societas Goerresiana (Freiburg: B. Herder, 1911), pp. 332–36. All references are to volume 5. The translations are mine. Pas argues that Seripando, a Thomist until 1538, traced the theory to the work of Gropper and Contarini (see Pas, "La doctrine," p. 11). McGrath disputes the common judgment that Gropper's *Enchiridion* (1538) marked the beginning of the doctrine of a twofold *formal* cause of justification (see McGrath, *Iustitia Dei*, pp. 246–48). Perhaps one might wish to qualify Pas's judgment; still, Seripando himself traced the doctrine to Gropper and Contarini.

30   See Pas, "La doctrine," p. 12, and Jedin, *Council*, p. 156.

31   See Jedin, *Council*, pp. 146–47, and Pas, "La doctrine," pp. 6–8.

32   See Pas, "La doctrine," p. 12.

33   See CT, pp. 384–91.

34   See CT, p. 518, note 6. Cf. Jedin, *Council*, pp. 193–94, and Alister McGrath, *Iustitia Dei*, p. 258 and p. 476, n. 18.

35   See CT, p. 386: 12–42.

36   Si quis dixerit, iustitiam, quae in hac iustificatione donatur, esse solam illam iustitiam Christi...anathema sit. Promeruit quidem solus Christus Iesus sua illa magna iustitia, ut homo per eum iustus efficiatur, sed iustitia, quae in illo ipso sit, non in Christo; actus iustitiae illius Christi in eo est, non in nobis. Iustitia, qua iusti sumus, habitus est divinae gratiae, quae in nobis est, quamquam non per nos, sed per eum, per eum et a Deo; a Deo ut qui efficit, per eum ut qui meruit (CT, p. 386: 25–32). For a discussion of the words "promerere" and "merere," see McGrath, *Iustitia Dei*, pp. 274–76. In short, in opposition to the early scholarship on these terms, it has been shown that the fathers used these terms synonymously. The distinction between "condign" and "congruous" merit can be detected primarily by use of the phrases "*vere mereri*" or "*proprie mereri*," which is meant to signify condign merit.

37   See CT, p. 392: 30–33.

38   In one of his works on Thomas Aquinas, Pesch recapitulates his research on the historical development of grace as a quality, arguing that the conception of grace as a "quality" was motivated both by concern for the creaturely conditions necessary for spontaneity and joy and also by the concern to fight off the reemergence of Pelagianism; hence the key qualifier "infused." See Otto Hermann Pesch, *Thomas von Aquin: Grenze und Größe mittelalterlicher Theologie* (Maiz: Matthias-Grünwald-

Verlag, 1988), pp. 244–45.

39   See Jedin, *Council*, p. 194.

40   See Pas, "La doctrine," pp. 16 and 19.

41   See the comments of the bishops themselves in CT, pp. 392–415.

42   See Jedin, *Council*, p. 196.

43   See Pas, "La doctrine," pp. 15–17.

44   Nihil aliud esse quam eius translationem per novam quandam et spiritualem nativitatem, ab eo statu, in quo secundum carnem natus est, filius primi Adae, sub ira et inimicitia Dei, in statum adoptionis filiorum Dei per secundum Adam Iesum Christum (CT, p. 823: 6–9). See also McGrath, *Iustitia Dei*, p. 260.

45   See CT, p. 825: 11–20.

46   Fenlon, *Heresy*, p. 163.

47   See Pas, "La doctrine," p. 19.

48   I can find no discussion of the August 11 in the Acta. See McGrath, *Iustitia Dei*, p. 261.

49   McGrath notes that the date given in the Acta, August 19, is incorrect and should be changed to August 29 (See McGrath, *Iustitia Dei*, pp. 476–77, n. 33).

50   Seripando's presence at Trent was surely not that of a mere foil for the opponents of double justice. In addition to the above-mentioned contributions, he made other distinctive contributions to the tridentine expression of faith. Most notably, he was responsible for the salutary reminders in chapter 16 that inhering justice is not produced by man but only by God and that it comes to us through Christ as though from its fontal source.

51   See Pas, "La doctrine," p. 17.

52   See Fenlon, *Heresy*, p. 164.

53   Praeter purissimam illam et integerrimam Christi servatoris et capitis nostri iustitiam, quae in omne corpus suum, hoc est, ecclesiam omnem diffunditur, omnibus suis membris per fidem et sacramenta communicatur et applicatur: eiusdem nostri redemptoris merito gratia seu caritas diffunditur in cordibus eorum, qui iustificantur per Spiritum Sanctum, qui datur eis (CT, p. 829: 41–45).

54   Si quis dixerit docueritve, sola fide iustificari hominem, aut solius Christi iustitiae imputatione cum exclusione omnis iustitiae in cordibus nostris diffusae; aut fidem iustificantem fiduciam esse divinae misericordiae peccata remittentis gratis propter Christum, eamque unam ad iustificationem sufficere ... anathema esto (CT, p. 832: 27–32).

55   See Pas, "La doctrine," p. 17.

56   See Fenlon, *Heresy*, p. 164.

57   "Non esse tutum arbitrantur respondere speculative, sed practice, ut serio se quisque statuat ante iustum iudicem habentem clavem mortis et inferni" CT, p. 486: 40–41.

58   See Jedin, *Council*, p. 253. This is a point that, as Pas rightly notes, is to be underscored. See Pas, "La doctrine," p. 31.

59   See Jedin, *Council*, p. 249.

60   See Hans Küng, *Justification: the Doctrine of Karl Barth and a Catholic Reflection*, trans. Thomas Collins, Edmund E. Tolk, and David Granskou (New York: Thomas Nelson & Sons, 1964), p. 219. For the German, see *Rechtfertigung: Die Lehre Karl Barths und eine Katholische Besinnung* (Einsiedeln: Johannes Verlag, 1957). Also, one of McGrath's statements might lead some to misinterpret double justice. Gropper avoids double justice by excluding "the possibility, necessarily associated with a doctrine of 'double justification', that the believer is justified on account of (*propter*) his renewal" (McGrath, *Iustitia Dei*, p. 246). In fact, however, Seripando did not think

that the renewal preceded God's grace. For a reading similar to McGrath's, see O'Callaghan, *Fides Christi*, pp. 82–83.

61 Nam non alia ratione primam Dei misericordiam seu praevenientem gratiam optamus, nisi ut qui nostra libera voluntate et mala a Deo per peccata avertimur, per eius excitantem atque adiuvantem gratiam ad convertendum nos, hoc est, ad nostram iustificationem per bonam voluntatem libere etiam praeparemur atque disponamur (CT, p. 824: 4–8).

62 See CT, p. 336: 18–26.

63 My reading of the Colloquy of Regensburg is corroborated by a comment in the American dialogue on justification about this colloquy as the proximate inspiration for the theory of double justice. According to the dialogue, the Regensburg agreement insisted that "one may not depend upon communicated, inherent righteousness. Assurance of salvation lies only in the righteousness of Christ by which one is accounted righteous" (USA, par. 47).

64 See Pas, "La doctrine," p. 31.

65 See Pas, "La doctrine," p. 32. I must disagree with Jedin's formulation that "in [Seripando's] view it is not sanctifying grace that is inadequate and in need of further perfecting, but rather those actions which the justified has performed by a spontaneous use of the energy derived from grace . . ." (Jedin, *Council*, p. 253). As Pas indicates, it is not as though Seripando held that grace does suffice, which one might conclude from reading Jedin.

66 Jedin, *Council*, p. 246.

67 Et ideo iustitia, quae in nobis est, dicitur iustitia Dei, quia gratis ab ipso solo eam accepimus. Dici etiam potest iustitia Christi, quia ut ea nobis daretur, ipse solus meruit....Ita non sunt duae iustitiae, quae nobis dantur, Dei et Christi, sed una iustitia Dei per Iesum Christum, (hoc est caritas ipsa vel gratia), qua iustificati non modo reputamur, sed vere iusti nominamur et sumus (CT, p. 423: 31–36; the clause in parentheses was added in the margin).

68 See Fenlon, *Heresy*, p. 174.

69 Jedin, *Council*, p. 243.

70 See Pas, "La doctrine," p. 19.

71 See Jedin, *Council*, pp. 243 and 245. Here, Fenlon appears to belabor and exaggerate Jedin (see Fenlon, pp. 174–76).

72 See Fenlon, *Heresy*, pp. 177–78.

73 See Mayer, *Pole*, p. 157–58.

74 Si quis dixerit, impium iustificari *solius* iustitiae imputatione (CT, p. 427: 1, emphasis mine). See the whole canon: CT, p. 427: 1–7.

75 See CT, p. 505: 26–27.

76 See CT, p. 829: 41–45.

77 Eius enim iustitia proinde nobis, quando iustificamur, communicatur et imputatur (CT, p. 423: 29–30).

78 See CT, p. 446: 37–49, and Pas, "La doctrine," pp. 21–22.

79 See CT, p. 464: 10–43, and Pas, "La doctrine," p. 22.

80 Chap. 7, DE 673: 33–36, translation by DE.

81 See CT, p. 481: 34–40.

82 See CT, p. 482: 42–51.

83 See CT, p. 486: 29–44.

84 See CT, p. 487: 9–15.

85 See CT, p. 487: 33–34.

86 He made appeals throughout the debates; one of the more forceful appeals to Cajetan

came in his late November speech (see CT, p. 672: 9–31, and Pas, "La doctrine," p. 10, note 22 and pp. 14–15).

87 Seripando defended himself by appeal to the work of Cajetan. He rightly drew attention to Cajetan's reflections on the intimate union of the justified with Christ as with their head. However, he took this to mean that the members do not so much merit eternal life as does Christ, who works within them. Cajetan's point was not to minimize human merit but to underscore it by showing precisely how intimate the union is between Christ and his members (see CT, p. 672: 21–35). Seripando went on to discuss a theme known to Cajetan, namely, the significance of the difference between adults and children with respect to merit. Seripando argued that children under the age of discretion cannot present God any merits of their own (see CT, p. 672: 38–48). Instead, they present the merits of Christ. Miranda, it should be noted, referred to this very difference between children and adults as well (see CT, p. 551: 10–22). The Thomist Miranda's reading of the significance of this difference more closely resembles that of Cajetan than does Seripando's. Seripando wanted to draw a distinction between the "application" of Christ's merits by way of faith and the grace actually bestowed upon (or infused into) the justified person, that which enables the justified to perform good works. Miranda had no room for this distinction. To present our inhering justice is to present the merits of Christ, for those merits are truly communicated to us in the grace of justification. Cajetan, too, eschewed any idea of a forgiveness that is not achieved precisely through the infusion of grace. Cajetan followed Thomas faithfully in distinguishing the two effects of grace: first, in the order of being, grace makes its subject deiform and free of damnable sin; second, in the order of free action, grace makes its subject capable of properly meritorious deeds. In fact, the reason Cajetan spoke of "two" justices, that of grace and that of works—for this is really the distinction to which Seripando alluded—was that he, unlike Scotus, followed Thomas in distinguishing between grace and charity, between the elevation of essence and the elevation of will. Children under the age of discretion have no free power over their wills. Hence, the very place in which the distinction between the effects of baptism in adults and in infants is treated is in the article Scotus derided (see Thomas Aquinas, ST IaIIae, q. 110, art. 4, and Cajetan's commentary: Cajetan, *Commentary on the Summa Theologiae*, in Thomas Aquinas, *Summa theologiae*, vol. 7, *Sancti Thomae Aquinatis doctor angelici Opera omnia iussu Leonis XIII. P.M. edita* [Rome: Ex Typographia Polyglatta, 1882], pp. 315–16).

88 Scotus considered forgiveness through extrinsic denomination to be possible according to God's absolute power. He held, however, that this way of forgiveness does not obtain according to God's ordained power. Against even the hypothetical possibility of forgiveness by extrinsic denomination, Cajetan echoed Aquinas's statement: "Non potest intelligi remisio culpae, nisi adesset infusio gratiae." Cajetan rightly noted the unpalatable corollary of Scotus's position: sin itself is held against the sinner only by the divine will. If sin is reckoned by the divine will, then of course forgiveness can be simply reckoned by that same will. It is most unlikely that Lutherans would digest the idea that sin is merely "reckoned" to the sinner (see Cajetan, *Commentary*, ST, IaIIae, q. 113, art. 2, p. 331).

89 Cajetan writes, "And hence, it is required that [the sinner] be changed from [having a] sinful privation to [having the] opposed habit…. From this it is obvious that, since the remission of guilt cannot be understood except by the newly arriving conversion to God, the object of charity, which conversion is the formal effect of charity—therefore it is not intelligible that there be a remission of guilt without the infusion of grace" (Et propterea oportet illum mutari ab impia privatione ad habitum oppostium…. Et ex hoc

patet quod, quia non potest intelligi remissio culpae nisi adveniente conversione ad Deum caritatis obiectum, quae est effectus formalis caritatis; idea non est intelligibile quod fiat remissio culpae absque infusione gratiae [Cajetan, *Commentary*, ST IaIIae q. 113, art. 2, pp. 331a]). In contrast, see Seripando's reading of him (see CT, p. 335:14–41). We see Cajetan's distance from the later-developed theory of double justice in his response to early Lutheran doctrine: "Their assertion that a conviction of this type [i.e., certitude of forgiveness] attains the forgiveness of sins can be said and understood both rightly and wrongly. If it is said and understood that this conviction informed by faith and charity attains forgiveness of sins, this is true.... It is intolerable that one's sins would be forgiven before charity is infused in the person forgiven.... Since friendship consists in mutual love, the forgiveness of sins takes place essentially through charity. Hence what we call the righteousness of faith is identical with charity" (Quod autem dicunt, quod huiusmodi credulitas assequitur remissionum peccatorum, potest & bene & male dici & intelligi. Nam si dicatur & intelligatur, quod haec credulitas formata fide & charitate assequitur veniam peccatorum, verum est.... Intolerabilius autem est dimitti peccata ante charitatem infusam illi, cui dimittuntur peccata.... In mutuo enim amore consistit amicitia: ergo per charitatem formaliter sit remissio peccatorum. Ita quod una atque eadem res est, quae vocatur iustitia fidei, & charitas: sed iustitia fidei, & charitas [Cajetan, *De fide et operibus*, in *Opuscula omnia* {Lyon: Ex officina iuntarum: 1587; reprint: New York: Georg Olms Verlag, 1995}, pp. 288–89]). See also Cajetan *Peccatorum summula*, Novissime Recognita (ex Typographia Baltazaris Belleri, 1613), pp. 557–58.

90   See CT, p. 489: 24–30.

91   See CT, p. 489: 31–33.

92   See chapter 1, and McGrath's excellent presentation in McGrath, *Iustitia Dei*, pp. 27–33.

93   See Mayer, *Pole*, pp. 158–60.

94   Pacem autem istam dicimus in Dei amore consistere, quo nos diligit. Quae quidem dilectio sive amor, quantum ex parte actus Dei, est aeternus et immutabilis, quantum tamen ex parte effectus, quem in nobis operatur, quandoque interrumpitur, sicut patet in his, qui per peccatum ab ipso quandoque deficiunt et iterum per gratiam in ipsum Deum reducuntur. Effectus autem divinae [dilectionis] in nobis, qui per peccatum tollitur, nihil aliud est quam gratia, qua homo dignus fit vita aeterna, a qua per peccatum mortale excluditur, et ideo sequitur, ad remissionem peccati requiri gratiae infusionem (CT, pp. 493:38–494:3; CT has, for the word in brackets, "delectationis"). This argument is, quite clearly, taken from Thomas Aquinas, ST IaIIae, q. 113, art. 2.

95   Ergo cum iustitia inhaerens non sit alia a iustitia Christi, ex quo fluit et dependet ab ea, licet sit propria iustificatis: sequitur quod praesentantes se ante tribunal Christi, retinentes iustitiam inhaerentem non indigent alia nova et speciali applicatione iustitae Christi (CT, p. 527: 15–17). The context of "alia" justifies the translation "alien," though the literal rendering is "other." Vincente calls inhering justice "proper to the justified," implying a personal participation in the justice. It is not as though Christ's justice itself simply dwells in the man who remains in part a mortal sinner. This would be analogous to the Lutheran notion of consubstantiation (see pp. 376–77). Vincente himself upholds the dependence of "iustitia inhaerens" upon the "iustitia Christi" (see CT 527: 10–11). He states, "Guilt from mortal sin cannot remain together with inhering justice." Quia culpa mortalis non stat cum iustitia inhaerente (CT, p. 528: 45–46). If one translates "alia" as "other," it should be understood as meaning "not connected with," as is evident throughout his discussion on CT, pp. 527–28.

96   Jedin labels Miranda as "the only advocate of double justice" (Jedin, *Council*, p. 245).

It would seem strange that Miranda, a Dominican, would be a proponent of double justice; Jedin only pages later describes Miranda as an "opponent" of double justice (ibid., p. 256).

97   Quod sicut aer quamvis illuminatur a sole, non tamen lucidus est formaliter per lumen solis, sed per lumen in eo existens causatum a lumine solis, sic et nos iustificamur a Christo, effective et meritorie, et tamen non sumus iusti formaliter per iustitiam, quae in Christo est, sed per illam, quae in nobis est, quam ex Christo participavimus et quae perpetuo pendet ab illo (CT, p. 550: 37–40). In this quote Miranda draws a distinction and connection between the exemplar and formal causes. It should be noted that Miranda, though a Thomist, does not shrink from using the Scotistic language of "divine acceptance" (see CT, p. 550: 10–35). The inequality between God and man is so great, i.e., infinite, that unless God had established a covenant with us, there would be no parity between our justice and God's demands. But unlike some Nominalists (e.g., Ockham and Biel), Miranda does not propose a possible divorce between covenant, or pact, and the divine ordering through divinely bestowed natures (and second natures). Aquinas himself does not labor over the (monstrous) possibility that God would bestow created grace on a person whom he did *not* order to glory. Nor does he consider it a possibility for the God of wisdom *not* to bestow grace upon a person whom he orders to supernatural glory. The very presupposition of the need for supernatural revelation, as such, is human cooperation in the journey home (see Thomas Aquinas, ST Ia, q. 1, art. 1). St. Thomas conceives the "divine ordering" of all things as inseparable from the intrinsic teleology of the things so ordered, a teleology inscribed in their natures. Formal causality and final causality cannot be rent asunder for him. Consequently, Thomas locates this ordering in the natures (essence and, by extension, the "second nature" of grace) that God gives to things (see Thomas Aquinas, ST IaIIae, q. 114, arts. 1 and 2). For an illuminating statement on the differences between Thomas and Scotus on divine ordering, see Joseph Wawrykow, *God's Grace and Human Action: 'Merit' in the Theology of Thomas Aquinas* (Notre Dame: University of Notre Dame Press, 1995), p. 189. There appears no outstanding reason to think that Miranda espoused a radically Scotistic understanding of divine ordering. In any case, Miranda's chief point was to underscore the dependence in distinction between Christ's justice and our justice. Finally, Cajetan himself rejects the notion of a merely "superadded" ordination not rooted in the nature (or second nature) of the being so ordered. Cajetan follows Thomas in maintaining that God ordains things precisely through their natures (see Cajetan, *Commentary,* ST, IaIIae, q. 114, art. 3, p. 348).

98   See CT, pp. 550: 36–45 and 551: 18.
99   See CT, p. 550: 47–56.
100   See CT, p. 551: 25.
101   See CT, p. 551: 29–46.
102   See Bartolomé Carranza de Miranda, *Comentarios sobre el Catechismo Christiano; edición crítica y estudio histórico*, vol. 2, ed. José Ignacio Tellechea Idígoras (Madrid: Biblioteca de Autores Cristianos, 1972). Miranda emphasizes that the *first* effect of baptism is the forgiveness of sins. He describes forgiveness in terms of cleansing, "limpiado," for as the body is washed with water so the soul is washed by grace (see ibid., p. 182). Once again, he draws out the importance of union with Christ, for the fourth effect of baptism is that, by grace, the baptized become children of God and spouses of Christ (see ibid., p. 184). Again, in the context of the discussion of sacramental reconciliation, Miranda states that the first effect of penitence is the destruction of all sins (see ibid., p. 241). In this way, he weaves into sacramental

reconciliation the necessary hatred for sin: penitence, which is pain for having offended God, leads the penitent to be sorry for all sins (see ibid., p. 242). The grace of the sacrament is contrary to all sins and destroys all mortal sins. He thus does not entertain a forensic forgiveness of sins. Further, in the same work, Miranda specifies charity as the greatest of the virtues and as the *gift* infused by the Holy Spirit. That is, it is distinct from the Holy Spirit. Further, he teaches three degrees of charity in the Christian wayfarer (Bartolomé Carranza de Miranda, *Comentarios sobre el Catechismo Christiano*, vol. 3, ed. Jose Ignacio Tellechea Idigoras [Madrid: Biblioteca de Autores Cristianos, 1999], pp. 41–43). For a view to the contrary, see José Ignacio Idígoras Tellechea, *Melanchthon y Carranza: Prestamos y affinidades* (Salamanca: Centro de Estudios Orientales y Ecuménicos, 1979).

103   See Pas, "La doctrine," pp. 39–40 and 53.

104   Jedin, *Council*, pp. 255–56.

105   See McGrath, *Iustitia Dei*, p. 263.

106   Cardinal Cervini was instrumental in introducing these causes. He even thought of introducing a "material cause." See his proposal for chapter 7 in Marcello Cervini, "Briefe und Traktate aus den Carte Cervniane," appendix to *Briefwechsel Johannes Gropper*, arranged by Reinhard Braunisch, vol. 32, Corpus Catholicorum (Münster: Aschendorff, 1977), pp. 127–28. For the authorship of this draft, see CT, p. 518, note 6.

107   Formalis iustitia una Dei, qua renovamur spiritu mentis nostrae et non modo reputamur, sed vere iusti nominamur et sumus (CT, p. 512: 19–20).

108   McGrath, *Iustitia Dei*, p. 264.

109   See McGrath, *Iustitia Dei*, p. 264, and CT, p. 658: 24–26.

110   CT, p. 700: 25.

111   Demum unica formalis causa est iustitia illa Dei, non qua ipse iustus est, sed qua nos coram ipso iustos facit, qua videlicet ab eo donati renovamur spiritu mentis nostrae et non modo reputamur, sed vere iusti nominamur et sumus, iustitiam in nobis recipientes unusquisque suam, secundum mensuram, quam Spiritus Sanctus partitur singulis prout vult, et secundum propriam uniuscuiusque dispositionem et cooperationem (CT, p. 700: 25–32).

112   Ut ostenderetur, unam esse iustitiam, qua formaliter iustificamur (CT, p. 701: 22).

113   Carl Peter responds to a suggestion by Peter Brunner that Trent's treatment of merit leaves open the possibility that Seripando's theory of double justice was not condemned. Peter cites Jedin in support of his judgment that Brunner was mistaken, since Trent's positive decree rejects double justice. Peter states, "But Trent said the formal cause was *unica* (one and one alone) and identified it with the *iustitia inhaerens*" (Peter, "Decree," note 47, p. 365).

114   "Diese sei nicht die 'gratia increata', sondern der von Gott geschaffene, durch den Hl. Geist der menschlichen Seele eingegossene und ihr inhäriende Habitus der Gnade oder Gerechtigkeit" (Anton Prumbs, *Die Stellung des Trienter Konzils zu der Frage nach dem Wesen der heiligmachenden Gnade: Eine dogmengeschichtliche Abhandlung*" [Paderborn: Druck und Verlag von Ferdinand Schöningh, 1909], p. 59).

115   See the entire essay for more subtle distinctions. Incidentally, Prumbs believes that the decree and the majority of the bishops leaned in favor of the Scotist notion. However, by this he does not mean the Scotist notion of charity as the uncreated indwelling of the Holy Spirit; rather, he means the infused habit of created charity (see Prumbs, *Die Stellung*, pp. 60–62).

116   See Hefner, *Die Entstehungsgeschichte*, p. 263.

117   Michael Schmaus, *Justification and the Last Things*, vol. 6, *Dogma* (Westminster, MD:

Christian Classics, 1984), p. 71.

118 See Peter, "Decree," p. 226.

119 Ohne daß das Konzil hier die Fachausdrücke "Qualität" oder "habitus" für die heiligmachende Gnade gebraucht, vertritt es doch deutlich die Überzeugung, daß der Mensch durch "die Gnade und Liebe" gerechtfertigt werde, die *"durch den Heiligen Geist ausgegossen wird"* (DS 1561), wobei die Person des Heiligen Geistes auch deutlich von dem Geschenk der Gnade, das dem Menschen anhaftet, unterschieden ist (Scheffczyk, "Gemeinsame [Teil I]," p. 64).

120 Hier ist sachlich die Rede von dem, was die Gnadentheologie als *gratia creata* benennt, als "geschaffene Gnade", die den Menschen innerlich erneuert, in ihm wachsen und abnehmen kann; zu unterscheiden ist sie von der *gratia increata*, der "ungeschaffenen Gnade", womit gemeint ist der dreifaltige Gott selbst, der dem Begnadeten innewohnt als Geber aller Gnade (Manfred Hauke, "Die Antwort," p. 91). I would make one qualification here: grace can be present to a greater or lesser degree. Whether it can "be decreased," or rather whether the human person in grace can simply be disposed more or less to its being taken away, is a matter of dispute among Catholics.

121 See DTC, vol. 8.2, col. 2221–22.

122 See Matthias Scheeben, *Handbuch der Katholischen Dogmatik*, vol. 3, ed. Wilhelm Breuning and Franz Lakner (Freiburg: Herder, 1961), pars. 791–915. For a recent reflection on Scheeben, see Richard White, "Justification in Ecumenical Dialogue," pp. 203–08.

123 See Scheeben, *Handbuch*, par. 838.

124 "Obwohl die geschaffene Gnade *einzige* causa formalis des übernatürlichen *Gerechtseins* im Sinne des Tridentinum ist, obwohl sie auch echte Gottes-kindschaft mit wirklicher und eigentlicher Verdienstlichkeit begründet und überhaupt in *vollstem* Masse alles das leistet, was eine *geschaffene* Qualität *je leisten kann*—die Adoptivkindschaft in ihrer *idealen* Fülle, in ihrer tatsächlich gegebenen konkreten und von der Offenbarung bezeugten Gestalt vermag sie nicht adäquat zu begründen" (Norbert Hoffmann, *Natur und Gnade: Die Theologie der Gotteschau als volendeter Vergöttlichung des Geistgeschöpfes bei M. J. Scheeben*, Analecta Gregoriana, no. 160 (Rome: Gregorian University Press, 1967), pp. 266–67.

125 He refers to two condemned propositions of Baius (13 and 15, in DS 1913 and 1915).

126 See Scheeben, *Handbuch*, pars. 874–77.

127 See Scheeben, *Handbuch*, par. 879. This point is at odds with John Henry Cardinal Newman's reading of Petavius and the Catholic tradition as leaving room, within a broader interpretation of Trent, for the opinion that created grace does not suffice unless it is sprinkled with the forgiving mercy of God through Jesus Christ (see John Henry Cardinal Newman, *Lectures on Justification* [New York: Longmans, Green, and Co, 1900]). The reader is hard pressed to distinguish Newman's proposal from the compromise constituted by the theory of double justice. Scheeben, who wrote this work between 1873 and 1887, may have had in mind Newman's *Lectures*, which were re-published in 1874. Newman added an Advertisement to the third edition in which he formally retracted anything that might contradict the tridentine decree on the *unica causa formalis*. The retraction is too formal to be of assistance. Moreover, he reads the tridentine decree as so open-ended that he takes it as leaving him license to espouse the theory of double justification. He gathers this openness from his reading of the intra-catholic disputes about whether charity or created grace or both are the only formal cause of justification (see ibid., pp. 348–54 and 367–71). These intra-catholic disputes do not warrant his conclusion, as the whole thrust of the tridentine decree makes manifest: the clear teaching of chapter 16 is that those who die justified have satisfied

the divine law. To speak of an additional sprinkling of mercy is to undermine this teaching.

128   Let us leave aside the consideration of whether the definition is "de fide divina" or "ad fidem pertinens." In either case, it is binding on the faithful.

129   In JF, the German dialogue appears to do this. I agree with the judgment of the Göttingen faculty that the dialogue fails to do justice to the Lutheran teaching because it restricts itself to a consideration only of the condemnations. I disagree, however, that a full and adequate presentation of Catholic faith can be gathered merely from the canons. See Göttingen, "An Opinion," pp. 11–12. See also Erwin Iserloh, "Luther and the Council of Trent: The Treatment of Reformation Teaching by the Council," chap. in JF, pp. 161–73. Iserloh writes, "Only the canons, not the doctrinal chapters presented before them, are actual definitions in the sense of infallible decisions.... They are indeed binding, but they do not have the magisterial significance of the carefully prepared canons; they are valid as far as their arguments go" (Iserloh, "Luther," p. 170). One wonders if Iserloh has read the warnings at the beginning and end of the positive teachings. Moreover, he seriously errs in maintaining that doctrinal teachings are valid only "as far as their arguments go." The Magisterium puts forth arguments precisely for the benefit of theologians and believers, but these arguments are not to be burdened with establishing the evidential weight determinative for the level of assent required. Faith is of things not seen. In contrast to these attempts to limit the doctrinal teaching to the canons, Tavard appears to limit it to the chapters (see Tavard, *Justification*, p. 128, note 14). Jedin argues for the importance of the doctrinal chapters in setting forth the positive content of Catholic faith. The canons mark the definitive boundaries, especially those between Catholicism and Protestant (especially Lutheran) doctrine, but the content of faith can be derived from the chapters (see Jedin, *Council*, pp. 309–10).

130   Introduction, DE, 671:12–17, translation by DE.

131   Post hanc catholicam de iustificatione doctrinam, quam nisi quisque fideliter firmiterque receperit, iustificari non poterit, placuit sanctae synodo hos canones subiungere, ut omnes sciant, non solum quid tenere et sequi, sed etiam quid vitare et fugere debeant (chap. 16, DE, 678: 35–38).

132   Albert Lang offered a very lucid account of this in the midst of a dispute at mid-century. He wrote, "Die abschließenden Entscheidungen des Konzils, mögen sie in den Kapiteln ausgesprochen werden oder in den Canones niedergelegt sein, *stellen unfehlbare Äußerungen* des kirchlichen Lehramtes dar, die den Zweck verfolgen, die Irrlehren einzudämmen und ihnen gegenüber die katholische Lehre, die veritates catholicae klar und präzise zu formulieren [emphasis mine]" (Albert Lang, "Der Bedeutungswandel der Begriffe 'fides' und 'haeresis' und die dogmatische Wertung der Konzilsentscheidungen von Vienne und Trient," *Müncher Theologische Zeitschrift* 4 [1953]: 146). Lang warned against interpreting everything as de fide divina, but he also held that the Church's intention was to make certain to the faithful the consequences of divine faith, what has been called the indirect objects of teaching.

133   See Profession of Faith, First Vatican Council, in DE, 803:13–15. Further down in the same profession, the council refers to "all that is defined and declared by the sacred canons and ecumenical councils" as well as everything contrary to these teachings (DE, 803: 33–37).

134   See John Paul II, *Ad tuendam fidem*, arts. 3 and 4.

135   See CDF, "Commentary on Profession of Faith's Concluding Paragraphs," *Origins* 28 (1998): 116–19.

136   See, e.g., Benedict XII's declaration, DS 1000–02.

137 "It is only at this point that the rejection of Seripando's concept of *duplex iustitia* may be considered to be complete and unequivocal" (McGrath, *Iustitia Dei*, 264).

138 Si quis dixerit, homines iustificari vel sola imputatione iustitae Christi, vel sola peccatorum remissione, exclusa gratia et charitate, quae in cordibus eorum per Spiritum sanctum diffundatur atque illis inhaereat, aut etiam gratiam, qua iustificamur, esse tantum favorem Dei: a. s. (canon 11, DE, 679: 37–40).

139 McGrath, *Iustitia Dei*, p. 272.

140 See Chemnitz, *Examination*, pp. 516ff.

141 See *Apology*, IV: 71–72.

142 *Epitome*, III: 12 and 21. See also ibid., III: 20 and *Solid Declaration*, III: 49 and 50.

143 See CT, p. 687: 3–7. See also CT, p. 684: 48.

144 See CT, pp. 687–90 and 692: 2–4. For the decision to add a clearer condemnation, see CT, pp. 691: 5.

145 For text and notes about the development of this canon, see CT, pp. 691: 5–6; 714: 16–18 and note 1; 718: 9–12 and 25–42; 719: 8–9 and 14–18; 720: 23–25 and 50–51; 722: 37–43; 759: 39–44; and 760: 1–21.

146 See Jedin, *Council*, p. 293.

147 See CT, p. 692: 2–4.

148 See CT, p. 700: 25.

149 See CT, pp. 709–10.

150 Una enim est iustitia Dei et nostra per Christum Iesum, qua iustificamur: Dei, quia a Deo, nostra, quia in nobis, Christi, quia per Christum (CT, p. 710: 14–16).

151 See CT, p. 711: 49–50.

152 See CT, p. 711: 51–52.

153 See CT, p. 712: 3–4.

154 See CT, p. 712: 18–19.

155 See CT, p. 712: 34–36. The Acta depict him as wanting the addition of the phrase, but the phrase was already in place. A glance at the odd placement of the phrase, however, leads me to believe that Castiglione simply desired better word order.

156 See CT, p. 714: 16–18.

157 See CT, p. 718: 10–12.

158 The dispute erupted between Cornelio Musso, bishop of Bitonto, and (it appears to me) Balthasar Lympus, bishop of Porto. The legate Cardinal Giovanni Maria del Monte, bishop of Palestrina, called for a recess from the discussion, instructing all present to think over the issue for the next meeting. See CT, p. 718: 24–42 for the initial dispute on December 15. It continued the next day (see CT, pp. 719: 8–10, 14–18, and 28–29; and 720: 1–2, 9–10, 23–24, and 50–51). The suggested revisions are summarized later (see CT, p. 722: 37–43).

159 See CT, p. 720: 23–24.

160 Some employed the term "formal cause" and others utilized circumlocutions that conveyed the same point.

161 By "organic relation" I am alluding to the dependence of inhering justice upon the capital grace of Christ; as specified earlier in this work, Christ is not merely the meritorious cause but also the exemplary and fontal cause.

162 *Quae enim iustitia nostra dicitur, quia per eam nobis inhaerentem iustificamur, illa eadem Dei est, quia a Deo nobis infunditur per Christi meritum* (CT, p. 758: 28–29, emphasis original; see also p. 758: 31–33).

163 See CT, p. 758: 31–33.

164 Both Hefner and Prumbs see fit to express this "inhering" nature of justifying grace by the term "habit of grace." See their works, passim.

165   See CT, pp. 759: 39–760: 21.

166   Cum de duplici iustitia accipi possit (CT, p. 760: 4–5).

167   See Marcello Cervini, "Briefe und Traktate aus den Carte Cerviniane," pp. 125–26.

168   Si quis dixerit, homines sine Christi iustitia, per quam nobis meruit, iustificari, *aut per eam ipsam formaliter iustos esse: a. s.* (canon 10, DE, 679: 35–36, emphasis mine).

169   The phrase "eam ipsam" helped address the concerns of those who wanted to avoid separating inhering justice from its fontal source in the capital grace of Christ. They had suggested adding "quae in Christo est."

170   Hefner states that canon 10 was designed in order to condemn more explicitly the theory of an imputation of Christ's righteousness (see Hefner, *Die Entstehungsgeschichte*, pp. 264–65).

171   McGrath attends not to canon 10 but only to canon 11 (see McGrath, *Iustitia Dei*, p. 272). Also, CRE refers to the former only in a dismissing way, while focusing on canon 11 (see CRE, pp. 48–49). Küng likewise addresses only canon 11 and dismisses its relevance (see Küng, *Justification*, pp. 217–18). Jaroslav Pelikan emends canon 10, claiming that it anathematizes "both the idea 'that men are justified without the righteousness of Christ, by which he merited for us,' and the teaching (attributed to Luther) that the righteousness of Christ *alone* could make them 'actually [formaliter] righteous'" (see Jaroslav Pelikan, *Reformation of Church and Dogma* [1300–1700], vol. 4, *The Christian Tradition: A History of the Development of Doctrine* [Chicago: The University of Chicago Press, 1984], p. 285, emphasis mine). The term "alone" does not appear in canon 10.

172   The Göttingen Faculty rightly states, "The second part of canon 10 applies to the Reformation doctrine which insists exactly on this, that the essence of man's righteousness before God is the righteousness of Jesus Christ imputed to man and appropriated by him in faith" (Göttingen, "An Opinion," p. 38).

173   Jedin and Pas point out that there is no explicit condemnation of either double justice as such or the authors of double justice (see Jedin, *Council*, p. 308, and Pas, "La doctrine," p. 51). Nevertheless, both rightly claim that the positive decrees of the council exclude the possibility of one to maintain double justice (see Jedin, ibid., p. 308, and Pas, "La doctrine," pp. 47 and 52). Seripando himself never again spoke of two justices, showing his authentic Catholicity (see Pas, "La doctrine," p. 51). Ehses states emphatically that double justice is excluded: "Da der Mensch ausser der innewohnenden keine andere bedürfe" (Ehses, "Johannes Gropers," p. 181). He rightly links this exclusion with chapter 16 on merit, wherein the council maintains that the justified person who has obeyed the commandments "does not stand in the least need of an imputation of Christ's righteousness" (dass es der Annnahme einer *Iustitia imputata* durchaus nicht bedarf [Ehses, "Johannes Gropers," p. 187]). Jedin also notes that the assertion in chapter 16 excludes the theory of double justice, while at the same time upholding the dependence upon Christ of the human person's share in God's justice. Maxcey concludes, similarly, that Trent's teaching on merit excludes the theory of double justice (see Maxcey, "Double Justice," pp. 276–78). We can recall that McGrath considers the rejection of double justice to be unequivocal (see McGrath, *Iustitia Dei*, p. 264), even though there is no explicit condemnation of "*iustitia imputata*" (see ibid., p. 270). That there is no condemnation of the authors of double justice is of no consequence, since the council in its sixth session omits mention of any names whatsoever.

174   See Philips, *L'Union personnelle*, pp. 202–08.

175   Celle que nous appelons notre *justice*, parce que par son *inhérence* en nous, nous sommes justifiés, celle-là même est la *justice de Dieu* parce qu'elle nous est *infuse* par

le mérite du Christ (ibid., p. 207).

176 Quae enim iustitia nostra dicitur, quia per eam nobis inhaerentem iustificamur, illa eadem Dei est, quia a Deo nobis infunditur per Christi meritum (chap. 16, DE, 678: 18–20).

177 See Otto Hermann Pesch, "The Canons of the Tridentine Decree on Justification: To Whom did they apply? To Whom do they apply today?" chap. in JF, pp. 175–216.

178 Pesch, "The Canons," p. 183.

179 Pesch, "The Canons," p. 184.

180 Pesch, "The Canons," p. 184.

181 Pesch, "The Canons," p. 185.

182 See Pesch, "The Canons," p. 207, note 32.

183 See Pesch, "The Canons," pp. 194–95.

184 McGrath, *Iustitia Dei*, p. 270. See also O'Callaghan, *Fides Christi*, p. 82.

185 See McGrath, *Iustitia Dei*, pp. 145–54.

186 See John Duns Scotus, *In Lib. I. Sententiarum*, vol. 2, *Opera omnia* (Hildesheim: Georg Olms Verlagsbuchhandlung, 1968), dist. 17, q. 3, pp. 960–969. William of Ockham, *Quodlibet VI*, q. 1, art. 2, vol. 9, *Opera theologica* (St. Bonaventure, N.Y.: Editiones franciscani, 1980), pp. 588–89.

187 See William of Ockham, *Quaodlibet III*, q. 10, art. 2, vol. 9, *Opera Theologica*, p. 241.

188 See Richard Cross, *Duns Scotus*, in *Great Medieval Thinkers*, ed. Brian Davies (New York: Oxford University Press, 1999), pp. 107–11. Cross believes that Scotus's theory even has a Pelagian counterpart, as far as God's absolute power goes, for God could have decided to justify persons precisely on the basis of their own efforts. Although there are undoubted similarities between Luther and Scotus, are not many of Luther's criticisms of Catholicism criticisms of the Pelagian bedrock of some nominalists, especially that of Gabriel Biel?

189 See William of Ockham, *In I Dist.*, q. 17, art. 2, vol. 3, *Opera theologica* (St. Bonaventure, N.Y.: Editiones franciscani, 1977), p. 479.

190 Heiko Augustinus Oberman, *The Harvest of Medieval Theology: Gabriel Biel and Late Medieval Nominalism* (Durham, NC: The Labyrinth Press, 1983), pp. 172–78.

191 Pas writes, "Il n'est pas nécessaire de faire ici la distinction entre thomistes et scotistes. Les uns comme les autres jugeaient que, dans l'ordre actuel des choses, les œuvres du juste aboutissent au ciel. D'après les derniers cependant, elles ont encore besoin d'une acceptation divine. Comme celle-ci est promise et confirmée par un pacte, les œuvres du chrétien lui donnent concrètement un droit au ciel" (Pas, "La doctrine," p. 15).

192 For these, "no created grace, whether actual or habitual, *can* render a man *gratus*" (McGrath, *Iustitia Dei*, p. 153, emphasis mine).

193 De facto die Sünden nicht ohne Gnade vergeben werden (Hefner, *Die Entstehungsgeschichte*, p. 258, n. 1).

194 Die inhärierende Gerechtigkeit, der Gnadenhabitus ist und bleibt von Gott als seiner Wirk- und von Christus als seiner Verdienstursache abhängig (Hefner, *Die Entstehungsgeschichte*, p. 263).

195 I am grateful to my colleague, Prof. Mark Lowery, for his insights on this matter.

196 Iustitia, qua iusti sumus, habitus est divinae gratiae (CT, p. 386: 30).

197 See CT, p. 392: 30–33.

198 Ubi dicitur *iustitia qua iusti sumus, habitus est*, desiderarem, quod loco illius vocabuli *habitus* apponeretur *donum* vel aliud simile, ne adversarii nobis impingant, quod nescimus loqui nisi figmentis ut ipsi aiunt scholasticis (CT, p. 414: 3–5).

199 Praeter verbum inhaerentiae desideratum est et aliud verbum sc. *tamquam habitus infusus*. Quod videretur superfluum, cum verbo *inhaeret* intelligatur habitus, et apud

omnes constat, caritatem de qua sermo est, diffundi per Spiritum Sanctum, non a nobis acquiri (CT, p. 521: 15–18).

200   Thomist that he was before his "conversion," Seripando would know this to be a grievous misreading.

201   This was the point Lainez wished to make (see Hefner, *Die Entstehungsgeschichte*, pp. 234–35).

202   Accepta iustificationis gratia per peccatum exciderunt (chap. 14, DE, 676: 38). Acceptam iustificationis gratiam amitti (chap. 15, DE, 677: 25–26).

203   Qua videlicet ab eo donati renovamur spiritu mentis nostrae, et non modo reputamur, sed vere iusti nominamur et sumus, iustitiam in nobis recipientes unusquisque suam, secundum mensuram, quam Spiritus sanctus partitur singulis prout vult, et secundum propriam cuiusque dispositionem et cooperationem.... per Spiritum sanctum charitas Dei diffunditur in cordibus eorum, qui iustificantur, atque ipsis inhaeret.... Unde in ipsa iustificatione cum remissione peccatorum haec omnia simul infusa accipit homo per Iesum Christum, cui inseritur: fidem, spem et charitatem (chap. 7, DE, 673: 27–38).

204   Per Christum Iesum illis donatam (chap. 7, DE, 674: 8–9).

205   In ipsa iustitia per Christi gratiam accepta...crescunt atque magis iustificantur (chap. 10, DE, 675: 5–7).

206   Quae enim iustitia nostra dicitur, quia per eam nobis inhaerentem iustificamur, illa eadem Dei est, quia a Deo nobis infunditur per Christi meritum (chap. 16, DE, 678: 18–20).

207   Gratia et charitate, quae in cordibus eorum per Spiritum sanctum diffundatur atque illis inhaeret (canon 11, DE, 679: 38–39).

208   DS, 904.

209   See Hefner, *Die Entstehungsgeschichte*, p. 260, note 3. See also Pas, "La doctrine," p. 51.

210   See Bellarmine, op. cit., pp. 210–11. Of course, Bellarmine's opinion that grace is identical with charity is a free theological opinion.

211   Est autem gratia, quemadmodum Tridentina Synodus ab omnibus credendum pœna anathematis proposita decrevit, non solum per quam peccatorum sit remissio, sed divina qualitas in anima inhaerens, ac veluti splendor quidam, et lux, quae animarum nostrarum maculas omnes delet, ipsasque animas pulchriores et splendidiores reddit (Bellarmine, op. cit., p. 242). For an English translation of the Catechism, see *The Catechism of the Council of Trent*, trans. John A. McHugh and Charles J. Callan (Rockford, IL: Tan, 1982), p. 188.

212   See Ruard Tapper, *Article 8, De Iustificatione*, in *Opera omnia* (Cologne, 1582), tom. 2, p. 1a.

213   Sit qualitas à qua intrinseca denominatione, verè iusti dicimur, quodque haec qualitas vera sit iustitia (ibid., p. 10b).

214   See ibid., p. 10b.

215   See ibid., p. 10b, and pp. 26a–28a.

216   See ibid., p. 11a and pp. 21b–22a.

217   Ibid., p. 13.

218   See Dominic de Soto, *De natura et gratia* (Paris: John Foucher, 1549), book II, chap. 19, p. 176a and p. 177a.

219   See ibid., chap. 18, p. 169b.

220   See ibid., p. 170a.

221   See ibid., p. 171a. That there is warrant for the claim that the possibility of forgiveness without grace is related to the possibility of the creation of man in the state of pure nature can be gleaned from Ockham's treatment of Mary. In a question about the

Virgin, Ockham maintains that God could forgive sins without an infusion of grace because he could have ordained man to his end without bestowing created grace; the habit of original justice, in such a situation, would not be necessary. Therefore, the lack of it would not be considered guilt; both sin and righteousness would not be a matter of possession or non-possession of the habit of grace. See William of Ockham, *Quodlibet* III, q. 10, art. 2, p. 241. It is apparent, in this respect, that Soto would not have followed Cajetan's reading of Thomas on divine ordination.

222 See de Soto, *De natura*, book II, chap. 19, pp. 174a–75a.

223 See ibid., p. 181b and p. 182.

224 See ibid., chap. 20, pp. 179a–80a.

225 "Formalis enim causa, ut inter philosophos & theologos probatissimum est & receptissimum, est res illa, vel qualitas, quae inest subiecto: sicuti anima est forma hominis: lumen, forma aeris" (ibid., p. 178b).

226 "Et [quamvis] hoc optimè intelligitur ab iis, qui agnoscunt, gratiam habitum esse infusum, tamen ut quisque pertinacissimè abnegaverit habitus, nihilofecius, nisi velit errare, fateri debet pro modulo suae cuiusque cooperationis" (ibid., p. 179b).

227 See ibid., p. 181a and p. 182a. For a superb and thorough study, see Karl Josef Becker, *Die Rechtfertigungslehre nach Domingo de Soto: Das Denken eines Konzilsteilnehmers vor, in und nach Trient*, vol. 156, Analecta Gregoriana, Series Facultatis Theologicae (Rome: Verlagsbuchhandlung, 1967), esp. pp. 313–36. Becker demonstrates Soto's rejection of the theory of imputation and his adherence to grace as the reality of divine participation. Grace as participation exists in the human person (see ibid., pp. 328–29).

228 McGrath, *Iustitia Dei*, p. 257.

229 McGrath, *Iustitia Dei*, p. 270.

230 "Quod non inest alicui subiecto, neque potest ipsum formaliter denominare, praesertim denominatione absoluta" (Andreas de Vega, *De Iustificatione*, vol. 1, *Opera omnia* (Cologne: 1572), chap. 22, p. 162b. On this page, he accepted Trent as defining the formal cause definitively. He made the content of that definition clear in the pages that follow, as will be evident in the text. It should be noted that St. Peter Canisius, S.J. held this text in high esteem.

231 "Factus quidem dicitur esse nostra iustitia, non quòd ille sit nostra formalis iustitia, sed quae per illum iustificamur meritoriè & efficienter" (ibid., chap. 23, p. 162b).

232 Sed iustitia nostra, est ex sua ratione aliquid nobis intrinsecum, & verè nobis inhaerens. Et ideò non potest nisi figuratè, neque Deus, neque Christus, neque aliqui Dei aut Christi actus, dici nostra iustitia formalis, sed oportet eiusmodi omnes propositiones causaliter interpretari (ibid., p. 163b).

233 Tametsi non sub nomine habitum.... Quod ne intelligi potest, si non sit aliquid creatum nostra iustitia.... non dubitaremus caritatem esse accidens quoddam creatum (ibid., chap. 24, p. 265b).

234 See Lawrence of Brindisi, "Lutheranismi hypotyposis," vol. 2, pt. 3, *Opera omnia* (Fribourg, 1933), p. 214.

235 See ibid., p. 215.

236 See ibid., p. 232.

237 See St. Francis de Sales, *Troisième Série—Controverse*, vol. 23.2, *Œvres de Saint François de Sales* (Annecy: Monastery of the Visitation, 1928), p. 114.

238 See ibid., pp. 114–15.

239 See ibid., pp. 115–16.

240 Iustitia, qua iustificatur per fidem ipius, consistit formaliter in oboedientia mandatorum, quae est operum iustitia; non autem in gratia aliqua animae infusa, qua

adoptatur homo in filium De et secundum interiorem hominem renovatur ac divinae naturae consors efficitur, ut, sic per Spiritum Sanctum renovatus, deinceps bene vivere et Dei mandatis oboedire possit (DS 1942).

241   See DS 1942 and 1969. These papal condemnations were preceded by several condemnations by theological schools: by the University of Paris in 1560 and by the Universities of Alcala and Salamanca in 1565.

242   See Jean-Miguel Garrigues, "La doctrine de la grâce habituelle dans ses sources scripturaires et patristiques," *Revue Thomiste* 103 (2003): 179–202. Philips is working with the traditional scholarly reading that Philip the Chancellor was the first to describe grace as "sanctifying grace," a created grace residing in the human person as a habit. See also Jedin, *Council*, p. 166.

243   See, esp., Garrigues, "La doctrine," p. 196.

244   Origen of Alexandria, *On First Principles* I, 5.5, trans. G. W. Butterworth (Gloucester, MA: Peter Smith, 1973), p. 50. For the Greek, see PG 11, 164 C.

245   Gregory of Nyssa is perhaps the most noteworthy; citations would be so abundant as to be unnecessary.

246   David Balás, *ΜΕΤΟΥΣΙΑ ΘΕΟΥ: Man's Participation in God's Perfections according to Saint Gregory of Nyssa*, Studia Anselmiana, no. 55 (Rome, Libreria Herder, 1966), p. 9.

247   St. Athanasius, *Four Discourses Against the Arians*, discourse 1, chap. 10, par. 36, in *Athanasius: Select Works and Letters*, trans. John Henry Newman, vol. 4, *Nicene and Post-Nicene Fathers*, second series, ed. Philip Schaff and Henry Wace (Peabody, MA: Hendrickson Publishers, Inc., 1999), p. 327. See the ensuing discussion as well. For the Greek, see PL 26.2, c. 88. There we encounter the epxressions "en ousia sumbebêkos" and "sumbebêkena tina charin kai hexin aretês." See also Athanasius's "To the Bishops of Africa," pars. 7–8 in ibid., pp. 492–93.

248   Ibid., *De Synodis*, par. 53, pp. 478–79.

249   St. Basil of Caesarea, *On the Spirit*, in *Basil: Letters and Select Works*, trans. Blomfield Jackson, vol. 8, *Nicene and Post-Nicene Fathers*, second series, ed. Philip Schaff and Henry Wace (Christian Literature Publishing Company, 1895; reprint, Peabody, MA: Hendrickson Publishers, Inc., 1999), chap. 9, pars. 22 and 23, p. 15.

250   Basil of Caesarea, *On the Spirit*, chap. 16, pars. 39 and 40, p. 25.

251   Balás, *ΜΕΤΟΥΣΙΑ ΘΕΟΥ*, p. 122.

252   See ibid., p. 124.

253   Thus, against the subordinationist Eunomius, Gregory insisted that neither the Son nor the Spirit "participate" in divinity (see ibid., p. 125).

254   See ibid., p. 129.

255   Ibid., p. 130.

256   See ibid., p. 128. Garrigues helpfully contends that, for all his energy fighting the scholastic "created grace," Gregory Palamas (1296–1359) would never have denied that the uncreated energies actually transform the human person into a just and divinized person. Thus, Palamas gives no shelter to the theory of "imputation" (Garrigues, "La doctrine," pp. 180–81).

257   See ibid., pp. 130–40.

258   Ibid., p. 56.

259   See ibid., p. 133.

260   Walter Burghardt, *The Image of God in Man According to Cyril of Alexandria*, Studies in Christian Antiquity, no. 14, ed. Johannes Quasten (Woodstock, MA: Woodstock College Press, 1957), p. 71; see the whole discussion, ibid., pp. 35–83.

261   Bonaventure, Aquinas, and other great medieval theologians did not shy away from

criticizing Lombard on this point. Thomas's arguments do not "minimize" the gift of grace, reducing it to a "mere quality." On the contrary, Thomas insisted that the Holy Spirit does dwell within the justified. He held that this indwelling is the very end or goal of grace, the very end of human life. It is this indwelling which is the "first fruits" of the beatific vision, the eschatological consummation of the earthly taste of the divine. Thomas also argued, however, that when God moves creatures, he moves them according to movements proper to them. If he does this in the order of nature, much more so in the order of grace, since he loves his children with a special love. Therefore, God moves the justified according to a supernatural form by which the movements of faith, hope, and love become "connatural" to them. Their earthly journey is not a mere "passage" into the divine but an active journey; the just are not passengers on a train, but sojourners with God. See Thomas Aquinas, *De caritate*, art. 1.

262   See Karl Rahner, "Some Implications of the Scholastic Concept of Uncreated Grace," in *God, Christ, Mary and Grace*, trans. Cornelius Ernst, vol. 1, *Theological Investigations* (Baltimore: Helicon Press, 1961), pp. 319–46. Rahner states his initial position that the formal cause of justification is sanctifying grace (ibid., p. 342). The position laid out here does not appear inimical to his later insistence upon a "quasi-formal" causality exercised by the Holy Spirit who adopts the human person, dwells within him, and *thus* infuses into him a created gift of sanctification. See also idem, "Nature and Grace," in *More Recent Writings*, trans. Kevin Smyth, vol. 4, *Theological Investigations* (Baltimore: Helicon Press, 1966), pp. 169–78.

263   I have already referred to the work of Scheeben. For his disputant's opinion, see T. Granderath, "Die Controverse über die Formalursache der Gotteskinschaft und das Tridentinum," *Zeitschrift für Katholische Theologie* 5 (1881): 283–319; and idem, "Die Controverse über den Formalgrund der Gotteskindschaft zum letzten Male," *Zeitschrift für Katholische Theologie* 8 (1884): 545–79.

264   Scheffczyk expresses the subtle balance between created and uncreated grace excellently (see Scheffczyk, "Ungeschaffene," pp. 81–97). Scheffczyk resists the attempts of contemporary Catholics to usher created grace out the backdoor. To rediscover grace as the self-gift of God, uncreated grace, is to make all the more intelligible the notion of created grace. God grants us this created disposition so that we can be his children and so that we can tend to him as intelligent agents (see ibid., pp. 90–91). To conceive of created grace as an agent is to misunderstand the Catholic teaching (see ibid., pp. 91–92). The whole point of the Catholic emphasis on created grace is, paradoxically, to emphasize the greater importance of uncreated grace, the indwelling of the Holy Spirit. The Catholic teaching *emphasizes* created grace only in response to a denial of its fundamental role in the indwelling, for unless man is disposed (by God), he cannot enjoy God.

265   Perhaps this explains the different emphases in Leo XIII's and Pius XII's descriptions of indwelling (see DS 3329–31 and 3814–15). It would seem that Pope John Paul II expresses himself more in the terms of Pope Leo than in those of Pius XII, but it should be noted that these positions are not antithetical. It may be a question of emphasis; it may be a matter of different questions at stake. One can say that the indwelling is "first" since it is the final end of grace and since the Holy Spirit is the efficient cause of the infusion of grace. On the other hand, it might be said that the infusion of sanctifying grace is first in the sense of a (material) condition for the possibility of indwelling, since God dwells within the human person inasmuch as the human person attains to God and since no human person can attain to God without that grace.

266   Henri de Lubac, *A Brief Catechesis on Nature and Grace*, trans. Richard Arnandez (San Francisco: Ignatius Press, 1984), pp. 41–42, citing at the end, Louis Bouyer, *Le*

Père invisible (Paris: Cerf, 1976), p. 288.

267   Ibid., p. 47.

268   See John Paul II, *Dominum et Vivificantem* (Washington, D.C.: USCC, 1986), art. 34.

269   See John Paul II, *Dominum*, art. 34.

270   See John Paul II, *Dominum*, arts. 42–45.

271   See John Paul II, *Dominum*, art. 45.

272   John Paul II, *Dominum*, art. 52.

273   See Bonaventure, *Breviloquium*, V, chap. 1, and Schmaus, *Justification and the Last Things*, 72–73. Rahner puts it eloquently: Grace "is something that is only 'put at man's disposal' in that act of 'letting oneself be disposed of' which is the proper gift of the freest grace, the miracle of love. Ontic categories are only maintained here (even by Catholics) because and insofar as a Catholic philosophy does hold that the real (and what could be more real and effective than the love of God?) must be thought of as 'real' and 'being', that the highest must be expressed in the most abstract words, and that therefore the act of divine love toward us—God's act, not ours, though enabling us to act, and not just submit—previous to our act, must be considered as that which renders possible our moral and religious decisions. It cannot therefore be expressed except in categories of being such as state, accident, habit, infusion, etc." (Rahner, "Nature and Grace," p. 177). Despite Schmaus's contribution, does he not overstate the legitimate plurality open to theologians? He rightly sums up the state of justification as a "resemblance" to God. Can we follow him when he adds, "The Council of Trent did not formally propose the teaching that God brings about the act of justification through the inpouring of sanctifying grace" (Schmaus, *Justification*, p. 74)? Athanasius's sound analysis of resemblance and likeness, cited above, shows clearly that it is a participation in the divine goodness, capable of augmentation and diminution. Are such characteristics attributable to uncreated reality?

274   See Hans Urs von Balthasar, *The Dramatis Personae: Man in God*, vol. 2, *Theo-Drama: Theological Dramatic Theory*, trans. Graham Harrison (San Francisco: Ignatius Press, 1990), p. 315, note 2.

275   Peter, "Decree," p. 221.

276   Ita neque propria nostra iustitia tamquam ex nobis propria statuitur ... (chap. 16, DE, 678: 16–17).

277   USA, par. 111.

278   Peter, "Decree," p. 225.

279   See canons 22 and 23, DE, 680: 28–34, and chap. 16, DE, 678: 1–34.

280   Though in itself such love is good (not in its imperfection but in the measure that it strives for a true good, namely one's own well-being), it falls far short of the charity that loves God for his own sake. The American dialogue states, "Meritorious works, moreover, cannot derive from a mere desire to accumulate spiritual treasures for oneself. Such works presuppose a charity that proceeds from God and goes out to God" (USA, par. 111).

281   Si quis dixerit, per hanc doctrinam catholicam de iustificatione, a sancta synodo hoc praesenti decreto expressam, aliqua ex parte gloriae Dei vel meritis Iesu Christi domini nostri derogari, et non potius veritatem fidei nostrae, Dei denique ac Christi Iesu gloriam illustrari: a. s. (canon 33, DE, 681: 25–28, translation by DE).

282   See UUS, art. 36.

PART TWO

Contemporary Attempts at Rapprochement

SWISS CATHOLIC theologian Hans Küng (1928–), several Finnish Lutheran theologians, and German Lutheran theologian Wolfhart Pannenberg (1928–) each present theological treatments of justification that promise ecumenical fecundity. Küng's work "marked the dawn of a new era of positive ecumenical discussion of a doctrine which had hitherto been seen largely as an insuperable obstacle to such dialogue."[1] Comparing Karl Barth's work with Trent, Küng argues that in substance there is no real divergence between Protestant and Catholic theories of justification. A school of Finnish Lutheran theologians contends that Luther's theology of justification is laden with notions of ontological sanctification and participation in Christ. They critique some elements of *The Book of Concord* as failing to measure up to Luther's insights; they likewise critique certain articulations of Catholic teaching that depict justifying grace as a habit infused into the soul. Pannenberg culls from the scriptural witness, which he interprets with the aid of philosophical rigor, in order to qualify what he sees as extreme elements in both the Lutheran and the Catholic traditions. He suggests that the basic intent of each tradition is harmonious with the other but that extreme formulations in both are in need of change. Of these, Küng alone contends that no doctrinal alteration is needed by either Protestants or Catholics. Pannenberg and the Finns imply the necessity of doctrinal change for an adequate establishment of consensus.

CHAPTER 3

Hans Küng

KÜNG'S WORK *Justification*, originally a dissertation, has been widely recognized as the stimulus of the "new willingness on the part of Roman Catholic theologians to discuss the controverted issue of justification."[2] Küng himself owes a debt to Johannes Lortz's historical work, which brought to light the Pelagian character of the Nominalism in which Luther was educated and against which he understandably reacted. Exposing this and other mitigating factors, Lortz helped Catholics assess the Reformation movement afresh.[3] Küng published his *Rechtfertigung* in 1957 (the English translation was printed in 1964). Although for the most part well-received, *Justification* has had some critics.[4] Regardless of one's opinion of the work, its indisputably great influence warrants attention to the argument.[5] *Justification* outlines the thought of Karl Barth and offers a fair-minded Catholic response. Küng praises Barth's work and criticizes only the latter's one-sided, and arguably misguided, attacks on Trent and Catholic theology. Since Karl Barth was a Reformed theologian of a particular sort, there are limitations to the use of Küng's work in relation to the Lutheran-Catholic dialogue; still, the very "success" of this work in furthering the Lutheran-Catholic dialogue attests to its relevance.[6]

Presentation

Küng begins his Catholic response to Barth with a methodological reflection, following Karl Rahner's lead in recognizing that every doctrinal formula is just as much a beginning as an end (*Justification*, 102–03 and 117). Doctrinal formulas, being necessarily finite, cannot exhaust the mystery. To limit oneself to rigid formulas would obscure the mystery to which the formulas bear witness against the one-sided rigidity of heresies. Küng draws attention both to the perfectibility of doctrines—although not flawed in themselves, they can be improved and refined over time—and to the context within which doctrines are formulated—the pressure of heresy.[7] Given the de facto setting of councils (before Vatican II), Küng concludes, doctrines can unwittingly conspire against the balance of the *depositum fidei* they are meant to defend

(*Justification*, pp. 107, 217–18, and 235). One-sided responses to heresy can lead to a neglect or practical denial of the grain of truth heretics rightly affirm. For instance, an overwhelming emphasis on tradition as an interpretative milieu for scripture might be erroneously taken by Catholics as "permission" to neglect the use of scriptures for prayer, contemplation, and theological reflection. In the case of justification, Catholic emphasis on sanctification bears the potential for an adverse, albeit indirect, effect on the lived appreciation of God's mercy in Christ Jesus. Not without cause, Protestants ceaselessly point to a practical Pelagianism and moralism in Catholic sermons and pastoral ministry. Küng admits, with Barth, that this much is often the case with the Catholic *reception* of Trent. He chides Barth, on the other hand, for failing to recognize that the actual intention of the Council of Trent was not to deny the prevenient grace of God but to respond to the perceived Protestant denial of the real power of God's sanctifying work. Trent, Küng insists, must not be read in isolation either from its basic intention to reject this perceived error or from the thrust of Catholic teaching as a whole, which irrevocably includes the anti-Pelagian condemnations from the first millennium (i.e., the Second Council of Orange).

After sketching these and other methodological considerations, Küng turns to scripture, discussing the terms "grace" and "justification" in order to establish the parameters of his proposal. Scripture scholars discern several meanings of the term "grace" in both Testaments: a created gift, the response of thankfulness, and, chiefly, divine mercy or favor (*Justification*, pp. 197–200). The referential breadth of "grace" must be retained, against both Catholic and Protestant tendencies to isolate one meaning from the multiform scriptural witness (*Justification*, pp. 201–07 and 214–16). Theological traditions reflect this scriptural polyvalence with respect to justification, which some traditions depict as a declaration of justice and which others depict as a "making just" of the sinner. Neglect of such terminological differences hinders inter-confessional communication. Return to the ordered differentiation of the scriptural testimony is paramount. The primary sense of "justification" in scripture is that of a declaration: "The term 'justification' as such expresses an actual declaration of justness and not an inner renewal" (*Justification*, p. 213). Notwithstanding the primacy of the "declarative" aspect, a purely forensic reading of "justification" does not adequately cover the breadth of the scriptural data. Küng asks, "Does it follow from this that God's declaration of justice does not imply an inner renewal?" (*Justification*, p. 213). The answer is a resolute, "No." God's word is effective. The "declarative" connotation simply prevents any illusion of human self-justification, any illusion that God recognizes (declares just analytically) the person who is righteous by works: "It all comes down to this, that it is a matter of *God's* declaration of justice and not of man's word" (*Justification*, p. 213).[8] Notwithstanding the primacy of divine mercy, the effects of God's word must not be underestimated: "The sinner *is* just, really and truly, outwardly and inwardly, wholly and completely. His sins *are* forgiven, and man is just in his heart" (*Justification*, p. 213).

Since the scriptures proclaim *both* the declarative and the ontological aspects of justification, is there any cause for disputes about forensic versus ontological notions of justification? Does not each communion simply highlight one aspect of this twofold reality, Catholics emphasizing the passive aspect of the sinner's becoming just and Protestants emphasizing the active sense of God's justifying act? Is not each communion in principle willing to accept that which the other emphasizes? Are not the condemnations of the Reformation era merely one-sided stances, albeit truthful in themselves, taken against perceived exaggerations of the "opponent"? Küng replies in the affirmative. He then throws down the gauntlet against apologists and controversialists who fan the tinder of discord and disunity: "Protestants speak of a declaration of justice and Catholics of a making just. But Protestants speak of a declaring just which includes a making just; and Catholics of a making just which supposes a declaring just. Is it not time to stop arguing about imaginary differences?" (*Justification*, p. 221).

After setting forth the parameters of his investigation, Küng supports his claim with theological arguments. Only a difference in terms, concerns, and approaches distinguishes the doctrines; both communions affirm the same essential truths. The claim that Küng most carefully works out here is that of the terminological differences between Catholics and Protestants. This clarification was much-needed at the time. Although not too difficult to grasp, the clarification demands a complexity in its presentation. The reader must keep in mind the different uses of terms, the realities to which they refer, and the proposed new ways of expressing these same realities. In order to simplify my presentation, I will discuss Küng's analysis with reference to three things: the reality to which the terms refer (also designated by a term!), the Protestant term for this reality, and the Catholic term for this reality. The reader can refer to the table on the next page for ready comparison of terms and those realities to which they refer. I would only ask that the reader not take this table as fully adequate either to the mystery of justification or to either communion's perception of that mystery; it is meant only to serve as a point of departure for discussion of Küng's own proposal. Furthermore, for purposes that will become evident in the "Critical Analysis," the chart also makes a further distinction (not drawn by Küng) in the second item of this schema.

Table: Terms and Realities

	1. Reality Signified	2. Lutheran Terms	3. Catholic Terms
A.	God's mercy through Jesus Christ *Küng: Objective Justification*	Divine Favor Forgiving Love Grace	Efficient Cause Meritorious Cause Redemption
B.	Effect of God's mercy *Küng: Subjective justification or* *Objective sanctification*	B: Justifying faith B': Regeneration	B: Forgiveness B': Sanctification
C.	Inner moral rectitude and good works	Renewal of life	Meritorious works

Implicit in Küng's reflection is a distinction between three aspects of the mystery of salvation: God's mercy towards sinners (A), the ontological effect of this mercy (B), and the good works that can follow from this ontological effect (C).[9] The two ecclesial bodies label these realities differently, but despite differences in nuance, both esteem the same truths. With careful discernment, Küng argues, Catholics can come to recognize their doctrine in Protestant theology, and vice-versa. Unfortunately, the reader encounters a difficulty in understanding Küng's thesis because the three aspects of the mystery of salvation are not consistently distinguished with care. As the reader will see, Küng attends predominantly if not exclusively to only two of the three aspects at any given point.

As stated above, scripture employs the term "justification" primarily to signify a "declaration of justice." This declaration occurs not because of any created habit or good work in the one to be justified. It occurs simply because, while we were yet sinners, the innocent Son of God took on human flesh and suffered the fate of the worst of sinners, an agonizing death on the cross (Rom 5:8). Because God so loved the world, he gave his only Son (Jn 3:16). God redeemed the world in Christ Jesus, who died and rose again. Catholics often identify this divine initiative as the "redemption." Protestants refer to the same reality as "justification." Küng notes the importance of drawing a distinction between, this "objective" sense of justification through the death and resurrection of Christ and the "subjective" realization of justification (*Justification*, pp. 223–26). Whereas the former takes place once for all and for all people, the latter takes place only in given individuals, i.e., in those who have true faith: "What Barth and with him many Protestants call 'justification' largely coincides with what we Catholics call 'redemption' [so that] many expressions that sound heretical [i.e., to Catholics] ought to be understood as completely orthodox (e.g., '*all* men are justified in Christ…')" (*Justification*,

p. 227).

Küng places the emphasis on the redemption itself (A), contending that this—not the subjective appropriation of it—is the heart of the mystery of salvation (*Justification*, p. 231). A difficulty in his presentation appears. On the one hand, as noted above, Küng distinguishes objective justification—God's mercy in Christ by which all are declared just (A)—from the subjective appropriation of this justification (B). The first aspect takes place for all, but the second takes place concretely for each person through faith. This would seem to suggest that all are declared just but that only those who have genuine faith—which, most readers will agree, need not be limited to those explicitly confessing Christian faith—in fact become just, whatever "becoming just" might mean for the respective communions. In this regard, objective justification is that to which Catholics refer by the term "redemption" and is identical with the declaration of forgiveness that Protestants label "justification." So I read this line of thought in Küng.

On the other hand, Küng elsewhere makes it ambiguous whether the objective declaration itself *is* the divinely wrought transformation of sinners into just persons: "The justification of the sinner means the declaration of justice by God who at the cross and in the resurrection of Jesus Christ declares all sinners free and just, *and thereby makes them just*, though this act can, for the Church, have its consequences in the individual only if the individual submits in faith to God's verdict" (*Justification*, p. 230, emphasis mine). What does he mean by "and thereby makes them just"? How can this clause be squared with the final qualification, "though this act can, for the Church, have its consequences in the individual only if the individual submits in faith to God's verdict"? To what "consequences" is he referring? Is he referring to the divine transformation of the sinner, or is he referring to the good works of the sinner made just, or, finally, is he referring indiscriminately to both? His treatment of faith and works, to be presented below, inclines toward relegating the "consequences" to the renewal of life in good works (C), that is, to faith working out what God has already accomplished for the sinner, i.e., declaring and thereby "making" him just (whatever that might mean). In this second line of thought, Küng appears to speak of objective and subjective justification not so much as redemption (A) and its subjective realization (B) but as the two inseparable aspects of God's single act: "These two [objective and subjective justification] do not exclude but rather include one another" (*Justification*, p. 232). According to Küng, Barth failed to observe that the different aspects of this mystery are two sides of the same reality. Barth faltered because he compared his own notion of justification (2A) to the Catholic notion of justification (3B and 3 B'). Instead, Barth should have perceived "active and passive justification as two complementary sides of one reality" (*Justification*,

p. 232).

Admittedly, Küng does at times express his position with the requisite subtlety. For instance, his praise of Karl Rahner's emphasis on uncreated grace occasions a balanced treatment of the indwelling of God and the requisite effect (or condition) of this indwelling:

> If God is to be able to do man this favor, if the triune God is to be able to dwell in man in this marvelous way, man must be properly prepared for it. He must have been prepared for it by God Himself. God does this through His own indwelling, but in such a way that in the sphere of created being something actually happens and becomes reality. In Catholic tradition this reality is called created grace (gratia creata). The gratia creata is not the main thing. (*Justification*, p. 201)

It is to be regretted that this balance is not consistent and that Küng does not consistently integrate these two lines of thought.

To continue, his first line of thought is a comparison of and thus a distinction between the declaration of forgiveness and its subjective appropriation through faith. What is the nature of this appropriation? Does it consist in the "effect" of the declaration in the life of the individual (B)? It might seem that this is the case in the following recapitulation of this line of thought:

> Thus the accent is not on the "subjective" but on the "objective" aspect of justification. [Nevertheless, it] is true that everything depends on this having its effect within individual men, on its realization in the individual, on human participation in it. It is true, too, that only he who believes is actually (subjectively) justified. (*Justification*, p. 231)

He here equates subjective justification with the individual appropriation of God's redeeming work. However, in the second line of thought, Küng links both objective and subjective justification together in the same act of God, understood from two points of view: from that of God's objective, saving action and from that of the very effect of this same act, which "thereby makes them just." This second line of thought portrays all men as "made just" in Christ. Is this "being made just" in Christ the corollary of God's saving action, the passive side of the objective event of salvation? Yet here, the objective and subjective, the active and passive, sides of justification are knitted together so closely that it would appear that "all men" are ontologically justified in the redemption. But according to the first line of thought, the declaration of forgiveness has its effects on sinners only individually, through faith.

As we shall see, the ambiguity arising from the neglect of consistent integration of these two lines of thought obscures the need to assess the distinctions between and relations among redemption (A), the effect of

redemption (B), and good works (C). Consequently, the focal issue at stake between Catholic and Protestant perspectives—the nature of the effect of redemption (B), what Trent labels the formal cause of justification—is only inadequately addressed.

Küng's treatment of faith, moreover, bears the marks of a similar obscurity. When discussing whether or not one is justified through "faith alone,"Küng compares merely two terms: God's act (presumably A) and the human response (A or B?): "The justification of the sinner is the work of God, but it is accomplished in man. How does man behave in this work? What is man's attitude in God's justification?" (*Justification*, p. 249). There are but two references in this question: God's work (A) and the human response. God's work falls on the extrinsic side (extrinsic in the good sense, that is, in the sense of its source, as indicated in Rom 10:3); the human response most likely falls on the side of renewal through good works (C).Küng asks this question from the perspective of the Reformers' concerns about the synergism and Pelagianism of the errant Catholic theology under which they were educated. The reader should notice, however, that the distinctively Catholic insistence on a mediating term, infused grace (B), is missing. Küng compares only God's action (A) and human action (C). Obscured from view at this point is the actual effect of God's action (B), the infusion of which is not due in any way to human potential or creativity.[10] Omitting consideration of this middle term, the chapter proceeds to claim a total compatibility between Catholic and Protestant teaching on the doctrine "by faith alone [*sola fide*]." The Reformation phrase "sola fide" underscores the total incapacity of the human sinner, because "man achieves nothing; there is no human activity" (*Justification*, p. 252; see also pp. 259 and 265). The believer simply accepts God's objective deed in faith and through faith receives the effect of God's salvation. Far more than barren "historical knowledge" or "intellectual assent," the faith prized by the Reformers resembles the characteristics Catholics attribute to faith and hope (*Justification*, p. 255).[11]

So, Küng embraces the dictum "faith alone justifies," defining faith as both acceptance of kerygma and confident trust in God's saving action (*Justification*, pp. 252–53).[12] Although he adds that it is *living* faith "which alone justifies," he does not clearly specify that faith "lives" precisely by charity; he rather joins the Reformation chorus that although faith alone justifies, faith ought never and can never be alone (*Justification*, p. 256). Küng cites Möhler, who described living faith as "faith formed by charity [*fides caritate formata*]," in support of his judgment but inadvertently casts a shadow over Möhler's crystalline presentation in his subsequent observations, at one point ascribing the character of love to faith and later relegating everything but faith alone to a "sign for the genuineness of faith" (*Justification*, pp. 256–57). His depiction of faith differs little from the Reformation perspective, greatly from Möhler's own view.[13]

Notwithstanding this difficulty, Küng rightly observes that Barth shares the typically Catholic recognition of the necessity of human appropriation of God's saving action and that Catholics share the Protestant insistence that all righteousness comes from God and ever depends upon God's faithful commitment. He concludes: Terminological differences ought not blind the communions to this concurrence. Though Barth uses "justification" in a restricted sense, distinguishing it from sanctification, which he calls the "new being," he does not thereby deny the latter. Conversely, Catholic esteem for sanctification, an element of "justification" in the broad sense, does not imply denial of the merciful source of this gift (*Justification*, pp. 260–61). For all of their terminological differences, that to which Catholics refer as "created grace" is more or less what Barth means by the "new being" of the sinner in grace (*Justification*, p. 261). Inasmuch as Barth offers a genuinely Protestant description, therefore, there seems to be no real dispute between Catholics and Protestants.

After his analysis of justifying faith, Küng turns to human cooperation with God in order to articulate the relationship between justification and sanctification. Here again, he does not align all three items noted in the chart. He begins with a discussion of the second and third items, the ontological effect of God's mercy (B) and good works (C): "The Catholic understands by 'sanctification' primarily the objective and ontological holiness (*heiligkeit*) achieved in man by God. The Protestant emphasizes the subjective and ethical sanctification (*heilung*) brought about by man. Both are valid provided the differences are seen in their unity" (*Justification*, p. 268). As he continues, he brings in the first item, redemption (A), but relates it to the third item, not to the second: "Inasmuch as justification occurs through faith alone, and not through works of man, it is *not* identical with sanctification (in the strictly [subjective] and ethical sense). Otherwise, divine justification would become the self-justification of man.... In this sense sanctification *follows* justification" (*Justification*, p. 268).[14] Both sentences are clearly true, but together, they do not address the divergent confessional conceptions of "objective sanctification" (B). Granted, a life of holiness, including prayer and deeds of love and thankful praise (C), *follows* justification. But what, if any, is the inner ontological basis or principle for this life of gratitude? The reader is left in doubt.

Küng then compares the first term with the second term but omits the third term: "Insofar as justification, considered as the efficacious divine just judgment, makes man really just or holy, it is *identical* with sanctification (in the sense of an objective and ontological making holy brought about by God)" (*Justification*, p. 268).[15] Is the identity portrayed here another way of expressing the *Barthian* conception of justification, strictly speaking, as both active (on

God's side) and passive (on the creaturely side)? Or, in contrast, is this an identity between the "passive" side of justification and the objective side of sanctification (*heiligkeit*)? The text is not clear. It is, consequently, not clear whether this "objective" side of sanctification is simply the virtual sanctification possible for anyone because of Christ's death (as Küng stated earlier, "all men are justified" [A]) or whether this objective side of sanctification is the very infusion of sanctifying grace (3B) that really and truly makes a person just, "really and truly, outwardly and inwardly, wholly and completely" (*Justification*, p. 213).[16]

Finally, Küng subsequently relates the second and third items of the mystery of salvation without attending to the distinction between the first and second items. "Justice or holiness given to man through the justification of God," he states, "is the necessary foundation for any moral sanctification of man and vice versa. Sanctification is holiness as established through justification becoming operative and real" (*Justification*, p. 269). The statement is indisputably true: There can be no moral or behavioral change worthy of the name "sanctification" unless the sinner first receives God's grace. Yet what does it mean to receive God's grace? What is the "justice or holiness given to man"? Is it simply the declaration of forgiveness that in turn, through gratitude rooted in faith, enables a justified sinner to respond with deeds of love? Or is it a participation in the grace of Christ, infused into the human person, making him Christ's possession and enabling good works to follow? The answers to these questions are crucial for an evaluation of Küng's thesis. The text is not terribly clear. Perhaps unaware of the ambiguities in his argumentation, Küng confidently concludes, "It is undeniable that there is a fundamental agreement between Karl Barth's position and that of the Catholic Church in regard to the theology of justification seen in its totality" (*Justification*, pp. 277–78). If Catholics can agree fundamentally with Barth, then perhaps they may also agree with Protestants in general and with Lutherans in particular.

Critical Analysis

Of Küng's contributions to the ecumenical dialogue, I would highlight the following. First, the terminological clarification is quite helpful: The Catholic sense of redemption is on its surface roughly parallel to the Protestant phrase "favor of God." Similarly, Catholics use the term "sanctification" to signify a divinely wrought regeneration, whereas Protestants usually link the term "sanctification" to the ethical renewal observable in human life. Second, following out this clarification, Küng justly begs Protestants to acknowledge that Trent distinguishes between God's unmerited mercy in Christ (3A) and the effect of this mercy (3B). Thirdly, again following out this clarification, he rightly distinguishes the effect of God's mercy (3B) from human cooperation (3C). Notwithstanding these and other contributions, there appear at least two deficiencies.[17] First, the book *Justification* seems to presuppose too rigid a distinction between nature and grace; second, it does not penetrate to the heart of the dispute between Catholics and Protestants—the issue of the formal cause.

With respect to the first apparent deficiency, I would ask whether the divisions between holiness (1B) and inner moral rectitude (1C) unwittingly imply a too-pronounced distinction between nature and grace. Küng describes holiness (1B) as the necessary foundation for moral renewal (1C). This statement is perfectly true on its surface, but a qualification must be made. In Catholic tradition, moral rectitude—not in the form of deeds but in the form of interior disposition—is a proper, concomitant effect of sanctifying grace. Thus, Catholic tradition locates moral rectitude—in the form of interior disposition—as an integral, albeit secondary, part of ontological sanctification (3B').[18] In describing moral rectitude as an effect of holiness Küng may be implying that moral rectitude is not structurally integral to the content of holiness. That is, he may be portraying moral rectitude as *merely* the gradual working out of God's once-for-all fashioning the sinner as just. No doubt, all virtues, moral and theological, can be ever perfected on earth. No doubt, no virtuous *deed* of us wayfarers constitutes interior "rectitude," supernatural or natural.[19] Still, Catholic tradition favors conceiving moral virtues as already present in justification, gifts tumbling out from the love of God imparted to the believer. *Inner* moral rectitude—i.e., the cardinal virtues and the subjection of appetite to reason and reason to God—is structurally integral to divine sonship.[20] Though it surpasses a merely moral rectitude, divine sonship cannot coexist with a serious disorder related to the cardinal virtues. As the Church teaches, the baptized person, made spotless through the laver of regeneration, forfeits sonship through serious sin, even in merely "moral matters."[21] Thus, it would accord better with Catholic tradition to locate inner moral rectitude (part of 1C) under divine sonship (3B'). Such an adjustment would not imply any "work (*ergon*)" in the reality referred to in Row B, because the divine establishment of moral rectitude is not a human work, even though it requires a certain receptivity. Such an adjustment, furthermore, would not conflict with Küng's insight that good works (C) only follow from ontological holiness (3B'). Positively, the adjustment would both better reflect the progress of Catholic theology in the past sixty years (à la *Nouvelle Theologie*) and also expose the necessity of confronting apparently divergent perspectives on the effect of God's mercy (B). This leads me to my second, more substantial criticism.

Küng's suggestion begs the question: What is the nature of the actual work of God in the sinner? What is "objective sanctification"? The precise issue at stake between Catholics and Protestants is the effect or formal cause (B) of God's mercy towards sinners (A).[22] If Protestants (for our purposes, Lutherans) accept that gifts constituting the effect of God's mercy (B) render the believer truly just before God, so that no damnable sin remains, then there is agreement. If, however, Lutherans believe that these gifts (2B) do not truly constitute the believer as just, then they and Catholics do not share an understanding of redemption (1A) and its effect (1B). Now, Lutherans do maintain the sufficiency of faith (2B) for salvation, but they disagree with Catholics about the meaning of this sufficiency. The confessional Lutheran documents do not describe faith as justifying because it makes one inwardly righteous through charity. Faith (2B) justifies because, on account of it, God reckons the believer worthy through the non-imputation of sins and the imputation of Christ's alien righteousness (2A).[23] Although God begins to transform the believer so that renewal of life may follow (3C), yet the believer remains in truth "totally sinner." The Reformers are careful to distinguish the alien righteousness of Christ (2A) from that which is *in the believer*: faith (2B), regeneration (2B'), and renewal (2C). Faith (2B) and regeneration (2B') do render the believer worthy to stand before God's tribunal. Although Küng rightly sees some parallel between the Protestant notion of faith and the Catholic notions of faith and hope, the confessional Lutheran documents explicitly deny that the justifying power of faith intrinsically depends upon charity; instead, Christ's righteousness is mercifully reckoned (2A) as the sinner's on account of faith alone (2B).[24]

For Catholics, on the contrary, infused grace and gifts (3B') render one "truly just," so that, by cooperating with God's constant help, one can actually merit eternal life through good works (3C). The believer is not merely reckoned righteous (2A through 2B); nor is the believer reckoned righteous (2A through 2B) *and* given gifts that do not expel all damnable sin (2B'); rather, the believer is truly made just (3B'). What the Reformers understand by (2B) and (2B') does not amount to what Catholics mean by sanctifying grace and the theological virtues flowing from it (3B'), not to mention the different evaluations of the quality and efficacity of meritorious works (C).[25] American Catholic theologian Richard White accurately notes, "Unfortunately, Küng has again confused the issue. The so-called 'objective' aspect of justification has never been a point of dispute between the two sides in and of itself. Both agree that justification is established and made possible by the death and resurrection of Christ."[26] The missing link in Küng's argument is, again and again, adequate discussion of the formal cause of justification.

Küng's failure to address this issue can be seen in summary by a return to two of Küng's key statements, rephrased and conjoined for purposes of clarity:

"Justification through faith (M) is not identical with subjective or ethical sanctification (N),"[27] but "the efficacious divine judgment (O) is identical with objective or ontological sanctification (P)."[28] A transposition of these two claims into logical form shows how puzzling Küng's claim is: M≠N, but O=P. The presence of four terms obscures the need for clarification of the three central aspects in question between Protestants and Catholics: God's mercy (A), the ontological effect of God's mercy (B), and good works (C).

There are two ways to read this statement. On the one hand, the reader can assume that Küng does not distinguish justification by faith (M) and effective justification (O).[29] If justification by faith and the efficacious divine judgment are identical, the statement would read: M≠N, but M=P. This statement is less ambiguous. The logic is as follows: If justification by faith (M) is identical with the efficacious divine judgment (O), and if the efficacious divine judgment (O) is identical with ontological sanctification (P), then justification by faith (M) is identical with ontological sanctification (P). What follows? If justification by faith is identical to ontological sanctification, then the gifts wrought by God in the human person formally constitute the righteousness of faith. Faith and infused gifts, more precisely, constitute justifying righteousness. It is clear, however, that the Lutheran confessional documents—if we are to apply Küng's effort to the case at hand—deny that faith and the other gifts constitute the believer's righteousness by faith. According to these documents, objective sanctification (P) does not expel all damnable sin and cannot, therefore, be that which constitutes justifying righteousness. That righteousness is constituted by Christ himself as distinct from the person's ontological status before God (*coram Deo*), even though this ontological status is fashioned by God. For Lutherans, at least, justification by faith (M) cannot be identical to objective or ontological sanctification (P). Although earlier in his work Küng appeals to numerous Catholic theologians in support of this logic, he does not read them aright.[30]

There is a second possible reading of Küng's ambiguous claim: "Justification through faith (M) is not identical with subjective or ethical sanctification (N), but the efficacious divine judgment (O) is identical with objective or ontological sanctification (P)." If the phrases "justification through faith" (M) and "the efficacious divine judgment" (O) refer to distinct realities, then justification by faith (M) is not identical with the efficacious divine judgment (O). The efficacious divine judgment (O) is identified with ontological sanctification (P). Consequently, justification by faith (M) is not identical with ontological sanctification (P);[31] therefore, the justifying faith that "saves" is not identified with an inhering grace that truly makes one pleasing to God. More precisely, faith is not considered "justifying" by its very inclusion of that reality to which Catholic tradition refers as "sanctifying grace" or charity.[32] Yet, this identity between justifying faith and sanctifying grace is precisely Catholic doctrine.

The reader will note that, in the table above, I have distinguished the first and second elements of justification in Catholic thought, forgiveness (3B) and sanctification (3B'). These of course must be seen as integrated by the single formal cause of justification, sanctifying grace, as Küng appears to acknowledge when discussing double justice (*Justification*, pp. 219–20). The complex reality to which Lutherans refer under the terms regeneration (2B') and justifying faith (2B) is not identical to that to which Catholics refer as remission of sins (3B) through sanctifying grace (3B'). According to Catholic teaching, faith has no justifying power apart from charity. The Lutheran notion of faith is therefore not equivalent to the Catholic understanding of faith, hope, *and love*. According to Lutheran teaching, faith's saving power is distinct from sanctifying grace and the charity flowing therefrom.[33] It is these latter, however, that Catholics believe formally justify the human person.

Küng justly draws the necessary distinction between God's eternal mercy (uncreated grace) and its temporal effect (sanctifying grace and actual graces). It is not this distinction that doctrinally separates Catholics and the Reformers (i.e., the Lutherans). Not just Barth, but Luther, of course, recognized real and sanative effects in the justified. Luther developed a sense of "faith" as lively trust in God's redeeming work, a personal adhesion to the merciful God. Trent's difficulty with Lutheranism (and with double justice) was the latter's denial that the effects of God's own action in the human person eradicate all damnable sin, qualify the person as a true child of God, and enable the person to merit eternal life.[34] In short, for Lutherans, the formal cause of forgiveness is not sanctifying grace. Though from a fundamentally different perspective, Hampson's conclusion concurs with mine: "It is perfectly clear. Küng agrees that Trent wishes to speak of an 'inherent' justice. Protestants however look to Christ's justice which is imputed to them! How could this be reconcilable with Trent?"[35] McGrath, too, while recognizing the positive impulse Küng's work provided for the recent ecumenical movement, charges that Küng "does little more than demonstrate that Roman Catholics and Protestants share a common Christocentric anti-Pelagian theology of justification."[36] Such concerns are too rudimentary to constitute a consensus. Though his readers may cite Barth's "approbation" of Küng's work, included in the front matter, Molnar is right in cautioning, "There can be little doubt that Barth's response to Küng was, to a certain extent, tongue in cheek."[37]

I should note in closing that in his treatment of "at once justified person and sinner [*simul iustus et peccator*]," Küng amasses many statements from the living tradition of Catholic faith that proclaim the sinful character of the justified and the constant need the justified have for mercy. These statements and Küng's reflections do offer a much-needed antidote to misconceptions of authentic Catholic piety. He refers to the following elements of Catholic tradition that manifest what he calls the Catholic form of "simul iustus et peccator." First, at Mass, the priest (who ought to be in a state of grace) pleads for God's mercy, as do those who receive communion, even though the reception of communion implies (for Catholics) the lack of awareness of mortal sin not yet forgiven in penance (*Justification*, p. 237). Second, in good Augustinian fashion, Küng points to the "not yet" character of earthly justification. Although the baptized are already sanctified, they are "not yet" fully sanctified and justified, for the consummation of God's saving work awaits eschatological fulfillment (*Justification*, pp. 239–42). Nonetheless, the "futurity" of Catholic hope that Küng likens to the character of Reformation faith in God ought not to be misunderstood as though the chief effect of God's justifying act has not already been accomplished; Catholics believe that the indwelling of the Trinity, the noblest fruit of justification, differs only in degree from that glory for which all believers "groan." Third, although sinners become just, their past remains their own past. Thus, sinners can always recall their own lack of merit before God and the fact that they do not deserve to be blessed with baptismal grace and God's constant assistance (*Justification*, p. 244). Finally, the very justice that God pours upon the justified—that which makes him formally just—never becomes a human possession such that the justified can do with it what he pleases. One's "possession" of grace is, more accurately, one's being possessed by God. The justified person is not the creator of this justice; the substantial being of the justified person is not the source, even proximate, of inhering justice; rather, the justified person ever receives it from God as an influx of grace, the constancy of which is due to God's faithful and just love.[38]

Many of these aspects of Catholic liturgical and theological life might surprise some Lutherans in an edifying way. They certainly point to some practical points of contact between Lutheran piety and Catholic piety. These practical points of contact might indeed form bases for dialogue if treated aright and if other necessary elements of Catholic piety not immediately palatable for Lutheran piety are not neglected. One of the most important practical differences between the two communions is the Catholic insistence upon much more than the relationship of a wretched sinner to a merciful mediator (*Mittel*). Such a relationship is indeed the starting point for authentic piety, but the journey continues, and progresses. Jesus washes the disciples' feet (Jn 13:1–10) and subsequently commands them to join him in solidarity (Jn 14:31). They are to abide in him (Jn 15:4) as he takes his exodus from "the world" to the Father (Jn 13:1). They frequently fall away from him and must receive forgiveness anew. But if they make steady progress, they are commissioned to enter continually into his death so as to receive life. It is the new life in the Spirit, by which Christians are conformed to Jesus, that is the heart of Christian life. In the words of Vatican II: "All are called to holiness."[39] The preservation of the importance of this call and of the meaningfulness of the "holiness" to which all are called is supported by the Catholic doctrine on the formal cause, which remains a point of conflict in spite of the aforesaid practical points of contact.[40]

NOTES

1 McGrath, *Iustitia Dei*, p. 389.
2 Ibid., p. 388.
3 See Tavard, *Justification*, pp. 99–101. See also Vercruysse, "Luthers Reformation," pp. 26–31.
4 Hampson laments, "If one thinks as I do that this book is profoundly mistaken, one must be aghast at the influence which it has clearly had in Catholic circles" (Hampson, *Christian Contradictions*, p. 129).
5 See Hampson, *Christian Contradictions*, p. 129.
6 Tavard writes, "While Küng dealt with Karl Barth and not with Luther, he identified Barth's thought as the purest systematization of Protestant theology today, thus implying that his own conclusion could apply to the teaching of the reformer" (Tavard, *Justification*, p. 100). Catholics received the work more readily than Protestants. Still, Protestants for the most part did not take issue with his presentation of Barth as *representative* of Protestantism; rather, they suspected his presentation of Catholic doctrine (see Tavard, *Justification*, p. 101).
7 Before Vatican II, no ecclesial council had refrained from issuing condemnations. Küng's book, which was published five years before the first session of Vatican II in 1963, must be read in its pre-Vatican II context. All councils before Vatican II addressed pressing threats from heretical movements. Doctrines were issued to defend against these threats.
8 Das Wort 'Rechtfertigung' als solches besagt also wirklich Gerechtsprechung und nicht innere Erneuerung. Folgt daraus, daß die Gerechtsprechnung Gottes keine innere Erneuerung bedeutet? Das Gegenteil! Alles kommt darauf an, daß es get um die Gerechtsprechung Gottes: Nicht Menschenwort ist's, sondern die vox Domini, potens in virtute (*Rechtfertigung*, p. 210).
9 For presentation that is somewhat similar, see CRE, pp. 47–53, to be considered in chapter 6.
10 By "not due in any way" I do not mean to convey an opinion about that which Trent left open to discussion, namely, congruous merit; rather, I mean to underscore the sovereign divine (efficient) causality. The infusion of grace is operative, not cooperative, grace
11 The reader will note that Küng reads the council's understanding of "hope" as referring to the future and not to an already-granted justification. This much is true, but the context of this description of hope is chapter 6 of the Decree on Justification, a chapter devoted to the "preparation" for justification. Consequently, the futurity Küng ascribes to hope is actually the futurity of an unformed hope. Thus, the "not yet" is not eschatological but this-worldly: it pertains to those not yet recreated by grace. To discuss more fully the tridentine concept of hope as such, one would need to have

recourse to other chapters, such as those on perseverance. Moreover, at least on a theological plain, one would need to address charity's transformation of hope.

12 Kerygma, in contrast to doctrinal teaching or instruction, refers to the Gospel as preached for the conversion of hearers (see *The Oxford Dictionary of the Christian Church*, ed. F.L. Cross and E.A. Livingstone [Oxford: Oxford University Press, 1997], p. 924).

13 Küng briefly recounts the tridentine debates, wherein a number of fathers defended the legitimacy of the formula *sola fide*, provided one maintain a correct understanding of it. Few of the fathers, however, agreed with the Protestant interpretation of the formula. Möhler himself exhibited keener perception than Küng's indelicate interpretation. Möhler stated, "As justification now, in the Catholic sense, consists in a total change of the whole inward man, we can understand why the Catholic Church should so urgently insist, that faith alone doth not justify before God; that it is rather only the first subjective, indispensable condition to be justified; the root from which God's approval must spring; the first title whereon we can establish our claim of divine filiation. But if faith passes from the understanding, and the feelings, excited through the understanding, to the will; if it pervades, vivifies, and fructifies the will, through the new vital principle imparted to the latter, and engenders, in this way, the new man created after God; or (to make use of the expression of Seripandus at the Council of Trent), if love is enkindled out of faith, as fire out of brimstone, then, only after faith and love doth regeneration or justification ensue" (Johann Adam Möhler, *Symbolism or Exposition of the Doctrinal Differences between Catholics and Protestants as Evidenced by their Symbolical Writings*, trans. James Burton Robertson, 5th ed. [New York: Benzinger Brothers, 1906], p. 121; for the German, see *Symbolik oder Darstellung der dogmatischen Gegensätze der Katholiken und Protestanten nach ihren öffentlichen Bekenntnisschriften* [Cologne: Jakob Hegner, 1958]). I would also like to note a strange statement later in this same chapter that might cause considerable difficulty for Protestants: "Yet, faith is indeed a condition [of justification]..., inasmuch as it is man *alone* who has subjectively realized in himself the 'objective' justification, who actively submits to divine justification" (Küng, *Justification*, p. 259). Whereas Küng reads Barth as describing faith as a human activity that does not merit salvation but that is the trust by which God allows the individual to appropriate justification, most Protestants see faith as the work of the Holy Spirit in man, lest faith itself be turned into a work that justifies.

14 Insofern Rechtfertigung durch den Glauben allein geschieht, und nicht durch Werke des Menschen, ist sie nicht gleich Heiligung (im streng 'subjektiv'-ethischen Sinn) (*Rechtfertigung*, p. 260).

15 Insofern aber Rechtfertigung als wirksamer göttlicher Richterspruch den Menschen seinsmäßig gerecht oder heilig macht, ist sie gleich Heiligung (im Sinne der von Gott gewirkten 'objektiv'-ontischen Heiligmachung) (*Rechtfertigung*, pp. 260–61).

16 Karl Rahner critiques Küng on a similar point (see Karl Rahner, "Questions of Controversial Theology on Justification," in *More Recent Writings*, vol. 4, *Theological Investigations* [Baltimore: Helicon, 1966], pp. 199–205). I agree with Rahner for the most part in his reading of justification by faith. He shows that "love," not as a work but as a gift from God that formally situates the *believer* in a salvific relationship with the God who already loves him, is a necessary constituent of justification properly so-called (i.e., what in Barth's terms might be called subjective justification). Justification and sanctification are linked through this faith formed by love. Perplexingly, Rahner chafes against his own claim in asserting only a material, not a formal, identity between sanctification and justification. While he is indisputably correct that no work

whatsoever merits the grace of justification, he must admit, as he appears to do in his claim that justifying faith includes supernatural charity, that there is an identity between justification and sanctification in terms of their formal cause. Admittedly, the *ratio* of sanctification includes something not proper to justification, namely, works of righteousness. In addition, the *ratio* of justification includes the remission of sins through the introduction of grace, but the simple introduction of grace does not necessarily involve the remission of sins, since the first ancestors of the human race and also the Blessed Virgin were blessed with an infusion of grace but had no sins to be remitted. To return to the connection between justification and sanctification, I would simply recall Thomas Aquinas's insight that, although the habit of grace can be distinguished into operative grace (justification) and cooperative grace (sanctification), it remains one habit of grace (see Thomas Aquinas, ST IaIIae, q. 111, art. 2, and Avery Dulles, "Justification in Contemporary Catholic Theology," in USA, pp. 256–77, esp. p. 257).

17   For a bibliography on critiques of Küng's work on justification, see the lengthy list in Manfred Hauke, "Die Antwort," pp. 101–02, note 70.
18   See John Paul II, *Veritatis splendor*, arts. 37 and 88. John Paul insists that it is erroneous to distinguish an ethical order as hermetically isolated from the order of salvation. The Church, he asserts, can teach on the ethical plane since this plane is not removed from the order of salvation. The converse implication of this teaching, in light of the necessity of keeping the commandments for salvation, is that justification establishes within the human person, who is so poor when living by purely human effort, the capability of living a truly ethical life.
19   At least, not according to Thomists.
20   See Pope Leo XIII, *On Jesus Christ Our Redeemer* (Boston: St. Paul Editions, 1978), p. 16.
21   The notion of a merely "philosophical sin" that is grave but not destructive of charity contradicts Catholic tradition (see DS 2291, and John Paul II, *Reconciliatio et Paenitentia*, art. 17).
22   For a similarly critical analysis, see Richard White, "Justification in Ecumenical Dialogue," pp. 123–42. White helpfully shows that Küng does not do justice to the subtlety of Rahner's call for a renewal of appreciation for and emphasis upon uncreated grace. He strikes right to the heart of the matter when he states, "Again, it is not a question of whether Lutheran and Reformed theologians admit of the reality of sanctification, or whether Catholics admit that justifying righteousness is supplied by God alone; both Küng and the ecumenical dialogues have done a good job of clarifying these misunderstandings. The problematic question has to do with the nature of justifying grace: is it inward righteousness or the alien righteousness of Christ?" (ibid., p. 130).
23   In the following two chapters, I discuss Pannenberg's reading and also the Finnish school's reading of Luther's notion of faith as *per se* including either a saving fellowship with Christ or an indwelling of Christ. See also Richard White, "Justification in Ecumenical Dialogue," pp. 138–42.
24   There is debate about whether faith is the object of God's decree of righteousness or whether faith grasps that decree, which is logically prior. In either case, the righteousness of faith is not saving precisely by its inclusion of charity, although charity always follows. See my discussion in the following section. See also Wolfhart Pannenberg, "Theses to the 'Joint Declaration' about Justification," *Pro Ecclesia* 7 (1998): 136. Cf. *Apology*, IV: 86.
25   For a foundational critique of Küng, see Hampson, *Christian Contradictions*, pp.

129–36. Hampson applies her insight that Catholics and Lutherans operate within wholly divergent "structures of thought" to Küng's thesis, finding the well-meaning Küng to be yet one more perpetrator of the "Catholic incomprehension" of Luther (and of orthodox Protestants). Küng attempts to render the Lutheran "*simul*" into the Catholic conception of the justified as a single subject *in via ad patriam*. Her critique of Küng is no less forceful than mine, but whereas I deal with his thesis on its own (attempted) terms, she cuts through the very foundations of his endeavor.

26   Richard White, "Justification in Ecumenical Dialogue," pp. 134–35.

27   "Inasmuch as justification occurs through faith alone, and not through works of man, it is *not* identical with sanctification (in the strictly [subjective] and ethical sense).... In this sense sanctification *follows* justification" (Küng, *Justification*, p. 268).

28   "Furthermore, insofar as justification, considered as the efficacious divine just judgment, makes man really just or holy, it is *identical* with sanctification (in the sense of an objective and ontological making holy brought about by God)" (Küng, *Justification*, p. 268).

29   The reader might wonder why, if the distinction is only terminological, Küng does not use the same term, comparing it with each of the two types of sanctification, objective and subjective.

30   He cites Bellarmine, Vasquez, Prat, and Knabenbauer (see Küng, *Justification*, p. 220). Just after citing these, he asks, "Is it not time to stop arguing about imaginary differences?" (ibid., p. 221). But on the contrary, these sources evaluate the divine declaration in terms of efficient causality, bringing about an effect not previously present. They thus evade the "either-or" of the "analytic" or "synthetic" conceptions of the divine declaration, unlike their Protestant interlocutors. When asking what their understanding of the effect of the divine declaration is, they respond that God's judgment is *true* and truly efficacious, so that no damnable sin remains in the sinner before God. Now, I grant that there is a sense in which certain Lutherans would state that objective sanctification does remove the harmful effects of sin because it renders sin controlled and incapable of breaking the relationship of faith to God. In this sense, however, sins are seen to be "removed" by being no longer considered on account of Christ. So, if Lutherans were to say that objective sanctification (P) does remove the damning effect of sin, they would in turn equate objective sanctification with the declaration of forgiveness, not *as ontologically effective* in the human person but as forensically established through faith. Küng may unwittingly espouse this as well: at the cross and resurrection God "declares all sinners free and just, and thereby makes them just" (Küng, *Justification*, p. 230). It should be clear that Catholic teaching does not permit this reading of justification.

31   Perhaps one might object that in this case "ontological sanctification" *is not* to be read as "sanctifying grace," which is a Catholic notion. Instead, the "ontological sanctification" that is identical with "effective justification" is rather the sense of making just by declaration. This is quite possible, but the reader will note that if this were the case, my argument need go no further, since ontological sanctification would be limited to the either-or disjunction of "analytic" and "synthetic" interpretations of the divine declaration. The formal cause of justification, in such case, could not be the grace and gifts poured forth from God.

32   It should go without saying that neither would the declaration of forgiveness (M) be considered identical with the divinely wrought effect of this forgiveness, the infusion of sanctifying grace (P).

33   Recent ecumenical dialogues draw attention to the places in which the Lutheran confessional documents refer to faith as the "grace that makes pleasing." Close analysis

shows that the phrase "sanctifying grace [*gratia gratum faciens*]" is used equivocally: Catholics use it to signify the infused justice that inheres in the justified and Protestants use it to signify forensic righteousness through faith. According to the latter notion, faith "makes pleasing" by being the instrument on account of which God extrinsically imputes Christ's alien righteousness to the person who, in himself, remains totally sinner. See CRE, p. 51 and *Apology*, IV: 116.

34   See *Solid Declaration*, III: 24–31.
35   Hampson, *Christian Contradictions*, p. 135.
36   McGrath, *Iustitia Dei*, p. 389.
37   Paul Molnar, "The Theology of Justification in Dogmatic Context," in *Justification: What's at Stake in the Current Debates*, ed. Mark Husbands and Daniel Treier (Downers Grove, IL: InterVarsity Press, 2004), p. 228.
38   See Küng, *Justification*, p. 241, citing Schmaus.
39   *Lumen gentium*, chapter 5.
40   See also Richard White, "Justification in Ecumenical Dialogue," pp. 137–38.

CHAPTER 4

The Finnish School

AN EXTRAORDINARY development in scholarship on Luther has recently taken place. "Beginning in the late 1970s, a new school of Luther studies [arose] in Europe, under the leadership of Tuomo Mannermaa, now Emeritus Professor of Ecumenics at the University of Helsinki."[1] Mannermaa, a Finnish Lutheran theologian, spearheaded the Finnish research into Luther with his work *In ipsa fide Christus adest* (*In Faith Itself Christ is Present*).[2] The Finns claim that much of Lutheran theology neglects Luther's insights about the transformation of the sinner that takes place through Christ, who is present in faith. Their groundbreaking research underlies key elements of the differentiated consensus of the *Joint Declaration*.

Presentation

One of the chief elements of the Finnish research is a critique both of the excessively Kantian reading of Luther in 19th and 20th century Lutheran theology and also of certain tendencies in the *Apology* and the *Formula of Concord* towards a purely forensic account of justification. A student of Mannermaa, Risto Saarinen published his dissertation in 1989, tracing much of the extrinsicist flavor of 20th century Lutheran theology to the philosophical work of Hermann Lotze (1817–1881). In his work on ontology, Lotze denied that there is such a thing as "being in itself." Being is constituted simply by relations, the contents of which are merely actions and passions. With respect to epistemology, Lotze denied that we can know "things in themselves." Instead of knowing things or their natures, we can know only the effects of things on us. As a result, when we know something, we do not enjoy a participation in the very "form" of the thing known; instead, we merely recognize the effects that this or that thing has upon us. This epistemology and ontology have implications for theology. If faith has a cognitive content, that content cannot include the very being of God or of Christ, because the object known is not present in the knower. Rather, only God's action is present in the knower. More specifically, only the humanly perceptible aspect of God's action is present in the knower.[3] There is a separation between God in himself and God's action in the believer. In "giving" his qualities of righteousness and wisdom, God does not give himself. Neither is Christ truly present in faith. Faith does not justify, therefore, because God finds the sinner already in Christ (or Christ already in the sinner). Christ's own righteousness remains extrinsic to the believer's identity. In this sense, the *alien righteousness* of Christ is merely attributed to the believer but does not inform the very constitution of the believer, making the believer to be truly righteous.

According to Saarinen, the Kantian presuppositions of this line of thought made it difficult for many Lutheran theologians to escape this extrinsicism.[4] Still, long before the Kantian movement in Lutheran orthodoxy, as early as Melanchthon's 1531 *Apology*, the seeds of the extrinsic reading of the righteousness of faith were planted. The appropriation of Kantian philosophy did not cause but only confirmed the problem.[5] The Finns, accordingly, level a severe critique against both Melanchthon's forensic reading of justification by faith and also the *Formula*'s purely extrinsic formulation of the "imputation" of righteousness through faith. These confessional documents lost sight of the integral unity between gift and grace in Luther. Simo Peura writes, "Contrary to Luther,...the [*Formula of Concord*] excludes gift, the renewal of a Christian and the removal of sin, from the doctrine (*locus*) of justification." The *Formula* mentions gift but "defines the gift in a radically limited sense compared with Luther."[6] Again and again, the Finns claim that Luther's own theology and the confessional Lutheran documents are at odds with, at times contradicting, one another.[7] Mannermaa astonishes his reader with the following remark:

> One must ask here whether what Luther considers damning for the believer to think is exactly what the *Formula of Concord* calls sound doctrine: in the locus of justification the divine person of Christ is separated from the believer, because justification is only a forensic imputation and does not presuppose the divine presence of Christ in faith.[8]

Against much of 20th century Lutheran theology, the Finns contend that Luther himself was an epistemological realist, regardless of his preference for nominalist philosophy in other areas. A realist believes that the thing known is present in the knower. Thus, the Finns argue, Luther contended that Christ himself is present in faith. Through faith, the believer is united in fellowship with Christ, whose very being and work are present in the believer. Christ is present both as gift and as grace. Simo Peura develops the ontological aspects of Luther's view of justification in his treatment of the theme of grace and gift, especially as it was articulated in the *Confutation of Latomus* (1521).[9] Luther indeed distinguished gift and grace, but he never separated them. The "gift" associated with justification clearly implies something given or bestowed, something present in the believer. In removing gift from the article of justification, the *Formula of Concord* separated what Luther merely distinguished. The *Formula* thus removed from justification any mention of the "being" of the believer; justification is solely an extrinsic imputation. Although the *Formula* affirmed that gifts are given to the believer, it also affirmed that these gifts are separate from the grace of Christ, which is imputed to the believer. Contrary to the *Formula*'s separation of gift from grace, Luther maintained that Christ—who is present in faith—is in his very person both grace and gift. Christ as grace is opposed to the divine wrath and is thus that grace by which God declares the sinner to be just. Christ as gift is that renewing power that transforms the believer into the very image of the Son of God: "According to Luther, then, grace is God's favorable mood effecting in a sinner confidence in God's forgiveness and benevolence.... Gift, however, constitutes the Christian's internal good, and it opposes his internal evil, that is, the corruption of human nature."[10]

How, for the Finns, does a sinner come into contact with Christ as grace and gift? Through divine faith, the sinner enjoys the presence of Christ as grace and gift. Christ himself *is* grace and gift, which become operative for a person who believes since by faith the believer is united to Christ.[11] Union with Christ is thus the fundamental reality in justification. This union with Christ flowers in the believer's transformation into Christ, which begins on earth and is consummated in glory: "The work of the Holy Spirit continues throughout our whole life until death, when we become totally transformed into Christ and thus possess within us the complete form of Christ."[12]

How are grace and gift united but distinguished in their operations? Grace and gift work together to justify human persons. The former is fundamental, although the latter is also a *sine qua non* condition of the former.[13] There is, therefore, a mutual conditioning of grace and gift. Christ as grace is absolutely necessary since the power of Christ as gift does not immediately destroy sin in the human person. The power of Christ as gift indeed begins a real, internal renewal of the human person, a renewal that consists both in growing trust in and love for God and in growing love for neighbor. Still, the believer who enjoys the gift of Christ's own person through faith remains "more or less sinful (Rom 8:1)."[14] This residual sin would of itself bring eternal condemnation upon the believer.[15] Gift of itself does not suffice to placate God's wrath. Christ as grace is thus also necessary: "Because of residual sin a Christian can stand before God's judgment only if he puts the righteousness of the innocent Christ against his own condemnation."[16] Christ as grace works against the wrath of God. It is not as though the believer is sinless in his very person because of Christ's grace; rather, the sinner is freed from God's wrath because he is united to Christ in faith. The as yet imperfect nature of the believer's transformation into Christ calls for an interpersonal situation of acceptance within which the transformation into Christ can unfold without the debilitating and self-oriented anxiety of moralism. To illustrate, Luther drew on the metaphor of Christ as the mother hen who shields her chicks while they are yet helpless, in order that they may mature.[17] While the Christian is on the way towards eschatological salvation, only the complete righteousness of Christ renders him truly secure: "The firmness of salvation can by no means be based on a Christian's own righteousness, even though God has given it to him and made him righteous and even when the gift has already to some extent expelled residual sin."[18] The very righteousness that is a Christian's, furthermore, is "his own" only if he remains united with Christ in faith and trusts in him alone, so that he can continually receive from Christ, the font, all of his "own" righteousness. So it is only by abiding in union with Christ that the believer can live serenely with God and be ontologically transformed by him. Moreover, and more importantly, it is only by rooting his attention solely on Christ through faith that the believer is relieved of his miserable self-contemplation and brought into a relationship with God that is salvific. Paradoxically, then, the residual sin that still afflicts believers actually serves as a goad to union with Christ: Insofar as one acknowledges oneself as sinner, one is thrown upon the grace of Christ and trusts even less in oneself. Of course, the Finns would not want to locate the primary reason for such dependence in the abiding sinfulness of the justified; rather, they would locate the chief reason in the authentic humility that even the saints are to possess, for even the perfect righteousness of the saint is not independent of Christ's own righteousness. On the contrary, at all times, "The Christian's own righteousness is sufficient for salvation only when it is linked to the righteousness of Christ and flows as a continuous stream from it."[19] On earth, however, the abiding sinfulness of the believer makes more pressing the distinction between Christ as grace and gift, which nonetheless remain united in Christ who is present in faith.[20]

In manifest contradiction of Lutheran orthodoxy, the Finns do not read the distinction between gift and grace as one between intrinsic and extrinsic righteousness. Both grace and gift are the intrinsic righteousness of the believer. However, the "intrinsic" righteousness of the believer must not be misunderstood as though it were a quality infused into and inhering in the believer, as scholastic theology maintained. The Finns adamantly oppose this "scholastic" notion of grace.[21] They strive to navigate a middle path between the traditional Catholic estimation of sanctifying grace and the traditional Lutheran divorce between God and his saving work (i.e., the traditional Lutheran tendency to consider the believer's contact with God as merely contact with God's saving work, which is not identified with God). On the one hand, the Lutheran confessional documents fail to appreciate the ontological union of God and the believer through Christ. Similarly, both dialectical Protestant theology and Lutheran renaissance theology failed to perceive that the Christian's relation to God involves more than action or will. In contrast to these tendencies towards reductive extrinsicism, Mannermaa focuses on the union of being.[22] In giving his wisdom and righteousness, God gives himself to the Christian, for he is his own wisdom and righteousness.[23] Justification is the reception of and participation in the very attributes of God; therefore, the Christian is truly just and righteous, for God is his.[24]

The Finns equally distance themselves from what they consider the reductive intrinsicism of Catholicism. Against the latter's conception of grace as a quality, the Finns maintain that grace is both more excellent and less self-absorbing:

> Luther abandons the concept of created grace. The scholastic understanding of grace as created held that habitual grace was, according to its ontological status, a quality, an accident adhering to the human being considered as substance. This doctrine did not go far enough to stress the ontological points that Luther wished to maintain. He preferred the interpretation of Peter of Lombard, who claimed that the Holy Ghost himself is the love (*charitas*) of a Christian. This standpoint is very important for Luther's view of justification.[25]

The Finns perceive the notion of "grace as quality" to promote, firstly, a solipsistic complacency. Those who conceive of the gift as an accidental modification of a subject that remains the same can be tempted merely to gaze at themselves instead of on Christ.[26] Such perceived self-sufficiency was the substance of the serpent's temptation: love of self unto hatred of God (*amor sui ad contemptum Dei*). Luther warned against such idolatry in his *Lectures on Romans* (1515).[27] It is only after we are gratuitously accepted by God and suffused with his goodness that we can kenotically undertake genuinely benevolent love of neighbor. Secondly, Christ as "gift" ought not to be reduced to something other than Christ that Christ merely gives. Christ himself is the gift present in faith. Mannermaa sums up the critique of the traditional Catholic notion:

> The form (i.e., the living reality) of faith is not divinely elevated human love, as in the scholastic program of *fides charitate formata*, but is in reality Christ himself.... According to Luther, faith is not such a "dead quality" in the soul, but rather contains the divine reality (*forma*), which is Christ himself, who is present in faith.[28]

Related to this critique of gift or grace as a quality is Luther's reading of the original state of mankind: "According to Luther, both the *imago Dei* and the *similitudo Dei* belong to Adam's created constitution."[29] Luther recognized a distinction between being in the image of God (*imago Dei*) and being in the likeness of God (*similitudo*), but he did not perceive this, as did western Catholics, as being a distinction between nature and the "supernatural."[30] Being in the image of God refers to the good state of man, especially in his intellect and will, whereby he *can* know and love God. Being in God's likeness refers to the human person *qua* one who concretely and progressively lives in accordance with his character as "image of God."[31] Both of these blessings, however, remain *within* the natural constitution of Adam. Sin, blotting out both, cannot be considered a mere "accidental evil" (à la scholasticism), which leaves human nature in tact. Sin is not extrinsic to fallen creatures; it is their very essence. As evil is essential to postlapsarian man, so "likeness to God" was essential to prelapsarian man.[32] The scholastic reduction of grace to the category of accident led to errors about both sin and grace.

Given his critique of the gift as an infused quality and the formula "faith formed by charity," Luther was challenged to express this mystery of Christ's presence in faith without stumbling into the errors of extrinsicism—separating Christ and the believer—and intrinsicism—making Christ part of the essence of the believer. Sammeli Juntunen observes Luther employing several complementary metaphors, each at once manifesting and distorting the truth.[33] Avoiding extrinsicism, Luther spoke of Christ as the new form (*forma*) or substance of the Christian, rendering the latter righteous precisely by his indwelling through faith. That is, Christ is the "substantial form" that establishes and in fact *is* the believer's new identity. Going further than imaginable according to the Catholic model, Luther argued that Christ is not merely an accident but the very *essence* of the "new man." This metaphor captures the truth that Christ gives the believer his identity, but it distorts the truth that Christ does *not* become part of the believer. Luther also had to employ images that highlight the distinction between Christ and the believer. Drawing on Peura's work, Juntunen follows out Luther's thought, depicting Christ as the "second substance" of the believer: "Believers have two substances, the human substance and that which is united with it (though not mingled with it) as a substantial reality in it, i.e., Christ's substance."[34] The notion of two substances has the merit of preserving both righteousness through faith and residual sin. As Mannermaa states, all "true righteousness" is God's property, for "In himself [the believer] always finds the opposite of divine qualities."[35] Still, although the metaphor of two substances preserves the distinction between the believer and Christ, it can be misunderstood as conveying the idea of "some sort of schizophrenic reality that is not Luther's idea."[36]

The union in distinction between the believer and Christ has a certain parallel with the doctrine "at once just and sinful." Mannermaa finds a

Christological parallel for the justified person's twofold identity—in himself as sinner and in Christ as righteous. In himself, the believer remains sinful, but through faith he comes to share in the qualities of Christ. Like Christ, "The Christian, too, has in a certain sense 'two natures'—in the theological sense of the concept of nature. The 'divine nature' of the believer is Christ himself."[37] Mannermaa does not identify the "human nature" of the believer, theologically considered. Might it be that he conceives it to be the "sinfulness" that is the "opposite of divine qualities"? One is not certain. For his part, Peura avoids the thesis that all human powers were utterly annihilated in the fall. This much is welcome. Still, he emphasizes the radical corruption of these same powers.[38] In fact, postlapsarian man is so corrupted that he "hates God" and "seeks to live and to be without God."[39] He cannot recognize the sinful character of these actions by his natural powers. Significantly, the renewal of the human person does not change this state of affairs, for according to Luther natural powers are wholly irreparable in this life.[40] Despite this, through faith Christ dwells in believers so that they come to participate in him.

Underscoring the union of the Christian with Christ, Mannermaa claims that, because of the union of the two natures in one person, the Christian truly "partakes" in the treasures of Christ. Characteristically, the Finns employ the term "participation" in an effort, once again, to strike a middle path between the extrinsicism of the confessional Lutheran documents and the intrinsicism of scholasticism. Luther did not regard faith as merely the believer's confident trust in the merciful God who acquits from sin and imputes Christ's alien righteousness. Nor does faith justify because it is informed by supernatural charity. Christ himself is truly present in faith as gift and grace. Faith justifies *because* of Christ's indwelling through faith. Andreas Osiander (1498–1552), a Lutheran whose positions were condemned by the *Formula of Concord*, held that the sinner is truly justified by the indwelling of Christ's divine nature. Later Protestant theology would describe Osiander as perceiving God's declaration of justice to be an analytic judgment. The *Formula of Concord* condemned both Osiander's Christological error—his apparent divorce of the two natures or inadvertence to the human nature—and also his presumption that justifying righteousness resided within the believer. The Finns deny that Osiander erred "in his claim that justification was based on God's indwelling in a Christian." Instead, his error lay in the "christological presupposition of his claim," namely, the divorce of divine and human natures.[41]

Though Catholic tradition also speaks of Christ's indwelling presence, the Finns go further. Christ resides in the believer not simply as the "term" of the virtue of faith, à la Catholic tradition. If Christ were simply the object of faith, the Finns might have less ground to level criticism against the scholastic opinion on grace as a quality. For the scholastics, or at least for Thomists, the

Trinity becomes really present in the justified person as the term of infused faith and charity, as the object known and loved. For the Finns, on the contrary, Christ is not merely the object of faith; He is also the subject of faith. Christ is not merely what is believed but the agent believing in the believer. Mannermaa writes, "Christ, as the object of faith, is present himself; thus, he is, in fact, also the 'subject' of faith."[42] God is present in faith similarly: "God who illuminates and the illuminated heart, the present God and the God seen by us, are identical.... God is both the object and the subject, the actor and act, of faith."[43] Similarly, when the Christian empties himself towards his neighbor out of love, "It is not he himself who does this, in the sense that he should receive honor and thanks for it, but rather Christ, who is present in his faith." Consequently, "God alone receives the honor for all deeds of love."[44] It would be too little to consider the human person as the subject of faith, just as it would be too little to describe the gift as an infused, supernatural quality. Or perhaps more to the point, because the "image and likeness" have been totally corrupted, even though human faculties remain, "It is clear that Adam no longer participates in God on the basis of his nature."[45] Does participation in God *not* come about, then, by God turning fallen human faculties back to himself? If indeed not, then how does it come about?

In any case, God brings about a real participation with himself through faith. The reality of this participation cannot be doubted, though it is not seen; it involves a faithful *waiting* for the day in which God brings it to completion.[46] It can never be complete during this life since perfect righteousness would entail perfect fulfillment of the first commandment, which demands that God be loved purely above all things.[47] Sinners thus stand continually in need of the "the wonderful exchange [*wundersame Wechsel*]" between their sins and the blessings of Christ. Christ takes on all human sins; indeed, he is made to be sin, so that sin itself is conquered by his divinity. In exchange for the sins of sinners, Christ gives the blessings of his divine justice, peace, wisdom, power, etc.[48] The fact that we truly have these goods not in ourselves but in Christ—the fact that we await this in hope—enables us the better to live not from ourselves but from Christ.[49]

The following passage from Peura excellently recapitulates the balance of the Finnish reading of Luther:

> The complete righteousness of a Christian—God's favor as well as God's gift—depends permanently and throughout one's life on Christ and Christ's own righteousness. A Christian participates in Christ's righteousness on the condition that he has become one with Christ. Grace and gift presuppose each other, but both of them come to existence only because of the union with Christ.[50]

These among others are the marks of the Finnish reading of Luther: genuine union with Christ through faith, though a union in distinction; ontological transformation into Christ, though a transformation that awaits eschatological completion; liberation from the anxiety of despair and the self-righteousness of presumption, though a liberation leading to benevolent love of neighbor; appreciation of Christ as gift, though, in the face of residual sin, reliance only upon Christ as grace.

Critical Analysis

The Finnish reading of Luther promises ecumenical fecundity. First, the recovery of Luther's notion of Christ's transforming presence in faith has opened the doors to dialogue with Orthodoxy, which treasures deification, and with Catholicism, which prizes sanctification. The sinner is not merely covered by Christ's grace through extrinsic imputation but enjoys the sanctifying indwelling of Christ and thus undergoes transformation. This transformation is not a logically subsequent, albeit simultaneous, regeneration that remains distinct in nature from justification, à la the confessional Lutheran documents. The indwelling of Christ through faith, as Osiander rightly claimed, belongs to justification itself. Grace is indeed the favor of God, yet grace operates in virtue of the indwelling of Christ. The gift, moreover, is not something separable from Christ but is Christ himself. By faith the believer is united with Christ, who thus becomes both grace and gift. The Finnish appreciation for the transformation of the sinner resonates with the Catholic appreciation of mystical union with Christ, the very aim of Christian life. Catholic and Orthodox traditions are in full agreement with Peura's claim that "The purpose of justification is that a Christian be made righteous, be completely transformed in Christ."[51] Catholics and Orthodox also confess, as does Peura, that this transformation will be completed only in the heavenly kingdom. Second, the Finnish adoption of ontological terminology, with hints of "substance" metaphysics, may further a common linguistic and conceptual ground for coherent dialogue about Christian realities.[52] Third, notwithstanding these positions helpful for Catholics, the Finns retain the twin Lutheran positions about residual sin, which remains despite the presence of the gift, and about the character of authentic love as selfless giving exclusive of the anxious search for personal gain. I could mention other insights, but these suffice for my present discussion. Notwithstanding these and other contributions, the Finnish project includes at least three impediments to the JD's twofold claim regarding a differentiated consensus in the basic truths of justification.

Revision of Lutheran Confessional Documents

The Finnish critique of the confessional Lutheran documents poses a serious obstacle for many Lutherans. Whereas most Lutheran pastors are called to recognize the confessional documents as authentic exegesis of the Gospel, the Finnish research calls for serious critique of fundamental elements of both the *Apology* and the *Formula of Concord*. Mannermaa does not exaggerate when he ascribes, by way of critique, the following position to the *Formula of Concord*: "The *inhabitatio Dei* is distinguished conceptually as a separate phenomenon that is logically subsequent to justification.... Justification is understood here in a totally forensic manner."[53] But if this Finnish assessment is accurate and if the Finns opt for Luther in lieu of the purely forensic language of Melanchthon and the extrinsic language of the *Formula*, do not Mannermaa and the Finns insist upon revision of the Lutheran confessional documents? If what Luther thinks damnable the *Formula* confesses, is not renunciation of certain tenets of the *Formula* necessary? But if such renunciation is necessary, how can a proponent of the Finnish reading concur in the JD's assessment that neither communion need renounce its teachings of the Reformation era? Furthermore, the Finnish critique raises the question of authority for Lutherans. Does not the following question once raised by American Lutheran theologian Carl Braaten still want for an adequate response: "In case of fundamental disagreement between Luther's theology and the Lutheran Confessions on an issue so crucial as justification, which is normative?"[54] The same question was also posed indirectly by the Vatican's Official Response to the Joint Declaration.[55]

Implicit Denial of Tridentine Doctrine

Even the "Catholic Luther" of the Finnish school denies the Catholic teaching that the formal cause of justification is inhering supernatural justice, despite the pleasantly surprising employment of such "Catholic" concepts as "participation," "substance," and "transformation." The Finns speak of the believer's participation in Christ, who is present through faith and consequently transforms the believer into an image of himself. Nevertheless, the Finns remain vexed by the "iustitia inhaerens" of Trent. It is not "iustitia inhaerens," they say, but Christ himself that constitutes the justice by which the believer stands worthy of salvation. This calls for close examination.

Christ is grace and gift. As gift, Christ renews the believer by transforming the latter into himself. As grace, Christ shields the sinful believer from the condemning judgment of God. Peura writes, "Christ himself is grace and gift.

Christ himself is the grace that covers a sinner and hides him from God's wrath, and Christ himself is the gift that renews the sinner internally and makes him righteous."[56] Although grace and gift are distinguished, their distinction lies not in their formal constitution—which is Christ himself—but in their operative effects: protection from wrath and internal transformation into Christ to be progressively worked out but to be completed only in the eschaton.[57]

Precisely because sin remains in the believer until death, though Christ as gift battles against sin, the believer has need of Christ as protective grace. Luther insists, against Latomus, that sin remains in the baptized and that the remaining sin is *truly* sin: "The main purpose of Luther's critique of Latomus was to defend the notion of residual sin in the Christian after baptism."[58] Catholic tradition, too, confesses the "not yet" character of this earthly transformation into Christ but offers a manifestly different interpretation. Catholic tradition locates the "not yet" character of Christian hope in three aspects of existence: the Pauline "groaning" for the redemption "of our bodies" (Rom 8:23) that is composed of longing for the resurrection of the body and deliverance from concupiscence; the Johannine dichotomy between the "deadly sin" that no child of God commits (1 Jn 3:4–10) and the daily, venial "sins" that must truthfully be confessed (1 Jn 1:10); and the genuine expectation for a fuller transformation into the likeness of God at his glorious appearing (1 Jn 3:2).[59] The Finns, however, view the "not yet" character of transformation not merely as concupiscence, not merely as the persistence of venial sin, not merely as the incomplete character of adoptive sonship in this life, but primarily as remnant infidelity worthy of damnation.

Their chief argument for remnant infidelity is that the Law demands pure and unadulterated love of God for his own sake, with no mingling of desire for one's own welfare.[60] The Law demands such purity, and sober believers, Antti Raunio insists, recognize themselves as condemned by the Law because, "Empirically, what the Christian does is never so good as to be right and acceptable in the sight of God, for our sinful nature continues to contaminate everything we do."[61] For this reason, Christians must have recourse to God's mercy, which is available in Christ as grace, when he dwells within the sinner through faith. In short, because residual sin is truly sin, Christ as transforming gift does not justify the person without Christ as shielding grace. Christ as grace is necessary for the unfolding of Christ's power as gift. Peura sums it up well:

> Only Christ can be the righteousness that stands through God's judgment. Christ is completely holy and pure in the eyes of God. Where Christ is, there God directs his favor. Moreover, Christ indwells in the Christian's heart through faith. So, according to Luther, the righteousness that stands in front of God is based on the indwelling of

Christ.[62]

There are three notes to be kept distinct, though not separate, in evaluating the Finnish school: Christ as grace; Christ as gift; and the renewal of the Christian. Christ as gift and Christ as grace are linked by the union with Christ that the believer enjoys through faith, by which Christ is present in the believer. The renewal itself is divinely wrought; it is not a merely human activity, a synergistic "working" of the believer who is freed to work on his own power because he has been relieved of anxiety about salvation by grace.[63] The renewal is God-wrought: "That a Christian is really made righteous, although only partially so, is not his own achievement but is effected by Christ who indwells the Christian."[64] This is significant in that the renewal of which the Finns speak parallels the "inhering justice" of which Trent speaks, the formal effect of God's forgiving and transforming mercy upon the sinner. Though divinely wrought, the renewal of the believer through Christ as gift does not render the Christian worthy of eternal life. Therefore, justifying righteousness consists not in the divinely wrought renewal but in Christ himself, who becomes the Christian's righteousness through faith by his indwelling presence as grace. The Father has favor (*favor Dei*) on the believer because his beloved Son dwells within the Christian through faith.[65] With the *Formula* and the *Apology*, Antti Raunio avows, "God accepts me as righteous and looks upon me with favor even though I am and remain a sinner." Against both works, though, he describes "the alien justice of Christ" as "infused" justice. He writes, "The infused justice is also Christ himself who dwells and works in the Christian, and the Christian cooperates with Christ."[66]

The essence of justifying grace is, hence, none other than Christ himself, as grace and gift.[67] Veli-Matti Kärkkäinen, a Pentecostal theologian, accurately interprets the Finns on this point: "Christ in both his person and his work is present in faith and is through this presence identical with the righteousness of faith."[68] As a result, the Finns cannot brook the tridentine doctrine on the formal cause:

> Righteousness is not achieved by the help of works, of inherent habitual love, or of inherent grace. The righteousness valid in God's judgment is not an inherent quality of the Christian, that is, a substantially inherent quality of habitual grace in the Christian. Therefore, according to Luther, the doctrine of *fides charitate formata* is wrong.[69]

The Finns have situated themselves between Trent (though for ecumenical purposes and perhaps because of misinformation from their Catholic brothers, they cordially label it "scholasticism") and the Lutheran confessional documents. Critical of both, they rely on a reading of Luther rich with Catholic (and Orthodox) mystical depth but not wanting in fundamental Lutheran concerns, such as remnant sin and shielding grace. Not all Lutherans, however, remain convinced. Missouri Synod Lutheran theologian Burnell Eckardt (1955–), in an article comparing Luther's and Anselm's soteriologies, offers tacit criticism of the Finns:

> Some have misunderstood the *fröhlicher Wechsel* as immature Luther, with the mistaken premise that it occurs through the mystical presence of Christ, *propter Christum in nobis*, which would create a tension with forensic justification. That is, if the exchange is mystical, then it becomes in effect akin to the scholastic *gratia infusa*, according to which the righteousness by which the Christian stands before God has been made inhering in the Christian's nature. But Luther's preference for the *fröhlicher Wechsel* cannot be called supportive of this position; rather, for him the exchange is actually quite forensic.[70]

The promise of the Finnish program depends upon the double alteration of tridentine and confessional Lutheran doctrines. The honesty herein is to be applauded, but the failure of the ecumenical movement to come to grips with such honesty bodes ill for the future.

Insufficient Basis for Articulating Human Cooperation

Presupposing the Finnish reading of Luther, I find it difficult to perceive therein adequate grounds for human cooperation with grace. Christ as gift renews the human person. But *how* does Christ renew the person? If Christ is himself the gift that renews, then does he simply "effect" that which the Christian simply undergoes, merely passively? Juntunen inclines in this direction. He admits that, in the order of nature, the human person has an imminent principle of action: By human nature, a person can perform this or that action and is thus properly called an "actor," though totally dependent upon God. In this respect, Juntunen enjoys the company of Bonaventure and Thomas, who were at least in part influenced by Aristotle's understanding of nature (*physis*). In the order of nature, then, God does not move things merely extrinsically but by inclinations proper to them rooted in their nature. Juntunen thinks things are otherwise in the order of grace:

> The claim that the axiom "*agere sequitur esse*" is equally true in both *esse naturae* and *esse gratiae* is not altogether correct. One has a smaller role in the actions of the *esse gratiae* than in those of the *esse naturae*, where one is a *causa secunda*. Even in *esse naturae* the person is totally dependent on God, but here God's effect causes a *factura*, whose principle of action is the created human essence. In the realm of *esse gratiae* the principle of action does not belong to the created essence of the believer but is a

participation in the uncreated reality of Christ's person.[71]

Echoing Mannermaa's and Peura's repudiation of "fides caritate formata," Juntunen contends that the *esse gratiae* is much greater than a mere quality infused into the human person, inclining him towards faith and charity. The *esse gratiae* is Christ himself. He contends, moreover, that Christ does not move the believer merely extrinsically but intrinsically, since he dwells within him. At this point, Juntunen concludes his reflection, enigmatically asserting it to be "understandable" that Luther would therefore speak of the believer's "cooperation" with God even in the realm of grace.[72]

One can surely grant with Thomas Aquinas that even without recourse to "habitual grace" one can conceive of "cooperation" with God.[73] Still, Thomas insightfully considered human movements towards God, aroused by God, to be more spontaneous and delightful precisely because of the blessing of an *additional* inclination given to them in habitual grace. Thomas perceived Peter Lombard as a reductively excluding created habitual grace in his identification of charity as the Holy Spirit. Thomas argued for a real distinction between the love by which we love God (i.e., charity poured into our hearts) and the love by which God loves us (the Holy Spirit who is given to us).[74] The Finns expressly desire to follow Lombard, against the scholastic doctrine and the Council of Trent. It would appear, however, that they do not cling to the full scope of Lombard's thought.

Unlike Juntunen, Peter Lombard had no difficulty affirming that the Christian is *truly* made a "lover of God." This is how he read Augustine's distinction between the love of God for us and the love we have for God: the Holy Spirit makes us to be lovers of God.[75] The Holy Spirit so "heals" and sanctifies the soul that the Spirit's active indwelling truly has the *character* of virtue and, under the influence of his sanctifying power, the human person can merit an increase in participation in the Spirit and, ultimately, eternal life.[76] It goes without saying for Lombard, who so assiduously quotes Augustine, that the grace of the Spirit is absolutely necessary for any truly virtuous use of free will, let alone any meritorious use of free will. Still, for him, the movement of the free will is a *sine qua non* of true merit.[77] In fact, unless the Christian is truly moved to love God and neighbor, he has not been moved from the kingdom of the enemy to the kingdom of God: It is precisely the reception of this love that makes him to be justified.[78] This love that is God, this love that is the Holy Spirit, is "given" and "received" exactly when it makes the receiver a lover of God and neighbor.[79] Although Thomas found fault with Lombard's denial that charity is also a created habit, he acknowledged the latter's recognition of the creaturely reality of the acts by which the creature believes in and loves God. Lombard indeed held out an important and necessary place for the Christian to cooperate meritoriously towards his salvation. He already made the scholastic distinction, faithful to Augustine's insights, between operating and cooperating grace.[80] Juntunen would not be willing to affirm this. Moreover, the Finns generally would be unlikely to brook the basic depiction of justification as a change from sin to righteousness. Although Lombard defends his thesis that the Holy Spirit makes sinners into lovers of God without the medium of a virtue, he nonetheless clings to the Augustinian model of a subject undergoing change. The notion of a permanent dialectic of Law and Gospel does not have a home in Lombard.

Finally, Lombard would likely distinguish his own conception of things from Mannermaa's claim that God is both knower and known, subject and object, illuminator and illuminated. Granted, Lombard and the Finns do agree in considering the "charity of God" of Rom 5:5 to be a subjective genitive (the love by which God loves us). They agree, too, on the reason for this reading: The excellence of charity is that of the uncreated God, not that of a created gift.[81] However, because of his position that "to receive" the Spirit is "to be made" a lover of God and neighbor, Lombard had to face a difficulty regarding the divine immutability. If sinners, those who do not love God, are made into just people, those who do love God, then how can the charity that causes this change be the Holy Spirit? Would such change not render him mutable? Again, if a just person can become holier by partaking more and more of charity, which is the Spirit, how can the Spirit be immutable? That this question arose for Lombard shows his fidelity to the Christian tradition, both with respect to divine immutability and with respect to justification as the transformation of a subject. In contrast, the divine immutability has not had a uniform reception among Lutherans.[82] Nor would Lutherans be willing to accept the identification of justification as the change of a sinner into a just lover of God. Perceiving his own thesis on uncreated grace to be that of the minority, Lombard felt intellectually obliged to defend the divine immutability while faithfully retaining Augustine's observations about the *new* presence and the *increased* presence of the Holy Spirit in the souls of the just. The Holy Spirit changes, not in himself, but on the side of the creature, who partakes more and more of the Spirit's renewing power.[83] Unfortunately, he did not offer any explicit defense of this position. Recently, German philosopher and scholar of the middle ages Philipp Rosemann, who lives and teaches in the United States, has suggested a possible defense of Lombard's position. The Holy Spirit remains in himself unchanged and yet pours himself out into a lower, created realm of reality and thus limits *himself* in that reality. Somewhat as the One in Neoplatonism, the Holy Spirit is limited outside of himself not by something already out there that limits him. Rather, by the richness of his own being he limits himself.[84]

It is well known that the majority of Lombard's disciples did not follow him on this point. Following an already active tradition on grace as a quality and charity as a created habit, Thomas accepted and forwarded Lombard's chief concern about the excellence of charity. Thomas in no way denied the indwelling of the Holy Spirit. He simply plumbed the mystery more profoundly, supposing it not fitting that God provide *less* for those whom he loves in a special way (his adopted children) than he does for those whom he loves in a general way (his creatures).[85] Since he provides natural inclinations for the latter to attain their proper ends, it is fitting—for Wisdom disposes all things sweetly (from the Vulgate, Wisdom 8:1)—that God's children be given a "second nature" qualifying them as God's children (1 Jn 3:2) and inclining them sweetly towards their final end. Thomas won the day among Catholics. In any case, it should be clear that both Thomas's and Lombard's estimations of the effects of the Spirit's indwelling exceed the Finnish estimation of the earthly realization of the Christian renewal through union with Christ.

In his desire not to reduce Christ to an "accident" that can be manipulated, Juntunen claims that grace "is realized in the person as a participation in something, something present in the person that still has its own substantial reality."[86] To this one can ask another question from a different perspective. Thomas's recourse to the Aristotelian categories "accident" and "quality" in expounding the Gospel also helped him preserve the continuity of the subject that undergoes God's transforming work. In light of this, I would ask the following question: If the very person who was a sinner is to become the one who is justified, must not he undergo change? How can the same person undergo change and yet not simply be replaced or displaced by that which is intended to "change" him? This is the mystery of justification: The sinner must *become* righteous. The issue is not whether we are dealing with an analytic or a synthetic judgment; the issue is the kind of transformation (*translatio*) at hand. The Finns rightly admit that this transformation is the very goal of justification, but they hold the transformation in abeyance. If Christ is the new "substantial form" of the Christian, and if the Christian somehow remains truly damnable, what in fact has actually changed? Has the old man become the new man or is the new man simply a guest of the old man? Has the old man been assumed so as to be healed, in the words of Gregory of Nazianzus? William T. Cavanaugh, although sympathetic with the Finnish critique of grace as a quality, raises the following pertinent and challenging question: "Does Luther's notion of the 'happy exchange' of the person of Christ for the person of the sinner—and his emphasis on the passivity of the sinner in justification—run counter to Aquinas's foundational presupposition that grace builds on, and does not destroy, nature?"[87]

Delay of Transformation

Finally, I must ask the Finns a question that von Balthasar once posed to Karl Barth. If at the end of time those who truly believe in Christ are transformed into vessels fitted for God's triune love, could not this transformation take place now, in a satisfactory albeit not yet eschatologically perfected manner?[88] Granted that definitive peace shall dawn only after every just person has been raised and all tears have been washed away, granted too that before death even the greatest saint is able to sin (*posse peccare*) and does sin venially, still, must sinners await until death the reception of the grace that will cleanse them from the inner darkness of damnable sin and constitute them as living branches of the true vine? Must the earthly spouse remain a harlot her life long, chasing after foreign gods? If she with simplicity pines for her divine lover's glance, can she be said *truly* to be an adulteress, even though she could await him more steadfastly and vigorously? If in the heavenly kingdom even the most righteous person could not think of boasting in inhering righteousness and if the guarantee of this proper humility is located *not* in the non-attainment or only partial attainment of righteousness but simply in trusting love of God, in humility, then why must all justified believers be sentenced to labor under the burden of still-remnant, damnable sin? Is it so inconceivable that a saintly person, washed with the blood of Christ, could dedicate herself wholly to God's glory and, while not guilty of any mortal sin her entire life, could cry out, "It is not because God, in His anticipating Mercy, has preserved my soul from mortal sin that I go to Him with confidence and love"?[89] And yet this same saint wished to "give the lie" to those who interpret Jesus' saying "It is those who are forgiven much who can love much" (Lk 7:47) to mean that one must first sin much in order to love much. She writes, "I have heard it said that one cannot meet a pure soul who loves more than a repentant soul; ah! how I would wish to give the lie to this statement!"[90] Hans Urs von Balthasar praised this humbly audacious saint, Thérèse of Lisieux, as the "Catholic answer" to the Lutheran question.[91] His prognosis is well-taken, if one consider the genuine piety of Lutherans. Much of her life is readily imbibed by Lutherans. Still, a well-balanced assessment of her "little way" must include her distinctly Catholic exclamation: "Ah! Since the happy day, it seems to me that *Love* penetrates and surrounds me, that at each moment this *Merciful Love* renews me, purifying my soul and leaving no trace of sin within it, and I need have no fear of purgatory."[92] Thérèse recognizes her poverty and confesses that she cannot merit anything of herself without God; however, she does not let this inhibit a bold confession of the really efficacious power of God's sanctifying love.

Peura is right to perceive that the Finnish reading of Luther invites Catholics and Lutherans closer together, but his vehement denial of the

Catholic teaching on faith formed by charity exposes the remnant gulf between Catholic and Finnish-Lutheran thought on justification. The Finnish reading has not provided the fundamental breakthrough necessary for Catholics and Lutherans to achieve a consensus, even a legitimately differentiated consensus, in basic truths.

NOTES

1   Veli-Matti Kärkkäinen, "Justification as Forgiveness of Sins and Making Righteous: The Ecumenical Promise of a New Interpretation of Luther," *One in Christ*, 37 (2002): 32–33.

2   His works include: T. Mannermaa, *In ipsa fide Christus adest* (Finnish edition, 1978); German edition: *Der im Glauben gegenwärtige Christus. Rechtfertigung und Vergottung. Zum ökumenischen Dialog. Arbeiten zur Geschichte und Theologie des Luthertum,* Neue folge Bd. 8 (Hannover, 1989); English edition: *Christ Present in Faith: Luther's View of Justification* (Augsburg Fortress Publishers, 2005); idem, "Theosis als Thema der finnischen Lutherforshung," in *Luther und Theosis: Vergöttlichung als Thema der abendländischen Theologie*, pp. 11–26, ed. Simo Peura and Antti Raunio (Helsinki, Finland: Luther-Agricola-Gesselschaft, 1990); idem, "Hat Luther eine trinitarische Ontologie?" in *Luther und Ontologie. Das Sein Christi als strukturierendes Prinzip der Theologie Luthers* (Erlangen: Martin-Luther-Verlag, 1993); idem, "Über die Unmöglichkeit, gegen Texte Luthers zu systematisieren. Antwort an Gunther Wenz," in *Unio. Gott und Mensch in der nachreformatorischen Theologie* (Helsinki: Schriften der Luther-Agricola-Gesellschaft, 35), pp. 381–91; idem, "Why is Luther so Fascinating?" and "Justification and *Theosis* in Lutheran-Orthodox Perspective," in *Union with Christ*, pp. 1–20 and 25–41; the first of the preceding chapters was based on his article in *Luther und Theosis*; which was translated into English by Norman M. Watt (idem, "Theosis as a Subject of Finnish Luther Research," *Pro Ecclesia* 4 [1995]: 37–48).

3   It is understood that this "human perception" is not merely of the natural order but is of a supernatural order. It is, nonetheless, a creaturely perception.

4   Of course, Saarinen would recognize that many Lutherans consider such extrinsicism to be integral to the Pauline witness.

5   See Simo Peura, "Christ as Favor and Gift," in *Union with Christ*, pp. 45–47.

6   Peura, "Favor," p. 45.

7   See *Union with Christ*, pp. 20, 27–29, 38–39, 45, and 72.

8   Mannermaa, "Justification," p. 38. See also the recent presentation of Finnish thought on this issue by Reinhard Meßner, "Rechtfertigung und Vergöttlichung – und die Kirche: Zur ökumenischen Bedeutung neuerer Tendenzen in der Lutherforschung," *Zeitschrift für Katholische Theologie* 118 (1996): 25 and 35. Meßner draws out the ecclesial implications of the Finnish program, citing Luther's view of the Church as a house for sick people (ibid., pp. 30–32). While the image is certainly attractive, and no less useful, still, the interpretation of *simul iustus et peccator* Meßner provides hardly amounts to the Orthodox and Catholic view of deification achieved on earth through the sacraments, even though that process is never perfected this side of the grave. The Finns still retain an inadequate view of what integration into Christ means, although Meßner is certainly right to note the profound ecumenical promise in the Finnish

program.

9   See Peura, "Favor," pp. 43–48.

10   Ibid., p. 44.

11   See ibid., pp. 53–55.

12   Peura, "What God Gives Man Receives: Luther on Salvation," in *Union with Christ*, p. 91; see also Peura, "Favor," pp. 60–63.

13   See Peura, "Favor," pp. 52–60.

14   Ibid., p. 55.

15   See ibid., pp. 55–57.

16   Peura, "Favor," p. 57.

17   See ibid., p. 56, and LW 32: 239.

18   Peura, "Favor," p. 59.

19   Ibid., p. 59. See also Bruce Marshall, "Justification as Declaration and Deification," p. 16.

20   See Peura, "Favor," pp. 60 and 62.

21   See the following: Mannermaa, "Fascinating," p. 17; idem, "Justification," p. 36; Peura, "Favor," pp. 48 and 59–60; and Sammeli Juntunen, "Luther and Metaphysics: What is the Structure of Being According to Luther?" in *Union with Christ*, pp. 141–43, 147, and 154.

22   See Mannermaa, "Fascinating," pp. 11–12.

23   See Mannermaa, "Fascinating," pp. 15–16; idem, "Justification," p. 35; and Peura, "Favor," pp. 49–50.

24   See Marshall, following the lead of the Finns, also treats this element in Luther (Marshall, "Justification as Declaration and Deification," p. 6).

25   Peura, "Favor," p. 48. In this passage, Peura refers to Luther's comments on Rom 5:5. It is worth noting, however, that in his 1515–16 *Lectures on Romans* (Latin edition), Luther described the love poured forth into our hearts as the love itself by which the Christian loves God, at one point seemingly distinguishing this from the love by which God loves the Christian. Luther's discussion of 5:5, which draws a distinction between the gift (the love by which we love God) and the giver (the Holy Spirit), thus appears to be in some tension with the discussion of 5:15, wherein the gift and grace of Christ are closely united and perhaps identified (see Martin Luther, *Lectures on Romans: Chapters 3–16*, trans. Jacob A.O. Preus, vol. 25, *Luther's Works*, ed. Hilton C. Oswald [St Louis: Concordia Publishing House, 1972], pp. 293–96 and 305–06 [LW 25: 293–96 and 305–06]). Luther's description of the gift of righteousness as coming from God through Jesus Christ (see ibid., p. 306), might be an indication of a lingering (Catholic) distinction between the favor of God and the effect of that favor wrought in the believer. Perhaps Luther's thought at this time still waivered between his scholastic upbringing and his nascent understanding of the "righteousness of God." It is also interesting that in his comments on 5:5, Luther distinguished love for God in himself from a secondary love, a love of neighbor for God's sake (see LW 25: 295). Pannenberg contradicts this hierarchical distinction of objects of love. Pannenberg argues that Paul identifed the "love of God" in Rom 5:5 with the Holy Spirit himself; he concludes that a hierarchical orientation of loves aiming at the true good, God, and aiming at other goods only in virtue of this true good is not compatible with the valid Lutheran insight on justification (see Wolfhart Pannenberg, *Systematic Theology*, vol. 3, trans. Geoffrey W. Bromiley [Grand Rapids, MI: Eerdmans, 1998], pp. 184 ff.; for the German, see *Systematische Theologie*, Band III [Göttingen: Vandenhoeck & Ruprecht, 1993]). Pannenberg does recognize, however, that Luther was struggling in the Latin edition of his *Lectures on Romans* to relate the notion of grace as a quality

(gift) and grace as favor (see ibid., p. 198). Sammeli Juntunen concurs with this assessment (see Juntunen, "Luther," 134, esp. note 22).

26   It should be noted that, according to Mannermaa, Luther would agree that there is no change of substance in this union of God and man, for each remains the same being (see Mannermaa, "Fascinating," p. 11).

27   "'God's love,' which is the purest feeling toward God and alone makes us right at heart, alone takes away iniquity, alone extinguishes the enjoyment of our own righteousness. For it loves nothing but God alone, not even His gifts, as the hypocritical self-righteous people do" (LW 25: 293).

28   Mannermaa, "Justification," p. 36.

29   Sowohl die *imago Dei* wie auch die *similitudo Dei* nach Luther zur geschaffenen Konstitution Adams gehören (Simo Peura, "Die Teilhabe an Christus bei Luther," in *Luther und Theosis: Vergöttlichung als Thema der abendländischen Theologie*, ed. Simo Peura and Antti Raunio [Helsinki, Finland: Luther-Agricola-Gesselschaft, 1990], p. 124).

30   See ibid., p. 126.

31   See ibid., p. 127.

32   See ibid., pp 128–29.

33   See Juntunen, "Luther," p. 154, note 83.

34   Ibid., p. 154, note 83.

35   Mannermaa, "Theosis as a Subject," p. 44.

36   Juntunen, "Luther," p. 154, note 83.

37   Mannermaa, "Theosis as a Subject," p. 48.

38   See Peura, "Die Teilhabe," pp. 138–39.

39   Haßt Gott und versucht, ohne Gott zu sein und zu leben (Peura, "Die Teilhabe," p. 139).

40   See ibid., p. 140.

41   Peura, "Favor," p. 46.

42   Mannermaa, "Justification," p. 36.

43   Mannermaa, "Fascinating," p. 12.

44   Mannermaa, "Theosis as a Subject," p. 45.

45   Es ist klar, daß Adam nicht mehr aufgrund seiner Natur an Gott partizipiert (Peura, "Die Teilhabe," p. 140).

46   See ibid., p. 141.

47   See ibid., p. 144.

48   See ibid., pp. 148–55.

49   See ibid., p. 159.

50   Peura, "Favor," p. 62.

51   Ibid., p. 63.

52   Although Sammeli Juntunen denies that Luther can accept the terms "substance" and "quiddity" because they seem to obscure the creature's constant dependence upon God, his essay teems with a defense of the "realistic" theological ontology of Luther. "To be" most essentially means to be in relation, yet there is always an "inward" aspect to that which stands in relation (see Juntunen, "Luther," p. 141).

53   Mannermaa, "Justification," pp. 27–28.

54   Carl E. Braaten, "Response," p. 72.

55   See OVR, 6.

56   Peura, "Favor," p. 53.

57   See Raunio, "Natural Law and Faith: The Forgotten Foundations of Ethics in Luther's Theology," in *Union with Christ*, p. 122.

58 Peura, "Favor," p. 63.

59 I am working with Brown's opinion that the Johannine expectation consists not merely in a noetic enlightenment, but rather, against the secessionists who contented themselves with the ceremony of initiation and entered not upon the way of the commandments (also contrary to Jn 15), in an ontological transformation, which calls for preparation: "And every one who thus hopes in him purifies himself as he is pure" (1 Jn 3:3). See Raymond Brown, *The Epistles of John*, vol. 30, *The Anchor Bible* (New York: Doubleday, 1982), pp. 426–27 and 434.

60 See Peura, "What God Gives," p. 76, and Raunio, "Natural Law," pp. 102–10.

61 Raunio, "Natural Law," p. 111.

62 Peura, "Favor," p. 66. See also Peura, "What God Gives," p. 91.

63 Pannenberg keenly observes a difficulty in the *Apology* and the *Formula of Concord* in the rejection of the notion of faith as fellowship with Christ. This rejection sent the Lutheran world into a quest to link up the "objective" side of forensic justification with a supposedly "subjective" side of appropriation through renewal. Pannenberg detects in the trajectory of these confessional documents, a trajectory borne out by later Lutheran theology, a misguided effort to link these two. There at times emerged theories that had the appearance of synergism (see Pannenberg, *Systematic Theology* 3: 215–19).

64 Peura, "Favor," p. 59.

65 See Peura, "What God Gives," pp. 89–90.

66 Raunio, "Natural Law," pp. 111 and 114.

67 See Peura, "What God Gives," pp. 90–91. Peura takes Luther's radical notion of the *commercium admirabile* to heart, identifying the gift with Christ himself who gives us his divine attributes so that we become these attributes. Whether the Finns can integrate this notion of deification (*theosis*) with the necessary Hebrew distinction between creator and created effect is another matter.

68 Kärkkäinen, "Justification as Forgiveness," p. 35. He rightly calls this a "real-ontic" participation; he then likens the Finnish thought to that of Athanasius. I would note, however, that the great combatant against Arianism drew upon the category of "participation" in order to express the possibility of different degrees of "wisdom" and "holiness" in those who participate. Holiness is in the creature as an accident in essence and can be present to a greater or lesser degree, even entirely removed. The Finnish hesitancy to admit different degrees of participation in the *grace* of Christ rubs against Athanasius's notion of participation.

69 Peura, "Favor," p. 65.

70 Burnell Eckardt Jr., "Luther and Anselm: Same Atonement, Different Approach," in *Ad Fontes Lutheri: Toward the Recovery of the Real Luther: Essays in Honor of Kenneth Hagen's Sixty-fifth Birthday*, ed. Kenneth Hagen, Franz Posset, and Joan Skocir, Marquette Studies in Theology, no. 28 (Milwaukee: Marquette University Press, 2001), pp. 59–60.

71 Juntunen, "Luther," p. 155.

72 Ibid., p. 156.

73 Thomas Aquinas, ST IaIIae, q. 111, art. 2.

74 Thomas Aquinas, *De caritate*, art. 1.

75 "Cum ergo ab Apostolo dicitur caritas Dei diffundi *in cordibus nostris*, non est dicta caritas Dei qua diligit nos, sed qua facit nos diligere: id est non ibi appellatur 'caritas Dei' eo quod Deus nos ea diligat, sed eo quod nos ea sui dilectores facit" (Peter Lombard, *Sententiae in IV libris distinctae* [Grottaferrata {Rome}: Collegii S. Bonaventurae ad Claras Aquas, 1971], Book I, dist. 17, chap. 6.4, p. 150).

76 See ibid., Book II, dist. 27, pp. 480-87. Consider, for instance, the following: "Et illa gratia 'virtus' non incongrue nominatur, quia voluntatem hominis infirmam sanat et adiuvat" (ibid., chap. 2, p. 482).

77 See ibid., chap. 3, pp. 482–83.

78 See ibid., chap. 4.2, p. 483.

79 See ibid., Book I, dist. 17, chap. 4, pp. 145–46.

80 See ibid., Book II, dist. 27, chap. 2, pp. 481–82, and Philipp Rosemann, "*Fraterna dilectio est Deus*: Peter Lombard's Thesis on Charity as the Holy Spirit," in *Amor amicitiae = On the Love that is Friendship: Essays in Medieval Thought and Beyond in Honor of the Rev. Professor James McEvoy*, ed. Thomas A. F. Kelly and Philipp W. Rosemann, Recherches de Théologie et Philosophie médiévales, no. 6 (Dudley, MA: Peeters, 2004), p. 427.

81 See ibid., Book I, dist. 17, chap. 6.7–9, pp. 151–52.

82 Of course, of late the divine immutability has become otiose in most circles, even Catholic ones. References are too abundant to be necessary or useful. The doctrine has been rejected for various reasons. I must ask: Have any of the proponents of divine mutability seriously faced the philosophical difficulties associated with divine mutability? Indeed, to mention such difficulties is today to invite the label "onto-theology." Although indeed what really falls under the genus "onto-theology" ought to be abandoned, does this mean that any attempt at a rational demonstration is a priori theologically tendentious? Does the notion of a rationally demonstrable truth "infringe" upon God's freedom and personal capacity? Or, on the contrary, are we today facing an increasingly popular fideism that warms itself by burning books that dare to include the "preambles" of faith? This fideism has gone unchecked because it offers an intuitively accurate rejection of rationalism, but its bite has yet to be felt.

83 See Peter Lombard, *Sentences*, Book I, dist. 17, chap. 5, pp. 146–48, and Rosemann, "Lombard's Thesis," pp. 427–28.

84 See Rosemann, "Lombard's Thesis," p. 428.

85 Thomas Aquinas, ST IaIIae, q. 110, arts. 1 and 2.

86 Juntunen, "Luther," p. 153.

87 William T. Cavanaugh, "A Joint Declaration?: Justification as Theosis in Aquinas and Luther," *The Heythrop Journal* 41 (2000): 278.

88 See Hans Urs von Balthasar, *The Theology of Karl Barth: Exposition and Interpretation*, trans. John Drury (New York: Holt, Rinehart and Winston, 1971), esp. pp. 271–76. See the discussion of this work in Hampson, *Christian Contradictions*, pp. 124–26. Hampson's incisive critique of Catholic readings of Lutheran theology cannot be easily dismissed. I should like to note that the "already/not-yet" duality that requires the covering of the grace of Christ is not simply a Finnish misreading of Luther. Luther himself in his 1535 (1531) *Lectures on Galatians* defended the necessity of faith as trust because of which God does not impute still-present sin unto damnation. Luther claims that faith is necessary now because of this still-present sin but that faith will not be necessary in the heavenly kingdom because the saints shall love God purely and perfectly (Martin Luther, *Lectures on Galatians [1535]: Chapters 5–6*, trans. Jaroslav Pelikan, vol. 27, *Luther's Works*, pp. 1–149, ed. Jaroslav Pelikan [St. Louis: Concordia Publishing House, 1963], p. 64 [LW 27: 64]; see also Martin Luther, *Lectures on Galatians [1519]*, trans. Richard Jungkuntz, vol. 27, *Luther's Works*, pp. 151–410, ed. Jaroslav Pelikan [St. Louis: Concordia Publishing House, 1963], p. 363 [LW 27: 363]).

89 St. Thérèse of Lisieux, *Story of a Soul*, trans. John Clarke, O.C.D. (Washington, D.C.: ICS Publications, 1996), p. 259. See also ibid., pp. 149–50, in which she relates her discovery that she had not committed any mortal sin her entire life.

90   St. Thérèse of Lisieux, *Story of a Soul*, p. 84.

91   See Hans Urs von Balthasar, "Thérèse of Lisieux," trans. Donald Nichols and Anne England Nash, in *Two Sisters in the Spirit: Thérèse of Lisieux and Elizabeth of the Trinity*, pp. 13–362 (San Francisco: Ignatius Press, 1992); see esp. pp. 256, 259, and 283–84.

92   St. Thérèse of Lisieux, *Story of a Soul*, p. 181.

CHAPTER 5

Wolfhart Pannenberg

GERMAN LUTHERAN theologian Wolfhart Pannenberg makes perhaps the strongest case for the ecumenical dialogue between Catholics and Protestants. In this section, I limit myself to his work as a theologian in volume 3 of his *magnum opus, Systematic Theology*. In my analysis of the Joint Declaration, I will treat his work for the dialogues themselves, especially his work with Karl Cardinal Lehmann. Though Pannenberg's reading of the Gospel resembles the Finnish reading of Luther in many respects, it differs from the latter in significant ways.

Presentation

Because of its complex historical and systematic nature, the thought of Wolfhart Pannenberg is not easily put in pithy form. I cannot convey all the refined aspects of his insights here but must restrict myself to the most pertinent elements of his work regarding justification and salvation. I shall follow his order of presentation: law; faith and love; justification and adoption; baptism; and eschatology. Pannenberg's basic *modus operandi* is to retrieve and critique ecclesial and theological texts on the basis of the principles of historically situated human reason (not excluding theological reason) and the normative theological articulations of the mystery of salvation in scripture. He discovers problematic elements in both Trent and *The Book of Concord*. He considers Luther to be one of the most accurate exegetes of Paul, though not without shortcomings. Pannenberg operates somewhat freely with regard to his own tradition. After an extended analysis of justification, he concludes that although there is a "profound" difference between Catholic and Lutheran expressions of the mystery, both are fundamentally united in their intention to root justification in the "incorporation of believers into Christ" (*Systematic Theology*, vol. 3, p. 220). He suggests that this common feature "largely relativizes the earlier antitheses as simply different interpretations of the one event to which many mutual misunderstandings and misjudgments were linked" (*Systematic Theology*, 3: 220–21). On the basis of this common intention,

Lutherans and Catholics ought to be able to recognize the inner defects in their own traditions and accept criticism from the biblical witness. Pannenberg thus maintains that both communions stand in need of correction on specific points of doctrine and that acceptance of such criticism with a view to their common teaching can pave the way towards a doctrinal rapprochement (*Systematic Theology*, 3: 221).

Pannenberg frames his discussion with respect to the Law-Gospel distinction so fundamental to Lutheran thought. According to Pannenberg, Paul's polemic against justification by works of law is grounded in the conviction that "no one at any time will keep the law in every part (Gal. 3:10). This does not have to mean that we cannot keep the individual statutes" (*Systematic Theology*, 3: 65). We can obey them piecemeal, but we cannot observe satisfactorily the entire law. This claim alone makes justification by works of the law impossible. But there is a difficulty one must face: If law or natural law is a "normative expression of God's eternal will for us" (*Systematic Theology*, 3: 90), then Christians are obligated to keep the law. In contrast to Paul's insistence on justification by faith apart from works,

> There can be no avoiding the contrary implication that no one can partake of salvation without keeping the law.... If the law as the eternal law or natural law is the criterion by which works are assessed at the last judgment, then it seems there must also be a righteousness of works for us even if on the basis of baptismal grace and the related forgiveness of sins. (*Systematic Theology*, 3: 90–91)

This seemingly inevitable implication (Rom 2) is clearly not tolerable, since it conflicts with Paul's continuing argument in Rom 3 and 4. There must then be another way of viewing the law. "The law," Pannenberg asserts, "is not the direct, unchangeable, definitive expression of the will of God" (*Systematic Theology*, 3: 66). It was given by angels (Gal 3:19) only for a time, to keep sinners in custody and to "multiply transgressions" (*Systematic Theology*, 3: 67) until the coming of Christ, whose saving work made void the *entire* law: "The saying about the end of the law in Rom. 10:4 certainly pertains to all the law in every part, not just to the ritual law, but to the moral law as well" (*Systematic Theology*, 3: 68, brackets mine).

This annihilation of the law does not, however, entail an antinomian chaos or hedonism. On the contrary, Jesus calls for certain responses from his followers, many of which have a material similarity to the Mosaic and natural laws, such as worshiping one God and honoring parents; further, the core of the Jewish law is retained, i.e., love of God and neighbor (*Systematic Theology*, 3: 68–69). Nonetheless, the Gospel of Jesus Christ does not come in the form of *demand*. That which comes in the form of demand is issued under threat of condemnation, exposing the addressee to anxiety. Jesus is not a new legislator, but he invites his followers to a life of love based upon the gratuitous love he has shown them in his death and resurrection. The Lutheran insight does not deny Jesus' invitation to loving action but rejects the interpretation of this invitation as setting up conditions for the righteousness of the sinner: "Reformation teaching does not surrender the obligatory nature of God's demand. Instead, pronouncement of the forgiveness of sins enables us to do the will of God freely and without anxious striving for works righteousness" (*Systematic Theology*, 3: 75).

Then what becomes of the law? For Pannenberg, law is by definition a fixed formulation of human conduct; as such, it can become ossified. Contexts change, and situations of interpersonal interaction might demand creative responses that, though faithful to God's Spirit, violate the letter of some past law. God's will never changes, Pannenberg grants, but the temporal expression of his will in various cultures and in various epochs of salvation history can change. Christians are charged with doing what is right, but they are not necessarily obligated to fulfill every particular expression of God's will. It must be possible "to regard God's righteous will as binding and yet to view its identification with the form of law as transitory, namely, as a specific phenomenon in the history of God's OT covenant people (and analogously in other cultures) that Jesus Christ has set aside" (*Systematic Theology*, 3: 93). The entire Mosaic law, he contends, is a transitory expression of God's immutable will, an expression that has come to an end in Jesus Christ. Obedience to the law is not a condition for salvation, since the law can never be kept in its entirety: "For no human being will be justified in his sight by works of law" (Rom 3:20). Pannenberg does *not* circumscribe this inability to obey the law satisfactorily with reference simply to the Mosaic law, a particular expression of God's will. More broadly, he contends that no believer can at all times obey *God's righteous will* (of which the law is but an expression), although authentic faith provides ample motivation for observance of it.

Since justification is not by works, it is by faith. According to Luther's reading of Paul, faith really unites the Christian to God. Through confident trust in God's promise, the believer enjoys a real fellowship with God. Melanchthon and others obscured this, Luther's key insight: "In Melanchthon we look in vain for Luther's basic thought that faith unites with God himself and his Word" (*Systematic Theology*, 3: 141). In the *Apology* and in the *Formula of Concord*, there is a one-sided emphasis on the forensic or imputed aspect of justification. According to these documents, faith does not make the sinner righteous. Instead, faith simply recognizes God's act of mercy in acquitting the sinner of his sins. Pannenberg would not dispute the confessional documents' contention that "Christ is our effective righteousness." But he disputes the way in which these documents, chiefly, the *Formula of Concord*, depict Christ as becoming our righteousness. Lutheran theologians who follow the *Formula* teach that "The formal righteousness of believers is by way of the imputing of Christ's righteousness" (*Systematic Theology*, 3: 228). Pannenberg insists that these interpretations of Paul miss the mark. According to Pannenberg, faith actually takes the believer outside of himself and into Christ. By faith, the believer no longer stands within himself but lives from Christ. In virtue of this fellowship with Christ outside himself, the believer is truly righteous.[1] Still, he finds Melanchthon and Luther in agreement that one ought to consider faith justifying not because it has characteristics of righteous works but rather because "it alone is the appropriate form of accepting the promise" (*Systematic Theology*, 3: 142).

At this point, I would like to note the principle difference between the Finns and Pannenberg. Whereas the former see the sinner as being righteous because of the "indwelling" of Christ, the latter sees the sinner as being righteous in virtue of an ecstatic (ec-centric) relation to Christ. The Finns struggle to express the mystery of God's indwelling without either making God a constituent part of the human (accidental form) or implying a schizophrenic conjunction of the sinner and God (i.e., two juxtaposed substances). Pannenberg is well aware of these difficulties (especially the former), and his theory of ecstatic faith-fellowship with Christ offers a promising alternative. He notes that the scholastics also worried that the notion of the Holy Spirit's indwelling might be mistakenly conceived as reducing the Spirit to part of the created world. The scholastic's worry, he suggests, can be expressed as follows: if the Holy Spirit were the very love shed abroad in our hearts (Rom. 5:5), then the Holy Spirit would become part of the human person. The scholastics opted to deny that the love infused into the human heart is formally identical to the Holy Spirit. They insisted that the Holy Spirit is the efficient and exemplar cause of the infusion of created charity, which is infused into the human person (*Systematic Theology*, 3: 199–200). The Finns, as I noted above, claim that the Holy Spirit is the very love by which one loves God, the very love shed abroad. Pannenberg sides with the Finns on the identity of the love "shed abroad"; however, he articulates the union of the believer with the Holy Spirit (and with Christ) not primarily by way of indwelling but by way of the outwardly directed thrust of faith: "Only the ecstatic structure of faith enables us to understand that the Spirit of God and therefore also the love of God that is poured into believers' hearts do not become part of our creaturely reality when God's Spirit is imparted to us as a gift and he pours God's love into our hearts" (*Systematic Theology*, 3: 200).

As the Finns do, Pannenberg strives to avoid the one-sided tendencies of a Catholic intrinsicism—grace as quality—and confessional Lutheran extrinsicism—merely forensic justification. On the one hand, he repeats that the "love of God" shed into our hearts is not the love by which we love God but the love by which God loves us, first rooted in the love by which the Father loves the Son: "Above all…the love that is poured into believers' hearts by the Holy Spirit (if the genitive in Rom. 5:5 is a subjective genitive) cannot be a habit of virtue related to the creaturely soul but has to be the divine love itself that dwells in believers by the Holy Spirit" (*Systematic Theology*, 3: 194).[2] Although not enamored of the Catholic position on grace as a quality, Pannenberg affirms, with the Finns, that believers participate in Christ and thereby become righteous before God. But, without explicitly distancing himself from the Finns, he links participation not so much to indwelling conceived in some sort of metaphysical light but rather to the "ecstatic nature of the dynamic of faith, hope, and love" (*Systematic Theology*, 3: 194). Only this "enables us to think of the participation of the creature in God without injury to God's transcendence, namely, by means of the idea of an ecstatic participation of the creature in the divine life outside the self in Christ (*extra nos in Christo*)" (*Systematic Theology*, 3: 194). Together with the Finns, he wishes "in some sense [to rehabilitate] Lombard's teaching about the identity of *caritas* and the Holy Spirit (*Systematic Theology* 3:194). He adds a simple but noteworthy qualification: the theologian should describe the Holy Spirit as Christian charity not by reference to the "indwelling" but "by reflection on the ecstatic structure of faith in keeping with the eccentric character of the spiritual life in general" (*Systematic Theology*, 3: 194). Pannenberg even takes issue with the suggestion that the perichoretic dance of the two natures in Christ can provide a model by which one can integrate both Christ's intimate presence to the believer (e.g., the Finnish talk of Christ as "substantial form" of the believer) and also God's independence from the creaturely realm.[3] Only the ecstatic structure of faith ensures that God is not made *part* of creation. *A fortiori*, contrary to the prevailing scholastic view, grace is not a quality in the soul.

The eccentricity of faith pervades Pannenberg's discussion of justification, yet he does not list the specific characteristics that manifest this quality in one place. One can glean his thought from various hints. First, living beings manifest a relation to "external" things in their very existence. Nothing subsists by itself; things thrive only in interaction with other things: "Every living thing lives its life by existing outside itself, namely, in and by the world around it" (*Systematic Theology*, 3: 135). Second, human beings manifest this ecstatic structure in a unique way, by being lifted "above their particularity and finitude" (*Systematic Theology*, 3: 135). Life would not be possible without a basic trust "with which, in spite of all disillusionment, we constantly open ourselves to what is around us, to the world" (*Systematic Theology*, 3: 135).

Third, faith itself is the supreme human experience of ecstatic fellowship with another, since by faith the believer is no longer isolated within himself, trusting in his own capacities, but entrusts himself entirely to Jesus Christ.

Pannenberg's notion of the ecstatic character of faith-fellowship with Christ has ontological, eschatological, Christological, and Trinitarian overtones. The ecstatic character has ontological overtones in that there is a twofold identity of the believer: outside the self with Christ and within the empirical reality of the self. The believer's empirical reality is already being transformed in Christ, but this transformation is not yet completed. Nevertheless, the believer already "touches" a complete righteousness by his present relationship to Christ through faith. The believer is already truly righteous by an ecstatic fellowship with Christ. In this sense and in a secondary sense because of the consequent yet gradual inner transformation, the believer might be described as being "ontologically righteous," to use my own phrase. But there is also an eschatological sense in which the believer is righteous. Faith links the believer to God not simply as a virtue taking him ontologically outside himself into Christ. Faith links the believer to his own history in God; that is, "This faith lifts us above our particularity inasmuch as God is powerfully present to us as the light of our final future and assures us at the same time of our own eternal salvation" (*Systematic Theology*, 3: 135). God knows the believer's future, which is the truth of who he really "is." Because who he will be is most who he is, he cannot know yet who he really is. This not knowing can give rise to a lack of self-certainty. By faith, however, the believer hears and accepts God's promise of eternal salvation. This future salvation is integral to the believer's very selfhood. Therefore, the assurance of faith is central to the believer's identity: "It has to do with an assurance that constitutes our actual personhood" (*Systematic Theology*, 3: 163).[4] Faith is ecstatic not simply in an "ontological" way but also in an "eschatological" way, linking the believer up to his future in God.

Both the ontological and eschatological aspects of faith's ecstatic structure have a Christological and Trinitarian resonance. Faith unites believers with the history of Jesus. Believers enjoy an unbreakable bond with Christ and participate in his life by their lives of discipleship: as he suffered and died, so they will suffer and die (*Systematic Theology*, 3: 201–02 and 231–32). Faith establishes the Christian on a trajectory of dying to self and rising to Christ. This is a life-long endeavor, which faith proleptically anticipates. Faith's ecstatic nature also has a Trinitarian overtone because it is a participation in the relation of the Son to the Father. As the Son is constituted precisely by his self-distinction from the Father, so Christians are constituted in their new identity precisely in their self-distinction from the Father through faith and, simultaneously, in their self-distinction from the Son. Whereas the Son is Son by nature, believers are children by adoption.

So much for an account of faith's structure and characteristics. The question now is, how does faith function in justification? On account of faith, God pronounces the believer just. Pannenberg agrees that this Lutheran statement accurately describes Paul's teaching, but he disagrees with the 19th and 20th century interpretation of this pronouncement as being *contra factum*. The 19th century Lutheran theologian Albrecht Ritschl (1820–1914) used Kantian categories to describe this pronouncement as being utterly forensic. God pronounces forgiveness not upon a righteous person but upon a sinful person. Ritschl, who went against the grain of the liberal Protestant theology of his day, therefore considered the pronouncement "synthetic" rather than analytic, since God calls just the person who is in fact ungodly—God brings together, synthesizes, what are in themselves alien, the sinner and righteousness.

Most orthodox Lutheran theologians have agreed with Ritschl's claim, until recently. Pannenberg maintains that justification is not by human works or by anything inherent in the justified, yet he rejects the Ritschlian reading of Paul. For Pannenberg, God's declaration "presupposes" a righteousness in the believer, but this righteousness is not one of obedience to the law. God's judgment is analytic in that it is a true verdict based upon the believer's identity through faith. Because faith brings about an ecstatic fellowship with Christ, the believer is truly just in Christ (*Systematic Theology*, 3: 223–25). This reading, Pannenberg recognizes, diverges not only from Ritschl but also from the *Apology* and the *Formula*, since for the latter two the notion of "the indwelling of Christ in believers is a *consequence* of justification linked to the gift of the Holy Spirit" (*Systematic Theology*, 3: 227). The *Formula* was written with an eye to refuting Osiander's notion that justification presupposes the indwelling of God's essential righteousness. The authors did not merely dispute his Christological implication that only the divinity dwells within believers. In addition,

[They] reversed the sequence of Christ's indwelling and the imputing of faith for righteousness, viewing the indwelling of Christ (and the trinitarian God) in believers as a *result* and not, like Osiander, as the *basis*, of pronouncing righteous. In this matter Osiander had on his side not only Luther but the priority Paul gave to the righteousness of faith over the pronouncing of believers as righteous. (*Systematic Theology*, 3: 227)

Pannenberg distances himself from this notable defect of the confessional Lutheran documents.

On the other hand, Pannenberg also takes the tridentine declaration to task for describing the infusion of divine charity as a necessary element of justification:

> There is no exegetical support for the view of faith in what the council says about the righteousness of faith and the justification of believers when it links faith only to the beginning of justification and then ascribes its completion to the infusing of love into the hearts of believers by the Holy Spirit, which Paul mentions in another context (5:5), not in relation to justification.... The council's defective exegetical judgment may well be understandable because it was seeing Paul's statements through the spectacles of the Scholastic doctrine of grace, but its judgment was defective nonetheless. (*Systematic Theology*, 3: 222–23)

Not infused grace and charity but "faith is itself the righteousness that counts before God" (*Systematic Theology*, 3: 223). Again, this is not to deny the necessity of the "gift" that comes with God's grace. For Pannenberg, the Lutheran confessional documents present too rigid a division between grace—the favor of God—and gift—that which God pours forth. He writes, "It will not do to set personal grace, as the favor of God in his condescending to us, in antithesis to the idea of a gift of grace that is granted to us. Rather, the two belong together. This is why Melanchthon, too, abandoned the antithesis in the later 1559 *Loci*" (*Systematic Theology*, 3: 199). In Chapter 6, the reader will see that Melanchthon's 1559 *Loci* do not go as far as Pannenberg claims here. The gift, Pannenberg holds, is really given and belongs inseparably to grace. However, "The thesis of created grace does not follow from this" (*Systematic Theology*, 3: 199). According to Pannenberg, the Catholic (Pannenberg diplomatically labels it the "scholastic") position on the formal cause as an inhering gift bestowed upon the creature is not acceptable. Gift is not something created and infused: "Precisely as a gift grace is identical with God himself, namely, with the Holy Spirit who is given us (Rom. 5:5)" (*Systematic Theology*, 3: 200). Accordingly, "not the grace identical with the gift of the Holy Spirit but only its effects, the new human impulses generated by it, count as part of our human reality" (*Systematic Theology*, 3: 200).

Pannenberg by no means denies the regeneration of the human person in his faith-fellowship with Christ. In a sense, fellowship with Christ constitutes the regeneration of the human person, if we are to read "regeneration" as a "revivification," because as the sinner finds himself in Christ, who is life, so he finds life. In himself dead, the sinner can be alive in Christ if he trusts in Christ rather than resting solipsistically in himself. Notwithstanding this revivification,

> Grace is not a quality or power that is different from Jesus Christ and that is imparted to us; it is Jesus Christ himself as the gift of divine love to whom believers are conformed by the Spirit as they are drawn into his filial relation to the Father and thus reconciled to God and freed to participate in God's love for the world. (*Systematic*

Theology, 3: 202)

Pannenberg describes a chief element of what Catholics hold—that believers participate in Christ's Sonship—but carefully denies the tridentine articulation of how this adoptive sonship transpires, namely, through the infused grace which serves as the principle of sonship and the actions belonging thereto.

In his argument, Pannenberg is not reacting against a strawman; he is not merely denying charity's justifying role because he conceives of it as a "work" wrought by natural human powers. He understands the Catholic perspective that this "habit" is infused by God, and he denies that this infused habit—grace or charity—is that by which one is justified: "Scholastic theology regarded love as a basic virtuous attitude of the soul or the will, though deriving not from *acquired* habit but from habit *infused* by God" (*Systematic Theology*, 3: 198). For Pannenberg, justified persons share in Christ not because of a created habit by which they are united to Christ, but rather because of the ecstatic power of faith by which they acknowledge and live their own "distinction" from Christ and yet thereby maintain their union with him outside themselves. By this union in distinction, believers enjoy Christ's indwelling. The union itself of the believer with Christ constitutes the "ontic" aspect of justification that Luther eventually came to distinguish, not separate, from the "forensic" aspect of divine verdict. Pannenberg cites the 1535 Galatians commentary as the prime locus in which one witnesses this distinction. He then raises a question about the relation of the ontic fellowship with Christ to the empirical reality of believers, i.e., that which they are, considered in themselves: "Since the ontic sharing of believers in Christ's righteousness rests on a union with Christ 'beyond the self,' the question arises as to how this matter relates to the empirical reality of believers 'in themselves'" (*Systematic Theology*, 3: 217). The reader must keep in mind that the question already presupposes Luther as drawing a distinction, albeit not a separation, between the forensic and ontic aspects of justification. The question therefore does not regard the relation between the forensic and ontic aspects of justification but rather the relation of the "ontic" aspect of fellowship with Christ through faith and the believer's empirical identity. How, he is asking, is the believer "made righteous"?

The reader must not lose sight of the fact that for Pannenberg there is a double sense of "being righteous" or "being made righteous." The first and primary sense is the righteousness that believers enjoy through fellowship with Christ: they partake in Christ by existing outside of themselves. This is not a creaturely habit or an internal renewal, but it does (somehow) affect the very identity of the believer. The secondary sense is the internal renewal that begins in this life and is consummated in eternal life. Internal renewal involves the "empirical identity" of the believer. Pannenberg insists that residual sin still so

affects believers that they cannot be called truly righteous, despite their
incipient renewal, except inasmuch as Christ's righteousness is attributed to
them: "In their empirical existence, then, believers share in the righteousness
that is theirs in Christ outside themselves only inasmuch as there is imputed to
them, as regards their empirical constitution, that which they are in Christ"
(*Systematic Theology*, 3: 218). Pannenberg follows Luther closely here, as is
evident by his reference to certain passages in the great Galatians commentary.
Turning to Luther's work, we find that one's empirical reality can be
considered *truly* righteous only by imputation, since sin still remains. God has
mercy on those who have faith and considers this imperfect faith to be perfect
righteousness, so that although believers are in themselves worthy of eternal
death, he does not charge their remnant sin to their account. Although God
begins to cleanse believers internally, Luther confessed, "We are not yet purely
righteous, but sin is still clinging to our flesh during this life."[5] Indeed, the sins
that remain are even "great ones" that the believer ought to consider "worthy
of wrath, the judgment of God, and eternal death."[6] There is no escape from sin
by way of a "quality that is first infused into the soul and then distributed
through all the members." Against the sophists' appeals to righteousness as a
quality that expels sins, Luther maintains that "Sins remain in us, and God hates
them very much." Therefore, "it is necessary for us to have the imputation of
righteousness...."[7] By anticipation, Luther categorically denied that which
Trent defined as binding for Catholics:

> Righteousness is not in us in a formal sense, as Aristotle maintains, but is outside us,
> solely in the grace of God and in His imputation. In us there is nothing of the form or
> of the righteousness except that weak faith or the first fruits of faith by which we have
> begun to take hold of Christ. Meanwhile sin truly remains within us.[8]

Pannenberg, like Luther, maintains both the incipient renewal and the
remnant sinfulness of the believer's empirical identity. The double status of the
believer is not an outright contradiction. The Christian is truly sinful in his
empirical identity and imperfectly righteous by the incipient renewal. In
proleptic anticipation of his future identity, the believer is righteous by
"imputation" in his empirical identity and is perfectly righteous in his ecstatic
existence in Christ. Through faith, the believing sinner already takes hold of
Christ and in that sense enjoys the plentitude of Christ's righteousness outside
himself and keeps "all the commandments through him" (*Systematic Theology*,
3: 216). The conceptual difficulty lies in the relation of the empirical reality of
believers (in themselves) to their "righteous identity" (outside themselves)
through faith in Christ. How can these two characteristics be aspects of one
person (*Systematic Theology*, 3: 217–19)? Pannenberg notes that this relation

poses a difficult question. He locates the source for an answer in the mystery of baptism, the sacrament of faith that unites believers to Christ, specifically to his death and resurrection, and that promises the hope of eternal salvation. Baptism makes believers adopted children of God, once for all, if they do not allow sin definitive control of their lives.[9] Hence, "Only the connection with baptism could really clarify the relation between the being of believers *in Christ* and their *earthly existence*" (*Systematic Theology*, 3: 233). The lack of discussion of baptism in much of Reformation theology of justification obscured Luther's insights on faith fellowship with Christ. Because baptism is the locus of justification, however, Pannenberg argues that reflection on its role can help Protestants and Catholics accept their doctrinal limitations as "serious defects when compared to the Pauline witness" (*Systematic Theology*, 3: 234). The two communions can come to see that their descriptions of justification are partial, albeit necessary, aspects of the whole mystery. The specifically Protestant insight that justification involves a pronouncement of forgiveness is meant not to deny the baptismal call to filial obedience but rather to underscore that a believer's righteousness, because imperfect, is not part of the object of the divine verdict. Only faith fellowship forms the object of that verdict (*Systematic Theology*, 3: 231). This fellowship includes or entails hope and love, "but always in such a way that participation in the life of divine love is sustained by ecstatic faith and only thus protected against corruption into human self-relatedness" (*Systematic Theology*, 3: 236). Faith alone guarantees the true freedom of the Christian to relate to Christ. Pannenberg, then, denies that faith's justifying power depends upon infused charity.

Pannenberg's suggestion that baptism ought to be the point of departure for a discussion of justification is not intended as a repudiation of the perennially valid critical role of the notion of justification as a declaration of forgiveness. Pannenberg does not attribute to baptism an efficient, albeit secondary, causality that already delivers its effect in the present empirical reality of the baptized. Rather, baptism is an effective *sign*. Though not merely an empty sign, it is not an instrumentally causative sign already delivering what is promised through it. Baptism and the Lord's supper "effect what they signify. But they do so only in the form and on the level of signs.... The significatory nature of the effecting distinguishes the present form of the saving participation of believers from the future consummation of the church's fellowship with its Lord at his return for judgment..." (*Systematic Theology*, 3: 238).[10] With his discussion of baptism, Pannenberg pinpoints the eschatological nature of his interpretation of the Pauline kerygma on justification. The baptized are already brought into an ecstatic relationship with God, a relationship that is in itself unbreakable and permanent, although an individual might choose permanently to forgo the grace of this relationship. This relationship is also a proleptic sign of what is to come for the believer in his empirical identity. In addition, the ecstatic relationship presently established sets the Christian on his way towards dying with Christ so as to rise with Christ, for the old man must whither away and the new man must gradually take its place. Empirical human life involves the process of transformation into Christ, guarded by the promise that God will faithfully confirm and fulfill this living relationship to himself in its perfection at the believer's death (*Systematic Theology*, 3: 239–43).

On this basis, Pannenberg critiques the Catholic use of the sacrament of reconciliation as a "second plank" by which those who have sinned and thus lost baptismal grace supposedly regain it. Catholic practice obscures the "once for all" nature of baptismal grace, making it look as though this grace were something "in" the justified that could therefore also be lost. Luther also attacked "the idea of Jerome that Christians lose baptismal grace by serious sins" (*Systematic Theology*, 3: 249). Although at times Luther may have lost sight of the "once for all" nature of baptism, Pannenberg approves him for refusing to conceive of baptismal grace as something infused. The notion of losing and regaining baptismal grace, Pannenberg contends, is inextricably linked to the "scholastic" idea of created grace: "If we view grace, with Scholasticism, as [a] created [even though] supernatural reality that is infused into the soul by baptism and inheres in it, then it is natural enough to think that mortal sin can mean the loss of this state of grace, since sin and gracious acceptance by God are incompatible" (*Systematic Theology*, 3: 252).[11] But the scholastic view is erroneous: we do not lose our baptismal identity, since it is established "once and for all." Pannenberg endeavors to strike a delicate balance here: on the one hand, baptismal grace is not lost and regained; on the other hand, one can "fall" from this grace and return. The believer does not lose this grace since it is not an inhering quality that can be lost by a single, willful turning away from God in a concrete act of sin. This grace is, rather, "set 'outside' the old humanity but is lived out physically in it, so that our lives are destined to be absorbed by the new identity and transformed into it" (*Systematic Theology*, 3: 253). The eschatological thrust of life ties together these two aspects. The believer is already identified by that which he is destined to become, by and in God's grace, yet because he is not yet "there," his life is "in motion" towards that end. His life is a daily dying to the old self and rising to the new self. Meanwhile, concupiscence remains within him until he dies, and it remains "sin in the proper sense" (*Systematic Theology*, 3: 254).

Now, if sin remains even in the justified, how can one distinguish those who are justified through sincere faith from either complacent hypocrites (the self-righteous) or lascivious wretches (unbelievers)? Pannenberg retains the basic Lutheran position that a genuine believer must wage a battle against sin. Even if he sins daily, and even though every sin is grave, the very waging of the battle—not as works righteousness but as a response of faithful gratitude—attests that justifying faith is never alone. It is inconceivable that a genuine believer convinced of God's gracious love would forgo this battle. To sin in a truly damning way, in the Lutheran sense, is to *surrender* to sin: "Falling away of this kind takes place when sin gains the mastery again in the lives of the baptized" (*Systematic Theology*, 3: 256). So there are baptized people who no longer strive to live in holiness and thus (most likely) do not look to Christ's coming as the hope of righteousness. But those who do not surrender to sin constantly return to the very grace gained in baptism. Pannenberg thus distinguishes between two types of Christians: ardent sinners and those who believe and set out daily to live in the Spirit. Obviously, both are sinners, but one set surrenders to sin while the other set fights against it. This distinction does *not* parallel the Catholic distinction between persons who often sin mortally and those who sin merely venially, since "every sin is of infinite weight before God" (*Systematic Theology*, 3: 256). All sins, that is, are "mortal" as *Catholics* understand the word "mortal," but those who believe in Christ and strive to fight concupiscence are not struck by such sins mortally, since such persons are bound with Christ outside themselves.

Original sin (i.e., remnant sin) "is not yet fully expunged in our empirical reality through baptism but is not imputed to those who are regenerated by baptism" (*Systematic Theology*, 3: 254). So why strive for holiness? There are two main reasons. First, as stated above, it is not thinkable that one who has a fellowship with Christ would neglect that fellowship maliciously throughout life. If redeemed through Christ, the sinful believer spontaneously desires to thank his Savior and publish his praises. Second, the call of baptism is a call to live towards one's eschatological goal: salvation in God through Jesus Christ. At the end of life, all will meet the Lord, the Merciful Judge. This meeting shall establish *in nobis* the eschatological identity proleptically anticipated in baptism. So, this meeting will entail a "change, the fire whose burning makes us the faultless ones that can be receptacles of eternal joy" (*Systematic Theology*, 3: 619). Remnant sins are not rendered neutral because forgiven. They are harmful, although they do not threaten the eternal security of the baptized who remain in God's grace. When Christ comes, he will execute judgment against all sin and every sinner. However, his judgment against believers will be one of purifying fire, not one of destructive force (1 Cor 3:12–15). "Judgment is thus the purifying fire of the smelter. It is the fire that purges out everything in the life of the creature that is incompatible with the eternal God and with participation in his life" (*Systematic Theology*, 3: 611).

The fact that the judgment is different for believers and unbelievers is not a matter of merely extrinsic mercy. Pannenberg has already shown that true faith supplies a real relationship with Christ. In virtue of this relationship, believers are already those whom God wants to save, for he sees them in Christ. In addition, believers live lives rooted in this holiness and make efforts to fight sin and express their loving gratitude. God's judgment purges away everything in believers not already taken up into their eternal (i.e., eschatological) identity. In the end, they will become what God promises them in baptism.

Critical Analysis

Pannenberg's numerous contributions to Luther research and to the ecumenical movement should be clear from the forgoing presentation. They include, among others, the ecstatic structure of faith, the centrality of baptism, the return to the Pauline kerygma, and attention to the continuity between earthly life and heavenly beatitude. His central role in the contemporary ecumenical movement is indisputable. I wish, now, to highlight four points that render his work in tension either with the JD's twofold claim or with Catholicism.

Evaluation of the Reformation-Era Teachings

Pannenberg finds numerous faults with both the Lutheran confessional documents and the tridentine decree. For example, the Lutheran confessional documents fail both to link justification and baptism and also to recognize as integral to justification the "ontic" side of faith as fellowship with Christ that truly makes the believer righteous outside himself. If Pannenberg's exegesis of the scriptural data is correct, then both traditions have misread key elements of revelation. Granted, Pannenberg does not condemn each side for these misreadings; the Reformation-era documents were attempts to express the mystery of salvation and to defend the Gospel against error. Still, each communion was partially mistaken; therefore, neither must so cling to its past that it continues to condemn the other communion on the basis of its own one-sided formulations: "Faced with these theological shortcomings the churches have little reason to condemn, for the sake of the gospel, the views on the opposite side that diverge from their own doctrinal model as though their own teaching were perfectly and completely identical with that of the gospel..." (*Systematic Theology*, 3: 235). He concludes that the ancient formulations, which appear to be antithetical, should be interpreted as different efforts to preserve that same Gospel:

> A modern view is that the differences in teaching about justification are the antitheses of two theological schools, both of which are trying to describe fellowship with Jesus Christ as decisive for partaking of salvation, and that in their attempts to do this both stand in need of correction by the witness of scripture. (*Systematic Theology*, 3: 235)

This viewpoint recognizes neither set of Reformation-era teachings as doctrinally definitive. For Catholics, this poses a considerable obstacle. Though the tridentine articulations of faith do not exhaust the mystery—scripture itself avoids such a claim (Jn 21:25)—the Decree on Justification includes, from the perspective of Catholic self-understanding, infallible definitions and condemnations. No ecumenical council has arrogated to itself the role of exhausting the scriptures. Still, solemn proclamations of faith are believed to be free from error. Pannenberg sees Trent as the articulation of a theological *school*, standing in need not merely of development and complement, but also of alteration. Few Lutherans if any would view their confessional statements in the same light as Catholics view Trent. Still, inasmuch as the Lutheran confessional statements are professed as accurate exegesis, and therefore as authoritative, Pannenberg's critique of them calls into question the interpretation of the Gospel to which most Lutherans are called to remain faithful. Not a few contemporary Lutheran theologians would dispute Pannenberg's reading of Paul. His thesis thus challenges fundamental Catholic assumptions about the Magisterium and Lutheran convictions about the authoritative status of *The Book of Concord*, raising the specter of how Lutherans are to determine authentic exegesis.

Obedience to Law

Pannenberg's denial that the law, whether it be Mosaic or natural law, is a binding expression of God's will conflicts with Catholic moral teaching.[12] Pannenberg and Catholics concur that the heart of law is love and that love, not the letter of the law, ought to provide the basis for a recognition of persons and ground the assessment of what "doing right" means.[13] Notwithstanding this, the Catholic Magisterium sees the ten commandments as a permanent expression of God's will. This law does not inhibit human creativity; it is not an imposition upon free persons. Law has two sides, positive and negative. In its negative aspect, law draws a limit beneath which one cannot go without doing serious damage to other persons and mortal damage to one's relationship with God.

This limit constitutes the so-called "negative moral norms." Obedience to these is a *sine qua non* condition for salvation as John Paul II teaches: "Jesus himself definitively confirms them and proposes them to us as the way and condition of salvation."[14] Pope Leo XIII, similarly, wrote, "It will be understood that in the Christian religion the first and most necessary condition is docility to the precepts of Jesus Christ, absolute loyalty of will towards Him as Lord and King."[15]

In the face of contemporary debate, John Paul II remains steadfast: "The negative moral precepts, those prohibiting certain concrete actions or kinds of behavior as intrinsically evil, do not allow for any legitimate exception. They do not leave room, in any morally acceptable way, for the 'creativity' of any contrary determination whatsoever."[16] These negative norms are truly liberating, the Pope argues. For instance, to be bound not to kill an innocent person is not to be restricted in one's sphere of authentic freedom. Instead, this negative limit salutarily warns the Christian not to renounce his dignity as a child of God by taking up Cain's hatred for his brother.

But the warning also points towards a positive challenge: love your neighbor as yourself. Love itself is the positive side of the law, and there is no limit to love (1 Cor 13; Jn 15). By proscribing deadly deeds in its negative aspect, the law, which is summed up in the twofold commandment of love, has a limitless positive dimension, for it points the way towards authentic human flourishing. Love's creativity enables Christians to respond to new situations in personally apt ways that offend neither human nature nor the orderly establishment of God's creation.[17] However, if love's creativity were taken to imply the need to find "new solutions and modes of action" (*Systematic Theology*, 3: 76) that in fact conflict with the law (Mosaic or natural) because the law is simply a "transitory" (*Systematic Theology*, 3: 93) expression of God's righteous will, then the negative moral norm contained in the law would be violated.

One of Pope John Paul II's chief intentions in *Veritatis splendor* is to defend the perpetual validity of negative moral norms within a context of the upward thrust of law in the call to love. He writes,

> The commandment of love of God and neighbor does not have in its dynamic any higher limit, but it does have a lower limit, beneath which the commandment is broken…. The Church has always taught that one may never choose kinds of behavior prohibited by the moral commandments expressed in negative form in the Old and New Testaments. As we have seen, Jesus himself reaffirms that these prohibitions allow no exceptions.[18]

The negative moral norms are permanent. Under no circumstances can the actions prohibited by these commandments be performed righteously. However, the commandments are primarily positive, not negative. They draw attention to behaviors compatible with human dignity and the grandeur of God. Because love of God and neighbor has no limit, there is no limit to the upward thrust of law. For this reason, John Paul II's representation of the rich young man in his *Veritatis splendor* is so appropriate. The young man and Jesus understood that keeping the commandments in minimalist fashion could not quench a deeper thirst. Jesus called him to "sell everything" and "follow me." John Paul II's appeal to this dramatic scene strikes at the heart of the modern distaste for law and reveals the personal dimension behind discipleship: Jesus wants the whole person. The Decalogue, whose true end is Christ (Rom 10:4, read teleologically), remains valid but is only the beginning. Though the young man's thirst incites him to follow Jesus, his riches yoke him down; he will not follow the ecstatic call of love.[19] Long ago, St. John Chrysostom called attention to this double-edged character of law. Both fornicator and virgin "pass the bounds of the Law, but not in the same direction; the one is led away to the worse, the other is elevated to the better; the one transgresses the Law, the other transcends it."[20]

Theologians may recognize some similarity in Pannenberg's treatment of law with the view of certain Catholic moral theologians who have dissented from the teaching on the permanent validity of negative moral norms. Some theologians detect an inconsistency between John Paul II's magisterial teaching and his public but non-magisterial praise of the Joint Declaration.[21] Only the former commands submission of intellect and will: obedience to the law of love is a necessity for salvation, and this obedience is made possible by the radically sanative and deifying effects of grace, which Christ by his passion and death has won. I will return to this point below.

Essence of Justifying Righteousness

Pannenberg discards the tridentine teaching that justifying grace is not the grace by which God himself is just but that which he pours forth into the human person, which truly makes the person righteous by inhering in him, and which includes charity in its power to justify. For Pannenberg, the "formal righteousness" of believers is the very righteousness of Christ that remains "outside" the human person. It is grasped through faith in an ecstatic way, but it is not so communicated as to remove all damnable sin from the believer. Damnable sin remains, for all sin is of infinite weight, even though remnant sin is not imputed to the empirical reality of persons who believe in Christ. Granted, Pannenberg's exegesis of scripture and reading of Luther provides

Lutherans and Catholics with grounds for communication and progressive rapprochement. Lutherans who read Elizabeth of the Trinity or Thérèse will likely discover the Catholic mystical emphasis upon ecstatic other-centered trust and love. If what Pannenberg describes as the ecstatic structure of faith is what Catholics want to hold about the charity requisite for justifying righteousness, then there are indeed noteworthy grounds for ecumenical progress. It should be clear to the discerning reader, however, that serious obstacles remain even on this issue, for Pannenberg denies that faith receives its justifying power from the charity infused by the Holy Spirit, and, correlatively, he does not acknowledge obedience to the commandments as a *sine qua non* condition for salvation.

This point becomes all the clearer in Pannenberg's denial that one can lose baptismal grace and subsequently regain it through sacramental reconciliation: "Since we ourselves have our new identity outside ourselves, our baptism according to Luther is never lost, while the medieval [sic] doctrine thought that the state of righteousness, acquired by baptism, is lost by the first mortal sin afterwards and must be restored by the sacrament of penance."[22] I do not intend to discuss the properly sacramental mediation involved in reconciliation; I simply wish to note his criticism of the Catholic practice—inextricably linked with Catholic doctrine—of seeking reconciliation in order to regain the grace lost through mortal sin. Pannenberg does recognize that some baptized persons can permanently choose to exclude themselves from the fruits of this grace; such persons let sin gain mastery over themselves (*Systematic Theology*, 3: 256). But others remain faithful, although they are still sinners. The distinction he draws is not, however, parallel to the Catholic distinction between mortal and venial sin. Every sin is of "infinite weight," and therefore of itself deserves condemnation. Despite this, for those who through faith remain united with Christ, this remnant sin is not imputed to their account (*Systematic Theology*, 3: 254). Pannenberg opines that Trent's insistence that the baptized are without sin can be seen to be compatible with his own account of faith's fellowship with Christ, because he can say that the ecstatic faith fellowship is a new identity that "is as such actually without sin" (*Systematic Theology*, 3: 254). However, he articulates baptismal causality in terms of a "sign."

Baptism causes *as a sign* that *anticipates* the future. Therefore, although by anticipation, the following is true: "There is nothing to condemn in those who are born again in Christ" (*Systematic Theology*, 3: 254). Still, a real contradiction to God remains in the form of the old man's self-seeking, called concupiscence, which Luther rightly defined as "sin in the proper sense" (*Systematic Theology*, 3: 254). In *this sense* Pannenberg regards the loss of baptismal grace as self-contradictory. A person may wander from the life of the grace thus promised, Pannenberg believes, but he does not thereby remove himself from this baptismal grace because baptismal grace is not an infused quality that can be lost and regained. So, although the new identity of the baptized "*as such* is without sin," still

> Because this new identity rests on anticipation of the death that is still ahead for us in this earthly life, in the course of this earthly life the old humanity must constantly be "absorbed" both body and soul by the new until at the last day that which in "sign" is done already in baptism is fully caught up with and fulfilled. (*Systematic Theology*, 3: 255)

Pannenberg makes the dubious assumption that conceiving sacramental causality "after the manner of a sacramental sign" is not "alien to Roman Catholic sacramental theology" (*Systematic Theology*, 3: 255). Catholics conceive of sacraments as *efficacious* signs; Pannenberg's thought does not adequately reflect the efficacity Catholics attribute to these signs. Moreover, Catholic sacramental practice—where it has not been corrupted—indicates the contrary of Pannenberg's thesis. Pannenberg concludes that there must be a constant return to baptismal grace; here, he attempts to return to a practice now otiose among Lutherans, who by and large emphasize merely a return to an *act* of faith. The Lutheran loss of the sense of baptismal grace has led to a discontinuity in the Christian life, which is broken up into discreet acts. Pannenberg's recovery of baptism is no doubt to be welcome. What is not welcome is his understanding of the effects of baptism:

> Contrary to the medieval [sic] doctrine of baptism, the act of baptism does not transform the life of the sinner into a righteous one. Rather, the sinner must die. The act of baptism anticipates the future death of the baptized person, and it is only beyond this death-bound life that we participate in a new life. In this sense, our life is reconstituted "outside ourselves" in Christ.[23]

Transformation and Judgment

I would like to conclude this analysis with a reflection on the relevance of the Balthasarian challenge to Barth. Is it impossible for God to take the earthly believer's heart of stone, replace it with the heart of flesh (Ez 36:26), newly create him a child of God (Gal 6:15; Jn 1:12; 1 Jn 3:2), and equip him both to walk in the Spirit (Rom 8:3–9) and to obey the commandments (Ez 36:27; 1 Cor 7:19; 2 Cor 6:16–7:1)? I am not asking whether God should already glorify the believer and make him so perfectly justified that he would not be able to sin (*non posse peccare*) by eliminating not only concupiscence but even the sacramental veils under which creation groans. That would drag down the eschatological pull of our calling, stripping earthly life of its character as a temporal journey towards authentic identity in Christ. Human beings, including Christians, are creatures of the way. As Pannenberg himself notes, human nature as creaturely must be distinguished from the divine nature. For Pannenberg, this distinction involves "some degree of independence" as "an essential condition of the existence of the creature alongside the eternal being of God" (*Systematic Theology*, 3: 642). I believe it is safe to assume that the "independence" of which Pannenberg writes is not to be taken either in a Pelagian sense or in the manner of the onto-theology, which Heidegger rightly criticized (i.e., making the "First Being" the "first" among many *beings*).[24] This assumed, I agree with Pannenberg. He insists, furthermore, that "temporality" is a necessary form of this creaturely independence: the believer works out his identity over time through an "active fashioning of that existence" (*Systematic Theology*, 3: 643). Is it not possible, then, for God to communicate grace so profoundly that Christians, who have "grown together in union with him" as living branches of the living vine, can undertake that salvific Passover to the Father that Jesus himself undertook (Jn 13:1) and thus be qualified as righteous?[25] Is it not possible for earthly life to be the locus for the believer's cooperative fashioning of his identity—under the influence of divine grace—so that he becomes a vessel fit for divine glory (Heb 12:14)?

I ask this question with pointed force, given that Pannenberg himself offers an edifying account of the last judgment that seems to call for the question. For those who are in Christ, he states, judgment is not one of rebuke but one of purifying love, a cleansing "fire."[26] Pannenberg remarks that there are "conditions" formally intrinsic to the state of glory. For this reason, the whole tradition "enables us to say that the light of the divine glory is the fire of purifying judgment" (*Systematic Theology*, 3: 625). Of its very nature, the light of glory is a purifying fire. The transformation of one's empirical existence into Christ is thus a *sine qua non* condition for glory. Penitence, first awakened in the baptismal call, constitutes in the empirical life of believers a dying to self and rising to Christ, a progressive unfolding on earth of one's eschatological identity. The purifying fire of judgment thus "involves the completing of penitence" by which one can be fully integrated into the new life with Christ (*Systematic Theology*, 3: 619). Nothing of sin, nothing contrary to the righteous will of God, can remain in those who undergo the transforming power of Christ's judgment (1 Cor 3:10–15).

Given the forgoing, can we not return to the question, slightly reformulated, that Pannenberg finds difficult? What is the relationship between the empirical identity of believers and the person who emerges from the purifying fire?

Surely it is precisely the empirical identity of believers that is purified. The course set out for the baptized is that of growth into their eschatological identity in Christ, an identity already established by anticipation of what is to come. Inasmuch as the old humanity, however, has not been "'absorbed' both body and soul by the new" (*Systematic Theology*, 3: 255), the believer is to be judged by fire; that which has not been absorbed is to be burned up in the "fire that purges out everything in the life of the creature that is incompatible with the eternal God and with participation in his life" (*Systematic Theology*, 3: 611). However, inasmuch as the new man has penetrated into the believer's empirical life, the empirical reality of the believer shall survive the purifying fires and be readied for glory. Is it not the case all along, then, that the very empirical reality of believers is the object of divine judgment? Is it not the case that the transformation of the empirical reality into Christ is exactly the measure of one's receptivity for eternal salvation? Is it not the case that the creaturely "effects" of divine grace constitute the formal righteousness of believers that is ultimately preserved, purified, and blessed (elevated) by the light of divine glory? Does Pannenberg not, in fact, espouse a Catholic theological structure of thought, the Augustinian model of "transformation of sinners into righteous persons," rather than simply the transformation of "sinners into *believers*" (*Systematic Theology*, 3: 223)? If so, the logic of the intrinsic necessity of the transformation of the human person into God's child makes my question more pointed: why cannot the principles of this transformation be given through baptism in such a way that damnable sins are destroyed and a life of cooperation with God is established or enabled? If in the end nothing that is not already purged is to enter heaven, then what is the purpose of maintaining the reality of residual sin and the distinction between the *in nobis* and *extra nos* identity of believers implicit in the ecstatic structure of faith-fellowship?

One motivating reason to maintain such a distinction could be to establish the intelligible grounds for a promise (a guarantee) of salvation to those who commit grave sins and yet are supposedly not enslaved to these sins because of their faith in Christ and their effort to fight sin. In other words, this theory lends systematic support for what some Catholic theologians have called the "fundamental option."[27] According to certain forms of the "fundamental option" theory, violations of negative moral norms do not destroy baptismal grace if they are not accompanied by a permanent and malicious refusal of God's grace, even though such a decision would usually be unthematic (i.e., not chosen on the level of "things" that can be explicitly chosen). Without entering into the quagmire of Catholic moral theology, I simply wish to note a consequential similarity of Pannenberg's treatment of law and justification with certain Catholic attempts to evade negative moral norms. Just as Pannenberg would say that one cannot have true faith and thus retain an ecstatic fellowship without fighting concupiscence and refusing to surrender to sin, so too Catholic proponents of "fundamental option" maintain that an individual must in his heart assent to God's grace if he is truly to "opt" for God in the core of his being. To be in grace, one must accept grace through faith, be drawn towards Christ, and (provided one is above the age of discretion) show signs of that new relationship. Similarly, both Pannenberg's theology and the "fundamental option" theory hesitate to picture individual human acts as determinative of the loss or attainment of baptismal grace. Both approaches point to general trends in the human person rather than to specific acts of generosity or selfishness. Trends of human action, however, presuppose individual human acts. In bypassing the substance of human acts and indistinctly "focusing" on trends, both of these approaches might be described as offering a kind of "meta-ethic" of basic intention rather than an ethics of virtuous action. In any case, Catholic teaching does not admit Pannenberg's (repeated) denial that the heart of the mosaic law, the ten commandments, is a definitive expression of God's eternal will. Vatican II's description of faith as a free self-commitment of the entire self to God (LG, art. 5) does not dissuade Pope John Paul II from distinguishing this free self-commitment from the faith informed by charity without which no one is justified:

> In point of fact, man does not suffer perdition only by being unfaithful to that fundamental option whereby he has made "a free self-commitment to God." With every freely committed mortal sin, he offends God as the giver of the law and as a result becomes guilty with regard to the entire law (cf. Jas 2:8–11); even if he perseveres in faith, he loses "sanctifying grace," "charity" and "eternal happiness."[28]

Not surprisingly, the Pope goes on to cite Trent and then takes up the distinction between mortal and venial sins, a distinction drawn in a manner foreign to Pannenberg's Lutheranism. There is a rift between the Pope's teaching and Pannenberg's own position.

The four critical points noted in this section bear upon the relevance of Pannenberg's work to the Lutheran-Catholic Joint Declaration. While I agree with Pannenberg that the Lutheran confessional documents warrant emendation from a biblical perspective, I disagree that Luther's theory of ecstatic faith-fellowship *suffices* for an articulation of the formal righteousness of believers. Nevertheless, Pannenberg's recovery of this theme, and the recent work of the Finnish school, illuminate some roads that might be journeyed in hopes of ecumenical progress.

My assessment thus far in the book demonstrates primarily that a legitimately differentiated consensus in basic truths that does not conflict with the Reformation era condemnations of either communion is not possible.

NOTES

1 Contrast this with Gerhard Ebeling "Die Anfänge von Luthers Hermeneutik," *Zeitschrift für Theologie und Kirche* 48 (1951): 172–230. Pannenberg, like the Finns, seems to imply the *necessity* of faith for justification, not merely as an instrument that receives the promise but as a *sine qua non* condition of the pronouncement of forgiveness. See also idem, "The New Hermeneutics and the Young Luther," *Theology Today* 21 (1964): 34–45.

2 "The genitive 'love of God' relates strictly to God himself as the subject and hence not to our love for God" (Pannenberg, *Systematic Theology*, vol. 3, p. 183).

3 See Pannenberg, *Systematic Theology*, vol. 3, p. 200. Cf. Dennis Bielfeldt's suggested qualification of the Finnish penchant for "participation" with "perichoresis" (Dennis Bielfeldt, "Response to Sammeli Juntunen, 'Luther and Metaphysics,'" in *Union with Christ*, p. 165).

4 See the discussion on the preceding pages as well.

5 Martin Luther, *Lectures on Galatians (1535): Chapters 1–4*, trans Jaroslav Pelikan, vol. 27, *Luther's Works*, ed. Jaroslav Pelikan (St. Louis: Concordia Publishing House, 1963), pp. 132–33 (LW 26: 132–33).

6 LW 26: 234–35.

7 LW 26: 233 and 235.

8 LW 26: 234.

9 I shall return to the theme of "definitive control" of sin. On its surface, this notion appears to function in Lutheran thought in a way similar to that of mortal sin in Catholic thought. Those who renounce the fight against concupiscence surrender completely to sin and thus lose their justification. Lutherans would contend, however, that given acts of grave sin (for all sin is grave) do not function in a mortal way. That is, such sins do not necessarily expel faith, by which even such hypothetically mortal sins are forgiven.

10 Pannenberg's discussion of the Eucharistic presence of Christ is, not surprisingly, hardly reconcilable with Catholic faith. Comparison of *Systematic Theology*, vol. 3, pp. 315–24, with the recent encyclical of John Paul II, *Ecclesia de Eucharistia*, esp. art. 15, shows this amply.

11 Translation in brackets is mine. The German reads, "Wenn man allerdings mit der Scholastik die Gnade als eine geschöpfliche, wenn auch übernatürliche Realität auffaßte" (*Systematische*, b. 3, p. 282).

12 See the discussion in John Paul II, *Veritatis splendor*, Vatican translation (Boston, St. Paul Books & Media, 1993), arts. 12 and 95.

13 See Pannenberg, *Systematic Theology*, vol. 3, p. 77. See Pannenberg's thought on the possible rigidity of law (ibid., pp. 76–96).

14 John Paul II, *Veritatis slendor*, art. 12.

15 Pope Leo XIII, *On Jesus Christ our Redeemer*, p. 11.

16 John Paul II, *Veritatis splendor*, art. 67.

17 See ibid., art. 96.

18 Ibid., art. 52.

19 See ibid., art. 13, and Mt 19:16-21.
20 St. John Chrysostom, *Homilies on Galatians*, trans. Gross Alexander, in vol. 13, *Nicene and Post-Nicene Fathers*, first series, ed. Philip Schaff (Peabody, MA: Hendrickson Publishers, Inc., 1994), V: 13, p. 39.
21 See Aidan Nichols, "The Lutheran-Catholic Agreement on Justification: Botch or Breakthrough?" *New Blackfriars* 82 (2001): 379.
22 Wolfhart Pannenberg, "Luther's Contribution to Christian Spirituality," *Dialog: A Journal of Theology* 40 (2001): 289.
23 Pannenberg, "Luther's Contribution," 289.
24 I mean that it is presumably safe to assume that a Lutheran would want to avoid Pelagianism. On the literal level, of course, Lutherans wish to avoid onto-theology. However, whether on the level of implication or presupposition they do so is another matter.
25 See Fitzmeyer, *Romans*, p. 435. On the Passover imagery, see St. Bonaventure, *Itinerarium mentis in Deum*, chap. 1.9.
26 This is clearly reminiscent of Gregory of Nyssa's thought.
27 At this point, I do not wish to discuss whose theory of "fundamental option" in fact allows for a concrete violation of negative moral norms that is not, in fact, mortally detrimental to one's eternal welfare. Karl Rahner was himself especially careful to qualify his own theory. Still, even in Rahner's work, one can detect a certain transference of existential weight from human action intelligently intended to basic options not thematically chosen. While certainly one must grant that no man understands himself fully, the trajectory Rahner established for Catholic thought was not healthy. One must grant that in the spiritual life man is a mystery; however, what is distinctive of man is his ability to know and to choose. Theories that downplay the central, determining role of knowledge and choice in human action undermine the very "specificity of what it means to be human" (a delightful line delivered by Marc Ouellet in a public lecture in the Fall 1998; the lecture touched upon the need to evangelize).
28 John Paul II, *Veritatis splendor*, art. 68.

PART THREE

Critical Analysis of the Joint Declaration

CHAPTER 6

Background Dialogues

THE JOINT Declaration on the Doctrine of Justification must be read in the context of the ecumenical dialogues between Lutherans and Catholics that have taken their impetus from the renewal of Vatican II and the invitation of Pope John Paul II. The JD aims "to show that on the basis of their dialogue the subscribing Lutheran churches and the Roman Catholic Church are now able to articulate a common understanding of our justification by God's grace through faith in Christ" (JD, 5). Because it is "not a new, independent presentation" (JD, 6), it must be read in its larger context.[1] In this chapter, I propose to analyze two of the chief resources for the JD: the American and German dialogues.

American Dialogue

In 1983 the American Lutheran and Catholic partners in dialogue determined to publish a volume on justification entitled *Justification by Faith* (USA). The published volume was considered to be a major breakthrough in ecumenical relations and a successful attempt to move past the divisions of the past.[2] The work begins with a common affirmation: "*Our entire hope of justification and salvation rests on Christ Jesus and on the gospel whereby the good news of God's merciful action in Christ is made known; we do not place our ultimate trust in anything other than God's promise and saving work in Christ*" (USA, par. 4, emphasis original). The dialogue builds upon this common Christological and soteriological affirmation, acknowledging that Lutherans and Catholics express their insights differently and asking whether the differences are Church-dividing or merely complementary expressions of an inexhaustible mystery.

Two Approaches

USA thematically distinguishes between two approaches to justification:

a transformationist scheme, à la Augustine, and a "simultaneously just and righteous [*simul iustus et peccator*]" scheme. I have already presented the basic differences between these two schemes. With this background in mind, the reader can understand USA's claim: "At issue in the debate with Pelagius and the Pelagians was the extent to which God's grace is necessary and sovereign in this soteriological process of individual transformation" (USA, par. 7). Grace, for Augustine, means the power of God transforming the sinner. Later theologians drew further distinctions, such as those between created and uncreated grace. The charity "poured forth" (Rom 5:5) came to be seen as the gift of charity, an infused habit formally distinct from the Holy Spirit himself, who nevertheless remains inseparable from the gift (USA, pars. 9–10). Most of the debates within western Christendom, before the Reformation, revolved around differing understandings of how the transformation from sin to righteousness takes place. Despite noteworthy differences among the schools, before Luther, there was general agreement that justification, in the concrete order of things, is the process of transformation of a single subject. Within such a perspective, the more "just" the subject is, the less "sinful" he is. Justice and sinfulness obtain in an inverse proportion within the same subject.

The transformationist model was challenged and even rejected by the Reformers. The rejection was not based simply on theological grounds. Other contributing factors to the Reformation insight on "faith alone" included ecclesial trafficking in indulgences, practical Pelagianism, corruption, intrigue, and, most importantly, the phenomenon of the "terrified conscience." For the Reformers, "The major function of justification by faith was, rather, to console anxious consciences terrified by the inability to do enough to earn or merit salvation" (USA, par. 24). Luther sought an answer to his chief question: "How can I find a gracious God?" To hear that grace is gratuitous and that God loves all did not alleviate Luther's anxiety. He needed something more radical than a greater emphasis upon the primacy of divine causality, because if justification required an infused grace, then, since human experience attests to the ever-present danger and reality of sin, those seeking to be righteous must burden themselves with anxious self-examination.

Luther therefore broke away from Augustine's transformationist model, without rejecting Augustine's emphasis on the primacy of grace. In order to find God as gracious, one must add,

> It is not on the basis of [God's] gifts of infused grace, of inherent righteousness, or of good works that God declares sinners just and grants them eternal life, but on the basis of Jesus Christ's righteousness, a righteousness which is "alien" or "extrinsic" to sinful human beings but is received by them through faith. (USA, par. 24)

This break marks the chief locus of the tension between the medieval and Reformation outlooks. According to the latter, men are both totally righteous and totally sinful simultaneously. One should not look at justification in terms of a process by which one moves from sin to righteousness, no matter how much one emphasizes God's efficacious power. According to Luther's reading of Paul, on the contrary, the believer is at once both righteous and sinner at the same time. Justification is not a process in which the old man is transformed into the new man, but rather the act of God by which a new situation arises. God justifies the *ungodly*, who remain ungodly in themselves but who are now placed in a new situation, that of God's favor. God's justifying act is a twofold sword by which the believer's sinfulness is uncovered and a new realm of forgiveness in Christ is opened up. Sin is both revealed and abolished in its destructive power because through faith the sinner is righteous in Christ (USA, par. 25–26).

The Reformers, especially Melanchthon, attacked the Catholic teaching that faith is justifying because of its inclusion of charity. "Saving or justifying faith, to be sure, is never alone, never without works; but it does not justify for that reason" (USA, par. 40). The authors of USA reiterate a scholarly opinion that Melanchthon saw "love" or charity as a work of the law, unlike the scholastics, who saw charity as an infused disposition that is not due to human creativity. USA thus hints, by way of implication, that if Melanchthon had encountered a more nuanced version of "faith formed by charity [*fides caritate formata*]," he would not have rejected it. I have already granted that in much of the *Apology* this is the case, for no one can deny that Melanchthon's depiction of the Catholic perspective is frequently indebted to an aberration rooted in nominalism.[3] However, I must repeat that Melanchthon also rejected the authentically Catholic teaching. He did not limit his rejection of "fides caritate formata" merely to a conception of charity as a work. It is not as though Melanchthon would have accepted the formula if he had known (as though he did not) that Catholics believe that charity is infused by God gratuitously. His insistence that faith justifies apart from works includes the very virtue of faith, which is not of itself worthy to render us just. Faith justifies only because it receives the promise.[4] Even Melanchthon's 1559 *Loci* show how little his thought was amenable to Osiander's proposal:

For when it is said that we have forgiveness through grace, if you understand this to mean that on account of the virtues given us we have forgiveness, you thoroughly overturn Paul's whole intention and deprive consciences of true consolation. For we ought not to regard our qualities when we are tormented about forgiveness, but we ought to take refuge in the Mediator.... Wherefore, the donation of the Holy Spirit is conjoined to this acceptation, but it does not follow that we have reconciliation on account of these new virtues.[5]

The gift of the Holy Spirit himself, transforming by his presence, does not constitute the believer as righteous before God even though it is concomitant with the divine acceptance. Therefore, although Christians are called to observe the commandments, they do not satisfy the divine law even under the influence of the Spirit but stand in need of the imputation of Christ's righteousness.[6] Luther also rejected the formula "fides caritate formata" even insofar as it referred to a gift infused by God:

> Thus you see that Christian righteousness is not an "inherent form," as they call it. For they say: When a man does a good work, God accepts it; and for this work He infuses charity into him. This infused charity, they say, is a quality that is attached to the heart; they call it "formal righteousness." (It is a good idea for you to know this manner of speaking.) Nothing is more intolerable to them than to be told that this quality, which informs the heart as whiteness does a wall, is not righteousness.[7]

Once again, it is true that Luther and Melanchthon frequently relegated love to a work. They frequently applied the Pauline exclusive terminology—faith apart from works—in order to counteract "works righteousness." At times they received the bad fruits of a semi-Pelagian nominalism, as might be gleaned within the text just cited. Notwithstanding these observations, one observes Luther, even in the text just cited, referring to his opponents' understanding of charity as a gift from above by which the soul becomes truly righteous. Sufficient data show that Luther knowingly rejected not merely the semi-Pelagianism of the nominalists but also the Thomistic version of "fides caritate formata," which expressly avows that God's causality is absolutely primary. This conclusion is further supported by the Lutheran evaluation of faith itself. Neither Luther nor Melanchthon held faith to be an infused gift *that* intrinsically qualifies the believer for salvation, even if Luther spoke of an ecstasy of faith outside the believer. For this reason, the American dialogue does not adequately address the dispute about faith's justifying power. Indeed, the very thought attributed to Luther, whereby he broke from the Augustinian model, expresses this plainly: "It is not on the basis of his gifts of infused grace" (USA, par. 24).

If Luther and Melanchthon denied that faith's justifying power is dependent upon charity, much more did the authors of the *Formula of Concord*. The latter work, therefore, presents the greatest obstacles to reunion, as is attested by Pannenberg, the Finns, and others.[8] In order to deal with this difficulty, the authors of USA claim that the *Formula* and confessional documents "were not replies to [Trent] but were concerned with intra-Lutheran problems" (USA, par. 58). The apparent implication is that these documents are not directly relevant for inter-confessional dialogue. German theologian Gunther Wenz dismisses such a suggestion: "This historical reality cannot theologically be suppressed;

one cannot in ecumenical dialogue with the Roman Catholic church avoid dealing with the severe condemnations that are present in the FC as well as in the SA."[9] Besides, this claim in USA hardly resolves the church-dividing power of the condemnations in the *Formula*. If the *Formula* excludes from Lutheran orthodoxy those Lutherans (the Osiandrans) who emphasized the divine indwelling and who failed to draw a strict enough distinction between justification and sanctification, then this work *a fortiori* condemns the doctrine of Trent. Perhaps in light of this, the authors of USA even admit the need for qualification of an extreme element in the *Formula*:

> The authors of the Formula increasingly moved towards a purely forensic understanding of justification as the divine reckoning which must be carefully distinguished from any intrinsic human righteousness.... The Formula...insisted strongly on the distinction between the "imputed righteousness of faith" (*imputata fidei iustitia*) and the "inchoate righteousness of the new obedience of faith" (*inchoata iustitia novae obedientiae seu bonorum operum*). Only the former counts before God, whereas the latter follows justification. (USA, par. 59)

The dialogue goes on to confess that the opposition between the *Formula* and Trent is unmistakable. One might ask whether this stands in tension with the suggestion that the *Formula* is irrelevant to inter-confessional dialogue.

After tracing some of the disputes that lingered into the 20th century, USA turns to the beginnings of the ecumenical movement. In 1963 in Helsinki, the LWF recognized and approved the movements afoot in the Catholic Church. At this assembly, some theologians claimed that the alternative between forensic and intrinsic righteousness in justification is a false one. To cling to one side exclusively begs the question, since "God's action brings about 'rebirth'" (USA, par. 84).

The authors of the dialogue then present a contemporary reflection on the dispute about justification. They begin with a methodological reflection and proceed to consider several issues traditionally deemed divisive. Methodologically, USA traces apparently diverse doctrines back to distinct thought structures and terminologies. Different structures of thought "gave rise to fears and were interpreted as conflicts" (USA, par. 94). Contemporary theology has found, they maintain, that these thought structures might in fact be complementary, just as at Helsinki it was suggested that the alternative modes of expression are not exclusive of each other (USA, par. 94). The differing patterns of thought are rooted in distinct "concerns," both theological and practical. Whereas Lutherans are concerned to preserve God's primacy in his word in order to exclude any possibility of human self-trust, Catholics are "generally speaking more concerned with acknowledging the efficacy of God's saving work in the renewal and sanctification of the created order" (USA, par.

95). Despite these differences, neither communion rejects the concerns of the other. The Lutheran concern is most at home expressing a "discontinuity" between the person without faith and the person with faith, whereas Catholics emphasize the transformation of a single subject from one condition to another condition.

Divisive Doctrines

Having noted these methodological points, the dialogue turns first to a consideration of forensic justification. Lutherans defend the gratuity and unconditional character of God's grace by describing justification as the extrinsic imputation of righteousness to faith. At the same time, Lutherans do not deny that sanctification must follow justification (USA, par. 98). Catholics, similarly, do not deny that God's will is caused by nothing other than itself and is thus unconditional. However, Catholics stress that, in the order of created effects, some of the effects of God's power are conditioned upon others. The authors allude to faith, sacraments, scripture, and receptivity (USA, par. 99). Unfortunately, infused grace does not appear among these conditions. Catholic faith is depicted as simply calling for "images" complementary to the forensic model. Catholics "hesitate to trace everything to justification considered simply as a forensic act. They are often inclined to emphasize other images or concepts" (USA, par. 99). USA attributes the hypothesis of "infused justice" to a *theological* approach: "Catholics *have tended* to look on the infusion of grace as a cause of the forgiveness of sins and sanctification" (USA, par. 101, emphasis mine). Does this mean that USA considers that the notion of justifying grace as infused grace is not a doctrinal element that Catholics must hold? USA cautions that neither perspective ought to exclude the other but rather that both are complementary. Lutherans fear that the Catholic insistence upon infused grace could "tend to throw believers back on their own resources" (USA, par. 100), and Catholics fear that the Lutheran insistence upon forensic justification could "unintentionally encourage a certain disregard for the benefits actually imparted through God's loving deed in Christ" (USA, par. 100). Both fears are held to be legitimate; their apparent divergence does not render them contradictory. Remarkably, we find the following concession from the Lutherans with regard to justifying grace as infused:

> Lutherans can admit that this Catholic understanding of the infusion of grace does not necessarily imply that justification is dependent on sanctification in such a way as to undermine confidence in God and induce an anxiety-ridden reliance on the uncertain signs of grace in one's own life. (USA, par. 101)

Had this admission found its way into the JD, it would have been of enormous benefit. Sadly, it did not. Moreover, USA's presentation of the Catholic concern about "forensic justification" is not adequate. Catholics who take Luther and Melanchthon seriously are not merely "concerned" about a narrow focus among Lutherans on forensic justification.

USA next considers the related issue of the simultaneity of righteousness and sinfulness. For Lutherans, the act of justification reveals both the sinfulness of the justified and the forgiveness of God. Therefore, "Sin...remains and is in need of continued forgiveness" (USA, par. 102). Justification attacks sin, but the renewal of the human person is a lifelong process intertwined with sinfulness. USA notes that Catholics, on the contrary, see concupiscence as not truly sin and that Catholics distinguish between mortal and venial sins. Despite these considerable tensions, the authors of the dialogue find that Catholics and Lutherans have unjustly reproached one another with regard to the question of remnant sin. Lutherans do not, contrary to Catholic fears, underplay sanctification in the Holy Spirit. Catholics do not deny the "abiding effects of sin in the baptized" (USA, par. 104). Moreover, the Lutheran fear that Catholic emphasis on "inherent righteousness" leads to self-complacency does not reflect the Catholic intention. Catholics do not emphasize created grace (an inhering quality) at the expense of uncreated grace (God's mercy). Rather, Catholics hold that the "'inherent righteousness' of believers is primarily God's gift of himself, i.e., primarily God himself, *gratia increata,* and only secondarily his gift, *gratia creata*" (USA, par. 103), for created grace is given so that God may dwell within the person whose sins are removed by grace. Catholics are bidden to trust not in themselves or in their inherent qualities, even if these are bestowed gratuitously, but in the saving God. The dialogue concludes that the two communions offer compatible teachings on justification.

It may now be asked whether USA demonstrates its conclusion. I would argue that it does not. In addition to criticisms I have noted above, I would add three more. First, the *reduction* of tridentine doctrine to basic "concerns," expressed according to certain "imagery," within the structure of the Augustinian model, obscures the "crux" of the Reformation era dispute. This reduction uses the sound principle of doctrinal development in a way that undermines authentic development. As I have shown by way of dogmatic theology in chapters 1 and 2 and as I will argue by way of systematic reflection in chapter 10, the tridentine doctrine and the Protestant doctrine actually contradict one another. Thus, the two doctrines do not legitimately complement one another. They cannot be brought together and united by a higher synthesis without violence. This is manifest in that the aggregate of properties intrinsically associated with the tridentine teaching run counter to the aggregate of properties intrinsically associated with Protestant doctrine. USA appears to seek a dynamic equivalence of meaning, but none can be found short of doctrinal alteration. This brings me to a second criticism.

USA's claims cannot be supported by appeal to the historical conditioning of doctrine, such as that referred to by the Catholic document *Mysterium ecclesiae*, published by the CDF. USA appears to relegate Trent's use of the "scholastic" system of causes to a transitory philosophical school. The implication is that what was scholastic in Trent does not actually constitute part of Catholic teaching. This implication in place, USA further contends that only the basic "concerns" behind the stated doctrine are in fact binding. USA identifies these concerns in minimalistic fashion: The chief concern for Catholics is that God indeed transforms the individual, though Catholics do not deny the Lutheran concern. Lutherans, for their part, acknowledge the Catholic concern even though they emphasize God's priority through the category of forensic righteousness, the two doctrines therefore do not conflict. These concerns, as I have argued, are too minimal for the genuine teachings of each communion to be preserved. Unfortunately, the National Conference of Catholic Bishops (NCCB), in its commentary on USA, appealed to *Mysterium ecclesiae* as support for jettisoning the scholastic element of Trent. The NCCB affirmed that doctrines "do not remain completely suitable for communicating revealed truth in another historical period, e.g., Trent's use of scholastic causal categories in explaining justification."[10] Reading this statement as relevant to popular catechesis, one might accept this claim, but it does not appear to be limited to a catechetical recommendation. The Evangelical Lutheran Church of America (ELCA), similarly, stated that USA does not suggest "that these [scholastic] categories themselves are permanently normative for a right understanding of justification."[11]

Mysterium ecclesiae does not supply warrant for these claims. In this document, the CDF acknowledges the necessarily historical character of revelation and its magisterial articulation. Yet the CDF is at pains to emphasize two aspects of development of doctrine. It emphasizes a) the dynamic continuity of doctrinal development wherein the protean character of an earlier epoch (chiefly, of the scriptural witness) receives elucidation on a matter of doubt; and it emphasizes b) the permanent validity of the sense and formulations of irreformable teachings. Defined doctrines retain their intrinsic ability to communicate the faith, provided they are properly understood. Thus, theological education must include, among other elements, an induction into the approaches that have enjoyed favored in one's tradition, so that the theologian can be equipped to understand and to communicate the same doctrine, with the same sense. Authentic preservation of defined doctrines is a prerequisite for the development of newer insights, insights that might one day lay the foundation for doctrinal development. In this regard, it should be recalled that Pope Paul

VI in his encyclical *Mysterium fidei* had already strongly censured those who would replace tested doctrinal formulas with novel and passing expressions: "Who would ever tolerate that the dogmatic formulas used by the ecumenical councils for the mysteries of the Holy Trinity and the Incarnation be judged as no longer appropriate for men of our times and therefore that others be rashly substituted for them?"[12] Although development is indeed to be desired, still, "It would be wrong to give to these expressions a meaning other than the original."[13] In harmony with Paul VI's exhortation, *Mysterium ecclesiae* suggests that ancient formulas be *explained* in manners suitable to communicate the perennial truths they enshrine. That is, such formulas ought to be retained yet explained. There may come a time in which a greater mind, working in organic continuity with the tradition, can offer a higher viewpoint from which to articulate the same mystery in a way that more adequately accounts for an even larger set of the data. Yet it is certain that such an articulation will not make void the very sense of the older formulas. Rather, it will lend even greater depth to that sense, without in any way diminishing prior content.[14] What is seldom noticed is that *Mysterium ecclesiae* cites Vatican I's teaching on the permanence of doctrinal content itself, a teaching echoed in the words by which Pope Bl. John XXIII opened the Second Vatican Council.[15] Most recently, John Paul II has reaffirmed the enduring validity of dogmatic statements against the one-sided relativism of historicism.[16]

Second, USA's treatment of the *simul* doctrine leaves too many questions unanswered. If Lutherans believe that "remnant sin" needs to be forgiven, do they not consider it to be worthy of judgment? But Catholics, as USA states, maintain that concupiscence is not in need of mercy. Venial sins, though in need of mercy, do not expel justifying grace. USA's discussion of the distinction between mortal and venial sins is welcome indeed. It is lamentable that this distinction found no home in the JD. If one party insists, however, that remnant sin is in need of forgiveness while the other does not, how can they not really be at odds? It is not merely "concerns" but rather the truth of the faith that is in question. Finally, a pastoral disharmony remains: Catholic priests console penitents that tendencies to sin are not sinful. In this way, priests help Christians avoid a scrupulosity that would impede psychological maturity and spiritual growth. Over and above the obvious defects of such scrupulosity would be the inadvertent masking of the penitent's actual sins.

German Dialogue

At about the same time as the American dialogue was approaching a consensus on the doctrine of justification, Lutherans and Catholics in Germany had also taken up John Paul II's request to revisit the condemnations of the Reformation era. The results of the German response to the Papal request are recapitulated in *The Condemnations of the Reformation Era: Do they Still Divide?* (CRE). The summary results are based upon years of theological work and oversight by pastors of both communions. Some of the original papers have been published in English in the volume entitled *Justification by Faith* (JF). Since CRE constitutes the chief basis for the differentiated consensus presented in the Joint Declaration, I wish to focus on it in this section.[17]

Basic Methodology

From the outset, CRE pledges fidelity to the doctrines of both communions. Each communion must remain faithful to its binding doctrines and also be open to new insights and further developments (CRE 5, 6, 14, and 19). In service of this desire, CRE initially presents seven points, traditionally held to be church-dividing, called "distinguishing doctrines." After noting these differences, the dialogue poses a series of questions in order to establish whether any condemnations were accurately directed against the "opponent," whether they apply as a condemnation to today's partner, and what significance such remaining differences may have. As the investigation progresses, many of the past condemnations are said to have been based on somewhat faulty grounds: misunderstandings, terminological differences, different modes of thought, undue fears of extreme theological positions, and narrowness of context. CRE leaves open the possibility that some of the condemnations may have originally hit their mark accurately.[18] In these cases, it is urgent to ask whether or not the original condemnation actually touches upon the teaching of the partner in dialogue today. If the partner today no longer clings to the rejected position, then the condemnation, though perennially valid, can be said no longer to apply because "Today's doctrine is no longer determined by the error that the earlier rejection wished to guard against" (CRE, 8). This methodological procedure takes no cognizance of the implication that if the condemnation was once accurately directed but is no longer applicable, then today's partner has departed from its original position. The hope of dialogue is that all the condemnations, while remaining salutary warnings, no longer apply to today's partner (CRE, 27–28). One wonders how the original teachings of *both* sides can actually "remain in force" in their entirety if one or both communions no longer cling to positions accurately condemned by the other. After this consideration of methodology, the dialogue turns to a discussion of justification.

Initial Presentation of One Distinguishing Doctrine

CRE first presents deliberately attenuated accounts of seven points on which there has traditionally been dispute: total depravity, concupiscence, total passivity, the essence of grace, faith alone, assurance of salvation, and merit. CRE returns, in the end, to a more serious consideration of these same points of apparent divergence. To take the most important issue as an example, I would like to cite CRE's presentation of the differing notions of justifying grace:

> The Reformers teach that *justifying grace* is completely identical with God's forgiving love and his ever-new commitment. It is therefore *a reality on God's side alone.* Roman Catholic doctrine, on the other hand, insists that justifying grace is by its very nature (*formaliter*) a reality in the soul of the human being. (CRE, 33)

In support of the Catholic position, the authors cite canon 11, the canon Seripando introduced. Canon 10 is not mentioned at this point. I shall return to the issue of justifying grace momentarily.

Common Return to Scripture

Before examining the condemnations more thoroughly, CRE draws upon the fruits of recent theological and biblical studies. The dialogue proposes that in order to overcome the ancient antitheses, each partner must look to the common foundation of faith with an openness to new insights and to the concerns and ways of thinking of the other partner. Stressing the Christological basis of justification, the Catholics and Lutherans involved in CRE agreed to read scripture together in hopes that the formulations of the Reformation era might be seen as partial and complementary witnesses to scripture. Through common investigation, they found that their doctrines are but compatible ways of expressing the "fundamental biblical assertion about justification of the sinner" (CRE, 37). CRE sums up the guidelines of the procedure as follows: Doctrine does not critique scripture; rather, "The scriptural witness, because it is primal and normative, remains a critical, and a dynamic, criterion for the doctrine" (CRE, 37). This guiding instruction is questionable in light of Catholic faith. Granted, Catholics are free to see in the scriptures the privileged expression of revelation.[19] Still, Catholics accept the Magisterium as the sole authentic servant-interpreter of revelation. The Magisterium is both a living reality and a patrimony enshrined in conciliar and papal decrees. Catholics distinguish between the inspired expression of revelation and the proximate norm of interpretation, expressed in magisterial documents, which guide an accurate reading of the former. Hence, Catholics cannot suppose that an investigation of scripture will contradict that which is taught by their Magisterium. In wishing to communicate more fruitfully with western partners in dialogue, Catholics do nonetheless find a common return to scripture to be of great importance. CRE focuses, understandably, on the Pauline message.

According to the Pauline kerygma, justification is "a totally unmeritable, divine act on behalf of sinful men and women. These receive the gift of justification solely through faith in Jesus Christ, who was crucified for us and is risen; and through this very faith they are also totally claimed by God" (CRE, 37). On the basis of this common reading of Paul, CRE contends that the extreme positions of either side recede into the background. First, though, some initial obstacles must be countenanced. Contrary to what might appear to be the case, Trent did not canonize the late scholastic position on grace. In fact, Trent located the sole source of justification in faith, just as did the Reformers. This remains the case, notwithstanding the fact that Trent "rejected the postulate that the righteousness of Christ was *formaliter* ('formally,' in the sense of its essential nature) the believer's righteousness also" (CRE, 37–38). CRE thus pays some attention to canon 10. Now, the Reformers did teach Christ as the righteousness of the justified person. Still, "There does not have to be any exclusive antithesis here" (CRE, 38). Historical studies show that Lutherans generally adopted a framework decisively different from the Aristotelian framework of the scholastics. Differences in framework, CRE contends, gave cause for misunderstandings when there was no genuine antithesis. If one framework is used, both can agree in substance. CRE defends this claim with reference to the adoption, by Melanchthon and by Lutheran scholastics, of the Aristotelean framework and terminology in order to articulate Luther's insights (CRE, 38).

I would contend that appeal to Lutheran scholastics not only shows that the doctrines of the Lutheran communion can in some measure be expressed in the scholastic framework but also sets divergences into relief: especially those between Catholic and Protestant thought but also those between Lutheran and Reformed thought.[20] Chemnitz, for instance, entered the scholastic framework precisely to criticize Trent. Contrary to the CRE's intention in this appeal, when Lutherans and scholastics communicated within the same framework, the incompatibility of the two doctrines became all the more evident. The American dialogue concurs with this assessment: "This was a partial return to transformationist modes of thought, but it tended to sharpen the remaining differences over the specifically forensic character of justification as an act distinct from sanctification" (USA, par. 65). Pannenberg astutely observes that this sharpened distinction led some Lutherans, paradoxically, to emphasize the subjective aspect of moral renewal, especially as they attempted to respond to internal criticism.[21] The *Formula*'s occasional use of scholastic terminology coincided neatly with its heightened antithesis to tridentine teaching. That this is the case is not surprising, since the adoption of the distinctions between formal and meritorious causality and between God's favor and the gift wrought in the human person by that favor enables the Lutheran theologian more easily to communicate his dispute with Catholics.

Notwithstanding these reservations CRE's call for each partner to respect the internal integrity of the other's doctrinal structure can be explored:

> From a given point within a theological "doctrinal structure" (insofar as any structure is aimed at) down to the final single assertion, everything is, fundamentally speaking, interlocked. This means that we must not make any attempt to break up this unity into individual, isolated elements, which we then go on to compare in equal isolation, discovering harmony or continued dissension, as the case may be (CRE, 39).

Now, if the doctrinal frameworks themselves were theologically neutral matters, perhaps one could even insist that, in order for authentic communication to take place, theologians of one side must be able to articulate their position in the framework of the other side. But if these are not theologically neutral matters, then such a demand might not be doctrinally palatable for either partner. As we have seen, when Lutherans attempt to enter the Catholic structure of thought, differences become pronounced.

It seems to me that Catholics have little difficulty acknowledging the ontological or "metaphysical" character of the framework within which the teachings of Trent are articulated. Rather than being a descriptive statement of the sinner's experience, Trent's Decree on Justification is an explanatory account of what happens in this event.[22] Nor would Catholic doctrine fail to stomach the person who experiences himself as a sinner and yet trusts in God's great mercy.[23] The question is, would Lutherans honestly allow their teachings to be characterized simply as "experiential" or as sets of statements about experience? Does the dilution of Luther's poignant theology to an experiential frame of reference do him and his followers justice? Moreover, must not a metaphysical realist maintain that reality itself should serve as the common point of reference for two apparently divergent accounts of it?

Hermeneutical Principles for Revisiting the Condemnations

CRE proposes four hermeneutical principles by which to reread the condemnations of the past. First, one must recognize that each condemnation and definition has "*a specific background and a practical reference to Christian life in the Church*" (CRE, 39, emphasis in original). With regard to background, Protestant doctrine emerged from the experience of penitential practices, but Catholic doctrine was rooted in the renewing power of baptismal grace. With regard to practical issues, Catholics were worried that an underemphasis on renewal could lead to neglect of the call to love one's neighbor, whereas Lutherans worried that to stress any human conditions associated with justification could lead either to prideful complacency or to anguish. Evidently, CRE traces doctrines to their roots in specific concerns and emphases, from which distinct terminologies and thought-structures emerged. One of the aims of CRE is to discover the core concerns and emphases of each partner so that both can strike a common ground by recognizing the validity of the other's concerns. Second, the goal of ecumenism is not uniform expression of faith, let alone the same mode of thought, but rather a mutual recognition that the chief concerns of both communions are adequately upheld by the other. Complementarity within a common horizon, not uniformity, is the goal. Third, the experiences predominant in both communions cannot be condemned. Namely, no one (i.e., no "Catholic") can condemn anyone (i.e., any "Lutheran") who experiences the weight of his sin and thus puts his whole trust in the saving God and makes an effort to live accordingly. Likewise, no one (i.e., no "Lutheran") can condemn "*those* [i.e., 'Catholics'] *who, deeply penetrated by the limitless power of God, stress above all, in the event of justification also, God's glory and the victory of his gracious acts on behalf of men and women, holding human failure and halfheartedness toward these gracious acts to be, in the strict sense, of secondary importance...*" (CRE, 40, emphasis in original). Fourth and last, in case of doubtful passages, Trent ought to be interpreted as closely to Augustine as possible in order that the original intention of the authors might be understood.

These four principles leave much to be desired. The first and second principles have the merit of pointing out the divergent thought-structures but have the unfortunate tendency to reduce doctrine to basic concerns. It should be evident from the American dialogue that Luther wished to break with the Augustinian transformationist model precisely *because* he wished to exclude absolutely any human conditions upon God's justifying act. This break was the chief *sign* of the incompatibility of Catholic tradition with his own opinions.[24] It is therefore not likely that averting to these divergent frameworks will unearth some common ground long buried by the rubble of the rabble. CRE portrays Catholics as having a concern to uphold the efficaciousness of God's power and Lutheran as having a concern to uphold the gratuity of grace in the face of sin. It may be asked whether the comparison of these portraits is unwittingly rendered according to the Augustinian model of transformation,

Catholics focusing chiefly on the effects, and Lutherans on the source, of grace? Moreover, can we sincerely state that Luther and Trent "oversimplified" the dispute? Is there no oversimplification in CRE? Is there no danger that the reduction of doctrines to basic "concerns" could equally service the reunion of semi-Pelagians with mainstream Christians? Would not a semi-Pelagian recognize that no one can merit heaven without God's assistance, thus upholding God's mercy? Would not the same person insist, by way of qualification, that human responsibility must be taken seriously? But neither Lutherans nor Catholics can responsibly confess an agreement in basic truths with semi-Pelagians. In short, one can ask whether it is intellectually viable to reduce carefully crafted doctrinal formulations of the past to basic "concerns" to which nearly anyone remotely associated with Christian tradition would assent? The Göttingen faculty justly complains, "The 'innermost centers' are talked about in the framework of rules for historical relativizing, but not at the beginning of the discussion of content. And this is the reason why nowhere an effort is made to determine what that 'innermost center' is supposed to be."[25] American Catholic theologian Richard White concurs with this judgment.[26]

The third principle is but a specification of the first two. Again, this principle is so generic as to be both true and unhelpful at the same time. Of course, no one can be condemned for experiencing the weight of sin while still trusting in God. Of course, no one can be condemned for stressing God's saving power. Does the truth that persons with these experiences ought not be condemned in any way settle the Reformation disputes? Trent exhorted Catholics not to boast in themselves, and the *Formula* exhorted Lutherans not to neglect good works; these exhortations appeared in the Reformation era documents. Trent and the authors of the *Formula* were hardly content with these warnings.

To make matters worse, CRE's articulation of the basic Catholic "experience" does not appear to be sufficient. I will cite the statement again: We cannot condemn "*those who, deeply penetrated by the limitless power of God, stress above all, in the event of justification also, God's glory and the victory of his gracious acts on behalf of men and women, holding human failure and halfheartedness toward these gracious acts to be, in the strict sense, of secondary importance...*" (CRE, 40). Is this citation not equally or even more applicable to Lutheran concerns about God's victory? Is not concentration on fear about sin precisely *not* Lutheran, at least not that which a Lutheran *qua believer* ought to do? Of course, the law pronounces judgment upon the Christian *qua* sinner, but if the Christian simply fears his sinfulness and God's wrath, he shows little if any faith. For Lutherans, faith *is* assurance of salvation. Faith *is* complete trust in God's victory. Do not Lutherans trust in God's victory? Moreover, the passage is not distinctively Catholic because there is no mention in this passage of God's victorious bestowal of the grace that inwardly renews the human person and removes all damnable sin. To say that human weakness and sinfulness ought to be of secondary importance is not specifically Catholic. Luther urged people to believe in God and to base their confidence not in their own half-hearted faith, which of itself is not sufficient to placate God's wrath, but rather to look to the object of faith. In sum, the very "concern" to which CRE tacitly traces Catholic doctrine is in fact not distinctively Catholic, even if one were to grant the presupposition that this concern is compatible with Lutheran doctrine.

The weaknesses convergent in these first three hermeneutical principles impinge upon the JD, since CRE's methodology forms the basis of the JD's "differentiated consensus." As Scheffczyk accurately observes, the authors of the JD do not attempt so much to achieve agreement in things believed as they seek mutual affirmations of experience. They pursue what Pöhlmann has called a "hermeneutic of empathy." This can hardly suffice to establish lasting reunion. The methodological weaknesses of CRE, consequently, are echoed in the JD itself.[27]

The fourth principle might not be problematic, although to impose it dogmatically upon Catholics would be unacceptable.[28] Augustine is the doctor of grace, but he is not the last authority for Catholics. Moreover, this very principle, if faithfully followed, would lead to the conclusion that the "justice of God" by which one is justified is a participation in God's own justice. It was for this reason that Lutherans found it necessary to depart from Augustine's very framework of thought.[29]

The Distinguishing Doctrines Revisited

After laying out these four hermeneutical principles, CRE revisits the seven "distinguishing doctrines" in an attempt to discern whether or not there exists a basic harmony within these different emphases. I will consider the first doctrine briefly and the fourth in detail. The first distinguishing doctrine is the different articulations of human sinfulness before justification and the consequent assessment of the "continuity" or "discontinuity" of the identity of the person to be justified. Lutherans speak of a "total depravity" that so afflicts human nature that everything inherently open to human powers is but sin, in the theological sense.[30] CRE claims that Lutheran doctrine does not reject the Catholic concern that God's original work in creation is not entirely obliterated but is rescued from the power of sin, even though this is due to God's unmerited grace. The Catholic view of justification "shows at the same time the inner theological connection between 'creation' and 'redemption': the justifying act of God is directed toward the man or woman in need of redemption, who is not totally 'replaced' by God's grace, but who is *awakened* to a new life…" (CRE, 42).

CRE upholds, on the one hand, a total depravity of the sinner and, on the other hand, some continuity of the person to be justified, who is not "totally replaced" by grace. Can these two contentions be held consistently? I would like to make two observations about these two claims. First, the assertion that the sinner is not "totally replaced" by grace can be put forth as a Catholic concern only tendentiously. The claim must come as a surprise to Catholic theologians used to the refrain, "Grace does not destroy nature [*gratia non destruit naturam*]," because this refrain is meant to underscore the radical continuity of the sinful person, who himself stands in need of a forgiving and divinizing transformation. Yet CRE manipulates the refrain: Grace does not "totally replace" nature! How can such a phrase be an expression of distinctively Catholic sentiment? The Catholic insistence on the inner connection between creation and redemption preserves the belief that it is the sinner who is rescued from sin. The statement in CRE fails to express this concern adequately.

Second, the passage is in tension with the work of a number of Lutheran scholars. Granted, the text itself is attenuated in expression, minimizing the continuity: The sinner "is not *totally* replaced" (emphasis mine). Some Lutherans will find this minimization consoling, since it suggests that Catholics are a step closer to affirming the discontinuity central to Lutheran thought. For others, the suggestion of continuity may hint too much of Catholic continuity.[31] These theologians recognize that if they were to uphold the Catholic concern for continuity, they would risk subjecting their doctrine to the Augustinian transformationist scheme. But should this happen, Lutheran theologian Gerhard Forde warned in his paper for the American dialogue, the doctrine of "simul iustus et peccator" would become senseless. He defended a radical discontinuity in the event of justification:

> The significance of Luther's view on justification in this regard is that it can be understood only as a complete break with the attempt to view it as a movement according to a continuous scheme of law or progress…. Since righteousness comes by imputation only, it is not at all a movement on our part…. That means of necessity for Luther that in place of all schemes of movement from sin to righteousness we must put the *simultaneity* of sin and righteousness….
>
> The divine imputation thus exposes us as sinners at the same time as it imparts righteousness. And Luther was insistent that these be understood as total states. If one does not so understand the matter and persists in thinking in terms of a continuous scheme or process, the *simul iustus et peccator* will simply turn to poison, a false comfort for lazy sinners.[32]

If Forde is right, how ought one to read the passage in CRE that the sinner is "not 'totally replaced'" by grace? An official statement of the American dialogue lends support for Forde's contention, at least from the "hermeneutical" approach within Lutheran theology: "Salvation as a product of God's creative word is, in this perspective, radically discontinuous with fallen nature. It is a new creation, not a transformation or perfecting of the old."[33] What is one to make of the contrast between this "hermeneutical" reading of Luther and the implication in CRE that Lutherans accept the Catholic concern that the same subject is transformed from sin to righteousness?

The fourth "distinguishing doctrine" is the dispute about the essence of grace. The dispute about this issue is so palpable that it presents an apparent fissure:

> When *the essence of grace or righteousness* before God is defined on the one hand as an objective *reality* on God's side "*outside ourselves*," and on the other hand as *a reality in the human soul*, a "quality" intrinsically "adhering" to the soul, this does not seem to be merely a misunderstanding, or even a different mode of expression or another use of words. It is evidently a clear difference, indeed an antithesis in the interpretation of the actual matter under discussion (and this becomes especially clear when we look at the history of the two views, and their impact). (CRE, p. 47)

If the very essence of grace is understood differently, then the purported agreements on other issues could be uncovered as examples of misunderstandings. The authors thus ask, "But does this really bring us up against an antithesis which cuts through everything we have in common, and makes mutual condemnation compellingly necessary?" (CRE, 47). The authors then sum up the results of the theological labor of the German dialogue, which concluded that the two views on the essence of grace can be seen as complementary.

New Testament exegesis supports the concerns of both sides, revealing that talk about forensic or alien righteousness "has a proper biblical foundation" (CRE, 48). In addition, "The idea of grace 'poured into' the soul and 'adhering' to it (*adhaerens*) clearly also has a sound biblical basis" (CRE, 48). CRE argues that these new exegetical insights provide a common foundation upon which to build. Created grace and uncreated grace cannot be separated; forensic and effective justification cannot be separated. Because these two pairs of terms, or the realities to which they refer, cannot be separated, the basic concerns of one communion are not contrary to those of the other. Faced with historical research, Catholics are no longer permitted to deny that Protestants adequately "take into account the fact that justification issues, and must issue, in a new life" (CRE, 48). Applying this lesson to a reading of Trent, the authors warn that canon 11, which condemns only those who hold "that grace is merely the favor of God" (CRE, 48), does not condemn Lutheran teaching. The reason is that Lutherans have always held that grace is accompanied by gift; God's favor delivers what it promises, albeit inchoately, even in the present age. Christ himself is our righteousness, and he is outside of us, but precisely as outside of us, his righteousness becomes ours. The authors refer to Luther's thought on grace and gift:

> The pregnant distinction that Luther makes (especially in *Antilatomus*) between "grace" and "gift" is intended to preserve the insight that "external" grace touches and claims the person of the believer himself. Through the Holy Spirit it makes sin "controlled sin" (*peccatum regnatum*), impels its expulsion, and thus determines the believer's whole practical conduct. (CRE, 48)

This distinction and union between grace and gift, CRE argues, is analogous to the Catholic insistence that God's love always accomplishes its salvific effect. If one were to reduce the Catholic teaching on the formal cause to this insistence, thus vaguely formulated, perhaps CRE's conclusion would be justifiable. Catholic teaching cannot be so reduced. Moreover, Luther's *Confutation of Latomus* exhibits lucidly a description of justifying grace as formally forensic. The gift of inhering righteousness must accompany this "extrinsic grace," but the gift Luther lauds as necessary does not compare with the Catholic understanding of the gift of sanctifying grace, for Luther's gift does not expel all damnable sin, whereas sanctifying grace does. For further treatment of this important work by Luther, I refer the reader to the next chapter.

CRE then turns to a rereading of Trent on the formal cause of justification. There are two strains of thought in this reading: First, the authors insist that the Catholic doctrine of grace as *habitus* does not entail "trust in one's own strength." If Protestants acknowledge this, CRE promises, then they have little reason to condemn the doctrine. This would seem to have sufficed, but the authors add that Trent "deliberately did *not* say by definition that justifying grace was to be understood as *habitus*" (CRE, 48–49). They then assure Protestant readers that Catholic faith does not "maintain what Protestant theology is afraid of: grace as an objective 'possession' (even if a conferred possession) on the part of the human being—something over which he can dispose" (CRE, 49). CRE's attempt to assure Lutherans that Catholics do not perceive grace as a "possession" may be a legitimate assurance, but it does a disservice. It dispels the illusion of an extreme caricature of Catholic doctrine but does not couple this service with a clear articulation of the genuine contents of Catholic doctrine on the essence of justifying grace. This surely does not further communication between the partners. Moreover, if the initial strain of thought is genuine, then Protestants should already be assured that Catholic teaching on grace as an inhering participation in Christ does not lead to trust in oneself. Why add the misleading suggestion that Trent did not define justifying grace as an inhering reality in the soul, that to which the term *habitus* refers?

Perhaps the Göttingen faculty has the answer. It recognizes in CRE "a clear correction of the statements of the Council of Trent."[34] This correction represents a substantive alteration, not an organic development, of doctrine. The statement of the Göttingen reaffirms this assessment later:

> The Formula of Concord, Solid Declaration, condemns the doctrine that according to its essence our righteousness before God (*iustitia formalis*) is love that adheres to us or new quality. The Council of Trent (canon 10; cap. 7 [DS 1529]) is directly condemned since it teaches exactly that and since it rejects the Reformation counterposition which insists that our righteousness before God essentially is the righteousness of Christ. Does *The Condemnations* [CRE] overcome the difference? As shown, the document at this point clearly corrects the Council of Trent, which represents a remarkable rapprochement.[35]

The same faculty laments that this correction of tridentine teaching was not integrated into the document as a whole. I concur with the judgment that CRE implies a correction and alteration of Trent, although I lament the presence of this correction and not the lack of its integration into the text. Richard White rightly accepts the literal accuracy of CRE in its claim that Trent never expressed itself in terms of "*habitus*." However, he attentively remarks, "This seems like an odd way to put it. According to the doctrine of Trent, justifying grace is sanctifying grace — and consists of the supernatural habitus that are the infused virtues (faith, hope, and love)."[36] He justly charges that the authors of CRE can conclude that the doctrinal differences are non church-dividing *only* "because they have neglected the important issue of the 'formal cause' of justification."[37]

CRE carries this neglect into other issues. The Lutheran doctrine *sola fide* supposedly harmonizes with the Catholic triad of faith, hope, and love. CRE cites Catholic Cardinal Willebrand's famous yet misleading statement: "In Luther's sense the word 'faith' by no means intends to exclude either works or love or even hope. We may quite justly say that Luther's concept of faith, if we take it in its fullest sense, surely means nothing other than what we in the Catholic Church term love" (CRE, 52). This contention is frequently found on the lips of Catholics, but many Lutherans do not find this to be an accurate comparison.[38] CRE considers faith "sufficient for righteousness before God, so that the renewal of the human being, without which there can be no faith, does not in itself make any contribution to justification" (CRE, 52). This reader would like to know the identity of the renewal that "makes no contribution to justification"? Is renewal the life of concrete deeds lived in gratitude for mercy? If so, then this statement may resonate with Catholic piety and teaching with respect to the initial event of justification itself (first justification). But if "renewal" is or includes the infusion of grace and charity, then this statement is contrary to Catholic faith. The dialogue leaves the answer to this question somewhat ambiguous, although it hints at a distinctively Lutheran answer in its articulation of the Catholic concern: While Catholics stress the renewal of the human person through justifying grace, CRE admits, "This renewal in faith, hope, and love is certainly nothing but a response to God's unfathomable grace" (CRE, 53). Faith, hope, and love are said to constitute the human response to God, also called "renewal." If this renewal contributes nothing to justification, does this imply that infused love contributes nothing to justification? If nothing, then what has become of the Catholic belief that "The grace that makes one acceptable to God...is sanctifying grace"?[39]

Finally, the ambiguity appears again in the discussion of baptismal grace. Reminiscent of Pannenberg's remarks, CRE notes the appearance of an antithesis when "Roman Catholic doctrine assumes that baptismal grace can be lost [but] Protestant doctrine assumes that it *cannot* be lost as such, although a person can no doubt 'fall out of it'" (CRE, 60). The authors find the solution in the distinctions between created and uncreated grace and between gift and grace: "Baptismal grace can be lost only insofar as it is *also* a gift bestowed on human beings. But the unfathomable forgiving love of God, which never repents of itself, cannot be lost" (CRE, 60, emphasis mine). This apparent solution is evasive, for it obscures Trent's position that *justifying* grace can be lost. The "also" bespeaks the authors' intentions to distinguish justifying grace and sanctifying grace. The reader may recall Pannenberg's correct observation that the opinion that justifying grace can be lost is the corollary of the position that grace truly inheres in the soul, much as a quality inheres in its subject. Pannenberg, the chief Lutheran proponent of the German dialogue, ascribed both positions merely to the "scholastic heritage," but they in fact belong to Trent, which holds baptismal grace to be that "spotless robe" believers are called to preserve and to present before God.

Evidently, CRE does not satisfy the rigors of analysis requisite to establishing a lasting, genuine reunion of Lutherans and Catholics. This is especially clear in its treatment of the essence of justifying grace and the consequent divergences that issue therefrom. Corroborating my critique, the United Evangelical Lutheran Church in Germany welcomed CRE as a step forward but also confessed that differences yet remained, especially with regard to "The understanding of grace as God's turning toward men (extra nos), or as a 'reality in the human soul' (qualitas in nobis)."[40] Many of CRE's limitations can be found in the Joint Declaration as well.

NOTES

1   See JF, 3.

2   The Catholic bishops heralded it as a "significant step toward reconciliation," judging it to be "thoroughly researched, comprehensive, [and] constructive" (National Conference of Catholic Bishops, "An Evaluation of the Lutheran-Catholic Statement *Justification by Faith," One in Christ* 29 [1993]: 336). The Catholic bishops showed an appropriate caution, however, and were attentive to USA's admission that "some of these differences seem to be irreconcilable" (ibid., 337). The ELCA was more optimistic, declaring, "[USA] does constitute a fundamental consensus on the gospel between Lutherans and Catholics" (Evangelical Lutheran Church in America, "Response to *Justification by Faith," One in Christ* 29 [1993]: 343).

3   This can still be detected in his 1559 *Loci*, wherein, in articulating an argument of his opponents, Mclanchthon cited a major premise that smacks of a Pelagian character: "Justice signifies obedience" (see Melanchthon, *Loci*, p. 417).

4   See *Apologia*, IV: 56.

5   Nam cum dicitur, per gratiam habemus remissionem, si sic intelligas, propter donatas virtutes habemus remissionem, plane evertes totam Pauli sententiam et conscientiis adimes veram consolationem. Non enim nostras qualitates intueri debemus, cum anguimur de remissione, sed confugere ad Mediatorem.... Quare cum illa acceptatione coniuncta est donatio Spiritus sancti, neque tamen sequitur nos propter illas novas virtutes habere reconciliationem (Melanchthon, *Loci*, pp. 420–21).

6   See ibid., pp. 428–29.

7   LW 26: 127.

8   George Lindbeck comes to a different judgment, observing that the *Formula*'s precise distinctions and careful methodology kept it from some of the hyperbole in Luther (see Lindbeck, "Compatibility," p. 232).

9   Wenz, "Damnamus," p. 101. Of course, Wenz goes on to suggest that the *Formula*, when read within the light of the Augsburg Confession, is not nearly as condemnatory as one might at first think.

10   National Conference of Catholic Bishops, "An Evaluation," p. 337.

11   ELCA, "Response," p. 344.

12   Paul VI, *Mysterium fidei*, St. Paul Books & Media, p. 11.

13   Ibid., p. 11.

14   See Frederick Crowe, "Doctrines and Historicity in the Context of Lonergan's Method," *Theological Studies* 38 (1977): 115–24, esp. pp. 119–20.

15   See *Mysterium ecclesiae*, art. 5.

16   See *Fides et ratio*, arts. 87 and 95–97. For an argument defending the enduring character of the propositions proposed by the Magisterium, see John Lamont, "The Historical Conditioning of Doctrine," *The Thomist* 60 (1996): 511–35.

17   In my analysis of the Joint Declaration itself, I make ample references to JF.

18   See Birmelé, *A Commentary*, p. 20.

19   I say "are free" because they are also free to see in the scriptures but one of two *loci* of revelation. Contemporary scholars rightly observe that Trent's expression "et...et" represented a deliberate decision to avoid declaring "two sources," which would have been the issue of Trent's decision if "partim...partim" had been retained. Nevertheless, Trent's indecision was but echoed in Vatican II's *Dei Verbum*. Many Catholics wrongly believe that the notion of two sources was simply rejected at Vatican II. They argue on the basis of the decision to jettison the original documents. No doubt, the final

text emphasizes the one Gospel of which scripture and tradition are inseparable expressions. But to claim that Vatican II *rejected* the idea that tradition might express some aspects of the Gospel not expressed in scripture is to ignore the Acta of that council. Of the carefully-worded options Paul VI gave the council on this point, the fathers chose one that would not decide the issue: "Consequently, it is not from sacred Scripture alone that the Church draws her certainty about everything which has been revealed" (*Dei Verbum*, art. 9, trans. R.A.F. MacKenzie, in Walter M. Abbott, gen. ed., *The Documents of Vatican II* [New York: Herder and Herder, 1966], p. 117). Thus, the material sufficiency of scripture is neither condemned nor taught by Vatican II. Who today reads this statement as simply leaving open the possibility of a material sufficiency of scripture? Is it not commonplace to read this formula as teaching, almost dogmatically, the material sufficiency of scripture? In this regard, what can one make of Abbott's note: "This careful formula was one of the last additions to the text, made at the Pope's request. It does not exclude [sic] the opinion [sic] that all revelation is in some way, though perhaps obscurely [sic], contained in Scripture" (Abbott, *The Documents of Vatican II*, p. 117, note 21). Some theologians offer a rhetorical "argument" that the inviolable unity of the Gospel a priori precludes the possibility that any genuine expression of the Gospel can materially lack anything. They contend that implicit in *any* genuine expression of the Gospel is the entire truth of the Gospel. The conclusion does not follow. Proponents of this a priori position gloss over the concrete contents of the Gospel. Indeed, on this thesis, one could take any of the four written Gospels and find therein a "materially sufficient" expression of the Good News. Thus, we would lose the stereoscopic approach to our Lord and also some of the contents of his teaching (if we choose Mark and not Matthew, we would lose crucial aspects of his authority). Granted that the one Word is present in the many words of scripture, we must yet remember that Christian faith is addressed to human beings, who reason discursively, and that therefore the "articles" of faith are not "one" in number. Since the articles are not "one" in number, our faith, so long as we are human *viatores*, involves a necessary multiplicity through which we arrive at the simplicity of the triune God. One can argue, then, that genuine expressions of the faith might not include all the articles of faith. Since it is possible that the books of scripture taken individually do not contain the entire deposit of faith, it is not impossible that the books taken together do not contain the entire deposit of faith. It is not, in short, a priori impossible that scripture is materially insufficient. No one should understand this to be an argument in favor of the material insufficiency of scripture; it is merely an argument against a facile argument in favor of the material sufficiency of scripture.

20 See McGrath, *Iustitia Dei*, pp. 226–40.

21 See Pannenberg, *Systematic Theology*, vol. 3, pp. 228–31.

22 I am drawing on Lonergan's distinction between description and explanation: description is the articulation of elements of the real with respect to the observer, and explanation is the articulation of elements of the real with respect to each other.

23 Seripando's piety was not condemned at Trent, although his attempt to translate that piety into doctrine at the council was condemned. The difference is important: in one case, we are dealing with sentiment; in another case, with truth claims.

24 See USA, par. 24.

25 Göttingen, "An Opinion," p. 22.

26 See Richard White, "Justification in Ecumenical Dialogue," esp. pp. 142–48.

27 See Scheffczyk, "'Differenzierter Konsens,'" p. 439.

28 See Göttingen, "An Opinion," pp. 23–24.

29 See, for instance, the following in St. Augustine of Hippo: *On the Spirit and the Letter*,

chap. 56; *On Nature and Grace*, chap. 84; and *On Man's Perfection in Righteousness*, chaps. 9 and 10. All of these are from the Antipelagian writings.

30   That is, the sinner takes himself or something other than God as his last end. God demands that he be loved above all things. All a sinner's actions are directed towards a lesser goal and, hence, are sinful.

31   See Göttingen, "An Opinion," pp. 25–26. Working in its favor, on the contrary, is CRE's reference to the *Solid Declaration*. The discussion therein upholds the notion of continuity of subject as well. Body and soul are the creation of God and thus remain continuous through the radical change that takes place in justification. The *Solid Declaration* even cautions that some of Luther's expressions—e.g., that human nature is sin—must be interpreted in light of the theological sense of nature as the negative characteristics of a thing, in this case the self-oriented love of man (*Solid Declaration*, I: 51).

32   Gerhard Forde, "Forensic Justification and Law in Lutheran Theology," in USA, pp. 281–82.

33   USA, par. 91.

34   Göttingen, "An Opinion," p. 28.

35   Ibid., p. 53.

36   Richard White, "Justification in Ecumenical Dialogue," pp. 108–09.

37   Ibid., p. 144.

38   See Göttingen, "An Opinion," pp. 30 and 60, notes 47–49.

39   Richard White, "Justification in Ecumenical Dialogue," p. 144.

40   UELC, "Comment," *Lutheran Quarterly* 9 (1995): 361.

CHAPTER 7

The Essence of Justifying Grace: Common and Lutheran Paragraphs

MANY HAVE praised the Joint Declaration, both academics and ecclesial officials, both Catholics and Lutherans, not excluding members of other communions. It is indeed remarkable that two communions once so bitterly divided could sit down together to discuss their differences and commonalities over a prolonged period of time. The communions have learned to listen to one another; they have attempted to enter into each other's structure of thought, stammering to communicate truths vital to Christian welfare. I find this very effort to be one of the most significant achievements of the ecumenical dialogue. Common prayer and common intellectual engagement—no mean accomplishment if one only considers the 30 Years' War or the practical rigidity during much of the post-tridentine era. Howsoever critical my opinion of the JD is, I take no exception to this living fruit of *dialogue*. Moreover, although I would argue that many theologians in both communions had already recognized a number of the commonalities said to be rediscovered only recently, still, the educational ministries in both communions stand to benefit considerably from the retrieval of this shared heritage: God's sovereign mercy, Christ's sole meritorious action in the atonement, the ecstatic nature of a salvific relationship with Christ, the powerlessness of sinful man even to beg for God's help without grace, the transformative effects of God's eternal love, and the necessity of identifying some kind of continuity between earthly and heavenly life. Too often the practice of members of the two communions has been to neglect or deny the commonality of these elements of shared heritage. How many a Catholic catechist has heard older students describe Luther's view of justification as "snow covering dung"! How many a Lutheran teacher has heard students describe Catholicism as goading sinners to labor to merit God's grace, as though God could be coerced by human action! Perhaps even teachers of both sides have joined in the chorus. It has long been time to do away with these irresponsible and libelous accusations.[1]

Notwithstanding the practical boon for both communions that has issued from these newly retrieved insights, the foundations of the JD are not certain.

Part I of my book argues against the validity of the twofold task the authors of the JD set themselves: (a) to accomplish a legitimately differentiated consensus on the basic truths of justification (b) that alters the substance of neither communion's teaching of the past. On the grounds of this argument, I agree with Cardinal Dulles's opinion: "The *Joint Declaration* tried to accomplish too much…. It went beyond the findings of the dialogues in asserting that the 'remaining differences' were 'acceptable.' No one should think that we have reached the end of the road."[2] The framers have strained credulity by the extent of their claims. These remarks touch upon the self-imposed task of the authors; they remain valid apart from any consideration of the contents of the agreement. Now, in light of the preparatory work in chapter 6, I intend in chapters 7 through 9 to investigate the contents of the JD itself.

The JD's doctrinal exposition is composed of sections, each of which involves a different topic, that consist in a common confession with distinct Lutheran and Catholic interpretations of that confession. Both communions are understood readily to subscribe to the contents of the common paragraphs. The "Lutheran" and "Catholic" paragraphs represent distinct interpretations of the common paragraphs, manifesting notably but legitimately different readings of the common confession, with the result that the differences are not held to be church-dividing.

The very structure of the declaration is at the service of the goal of attaining a "differentiated consensus." The method of "differentiated consensus" was intended both to surmount the obstacles perceived for centuries to be insurmountable and to secure the agreement necessary for full communion *on this issue*. The JD makes it quite clear that disputes about other issues may well still be in place. However, the framers' understanding of the accomplishments of this differentiated consensus is unequivocally clear in the JD and the OCS. American Lutheran theologian William Rusch characterizes the agreement as one of "reconciled diversity," which involves both agreement on a first level of "fundamental and essential content" and also "remaining differences" that "do not call into question the basic consensus on the first level."[3] Rusch takes his lead from Lutheran theologian Harding Meyer, who wishes emphatically to dispel the illusion that the consensus is "monolithic."[4] The notion of a monolithic consensus is not only outdated but also unfruitful. Instead, the ecumenical movement strives for both agreement in matters considered fundamental and also mutual understanding and acceptance in matters considered non-fundamental. This goal is the "differentiated consensus."[5] The JD reflects this approach to ecumenical dialogue. Thus, the JD encompasses an agreement on fundamental matters and mutual understanding and acceptance on non-fundamental matters. The common paragraphs represent affirmations of agreement without differentiation, and the Lutheran and Catholic paragraphs that follow articulate the really distinctive interpretations of that common confession and also the reasons why the distinctive character of these interpretations do not mitigate the agreement about the common confession.[6]

The notion of "differentiated consensus" allows one to countenance the difference between language and the reality to which it refers. There can be different ways of expressing the same reality. As long as the different conceptual articulations do not reflect a difference in substance, the differing articulations are not necessarily church-dividing.[7] We see in its inception, then, appeal to the reality which the formulas attempt to signify. The "non monolithic" character of this consensus is, at least on its surface, in harmony with Pope Bl. John XXIII's remarks at the commencement of the Second Vatican Council: "One thing is the deposit of faith and the truths contained in our venerable doctrine, another thing is the way they are announced, with the same meaning and the same content."[8] John XXIII's remarks echo the refrain of Vatican I: "with the same meaning and the same content." This is a significant qualification and an instructive light for the adventure of theological discovery. John XXIII did not give license to circumvent genuine obstacles. Has his caution been heeded?

Legrand triumphantly proclaims that the method of "differentiated consensus" marks a notable departure from the typical doctrinal approach of the last five centuries, according to which the distinct teachings uttered by the Magisterium are taken as obligatory.[9] He laments the fact that the 1989 Profession of Faith, which demands fidelity to "each and every" definitively taught proposition, succumbs to the ancient approach.[10] To him, this kind of thinking is the "enemy" of ecumenical thinking.[11] It is instructive to observe how Legrand believes this method might be used to resolve other disputes. As a test-case of future applications of the new method, he describes the Lutheran and Catholic views of ordained priesthood as complementary. The Catholic intention is simply to hold that ordination is not merely a "ritual"; it is not merely the "public recognition" of the spiritual aptitude of the ordinand. In addition, there is a "gift of the Spirit" given for the good of the Church. Lutherans, in contrast, simply want to avoid suggesting that the priesthood confers the kind of grace available in the Eucharist and baptism. In evaluation of Legrand's suggestions, I would concede that it is legitimate to emphasize doctrines as organically linked within a whole fabric. I would argue, nonetheless, that his summary assessment of the complementary differences between Lutheran and Catholic views of ordination leaves much to be desired.[12] Similarly, the JD's own differentiated must be tested in terms of its contents.

The test of the differentiated consensus is this: Does the consensus attained actually represent an agreement about the realities believed, an agreement sufficient for full ecclesial communion?[13] This is the question I wish to undertake to answer. Because I perceive a greater harmony between the common and Lutheran paragraphs than between the common and Catholic paragraphs, I will examine together, in the present chapter, the common and Lutheran paragraphs on the essence of justifying grace. Since my reading of the text will undoubtedly cause rancor among some Catholic readers (thought it may well be to the delight of Lutherans), I will consider two of what I take to be the weightiest objections to my reading. Chapter 8 treats the essence of justifying grace in the Catholic paragraphs.

The Identity of Justifying Grace

After an initial preamble, the JD briefly presents the scriptural witness to justification, focusing on St. Paul. The section consists for the most part of an ordered narration of the Pauline kerygma. The narration reflects Paul's Christocentricity. It is open to a Trinitarian reading, which could be more pronounced. Perhaps the strongest point of this narration is its linking of justification and its ultimately ecclesial dimension, namely, incorporation into the body of Christ. Faithful to its method of achieving a "differentiated consensus," the JD acknowledges that the biblical witness is varied, involving "diverse treatments" and, even within the Pauline corpus, "various ways" of expressing the mystery (JD, 9). The JD tacitly ratifies USA's claim that the New Testament, especially Paul, presents diverse and yet complementary images for justification. One must grant the rich and multifarious character of the scriptural imagery for this great mystery. Whether or not such diversity reflects indecision on Paul's part or even subtle contradiction among the Biblical authors is another matter.[14] Noticeably absent is any articulated sense that the Catholic Church does not draw the certitude of her faith from scripture alone but from scripture and sacred tradition.[15]

The common affirmation of the two communions is encapsulated in the following central confession. In this and other citations of the JD, I will be citing from the standard English translation of the official German text, at times making changes in brackets to reflect the German more exactly. I will supply the German and (frequently) the standard English translation when I make changes, usually in endnotes. It will become clear, to the chagrin of Catholics, that the German text frequently enjoys a more pronouncedly Lutheran ring than does the standard English translation. The central confession reads:

15. ... Justification thus means that Christ himself is our righteousness, in which [righteousness] we share through the Holy Spirit in accord with the will of the Father. Together we confess: By grace alone, in faith in Christ's saving work and not [on the

basis of our merit], we are accepted by God and receive the Holy Spirit, who renews our hearts while equipping and calling us to good works.[16]

This common confession is carefully structured. It resonates with both Lutheran and Catholic concerns. On the one hand, it declares that "Christ himself is our righteousness," that justification is "by grace alone," and that it occurs "not on the basis of our merit." On the other hand, it asserts that we participate in Christ's righteousness and that the Holy Spirit, whom we receive, renews our hearts. The first set of claims resonates especially with Lutheran thought; the second set, with Catholic thought. Moreover, both sets of claims, as articulated above, are amenable to each communion. Catholics agree that "Christ is our righteousness" and that (first) justification is not merited but utterly depends upon God's mercy. Lutherans agree that the Holy Spirit renews human hearts, that the justified become participants in Christ's righteousness, and that they are called to a life of good works. At this point, a question is in order.

Raising a Question

The heart of the common confession is rooted in the Pauline proclamation that God "has made [Jesus] our wisdom and also our justice, our sanctification, and our redemption" (1 Cor 2:30). Both communions submit to this proclamation as revelation. Both can agree to the above-cited common confession. Still, further questions can be asked to probe the depths of this confession.

Among these, the central question is, in what way is Christ himself a Christian's righteousness? Is he understood as the meritorious basis for justification? Is he understood as the fontal source through which infused righteousness flows? Or is this not to go far enough? Is Christ's own righteousness *also* taken to be that by which the sinner stands just before God? That is, is it understood as the formal righteousness of the Christian? If not, what is the essence of the Christian's justifying righteousness? No immediate answers present themselves. In the absence of the precision traditionally manifest among both communions, the reader of the JD must work by inference from the data that are both directly and indirectly pertinent to this issue.[17]

My procedure will be to discern and to link synthetically the meanings of the relevant affirmations in the JD. To assure greater reliability of the data for this synthesis, I will study the relevant affirmations closely, drawing upon both the background dialogues and the sources cited in the footnotes. What follows, then, includes a close study of important passages and a systematic attempt to discern their contextual intelligibility. My systematic endeavor is more pronounced in chapter 9, a consideration of the nexus of issues pertaining to the formal cause of justification. The interconnected discussions in chapter 9 witness that the scrutiny of texts in the present chapter is rooted in a synthetic vision of the overall impact of justifying grace in the life of the believer, as articulated in the JD.

Tracing an Answer

The first steps towards an affirmation of the identity of justifying grace appear in the paragraphs subsequent to the above-cited passage. They read:

> 16. All people are called by God to salvation in Christ. Through Christ alone are we justified, when [or while] we receive this salvation in faith. Faith is itself God's gift through the Holy Spirit, who works [in] word and [in the sacraments] in the community of believers and who at the same time leads believers into that renewal of life which God will bring to completion in eternal life.[18]

> 17. We also share the conviction that the message of justification directs us in a special way towards the heart of the New Testament witness to God's saving action in Christ: It tells us that [we sinners {*wir Sünder*} owe our new life solely to the forgiving and renewing mercy of God, which we only accept and receive in faith, but which we] never can merit in any way.[19]

Paragraph 16 speaks of justification as the reception of salvation in faith. It is stressed, in accordance with both communions' beliefs, that faith is not a merely "human work [*ergon*]" but a gift of the Spirit. "At the same time," the Spirit also leads those who believe into a renewal of life that awaits eschatological consummation. Highlighted here are the primacy of the Spirit's initiative in our lives, the centrality of faith in the event of justification, the inseparability of the renewal of life from the event of justification, and some degree of continuity between earthly and heavenly life. We begin to see the duality undergirding the consensus: both reception of salvation and renewal of life. The two elements are united in that they are both the Spirit's work, but the relationship between justification itself (reception of salvation) and renewal itself is not specified. It may fairly be asked, as well, to what the term "salvation" refers. In general, Catholics reserve this word for the eschatological consummation of a life justly lived in baptismal grace, whereas Lutherans frequently identify it as the gift promised in justification unconditionally. Thus, whereas Catholics speak of justification as a past event, most Lutherans speak of it in actualistic terms, as an ever-recurring event. The ambiguity of the duality in par. 16 does not tease out these significant differences. We will see this duality throughout the JD.

Paragraph 17 brings us closer to an affirmation of the identity of justifying grace: "We sinners owe our new life solely to the forgiving and renewing mercy of God." The duality of par. 16 resurfaces in par. 17 and raises the question about the identity of the "forgiving and renewing mercy of God" to which *alone* our new life is due. Noticeably different from the official German text, the English translation reads: "[The message of justification] tells us that *as sinners* our new life is solely due to the forgiving and renewing mercy *that God imparts* as a *gift* and we receive in faith, and never can merit in any way" (JD, 17, emphasis mine). Observe that the English "as sinners" does not correspond to the German "we sinners [*wir Sünder*]." The English would appear to leave some room for a different aspect of human identity, namely, the aspect of the sinner "as forgiven." Further, the English "that God imparts as a gift" misleadingly adds a distinctively Catholic connotation, namely, the connotation that the "forgiving and renewing mercy of God" is infused as a gift. The German does not have this connotation, for it lacks both the sense of "infusion" and the substantive term "gift." What, then, is the "forgiving and renewing mercy of God…which we never can merit in any way"? Is it, as the English translation but vaguely hints, infused, sanctifying grace? If so, how can the final clause, "which we never can merit in any way" be acceptable to the Catholic communion? Do not Catholics believe that the person *already justified* can merit an increase in sanctifying grace? But if, as is much more likely, the "forgiving mercy" refers to God's *favor*, then both communions can indeed accept the final clause. However, given this interpretation, can Catholics sincerely affirm the first statement: "We sinners owe our new life *solely* to the [favor of God]"? Is our new life not also rooted in the gift of infused, sanctifying grace? Does par. 17 implicitly identify "justifying righteousness" as the "favor of God"? Perhaps par. 17 was not intended to be burdened by such questions. Still, as CRE and USA affirm, this issue is precisely the crux of the matter to be resolved in the ecumenical dialogue. Thus, the question returns: What does par. 15 mean by the clause, "Christ himself is our righteousness"?

I now turn to the next section of the JD, "Explicating the Common Understanding of Justification," which begins with par. 19. It is in this section that the variegated structure of the JD begins in earnest. Since I treat pars. 19–21 in detail in my discussion of merit (chapter 9), I will pass immediately to the common (JD, 22) and Lutheran (JD, 23) paragraphs, under the subheading "Justification as Forgiveness of Sins and Making Righteous." They read:

22. We confess together that *God forgives sin by grace and at the same time frees human beings from sin's enslaving power and [grants] the new life in Christ.* When persons come [in] faith to share in Christ, God [does not impute their sins to them {or,

does not charge their sins against them}] and through the Holy Spirit effects in them
an active love. [Both aspects] of God's gracious action [may not be] separated. [They
belong together in such a way that] persons are by faith united with *Christ, who in his
person is our righteousness* (1 Cor 1:30): both the forgiveness of sins and the saving
presence of God [emphases mine].[20]

23. When Lutherans emphasize that *the righteousness of Christ is our righteousness*,
their intention is above all to insist that *the sinner is granted righteousness before God
in Christ through the declaration of forgiveness* and that only in union with Christ is
one's life renewed. When they [say] that God's grace is forgiving love ("the favor of
God"[12] [note 12 of JD, in text below]), they do not thereby deny the renewal of the
Christian's life. They intend rather to express that justification remains free from
human cooperation and [also] is not dependent on the life-renewing effects of grace in
human beings [emphases mine].[21]

[12] WA 8:106; American ed., 32:227.

Again, God's act has two aspects: forgiveness and renewal. The JD clearly
undertakes to emphasize the unity of these two aspects. This effort represents
a notable and laudable compromise on the part of the Lutherans in dialogue. At
least two reasons for the unity are given. The two aspects are granted "at the
same time" so that they "may not be separated"; and they "belong together" in
virtue of Christ, with whom believers are united. The JD thus presents a union
in distinction between forgiveness and renewal. The bond between the two is
both temporal and Christological. I would like to postpone my treatment of the
Christological character of the bond for the moment.[22] Here, I will treat the
"simultaneity" or the "inseparability" of the two aspects of God's act.

The JD stresses the "simultaneity" and "inseparability" of forgiveness and
renewal again and again. In addition to pars. 22 and 23, par. 24 (a Catholic
paragraph) insists, "God's forgiving grace always brings with it a gift of new
life, which in the Holy Spirit becomes effective in active love." Lutheran par.
26 is most explicit:

Because God's act is a new creation, it affects all dimension of the person and leads to
a life in hope and love. In the doctrine of "justification by faith alone [or through faith
alone]," a distinction but not a separation is made between justification itself and the
renewal of one's way of life that necessarily follows from justification and without
which [no faith can exist].[23]

This Lutheran paragraph depicts justification and renewal as inseparably
conjoined. The subsequent Catholic paragraph, manifesting a differentiated use
of terminology, declares, "The justification of sinners is forgiveness of sins and
being made righteous by justifying grace, which makes us children of God"
(JD, 27). In recognizing a differentiation of terminology, we can recall Küng's

point that Catholics employ the term "justification" more broadly than do Lutherans. Thus, the bond between "forgiveness" and "being made righteous," enunciated in par. 27, echoes that between "justification" and "renewal (or sanctification)" in par. 26.

It would appear to many that a happy middle has been reached, for the chief concerns of both communions are hereby tethered tightly together, not to be separated. This is the common judgment of many. The Institute for Ecumenical Research in Strasbourg considers that the JD has hereby resolved the once inveterate misapprehension of both sides: "It is thus clear that for both traditions, God's justification includes the renewal of the Christian's life. An old misunderstanding is here overcome."[24] Spanish Catholic theologian Josè Villar and Lutheran Harding Meyer assess the matter similarly.[25] Kärkkäinen states in summary, "Justification means both forgiveness of sins (forensic justification; *favour*) and inner renewal and change. In other words, justification and sanctification form one theological entity."[26] Birmelé sees the JD as having taken us far away from the "false alternative" of either intrinsic or extrinsic righteousness.[27] These and numerous other theologians perceive the concurrence of forgiveness and renewal as a retrieval, without renunciation, of the authentic teachings of both communions, which was obscured by the polemical *Zeitgeist* of the Reformation era. Other scholars detect a happy compromise at work.

British Methodist theologian Geoffrey Wainwright, now residing in America, is quite lucid in his interpretation. He detects a remarkable resemblance between the JD and the theology of John Wesley. Wesley, distinguishing himself from both Luther and Rome, taught a simultaneous union in distinction between justification and sanctification. Wainwright cites him: "[Justification] restores us to the favour, [sanctification] to the image of God. The one is the taking away of guilt, the other the taking away of the power, of sin. So that although they are joined together in point of time, yet they are of wholly distinct natures."[28] Wesley found a happy middle between the warring titans. He took justification by faith alone from Luther and a rich appreciation of sanctification from Rome. Wainwright comments,

> If continuance in the regrettably triumphalist vein of Wesley may be excused, Methodists might say that the Joint Declaration on the Doctrine of Justification has finally brought Lutherans and Catholics to affirm together the twofold truth that had been distorted from the one side or the other—the distinct but inseparable doctrines of sheer giftedness of the divine forgiveness of the sinner and the real change empowered and summoned in the recipient of grace.[29]

According to Wainwright, the JD resembles Wesley's thought, a *via media* between Catholicism and Lutheranism.[30] If a *via media*, the friendly concord struck at Regensburg would appear to have revisited us. Does the fate of the earlier accord toll the fate of the newer?

Questioning the Answer

Regensburg could not withstand the trials of either Luther's fiery mouth or Rome's slow but heavy hand. Can the JD's juxtaposition of forgiveness and renewal, so similar to that ill-fated colloquy, carry us beyond the burden of division that has proved so weighty, so long? Daphne Hampson thinks not. Among respectably neutral observers, she is the least content with the accord. Her remarks are on target:

> To say that Lutherans believe in newness of life resulting from justification is clearly the case (but this is not understood in the same way as the Catholic infusion of grace!). It is also true to say that for Catholics God's gift of grace is entirely free (but this is nothing like the Lutheran sense that we live by God's justice and not by our own!). It might then be said that this way of proceeding does little to reconcile the two structures [of thought].[31]

She likens the JD to an "umbrella document," generically affirming the basic concerns of each communion but failing to penetrate the substance of either. With good British reserve, not enamored of the "hermeneutics of empathy," she asks whether or not this "umbrella document" can actually hold together the two radically divergent doctrines and structural approaches of Lutheranism and Catholicism.[32] She concludes, "In view of the difficulties that there have been—on both sides—it would clearly be a rash person who would say that Catholics and Lutherans have now 'settled' their differences over justification!"[33] Eberhard Jüngel, before the publication of the Annex, reacted similarly: "This is one of the scandals in the history of theology which that *Declaration* will go on to serve as an example. To accept this amounts to a sacrifice of the intellect on the part of any theologian. But enough of these shameful attempts to excuse ecumenism from due intellectual honesty!"[34]

Wainwright's understandable delight about the conciliatory character of the declaration, if taken to be true, almost makes one stand back, aghast at the foolishness of the forefathers of both communions. Küng's gauntlet is apropos of such shock: "Is it not time to stop arguing about imaginary differences?"[35] The question is hardly new. In the latter half of the sixteenth century, Chemnitz, taking on the persona of the perplexed, wrote,

> But someone may say: If matters stand thus, then what is it about which you contend so sharply concerning the article of justification, so that you throw almost the whole

world into turmoil? Certainly, as you do not deny the renewal nor simply reject charity, so the papalists do not deny the remission of sins, but confess it. And if there is agreement concerning the matters themselves, there will then be only contentions about words or a war about grammar. For the papalists understand the word "justify" according to the manner of the Latin composition as meaning "to make righteous" through a donated or infused quality of inherent righteousness, from which works of righteousness proceed. The Lutherans, however, accept the word "justify" in the Hebrew manner of speaking; therefore they define justification as the absolution from sins, or the remission of sins, through imputation of the righteousness of Christ.... And yet they teach at the same time that renewal follows, that love and good works must be begun. Therefore there will be no contention about the matter itself, but only about the word "justification," which arises from this, that each understands and interprets that word differently.

However,...the dissension and strife in the article of justification is not only about words but chiefly about the matters themselves.[36]

Chemnitz, one of the chief authors of the *Formula*, spilled much ink in attempts to resolve lingering doubts about the importance of the differences between Rome and Augsburg. Martin Luther was his mentor.[37] For the very reason that this question has been raised before, eliciting sharply negative answers throughout the centuries (except among the British), I took pains in Part I to examine the gaping fissure that obstructed all past attempts to smooth over differences. Have the JD and its preparatory dialogues manifested the intellectual rigor necessary to breach the gap? I would have to concur with Jüngel's original answer, but obviously for very different reasons: He detected a problematic compromise with Trent, whereas I detect a problematic compromise with Augsburg. Lutherans themselves are divided about whether or not the JD represents a compromise, for good or for ill, with Trent. Not surprisingly, the Lutherans who welcome the document agree about the crux of the matter, the identity of justifying grace.

Specifying the Essence of Justifying Grace

It would appear that the JD specifies the essence of justifying grace as Christ's own righteousness. The affirmation is repeated several times, in quite fundamental paragraphs:

Justification thus means that Christ himself is our righteousness, in which [righteousness] we share through the Holy Spirit in accord with the will of the Father. (JD, 15)

[Both aspects] of God's gracious action [may not be] separated. [They belong together in such a way that] persons are by faith united with Christ, who in his person is our righteousness (1 Cor 1:30): both the forgiveness of sins and the saving presence of

God. (JD, 22)

> When Lutherans emphasize that the righteousness of Christ is our righteousness, their
> intention is above all to insist that the sinner is granted righteousness before God in
> Christ through the declaration of forgiveness and that only in union with Christ is one's
> life renewed. (JD, 23)

It may be surprising that none of these affirmations appeared in the first draft, issued in 1995. Neither did the two chief biblical inspirations for this affirmation appear, namely, 1 Cor 1:30 and 2 Cor 5:21. The 1996 draft laid the foundation for the final draft. It included 1 Cor 1:30 in the biblical section (JD 1996, par. 10) and the statements that appeared in the final draft in pars. 15 and 22 (same numbers for both drafts). The 1996 draft did not repeat the affirmation that "Christ is our righteousness" in its (Lutheran) par. 23. As we have seen, the final draft does repeat the affirmation in par. 23. The final draft clearly marks the goal of a consistent trajectory in the development of the declaration, a development due in large part to Lutheran criticisms of both the 1995 and 1996 drafts.[38]

Does the JD therefore affirm that Christ's own righteousness is the righteousness by which the human person stands just before God? A large number of respectable interpreters think this is the case. The Institute for Ecumenical Research at Strasbourg states,

> JD 23 elaborates two Lutheran conceptions in relation to (Catholic) misunderstandings:
> a) The statement that the righteousness of Christ is our righteousness seeks to
> emphasize that righteousness is given us before God in Christ through the *declaration*
> of forgiveness and that the life of the believer is renewed "only in union with Christ."
> b) That Lutherans conceive of the grace of God as forgiving love or as the favor of God
> and not as created grace (the Catholic conception of the created effect of the love of
> God within the person) does not mean that they believe that the grace of God remains
> external to the person or that they deny "the renewal of the Christian's life."[39]

According to this interpretation, the grace by which one stands just before God is God's favor through Jesus Christ, the effect of which, though necessary, does not constitute Christian justice. Kärkkäinen, similarly, perceives the JD identifying Christ as the human person's righteousness. He summarizes one of the chief points as follows: "Christ in his person is the human being's justification and righteousness."[40] Birmelé, too, holds that "Christ is their justice."[41] In relating the Catholic conviction that justification occurs in phases, he alludes to a distinction between justifying grace and sanctifying grace.[42] Whether this is a distinction between the habit of sanctifying grace and the declaration of justice is not immediately clear. His approbation of the Lutheran wariness of conceiving grace as a habit, however, makes it appear as though he does not consider the one formal cause of justification to be sanctifying grace. He observes as well that, due to Lutheran criticism of the 1995 Geneva text, Catholics distanced themselves in the 1997 draft from the notion of grace as a created quality that can be increased in man through good works. The Catholics thus allowed for accommodation of the Lutheran contention that justification is identical with the fulness of salvation and is perfect and complete. They did not wholly abandoned, however, the notion of stages of justification. He considers the difference in unity exemplary of a "differentiated consensus."[43]

Anthony Lane readily appreciates the concessions Lutherans have made in allowing a degree of ambiguity in the JD, but he discerns an implicit affirmation of the traditional Protestant insistence on the distinction between renewal and justifying grace. He asks, "On what basis is the converted Christian accepted by God? This question is not directly answered in the Declaration, but there are two relevant statements." Citing pars. 15 and 23, he comments:

> While this statement [par. 15] clearly (and rightly) holds together acceptance and renewal it seems to teach that the acceptance is on the basis of faith in Christ's saving work, not on the basis of the renewal—although that could be understood of initial justification rather than our ongoing status.... The *Joint Declaration* is not very explicit, but it appears to be more amenable to the idea that we are not accepted on the basis of imparted righteousness.[44]

Lane observes the ambiguity of par. 15, which does not clearly exclude the possibility that, after the event of baptismal regeneration, humans are accepted in virtue of the grace imparted to them. I would grant some degree of ambiguity, but I would side with his overall judgment that the JD is more amenable to the idea of *imputed* righteousness, even after the baptismal event. Lane does not see the ensuing Catholic par. 24 as contradicting the affirmation in par. 23 that we are justified by the *declaration* of forgiveness. Not surprisingly, Lane credits the agreement mainly to "Roman Catholics being willing to move beyond the positions of the sixteenth century." In contrast, "The dialogue documents have not required Protestants to go back on any of their traditional doctrines," even though the inherently Protestant doctrine of imputed righteousness does not come to the fore.[45] Regensburg again: "In this respect the situation is much the same as at Regensburg where Protestant substance was accepted in exchange for the acceptance of a measure of ambiguity."[46] Lane thus reads the general trend of the document as presenting Christ as the formal righteousness of believers, without explicitly affirming the imputation of an alien righteousness.[47]

American Lutheran theologian Michael Root rejoices that the Finnish critique of the early draft was heeded.[48] He sees the essential Reformation teaching preserved: The righteousness of the Christian is the very righteousness of Christ. We do partake of this righteousness, but justifying righteousness "is complete and perfect, even while the old person lives within us in such a way that we do not fulfill the central commandment to love God with all our heart, mind, and strength (the *simul iustus et peccator*).[49]

The Australian dialogue between Catholics and Lutherans reaffirms the Lutheran distinction between justification and sanctification: "Lutherans insist on the sanctification and regeneration that follow justification. They do not separate justification and sanctification, but they do distinguish between them in order to make it clear that justification comes entirely from God and not from what we do."[50] Catholics, as I have argued identify the formal cause of justification and sanctification, yet they do not see justification as a result of human activity. Thus the Australians' stated reason for the distinction does not suffice. Moreover, the Australians insist on using the language of imputation for forgiveness itself: "Our sins are no longer imputed to us, that is to say, they are no longer debited against us. This does not mean that we no longer commit actual sins, nor that we no longer struggle with sin in our lives. God's forgiveness means that, rather than the condemnation that our sins deserve, the righteousness of Christ is credited to us."[51] The Australians subsequently link this "crediting" to the first aspect of justification in the Catholic paradigm. They conclude that the "two dimensions" of justification in Catholic teaching are tantamount to the justification and sanctification in Lutheran teaching.

Polish Catholic theologian PaweŁ Holc raises some questions about the document but is fundamentally confident in its achievements. He raises questions about the declaration's Lutheran expression "simultaneously justified person and sinner," an expression to be treated in Chapter 9. He nevertheless accepts even the Lutheran description of justification as utterly "unconditional." Grace *never* becomes a human property about which the justified can boast.[52] Further, he reads the Lutheran paragraphs as teaching that sinners become "wholly just" because they are *pardoned* by God who *attributes* the righteousness of Christ to them.[53] Despite questions that remain, the agreement can be upheld, he claims, if both communions retain a reciprocal openness to different conceptions of "justice," i.e., transformative and declarative.[54] The two emphases, proclamation of forgiveness and genuine renewal, are complementary. This is true even of the most rigorously Lutheran documents: Although the *Formula of Concord* draws distinctions rigorously, it does not exclude renewal in the overall redemptive process.[55]

Scheffczyk notes the hesitancy of the JD to affirm the Catholic doctrine on the formal cause *even* in the Catholic paragraphs. This hesitancy, which would not in itself be false, leads in context to false statements. He thus charges the following statement in Lutheran par. 23, because of the absence of the Catholic doctrine, with error: "Justification remains free from human cooperation and is not dependent on the life-renewing effects of grace in human beings" (JD, 23). The statement is "plainly untridentine and false" because it implicitly denies the role of created grace.[56]

Wainwright appears to find something like the Regensburg compromise, à la Wesley, in the JD because of its linking both forgiveness and renewal together in the redemptive process. Recalling the theory of double justice, Wesley replaced the "*totus-totus* [totally just and totally sinner]" scheme with a "*partim-partim* [partially just and partially sinful]" scheme.[57] Understandably, many Lutherans will find it difficult to adhere to Wainwright's position, since it chafes against the *totus-totus* scheme, to which Lutherans are wed and which even appears in Lutheran par. 29, to be treated below.[58] Catholics, on the other hand, ought also to be chagrined when Wainwright observes:

> Wesley holds to Christ not only as (in his redemptive passion) the meritorious cause of justification (a point on which Lutherans and Catholics declare their agreement) but also as (in his transformative presence) its formal cause, a point that some Catholics have missed from the Joint Declaration.[59]

Christ is the formal cause of justification! If Wainwright is correct, then the JD opposes Trent's thunder (canon 10). His elusive remark—"a point that some Catholics have missed"—unwittingly offers a reason that the JD has enjoyed such remarkable acceptance among Catholics.

Bertram Stubenrauch remarks, "Justification and inner healing are harmoniously connected to one another."[60] The tethering does not preclude him from concluding that justifying righteousness is an alien justice. He claims that holding that the grace of justification is Christ himself poses no problem for Catholics.[61] He further differentiates between Christ's communication of grace and that of the sacraments. He holds that Christ's efficacious power and that of the sacraments ought not to be conflated. Doubtless, one can grant that Christ operates both in and outside of the sacraments. This is especially the case when one considers mystical graces, special callings, and gifts for the edification of the whole community. But when it comes to the communication of justifying grace through baptism, this differentiation poses a difficulty. Is Stubenrauch implying that the "res tantum," i.e., the effect common to every sacrament, is something *other* than sanctifying grace?[62] It appears that this is the case, for he contends that it is erroneous to believe that baptized persons "have" through the sacraments what they need to stand before God.[63] Faith justifies, he holds, because it *is* a relationship with Christ.[64] Still, it justifies sinners *outside of themselves*.[65] Stubenrauch then differentiates that through which humans touch God's saving power, justifying faith, from what results from this contact, a new creation or sanctification.[66] He concurs with the Göttingen statement, which was so critical of the elements of compromise in CRE: "The righteousness of Christ is human righteousness. However, it remains the righteousness of Jesus Christ: established outside of human beings (*extra nos*) and to that extent foreign (*iustitia aliena*)."[67]

Given the three emphatic statements in the JD, cited above, and the general consensus of interpreters, I find the principal weakness of the JD to be this: Its identification of Christ as the very righteousness by which the Christian stands just. The OVR overlooked this weakness and thus did not present an integrated diagnosis of the obstacles to consensus. Although the JD tethers together justification and sanctification, forgiveness and renewal, complete righteousness and good works, God's favor and active love, still, the declaration does not arrive at that essential unity on the level of the formal cause. The common and Lutheran paragraphs imply a distinction between the formal cause of forgiveness—let us call it justifying grace—and that of sanctification—let us call it sanctifying grace.

In response to this observation, some Catholics may well set against one another the rancor of the Missouri Synod and the rigidity of scholastic readings of Trent. They would hope to find themselves in the privileged "synthesis" of this dialectic. But this approach is not ecumenically helpful. We must pay due heed to the specific issues under contention and to the inviolable character of the principle of noncontradiction. The time has come to put the dialectics of caricatures aside and to peer into the abyss that once really divided the communions. If ignored, this abyss threatens to become a willfully ignored, inveterate wound.

Undoubtedly, numerous well-intentioned Catholic theologians will undertake hermeneutical gymnastics in order to retrieve this document on behalf of Catholic tradition. This effort is indeed understandable. Had the document magisterial force, I might have been more tempted to do the same. Notwithstanding the valiance of such efforts, I take it that few Lutherans will find such readings credible. Moreover, many will find such readings exemplary of an ecumenical disingenuousness. It is a safer course to countenance the possibility that the document itself is, from a genuinely Catholic perspective, fundamentally flawed. Having stated my thesis about the principle weakness of the JD, I now wish to defend it against two potentially weighty criticisms that might be leveled against it, especially by Catholics.

Anticipated Objections

The two weightiest arguments against my critique that remain are as follows: First, in harmony with the Finnish reading of Luther, justification and sanctification are ontologically linked, for they are linked through the believer's "union with Christ." Second, a subtler reading of the JD can justly interpolate the Catholic teaching on the "only formal cause," interpreting the justifying faith which alone justifies (*sola fide*) as constituted by the Catholic triad of faith, hope, and charity.

Justification and Sanctification Are "United in Christ"

When the JD declares Christ as our righteousness, it invariably includes the significant element that the believer is united with Christ. This ontological or genuinely personal union with Christ guarantees, so the argument may run, that the formal cause of forgiveness is not a merely extrinsic grace and that, in fact, it is identical with the formal cause of sanctification. The union with Christ appears as follows. Par. 15 suggests that believers participate in Christ's righteousness. Par. 22 insists that faith unites believers with Christ, who is himself both forgiveness and the saving or renewing presence of God.[68] Par. 23 maintains that only in union with Christ can one's life be renewed. Although it does not return to the formulation "Christ is our righteousness," par. 26 adds the important statement "Justification and renewal are joined in Christ, who is present in faith."

Quite happily, the theme of union with Christ came to have a prominent place in the dialogue. The JD describes the origin of this union in at least two ways. Union with Christ is a result of the indwelling of Christ. It can also occur through the believer's fellowship with Christ enjoyed through faith. These explanations of the "union with Christ" recall both Finnish research and Pannenberg's theology. Commenting on the final draft, Finnish Lutheran Bishop of Helsinki, Eero Huovinen, highlights the indwelling:

> The faith not only has Christ's work as its object, but in the faith Christ is present. Christ is not only "outside" of us, but comes "in" us. Through faith, Christ lives in the human being. Because Christ is our righteousness, we are not only declared righteous but we are also made righteous.[69]

Huovinen links the "union with Christ" to the insistence that Christ himself is our righteousness. Pannenberg's own theology anticipates the theme of union with Christ through faith, which brings sinners out of their old selves into

Christ.

The present formulations of the decree have been inspired chiefly by the Finnish critique of earlier drafts.[70] It is instructive to see why. Simo Peura critiqued the 1995 draft for failing sufficiently to *distinguish* the forensic and intrinsic aspects of justification. The draft stated, "God both declares and makes believers righteous" (JD 1995, par. 21). Peura offered this diagnosis:

> According to [the 1995 draft] the forensic aspect seems to characterize especially the Lutheran way of understanding justification, and the effective aspect explains specifically the Catholic point of view. The document indicates that the two aspects describe two different sides of the same thing.[71]

Resembling one of Küng's lines of thought, the draft described the forensic and intrinsic elements as but two sides of the same reality. Peura's diagnosis could apply equally well to both USA and CRE. Peura suggested the declaration take a different outlook: "Actually the two aspects are connected to each other so that we might properly say that they coexist side by side."[72] Peura intended a real distinction but not a separation. The union in distinction can be upheld, he urged, by recourse to the notion of "union with Christ." In this light his poignant criticism of the 1995 draft comes to light:

> Because of Luther's view of the real union with Christ, we can connect the effective aspect of justification to the forensic aspect. But this argument has not informed the method of [the 1995 draft of] the Joint Declaration. That document lacks totally the idea of union with Christ.[73]

The Finnish critique made its impact with the 1996 draft and certainly colors the final draft, enshrining Luther's saying and the title of Tuomo Mannermaa's work, *In Faith Itself Christ is Present*, in par. 26. Assuredly, Catholics can rejoice at the in-breaking of the Finnish school into the final draft, for attention to the multifarious richness of Christ's indwelling can draw Lutherans and Catholics closer together. The consequent fittingness of transformationist and ontological language supplies a greater basis for communication.

Notwithstanding the Finnish contributions, other forces are at work in the JD, some of which are in tension with the Finnish thesis. The extrinsic language savoring of expressions from the *Formula*, though not pronounced, is detectable. Indeed, it is sufficiently present to warrant Lane's judgment that Protestants have surrendered nothing in the decree. The traditional terminology associated with the extrinsic sense is present: "God does not impute their sins to them" (JD, 22); "The sinner is granted righteousness before God in Christ through the declaration of forgiveness" (JD, 23); "God's grace is forgiving love" (JD, 23); the enigmatic "God justifies sinners in faith alone (*sola fide*)";

the more emphatic "In the doctrine of 'justification by faith alone'" (JD, 26); and the explicit "by faith alone" (Annex 2–C); and "God [forgives them their sins through word and sacrament and awards or judicially grants the righteousness of Christ to them]" (JD, 29).[74] Moreover, a key passage referred to in the sources to section 4.2 is even more explicit:

> It is therefore no more than consistent when Protestant theology links the righteousness of the believer with the righteousness of Christ *extra se* ("outside himself"), in which the believer participates, and yet at the same time sees the justified person, as far as he himself is concerned, as still a sinner (*simul iustus et peccator*, at once righteous and as sinner); and when it also sees the heart of the event of justification as being a single, total (though continually new) divine act: in the forgiving pardon, in the non-imputation of sin, in the imputation of the righteousness of Christ—all of which are words for the same thing, namely, that the human person is again standing in a proper relationship to God.[75]

Bishop Huovinen comments that at least three Lutheran models for justification, present in the tradition, found a place in the final draft: "First, there is a 'forensic interpretation' of justification.... Second, there is a modern 'proclamationary-relational interpretation....' Third, there has also been within the Lutheran tradition an interpretation based on the real presence of Christ.... In the Joint Declaration there is an attempt to bring together elements of all these interpretations."[76] Bishop Huovinen observes that this diversity of Lutheran opinion makes the accord more complex, but he sees no reason to doubt its fruits. I would only note that according to the extrinsic sense, to which the above passages allude, the sinner is granted righteousness through a forensic acquittal by which sin is no longer imputed and Christ's own righteousness is imputed in its stead. Through faith, the believer appropriates this mercy of God in Jesus Christ.

This extrinsic approach does appear to be in tension with the Finnish reading, which promises a richer interpretation of the phrase "Christ in his person is our righteousness." The extrinsic reading manifestly contradicts Trent's teaching on inhering righteousness. Despite its numerous benefits, the Finnish reading also contradicts Trent, for it too implies that Christ, not infused grace, is the formal cause of justification.

Still, many remain eager to insist that there is no church-dividing division between the communions. Since Christ's righteousness as the formal cause of both justification and sanctification, Christ as both "grace and gift," does not supply the necessary evidence for consensus, some theologians will revisit the issue of the identity of that "through which" such righteousness comes to the sinner, faith.

Justifying Faith Includes Hope and Love: Catholic Interpolation

The Objection. The weightiest objection to my critique is the contention that one can interpolate in the JD the official Catholic teaching on the "only formal cause" in a roundabout manner. The case can be argued as follows, drawing upon the preparatory dialogues.[77] In the JD, the Lutheran notion of justifying faith appears not to differ in substance from what Catholics refer to as the virtues of faith, hope, and love. If faith, hope, and love can be considered to be "sanctifying grace," then Lutherans and Catholics concur that justification occurs precisely through what Catholics refer to as sanctifying grace. This being the case, the crux of the ancient dispute has finally been surmounted. One can detect direct and indirect evidence for this claim in the following texts:

> [Christians] place their trust in God's gracious promise by justifying faith, [in which are included] hope in God and love for him. Such a faith is active in love, and thus the Christian cannot and [may] not remain without works.... (JD, 25)[78]

> According to Lutheran understanding, God justifies sinners in faith alone (*sola fide*). In faith they place their trust wholly in their Creator and Redeemer and thus [are] in communion with him. God himself effects faith as he brings forth such trust by his creative Word. Because [this act of God] is a new creation, it [concerns or] affects all dimensions of the person and leads to a life in hope and love. In the doctrine of "justification by faith alone," [the renewal of one's way of life that necessarily follows from justification and without which no faith can exist is admittedly distinguished, but not separated, from justification. Rather, the basis is thereby] indicated from which [such] renewal of life [springs. The renewal of life proceeds from the love of God, which is given to the human person in justification]. Justification and renewal are joined in Christ, who is present in faith. (JD, 26)[79]

> The justification of sinners is forgiveness of sins and being made righteous by justifying grace, which makes us children of God. In justification the [justified] receive from Christ faith, hope and love and are [thus] taken into communion with him. (JD, 27)[80]
> Grace, as fellowship of the justified with God in faith, hope and love, is always received from the salvific and creative work of God. (Annex, 2–D)

> Protestant doctrine understands substantially under the one word *faith* what Catholic doctrine (following 1 Cor. 13:13) sums up in the triad of "faith, hope, and love." (Sources to 4.3)

In each of these paragraphs, justifying faith is linked to hope and love. Par. 25 hints at this: In justifying faith "are included [*eingeschlossen sind*] hope in God and love for him." Lutheran par. 26 offers a couple of interpretative guides to the common confession's "inclusion" of hope and love. On the one hand, it relegates these to the proper effects of God's justifying act: God's act "leads to a life in hope and love." On the other hand, it speaks of the "love of God" as "given" to the Christian in justification. Catholic par. 27 identifies both forgiveness and renewal as elements of justification, reading the term "justification" as both a divine pardon and an objective, ontological act. Again, it specifies that the justified person receives faith, hope, and love. The tenor of this excerpt of the paragraph is quite Catholic. The citation from the Annex, 2–D, characterizes grace as "fellowship" with God in the virtues of faith, hope, and love. This citation, too, appears to be quite harmonious with Catholic tradition. Finally, the citation from Sources to 4.3 is most explicit: Lutherans mean by justifying faith what Catholics mean by faith, hope, and love. In sum, these citations might appear to circumvent any dispute over "Christ as our righteousness" by drawing attention to the transformative character of the faith by which persons are justified. Though Lutherans insist that faith alone justifies, yet "faith alone" is not "only faith."[81] A good number of interpreters find the JD saying just this, and conclude that the dispute has been successfully overcome, locating remaining differences in the realms of terminology, concerns, emphases, and thought structures.

Nørgaard-Højen recognizes that the Lutheran paragraphs emphasize "in faith alone" but observes the Catholic paragraphs as holding, "Justifying faith is the *fides caritate formata*, no matter how much renewal in faith, hope and love is rooted in and dependent on 'God's unfathomable grace'...." He approves both the Lutheran doctrine and the Catholic hermeneutic. He pauses momentarily over the duality in par. 17, noted above, remarking, "Perhaps the Declaration is inconsistent—and more clearly Lutheran—when it states (no. 17) that 'as sinners our new life is *solely* due to the forgiving and renewing mercy that *God imparts as a gift and we receive in faith and never can merit in any way*' (italics mine [i.e., his])." Still, he bites at the bit of those who tighten the reins and strive too much for precision: "But here we encounter distinctions so subtle that it seems difficult, if not meaningless, to draw a clear border line between the confessions."[82] Notwithstanding the fact that these distinctions are, to the contrary, far from meaningless, his observations both about the tensions in the JD and about the attempted identification of justifying faith with *fides caritate formata* are on the mark.

Villar interprets "faith alone" in JD 26 to be a fiducial faith that includes hope in and love for God. He observes that in this Lutheran paragraph justification is compared to renovation as cause to effect. He sees in this comparison something complementary to the Catholic contention that the eternal love of God produces in the soul a created effect, namely, the created grace that justifies.[83] He argues that the term "created grace" was omitted from the decree in order to avoid the misimpression that Catholic faith maintains grace as some sort of "thing" in the human person.[84] It would seem that Villar considers the JD as containing the content, albeit not the traditional expression, of the Catholic teaching on created grace. I have argued that this is not the case; if Villar is correct, then the JD is more faithful to Trent than I have contended it is. Still, if this is the case, not only traditional Lutherans, but even the Finns and Pannenberg would have cause to question this element of the decree. Another Catholic, Fr. Michel Fédou, beautifully describes the gift of grace as impregnating the existence of the baptized and enabling the baptized to do good works. Surprisingly, he finds no substantial difference between the two communions.[85] Birmelé concurs, citing Vatican II's expansive reading of "faith" as a personal commitment.[86]

Kärkkäinen remarks of par. 26:

> This is a very carefully drafted explanation revealing the real struggle which the Lutheran Confessions bring to the question of forgiveness and renewal. The statement attempts to steer a middle course between the one-sided forensic view and the sanative view of Luther himself.[87]

Kärkkäinen reflects the intra-Lutheran disputes about justification as forensic and justification as restorative. He detects a compromise among the Lutheran party here. Moreover, and astutely, he relishes the diplomacy of the Lutheran party in employing Catholic language—the love of God *imparted* to the believer—to express the *Lutheran* concern: "The continuation of the Lutheran comment is interesting in that it dares to use the Catholic language of "impartation" of God's love."[88] Finally, the Institute for Ecumenical Research states, "As trust, this faith includes hope and love toward God" but adds the qualification, "This love toward God is to be differentiated from the love through which faith is active."[89] Similarly, Michael Root writes, "Faith *is* communion with God. Faith is thus itself regeneration." Still, although faith is itself regeneration, "That regeneration is not itself the Christian's righteousness." Christ alone is the Christian's righteousness.[90] Paweł Holc enigmatically adds that the document does not suggest "through (*per*) faith alone" but rather "by means of faith." Both communions agree that faith must not be and cannot be separated from love; it must be effective in works. The qualifier "alone," he maintains, enables us to distinguish between justification, which is unconditional, and salvation, which is its effect in our being; in the overall process, we are truly renewed.[91]

None of the above interpreters makes other than passing assertions that justifying faith is identical with what Catholics hold to be faith, hope, and love. I would like to undertake a serious argument on their behalf, in order that my responses to this counter-argument may be as responsible as possible.

An attempt must be made to avoid any detrimental inconsistency in the consensus. Nonetheless, as Nørgaard-Højen notes, an *apparent* tension cannot be denied. On the one hand, the JD attempts to link the Lutheran *sola fide* with the Catholic "faith, hope, and love," but on the other hand, it occasionally has a distinctively Lutheran ring. I would approach the tension with the following questions: Why does the JD distinguish sanctification—which for Catholics consists pre-eminently in sanctifying grace and the virtues of faith, hope, and charity—from justification—which the common and Lutheran paragraphs implicitly trace to Christ's righteousness as its formal cause? That is, why does the JD usually offer a merely twofold distinction between forgiveness through God's favor in Christ and the gift of new life? Why does the JD make no mention of the formal cause of justification as being "infused, inhering grace"?

Perhaps one can justifiably interpolate the tridentine teaching on the formal cause of justification. Perhaps the merely twofold distinction can be qualified by the subtle discernment of a more precise threefold distinction. That is, one can take the twofold distinction between justification and sanctification as an abridged expression for a *threefold* distinction between God's eternal mercy in Christ, infused grace or charity, and good works. Returning to the document, the reader could interpret the term "justification" (in the common and Lutheran paragraphs) as generally denoting God's action. The term "sanctification" (in the common and Lutheran paragraphs) could be taken as generally signifying the good works or "renewal of living" that follows God's action. Between these two terms, the reader could suppose a third factor lies latent in the common and Lutheran paragraphs but is nonetheless discernible. The Catholic paragraphs, the reader could argue, offer more explicit warrant for such a supposition. The somewhat latent factor would be sanctifying grace. In the common and Lutheran paragraphs, this factor often receives the name "faith" or "justifying faith," but its contents are not what Catholics mean by "only faith." Rather, justifying faith is said to contain (*enthaltet*, reading *einschliessen* emphatically) both hope and charity.[92] Indeed, Lutheran par. 26 even "dares to use the Catholic language of 'impartation' of God's love," as Kärkkäinen observes.[93] He is reading from the English, which states, "The renewal of life…comes forth from the love of God imparted to the person in justification." Sadly, the German is more accurately translated, "The renewal of life proceeds from the love of God which is given to the human person in justification." Kärkkäinen is correct to note that the word "imparts" has a Catholic ring, albeit not as emphatic as the word "infuses." Unfortunately, in the German we simply have "is given." In any case the clause is still noteworthy, for it is suggestive of Rom 5:5, a text with quite a *Wirkungsgeschichte* in Catholic tradition. The clause lends some credibility to the reading I am presently entertaining.

In the citations from par. 25, par. 27, Annex 2–D, and Sources to 4.3 listed above, the otherwise latent factor comes to the fore. The contention, then, is that the thrust of the JD is to identify justifying faith with faith, hope, and charity. This is an ecumenically potent possibility. Catholic faith holds that faith, hope, and charity render Christians truly pleasing to God, free them from all damnable sins, equip them to be more justified through good works, and enable them to merit eternal life. Therefore, faith, hope, and charity can be called the "grace that makes pleasing" and can be considered the "inhering grace" to which Trent refers in its definition of the "unica causa formalis." This third factor, both latent and expressed in the JD, could be said to "link" the distinguished terms "justification" and "sanctification." That is, it constitutes the precise effect of God's unchanging and eternal love—sanctifying grace—and in turn serves as an immanent principle of renewal. The phrases "Justification remains free from human cooperation" could be interpreted to mean that God, as first cause, operates without conditions and does not respond to the prior movements of man. Still, in light of this third factor intermediate between God's eternity and good works, the reader could assert that God operates through this gift, which he infuses, so that the justified human person is moved in the order of grace as one also inclined to good works. Moreover, as one made a child of God through adoption by the divine infusion of sanctifying grace, the Christian could truly be said to be worthy of eternal life, for "if children, then heirs" (Rom 8:17; Gal 4:7).[94]

Now if the JD actually admits of this reading in a consistent, albeit implicit, manner, then it indeed gives witness to a notable step forward in the ecumenical relations between Lutherans and Catholics. This, I take it, is the most incisive "Catholic" objection that can be leveled against my critique.[95] To examine it I would like to investigate, first, the Lutheran confessional teachings. It must be determined whether or not the reading is in concert with *The Book of Concord* and the mind of Luther, Melanchthon, et al. Any substantive tension here would imply that the contents of *The Book of Concord* have somehow been superseded on this most important point. Second, I will investigate more closely the common and Lutheran paragraphs in the JD; if the reading can withstand this attentive perusal, the JD is indeed a milestone.

Lutheran Teaching. This investigation falls into two parts. On the one hand, do the Lutheran confessions understand "sola fide" to include what Catholics mean by faith, hope, and charity? On the other hand, do the Reformers perceive the "granting" or "imparting" of the love of God that undergirds renewal in a manner compatible with the Catholic reading of Rom 5:5?

(1) Ecumenical dialogue has helped to show Catholics the richness of the Reformer's understanding of "faith," which is far from a merely intellectual assent to barren historical knowledge.[96] In addition, the Catholic Magisterium has adopted the personalist dimension in speaking of faith as a free, personal commitment to God (*Dei Verbum*, art. 5).[97] It is important to note, however, that

the living Magisterium distinguishes even this richer conception of faith from the triad of faith, hope, and charity, as John Paul II implies in the following citation (also cited in chapter 5): "In point of fact, man does not suffer perdition only by being unfaithful to that fundamental option whereby he has made a 'free self-commitment to God.'"[98] John Paul follows in the footsteps of Trent, which offers a clear emphasis on the essential role of charity in making the human person spiritually alive, that is, justified: "For faith, unless hope be added to it, and also charity, neither perfectly unites one with Christ, nor makes one a living member of his body."[99] Trent repeats this teaching in its treatment of reconciliation, the sacrament by which a baptized person who falls away can again be justified. By the grace of God, justification sometimes occurs before the sacrament is received, in anticipation of the sacramental grace. For Trent, though, regardless of when grace is received, justification always involves charity in the justifying power of faith, for the council admits that the event sometimes occurs before the reception of the sacrament, precisely when one's "sorrow for sin is made perfect by charity, and [he] is reconciled to God."[100]

As we have seen in Part I, Melanchthon's *Apology* describes justification in forensic terms and correlates "faith" with this justification. Faith, a work of the Spirit given to the sinner, reaches out and grasps the promise of forgiveness in Christ. Faith justifies in this way; it can be called "sanctify grace" in this way, not because it renders the believer truly pleasing to God. So, in another respect, faith does not justify:

> Since we also grant that love is the work of the Holy Spirit and since it is righteousness because it is the keeping of the law, why do we deny that it justifies? To this we must answer, first of all, that we do not receive the forgiveness of sins through love or on account of love, but on account of Christ by faith alone.[101]

Melanchthon excludes charity from faith's justifying power. Catholic scholars insist that Melanchthon was working with a notion of love or charity as a "work" of righteousness. They conclude that his understanding did not conflict with Trent, at least when Trent is interpreted as distinguishing the habit from the act of charity. Pfnür argued as much in his classic *Einig in der Rechtfertigungslehre*, which I have discussed in chapter 1. More recently, O'Callaghan, states the same: In Trent charity is "taken as the *infused virtue of charity*, which renews man's heart and animates Christian life and action from within." But Melanchthon understood charity differently: "Charity in this sense, as the *love of man for God resulting from the infusion of grace*, was considered by Melanchthon, a 'work', and therefore totally subordinate to faith."[102] I have shown in chapters 1 and 6 that although Melanchthon frequently took charity reductively as a work, he did not conceive of it as a merely human work, for it is the work of the Spirit. Moreover, he also understood it to be a gift bestowed by the same Spirit and yet denied that it qualifies the human person as just. Even the justified person is in himself condemnable, but God does not condemn him on account of his faith: "The incipient keeping of the law pleases God because of faith; because of faith our failure to keep it is not [reckoned] to us, although the sight of our impurity thoroughly frightens us."[103] Not even faith itself qualifies the human person as just. Now, if faith truly "made pleasing" in the Catholic sense, a believer would be able to fulfill the whole law of God (i.e., the New Law). According to the *Apology*, faith is a sinner's righteousness not because it is infused supernatural justice but because it is the instrument for the imputation of an alien righteousness.

The authors of the *Formula of Concord* intended to dispel lingering doubts about Melanchthon's meaning. According to this official Lutheran confession, faith apprehends the grace of God in Christ by which the believer is justified. Faith does this apart from charity: "From this office and property of application and appropriation we must exclude love and every other virtue or work." This does not mean that charity is excluded from Christian life; it does mean that charity constitutes no essential component of faith's justifying power:

> When we ask where faith gets the power to justify and save, and what belongs thereto, then it is false and incorrect to answer: Faith cannot justify without works; or, faith justifies or makes righteous in so far as it is associated with love, on account of which love the power to justify is ascribed to faith.... [Rather, faith] justifies solely for this reason and on this account, that as a means and instrument it embraces God's grace and the merit of Christ in the promise of the Gospel.[104]

Love is excluded from the justifying power of faith. Moreover, this love is not merely a work but a gift poured into the justified person. I would like to cite again an important passage from the *Formula*:

> We unanimously reject and condemn [the following error].... That when the prophets and the apostles speak of the righteousness of faith, the words "to justify" and "to be justified" do not mean "to absolve from sins" and "to receive forgiveness of sins," but to be made really and truly righteous on account of the love and virtues which are poured into them by the Holy Spirit and the consequent good works.[105]

Of course, as we have seen, the Finns, Pannenberg, and others beg to differ from these ossified distinctions in the *Formula*. They say Luther followed Paul more faithfully and manifested a more "Catholic" appreciation of the indwelling of Christ.[106] If they are right, Luther's work corrects the one-sidedness and even the errors of the *Formula*. But is this "correction" explicitly reflected in the JD? Moreover, was Luther himself wedded to the substance of the Tridentine teaching?

Writing in 1515, Luther asserted that no man can stand just before God, even if he is regenerated by the Spirit. Luther urged that, consequently, everyone should hope. His conception of hope even then fell short of the full scope of hope in Catholic tradition:

> That we are commanded to hope surely does not mean that we are commanded to do this in order that we might hope to have done it as we ought [i.e., to obey the commandments], but rather that the merciful Lord who alone can see into this abyss of ours (over the surface of which there are only shadows for us) does not account it to us for sin, as long as we confess it to Him.[107]

According to Luther, this confession must be perpetual, for even the regenerate are sinful: "They believe that they are always sinners, as if the depth of their evil will were infinite," for who would do good and avoid evil without fearing the law's thundering threats?[108]

He clung to this position throughout his career. In 1531, he still held all regenerate believers to be ever guilty of damn*able* sins, though these sins are (supposedly) not damn*ing* in their effect because of faith: "The Law and works do not redeem from the curse. On the contrary, they drag us down and subject us to the curse. Therefore love, which, according to the sophists, 'informs' faith, not only does not redeem from the curse but forces and wraps us into it even more."[109] Most Lutherans have perceived Luther as considering these sins truly mortal in themselves. They see them as not damning *only* in their effect; that is, they are "ruled sins." More progressive Lutherans identify "ruled sins" with venial sins and claim that Luther teaches that no mortal sins coexist with faith. Luther himself spoke not of the expulsion of all damnable sins but of their being not held against the sinner's account, of their not being imputed (*zugerechnet* or *angerechnet*). Although "There are still remnants of sin in the saints because they do not believe perfectly, nevertheless these remnants are dead; for on account of faith in Christ they are not imputed."[110] He concluded, "It is evident that faith alone justifies."[111] This is not a faith quickened by charity; faith's justifying power is independent of charity: "[Paul] says that works are done on the basis of faith through love, not that a man is justified through love."[112]

Although Luther too often lampooned charity as merely a human "work," he showed enough savvy to penetrate beyond the meager fodder that Biel served. He also tasted the better Catholic tradition on charity as an infused habit, and he stomached it none the more. He rightly chastised the aberrant Pelagians who held that fallen men can obey God's law as to the content of the law without grace, but this was not enough for him. He also protested against the claim that obedience to God's law out of supernatural charity is a necessary condition for salvation. Recounting the Catholic position, he wrote, "[God] requires in addition that you keep the Law in love—not the natural love that you have but a supernatural and divine love that He Himself confers. What is this but to make God a tyrant and a tormentor who demands of us what we cannot produce?"[113] Did not Pelagius serve up the same bilious question to Augustine, who prayed, "Give what you command, and command what you will." Luther indeed recognized this charity as a "quality that inheres in the will, granted by God over and above the love we have by our natural powers."[114] Luther nonetheless eschewed this view and substituted his own in its stead: "Our 'formal righteousness' is not a love that informs faith; but it is faith itself."[115] Because damnable sins remain even in the justified, despite the union with Christ established through faith, sins are forgiven not through a bestowed gift but through a sheer imputation.[116]

There is a twofold logic for justification through faith in these lectures on Galatians. As both Pannenberg and the Finns among others argue, only justification by faith rescues the human person from self-contemplation or prideful self-relation. This is the primary basis for the dictum "through faith alone." Luther subscribed to this view, but he also gave evidence of another logic behind the dictum: The insufficiency of Christian charity demands as much. Christ's own righteousness is that by which believing sinners stand just.[117] The latter logic is rooted in the Augustinian model of transformation. Faith's justifying power is independent of infused charity, even though it must issue in charitable deeds, precisely because *this side of the grave* charity cannot withstand God's wrath.[118] This role of faith is intimately linked with the virtue of hope, without which, Luther sometimes said, faith is of no great consolation. It is for this reason that Manns suggests that Luther perceived a double role for hope. First, hope carries the believer through the dark night of faith, in which the believer is hardly aware of the righteousness already present through faith. Hope makes the terrors of the believing sinner bearable. Second, hope also enables the believer to be confident that progress in sanctification is possible.[119] Faith is necessary so long as this process is not yet complete, since the incomplete character of this process can occasion terror. Manns thus sees Luther as linking, through hope, the righteousness attributed to the believing sinner on account of faith with the eschatological consummation of sanctification. In heaven, that process will be completed; therefore, the saints no longer need either faith or hope. "Consequently," Manns writes, "the primacy of faith is only provisional and temporary, lasting as long as the perfect and eternal righteousness of love is held back."[120]

Luther, Melanchthon, and the authors of the *Formula* agreed that "justifying faith" justifies apart from charity even though it issues in charity. The Lutheran insistence on justification through faith alone is therefore not compatible with the Catholic teaching that faith justifies a person and makes him a living member of Christ precisely by its inclusion of charity. Rather,

Lutheran faith is more akin to Catholic faith and hope. Pope John Paul II shares the Lutheran concern to recognize sin for what it is, especially in our time too chary to acknowledge sin and to trust in God. He recognizes that the law cuts to the quick, for no one can fulfill it without grace. Despite this, Christ is the hope of sinners. John Paul's exhortation to hope runs in a different direction that Luther's, urging that we pray with St. Augustine, "Grant what you command and command what you will." Augustine's prayer is urgent because obedience to the commandments is a necessary condition for salvation. Augustine's prayer cuts two ways: upholding the demands of law and recognizing human poverty before God. What offended Pelagius on account of God's injustice later offended Luther on account of our unrighteousness. If Pelagius gave way to pride, Luther gave way to despair and, subsequently, to a different form of presumption. John Paul II's magisterial teaching navigates the middle path of hope, reminding the flock that justifying righteousness is not something acquired but a gift. His work ushers the flock on by promising that this gift enables adequate and concrete obedience to all of God's commandments.[121] Though Lutherans can follow John Paul to a certain extent, they cannot follow him this far without severing themselves from the *sola fide* of the past.

The *Apology* and the *Formula* present insurmountable obstacles to the reading of the JD I entertain in the objection. For if the JD in fact espouses the idea that faith's justifying power is dependent upon infused charity, then the JD conflicts with the Lutheran confessions. But if it so conflicts, then it cannot rightly declare a "consensus" that renounces neither of the communions' Reformation era teachings. Even if the Finnish solution and that of Pannenberg lead in the right direction, they do not go far enough and they, too, imply the necessity of doctrinal alteration of past Lutheran and Catholic doctrines. Now, what of the Lutheran reading of "imparted love"? Do Lutherans understand "the love of God imparted to the person in justification" as Catholics do?

(2) For Catholics, the "imparted love" (Rom 5:5) that constitutes the essence of justifying righteousness is the infused grace or charity that renders the baptized pleasing to God, can increase through good works, and enables acts properly meritorious of eternal life.[122] The Reformers denied that inhering grace can justify. Logically, therefore, they could offer only two interpretations of imparted love, each of which contrasts with the Catholic reading. "Imparted love" can mean, on the one hand, the Holy Spirit's uncreated love, which is "given" to the sinner either through imputation or through an indwelling (and/or ecstatic faith fellowship) that does not purge away all damnable sins. On the other hand, "imparted love" can mean the inchoate righteousness that logically follows justification. In the former case, "imparted love" is the Holy Spirit's uncreated love, understood in a manner incompatible with Trent's

inhering justice. In the latter case, imparted love is not identified as the formal cause of forgiveness, because it is always deficient in this life. In both cases, the formal cause of justification is Christ's righteousness or the love itself of the Holy Spirit by which Christ's righteousness is imputed, for despite the indwelling, damnable sin supposedly remains.

Luther's work bears witness to this logical alternative. His thought followed a trajectory towards an explicit distinction between justifying faith and imparted love. As a Catholic, he spoke eloquently of the love of God imparted to the believer. He described this love as truly poured out and truly enabling one to love God above all things. It is the gift given through the Holy Spirit. Yet what precisely did he mean by this reading of Romans?[123] Is this gift the love itself of the Holy Spirit (a subjective genitive)? Or was Luther referring to the love by which humans love God? In this commentary, Luther did not clearly distinguish the imparted "gift" from the grace itself of Christ. He wrote, "But 'the grace of God' and 'the gift' are the same thing, namely, the very righteousness which is freely given to us through Christ."[124] This grace he earlier specified as that "by which He justifies us, which actually is in Christ as in its origin, just as the sin of man is in Adam."[125] Was this a Catholic rendering of the distinction between God's own or Christ's own justice and the imparted gift whereby God justifies sinners? It is not clear, but it might be possible to answer in the affirmative. On the one hand, Luther identified gift and grace; on the other hand, he seemed to locate the identity in the fact that Christ is the source of that gift.[126] We see a similar position, most beautifully articulated, in his early commentary on Galatians:

> This is a righteousness that is bountiful, given without cost, firm, inward, eternal, true, heavenly, divine; it does not earn, receive, or seek anything in this life. Indeed, since it is directed toward Christ and His name, which is righteousness, the result is that the righteousness of Christ and of the Christian are one and the same, united with each other in an inexpressible way. For it flows and gushes forth from Christ, as he says in John 4:14.[127]

There appears here something similar to the tridentine distinction between Christ's own grace and that which flows from him into the believer. This position holds promise. Regrettably, this realistic understanding of the communication of Christ's righteousness does not appear to remain in Luther's later works. Had he followed through the realism of Rom 5 and 6 on this point—that as by one man's sin all *became* sinners so by one man's righteousness all are *to be made* righteous—he might have had less reason to leave the Catholic fold.

Sadly, even in this commentary on Galatians, Luther acknowledged that despite the benefits of the imparted gift of charity, damnable concupiscence remains, but God "does not impute [this] sin but heals it; for if He wanted to impute it, as He could truly and justly do, it would be altogether mortal and damnable."[128] Moreover, concupiscence is an inclination not only of the flesh but of the "whole man," that is, spirit, soul, and body.[129] In marked contrast with the Catholic tradition (which has since become doctrine), Luther asserted that charity does not cast out damnable sin but abides with it, even though it fights against sin. How is it that Luther's praises of imparted love were so soon overshadowed?

Luther's thought culminated in his 1531 *Lectures on Galatians*. In this work, he clearly recognized that imparted or infused love cannot justify because it is too weak in this life. Luther distinguished gift and grace but noted the inadequacies of the former. He stated, "We do indeed receive the gift and the first fruits of the Spirit here (Rom 8:23), so that we do begin to love; but this is very feeble."[130] It is weak because "our corrupt love of ourselves is so powerful that it greatly surpasses our love of God and of our neighbor."[131] Therefore, we are saved only by the faith that, through the imputation of Christ's righteousness, makes up for the deficiencies of our charity on earth.[132] He concluded:

> If we believe in Him, sin is not imputed to us. Therefore, faith is our righteousness in this present life. In the life to come, when we shall be thoroughly cleansed and shall be completely free of all sin and fleshly desire, we shall have no further need of faith and hope.
>
> Therefore it is a great error to attribute justification to a love that does not exist or, if it does, is not great enough to placate God.... But meanwhile we are sustained by the trust that Christ ... covers us with His righteousness.[133]

That which justifies, then, is Christ's own righteousness, imputed to faith. Earlier in the same commentary, Luther insisted that obedience to the law would justify someone if his obedience were perfect and from the heart. Since there is no one that so obeys God, righteousness is by faith through an imputation:

> Where is the one who loves God with all his heart, etc., and his neighbor as himself? Therefore there is no one who keeps the Law.... Yet a believer does keep the Law; but what he does not keep is forgiven him through the forgiveness of sins for Christ's sake, and what sin there is left is not imputed to him.... Because of our faith in Christ what we do not keep is not imputed to us. But in the life to come believing will cease, and there will be a correct and perfect keeping and loving. For when faith ceases, it will be replaced by glory, by means of which we shall see God as He is (1 John 3:2). There will be a true and perfect knowledge of God, a right reason, and a good will, neither moral nor theological but heavenly, divine, and eternal. Meanwhile we must persevere here in faith that has the forgiveness of sins and the imputation of righteousness through Christ.[134]

Again, part of the logic employed here is that righteousness through faith is the only solution to the inevitable sinfulness of humankind. Once God thoroughly purifies human persons, the need for faith vanishes. Apparently, ultimate trust in oneself is no danger for those in glory! The saints do not need to rely on faith in order to be preserved from self-relatedness. The gifts divinely bestowed upon them, ever flowing from their source, so purify them that they actually love God as his righteous children. It is difficult to conceive of this logic in any other way than through the Augustinian scheme of transformation.[135] If one is not pure, one can be righteous only through imputation. Once righteous, one no longer needs faith. The ever-present *lack* of perfection in charity, while the pilgrim sojourns on earth, determines the need for another mode of righteousness. Once such love is established in its perfection, there is no need for another mode of righteousness. This logic remains intact even if Luther incessantly pled, as did the *Formula of Concord*, that the inchoate obedience of believers constitutes not even part of the imputed righteousness of faith. While sinners make their pilgrim way through this vale of tears, they must be protected from the *possibility* that they would even slightly trust in themselves or in that which God has done *within them*. But the very necessity of this protective measure vanishes when perfect love dawns in the heart of the saint. At that point, there is no need for a "second righteousness."[136]

Luther was not alone in his opinion that imparted love, considered as a gift distinct but not separate from grace, does not justify because damnable sin remains. Luther's followers adhered to the same idea, namely, that Christ's own righteousness is that righteousness by which sinners stand just because inhering righteousness remains too weak. Melanchthon wrote, "[Christ] himself is their propitiation, for whose sake they are now accounted righteous. But when they are accounted righteous, the law cannot accuse or condemn them, even though they have not really satisfied the law."[137] The corroborative evidence for this reading of Melanchthon is his refusal to admit an increase in justifying grace. Infused grace can increase, since it is a participation in God's perfect grace. So, if the formal cause of forgiveness were infused grace, it could increase. But Melanchthon denied that justifying grace can increase: "The forgiveness of sins is the same and equal to all, as Christ is one."[138] He likewise denied merit its proper significance, admitting, "Because our works do not merit our justification, which makes us sons of God and co-heirs with Christ, we do not merit eternal life by our works."[139] The justified can merit only bodily and spiritual goods that are "other" than eternal life itself.[140]

Finally, the *Formula of Concord* does not admit of a Catholic understanding of imparted or infused love, that which lies between God's mercy through Christ and a life of good works. The *Formula* usually draws a merely twofold distinction between justification and sanctification, describing the first as extrinsic and the second as intrinsic. When the *Formula* adverts to a threefold distinction (forensic justification, inner sanctification, and good works), it clearly conflicts with Catholic teaching. The *Formula* holds that only the first item of the triad justifies, though the other two follow: "Faith apprehends the grace of God in Christ whereby the person is justified. After the person is justified, the Holy Spirit next renews and sanctifies him, and from this renewal and sanctification the fruits of good works will follow."[141] The *Formula* does not admit of a Catholic reading of imparted love as the term that mediates between God's mercy and good works and as the term that refers to the reality by which people are formally justified.

In summary, if "imparted love" is read as the indwelling of the Holy Spirit or as the favor of God, it is not identifiable with what Catholics call the "formal cause" of justification. If it is read as "inchoate righteousness," it is deemed incapable of enabling the believer to escape hell and merit heaven. In either case, that by which one is justified is not infused, inhering grace or charity. Therefore, in either case, the Catholic teaching is not upheld. We encounter the difficulty again: If the JD is to reconcile the two communions, it must include admission of doctrinal revision. Leaving this difficulty aside, we can turn to the declaration itself.

The Joint Declaration. The question to be pursued now is, does the JD supply a consist warrant, without insurmountable obstacles, for the reading proposed above, according to which justifying faith includes the triad of faith, hope, and charity? I propose several related answers. First, the JD's common and Lutheran paragraphs show only passing signs that such a reading is admissible. Contrary to the English translation, par. 26 does not speak of the "love of God *imparted* to the believer" but rather of the love of God "given" to the believer. Similarly, par. 17 does not suggest that "God imparts as a gift" forgiving and renewing mercy. There is no substantive "gift [*Geschenk*]" and we only "accept and receive" this love. The language is hardly precise enough to suggest clearly the Catholic connotation of infusion. A similar absence of the substantive "gift," misleadingly present in the English, appears in par. 22. Second, nowhere in the JD is there an unambiguous teaching on the formal cause of justification itself. There often appears a merely twofold distinction, à la the Lutheran confessions, between forgiveness through God's favor and sanctification or renewal through God's effective power. At times, admittedly, the twofold distinction admits of some ambiguity, which might allow for a Catholic reading. Faced with these isolated, ambiguous statements, the reader must determine as best as possible the likely meaning. I will consider one key text and a set of parallel statements.

The following key text, a Lutheran paragraph already cited, deserves further study:

> When [Lutherans say] that God's grace is forgiving love ("the favor of God"[12] [note 12
> of JD, in text below]), they do not thereby deny the renewal of the Christian's life.
> They intend rather to express that justification remains free from human cooperation
> and [also] is not dependent on the life-renewing effects of grace in human beings. (JD,
> 23)
>
> [12] WA 8:106; American ed., 32:227.

What is the meaning of the second sentence: "Justification remains free from
human cooperation and [also] is not dependent on the life-renewing effects of
grace in human beings"? As noted above, Scheffczyk finds that it logically
entails the denial of the Catholic doctrine on inhering grace. But perhaps it is
a bit more ambiguous than Scheffczyk makes out. Perhaps the term "grace"
signifies infused grace. If so, the "effects" of which justification is said to be
independent would not be inhering grace. Justification would not, then, be
"independent" of inhering grace. Perhaps these effects, of which justification
is independent, are "good works." If this is what the Lutherans mean, they
might still be open to admitting inhering grace as the formal cause of
justification. Read in this light, the statement asserts not that justification is
(formally) independent of infused charity or grace but rather that justification
is independent of good works. The statement would, then, be harmonious with
Catholic faith, and Scheffczyk's complaint, unjustified.

This reading is clearly favorable from a Catholic point of view, but it is
most difficult if not impossible to maintain. The first statement in the above
citation discourages the reader from interpreting the text in this way: "When
[Lutherans] stress that *God's grace is forgiving love* ("the favor of God"), they
do not thereby deny the renewal of the Christian's life" (emphasis mine). For
those familiar with Reformation idioms, it should be evident that the phrases
"God's grace"; "forgiving love"; and "the favor of God" stand not for an
inhering grace that makes the justified person truly and inwardly pleasing to
God. Instead, the "favor of God" refers to God's mercy by which he declares
the sinner forgiven of still-extant sin that is incipiently purified through God's
gifts and human cooperation (if we can attribute cooperation to the justified).
Inner transformation logically follows this attribution of righteousness, remains
compatible with damnable sins, and is therefore unable to satisfy God's wrath.
Charity, accordingly, is simply that which logically follows faith and from
which faith's saving power is independent. This appears to be the sense in
which the Lutherans involved in the JD wish to affirm that faith "includes"
hope and love: "Because [this act of God] is a new creation, it [concerns or]
affects all dimensions of the person *and leads to* a life in hope and love" (JD,

26, emphasis mine). They accurately reflect the common paragraph: "Such a faith is active in love" (JD, 25).

It is instructive to consider the different emendations to the Joint Declaration that led to this final formulation. The 1995 draft reads: "When Lutherans understand the grace of God above all as forgiving love, they do not thereby deny the life-renewing power of grace" (JD 1995, par. 22). The text appears to leave some room, however small, that this is but one way in which Lutherans understand "the grace of God." The text does not necessarily exclude an understanding of infused grace as the formal cause of justification, even if such a reading rubs against Lutheran exegesis. As will be shown in chapter 8, moreover, the Catholic paragraph of this draft explicitly affirms created grace. The 1996 draft is less open-ended: "When Lutherans stress that God's grace is forgiving love, they do not thereby deny the life-renewing power of grace" (JD 1996, par. 23).[142] In the 1996 draft, it is not that Lutherans simply understand God's grace as being above all forgiving love. Rather, it is that Lutherans *stress* that God's grace *is* forgiving love. But the final draft removes all doubt about the identity of God's grace. The final draft includes the important addition of the following phrase in parentheses: "the favor of God." This addition identifies the grace as God's eternal mercy. The final draft includes, as well, the addition of an endnote (note 12), which is a reference to Luther's *Antilatomus*, written in 1521. The work was Luther's response to a Catholic theologian from Louvain named Latomus. Many of the ecumenically fruitful suggestions of Lutheran theologians make reference to this work. For instance, perhaps the most important ecumenical source for the JD, the German dialogue, refers to Luther's *Antilatomus* as a central source for grasping Luther's pregnant distinction between gift and grace. The distinction is identified as crucial to a resolution of the apparent antithesis between the teachings on the essence of justification. CRE rightly recognizes the issue of the essence of justification as the heart of the dispute and rightly pinpoints Luther's *Antilatomus* as the relevant source in which to investigate the ecumenically useful distinction between gift and grace.[143] The Finns also make abundant use of this text. Not surprisingly, a footnote to this text now appears in the final draft.

Given the consensus on the importance of this work, I hope the reader will pardon me for a lengthy citation. This passage should make Luther's position crystal clear:

> For the gospel also teaches and preaches two things, namely, the righteousness and the grace of God. Through righteousness it heals the corruption of nature. This is done by the true righteousness which is the gift of God, namely, faith in Christ.... Almost always in Scripture, this righteousness which is contrary to sin refers to an innermost root whose fruits are good works. The companion of this faith and righteousness is grace or mercy, the good will [*favor*] of God, against wrath which is the partner of sin,

so that he who believes in Christ has a merciful God.... Here, as ought to be done, I take grace in the proper sense of the favor of God—not a quality of the soul, as is taught by our more recent writers. This grace truly produces peace of heart until finally a man is healed from his corruption and feels he has a gracious God.... Faith is the gift and inward good which purges the sin to which it is opposed.... The grace of God, on the other hand, is an outward good [*externum bonum*], God's favor, the opposite of wrath....

We therefore have two goods of the gospel against the two evils of the law: the gift on account of sin, and grace on account of wrath. Now it follows that these two, wrath and grace, are so related—since they are outside us—that they are poured out upon the whole, so that he who is under wrath is wholly under the whole of wrath, while he who is under grace is wholly under the whole of grace, because wrath and grace have to do with persons. He whom God receives in grace, He completely receives, and he whom He favors, He completely favors....

Now we finally come to the point. A righteous and faithful man doubtless has both grace and the gift. Grace makes him wholly pleasing so that his person is wholly accepted, and there is no place for wrath in him any more, but the gift heals from sin and from all his corruption of body and soul. It is therefore most godless to say that one who is baptized is still in sin, or that all his sins are not fully forgiven. For what sin is there where God is favorable and wills not to know any sin, and where he wholly accepts and sanctifies the whole man? However, as you see, this must not be attributed to our purity, but solely to the grace of a favorable God. Everything is forgiven through grace, but as yet not everything is healed through the gift. The gift has been infused.... It works so as to purge away the sin for which a person has already been forgiven, and to drive out the evil guest for whose expulsion permission has been given. In the meantime, while this is happening, it is called sin, and is truly such in its nature; but now it is sin without wrath, without the law, dead sin, harmless sin, as long as one perseveres in grace and his gift. And as far as its nature is concerned, sin in no way differs from itself before grace and after grace; but it is indeed different in the way it is treated. It is now dealt with otherwise than before.... Now it is treated as non-existent and as expelled. Despite this, it is truly and by nature sin. Indeed, it is ingratitude and injury to the grace and gift of God to deny that it truly is sin....

I say and teach thus so that every man may know that he has just as much sin in every one of his own works as the amount of sin which has not yet been expelled from him.... Thus he will not boast before God of the cleanliness which he has in himself, but will rather glory in the grace and gift of God, and in the fact that he has a gracious God on his side who does not impute this sin and, besides this, has given the gift through which it is purged away. He therefore confesses the truth that if he must be judged according to the nature of his works apart from grace, he cannot stand before His face; but now, because he relies upon grace, there is nothing which can accuse him....

Therefore, since this opinion of mine favors godliness, agrees with the words of Scripture, and is simple and sound both in its expression and content, I will not let "sin"—as a term applicable to all men and to all their works in this life—be taken from me, even though I confess that there is nothing of sin or of evil works in them from the perspective of God's grace....

I reject [the Louvainian] opinion, and say that sin and trust [in God] are simultaneously present in us and in all our works as long as we are on this earth....

However, you may say that we seem to be tormented by a verbal disagreement over a matter on which we essentially agree, for neither party asserts that what remains after baptism—whether sin or penalty—deserves damnation. I answer that we agree on the end—namely, that it is harmless—but not at all on why this is so....

For, as I have said, true faith is not what they have invented, an absolute—nay, rather, obsolete—quality in the soul, but it is something which does not allow itself to be torn away from Christ, and relies only on the One whom it knows is in God's grace. Christ cannot be condemned, nor can anyone who throws himself upon him. This means that so grave a matter is the sin which remains, and so intolerable is God's judgment, that you will not be able to stand unless you shield yourself with him whom you know to be without any sin. This is what true faith does....

Then you shall know that you cannot make this sin great enough, for absolutely no man can ever discover or comprehend his wickedness, since it is infinite and eternal.[144]

There are four interrelated terms at work here: sin, wrath, gift, and grace. Sin is an internal evil, and gift, an internal good at war with sin. Wrath is in external evil, God's anger over sin and his threat of punishment. Grace is an external good warring against wrath; it is that by which God forgives the sinner. Grace and gift are distinguished, the former identified with God's eternal mercy and the latter with the transforming blessings God infuses into the sinner. Since the work of the gift remains incomplete, the sinner is ever actually damnable, but he is not damned because he is protected by God's favor. Grace and gift are inseparable, but gift does not remove all damnable sin.

There can be no doubt that Luther herein distinguished gift and grace and denied that the "gift" can formally justify someone before God's throne.[145] Since it cannot do so, the gift must not be considered one's justification. That is, only Christ's own righteousness is justifying righteousness, which on account of faith is attributed to the believer who remains a mortal sinner (i.e., guilty of damn*able* sin) until death. Mortal sin is not destroyed though the "gift" begins to war against it. Instead, mortal sin is not imputed if the human person, having faith, makes a sincere effort to struggle against it. This effort constitutes the individual's cooperation with the gift and the purgative effects thereof. Nevertheless, this effort is not that which Catholics describe as satisfactory obedience to the New Law, for sin remains and remains damnable.[146] German theologian Paul Althaus captures the essence of Luther's thought well, paying due heed to Luther's affirmation of a genuine beginning of sanctification but retaining the place of remnant sin: "For this reason [the Christian] cannot stand in God's judgment even with his new being. For he constantly has the old man beside him, and thus even with his new obedience remains completely a sinner and damnable before God."[147]

Let me return to the key text in JD, 23:

When [Lutherans] stress that God's grace is forgiving love ("the favor of God"[12]), they do not thereby deny the renewal of the Christian's life. They intend rather to express that justification remains free from human cooperation and is not dependent on the life-renewing effects of grace in human beings.

[12] WA 8:106; American ed., 32:227.

The final clause reads, "Justification...is not dependent on the life-renewing effects of grace." Read in its context and in accordance with the source to which the JD refers, the term "grace" must refer to the eternal mercy or favor of God by which the believer is considered just in his sight. This grace is not identifiable with what Catholics refer to as "inhering grace." Since it asserts that justification is "independent" of the effects of grace, par. 23 logically denies that justification consists formally in the transformation of the Christian through infused grace and charity. Now, Catholic doctrine can admit that (first) justification is independent of the effects of grace, but *only* upon the supposition that the term "grace" signifies inhering, sanctifying grace and that the term "effects" refers to good works. Since the Lutherans do not intend to use the terms in this way, this statement cannot fall under the rubric of "legitimate diversity." It is most unfortunate for the ecumenical situation that this use of the term "grace" is, at first sight, so obscure as to prevent clear communication about the sense of the text. The textual ambiguity inhibits a mutual recognition of the incompatibly divergent interpretations of this statement that each communion must render if it wishes to remain faithful to its heritage.

A set of parallel phrases on the necessity of "faith alone" is also worthy of note. The 1995 draft of the JD did not make reference to justification "through faith alone [*allein durch den Glauben*]." This was a noteworthy omission and was not well-taken by Lutherans. We may recall that the German faculty of Göttingen had criticized CRE for a similar omission.[148] The 1996 text added a statement approximating the precise "by faith alone" but still left matters sufficiently ambiguous: "According to Lutheran understanding, sinners receive righteousness before God [in] faith alone [*allein im Glauben*]" (JD 1996, par. 26). The same text also stated in passing, "'Justification by faith alone' entails a renewal" (JD 1996, par. 26). The 1997 draft retains the sense of these two passages from the 1996 draft but describes the phrase "by faith alone" as "doctrine." Despite these additions, a large number of German Lutheran professors still protested that the JD did not achieve a consensus on the fact that "the sinner is justified by faith alone."[149] Perhaps in light of strong criticism on this point from professors, the Annex includes the following statement: "Justification takes place 'by grace alone' (JD, 15 and 16), *by faith alone*, the person is justified 'apart from works' (Rom. 3:28, cf. JD, 25)" (Annex, 2–C, emphasis mine).[150] This addition in the Annex caught many an eye. It was a remarkable gain from the Lutheran perspective. Theologians vociferously critical of the lack of distinctively Lutheran thought in the JD received this statement with joy. Eberhard Jüngel, for one, exclaimed, "NB: through faith alone, sola fide.... It is worth holding your breath."[151]

Jüngel's delighted astonishment ought to be echoed by dismal wailing among Catholics. One noteworthy example of Catholic perplexity can be found in Avery Cardinal Dulles's subtly registered complaint. Pursuing a commonly known ecumenical claim, Dulles stated that Catholics can accept the phrase "faith alone" only if faith includes hope and charity. Dulles went on to note, however, that a Lutheran paragraph of the JD proposes, against the very teachings of Trent, that faith *cannot* exist without renewal and justification. Indeed, Dulles is right on the mark, and the German text makes this all the more clear. Whereas the English is stated factually, "without which (renewal) faith does not exist," the German is stated logically, "without which no faith can exist." That is, no faith can exist without renewal. Trent teaches the contrary, that true and supernatural faith can exist without justification. Dulles's remarks implicitly question whether or not the JD *really* includes hope and charity in the formally justifying power of faith.[152]

Even before the release of the Annex, Wolfhart Pannenberg, reading the JD alone, tacitly ascribed to the Catholic proponents of the JD a substantive modification of doctrine. He wrote, "The Catholic side no longer calls faith—as at the Council of Trent (DS 1532)—the mere 'beginning' of justification."[153] In light of my analysis in chapter 5 of Pannenberg's criticism of substantial elements of Trent, this statement is loaded. Pannenberg criticized Trent as being utterly unable to provide scriptural support for its contention that faith is merely the beginning of justification, a beginning in need of the quickening power of infused charity. Lane, in addition, ascribed substantive change to the Catholic Church, not to the Protestant traditions. Finally, the Lutheran World Federation declared, "The good news of justification refers to people's experiences and proclaims clearly that human beings are saved, not by works, but only by faith, through grace, on the merit of Jesus Christ alone.... *We do not need to do anything for our salvation*" (emphasis mine).[154] This remark, outrageous from a Catholic perspective, ought to sound the alarm or toll the funereal bell in all quarters of the Catholic world. It is clear that many a competent theologian is under the impression that the Catholic Church has substantially changed her doctrine in a manner far different from organic development. These interpretations further validate my concern that the JD's common and Lutheran paragraphs do not admit of an authentically Catholic interpretation. Now I turn to the Catholic paragraphs.

NOTES

1   George Lindbeck would not seem to share my assessment of the sobriety of past thinkers (see George Lindbeck, "Response to Gabriel Fackre on the Joint Declaration," section in *Story Lines: Chapters on Thought, Word, and Deed [For Gabriel Fackre]*, ed. Skye Fackre Gibson [Grand Rapids: Eerdmans Publishing Company, 2002], pp. 26–27).

2   Dulles, "Justification: The Joint Declaration."

3   William Rusch, "The History and Methodology of the *Joint Declaration on Justification*: A Case Study in Ecumenical Reception," in *Agapè: Études en l'honneur de Mgr Pierre Duprey M. Afr., Évêque Tit. De Thibar*, ed. Jean-Marie Roger Tillard (Geneva: Centre Orthodoxe du Patriarcat Œcuménique, 2000), p. 182.

4   Harding Meyer, "La 'Déclaration Commune sur la Doctrine de la Justification' du 31 Octobre 1999," in *Agapè: Études en l'honneur de Mgr Pierre Duprey M. Afr., Évêque Tit. De Thibar*, ed. Jean-Marie Roger Tillard (Geneva: Centre Orthodoxe du Patriarcat Œcuménique, 2000), p. 193. For his article on this issue before the final draft was released see idem, "Ecumenical Consensus: Our Quest for and the Emerging Structures of Consensus," *Gregorianum* 77 (1996): 213–25.

5   See Meyer, "Ecumenical Consensus," pp. 220–24.

6   See Meyer, "La 'Déclaration,'" pp. 193–94.

7   See Anneliese Meis, "El problema de la salvación y sus mediaciones, en el contexto de la *Declaración Conjunta* católico-luterana sobre la doctrina de la justificación," *Teología y Vida* 42 (2001): 90–93.

8   John XXII, "Opening Address," art. 6 [online, accessed July 8, 2004], available at www.ewtn.com/library/papldoc/j23v2adr.htm.

9   See H. Legrand, "Le consensus différencié sur la doctrine de la Justification (Augsbourg 1999): Quelques remarques sur la nouveauté d'une méthode," *Nouvelle revue théologique* 124 (2002): 30–39, esp. pp. 36–38.

10   See ibid., pp. 36–37.

11   "La pensée unitaire se révélant l'ennemie de la pensée de l'unité" (ibid., pp. 39).

12   See ibid., p. 51.

13   For lengthier discussion of the concept of "differentiated consensus," see André Birmelé, "La Déclaration Commune Concernant la Doctrine de la Justification," *La communion ecclésiale: Progrès œcuméniques et enjeux méthodologiques* (Paris: Les éditions du cerf, 2000), pp. 125–37.

14   Fernand Prat found a similar "interpretation of inconsistency" in his day (Prat, *Theology of St. Paul*, II, pp. 249–50).

15   *Dei Verbum*, art. 9. On this issue in the JD, see Scheffczyk, "Gemeinsame (Teil I)," p. 65.

16   The German "derer" refers to the *righteousness* of Christ. As an exception to the rule, the German "nicht aufgrund unseres Verdienstes" (GE, 16) less emphatically denies human merit than the English "not because of any merit on our part."

17   Because of this, the reader might be puzzled about the actual content of the agreement (see Scheffczyk, "Gemeinsame [Teil I]," p. 66).

18   The German "indem" more readily translates "while," which would appear to undercut the role of the believer even more. The German "im Wort und in den Sacramenten" (GE, 16) both specifies a multiplicity of sacraments and also mitigates the "instrumentality" of the role of sacraments, in contrast to the English "through."

19   The German reads, "daß wir Sünder unser neues Leben allein der vergebenden und neuschaffenden Barmherzigkeit Gottes verdanken, die wir uns nur schenken lassen und

im Glauben empfangen, aber nie – in welcher Form auch immer – verdienen können" (GE, 17). The English "as sinners" makes a qualification not apparent in the German. Moreover, the English "that God imparts as a gift" inaccurately adds an (albeit vague) connotation of "infused grace."

20 The German reads, "daß Gott aus Gnade dem Menschen die Sünde vergibt und ihn zugleich in seinem Leben von der knechtenden Macht der Sünde befreit und ihm das neue Leben in Christus schenkt. Wenn der Mensch an Christus im Glauben teilhat, rechnet ihm Gott seine Sünde nicht an und wirkt in ihm tätige Liebe durch den Heiligen Geist. Beide Aspekte des Gnadenhandelns Gottes dürfen nicht voneinander getrennt werden. Sie gehören in der Weise zusammen, daß der Mensch im Glauben mit Christus vereinigt wird, der in seiner Person unsere Gerechtigkeit ist (1 Kor 1,30): sowohl die Vergebung der Sünden, als auch die heiligende Gegenwart Gottes" (GE, 22). The English translation reads, "We confess together that *God forgives sin by grace and at the same time frees human beings from sin's enslaving power and imparts the gift of new life in Christ.* When persons come by faith to share in Christ, God no longer imputes to them their sin and through the Holy Spirit effects in them an active love. These two aspects of God's gracious action are not to be separated, for persons are by faith united with *Christ, who in his person is our righteousness* (1 Cor 1:30): both the forgiveness of sins and the saving presence of God himself" (JD, 22, emphases mine).

21 The English closely resembles the German in this paragraph. The word "stress" is actually only "say [*sagen*]" (GE, 23).

22 I will treat it in the section "Responses to Anticipated Objections."

23 The English accurately reflects the German "allein durch den Glauben" (GE, 26) here; because some Lutherans are disappointed that the JD often employs the ambiguous "im Glauben," I wished to draw attention to the more emphatic "durch den Glauben," which accurately conveys the Latin "sola fide." On the other hand, the English, "without which faith does not exist," does not reflect the more emphatic German, "ohne die kein Glaube sein kann" (GE, 26).

24 Birmelé, *A Commentary*, p. 12.

25 See Villar, "La Declaración," pp. 110 and 116–20 and Meyer, "La Déclaration," pp. 192–97.

26 Kärkkäinen, "Justification as Forgiveness," p. 42.

27 Birmelé, "La déclaration," p. 152.

28 Geoffrey Wainwright, "The Lutheran-Roman Catholic Agreement on Justification: Its Ecumenical Significance and Scope from a Methodist Point of View," *Journal of Ecumenical Studies* 38 (2001): 23, citing Wesley's *Works*, vol. 1 (1984), pp. 431–32.

29 Wainwright, "Methodist Point of View," p. 24.

30 In this respect, Wainwright's Wesleyan stance is similar to the thought of Newman (see Newman, *Lectures on Justification*). First as an Anglican, then later as a Catholic, Newman saw the English position as a *via media* between the extreme Romanist position, which he distinguished from the teaching of Trent, and the extreme Lutheran position. The *via media*, he wrote, "is in other words the doctrine of two righteousnesses, a pefect and imperfect; not of the Roman schools, that obedience justifies without a continual imputation of Christ's merits; nor of the Protestant, that imputation justifies distinct from obedience; but a middle way, that obedience justifies *in* or *under* Christ's Covenant, or sprinkled with Christ's meritorious sacrifice" (ibid., p. 374). Newman further claimed that the tridentine position is open to this *via media*, calling on Vasquez and other Catholic theologians for support. He concluded that in the end, there is no real basis for substantial disagreement between Catholics, Lutherans, and Anglicans. Newman's *Lectures* have had a mixed reception of late.

Thomas L. Sheridan intends to vindicate Newman's basic thesis that the intractable positions of extremists on all sides failed to represent the plasticity inherent in each communion's views. While Sheridan criticizes Newman for not recognizing in Luther the *via media* he took to be the essence of the Gospel, he contends that Newman's description of justification, because it so closely resembles authentic Lutheran and Catholic thought, promises ecumenical fecundity once it is removed from its polemical *sitz im Leben* (see Thomas L. Sheridan, "Newman and Luther on Justification," *Journal of Ecumenical Studies* 38 [2001]: 217–45). McGrath, on the other hand, levels a sharp criticism at Newman: "There is thus every reason to state that Newman's construction of a *via media* doctrine of justification unquestionably rests upon an historico-theological analysis of the dialectic between Protestantism and Roman Catholicism which is seriously inaccurate in the case of Luther, and may well be, although conclusive evidence may never be forthcoming, equally inaccurate in the case of Roman Catholicism" (McGrath, *Iustitia Dei*, p. 318). On this basis, McGrath contends, Newman's *via media* cannot serve as the avenue for ecumenical relations. Although Sheridan promises to return to McGrath's critique (see Sheridan, "Newman," p. 218), he merely returns to McGrath's summary conclusion that Newman likely did not obtain Luther's actual *Lectures on Galatians* and that Newman most likely did not receive the German. It is beyond the competence of this book to investigate Newman's *Lectures* in any greater detail; suffice it to say that his proposal, cited above, simply juxtaposes Baius's (condemned!) position with Lutheran orthodoxy (from the *Formula*). Baius hardly grasped Trent, as is evident in the condemnation of his many propositions, issued four years after the council's official promulgation. Also attesting to problematic elements of Newman's *Lectures*, John F. Perry, on the other hand, perceives in Newman's *Lectures* a deliberate attempt to deconstruct Luther in order to find in his work a witness amenable to his own theory of justification (see John F. Perry, "Newman's Treatment of Luther in the *Lectures on Justification*," *Journal of Ecumenical Studies* 36 [1999]: 303–17). Perry surely makes the stronger case, accounting for notable omissions in Newman's citations of Luther. Because the reader reads Luther less crucial omissions, he is mislead into understanding, *contra factum*, that Luther's position on justification by faith is in the end amenable to both the Anglican *via media* and the tridentine doctrine, provided the latter is interpreted in a broad (not strictly "Roman") sense. In any case, Sheridan does not grasp the tridentine teaching. He contends that Luther's doctrine of justification by faith alone and grace alone "exactly how Trent would describe justification in 1547" (Sheridan, "Newman," p. 227). He considers it erroneous for Catholics to think that after a person is justified, works are necessary for salvation (ibid., 243). He relates that even his Lutheran aunt was infected by this anxiety-provoking point of view. Against Sheridan, it must be stated emphatically that works indeed are quite necessary and that the anecdote about his aunt is unhelpful. A pastoral story more edifying and more faithful to Catholicism is that of little Luke John Hooker, who at the age of four died heroically of cancer, having refused all painkilling medicine in order to offer up his sufferings as a sacrifice for the sanctification of others. His understanding of justification? When "the bad guys become good again, so God will be so happy" (see the story on the web [online; accessed June 6, 2004], available at www.comealiveusa.com/LukeJohn.html).

31   Hampson, *Christian Contradictions*, p. 208.
32   Ibid., p. 207.
33   Ibid., p. 222.
34   Jüngel, *Justification*, p. 207, note 136. Jüngel reacted so severely to the Joint Declaration because it smacked all too much of Trent in his estimation. I do not

question Jüngel's judgment in this respect; he and other Lutherans give witness to the "other half" of the scandal of the Joint Declaration. I attend to the excessively *Lutheran* character of the JD. Wainwright's observations affirm the legitimacy of both Jüngel's and my observations.

35   Küng, *Justification*, p. 221.

36   Chemnitz, *Examination*, pp. 467–68.

37   See LW 27:30–31.

38   "On the Lutheran side, the churches responded to a first draft of the JD distributed to them in 1995 with much agreement, but also with important suggestions for improvement. These were worked into the present text" (Birmelé, *A Commentary*, pp. 14–15). Rusch notes the criticism of the 1996 draft (see Rusch, "The History," p. 177). Wendebourg, a participant, contends that the Finnish critique was among the most vociferous; it included discontent with the 1996 draft (see Wendebourg, "Zur Entstehungsgeschichte," pp. 156–59).

39   Birmelé, *A Commentary*, p. 36.

40   Kärkkäinen, "Justification as Forgiveness," p. 42.

41   Birmelé, "La déclaration," p. 139.

42   See ibid., p. 154.

43   Ibid., p. 174.

44   Lane, *Justification*, p. 167.

45   Ibid., p. 226.

46   Ibid., p. 226.

47   He does lament that the "Lutheran doctrine of imputed alien righteousness," explicitly accepted in USA, was not explicitly reaffirmed in the JD. On this score, his comments in the text and in the appendix are in some tension with one another (see ibid., p. 126).

48   See Michael Root, "The Implications of the *Joint Declaration on Justification* and its Wider Impact for Lutheran Participation in the Ecumenical Movement," in *Justification and the Future of the Ecumenical Movement: The* Joint Declaration on the Doctrine of Justification, ed. William Rusch (Collegeville: Liturgical Press, 2003), pp. 48–49.

49   Ibid., p. 49.

50   "A Common Statement of the Australian Lutheran-Roman Catholic Dialogue" [online; accessed June 19, 2002], available at http://www.home.gil.com.au/~stillerk/justif-ication.html], art. 3.

51   Ibid., art. 5.

52   See Holc, *Un ampio*, p. 332.

53   See ibid., p. 333.

54   See ibid., p. 358.

55   See ibid., pp. 80–90 and 166–74.

56   Was schlicht untridentinisch und falsch ist (Scheffczyk, "Gemeinsame [Teil II]," p. 126).

57   See Wainwright, "Methodist Point of View," p. 29.

58   See Jüngel, *Justification*, p. 207 note 136, and pp. 214–24. In defense of Wainwright, though, one might suppose that Wesley would accept the *totus-totus* scheme with respect to forgiveness and the *partim-partim* scheme with respect to the incipient renewal that bears an eschatological thrust. More to the point, Jüngel and others have difficulty with those elements of the JD that bear the marks of the Augustinian model of transformation, elements that Wainwright astutely observes as present in the JD.

59   Wainwright, "Methodist Point of View," p. 26.

60   Bertram Stubenrauch, "Consensus without Unity?" *Theology Digest* 47 (2000): 48.

61   See ibid., p. 50.

62   See ibid., pp. 50–51.

63   See ibid., p. 51.

64   See ibid., p. 48.

65   See ibid., p. 51.

66   See ibid., p. 52.

67   Ibid., p. 53.

68   If "or renewing" is a stretch, the reader will agree with me that the objection to my thesis would be weakened.

69   In an interview with *30 Days* (July, 1999): 20.

70   See the following sources that recognize the Finnish influence in the Joint Declaration: Wendebourg, "Zur Entstehungsgeschichte," pp. 164–65; Kärkkäinen, "Justification as Forgiveness," esp. 32–40; Wainwright, "Methodist Point of View," 26; Romanian Orthodox theologian Lucian Turcescu, "Soteriological Issues in the 1999 Lutheran-Catholic Joint Declaration on Justification: An Orthodox Perspective," *Journal of Ecumenical Studies* 38 (2001): 64–72; and see also the critique of Turcescu by George Vandervelde, "Justification and Deification—Problematic Synthesis: A Response to Lucian Turcescu," *Journal of Ecumenical Studies* 38 (2001): 73–78. Turcescu's only complaint is that the JD does not go far enough in integrating the Finnish thought (see Turcescu, "Soteriological," pp. 71–72).

71   Peura, "Favor," p. 64. As an aside, I might note that it would be tolerable for Lutherans loyal to their confessional documents to describe forensic and effective justification as two sides of the same reality only if the effective side (being made righteous, as even Melanchthon would state) consists in being made righteous through the acquittal, not through an infusion of grace and not even through the indwelling of Christ. No Lutheran who holds fast to the strictly forensic description of justification would consider the declaration of forgiveness to be an empty formula. But nor would any Lutheran think that the formula's "not being empty" implied the Catholic notion of infused righteousness; many Lutherans would not think it implied *per se* an indwelling of Christ.

72   Peura, "Favor," p. 64. For a critique of this very juxtaposition, see Vandervelde, "Justification and Deification," pp. 76–78. Vandervelde beautifully describes the utterly changed situation of the believer, who is affected "in the radix" of his being. Vandervelde still protests, however, the supposed consonance between the Lutheran conception of justifying faith and the Catholic triad of faith, hope, and love (or the Orthodox concept of synergy), though his reading of justifying faith at times resembles the Catholic notion of living faith.

73   Peura, "Favor," p. 64.

74   The German "zuspricht" (GE, 29) can be rendered either "awards" in the sense of gives or "grants" in a legal manner.

75   CRE, p. 47.

76   Bishop Eero Huovinen, "How Do We Continue? The Ecumenical Commitments and Possibilities of the Joint Declaration" (delivered in Ohio, Nov. 27, 2001, at a gathering entitled Unity in Faith).

77   See, for instance, Wolfhart Pannenberg's summary account of the differences within the overarching unity of faith (Pannenberg, "Can the Mutual Condemnations between Rome and the Reformation Churches be Lifted?," in JF, pp. 36–37). See also Harding Meyer, "The Text 'The Justification of the Sinner' in the Context of Previous Ecumenical Dialogues on Justification," in JF, 78–79. Beisser arrives at a similar result but shows more distinctly the Lutheran teaching that sanctification must be distinguished, albeit not separated, from justification. He thus leads the reader to an

accurate understanding of Lutheran thought. He fails, however, to compel this reader that Catholic teaching is not in conflict with that Lutheran thought (see Beisser, "Formula," pp. 156–57).

78 The German reads, "in dem die Hoffnung auf Gott und die Liebe zu ihm eingeschlossen sind" (GE, 25). The English reads, "justifying faith, which includes hope in God and love for him."

79 The German reads, "ist so in Gemeinschaft," and the English, "thus live in communion." Again, the German reads "diese Tat Gottes…betrifft." *Betreffen* can mean either "concerns, regards" or "touches, affects." The English opts for the latter connotation. I will cite the remaining German in full: "die Erneuerung der Lebensführung, die aus der Rechtfertigung notwendig folgt und ohne die kein Glaube sein kann, zwar von der Rechtfertigung unterschieden, aber nicht getrennt. Vielmehr wird damit der Grund angegeben, aus dem solche Erneuererung hervorgeht. Aus der Liebe Gottes, die dem Menschen in der Rechtfertigung geschenkt wird, erwächst die Erneuerung des Lebens. - Rechtfertigung und Erneuerung sind durch den im Glauben gegenwärtigen Christus verbunden" (GE, 26).

80 The German reads, "die Gerechtfertigten," whereas the English translation has "the righteous." Again, the German reads "und werden so" (GE, 27), not "dadurch," as is suggested by the English translation "thereby." I will discuss this in Chapter 8.

81 This more accurately reflects the line of argument I am pursuing than the more properly Lutheran expression "Faith is never alone."

82 Nørgaard-Højen, "No Return?" p. 213.

83 See Villar, "La Declaración," p. 119.

84 See Villar, "La Declaración," pp. 119–20. Villar gives a generous and edifying reading of this omission. It seems that Villar is inspired by Birmelé, *A Commentary*, p. 38.

85 See Michel Fédou, "L'accord luthéro-catholique sur la justification," *Nouvelle revue théologique* 122 (2000): 37–50, esp. pp. 46–47.

86 See Birmelé, "La déclaration," pp. 157–59.

87 Kärkkäinen, "Justification as Forgiveness," p. 40.

88 Ibid., p. 40.

89 Birmelé, *A Commentary*, p. 37. The unfortunate distinction can be read in several ways. First, it can be read as a distinction between the habit and individual act of charity. This would pose no difficulties for Catholics. Second, the text may mean that the "love" included in faith is really the "honor" that man ought to give God, precisely by letting God be God. However, Lutherans will insist that this "love toward God" cannot be that which Catholics label *caritas*, lest the doctrine of *sola fide* collapse into law.

90 Root, "The Implications," p. 49.

91 See Holc, *Un ampio*, p. 331.

92 Some readers might object that Trent does not identify charity and grace. This much is true. This observation—part of an intra-Catholic dispute—does not constitute an objection. If grace and charity are distinct (as I would contend they are, following Aquinas), they are not without one another. Together, they are incorporated in that which is called "sanctifying grace" in the sense that charity's "presence" in the will is that by which the will is united with God and therefore no longer sinfully alienated from God. The Catholic Church insists that grace and charity, if distinct, always come together, not in the way in which "forgiveness and renewal" are said to come together according to Lutheran teaching. Rather, both are inhering realities in the human person, one rooted in the other as its proper effect. Should one add the useful and yet tedious qualifications to each of the following statements in the text (charity and grace), the argument would hold the same.

93   Kärkkäinen, "Justification as Forgiveness," p. 40.

94   "The Christian, as such an adopted son, is not only admitted into God's family, but by reason of the same gratuitous adoption receives the right to become master of his Father's estate. Despite having no natural right to it, he acquires title by adoption through the Spirit" (Fitzmeyer, *Romans*, p. 502).

95   For one of the better sources by which such an argument might be constructed, see Vinzenz Pfnür, "The Condemnations on Justification in the Confessio Augustana, the Apology, and the Smalcald Articles," chap. in JF, 129–47, esp., pp. 136–38; see also his earlier work (Pfnür, *Einig*, pp. 193–97).

96   Catholics have increasingly discovered that for Lutherans faith "is not merely a knowledge of historical events but is a confidence in God and in the fulfillment of his promises" (Augsburg Confession, XX: 26). Luther links faith and hope very tightly together (see LW 27: 22–23).

97   See USA, par. 73.

98   John Paul II, *Veritatis Splendor*, art. 68.

99   Fides, nisi ad eam spes accedat et charitas, neque unit perfecte cum Christo, neque corporis eius vivum membrum efficit (chap. 7, DE, 673: 38–40).

100   Etsi contritionem hanc aliquando charitate perfectam esse contingat, hominemque Deo reconciliare, priusquam hoc sacramentum actu suscipiatur (Decree on Reconciliation, chap. 4, in DE, 705: 20–22).

101   *Apology*, IV: 147.

102   O'Callaghan, *Fides Christi*, p. 84. For this reason, I question the consistency of his reading of the formal cause of justification. Trent can be theologically coherent only if the "iustitia Dei" is conceived as infused justice.

103   *Apology*, IV: 177. Tappert has "imputed"; Kolb has "reckoned" (Kolb, octavo edition, p. 146). Though Kolb is working from the octavo edition, whereas the citation is found in the quarto edition, the word "reckoned" is perhaps more sober. See also IV: 179 and 308.

104   *Solid Declaration*, III: 43.

105   Ibid., 59 and 62.

106   See chapters 4 and 5 of this book, and also CRE, pp. 50–52.

107   LW 25: 222. "Quod Dominus misericors … non imputet nobis eam ad peccatum, dum ei confiteamur ipsam" (WA, 56: 236.26–28).

108   LW 25: 221.

109   LW 26: 286. In the Latin edition, Luther includes charity in this curse: "ergo lex, opera, charitas, Vota etc. non redimunt, sed magis involvunt et gravant Maledicto" (WA, 40, I: 446.34–447.13).

110   LW 26: 286.

111   LW 26: 287.

112   LW 27:28.

113   LW 26: 129.

114   LW 26: 130.

115   LW 26: 130.

116   See LW 26: 133.

117   See LW 27: 63–65.

118   See LW 27: 21–23.

119   See Manns, "Absolute and Incarnate," pp. 135–36.

120   Ibid., p. 145. Manns is drawing on Luther's commentary on Galatians.

121   See John Paul II, *Veritatis splendor*, arts. 23–24, citing Augustine's *Confessions*, X, 29 and 40.

122 Certainly, Catholic exegetes freely dispute the meaning of Rom 5:5, but that ought not touch the substance of their agreement with the Catholic doctrine on inhering grace.

123 See LW 25: 293–96.

124 LW 25: 306.

125 LW 25: 306.

126 Kärkkäinen thinks Luther identified grace and gift early in his career but distinguished them later in his career. However, Kärkkäinen insists that Luther nowhere separates the two but "always keeps them together." My work in the text will show that this "tethering" of grace and gift does not suffice (Kärkkäinen, "Justification as Forgiveness," pp. 37–39).

127 LW 27: 222.

128 LW 27: 362; WA, 2: 584.7–9.

129 See LW 27: 363.

130 LW 27: 65.

131 LW 27: 64.

132 The logic herein employed is remarkably similar to that of double justice. Even Contarini would agree, adding the qualification that, in some cases, it is possible for charity to reach perfection on earth.

133 LW 27: 64.

134 LW 26: 273–74.

135 See also the references cited by Wainwright, who observes the same phenomenon in Luther: LW 32: 229 and LW 41: 143–44 and 165–66. Wainwright discusses this phenomenon on pp. 29–30 of his "Methodist Point of View." I would add other texts as well, for instance, LW 27: 372. Though not intentionally responding to the argument about differing models, Manns observes this phenomenon in many passages (Manns, "Absolute and Incarnate," *passim*).

136 I thus disagree with Gerhard Forde's reading of Luther, for these passages fall under the logic of the Augustinian transformationist scheme (see Forde, "Forensic Justification," pp. 284–87).

137 *Apology*, IV: 179. See also Kolb's translation of the octavo edition (Kolb, octavo edition, pp. 146–49).

138 *Apology*, IV: 195, quarto edition.

139 Ibid., 196.

140 See ibid., 194.

141 *Solid Declaration*, III: 41.

142 The English translation of the German adds "this," whereas the German has simply "Kraft der Gnade" (GE 1996, par. 23).

143 See CRE, p. 48.

144 LW 32: 227–40; WA, 8: 106–15.

145 For a reading that finds Luther and Latomus in agreement, if one abstracts from the polemicism, see Erwin Iserloh, "Gratia und donum: Rechtfertigung und Heiligung nach Luthers Schrift 'Wider den Löwener Theologen Latomus' (1521)," *Catholica* 24 (1970): p. 73.

146 Peura's reading of the distinction and relation between grace and gift is faithful to Luther here. Consequently, his thought is also not compatible with the Catholic insistence that the justified person is no longer a person who commits damnable sins (see Peura, "Favor," pp. 56–60).

147 Paul Althaus, *The Theology of Martin Luther*, trans. Robert Schultz (Philadelphia: Fortress Press, 1966), p. 240. See the whole discussion (ibid., pp. 234–45). The delicate balance Althaus strives to retrieve from Luther is still *not* tantamount to the

Catholic position, for the "total righteousness" of the believer is, he maintains, still a righteousness by imputation (see note 61, p. 236), even though indwelling is emphasized (see ibid., p. 235). Although the new being of the justified is inseparable from God's imputation of righteousness, still, the "as if" Althaus rightly refers to (see ibid., pp. 238–39) forms the critical difference between the Catholic and Protestant readings of Rom 8:4. For Protestants, it is "as if" we obeyed the law, although we are merely on the way to this; for Catholics it is *that* we obey the law, although we are on the way to perfection in the upward call. The dividing line remains: "The beginning of the new creation and the battle against sin in the Christian in no way changes the fact that he still remains a sinner. And this means more than that he is not yet righteous: he is guilty before God" (ibid., p. 240).

148   See Göttingen, "An Opinion," pp. 19–21.

149   "GTP," p. 72.

150   The Annex implicitly makes its own the spurious emendation of Sacred scripture popularized by Luther.

151   Eberhard Jüngel, "Das neue Leben in Christus: Katholicken und Lutheraner verständigte sich über umstrittene Punkte der 'Gemeinsamen Erklärung' zur Rechtfertigunslehre," *Deutsches Allgemeines Sonntagsblatt*, no. 23, 4 June 1999, cited in Hampson, *Christian Contradictions*, pp. 221–22.

152   See Dulles, "Justification: The Joint Declaration."

153   Pannenberg, "Theses," p. 136.

154   Lutheran World Federation, "Implications of Justification in the World's Contexts," October 31, 1998; [online; accessed July 16, 2004], available at www.ecumenism.net/archive/justification-today.htm.

CHAPTER 8

The Essence of Justifying Grace: Catholic Paragraphs

THE CATHOLIC paragraphs of the JD contain some distinctively tridentine expressions, but whether they substantially cover "the basic truths" of justification in Catholic faith is another question. This chapter considers the formal cause and its effects.

Formal Cause

First, there is no unambiguous declaration that justifying grace, or the formal cause of justification, consists in the reality traditionally called inhering justice.[1] Whereas many distinctively Lutheran phrases appear in the text, some of which are mentioned above and many of which are mentioned below, this central Catholic hinge of the doctrine of justification is not mentioned. At best, it is vaguely discernible in the following two passages:

Statement P:
When Catholics emphasize [that the renewal of the inner person is given to the believer through the reception of grace[13] {note 13 of JD, below in text}, they wish to insist that the forgiving grace of God is always united with the gift of a new life, which is expressed (becomes effective) in the Holy Spirit in active love. But] they do not thereby deny that God's gift of grace in justification remains independent of human cooperation. (JD, 24)[2]

[13] Cf. DS 1528.

Statement P':
The justification of sinners is forgiveness of sins and [making righteous through the justifying grace that makes us children of God. In justification, the justified receive from Christ faith, hope, and love, and are thus taken into communion with him[14] {note 14 of JD, below in text}. This new personal relation to God is grounded totally in the graciousness of God and remains always dependent on the salvific-creative work of the merciful God, who remains faithful to himself and on whom one can therefore rely. Therefore, justifying grace never becomes a human possession, to which the justified person can appeal over against God. If according to Catholic understanding the renewal of life through justifying grace is stressed, yet this renewal in faith, hope, and love is always dependent on God's unfathomable grace and makes no contribution to

justification about which one can boast before God]. (JD, 27)³

¹⁴ Cf. DS 1530.

"Reception of grace," in P, might be taken to imply the reality signified by the traditional Catholic expression "infused grace." The English translation is even more suggestive: "grace imparted as a gift." The English adds to the official edition the substantive term "gift" and the participle "imparted." Moreover, whereas in the English it seems as though "grace" is what is given (or imparted), in the German it is very clear that it is the "renewal" that is given. But let us for the moment set aside these misleading translations. This passage might serve as evidence for the reader who wishes to interpret the twofold distinction between justification and sanctification as follows: not that between two formal causes, one extrinsic and one intrinsic, but that between a gratuitously established "formal cause" and the effects (good works or new life) springing therefrom. The Catholic teaching that inhering grace is the formal cause of justification would be preserved. This textual possibility seems to be further ratified by the two source notes that refer to the paragraphs in Trent that precede and follow the definition of the formal cause (DS 1529). Finally, the first sentence of the Annex, par. 2–D, might lend credence to such an interpretation, if it is read as an implicit description of the inhering quality of justifying grace: "Grace, as fellowship of the justified with God in faith, hope and love, is always received from the salvific and creative work of God."

Similarly, P' seems to imply that faith, hope, and charity are all necessary for the believer to have a justifying relationship with Christ. Perhaps the text even implies that faith justifies insofar as it includes "hope and charity." These two key texts from the Catholic paragraphs appear amenable to the tridentine definition of the sole formal cause as inhering grace. In any case, one must admit that these and other passages have a distinctively Catholic ring to them.

Nevertheless, there are some obstacles to reading P and P' in harmony with Trent. The following sets of correlations, each found in the above citations, can mislead the reader into interpreting justifying grace as God's favor in Christ. Let me paraphrase these statements and then transpose each into logical terms. Statement P reads, "When Catholics emphasize that the renewal of the inner person is given to the believer through the reception of grace, they insist that the gift of a new life is always united with God's forgiving grace." Statement P contains the following terms: (A) inner renewal, (B) reception of grace, (C) gift of a new life, (D) God's forgiving grace. P transposed reads as follows: When Catholics emphasize A through B, they insist that C is united with D. Statement P' reads: "If according to Catholic understanding the renewal of life through justifying grace is stressed, yet this renewal in faith, hope, and love is always dependent upon God's unfathomable grace."[4] Statement P' has four key terms: (A') renewal, (B') justifying grace, (C') this renewal in faith, hope, and love, and (D') God's unfathomable grace. Accordingly, P' reads as follows: While Catholics emphasize A' through B', this C' is dependent upon D'.

In statement P, renewal and new life appear to be synonymous. In statement P', renewal is used twice. Therefore, in P, C=A. In P', C' = A'. The two statements, basically parallel, can accordingly be simplified. P reads: "When Catholics emphasize that A comes through B, they insist that A is united with D." P' reads: "While Catholics emphasize A' through B', this A' is dependent upon D'.

Each statement consists in two sets of relations. In each statement, renewal (A/A') is related to two expressions signifying some type of grace (B/B' and D/D'). In P, (A) renewal is related to (B) reception of grace and to (D) God's forgiving grace. In P', (A') renewal is related to (B') justifying grace and also to (D') God's unfathomable grace. It is not clear in P, however, how (B) the reception of grace is related to (D) God's forgiving grace. Again, it is unclear how P' relates (B') justifying grace to (D') God's unfathomable grace. But precisely these relations between B and D and between B' and D' constitute the most thorny and divisive issue concerning justification! Can the reader glean any light from these passages?

Perhaps one ought to take a step back from the terms in the statements and reflect on the formal structure of each statement. Presumably, in each case the second clause is intended to illuminate the first, since the subordinate structure of the first clause leads the reader to expect a clarification in the second, main clause. In the first clause of each statement, one term is said to come through another: A/A' comes through B/B'. It would seem natural, then, that in the second clause further light would be shed on one of these two terms. Either A/A' or B/B' will be further elucidated by the main clause. The apparent repetition of A/A' in the second clause leads the reader to anticipate that "renewal" is to be further elucidated in the second clause.

The second clause could elucidate A/A' by referring it to a further source beyond B/B'. P/P' would then read: while A/A' comes through B/B', A/A' also comes through D/D'. To add common terms: "While David is fathered by John, David is grand-fathered by Tom." When the original terms are inserted into the text, P' reads as follows: "While Catholics emphasize (A) inner renewal through (B) justifying grace, they insist that (A) inner renewal depends upon (D) God's unfathomable grace." If understood correctly, this statement is certainly intelligible and true. Still, it is not particularly illuminating. Too many questions remain unanswered. First, what is justifying grace, and how does it justify? Secondly, what exactly is the relationship between (B') justifying grace and (D') God's unfathomable grace? Is justifying grace the gift infused into the believer by the unfathomable grace of God? Is justifying grace an inhering grace constituting the formal cause of forgiveness? Precisely because these questions remain unanswered—though they cry out for answers, from both the Lutheran and Catholic perspectives—this statement can only be described as odd: "While David is fathered by John, David is grand-fathered by Tom." The same analysis would apply to the statement P: What is the "reception of grace" (or, as the English has it, imparted grace)?

The evident way to circumvent this judgment is to consider both clauses of each statement as referring to the same two realities, the second clause clarifying the relationship incipiently described in the first clause. In the first clause, Catholics are said to emphasize the renewal, but in the second clause, Catholics confess that this renewal is always dependent upon God's unfathomable grace. The reader can surmise that, just as the two terms for renewal (A/A' and C/C') are used synonymously the terms used for reception of grace or justifying grace B/B' are used as synonymous with the terms for God's forgiving grace or unfathomable grace (D/D').

If the second term (B/B') is identified with the last term (D/D'), the second clause simply articulates the first clause with greater accuracy, by way of an adjusted emphasis: "While Catholics emphasize renewal (A') through justifying grace (B'=D'), they fully admit that this renewal (A') is dependent upon God's unfathomable grace (B'=D')." This statement is not awkward, and it is true. But once again, the crucial question must be raised: To what grace is the statement referring? The conflation of B/B' with D/D' leads to one likely reading: God's favor or forgiving grace. God's forgiving or unfathomable grace (D/D') signifies his favor, not an infused, inhering grace. The traditional Catholic interpretation of "reception of grace" (B) or "justifying grace" (B') as infused grace, then, is unlikely. Instead, for pars. 24 and 27, "reception of grace" and "justifying grace" appear as alternative expressions for God's forgiving favor.[5]

This judgment is confirmed by the editorial changes made between the first and second drafts and between the second and third drafts. The 1995 draft contained an explicit affirmation of the official Catholic position. This affirmation came in a paragraph that corresponds to par. 27 of the final draft. It reads:

> According to Catholic understanding justification as forgiveness of sins and being made righteous takes place through sanctifying grace (gratia gratum faciens). Thus the continuing dependence of this created grace on the "uncreated grace," the very graciousness of God, is stressed. Sanctifying grace therefore never becomes a possession at the disposal of human beings to which they might appeal before God. (JD 1995, par. 29)

This original draft, without using the phrase "formal cause," captured the substance of the Catholic doctrine and also accurately placed it in the hierarchy of truths: Christians are formally justified by grace that has a created character, but this grace is faithfully bestowed by and ever dependent upon the merciful God since it streams from God's constant mercy upon His children. The 1996 draft omitted all mention of grace as created and no longer identified justifying grace with infused grace.

As we have seen, the third and final draft tempts the reader to identify justifying grace with God's favor through Jesus Christ, for the two appear to be conflated. The fact that this draft was the result of a deliberate editorial removal of references to created, sanctifying grace confirms this reading. Furthermore, this temptation is magnified when the statements are read in their immediate context. The final draft, continuing from the passages cited above, rejects a caricature of the tridentine definition on justifying grace: "Therefore, justifying grace never becomes a human possession to which the justified person can appeal over against God" (JD, 27). The rejection of this caricature is also cited in the sources to section 4.2: "Nor does [Catholic doctrine] maintain ... grace as an objective 'possession' (even if a conferred possession) on the part of the human being—something over which he can dispose."[6] The Göttingen faculty rightly found the latter to be an explicit correction of the tridentine teaching.[7]

I would like to return to the issue of translation. I have already noted that in par. 24 the official German text is less suggestive of a Catholic reading than is the English. A similar phenomenon besets us in par. 27. The English text reads, "In justification the righteous receive from Christ faith, hope and love and are *thereby* taken into communion with him" (JD, 27, emphasis mine). The term "thereby" appears to locate faith, hope, and love as proper constituents of saving communion with Christ. Is love, therefore, partially constitutive of the communion with God by which the Christian is justified? This may well be the intent of the paragraph, and it may be that the Annex also intends this in the following statement: "Grace, as fellowship of the justified with God in faith, hope and love, is always received from the salvific and creative work of God (cf. JD, 27)." Nevertheless, the German text of par. 27 reads, "In justification, the [justified] receive from Christ faith, hope, and love and [are thus] taken into communion with him." I would note the following. First, the English text uses the word "righteous," whereas the German uses the word "justified." This is an apparently slight difference, but it might be significant. A Lutheran could interpret the German as meaning that, in the overall process of justification, those who are justified by God's favor *also* receive faith, hope, and love from Christ. The text does not say that faith, hope, and love are all intrinsically necessary to the "being justified" of the sinner. Rather, the text says that the justified receive these gifts. Second, the English translation's "thereby" suggests that it is "by" the gifts of faith, hope, and love that the human person is "taken into communion with God" or justified. The German "*und so*" translates more accurately "and thus," not "thereby," which would be, in German, "dadurch." This difference is significant, for had the authors chosen the term "thereby [*dadurch*]," one might discern greater evidence for the Catholic conception of inhering grace; as it is, the text is not suggestive of such a reading.

In summary, the Catholic paragraphs in the final document are ambiguous. They leave unstated the crux of the tridentine teaching. In light of the editorial work, the omission of the Catholic teaching on the essence of the grace by which sinners are made just cannot be seen as simple oversight.[8] Finally, the official German is less amenable to the Catholic "interpolation" suggested in chapter 7.

The Power of Baptismal Grace Insufficiently Affirmed

The description of the effects of baptismal grace in par. 30 does not adequately express the Catholic faith. Whereas the JD rightly declares that the sin that is "worthy of death" is taken away in baptism, the Catholic faith holds, further, that all venial sins are taken away. Correlatively, it is an understatement to affirm that concupiscence "does not merit the punishment of eternal death" (JD, 30). Indeed! It merits no punishment whatsoever, temporal or eternal. This statement is breathtakingly understated. It might be noted, though, that the two references to DS, 1515 in par. 30—notes 16 and 17—will hopefully guide the reader to a more adequate interpretation. I leave to the next section other criticisms of the Catholic paragraphs. It is now necessary to turn to the nexus of problematic affirmations that issue from the central error of the JD, that Christ's own righteousness is that whereby the sinner stands just before God.

NOTES

1   Anneliese Meis appears to observe something of a difficulty on this issue as well (see Meis, "El problema," p. 102). She notes Scheffczyk's complaint about this absence (see ibid., p. 104). Scheffczyk judges that, while the Catholic paragraphs are not certainly false, they are ambiguous; they can even be said to be insufficient on the issue of the formal cause of justification (see Scheffczyk, "Gemeinsame [Teil II]," p. 126).

2   The German reads, "Wenn die Katholiken betonen, daß dem Gläubigen die Erneuerung des inneren Menschen durch den Empfang der Gnade geschenkt wird, dann wollen sie festhalten, daß die vergebende Gnade Gottes immer mit dem Geschenk eines neuen Lebens verbunden ist, das sich im Heiligen Geist in tätiger Liebe auswirkt; sie verneinen damit aber nicht, daß Gottes Gnadengabe in der Rechtfertigung unabhängig bleibt von menschlicher Mitwirkung" (GE, 24). The English reads, "When Catholics

emphasize the renewal of the interior person through the reception of grace imparted as a gift to the believer, they wish to insist that God's forgiving grace always brings with it a gift of new life, which in the Holy Spirit becomes effective in active love" (JD, 24).

3   The German reads, "Die Rechtfertigung des Sünders ist Sündenvergebung und Gerechtmachung durch die Rechtfertigungsgnade, die uns zu Kindern Gottes macht. In der Rechtfertigung empfangen die Gerechtfertigten von Christus Glaube, Hoffnung und Liebe und werden so in die Gemeinschaft mit ihm aufgenommen. Dieses neue personale Verhältnis zu Gott gründet ganz und gar in der Gnädigkeit Gottes und bleibt stets vom heilsschöpferischen Wirken des gnädigen Gottes abhängig, der sich selbst treu bleibt und auf den der Mensch sich darum verlassen kann. Deshalb wird die Rechtfertigungsgnade nie Besitz des Menschen, auf den er sich Gott gegenüber berufen könnte. Wenn nach katholischem Verständnis die Erneuerung des Lebens durch die Rechtfertigungsgnade betont wird, so ist diese Erneuerung in Glaube, Hoffnung und Liebe immer auf die grundlose Gnade Gottes angewiesen und leistet keinen Beitrag zur Rechtfertigung, dessen wir uns vor Gott rühmen könnten" (GE, 27). The English reads, "The righteous receive from Christ faith, hope and love and are thereby taken into communion with him…. While Catholic teaching emphasizes the renewal of life by justifying grace, this renewal in faith, hope and love is always dependent on God's unfathomable grace" (JD, 27).

4   This statement is most likely based on a statement in the German dialogue (see CRE, p. 53, cited in Sources to 4.3).

5   If the reader affirms the distinction between justifying grace and God's unfathomable grace, the reader must also admit that the relation between the two is not specified and that the identify of the formal cause of justification is therefore also left uncertain.

6   CRE, p. 49.

7   See Göttingen, "An Opinion," pp. 39–40.

8   Birmelé notes that the change was issued in response to severe Lutheran criticism of the Geneva text. Lutherans wanted every trace of grace as a quality removed. They got their wish (See Birmelé, "La déclaration," p. 110).

CHAPTER 9

Consequent Difficulties

THE AFFIRMATION that Christ's righteousness is the sinner's justifying righteousness implies several additional theological positions, each of which is outside the parameters of Catholic faith. These include: the coexistence of damnable sin and infused grace, the independence of faith's salvific power from obedience to the commandments, the impossibility of an increase in justifying grace, insufficient distinction between mortal and venial sins, and the exclusion of eternal life from the proper scope of meritorious works. The presence of these positions in the JD would further corroborate my basic thesis. I propose to investigate whether the JD manifests these implications.

Simultaneously Just Person and Sinner

If damnable sin can exist within a "justified" person, the formal cause of justification cannot be simply sanctifying grace—which, according to Catholic faith, expunges all damnable sins—but must be or at least include something extrinsic, e.g., the imputed righteousness of Christ. Lutheran par. 29 asserts the antecedent and thus implies the consequent. Par. 29 reads:

[Lutherans understand this in the sense that the Christian is "at once a just person and a sinner." The Christian is wholly just because God forgives him his sins through word and sacrament and awards {judicially grants} him the righteousness of Christ, which becomes his own in faith and which makes him just in Christ before God]. Looking at themselves through the law, however, they [i.e., the justified] recognize that they remain also totally sinners. Sin still lives in them (1 Jn. 1:8; Rom. 7:17, 20), for they repeatedly turn to false gods and do not love God with that undivided love which God requires as their Creator (Dt. 6:5; Mt. 22:36–40 pr.). This contradiction to God is as such truly sin. Nevertheless, the enslaving power of sin is broken on the basis of the merit of Christ. It no longer is a sin that "rules" the Christian for it is itself "ruled" by Christ with whom the justified are bound in faith. [Thus, Christians, so long as they live on earth, can at least in part {in fits and starts} lead a life in justice]. Despite sin, the Christian is no longer separated from God, because in the daily return to baptism, the person who has been born anew by baptism and the Holy Spirit has this sin forgiven, [so that his sin no longer condemns him and does not bring him eternal death[15] {note 15 of JD, in text below}]. Thus, when Lutherans say that justified persons are also sinners and that their opposition to God is truly sin, they do not deny that, despite this sin, they are not separated from God and that this sin is a "ruled" sin. In these affirmations they are in agreement with Roman Catholics, despite the difference in understanding sin in the justified.[1]

[15] Cf. Apology II: 38–45; Book of Concord, 105 f.

According to this paragraph, the justified are "totally sinners" in themselves because there lives within them sin that of its nature deserves damnation and eternal death. This affirmation is discordant with the Catholic faith.

There is exacerbating evidence for this judgment in the editorial changes. The final draft represents a notable change from the 1995 draft in which the Lutherans confessed simply that "they [the justified] remain sinners ['*Sünder*' *bleibt*] in constant need of the justifying grace of God" (JD 1995, par. 25). The final draft adds the modifier "*totally* sinners [ganz *Sünder bleibt*]" (emphasis mine). This change in terminology was paralleled by another change with regard to the status of the remnant sin as "truly sin." The 1995 draft stated in par. 26:

> In terms of content, there is agreement with Lutherans when Catholics say that "concupiscence," which remains after baptism, is in contradiction to God and is the object of a lifelong struggle. And yet concupiscence no longer separates the justified from God. Properly speaking, it therefore is not sin.[2] (JD 1995, par. 26)

This statement appeared in a Catholic paragraph. The preceding, Lutheran paragraph of that draft did *not* call concupiscence "truly sin." The Catholic paragraph explicitly claimed that Lutherans were in agreement with it. Understandably, not a few Lutheran theologians took exception to the statement.[3] Expressing the disfavor of the Finnish school, Peura wrote:

> In my opinion this statement is inconsistent with the view represented by Luther and the Lutherans in common. Sin after baptism is real sin.... It appears that the Catholic partner as well as perhaps most Lutherans is claiming that the notion of the real character of sin *post baptismum* is in contradiction to the view that a Christian is made righteous. This is obviously a false conclusion in the light of the interpretation of Luther presented [in my article].[4]

This critique was heeded in the final draft, cited above, which states that concupiscence is "as such truly sin [*als solche wahrhaft Sünde*]." The qualifier "truly" is repeated towards the end of the paragraph.[5] Moreover, the 1996 draft retained a clear explanation, in the Catholic paragraph, as to why concupiscence is not sin: "It is not a morally wrong, free decision" (JD 1996, par. 30). The final draft leaves us with the following vague expression: "Human sin always involves a personal element and since this element is lacking in this inclination, Catholics do not see this inclination as sin in an authentic sense"

(JD, 30). Lutherans may still take exception to the Catholic statement that concupiscence is not "sin an authentic sense." German Lutheran theologian Reinhard Brandt complains that the tridentine teaching is still discernible: Although the newer expression "personal element" is vague, there still remains the warning, "But when individuals *voluntarily* separate themselves from God, it is not enough to return to observing the commandments" (JD, 30; emphasis mine). Brandt perceives the appeal to the qualifier *voluntarily* [*willentlich*] as an implicit definition of sin as volitional, a definition incompatible with the Lutheran definition.[6]

I do not disagree with Brandt's observations, which understandably make him wonder how par. 30 and par. 29 are reconcilable. Nevertheless, I wish to allay such fears with some of my own. One can rase objections to par. 30 from a Catholic perspective. First, no one can doubt that the editorial changes to the various drafts witness a trajectory towards vaguer expressions. The reason for the trajectory seems to have been appeasement of ongoing Lutheran concerns.[7] Second, par. 30 on one occasion specifies the proper character of sin in a Lutheran, not tridentine, way. This is best discerned in the official German. The English translation reads, "Catholics hold that the grace of Jesus Christ imparted in baptism takes away all that is sin 'in the proper sense' and that is 'worthy of damnation'" (JD, 30). The translation evades conveying a strict identity between sin in the "proper" sense and sin that is "worthy of damnation." The English translation thus appears amenable to the Catholic distinction between venial and mortal sin. The German text is less supple than the English. It is better translated as follows: "The grace of Christ which is conferred in baptism takes away all that is 'truly' sin, all that is 'worthy of damnation.'"[8] The German text leaves less room for the distinction between mortal and venial sins, both of which are truly sin. In this respect, the German text appears to be in greater continuity with CRE.[9] From a Catholic perspective, this is less than satisfactory.

The editorial development of the JD's three paragraphs on the "simul iustus et peccator" topic clearly moves in a Lutheran direction. What is most troubling about the final draft, from the Catholic perspective, is the "damn*able*" nature of the sin that remains. Par. 29 reads, "Sin no longer condemns him and does not bring him eternal death." Remnant sin is described as the idolatry that of its nature *can* bring eternal death: Because of concupiscence, the justified person continually fails to love God as he is commanded to do and thus deserves the wrath of God.[10] This sin is in itself damnable but does not damn because God constantly forgives.

In affirming the damnable nature of concupiscence, the JD departs from earlier drafts and draws instead upon earlier dialogues. A passage noted in "Sources to 4.4" affirms that concupiscence is in itself damn*able*, albeit not damn*ing*: "In Lutheran phraseology, [concupiscence] is *peccatum regnatum*, 'controlled sin,' which is only damnable hypothetically, as it were—that is, only if God were not to forgive."[11] Accordingly, God's act of forgiveness does not occur formally by the infusion of grace into the sinner by which grace the sinner is rendered no longer a mortal sinner. Instead, God's forgiveness is conceived in an actualistic manner, as the constant bestowal of declarative favor. Thus, the term "forgiveness" employed here does not denote the removal of sin from the sinner but rather the non-recognition of that sin, which remains, and which remains damnable.

Granted, this "non-recognition of sin" can be seen in two distinct ways, either along the lines of the strictly forensic interpretation of the *Formula* or along the lines of the Finnish interpretation: forgiveness on account of the indwelling of the person of Christ.[12] As Bishop Huovinen rightly noted, there seems to be some evidence for both interpretations. As to evidence for the first interpretation, one could argue that to maintain that still-extant, damnable sin is not mortal in its effect, one must understand justification as the non-imputation of sin and the imputation of Christ's righteousness—the formal cause of forensic forgiveness. The following sentences from par. 29, then, could be interpreted accordingly: "[The Christian is wholly just because God forgives him his sins through word and sacrament and awards {or judicially grants} him the righteousness of Christ, which becomes his own in faith and which makes him just in Christ before God]. In Christ [believers] are made just before God." They are "made" righteous because God's verdict is the only valid verdict, freeing them from sin's enslaving (demoralizing) power. Thus forgiven, sinners can begin to lead a new life, even though they continually fall short. Note 15 from par. 29 ratifies this interpretation. This note appears as a reference in explanation of the reason why remnant sin "no longer condemns him and no longer brings him eternal damnation." The following statement is found in that section of the *Apology*: "For [the fathers and Paul] clearly call lust sin, by nature worthy of death if it is not forgiven, though it is not [reckoned] to those who are in Christ."[13] We thus encounter the judicial language of Melanchthon. According to this interpretative line, justifying grace is not inhering grace; it is a forensic acquittal.

On the other hand, one might interpret the forgiveness of the remnant, damnable sin along the lines of the Finnish school. Peuro criticized the 1995 draft for lacking "totally the idea of union with Christ."[14] His remarks on this matter were also heeded; the final draft contains several references to the justified person's "union with Christ." In particular, the section on the simultaneity of sin and righteousness in the justified affirms this union as the basis for forgiveness. The sinner is made just *in Christ*: "[The righteousness of Christ] makes him just in Christ before God" (JD, 29). This statement finds fuller expression later in the same paragraph: "It is no longer a sin that 'rules' the Christian for it is itself 'ruled' by Christ with whom the justified are bound in faith." Christ's "ruling" of sin appears to be intimately bound up with the believer's communion with Christ: "the righteousness of Christ, which becomes his own in faith."

Catholics can surely agree that the second line of interpretation is more consonant with their doctrinal heritage. It would seem unlikely, however, that the Lutheran paragraphs are intended to be restricted to this interpretation. The juridical or forensic interpretation of forgiveness is also a legitimate reading of par. 29. In any case, neither interpretation substantially accords with Catholic faith, which holds that the venial sins that may remain after the reception of the sacrament of reconciliation are no longer damnable and since the concupiscence that remains is not even venially sinful. I need not repeat here my argument for the incompatibility of the Finnish reading of Luther with Catholic doctrine. Although the Finnish reading is more favorable from a Catholic perspective, it still remains divergent from the latter. Peura made this clear in his careful repudiation of the traditional Catholic interpretation of Gal. 5:6 "faith working through or informed by love."[15]

The Official Vatican Response to the final draft of the Joint Declaration found that the Lutheran affirmation of the simultaneity of sin and righteousness in the believer was "not acceptable."[16] Art. 2–B of the Annex was intended, in part, to address the Vatican's concern about the simultaneity of sin and grace. Nevertheless, one can legitimately ask whether this article has in fact resolved the problem. The Annex offers the following description of the Catholic notion of voluntary sin: "Sin has a personal character and as such leads to separation from God. It is the selfish desire of the old person and the lack of trust and love toward God."[17] The Annex also offers the following as a Lutheran position: "*Concupiscence* is understood as the self-seeking desire of the human being, which in light of the law, spiritually understood, is regarded as sin."[18] A comparison of the two descriptions, one of sin and one of concupiscence, shows little if any difference. The Catholic definition of voluntary sin includes the following elements: selfish desire and lack of love. Those of the Lutheran conception of concupiscence are selfish desire, lack of love, and repeated idolatry—a sin which, as stated in the JD, requires daily *forgiveness* (JD, 29). The Catholic definition of sin appears quite similar to the Lutheran definition of concupiscence. Granted, the Annex does not use the modifier "truly [*wahrhaft*]" in describing the sinful character of concupiscence, but neither does it deny the truly sinful character of concupiscence. Now, if Lutherans maintain that concupiscence remains after baptism, and if their definition of concupiscence matches the Catholic definition of sin, then the Annex itself betrays an ambiguity. Significantly, the Annex does not return to the formulation of the 1995 draft: "Properly speaking, [concupiscence] therefore is not sin" (JD 1995, par. 26). It is thus not at all apparent, despite its having been approved by the PCPCU and the CDF, that the Annex actually meets the substance of the Vatican's concerns.

The stated incompatibility between the Lutheran and Catholic notions of concupiscence cannot, moreover, be circumvented by describing the Catholic notion of sin as "univocal" and the Lutheran notion as "analogical," as American theologian David Yeago attempts to do. Yeago claims that whereas Catholics restrict the term "sin" only to voluntary acts, thus employing the word "univocally," Lutherans understand "sin" both as the action of an individual and as the basic tendency of the sinner's nature to violate God's commandments.[19] I would submit, with Susan Wood, that Catholics draw an analogy between two categories of voluntary sin, mortal (proper sense) and venial (extended sense).[20] At this point one encounters a dispute about principles so fundamental that argument appears quite difficult. Catholics claim that the true character (*ratio*) of sin is voluntary offense. Accordingly, one could employ the term "sin" for the phenomenon of concupiscence only in an extended sense, namely as signifying a "cause by way of occasion or inclination." Most properly, concupiscence is seen by Catholics as a type of temptation, *fruitfully* left by God in order that the justified might enter the struggle of obedience to God, so that by suffering with Christ, they might be raised with Christ. To be tempted is not "to sin" in this sense. Lutherans, however, consider the non-voluntary contradiction of God's will to be sin in the true sense of the word, something in need of forgiveness and demanding an attitude of repentance. Moreover, all sin is alike grave for the Lutheran. All sin is damnable. It would appear, then, that it is Lutherans who refuse an analogical differentiation between mortal and venial sin.

For three reasons, neither Catholic doctrine nor Catholic piety can brook this position. First, Catholicism teaches that concupiscence is not a willful act but only a tendency towards sin. It can be called "desire" only in the sense of a spuriously spontaneous, non-willed inclination. Second, Catholics believe that concupiscence incurs absolutely no punishment and that venial sins incur only temporal punishment.[21] Third, the Catholic Church recognizes that inhering justice can coexist with venial sins but not because these sins are "not imputed." Rather, sanctifying grace remains, even though venial sins hinder its effects in human action.[22] God forgives both kinds of sin not by ignoring them but precisely *by* washing them away. Venial sins can also be purged by good works wrought through grace: "Love covers a multitude of sins" (1 Pet 4:8). Thus, the Catholic Church teaches that Christ "rules" damnable sin precisely by eradicating it through the infusion of sanctifying grace.[23] This issue leads naturally to the next.

Observance of the Law not a Condition for Salvation

The law is summed up in two commandments: the love of God and the love of neighbor. Conscious and free disobedience of the commandments is damnable sin. Damnable sin cannot coexist with inhering grace, which unites one to God through the bond of love. Therefore, if one holds that a person can stand just before God despite disobedience to the commandments, one cannot hold justifying righteousness to be identical with sanctifying grace. The common and Lutheran paragraphs imply the antecedent and thus, the consequent.

Par. 29 states: "[Thus, Christians, so long as they live on this earth, can at least in part {in fits and starts} lead a life in justice."[24] Is it not possible for the justified to obey all of God's commandments satisfactorily? Here, we encounter a discrepancy between the English translation and the official German. The English reads, "Christians can in part lead a just life," leaving the answer to the question obscure. The German hints at "piecemeal [*stückweise*]" observance of the commandments. Moreover, the German does not speak of leading a "just life" but of leading of life "in justice [*in Gerechtigkeit*]." Does this mean that the Christian also falls out of true justice or, rather, that no Christian expresses in action adequate obedience to the commandments? Hinting at an answer, a Lutheran paragraph on the Law teaches that even the justified fail to obey the commandments satisfactorily: "Every person, even the Christian, insofar as he is a sinner, stands his entire life under the accusation of the Law, which exposes his sins], so that, in faith in the Gospel, [he] will turn unreservedly to the mercy of God in Christ, which alone justifies [him]" (JD, 32).[25] This would appear to mean that, by the standards of the Law, even the regenerated Christian stands damnable before the presence of God.

The Catholic paragraph in the same section ambiguously states, "Christ is not a lawgiver in the manner of Moses" (JD, 33). Instead, Jesus has "overcome [*überwunden*]" the law as a way to salvation (JD, 31 and 33). What is the meaning of this expression? No one would dispute that Christ is not merely another Moses. Christ gives grace, whereas the law, the Old Law, consists chiefly in commands (Jn 1:17). Nevertheless, from the Catholic perspective, adequate obedience to the law remains obligatory for salvation. After all, Christ promulgated an even more radical law: "Think not that I have come to abolish the law and the prophets; I have come not to abolish them but to fulfil them" (Mt 5:17). In this manner, Jesus began his discourse on the radical demands of God's will: "You, therefore, must be perfect, as your heavenly Father is perfect" (Mt 5:48). Indeed, unlike Moses, Jesus gives power to fulfill this law: "Come to me, all who labor and are heavy laden, and I will give you rest" (Mt 11:28). Thus, Jesus promises to answer pleas such as Augustine's: "Grant what you command." In essence, what the Father commands through Jesus is that all abide in Christ through love (Jn 15:9). It is thus that Christians prove themselves to be Jesus' brother, sister, and mother (Mt 12:50). Against Luther's thought, Trent taught definitively that Christ is a legislator, though he is not *merely* a legislator: "If anyone says that Jesus Christ was given by God to men as a redeemer in whom they ought to trust and not also as a legislator whom they ought to obey: let him be anathema."[26]

Granted, man is not for the law (Mk 2:27). Nor is the law for God.[27] But the law *is* for man.[28] The law represents God's will for human happiness. Pope John Paul II has taken great pains to express the true significance of the law, both that given on Sinai and the radically deeper call issued on the Mount: "From the very lips of Jesus, the new Moses, man is once again given the commandments of the Decalogue. Jesus himself definitively confirms them and proposes them to us as the way and condition of salvation."[29] Three things are clear from the context of this passage: First, John Paul II emphasizes the inseparable unity of both tables of the law, love of God and love of neighbor; second, he recognizes that the full flowering of the imitation of Christ (*sequela Christi*) awaits heavenly life and that the inchoate beginnings in this life are a participation in and preparation for the life to come; and third, he insists that attainment of the promised heavenly kingdom depends upon adequate and concrete obedience to the commandments, as they have been more deeply put forth by Jesus Christ.[30]

Obedience to the commandments is not alien to the life to come; it is not merely a trial that, once successfully passed, has no relevance to those who receive the reward. According to John Paul II, the human person *cannot* be happy without obeying the commandments; indeed, this obedience is not one merely of "avoidance of sin" but more importantly one of ever-greater intimacy with Christ. John Paul insists that the "negative moral norms" which derive from these commandments are merely the lower limits beneath which one cannot go without gravely offending God, seriously damaging one's own person, and threatening one's eternal salvation. The law in its positive aspect is an upward call, with limitless potential: It is the call of love. For this reason, those who fail to enter into that upward thrust find themselves forlorn, as did the rich young man with many possessions (Mt 19:22). They are left in Egypt while the true Israel follows the Passover of the Lord from this world to the Father (1 Cor 10:6–13 and Jn 14:31b).

The JD falls short with respect to the law's obligatory nature. It states merely that the commandments "retain their validity for the justified." They and the life of Christ are a "standard [*Richtschnur*] for the conduct of the justified" (JD, 31). The reader can easily avoid drawing the conclusion that satisfactory obedience to the commandments is a *sine qua non* condition for salvation. The

1995 draft, though similar to the final draft on this score, left greater scope for the ongoing importance of the law: "Christ in his teaching and life gave expression to the demands of God's will [*fordernden Willen Gottes*], to which also the justified owe obedience [*Gehorsam schuldet*]" (JD 1995, par. 34). This emphasis on the Christian's obligation to obey God's demanding will is not found in the final draft, even in its Catholic paragraph, which states merely that the justified are "bound (or held) to observance [*zur Beobachtung...gehaltung ist*]" (JD, 33) of these commands. The preparatory dialogues express a similar reservation about the necessity of such obedience. A Lutheran passage quoted in Sources to 4.5 states, "If however Canon 20 [see below] affirms that faith has salvific power only on condition of keeping the commandments, this [anathema] applies to us."[31] Lutherans deny observance of the law is a *sine qua non* condition of salvation.

While this Lutheran denial is rooted in the experience of sinful man's weakness, the explicit conclusion that God's laws cannot be fulfilled by the justified person is not reconcilable with the Catholic perspective. Trent strikes a balance between affirming the necessity of grace and the sufficient empowering that takes place through the gift of grace. Justified persons can obey the entire law, "For God does not desert those once justified by his grace unless he is first deserted by them."[32] Those are condemned who deny either the necessity or the efficacy of grace: "If anyone says that the justified are able to persevere in the justice received without God's special help or that they cannot do so with that help: let him be anathema."[33] For ages it has been anathema to say, "The precepts of God are impossible for the justified man to observe."[34] Since observance of the law is not impossible, it is not necessary for the Church to qualify the "ongoing validity" of the law as not constituting a necessary condition for salvation. For Trent, the Gospel is not a "bare and unconditional promise of eternal life without condition of observing the commandments [canon 20]."[35] Though believers fall into daily sins "which are also called venial ..., they do not on account of these cease to be just."[36] They remain just only if, by God's grace, they obey these commandments in charity. Nor ought this obedience be seen merely as "not" committing certain proscribed actions. Sins of omission can be as deadly as sins of commission, because sins of omission also affect the Christian's relation to God and neighbor. It is for this reason that spiritual sloth, which inhibits good action in light of a perceived burden, is so deadly.[37] This becomes apparent in the upward call in Christ (Phil. 3:14), for although the lesser good is not necessarily sinful, still, there is a certain minimum threshold of action (yes, *ergon*) without which no person with the use of free will can remain justified. Sins of omission can be every bit as deadly as sins of commission. Because what is at issue is a relationship, disobedience to the commandments entails the loss of that charity by which the human person relates to God in a saving way and without which no one can be saved. Grace and charity are in this way the "spotless robe" that God bestows in justification.[38] One can forfeit this baptismal robe through a single mortal sin.

With this in mind and with confidence in God's saving power, Trent declares, "Those reborn, receiving true and Christian justice for that which Adam lost for himself and for us in his disobedience, are ordered at once to preserve it as a best robe, bright and immaculate, that they might bear it before the judgment seat of our Lord Jesus Christ and have eternal life."[39] Given an acute experience of sin, inscribed in the tradition of the Lutheran communions, this statement might well appear an occasion for either self-righteous self-contemplation or terrified despair. It seems to leave the believer unto himself: work out your salvation in fear, without Christ! Yet this reading is quite far from the authentic intent of the council. Seripando entered the scene again, offering a contribution wholly acceptable to the council fathers: The righteousness of the justified streams from Christ, who also faithfully supplies them with that strength they need to persevere. He accompanies them before, during, and after each of their works. Thus, it is not a matter of an "either-or" dichotomy: either Christ alone or also (or only) the believer. It is a matter of the believer being engrafted into Christ by God the Father through the Holy Spirit. Having hinted at the Trinitarian dimension in chapter 7 of its decree, the council turned to a Christological focus in chapter 16: "For Jesus Christ himself continually imparts strength to those justified, as the head to the members and the vine to the branches, and this strength always precedes, accompanies and follows their good works, and without it they would be wholly unable to do anything meritorious and pleasing to God." The fathers then followed out the theological conclusion, which Seripando hesitated to do: If Christ's grace is indeed communicated to those justified as a power by which they become children of God (Jn 1:12), then they can indeed obey the entire law and merit eternal life. Therefore, "It must be believed that nothing more is needed for the justified to be considered to have fully satisfied God's law, according to this state of life, by the deeds they have wrought in him and to have truly [merited to obtain] eternal life in their time (provided they die in a state of grace)."[40]

This Catholic teaching is thus not alien to the genuine Lutheran concern that the experience of sin should lead the believer to trust in God alone for mercy. In proclaiming with Paul that the baptized are a "new creation" (Gal 6:15), the Catholic Church does not wish to dilute this trust. And yet there is another reason for trust, also not alien to Lutheran piety: filial devotion. The Johannine and Pauline teachings that believers become children of God thwarts the reduction of Christian life to a Law-Gospel dialectic. Children are without the law because they are a law unto themselves, having it etched into their hearts (Ezek 36:26–28). They are not his children, however, who do not follow that law (1 Jn 3:4–10). They who do "not submit to God's law" are still "in the flesh" (Rom 8:7).

Walking this narrow road of "filiation," evading Pharisaical pride, paralyzing despair, and presumptive trust, St. Thérèse proved herself a daughter of the Father and of the Church. She emphatically refused to "trust" in herself, despite the apparent fact that she committed no mortal sin her entire life. She flew simply to the Father through his Son, Jesus Christ, in whom she partook. Her life of loving trust still provides the world with ample proof that honest (humble) recognition of the reality of one's sanctity in no way distorts one's trusting relationship with Christ. Thérèse obeyed the commandments of God, but to say this hardly expresses the depth of her sanctity, let alone her mission, since faithful observance of the law is not merely a negative relation to some restrictive force. Rather, faithful observance of the law preserves and deepens the life of sanctity by which believers move from grace to grace, advancing in intimacy with their heavenly Father through their Savior, Friend, and Brother. Advancing in their filial relationship with God, the justified enjoy an increase in justifying grace.

No Increase of Justifying Grace

The JD does not appear to allow for an increase of justifying grace or that by which the Christian stands just before God. No one can doubt that Christ's personal righteousness is perfect and does not increase. From a Catholic perspective, however, sanctifying grace can always increase since it is the human person's spiritual participation in the divine perfection, by which that person is constituted a child and friend of God. As a participation in God's justice through Jesus Christ, sanctifying grace can increase. Since this increase pertains to spiritual perfection, it cannot occur to the detriment of its bearer's nature: It can make a person holier but it cannot render him a not-man. If, therefore, one holds that justifying righteousness cannot increase, then one must also hold that the formal cause of justification is not sanctifying grace. The section entitled "Good Works of the Justified" addresses the issue of sanctification and an increase in holiness.

The common paragraph states, "We confess together that good works—a Christian life lived in faith, hope and love—follow justification and are its fruits" (JD, 37). This statement would be acceptable both to the fathers of Trent and the authors of the *Formula of Concord*. It presents a twofold distinction between grace and works, leaving room for various interpretations.

The following Catholic interpretation has raised some eyebrows in the

Lutheran world: "According to Catholic understanding, good works, [which are accomplished] by grace and by the working of the Holy Spirit, contribute to growth in grace, so that the righteousness that comes from God is preserved and communion with Christ is deepened" (JD, 38).[41] The affirmation of an increase in grace seems strikingly tridentine. If this is so, then by its recognition of the JD, the LWF has taken a significant step towards the Catholic understanding. But this is not necessarily the case. The text speaks of a "growth *in* grace."[42] This growth is not necessarily an increase of the grace by which persons are justified. The explanation that follows refers to a "preservation of righteousness" and a deepening of communion with Christ, steering the reader away from conceiving of the growth as an increased presence of justifying grace in the justified person (or, in scholastic phraseology, an increased hold of the infused habit of grace upon the person justified). A number of Lutherans are comfortable holding a preservation of righteousness and a deepening personal relationship with Christ. They are not comfortable affirming an increase of justifying grace itself.[43] The "Catholic" articulation in par. 38 *can* be interpreted in accordance with the traditional Lutheran approach. Birmelé reads the document in this way, for he argues that the "in [*dans*]" disallows any increase of *grace*. He perceives herein a Catholic concession, for the *Formula of Concord* condemned Trent's teaching on an increase *of* grace. Moreover, numerous other Catholic passages exclude "with express words" all trace of an increase of grace; they even exclude the idea of an increase of faith by means of good works.[44] Birmelé draws attention to the closing clause in par. 38: "Justification always remains the unmerited gift of grace."[45] If *always*, then in no case is the grace by which sinners are made just ever merited, not even after baptism. One could add the following evidence to Birmelé's contention: The official German does not merely say that good works are "made possible" by grace and the Holy Spirit (as the English maintains) but that the Holy Spirit accomplishes (*erfüllt*) them. We have, then, a witness within the JD to the Catholic framers' understanding of the following ambiguous statement of the common confession: "[The message of justification] tells us that [we sinners {*wir Sünder*} owe our new life solely to the forgiving and renewing mercy of God, which we only accept and receive in faith, but which we] *never can merit in any way*" (JD, 17, emphasis mine). These statements lead logically to the contradiction of Trent's *unica causa formalis*.

The Lutheran paragraph in the section on merit also expresses a growth "in" grace, but it qualifies the assertion by denying that there is growth in the righteousness by which Christians are justified:

> The concept of a preservation of grace and a growth in grace and faith is also held by Lutherans. They do emphasize that righteousness as acceptance by God and sharing in

the righteousness of Christ is always complete. At the same time, they state that there
can be growth in its effects in Christian living. When they view the good works of
Christians as the fruits and signs of justification and not as one's own "merits," they
nevertheless also understand eternal life in accord with the New Testament as
unmerited "reward" in the sense of the fulfillment of God's promise to the believer.
(JD, 39)[46]

It is certainly a joyful surprise to witness a Lutheran affirmation of growth "in"
grace and faith. The Lutherans appear to see the possibility of compromise. It
is nonetheless difficult to interpret this statement as fully adequate to Catholic
teaching. The paragraph quickly qualifies this "growth" by its denial that
righteousness (*Gerechtigkeit*) increases. The underlying reason for this denial
is likely attributable to a conception of the essence of justification as being the
righteousness of Jesus Christ. According to this conception, justification is
God's acceptance of the sinner who "shares" in Christ's own righteousness
through faith. Since this acceptance and sharing are "always complete," they
cannot consist formally in infused grace. The Catholic reader is delightedly
surprised, as well, at the Lutheran use of the terms "sharing" or "participation
[*Teilhabe*]" but equally perplexed that such "participation" can be said to be
"always complete [*immer vollkommen*]." One of the purposes of the concept
"participation" has been, among other things, to allow for a greater or lesser
manifestation of some perfection in the participating subject. That which is "X"
by essence cannot coherently be said to increase in "X," but that which is "X"
by participation can surely enjoy an increase in "X," since the perfection "X"
is always in itself more perfect than some being's share in "X." It seems clear
that the Lutheran paragraph affirms the "increase in grace" to mean simply an
increase in the effects of grace in the Christian life and not an increase in
justifying grace: "At the same time, they state that there can be growth in its
effects in Christian living" (JD, 39).

A work cited in Sources to 4.7 corroborates this reading. The passage
referred to denies that justifying righteousness can increase, since it identifies
justifying righteousness with God's favor:

The Lutheran confessions stress that the justified person is responsible not to lose the
grace received but to live in it.... Thus the confessions can speak of a preservation of
grace and a growth in it. If righteousness [*iustitia*] in Canon 24 [see below] is
understood in the sense that it [a]ffects human beings, then it does not apply to us. But
if *righteousness* in Canon 24 refers to the Christian's acceptance by God, it applies to
us; because this righteousness is always perfect; compared with it the works of
Christians are only "fruits" and "signs."[47]

According to this source, the righteousness by which one is just before God
consists in Christ's own righteousness attributed to faith, either through

forensic acquittal or through Christ's indwelling or through faith's ecstatic fellowship.[48] Hence, the formal cause of justification is not identifiable with the formal cause of sanctification. A similar distinction appears also in the American dialogue, to which Sources to 4.2 also refers:

> Lutherans describe justification as the imputation to sinners of a righteousness which is that of Christ himself (*iustitia aliena*).... Lutherans also affirm the reality of sanctification and good works, but they regard these effects as fruits rather than parts of justification itself.[49]

Christ's righteousness attributed to faith, the saving power of which is not dependent upon charity, is held to be the formal cause of justification.[50]

The above-cited sources to the JD clearly distinguish the "growth" of sanctification from the essential righteousness of the believer, by which the believer is righteous before God. An important commentary on the JD reads both the Catholic and Lutheran paragraphs in precisely this manner. Although JD 38 "presents the Catholic understanding" of growth in grace, "This statement is made more precise by adding that through such works 'the righteousness that comes from God is preserved.'" The commentary continues, "The word 'preserved'…means that good works as works which correspond to the righteousness given and maintained by God prevent this righteousness from being lost through actions or omissions." But, the commentary concludes, righteousness itself does not increase: "This growth does not imply that less grace is present at first and then more later. Grace is either present as a whole or not present at all."[51]

Trent, on the contrary, identifies the formal cause of justification and the formal cause of sanctification. So, an increase in sanctification is *eo ipso* an increase in justification. As cited in Part One, Trent states,

> By mortifying the members of their flesh and by offering them as weapons of justice towards sanctification through observance of the commandments of God and of the Church, they increase in that very justice received through the grace of Christ, by faith cooperating in good works, *and they are even more justified.*[52]

Justification, i.e., first justification, is the first moment in which sanctifying grace is infused. Good works are indeed signs of justification, but they are not merely signs, for by them one can merit an increase in justifying grace, i.e., second justification. Good works are wrought through the power of inhering grace. The initial attainment of this grace is absolutely beyond human power. But once bestowed, this grace becomes an inner principle by which the human person can relate intimately with the triune God. When the just person acts from this principle, he preserves his being in grace, sometimes meriting and disposing himself to an increase of it. Sanctification as an increase of an infused gift might be compared, loosely, to the life of Lazarus after being raised from the dead. Although dead Lazaraus had only a "passive potency" to be raised from the dead, for *he* was raised, yet the life restored to him allowed him to act in concert with the end of human life. Through such action, he could live life "in greater abundance," becoming more vigorously active in virtue and thus allowing his concrete life to be more radicated in the principles of life restored to him: To live is life. The dynamic character and orientation of grace underlies the rationale in canon 24 of Trent's Sixth Session: "If anyone says that the justice received is neither conserved nor increased in the presence of God through good works but that the works themselves are only fruits and signs of the justification received and not also a cause of its increase: let him be anathema."[53] The JD and Trent are in manifest tension on this point and, consequently, on the matter of "cooperation" with God's grace. Before considering cooperation, I would like to consider the JD's neglect of the distinction between mortal and venial sin.

Insufficient Distinction between Mortal and Venial Sin

The preceding three sections discuss problematic teachings consequent to or correlative with a denial of sanctifying grace as the formal cause of justification. These three consequences logically prevent the theologian from offering a properly Catholic account of mortal sin. If a person is formally justified not by sanctifying grace but by the righteousness of Christ attributed to faith (whether synthetically *or* analytically), how could any sin except unbelief affect his status as justified? Is there any alternative to this conclusion? Proper discussion of the sacrament of reconciliation would include the distinctions between imperfection and venial sin and between venial sin and mortal sin. These distinctions are crucial to Catholic doctrine and piety. Imperfections are not sins; choice of the lesser good is not necessarily sinful. Although the JD makes passing reference to the sacrament of reconciliation (JD, 30), it does not take occasion to address these distinctions.[54]

Traditional Lutheran teaching avoids the distinction between mortal and venial sins, though Lutherans, unlike those in the Reformed tradition, admit that true faith can be lost and with it, justification.[55] Still, only the loss of faith, on account of which God justifies the sinner, is held to be truly damn*ing*. Such loss can be explained in one of two ways. In the first way, damning sin is always and only unbelief itself. Thus, the one who disbelieves—and *only* this one—forfeits the promised inheritance. All other sins, howsoever grievous, are "ever again granted forgiveness" in the "daily return to Baptism" (JD, 28 and

29). Even though sanctification and good works are necessary "fruits" of justification without which justifying grace is not preserved (JD, 37 and 39), sanctification does not include the eradication of mortal sin, for sanctification is inchoate. Because sanctification is inchoate, observance of the law is only piecemeal; therefore, sanctification coincides with sin—even hypothetically damnable sin. This sin is "forgiven" (not obliterated) as something not reckoned to the believer. In the second way, malicious sin always causes the loss of "justifying" faith. Wherever there is malicious unrighteousness, faith is always also destroyed.[56]

Both of these accounts of "damning" sin are contrary to Trent. The first is condemned as follows: "If anyone says that there is no mortal sin except unbelief, or that the grace once received is lost by no sin, howsoever grave and enormous, other than unbelief: let him be anathema."[57] About the second, Trent warns, "If anyone says that, if grace be lost through sin, faith is always at once lost, or that the faith which remains is not true faith, even though it is not living, or that he who has faith without charity is not a Christian: let him be anathema."[58] Avery Dulles notes that the JD does not seem to square with the Catholic teaching on this point, even though, he believes, the JD purports to assert that justification takes place alone through *living* faith, i.e., faith informed by charity. The JD denies that true, albeit not necessarily living, faith can exist without renewal and justification. Dulles comments, "Trent and the whole Catholic tradition maintain on the contrary that the gift of faith can exist in the absence of love and repentance. The Council of Trent taught this under anathema. The *Joint Declaration* fails to explain why canon 28 of Trent's *Decree on Justification* does not apply to Lutherans today."[59] Dulles thus critiques a formulation in the JD that was in part intended to placate Catholics.[60]

The two Lutheran explanations of "damning" sin are rooted in the understanding of justification through the attribution to faith of the righteousness of Christ. Because this "attribution" can be conceived to occur in at least two different ways, it would be useful to note how different schools might offer somewhat different accounts of mortal sin. First, the "attribution" can be seen as forensic and extrinsic (a synthetic judgment). Melanchthon in 1531 and the authors of the *Formula of Concord* held that justification occurs through a forensic imputation to faith. This imputation is by nature independent of inhering grace. In this line of thought, justification cannot be destroyed, except by loss of faith. Now this line of thought also includes an insistence that faith necessarily impels the believer towards gracious thanks to God and generous love towards neighbor. True faith cannot exist in a person without such attitudes and works, although the justifying power of true faith must be completely distinguished from these latter, which are mere fruits.

Second, the "attribution" can be seen to be rendered on account of the believer's union with Christ through faith (an analytic judgment). The gift of Christ in the believer makes the believer to be truly righteous, purging away the dross of sins and calling the believer toward an ever deeper union with Christ. This line of thought maintains that any fundamental failure of the believer to remain faithful to the gift of Christ results in the falling out of justification. If the believer does not accept the gift of Christ and its sanctifying work, then God will not protect the sinner from his wrath. For if the sinner is not united with Christ (by an indwelling or by an ecstatic relationship) through faith, how can God look upon him as righteous? And yet at the same time, this second line of thought openly avows that damnable sin remains within the justified person.

The Lutheran cannot subscribe to the Catholic notion that every concretely damnable sin committed by the believer renders him unjustified. Luther, Melanchthon, Chemnitz, and today, Peura and Pannenberg, have sought to find some *via media* between the Catholic notion of mortal sin and a complete disregard of anything that can be called mortally sinful; they seek a *via media* between the "moralists" and the "Epicureans." Each of these theologians maintains that the baptismal call includes loving obedience to Christ. They also maintain that true faith is incompatible with a deliberate and obstinate refusal of this obedience, all the while claiming that the willingness to obey (as well as actual obedience) is not the cause of faith's justifying power, even though this very willingness is itself the gift of God. They maintain that the believer can cast himself away from the inheritance by a willful opposition to God's grace. They do not identify this basic opposition to God's grace with what Catholics describe as concrete mortal sins. Rather, they restrict this opposition to a basic attitude of the whole person, maliciously directed against the covenantal grace of baptism. The Catholic phenomenon of "repeat offenders" who faithfully seek forgiveness for repeated mortal sins through the sacrament of reconciliation would seem possible, from this Lutheran perspective, only in virtue of the basic attitude of faithfulness, by which these believers truly strive to obey the commands of God.[61] The Lutheran will undoubtedly pity such believers for their attachment to this cycle and for the concomitant terrors that might accompany it. Nevertheless, the Lutheran will insist that this very cycle testifies to a *tertium quid* between what Catholics call mortal sin and a complete disregard of anything like sin that kills. If the believer truly commits "mortal sins" or "sins that kill," so it might be said, he would be unlikely to seek God's grace so faithfully, so consistently after having spurned it.

Moreover, Lutherans will insist that if the believer were truly to spurn God's grace, he would not turn back so quickly, for by really spurning God, one orients oneself away from God's grace. While it is not impossible for an obstinate sinner to repent, it is unlikely for this to happen in a cyclic manner, from true faith to infidelity to true faith to infidelity. To spurn God in this way is to refuse his grace and to sin in a way that is damn*ing*. Lutherans describe this damn*ing* sin as infidelity, as the willful opposition to God's movements within the sinner, such that the sinner actually forgoes true faith and, with it, the grace of justification. In contrast, the attitude that keeps the "Catholic cycle" going, Lutherans will maintain, can be described as the basic orientation of the human person to receive God's grace; it can be called a "fundamental option" for God's grace, i.e., faith. It is the basic acceptance of God's covenantal love. This basic attitude requires a constant struggle against sin, without which true faith is lost. To keep up this struggle is not to attempt "to achieve" salvation, but to preserve the salvation already given through faith. Lutherans insist, however, that if a person fails to fulfill the law by doing what is objectively damnable, he does not necessarily forfeit God's grace, because justification is through faith. True faith is lost by neglect of the struggle against sin, but this struggle is fraught with failure, even with failure that Catholics describe as damnable sin.[62]

It should be clear to Catholic moral theologians that this search for a middle ground between "mortal sin" and Epicurean antinomianism yields precisely the notion of a "fundamental option" that is capable of remaining basically the same despite concrete, freely-performed actions that violate the ten commandments. Such a notion of the fundamental option—and I am here avoiding reference to specific Catholic theologians, since the subtleties of the various positions are beyond the scope of this work—is clearly in violation of Catholic teaching.[63]

It is remarkable to find some pastoral equivalence between the general thrust of a Lutheran articulation of justification and the conclusions of Catholic moral theologians who conceive of the full depth of the fundamental option as disengaged from concrete action, except in rare cases. Through very different and even opposed approaches, Lutherans and these Catholic thinkers arrive at a very similar conclusion: Specific, freely and knowingly chosen violations of the ten commandments do not always render a person unjustified. It seems to me that the Lutheran conception has the advantage of a more honest evaluation of human action, for as John tells us, those who say they have no sin are liars (1 Jn 1:8). Whereas the Lutheran doctrine rightly encourages one to acknowledge sin, today's Catholic moralists undertake to call what is sin "no-sin" and to claim that through a supposedly good fundamental option one really does not sin mortally, except in the rare case of deliberate malice. Lutherans are encouraged to repent when God's Word strikes them, in harmony with Psalm 51, but the tickling lies of today's Catholic moralists make the "no-people" think they are "God's-people." Isaiah long ago decried such moralism: "Woe to those who call evil good and good evil, who put darkness for light and light for darkness, who put bitter for sweet and sweet for bitter…who acquit the guilty for a bribe and deprive the innocent of his right!" (Is 5:20, 23). Whereas Lutherans perceive themselves as the repentant tax collector, the Catholic moralists build their Babel and usher their hearers inside, up to the front seats, playing Nietzsche's *Zarathustra* ill.

Eternal Life not Truly Merited

The tridentine position on the formal cause of justification is organically linked with its teaching that persons endowed with grace can "truly merit" eternal life. The basis for this teaching is the genuine character of the Christian's union with Christ. The baptized person is "inserted" or "engrafted" into Christ and truly partakes in his righteousness, which flows from him as from its fontal source. Therefore, God the Father sees in the baptized the resemblance of Jesus. Their faithful actions, wrought in the grace of the Spirit, participate in the actions of his Son. Therefore, "If we have grown into union with him" (Rom 6:5), we are called to suffer with Christ so as to be glorified with him: "If we have died with Christ, we believe that we shall also live with him" (Rom 6:8).[64] For this reason, those persons who die endowed with a participation in Christ's righteousness through the Holy Spirit can be said to be worthy not of eternal damnation but only of eternal life: "When we cry 'Abba! Father' it is the Spirit himself bearing witness with our spirit that we are children of God, and if children, then heirs, heirs of God and fellow heirs with Christ, provided we suffer with him in order that we may also be glorified with him" (Rom 8:15–17). To claim otherwise is to deny that these persons share in Christ in such a way that they are truly children of God in whom there is no damnable sin (1 Jn 3:2, 9). As our Savior himself promised, if we abide in him, we will bear much fruit (Jn 15:5); however, just as no bad tree bears good fruit, so no good tree bears bad fruit (Mt 7:17–18).

Trent distinguishes between non-meritorious and meritorious cooperation. The former occurs before justification, and the latter, afterwards. Despite the greater importance of meritorious cooperation, it is expedient first to analyze non-meritorious cooperation. Since this analysis of the JD is quite involved, the relevant paragraphs will be cited and examined distinctly.

Non-meritorious Cooperation

Common Paragraph. The common paragraph relevant for non-meritorious cooperation reads:

> 19. We confess together that [human persons] depend completely on the saving grace of God for their salvation. The freedom they possess in relation to persons and the things of this world is no freedom in relation to [their] salvation, for as sinners they stand under God's judgment and are incapable of turning by themselves to God to seek deliverance, of meriting their justification before God or of attaining salvation by their own abilities. Justification takes place [by grace alone].... [65]

Par. 19 rightly denies that unjustified sinners can turn towards God for mercy without His saving help. No mortal sinner could ever turn towards God without divine assistance.

Closer scrutiny of this paragraph, in the context of the Declaration as a whole, leaves the reader wondering *who* it is that has "no freedom in relation to salvation." As an exception to the rule, the English—which reads, "all persons"—is more suggestive of the Lutheran perspective. The German has simply "the human person [*der Mensch*]." The second sentence refers to persons who "as sinners stand under God's judgment." We must read this second sentence in light of other passages. So read, it does refer to "all persons," the justified as well as the unjustified. We gather this from par. 32: "All persons, Christians also in that they are sinners, stand under [the Law's] accusation." Similarly, par. 29 describes all the justified "as sinners" in that sin still dwells within them. The denial of salvific freedom in par. 19 can be taken, then, to refer to "all persons," justified and unjustified. So, par. 19 affirms that all persons at all times are powerless to win their salvation. Does this imply that no one can truly merit the beatific life, even after being endowed with the gift of righteousness that God bestows, faithful to his promise? Those Catholics who wish to avoid this implication will appeal to the sentence that claims, rightly, that Christians cannot attain salvation "by their own abilities." In this way, these Catholics would seek to evade the possible implication that the human person has no freedom with respect to eternal salvation; they would insist that any freedom is upheld and nurtured by God's grace and that, on the presupposition of this grace, humans have salvific freedom and can truly merit eternal life. If Catholics wish to read the paragraph thus, will Lutherans follow suit?

Catholic Paragraph. The JD's Catholic interpretation of human powerlessness is ambiguous. Its statement with reference to the state of the sinner before justification appears to be satisfactory (JD, 20). However, a parallel statement in the section on justification as forgiveness leaves some questions unanswered (JD, 24). The two statements read:

> 20. When Catholics say that persons "cooperate" in preparing for and accepting justification by consenting to God's justifying action, they see such personal consent as itself an effect of grace [and as no human deed arising from immanent human powers].[66]

> 24. ... [Catholics] do not thereby deny that God's gift of grace in justification remains independent of human cooperation.

Par. 20 accurately attributes human powerlessness to the absolute need of the sinner for prevenient grace. This is perfectly acceptable. Par. 24 is problematic. It appears to reject the need for human cooperation antecedent to justification. In what way is God's grace independent of human cooperation? Is it, as Trent teaches, that no works whatsoever merit first justification? The meaning of par. 24 is not clear. One is left wondering whether this statement sufficiently accommodates the tridentine description of the existential process, involving arduous volitional activity, which terminates in God's merciful act of a free infusion of justifying righteousness.[67] Without a doubt, even from the tridentine perspective, this entire process is dependent upon God's merciful initiative of covenantal love and upon his moving power. Still, notwithstanding the absolute priority of prevenient grace, the justification of an adult cannot take place without active cooperation, for it is the human person that is converted; it is the old man that becomes new. The expression of Catholic teaching in the JD is ambiguous at best and might justly be labeled a distortion.[68] The ambiguity of the Catholic interpretation is compounded by difficulties that the Lutheran paragraph presents.

Lutheran Paragraph. Lutheran par. 21 offers the most problematic explication of par. 19:

> 21. According to Lutheran teaching, human beings are incapable of cooperating in their salvation, because as sinners they actively oppose God and his saving action. Lutherans do not deny that a person can reject the working of grace. When they emphasize that a person can only receive (mere passive [Latin terms]) justification, they mean thereby to exclude any possibility of contributing to one's own justification but do not deny [one's full personal involvement in faith], which is effected by God's Word.[69]

It is rightly stated that human persons can reject the working of grace, but the meaning of this statement unclear. More importantly, there are three elements in this paragraph that pose difficulties from the Catholic perspective. First, there is a categorical denial of human cooperation in salvation: "Human beings are incapable of cooperating in their salvation." The exclusion pertains not merely to justification, which Catholics agree cannot be merited, but also to salvation. Second, the insistence that Christians "as sinners actively oppose God and his saving action" calls to mind Luther's exaggerations about original sin. The JD here echoes the pessimism of the *Solid Declaration*, which declares that the will of an unregenerate sinner "is not only totally turned away from God, but is also turned and perverted against God and toward all evil."[70] The Catholic Church, while confessing that all men are due to be born without sanctifying grace on account of original sin, does not share this extreme pessimism about human sinners.[71] Third, the phrase "full personal involvement" does not sufficiently affirm the painstaking steps of cooperation that God requires of those adults who would be justified. In the context of traditional Lutheranism, "personal involvement" means a passive "undergoing." It is the believer's awareness that something is going on and his willing something in connection to it.[72] How do these intellectual and volitional operations relate to the sinner's own intellect and will? Must we say that they do "not proceed from our carnal and natural powers"? Does conversion belong "in no way to the human powers of the natural free will, be it entirely or one-half or the least and tiniest part, but altogether and alone to the divine operation and the Holy Spirit"?[73] If grace does not replace nature, how can these "new movements" not be movements of the sinner's own intellect and will? If they are not movements of the sinner's intellect and will, of what are they movements? The authors of the *Formula* affirm only two efficient causes of the preparation for justification: the Word of God (preached and heard) and the Holy Spirit.[74] The JD itself depicts the Holy Spirit as "effecting" or "performing"faith; this depiction tends away from conceiving the human person as a secondary efficient cause.

The JD's low estimation of cooperation is found also in the preparatory dialogues cited therein. A dialogue cited in Sources to 4.1 reads: "[We] exclude any cooperation in the event of justification itself. Justification is the work of Christ alone, the work of grace alone."[75] Remarkably, a Catholic source also cited in the JD critiques this exclusive assignment of action in justification to God:

> Where, however, Lutheran teaching construes the relation of God to his human creatures in justification with such emphasis on the divine "monergism" or the sole efficacy of Christ in such a way, that the person's willing acceptance of God's grace—which is itself a gift of God—has no essential role in justification, then the tridentine Canons 4, 5, 6, and 9 still constitute a notable doctrinal difference on justification.[76]

This citation would appear to call into question the very "compatibility" of doctrinal expression that the JD claims to enjoy. It is not clear in the JD that the Lutherans have qualified their traditional reluctance to admit the need for human cooperation, even cooperation inspired by God's prevenient grace, as preparation for justification. Avery Dulles's remarks about this paragraph remain pertinent: "These statements are intelligible only if one understands justification as a divine decree, prior to any human act of faith or love. The Catholic response [i.e., the OVR] quite understandably asks whether the Joint Declaration on this point can be harmonized with Trent, which…teaches a very different doctrine of justification."[77]

The Teaching of Trent. The tridentine decree begins with a confession of the sinner's absolute need for prevenient grace, yet this confession does not deny the necessity of preparation: "Through God's arousing and supporting grace, sinners are disposed to convert themselves to his justification of them by freely assenting to and cooperating with that same grace."[78] Chapter 6 maps out the laborious steps frequently involved in the conversion that precedes justification, including fear of punishment, hope in God's mercy, an incipient love short of charity, and the decision to obey the commandments.

The ultimate moment of justification is the infusion of grace through baptism, but the process leading thereto necessarily involves cooperation from adults, inspired and assisted by God. Those who have fallen through mortal sin must, likewise, actively cooperate with God before receiving forgiveness. This includes a contrition for sins that involves hatred for the perversity of sin, a tender sorrow of spirit, and the willingness to emend one's life.[79] Trent condemns the understanding of "*mere passive*" as found in traditional Lutheranism and, it seems to me, as found in the JD. Canon 9 states:

> If anyone says, that a sinner is justified by faith alone, understanding this to mean that nothing else is required by which he would cooperate for the attainment of the grace of justification, and that there is no necessity for him to be prepared and disposed by a motion of his will: let him be anathema.[80]

The thrust of Trent, both in the Decree on Justification itself and in the decrees on the sacraments, presents a picture of the Catholic perspective: The sinner who is to be justified must actively respond to God's grace, freely reject former sins, embrace God as the ultimate end, and begin to love God as the source of righteousness. The JD's shortcomings with regard to non-meritorious cooperation are replicated with regard to meritorious cooperation.

Meritorious Cooperation

The Joint Declaration. The elect who are admitted into eternal life consist solely in those who die justified, since justifying righteousness is the key that opens paradise for the just. If this righteousness is formally caused by sanctifying grace, the person who dies in grace can be worthy not of damnation but only of eternal life, a post-mortem purification of *venial* sins notwithstanding. This is what Trent confesses. If, however, the "justified" person is worthy of damnation but receives eternal life simply because of faith in the promise, justifying righteousness is not sanctifying grace. What does the Joint Declaration say?

The Catholic paragraph is somewhat evasive. It states nebulously,

> When Catholics affirm the "meritorious" character of good works, they wish to say that, according to the biblical witness, *a* reward [ein *Lohn*] in heaven is promised to these works. Their intention is to emphasize the responsibility of persons for their actions, not to contest the character of those works as gifts or far less to deny that justification [itself] always remains the unmerited gift of grace.[81] (JD, 38, emphasis mine)

Several questions are in order. First, *what* reward is promised? Is it eternal life itself, namely, the saint's participation in divine glory? Or is it some concomitantly bestowed blessing? Second, how are responsible actions connected to this reward? Are they properly meritorious, or are they, as Melanchthon held (see below), simply called meritorious because the gift of salvation given on the basis of the promise alone can be *considered* as a reward for works of love? Third, what is the meaning of the final clause: "[The Catholic intention is not] to deny that justification [itself] always [*stets*] remains the unmerited gift of grace"? The context—a paragraph about merit—suggests that this "unmerited character" is predicable not merely of the beginning of justification but of its increase—sanctification—and of its fruition—salvation. The statement seems to specify what remained ambiguous in an earlier Catholic paragraph: "[Catholics] do not thereby deny that God's gift of grace in justification remains independent of human cooperation" (JD, 24). Par. 24 left us wondering whether human cooperation never contributes to justification, either to first justification (in a way that would be, to say the *least*, not condign) or to second justification, i.e., to one's being "more justified" through cooperation. Par. 38 leads one to favor a reading of par. 24 that is, from a Catholic perspective, more problematic. So, the somewhat ambiguous claim in the midst of par. 38, "*A* reward [ein *Lohn*] in heaven is promised to these works" (emphasis mine), is mitigated by its final clause. Finally, the reader will recall that the German text begins with an affirmation that good works "are accomplished [*erfüllt sind*]" by grace and the Holy Spirit. There is little in this paragraph that genuinely conveys the distinctively Catholic doctrine on merit.

The Lutheran paragraph is clearer and more problematic: "[Lutherans also understand] eternal life...as an unmerited 'reward' in the sense of the fulfillment of God's promise to the believer" (JD, 39). Is the reader to surmise that eternal life itself is purely a gift, so that it is in no sense merited, even by those who walk in newness of life with Christ? The keyword is "promise." God promises eternal life to the believer. How is this term being employed? Melanchthon linked the Pauline term "promise" exclusively to faith, not to faith as quickened by charity, but simply to faith that "accepts the promise."[82] "We must," Melanchthon stated, "be accounted righteous by this faith for Christ's sake before we love and keep the law, although love must necessarily follow."[83] Faith's justifying power is, for him, independent of obedience to the commandments. Thus, although damnable sin remains, the justified person receives the promise of salvation unconditionally through faith. Granted, Melanchthon did suggest that the gift of eternal life can been seen as recompense for works performed in faith; this is how he interpreted Paul's "If a son, then an heir" (Gal 4:7). Still, whereas Paul's word is suggestive of a strict right to inheritance, a right *freely given* by God through adoption, Melanchthon would locate this "right" not in the status of the person made to be a child of God (Jn 1:12) but merely in the extrinsic favor of God. Is Melanchthon's "fit" between works and eternal life even tantamount to the scholastic notion of *congruous* merit? Did he even believe that works are "fittingly" rewarded? In any case, it is clear that he would not agree that the justified person who has the use of free will receives eternal life as merited by good works.[84]

The reader seeking clarity must further examine the sources of the ecumenical accord. The JD guides the reader to the following citation in Sources to 4.7: "We grant that eternal life is a reward because it is something that is owed—*not because of our merits but because of the promise*."[85] This statement is taken from *Apology*, IV: 362. The reader should consider its context: The statement appears in the midst of a discourse that excludes eternal life from the scope of merit associated with good works. Melanchthon linked eternal life solely to faith and justification—the forensic decree of righteousness. He admitted that God grants "rewards" for good works, but he denied that among these rewards is eternal life itself: "We also concede, and have often declared, that though justification and eternal life belong to faith, still good works merit other rewards, both bodily and spiritual, in various degrees."[86] Here we encounter a delicate balancing act. Melanchthon did not deny all sense of merit to good deeds. He did, however, restrict the scope of merit to only temporal and spiritual goods not identifiable with eternal life.[87]

Important papers in the American dialogue make explicit note of this distinction in objects that can be merited. Joseph A. Burgess reads Melanchthon at face value. Although even non-Christians can expect rewards, he claims, good works are "not for salvation, [but lead] to physical and spiritual rewards in this life and in the life to come."[88] However, this does *not* mean that the eternal life is merited. Nor does it mean that eternal life is measured out in degrees in any sense of the term. Burgess contends that it is inappropriate to read St. Paul's metaphor of reward "in order to try to demonstrate that there are degrees of reward in heaven.… The very idea that there can be degrees of glory is hyperbolic."[89] Logically consistent with his own position, Burgess denies that there can be degrees of incorporation into Christ: One is either in Christ or separated from Christ, but one cannot be "more" and "less" in Christ. This position is correlative with Burgess's judgment that degrees of glory are merely figurative expressions. For him, justification is all or nothing; so too salvation, which is linked exclusively to justification, is all or nothing. No human works, even those wrought in the power of Jesus Christ into whom the justified is engrafted, merit the essence of heavenly life.[90] Jill Raitt, similarly, denies that Lutherans admit works as meritorious for salvation. She emphasizes, moreover, that Melanchthon's perspective on works remained consistent even after the Council of Trent. Even in the conciliatory *Book of the Augsburg Interim* (1548), "Works are never the cause of justification or even of eternal life."[91]

The Annex. The Annex, drawn up in part to address the questions enunciated in the OVR, does nothing to ameliorate the attenuated sense of "merit" in the JD; it rather exacerbates the problem. The relevant section reads:

> By justification we are unconditionally brought into communion with God. This includes the promise of eternal life: "(I)f we have been united with him in a death like his, we will certainly be united with him in a resurrection like his" (Rom. 6:5, cf. Jn. 3:36, Rom. 8:17). In the final judgment, the justified will be judged *also* on their works (cf. Mt. 16:27; 25:31–46; Rom. 2:16; 14:12; 1 Cor. 3:8; 2 Cor. 5:10 etc.). We face a judgment in which God's gracious sentence will approve anything in our life and action that corresponds to his will. However, everything in our life that is wrong will be uncovered and will not enter eternal life. The Formula of Concord also states: "It is God's will and express command that believers should do good works which the Holy Spirit works in them, and God is willing to be pleased with them for Christ's sake, and he promises to reward them gloriously in this and in the future life" (Formula of Concord, SD IV, 38). Any reward is a reward of grace, on which we have no claim. (Annex, 2-E, emphasis mine)

This passage calls for careful analysis. I would like to raise three sets of questions.

First, why is it said that humans will be judged "also" on their works? What is the "other" criterion? Is the other criterion the gift of sanctifying grace, by which even infants without works are entitled to the divine inheritance? This would be perfectly acceptable from the Catholic perspective. On the other hand, is the other criterion faith alone, the justifying power of which is independent of charity, although it issues in charity? If the latter is the case, it would appear, yet again, that Regensburg has returned. If so, it would also appear that Trent's teaching on the "one formal cause" has fallen by the wayside. Yet we have seen that Trent's implicit proscription of double justice precludes Catholics from believing that inhering righteousness must be supplemented by another righteousness, e.g., the imputed righteousness of Christ.[92] Thus, from a Catholic perspective this inclusive "also" may well be problematic.

On the other hand, there is certainly something welcome in this statement, something that exhibits a remarkable openness on the part of Lutherans. It would represent a movement past the fear of including any human conditions with the gift of salvation. This inclusive "also" appears to mark a development from USA, which *identified* the gratuity of justification with that of salvation. USA stated that it is not admissible to assert that one who is already justified stands in a position to merit eternal life, even on the basis of the gift of justification:

> One should add that it is not on the basis of his gifts of infused grace, of inherent righteousness, or of good works that God declares sinners just and grants them eternal life, but on the basis of Jesus Christ's righteousness, a righteousness which is "alien" or "extrinsic" to sinful human beings but is received by them through faith. Thus God justifies sinners simply for Christ's sake, not because of their performance, even with the help of divine grace, of the works commanded by the law and done in love.[93]

For USA, salvation is not merited, even "after" the event of justification. Rather, justification and salvation together form a single gift. The Annex's affirmation that persons are judged "also" on their works appears, on its surface, to chafe against this traditional Lutheran teaching. In sum, it cuts between the genuinely Catholic and genuinely Lutheran teachings on salvation. Members of both communions can, in a certain sense, see this aspect of the passage as a welcome ecumenical advance.

I would make another positive observation. The sentence that follows the statement about judgment "also on their works" is suggestive of the Catholic understanding: Only that which in our lives corresponds with God's will shall enter eternal life. This statement resonates of Pannenberg's thought on eschatology. It also implicitly affirms the Catholic position on the intrinsic requirement of holiness (inhering justice) for eternal life (Heb 12:14). Might this subsequent statement be in some tension with the inclusive "also," since this statement appears to identify divine judgment with that purifying encounter with the Lord (1 Cor 3:13) in which what is not fit for the embrace of love simply cannot endure? The final judgment would reveal one's true identity: Insofar as one corresponds with God's will, one is raised up to eternal life; insofar as one fails to correspond with God's will, one is either purified or condemned. The question I raised in response to Pannenberg's thought is appropriate in this context as well: Is it not the case all along that the precise issue at stake is God's transformation of the individual and the individual's responsiveness to that transformation? Further ecumenical discussion on this point could yield a good harvest. I now turn to a second question about an apparent problem in this passage.

How is the reader to understand the "unconditional" nature of the promise? Can a promise of eternal life be described as "unconditional" when this promise includes the following conditions: active acceptance of grace, loving cooperation with grace, and hopeful perseverance in grace? Nowadays, Catholics frequently use the adjective "unconditional" in association with God's grace.[94] But it seems to me that the adjective can lead to understandings at odds with the substance of Catholic faith. Indeed, God's love is unconditioned by anything, for God is unconditioned, and God is love. Moreover, God's love is not given "in response" to created things, including human action. God's love is rather constructive of them: "We love because he first loved us" (1 Jn 4:19). God creates what he loves; God creates the very lovability of what he loves. Nevertheless, God has set up conditions that a creature must meet in order to obtain further blessings, the whole order of which is dependent upon God's wisely ordering freedom. O'Callaghan expresses this well: "Man can, the Council teaches, either adversely condition or generously accept God's efficacious will to justify him, and in that sense to a significant though not decisive degree condition the reality and depth of divine life in himself."[95] O'Callaghan intends this phrase "not decisive" to counter the semi-Pelagian error that man, not God, must take or can take the initiative. However, man can decisively cut himself *away* from the justifying grace of God, although God will pursue him lovingly until death. O'Callaghan rightly implies that no blessing—neither life itself, nor prevenient grace, nor sanctifying grace, nor eternal life—can be "exacted" from God. God bestows everything. This is why the condition is not "decisive." However, God can—and in the Catholic view God does—establish an order by which created things can move from one blessing to another. Within this order, creatures can "merit" further blessings.[96] Pope Leo XIII himself teaches at least three conditions necessary for the attainment of heaven, one of which is adequate obedience to the commandments: "Christ has not promised eternal bliss in heaven to riches, nor to a life of ease, to honors or to power, but to long-suffering and to tears, to the love of justice and to cleanness of heart."[97] The promise of eternal life is conditioned from the creaturely perspective: If the believer does not obey God's commandments, he cannot be saved. If the believer freely and knowingly disobeys even one of the ten commandments but once, he cannot be saved, unless, inspired by God, he repents. Loving obedience enables growth in justifying grace, but disobedience removes it. It is, therefore, improper to describe justifying grace as absolutely "unconditioned." If the description of the promise of life as "unconditional" does not allow room for these conditions on justifying grace, then the description of the promise misleads.

Third, does the following citation in Annex 2–E imply that God enables the justified person to merit eternal life: "'It is God's will and express command that believers should do good works which the Holy Spirit works in them, and God is willing to be pleased with them for Christ's sake, and he promises to reward them gloriously in this and in the future life' (Formula of Concord, SD IV, 38)"? This passage from the *Formula* is cited as an authority on meritorious cooperation. It seems at first sight that the passage affirms that humans are to cooperate with God in order to merit eternal life—an affirmation in harmony with Trent! Surprisingly, the source of this passage is the most conservatively Lutheran document. The Annex thus exhibits a rhetorically admirable stroke of genius: a distinctively Catholic teaching affirmed by the most rigorously Lutheran document. Observing matters from his "neutral" position, Wainwright is delighted in the strategy: The Lutheran will not be threatened, and the Catholic will be pleasantly surprised.[98]

Examined in its original context, the cited passage does not suggest that eternal life is merited; it suggests the opposite. The first sentence of IV: 38 reads, "But it does not follow herefrom that one may say *without any qualifications that good works are detrimental* to believers as far as their salvation is concerned" (emphasis mine). The affirmation of the importance of good works is couched in a paragraph that begins with a strange disclaimer: Good works are not without qualification detrimental. The bizarre character of this introductory sentence is understandable only in a yet wider context. Section IV: 38 concludes a lengthy condemnation of an Epicurean theory of salvation. According to the "Epicurean" notion of salvation faith can never be lost, regardless of the sinful deeds the believer might commit in a lifetime. The Epicureans concluded from this that good works themselves are deleterious to salvation. In striving to perform good works, the believer endangers the purity of faith and neglects the promise of forgiveness. Proud Pharisee, he mistakenly believes that good works merit eternal life, either entirely or in part. Wary of this presumption, the Epicureans condemned good works as dangerous to salvation. The authors of the *Formula* were rightly horrified by this theory and firmly rejected it. It is indeed central to the Lutheran viewpoint that good works are *necessary*, not as causes of salvation or justification but as concomitant fruits of true faith. True faith is never without works.

Now, the *Formula* rejected the said Epicurean delusion, but it did not affirm the Catholic understanding of eternal life as both gift and reward. Quite to the contrary, the *Solid Declaration* took great pains also to reject the Catholic notion of meritorious works. The condemnation of a Catholic understanding forms part of the wider context of the passage cited in the Annex. The *Formula* reads:

> Therefore we correctly reject the propositions that good works are necessary for the believers' salvation, or that it is impossible to be saved without good works, since such propositions are directly contrary to the doctrine of exclusive terms in the articles of justification and salvation (that is, they are diametrically opposed to St. Paul's words which exclude our works and merit completely from the article of justification and salvation and ascribe everything solely to the grace of God and the merit of Christ), as was explained in the preceding article.[99]

This passage unequivocally rejects the possibility that persons endowed with infused gifts can merit eternal life itself. The authors of the *Formula*, so wanting not to misguide their readers, repeated their critique of the Catholic position precisely in the context of their rejection of the Epicurean delusion. The following passage appears only four paragraphs above the passage cited in the Annex: "[Paul] attributes to faith alone the beginning, the middle and the end of everything.... It is evident from the Word of God that faith is the proper and the only means whereby righteousness and salvation are not only received but also preserved by God."[100] Although faith is never alone, faith alone justifies. Lutheran theologian John F. Johnson, in his paper for the American dialogue, writes, "Justifying faith produces good works. But faith never receives forgiveness of sins on account of love or works." Despite its concern to refute the enthusiasts or Epicureans, the *Formula* "hastens to reject the notion that faith cannot justify without works or that faith justifies insofar as it is associated with love.... [While] it is impossible to separate works from faith, such good works and merits are completely excluded from the article of justification."[101] It is clear that Johnson refers here not merely to the status of the unjustified person who faces justification but simply to the status of any person before God (*coram Deo*). No person stands before God worthy of salvation, and therefore no person can or ought to put any credence in the notion that good works merit salvation, either entirely or in part.

Before moving on to a discussion of the actual position of the Catholic Church on meritorious cooperation, I would like to make an observation about my approach in this section on merit. The distinction between the sinner who "faces" justification and the converted sinner who "is justified" can be understood in different ways. Catholics understand the distinction to involve the possession or non-possession of sanctifying grace: One is either in the state of grace or not. Lutherans, however, understand the distinction to refer to the status of the sinner as either "faithful" or "not faithful." The sinner always sins.[102] The sinner who believes begins not to sin or rather begins to walk with Christ. However, the believer still stands as helpless as the infidel before the mercy of God. Lutheran theologian Friedrich Beisser expresses this as follows:

> That there is a growth of the good in the Christian was asserted by Luther many times, as also by the [*Formula*]. This growth, however, constitutes no contribution to our status under grace. Good works do not effect salvation, neither before nor after justification. They do not form a supplement to the divine acquittal.[103]

The believer does not present to God any good works nor the gift of sanctifying grace. The believer presents only Christ through faith to appease the wrath of God. From the Lutheran perspective, it is not a matter of a single subject who "once was sinful" and "now is just." It is for this reason, I would surmise, that there is no clear distinction, in the JD's common and Lutheran paragraphs, between meritorious and non-meritorious cooperation. The very distinction is distinctively Catholic.

The Teaching of Trent. The Catholic Church teaches that Paul excludes works from first justification because God's call of the ungodly is absolutely unsolicited (Rom 3:28). An unregenerate sinner cannot merit the promise of eternal life that comes with first justification. Jesus Christ died for the ungodly, while we were yet sinners (Rom 5:6). Still, God's gracious acceptance and the promise of eternal life touch the sinner precisely through actual grace and the infusion of sanctifying grace. Just as the sin of Adam brought about real spiritual death in his bosom and in those of all his descendants, just as the sentence of physical death is real for each, so too the *gift* of righteousness brings about real life in the bosom of the justified (Rom 5:19), a first fruits of the promised resurrection, which in turn shall be real for each (Rom 5:17). This gift of righteousness, granted through God's promise, is the freely given basis upon which all merit rests. Moreover, even though endowed with this gift, the justified person is ever dependent upon God, who continually infuses a participation in Christ's life through the Holy Spirit.[104] But the justified can and does merit salvation as something truly owed, not because of his innate or natural powers but because he is a living member of Christ. He is engrafted into the vine, a son by grace, an heir by promise—a new creation. Eternal life is both a gift promised and a reward merited by works done in God's grace. And so, the fathers of Trent declare:

If anyone says that the good works of the justified man are the gifts of God in such a way that they are not also the good merits of the justified himself, or that the justified person himself—in the good works which are wrought by him through the grace of God and the merit of Jesus Christ of whom he is a living member—does not truly merit an increase in grace, eternal life, and the attainment of that eternal life (if he dies in grace) and even an increase in glory: let him be anathema.[105]

Trent is clear: The just can merit an increase in justifying grace, the attainment of eternal life, and an increase in eternal glory. This teaching rests upon the acknowledgment of only one formal cause of justification, the infused justice of God, by which the justified is bound to Jesus Christ, empowered by him to act as God's child, and entitled to receive the inheritance of a child.[106]

Inseparably linked to Trent's teaching that one can "truly merit" eternal life is Catholic teaching on "degrees" of participation in grace and glory. As stated above, Trent holds that the "very justice received" in justification increases in sanctification. This increase renders persons "more justified."[107] The whole order of salvation is upheld by God's generous and gratuitous love. Within this order, however, Christian's are called to preserve the inhering grace granted them in justification. It is the presence or absence of this gift of grace that distinguishes the saved from the reprobate at the end of time; for this reason, Trent urges all to preserve this "spotless robe," to cooperate so as to increase in it, and to present it before the judgment seat of God.[108] The council's twin teachings on both the possibility of different degrees of eternal life, not merely of "other rewards, bodily and spiritual," and also the capacity of the just to "truly merit" eternal life stand together with a reciprocal intelligibility. The Catholic teaching on justification reaches its crown here, rooted not simply in a "concern" about human responsibility but rather in an adequate appreciation of God's regenerative power and of his will to restore all things to himself (Col 1:19–20) in a way suitable to each. St. Bonaventure underscored the importance of merit in continuity with earthly perfection: "Free will, then, acquires through grace not only a just title to the growth of grace in the present life, but also an absolute right to its perfecting in heaven."[109]

The fathers of Vatican II also confessed that one is judged according to works wrought in grace.[110] The issue at stake is neither the freedom of God nor the helplessness of the sinner but God's radical communication of grace to the justified through the merits of Christ. To affirm the reality of the new creation diminishes neither God's glory nor the Cross of Christ, but shows forth God's power to save.

The Joint Declaration and the Annex stand opposed to this Catholic teaching on meritorious cooperation as well as on the whole nexus of issues discussed in the present chapter. The contents of the Joint Declaration, therefore, are not merely flawed in isolated cases; they are in organic fashion contrary to the integrity of Catholic faith.

NOTES

1 The German reads, "Das verstehen Lutheraner in dem Sinne, daß der Christ 'zugleich Gerechter und Sünder' ist: Er ist ganz gerecht weil Gott ihm durch Wort und Sakrament seine Sünde vergibt und die Gerechtigkeit Christi zuspricht, die ihm im Glauben zu eigen wird und ihn in Christus vor Gott zum Gerechten macht. Im Blick auf sich selbst aber erkennt er durch das Gesetz, daß er zugleich ganz Sünder bleibt, daß die Sünde noch in ihm wohnt ...; denn er vertraut immer wieder auf falsche Götter und liebt Gott nicht mit jener ungeteilten Liebe, die Gott als sein Schöpfer von ihm fordert.... Diese Gottwidrigkeit ist als solche wahrhaft Sünde. Doch die knechtende Macht der Sünde ist aufgrund von Christi Verdienst gebrochen: Sie ist keine den Christen 'beherrschende' Sünde mehr, weil sie durch Christus 'beherrscht' ist, mit dem der Gerechtfertigte im Glauben verbunden ist; so kann der Christ, solange er auf Erden lebt, jedenfalls stückweise ein Leben in Gerechtigkeit führen. Und trotz der Sünde ist der Christ nicht mehr von Gott getrennt, weil ihm, der durch die Taufe und den Heiligen Geist neugeboren ist, in täglicher Rückkehr zur Taufe die Sünde vergeben wird, so daß seine Sünde ihn nicht mehr verdammt und ihm nicht mehr den ewigen Tod bringt. Wenn also die Lutheraner sagen, daß der Gerechtfertigte auch Sünder und seine Gottwidrigkeit wahrhaft Sünde ist, verneinen sie nicht, daß er trotz der Sünde in Christus von Gott ungetrennt und seine Sünde beherrschte Sünde ist. Im letzteren sind sie mit der römisch-katholischen Seite trotz der Unterschiede im Verständnis der Sünde des Gerechtfertigten einig" (GE, 29).

2 See also Peura, "Favor," pp. 63–64.

3 See Birmelé, "La déclaration," p. 110, and Wendebourg, "Zur Entstehungsgeschichte," p. 166.

4 Peura, "Favor," p. 64.

5 See also *Lehrverurteilungen im Gespräch* (Göttingen: 1993), p. 82: 29–39, quoted in sources to 4.5 (hereafter, VELKD).

6 See Brandt, "Gemeinsame," p. 89.

7 Wendebourg notices that the 1997 draft is less pointedly Catholic in its concern about concupiscence than was the 1996 draft (see Wendebourg, "Zur Entstehungsgeschichte," p. 166 and note 101).

8 The German reads, "Die Gnade Jesu Christi, die in der Taufe verliehen wird, alles was "wirklich" Sünde, was "verdammenswürdig" ist, tilgt (Röm 8, 1)" (GE, 30).

9 See Wenz, "Damnamus," pp. 111–13.

10 One finds no such explanation of concupiscence as constant idolatry—the traditional Lutheran understanding of concupiscence—in the 1995 draft. For a remark on this part of the JD, see Birmelé, *A Commentary*, p. 40.

11 CRE, p. 46. The Göttingen faculty finds this statement to be insufficiently direct on the identity of concupiscence with sin that is certainly and always damnable (see Göttingen, "An Opinion," p. 26). A similar assessment appears in a paper delivered for the American dialogue by Joseph A. Burgess. The author cites an early statement of Luther to the effect that all our "good works" are in fact only mortal sins, worthy of damnation. Burgess agrees with Luther. He maintains that Luther did not exaggerate but simply clarified Paul's own teaching on sin (see Joseph A. Burgess, "Rewards, But in a Very Different Sense," in USA, p. 103). Burgess contends that Luther had no more

radical a view of sin than Paul. Because he took sin so seriously, he denied all notion of merit of eternal reward (see WA 7: 445).

12   At this point, I am not distinguishing Pannenberg's thought from that of the Finns.

13   *Apology*, II: 40. Tappert has "imputed" but Kolb has "reckoned" (Kolb, octavo edition, p. 118).

14   Peura, "Favor," p. 64.

15   See ibid., pp. 65–67.

16   OVR, art. 1.

17   Annex, 2–B.

18   Ibid., 2–B.

19   See David S. Yeago, "Interpreting the Roman Response to the *Joint Declaration on Justification*," *Pro Ecclesia* 7 (1998): 407.

20   See Susan K. Wood, "Observations on *Official Catholic Response to Joint Declaration*," *Pro Ecclesia* 7 (1998): 422–23.

21   According to Catholic faith, only mortal sins are damnable. The Lutheran paragraph, in contrast, suggests that believers repeatedly turn to false Gods, but this idolatry of its nature brings eternal death, although for those who have faith (JD, 29). "God no longer imputes to them their sin" (JD, 22). The implication is that believers repeatedly commit damnable sin. This implication resembles the following proposition condemned at Trent: "in every good work the just sin even venially. Or (which is more intolerable) that they sin mortally and therefore deserve eternal punishment. But they are not damned on account of this: that God does not impute their works to damnation" (In quolibet bono opere iustum saltem venialiter peccare dixerit, aut [quod intolerabilius est] mortaliter, atque ideo poenas aeternas mereri, tantumque ob id non damnari, quia Deus ea opera non imputet ad damnationem [canon 25, DE, 680: 38–41]). Luther also appears to fall under the condemnation when he writes, "All the saints fall short of [the Law] and thus commit sin in every work. Nor is it sin in an improper sense; but it is sin indeed, because it is not grace in an improper sense or God in an improper sense or God in an improper sense or Christ in an improper sense or the Holy Spirit in an improper sense who remits and purges away these sins" (LW 27: 362; WA, 2: 584.39–585.1). The proof of the reality of the sin is this: it needs forgiveness.

22   Venial sins wound but do not kill the spiritual life of the soul. One might compare venial sins to sickness, as opposed to death. Is there not an analogy for this in human friendships? Do not slights differ from serious offenses? See Möhler, *Symbolism*, pp. 111–13.

23   Villar rightly claims that the actual understandings of "simul iustus et peccator" will clarify whether or not the Lutheran reading of forgiveness through imputation (JD, 22) is compatible with the Catholic understanding. I disagree, however, with his reading of the "simul" controversy as it is presented in the JD (see Villar, "La Declaración," pp. 118 and 120–24).

24   The German "stückweise" (GE, 29) connotes a piecemeal observance of law. The Italian renders this, "in a discontinuous manner" (see Holc, *Un ampio*, p. 333). Catholics should find the expression "in part" insufficient. In contrast, the Evangelical Lutheran Church of Denmark finds it excessive. The representatives warn, "[It is] not only open to misunderstanding; rather, it is inconsistent with the Lutheran understanding of sin and righteousness" ("Response from the Evangelical Lutheran Church of Denmark," Copenhagen, 20 March 1998).

25   The German reads, "Das Gesetz in seinem theologischen Gebrauch ist Forderung und Anklage, unter der jeder Mensch, auch der Christ, insofern er Sünder ist, zeitlebens steht und das seine Sünde aufdeckt, damit er sich im Glauben an das Evangelium ganz

der Barmherzigkeit Gottes in Christus zuwendet, die allein ihn rechtfertigt" (GE, 32).

26 Si quis dixerit, Christum Iesum a Deo hominibus datum fuisse ut redemptorem, cui fidant, non etiam ut legislatorem, cui obediant: a. s. (canon 21, DE, 680: 26–27).

27 See Irenaeus, *Against Heresies*, in *The Apostolic Fathers with Justin Martyr and Irenaeus*, vol. 1, Ante-Nicene Fathers, ed. Alexander Roberts and James Donaldson (Peabody, MA: Hendrickson Publishers, 1999), IV, chap. 14, pp. 478–79.

28 See ibid., chaps. 15–16, pp. 479–82.

29 John Paul II, *Veritatis Splendor*, art. 12.

30 Manns has noticed that Luther too neatly distinguished love of God and love of neighbor, the former accomplished through faith and the latter through charity (see Manns, "Absolute and Incarnate," p. 143).

31 VELKD, p. 89: 28–36, quoted in Sources to 4.5.

32 Deus namque sua gratia semel iustificatos non deserit, nisi ab eis prius deseratur (chap. 11, DE, 675: 28–29).

33 Si quis dixerit, iustificatum vel sine speciali auxilio Dei in accepta iustitia perseverare posse, vel cum eo non posse: a. s. (canon 22, DE, 680: 28–29).

34 Dei praecepta homini iustificato ad observandum esse impossibilia (chap. 11, DE, 675: 15–16).

35 Nuda et absoluta promissio vitae aeternae, sine conditione observationis mandatorum (canon 20, DE, 680: 24–25). The necessity of obedience to the commandments should be qualified: what is necessary is not to infringe the commandments. Infants and those indisposed to action cannot properly infringe these commandments; they neither obey nor disobey them. For all others, the potentially mortal nature of sins of omission mandates, under certain circumstances, specific acts (see first Decree on the Sacraments, canon 6, DE, 685: 36–37).

36 Quae etiam venialia dicuntur … non propterea desinunt esse iusti (chap. 11, DE, 675: 22–23).

37 See Rebecca Konyndyk DeYoung, "Resistance to the Demands of Love: Aquinas on the Vice of Acedia," *The Thomist* 68 (2004): pp. 173–204.

38 There is no appeal to the alien righteousness of Christ as formally justifying; rather, there is an appraisal of one's very being (see chap. 7, DE, 674: 6–11).

39 Itaque veram et christianam iustitiam accipientes, eam ceu primam stolam, pro illa, quam Adam sua inobedientia sibi et nobis perdidit, per Christum Iesum illis donatam, candidam et immaculatam iubentur statim renati conservare, ut eam perferant ante tribunal domini nostri Iesu Christi et habeant vitam aeternam (chap. 7, DE, 674: 6–11). See St. Thérèse, op. cit., pp. 149–50.

40 Cum enim ille ipse Christus Iesus tamquam caput in membra et tamquam vitis in palmites in ipsos iustificatos iugiter virtutem influat, quae virtus bona eorum opera semper antecedit, comitatur et subsequitur, et sine qua nullo pacto Deo grata et meritoria esse possent: nihil ipsis iustificatis amplius deesse credendum est, quominus plene illis quidem operibus, quae in Deo sunt facta, divinae legi pro huius vitae statu satisfecisse et vitam aeternam, suo etiam tempore (si tamen in gratia decesserint) consequendam vere promeruisse censeantur (chap. 16, DE, 678: 7–14, translation by DE).

41 The German reads, "Werke, die von der Gnade und dem Wirken des Heiligen Geistes erfüllt sind" (GE, 38).

42 The German reads, "Wachstum *in* der Gnade" (GE, 38, emphasis mine).

43 The Göttingen faculty urge that the "human responsibility" linked to salvation "is not…a responsibility for obtaining salvation, but for the preservation of salvation already received" (Göttingen, "An Opinion," 33; see also p. 45).

44 Birmelé, "La déclaration," pp. 172–73.

45 Whereas Trent conceived of justification as the first step, Lutherans identify justification with salvation; so, the JD witnesses to a Catholic concession in this regard as well (see Birmelé, "La déclaration," p. 188).

46 That the JD describes even the "sharing" as perfect raises difficulties. It implies that the "sharing" is not the believer's own justice infused by God. It implies, instead, that the "sharing" is the righteousness of Christ imputed to or dwelling within the believer.

47 VELKD, 94: 2–14, cited in Sources to 4.7.

48 See also Beisser, "Formula," pp. 159–60.

49 USA, par. 98.

50 If it were asserted that Christ's presence in the believer does grow—not through justification but through sanctification—the problem would again arise. The formal notes of justification and sanctification would be distinguished. The former would not grow, but the latter would grow. This begs the question, what justifies? Is it one's sanctifying participation in Christ that grows through good works (i.e., intrinsic righteousness)? Or is it the perfect righteousness of Christ (i.e., extrinsic righteousness)?

51 Birmelé, *A Commentary*, p. 44.

52 Mortificando membra carnis suae et exhibendo ea arma iustitiae in sanctificationem per observationem mandatorum Dei et ecclesiae: in ipsa iustitia per Christi gratiam accepta, cooperante fide bonis operibus, crescunt *atque magis iustificantur* (chap. 10, DE, 675: 3–7, emphasis mine). See also chap. 7, DE, 673: 26–27.

53 Si quis dixerit, iustitiam acceptam non conservari atque etiam non augeri coram Deo per bona opera, sed opera ipsa fructus solummodo et signa esse iustificationis adeptae, non etiam ipsius augendae causam: a. s. (canon 24, DE, 680: 35–37).

54 Leo Scheffczyk links the JD's erroneous teaching on cooperation with grace to its neglect to tread the sacrament of reconciliation (See Scheffczyk, "Gemeinsame [Teil II]," p. 125).

55 See *Solid Declaration*, IV: 31–32.

56 See *Apology*, IV: 64 and 115.

57 Si quis dixerit, nullum esse mortale peccatum nisi infidelitatis, aut nullo alio quantumvis gravi et enormi praeterquam infidelitatis peccato semel acceptam gratiam amitti: a. s. (canon 27, DE, 681: 1–3).

58 Si quis dixerit, amissa per peccatum gratia simul et fidem semper amitti, aut fidem, quae remanet, non esse veram fidem, licet non sit viva, aut eum, qui fidem sine charitate habet, non esse christianum: a. s. (canon 28, DE, 681: 4–6).

59 Dulles, "Justification: The Joint Declaration."

60 If Lutherans assert that "faith alone" justifies, Catholics are supposed to be assuaged by the claim that faith is never alone, but always includes hope and love. Dulles asks whether true faith *can* exist without hope and love, discovering to his dismay a response in the negative.

61 Ecumenically minded Lutherans will interpret the actions of specific Catholics in a kindly light, ascribing to those who continually seek God's grace, though they routinely judge themselves to have fallen, as being sped on by true faith in God and trust in his mercy.

62 See a well-constructed account of this in Göttingen, "An Opinion," pp. 33 and 45.

63 See John Paul II, *Veritatis Splendor*, arts. 69–70.

64 For this translation, see Fitzmeyer, *Romans*, p. 435.

65 The German adds "sein" to "Heil" (GE, 19), showing specifically that this freedom is not freedom with regard to one's own salvation. The German does not qualify the final

reference to "grace" with the possessive "God's."

66 The German reads, "und kein Tun des Menschen aus eigenen Kräften" (GE, 20).

67 See all of chap. 6, DE, 672:35–673:12.

68 Leo Scheffczyk describes the JD's teaching on cooperation as a "corruption" and not a "development," borrowing from John Henry Newman's analysis of the notes of authenticity for doctrinal development (see Scheffczyk, "Gemeinsame [Teil I]," pp. 67–68).

69 The German reads, "Verneinen sie damit jede Möglichkeit eines eigenen Beitrags des Menschen zu seiner Rechtfertigung, nicht aber sein volles personales Beteiligtsein im Glauben, das vom Wort Gottes selbst gewirkt wird" (GE, 21). The English reads, "believers are fully involved personally in their faith, which is effected by God's Word."

70 *Solid Declaration*, II: 17. Cf. canon 7, DE, 679: 24–27.

71 See Denzinger, 1920, 1927, 1928, 1935, 1948–51, 1965, 1974, and 1975.

72 See *Solid Declaration*, II: 89.

73 *Solid Declaration*, II: 65 and 25, respectively.

74 See *Epitome*, II: 19 and *Solid Declaration*, II: 90.

75 Comments of the Joint Committee of the United Evangelical Lutheran Church of Germany and the Lutheran World Federation German National Committee regarding the document *The Condemnations of the Reformation Era. Do They Sill Divide?* in *Lehrverurteilungen im Gespräch* (Göttingen: 1993), p. 84.

76 Found in Sources to 4.1. Evaluation of the Pontifical Council for Promoting Christian Unity of the study *Lehrverurteilungen-kirchentrennend*? (unpublished), 22.

77 Dulles, "Two Languages," p. 27.

78 Per eius excitantem atque adiuvantem gratiam ad convertendum se ad suam ipsorum iustificationem, eidem gratiae libere assentiendo et cooperando, disponantur (chap. 5, DE, 672: 25–27).

79 Fuit quidem poenitentia universis hominibus, qui se mortali aliquo peccato inquinassent, quovis tempore ad gratiam et iustitiam assequendam necessaria, illis etiam qui baptismi sacramento ablui petivissent, ut perversitate abiecta et emendata tantam Dei offensionem cum peccati odio et pio animi dolore detestarentur (Decree on Reconciliation, chap. 1, DE, 703: 21–25). See also Decree on Justification, chap. 6, DE, 673:3, and Decree on Reconciliation, chap. 4, 705:11–13.

80 Si quis dixerit, sola fide impium iustificari, ita ut intelligat, nihil aliud requiri, quo ad iustificationis gratiam consequendam cooperetur, et nulla ex parte necesse esse, eum suae voluntatis motu praeparari atque disponi: a. s. (canon 9, DE, 679: 31–34).

81 The German has, "Rechtfertigung selbst" (GE, 38).

82 *Apology*, IV: 113. See also IV: 84–86.

83 *Apology*, IV: 114.

84 For a recent word on Melanchthon's notion of reward, in connection with the JD, see Michael Root, "Aquinas, Merit, and Reformation Theology after the *Joint Declaration on the Doctrine of Justification*," *Modern Theology* 20 (2004): 14–16. Root's reading of Melanchthon is promising. His reading of Thomas is questionable (see ibid., pp. 10–14). It is unclear whether he has taken Thomas's analysis of the *principles* of meritorious action, viz., free will and the grace of the Spirit, to imply a distinction of two actions, one simply human and one simply divine. This is not the distinction Thomas has in mind. There are indeed, from a broader perspective, two agents: the Holy Spirit and the human being. However, the Holy Spirit moves the human being not simply in an extrinsic way, nor even simply by his indwelling presence. With respect to the meritorious character of an action, Thomas contends, the Spirit moves the human

agent through the grace that has been infused. So, in the act called meritorious, there is a single action; there is one meritorious deed, which is *condignly* meritorious. It is the human person who condignly merits eternal life. Root's identification of the grace of the Spirit with the Spirit's indwelling is inaccurate (see ibid., p. 12); for Thomas, the grace of the Spirit refers to the gift of sanctifying grace, for the Spirit moves man towards meritorious deeds through the gift of this grace, so that the end of the action is attained by principles now immanent to the human agent, namely, free will—thanks to creation—and infused grace—thanks to the divine ordination.

85   VELKD, p. 94 (emphasis mine).
86   *Apology*, IV: 366, quarto edition. In the octavo edition, Melanchthon demonstrates greater subtlety of thought, but still refuses to ascribe merit to works of the justified. He contends that, because the adopted child of God does suffer, the free gift of eternal life can be considered compensation for his endurance (and action). Still, this adopted child does *not* act as God's child and is therefore not worthy of eternal life, except solely by God's promise (Kolb, octavo edition, pp. 170–71).
87   Such things might include a long life, health, good friends, spiritual consolations, and heavenly "crowns."
88   Burgess, "Rewards," p. 94.
89   Ibid., pp. 104–05.
90   Burgess proffers a tendentious alternative that might dupe the unvigilant reader: "A person cannot be partially in Christ or more than in Christ" (Burgess, "Rewards," p. 104).
91   Raitt, "Augsburg," p. 217.
92   Summing up the shared theological convictions of the bishops at the council, Prumbs writes, "Wenn aber auch die heiligmachende Gnade der Zunahme fähig ist, so ist sie deshalb an sich nicht unvollkommen, d.h. zur Erlangung der ewigen Glückseligkeit nicht unzureichend; sie bedarf vor dem Tribunal Gottes keiner Ergänzung durch eine neue und äußerliche Imputation der Gerechtigkeit Christi" (Prumbs, *Die Stellung*, p. 59).
93   USA, par. 24.
94   This claim is so commonplace that one example should suffice. Cardinal Walter Kasper observed, in harmony with the Malta Report, "Catholic theology, too, stresses in the question of justification that the saving gift of God to the believer is tied to no human condition" (Auch die katholischen Theologen betonen in der Rechtfertigungsfrage, dass die Heilsgabe Gottes für den Glaubenden an keine menschlichen Bedingungen geknüpft ist [*Malta-Bericht*, Nr. 26, ed. H. Meyer et al., *Dokumente wachsender Übereinstimmung*, vol. 1 {Paderborn, 1983}, p. 255, cited in Hauke, "Die Antwort," p. 106]).
95   O'Callaghan, *Fides Christi*, p. 87.
96   It seems to me that the American dialogue articulates *this* element of Catholic thought fairly well (see USA, par. 99).
97   Leo XIII, *On Jesus Christ our Redeemer*, p. 12.
98   See Wainwright, "Methodist Point of View," p. 32.
99   *Solid Declaration*, IV: 22.
100   *Solid Declaration*, IV: 34–35.
101   John F. Johnson, "Justification According to the Apology of the Augsburg Confession and the Formula of Concord," in USA, pp. 196–97.
102   It is noteworthy that the Göttingen faculty criticized CRE for making a distinction between the being of the baptized and that of those still in original sin: "Against precisely this notion the Reformation's position is that sin remains active also in the

baptized, and that the justified person is at the same time a real sinner. There can be no arguing, therefore, that his sin no longer separates him from God, since it is 'no longer sin in the real sense,' and that it is, as it were, 'only damnable hypothetically.' In itself, concupiscence is indeed sin and therefore damnable" (Göttingen, "An Opinion," p. 26).

103 Beisser, "Formula," p. 160.

104 Chap. 16, DE, 678: 7–10.

105 Si quis dixerit, hominis iustificati bona opera ita esse dona Dei, ut non sint etiam bona ipsius iustificati merita, aut ipsum iustificatum bonis operibus, quae ab eo per Dei gratiam et Iesu Christi meritum (cuius vivum membrum est) fiunt, non vere mereri augmentum gratiae, vitam aeternam et ipsius vitae aeternae (si tamen in gratia decesserit) consecutionem, atque etiam gloriae augmentum: a. s. (canon 32, DE, 681: 19–24; cf. *Epitome* IV: 15).

106 See Hefner, *Die Entstehungsgeschichte*, p. 271.

107 See chap. 10, DE, 675: 5–7.

108 See chap. 7, DE, 674: 7–11.

109 St. Bonaventure, *The Breviloquium*, trans. José de Vinck (Paterson, N.J.: St. Anthony Guild Press, 1963), V, 2. The translation is faithful to the Latin: "non tantum congrui, sed etiam condigni" (Bonaventure, *Tria opuscula*, vol. 5, *Opera theologica selecta*, ed. Augustini Sépinski. Florence: Quaracchi, 1964), p. 103.

110 See LG, art. 48, and USA, par. 74.

PART FOUR

Evaluating the Divide

For [Paul] loved Christ not for the things of Christ, but for His sake and things that were His, and to Him alone he looked, and one thing he feared, and that was falling from his love for Him. For this thing was in itself more dreadful than hell, as to abide in it was more desirable than the kingdom.

St. John Chrysostom, *Homily on Romans XV*

We would perhaps have disregarded corruption and been pleased with our evil unless this other evil, which is wrath, had refused to indulge our foolishness and had resisted it with terror and the danger of hell and death, so that we have but little peace in our wickedness. Plainly, wrath is a greater evil for us than corruption, for we hate punishment more than guilt.

Martin Luther, *Confutation of Latomus*

For if you object to my being rid of that corruption which is by nature, see that you object not to God's Word having taken my form of servitude; for as the Lord, putting on the body, became man, so we men are deified by the Word as being taken to Him through His flesh, and henceforward inherit life everlasting.

St. Athanasius of Alexandria, *Against the Arians*, III, 26

CHAPTER 10

Theological Reflections

THE CHIEF argument of this book is already accomplished. It is a largely critical argument, rooted in essentially doctrinal concerns. Here, I wish to close with some theological reflections on the divergent understandings of the essence of justification. It is no accident that Lutherans consider this article the crucial article, that upon which everything depends. Although Catholics do not place this article at the summit of the "hierarchy of truths," they can agree that any serious dispute on this point of faith has ramifications for the whole fabric of the deposit of faith.

The present chapter contains five interrelated investigations concerning the theological implications of divergent understandings of the nature of justification. Each of these investigations stands on its own; however, there is a discernible line of thought from one to the next. They are arranged to follow a point-counterpoint pattern. First, I investigate the eschatological implications of divergent understandings of the formal cause. Second, in a reflection on faith and self-trust, I present a Lutheran objection to this argument, followed by a Catholic response to this objection. Third, I consider the "retrospective" implications that the ineffable grandeur of eternal life bears for its "seed," the formal cause of justification. Fourth, I critically examine the theory that Catholics and Lutherans offer two complementary, non-conflicting languages for the same faith. Finally, in an essay on Christological soteriology, I discuss the demerits of the structure of thought fundamental to Lutheranism. Each of these reflections is meant to be a point of departure for further theological discussion, i.e., for vigorous but fraternal debate about these important issues. They cannot claim to be exhaustive, but it is my hope that they do strike chords, even falteringly, for both Lutheran and Catholic ears, since the original discord was no mean quibble.

Where Does this Justice Lead?

The relationship between beatitude and the seed of beatitude, justification, illuminates the deeper theological bases for the Catholic teaching on the formal cause of justification. Justification and salvation are intrinsically connected, the former admitting and equipping the wayfarer for the latter. This being granted, then the way in which one conceives of justification will have implications for the way in which one conceives of salvation or eternal life. So, if the Lutheran notion of justification reflects reality, to what beatitude does it lead?

From the Lutheran perspective, justification does not consist in the total eradication of damnable sin. Instead, justification consists in the attribution of the righteousness of Christ to faith, either by way of an extrinsic imputation or by way of the indwelling presence of Christ or by way of an ecstatic fellowship with Christ. In whatever a Lutheran finds this "attribution" to consist, justification is not constituted by an ennobling gift given by God to the sinner by which the sinner's willfully perverse alienation from God is destroyed. Justification is not constituted by an infusion of the justice that restores human powers to their rightful orientation, so that the pilgrim can accept God's truths and love him as Father. The Lutheran notion of the attribution of Christ's righteousness does not correspond to the Catholic perception of the sinner's ontological integration into Christ, in whom alone the human heart finds peace. Granted, one must admit that some of the different understandings of this "attribution" in Lutheranism show promise of ecumenical rapprochement: The Finnish notion of indwelling and Pannenberg's notion of ecstatic faith more closely approximate to Catholic thought than the forensic and extrinsic language found in the confessional documents. Here, there are grounds for continuing dialogue. Notwithstanding the promise of dialogue, each of these schools of thought insists that damnable sin remains in the justified: The justified is still in some real way a damnable sinner. Precisely because of this, one cannot say that the justified person is intrinsically fitted for a life of glory. Insofar as he is "considered" to be righteous, he is "fitted" for the remission of sensible punishment due to sin. But the sinner, in his empirical reality, is not made fit for the vision and love of God.

Therefore, justification as "attribution of righteousness" does not save *for* God's beatific espousal but precisely *from* the fires of hell.[1] Even so, justification saves only from the secondary punishment of hell, i.e., the pain of sense.[2] The primary punishment of hell is isolation from God (2 Thess 1:9–10) through utter and eternal loss of sanctifying grace, without which no one enjoys God's indwelling presence. The essence of hell is thus alienation from God's presence.[3] Descriptions of the bodily and spiritual torments of hell pale in comparison with this ominous thought: A human being that naturally yearns for God's presence—"You made us for yourself and our hearts find no peace until they rest in you"[4]—is torn from God and abandoned to himself for an endless succession of ages. Catholics have come to appreciate this dimension of hell much more, in large part because of the 20th century work of Henri de Lubac on the mystery of God's grace. Does not much of the weight of de Lubac's argument rest upon the contention that only the existence of a natural desire for God can account for the primary pain of hell? "This is why," he explains, "if I fail to achieve this which is my end it may be said that I have failed in everything; if I lose it, I am 'damned'; and to be aware of such a situation is for me the 'pain of damnation.' This *poena damni*, as I have said, can be explained in no other way."[5] He defines the pain of hell as the unveiled awareness of the perpetual loss of the vision of God. De Lubac presupposes that the essence of hell is isolation from God. From his perspective, the opposite of hell, i.e., salvation, is the presence of God to the human person or, in other words, the union of the human person with God. De Lubac implies that a proper conception of salvation does not focus primarily on the negative aspect, the remission of punishment, but rather on the positive aspect, beatific union with God.

Given the foregoing, is it not legitimate to ask the following question: If salvation consisted primarily in God's free decision not to inflict punishments, bodily and spiritual, would not the very foundation of de Lubac's argument be undermined? Since an affirmative answer seems unavoidable, it therefore seems that an acceptance of the Lutheran understanding of justification would have deleterious implications for de Lubac's accomplishments in 20th century theology. Conversely, an appreciation of the nature of the effect of human sinfulness upon the human relationship with God underscores de Lubac's argument and offers persuasive evidence that the Catholic understanding is preferable to the Lutheran understanding. It would be fruitful to sketch an argument to this effect, before returning to the properly Lutheran understanding of justification and its implications for the life of beatitude.

Only creatures and God exist. Since God is immutable, all change occurs only in creatures. The unchanging God does not need to be reconciled *to sinners* whom he still loves and calls. Sinners need to be reconciled *to God* whom they do not love. God reconciles sinners to himself by constituting them in newness of life, by which they are no longer willfully alienated from him. Two doctors of the Church expressed this particularly well. St. Augustine exclaimed, "And when you pour yourself out over us, you are not drawn down to us but draw us up to yourself: you are not scattered away, but you gather us together."[6] St. Bonaventure echoed,

> No conceivable man is worthy to attain this supreme Good exceeding in every possible way the limits of human nature, unless he is lifted up above himself through the action of God coming down to him. Not that God would come down in His immutable essence: He does so through an influence that emanates from Him; nor that the soul would rise above itself by physical ascent: it is lifted up through a God-conforming disposition.[7]

This God-conforming disposition, or habit of grace, is utterly lost to the one who commits mortal sin. Further, sin deforms the human person's skill in acting: It begets vice. Finally, as an offense against God (not against created grace), mortal sin merits eternal punishment, the atonement for which is adequately paid only by Jesus Christ. So, sin entails the deformation of human action, the stain of the loss of grace and fellowship with God, and the eternal punishment due to the offense. All damnable sinners are by definition *not* in a salvific relationship with God, for they have through free will removed themselves from a saving relationship with God by setting their hearts on some idol. This perverse action of itself disorders the heart and invites misery, since one thereby seeks rest in something that cannot satisfy the heart's yearning. The stain and the disorder constitute human misery in its depths; this misery is the *primary* defect of sin on the part of the sinner.[8] Stain and disorder constitute human alienation from God. The primary aspect of everlasting punishment is the unveiling of this alienation and the sinner's awareness that the alienation is to be everlasting. It is in this way that sin merits eternal punishment. The primary punishment of hell, then, is inflicted upon the sinner by himself.

Now, sin also fittingly entails a debt of "temporal" or "sensible" punishment to be inflicted retributively for past sins. The remission of sensible punishment can in some sense be described as extrinsic to the sinner.[9] Still, even such remission must involve something formal in the human person. One who is punished suffers harm to his bodily or psychic integrity. The absence of such punishment, e.g., the absence of sensible pain, implies the "absence" of this disorder or, in other words, somatic integrity (formal cause of the remission of sensible punishment). A formally extrinsic remission of sensible punishment would be meaningless to one who actually feels the punishment.

But the chief punishment of hell is *spiritual* pain, the loss of the vision and love of God. Now, how can such spiritual pain be remitted except precisely when the human person is endowed with the interior receptivity for a loving vision of God? Just as an extrinsic remission of physical punishment is meaningless for one who actually suffers, so an extrinsic remission of spiritual misery is meaningless for one who remains miserable. Spiritual misery is *not* the threat of punishment to be imposed; spiritual misery *is* alienation from God through the loss of charity.

The Catholic perspective on forgiveness, then, is that God freely extends his mercy to the ungodly on account of the infinite merits of his Son, who suffered, died, and rose for the salvation of all human beings. Short of the merits of Christ, it would be in some sense unjust for God to bring sinners back to a living relationship with himself. Eternal and sensible punishment is their due. However, eternal and sensible punishment are actually remitted, by definition, only by being removed. That is, God can liberate humans from sins and the punishment due to sins only by restoring them to life with himself and to somatic integrity. He restores sinners to life with himself by redirecting the sinner's heart and mind to himself in whom alone the sinner can find true happiness. Thus, sin and its forgiveness are formally constituted by the loss and recovery of friendship with God, a friendship not merely of moral depth but of spiritual and ontological depth, touching the very being of the human person.[10] The merciful remission of the eternal punishment for past sins occurs through a cleansing of the sinner's filth so that he no longer deserves eternal punishment, provided he perseveres in grace. God's mercy—his decision to remit the eternal punishment due to sin—is extrinsic in that it is not a response to something anterior in the sinner and in that it involves graciously rescinding the threat to "impose," as everlasting, the spiritual alienation from God merited by the sinner. God's mercy is extrinsic, then, in that the restoration of fallen creatures depends upon his initiative as covenantal Lord of those who have become ungodly.

However, given that the essence of hell is alienation from God, therefore, by definition, God's eternal mercy through Jesus Christ cannot be the forgiveness of sins itself, for alienation is not remitted unless it is taken away.[11] Insight on this point illuminates the Catholic belief that God does not pronounce forgiveness except upon those he also makes truly righteous. Genuine reconciliation occurs when, with the sinner's voluntary assent inspired by prevenient grace, God changes the his stony heart into a heart of flesh. Only thus does the human person no longer stray from God as the Final Good and incur the eternal loss of God and the debt of sensible punishment in hell. Forgiveness of sins thus necessarily involves the obliteration of the stain of sin, the restoration of right order in the rational faculties, as well as the remission of past guilt. These are formally caused by the grace that heals the sinner's will, unites him to God, and thus makes him truly pleasing.[12] The justified is not culpable for the disorder that remains (i.e., concupiscence). Indeed, God wisely leaves concupiscence as an occasion for arduous struggle, so that the justified may die into Christ's death by putting to death the deeds of the flesh.

At last, it is time to return to the consideration of Lutheran doctrine and its implications for eternal life. By upholding the "attribution of righteousness" as that by which the sinner stands just before God, Lutheranism undercuts the power of redemption and diminishes the splendor of beatitude. Granted, Lutheran theologians, in different ways, affix a personal righteousness to this attribution. Some Lutherans even speak of "rewards" in this regard, but these rewards are never identified with the essential reward of heaven, the beatific knowledge and love of the triune God. Lutherans always qualify these rewards as being "other" than eternal life. They admit no degrees of eternal bliss itself. The rewards of righteous works, according to the implication of Lutheran doctrine, must be peripheral to beatific friendship with God since this friendship is the very essence of salvation and since Lutherans deny the formally saving sufficiency of sanctifying grace, which, according to Catholicism, is the establishment of this friendship in the human person. The rewards of which Lutherans speak might include certain bodily and spiritual goods which are accidental to the nature and degree of one's divine friendship, one's participation in the Holy Trinity.[13] Nonetheless, if the Lutheran notion of justification were correct, then the "justified" person would still remain in some real way God's hostile enemy who was yet said "also" to enjoy certain attributes in common with the true friends of God, viz., the holy. How could such a person be said to be "fit" for salvation? Is it not necessary, on the presupposition of the truth of the Lutheran position, to diminish the essence of eternal beatitude? Would it not follow that eternal life is something other than or less than an everlasting friendship with God? What kind of divine friendship could one who is "totally just and totally sinner" enjoy? What sanctuary can the sinner, whose eyes are essentially unsound, find in God's transfiguring Light?

But perhaps this is not the end of the story. Perhaps the Lutheran need not abandon a lofty hope for eternal life. Perhaps every "saved" person, after having been "covered" by Christ's merits on earth and inchoately renewed, is also granted a thorough transformation of heart before entering paradise.[14] The Finns are keenly aware that the whole purpose of justification is this transformation of the human person. Pannenberg is equally aware that the encounter with Christ will be an encounter with the purifying fire of love. So perhaps God will radically complete, at the last judgment, the work he began on earth. Perhaps he will purify the souls of all those who die justified, eradicating their guilt, washing them clean, and bestowing on them the love by which they can love him above all things and for his own sake.

Such a "last-minute" purification of damnable sinners is hypothetically possible.[15] The fact that Lutherans deeply appreciate the need for purification is grounds for further dialogue. Still, two comments are pertinent. First, Catholic faith holds that God has not chosen this hypothetical possibility: Catholic faith holds that those who die without charity are damned and that charity cannot coexist with damnable sin.[16] Second, perhaps *this* hypothetical notion of a last minute purification must itself be purified. It seems to me that acknowledgment of such a hypothetical scenario would have a detrimental impact on the dramatic significance of earthly life. It would seem to sever the dynamic link between one's earthly progress in grace, so well-sung by the Greeks, and eternal participation in the triune life. It would, consequently, siphon away the dramatic energy of earthly life. One would lose sight of the intrinsic relevance of earthly life as a preparation for the final act of creation, the glorious praise of God in a mutual exchange of love. Granted, the vision of

God is an ineffable grace, the likes of which no eye has seen and no ear has heard. Beholding God, the saints must undergo an unspeakably great magnification of their earthly charity. Nevertheless, must there not be an essential continuity between a man's life on earth and his life of glorious love? How can Lutheran doctrine account for the integral continuity between earthly life, purgatory, and beatitude? May these questions stand as an invitation to further dialogue on the dramatic relevance of earthly life. If Lutherans can follow through on the promise of the Finns and of Pannenberg, our dialogue may step beyond the narrow horizon within which our conflict arose. The existential situation in which Lutheranism arose was the terrified conscience seeking solace in a gracious God. Would it not be too great a price to gain peace of conscience at the price of eternal life?

Faith and Self-Trust

Objection

The Lutheran will undoubtedly find the above argumentation objectionable, even if it may be persuasive for some Catholics. Lutherans worry that the Catholic conception of justification as a divinely infused gift leads to either presumptuous self-complacency or despair. The Lutheran evaluates Catholic thought as follows. I would only ask the reader to understand that I impute no judgment to Lutherans against Catholic persons; I am simply relating a Lutheran critique of what the Catholic doctrine does to human persons. Believing that God accepts him on the basis of infused gifts and cooperation, the (Catholic) sinner commences a routine self-examination, attempting to discern the (indiscernible) presence or absence of sanctifying grace and meritorious works. The penitent sinner worries whether or not God has infused grace and whether or not he has cooperated with God's action. At any stage of his religious "development," the penitent serves as his own focal point. He revolves around himself. Neither God nor Christ form the center of this person's life. Entrapped in the Catholic system of grace, the sinner can be tempted to despair, anxiously searching for elusive signs of grace. Those less conscious of sin are tempted to boast of their holiness, either openly or secretly, perhaps even unawares. These latter consider themselves clean before God. They approach the altar of the Lord's body with confidence, not confidence in Christ but confidence in themselves (Lk 18:11–12). They even presume that at the judgment, it will be right for Christ to serve them, since they are spotless and deserving of eternal life (Lk 17:7–10). They remain ungrateful for the divine gifts. They entirely forget that Christ died for them. They live in "glory,"

324 ENGRAFTED INTO CHRIST

unmindful of the Cross and of the Crucified. They constitute their own salvation, since they cling to nothing but themselves, and thus become nothing themselves. Having found themselves, they lose themselves, for they do not submit to Christ's teaching. On the contrary, the Lutheran insists, only those who lose themselves find themselves (Mt 10:39). One must accept one's nothingness by being made nothing in oneself; one must be humbled so that one can draw everything from the one who alone is Good.[17] Catholics suffering from pride extend no hand to plead for God's mercy; they offer no thanksgiving for his grace. Catholics suffering from despair arc not clatcd but suffer a similar solipsism, scratching around for signs of grace within their breasts. In summary, the very basis of Catholic thought leads either to presumption or to despair. Simo Peura deftly castigates the likes of such moralism and self-worship: "When a person seeks to merit salvation by works or achievement, nothing can be received as a gift from God. Instead, the person merely presumes that God is at once ready to give such gifts as salvation when they are earned by dint of self-approving work. Such idolatry ends up making God the servant of human beings."[18]

Catholic stress upon the category of created grace, grace as an infused "reality" in the soul distinct from the indwelling Spirit, detracts from the purpose of God's justifying action. For Lutheranism, on the contrary, God justifies sinners so that they may attend not primarily to his gifts but to him. Encumbered by the many distinctions drawn by scholastic theology and by an enslaving system of sacramental penitence, Catholics grasp for the "object" of their desire, imprisoned within their own limitations. Their attention riveted only upon the gift of grace, they are locked within their self-centeredness. Against this, Peura warns, "To trust in oneself is to unite one's heart with nothing at all. And this act further implies that the transforming power of love, when directed by self-love, unites the heart with nothing, so that the person becomes nothing."[19] Self-centeredness breeds pain and loneliness, not liberation. Therefore, it is the *Catholic* understanding of justification that leads to the solipsism of eternal self-isolation. It is the Catholic understanding that leads, or that can lead, to spiritual deprivation of God. In short, the Catholic notion of justification leads to hell. Luther himself alludes to this:

> For self-righteous people of this kind, who take everything very seriously…are never serene and peaceful. In this life they are always in doubt about the will of God and are afraid of death and of the wrath and judgment of God; and after this life they will suffer eternal destruction as punishment of their unbelief.[20]

The Lutheran finds a different perspective to be life-giving. Faith was meant to deliver the sinner from self-imposed isolation. Faith was meant to console the worries of the anxious and to eviscerate the boasting of the presumptuous. Faith was meant to buoy the hope of the despairing and to unplug the ears of the self-righteous, deaf to the incessant accusations of the law. Through faith, the believer knows both that he is ever a sinner and also that God is merciful. God extends mercy to the believer who abandons all futile attempts at self-justification and clings simply to God.[21] Faith is trust in God; faith is not blind trust, nor is it empty knowledge; it is lucid. Faith binds the human person to Christ in self-abandonment. In a sense, faith *is* this self-abandonment.[22] The believer does not relate to faith but rather to Christ: "True faith is what may be called colourless, like air or water; it is but the medium through which the soul sees Christ; and the soul as little really rests upon it and contemplates it, as the eye can see the air."[23] Through faith, the human person is slain and brought to life. The sinner is slain in his attempt to find something in himself that can please God: He abandons all folly. He is brought to life because God mercifully promises new life to those who trust in him. Faith is assurance of this promise; it is the beginning of eternal life. Because Catholics do not rightly appreciate faith and because they even denigrate faith by defining it as mere knowledge of God, they cannot as such be liberated by the promise of forgiveness. They cannot enjoy an ecstatic fellowship with Christ, which is really the essence of eternal life. Catholicism bids them attend to the beauty of their own souls and to the gifts that God pours forth. They plead against his righteous judgment that they are owed eternal life or they anxiously search for a pearl of little price, all the while enclosing themselves within themselves.

Response

Re-articulation. The preceding objection to Catholic thought preoccupies much of the Lutheran discussion of the intelligibility of Lutheran versus Catholic doctrines. Catholics too rarely countenance this weighty objection, which underlies the most fundamental and genuine Lutheran concerns. I believe that this very objection involves both promise and problem. If one follows out on its promise, it can further dialogue between the communions. The problem is that the objection rests upon a precarious substructure. I will present here only the preliminary outline of a counter-argument worked out precisely from *within* the Lutheran world of thought. What I am attempting to do here is to draw attention to self-destructive forces within the Lutheran framework that have heretofore gone too little noticed. One current of thought bears promise, while the conjunction of the two together threaten to undermine the very foundations of Lutheranism from within its own logic. The sketch is quite brief, especially for such an enormous claim. It is my sincere hope that this argument will be taken not as an attack upon persons (just as neither is a Lutheran critique of the

Catholic [scholastic] system of grace taken as a critique of persons) but as a fraternal critique of a body of thought that as a whole.

To undertake this task, I wish to revisit the above objection with an eye to an ineradicable fault line therein. The above Lutheran objection to Catholic teaching rests upon one chief premise. This premise leads to the search for a solution, but the solution contradicts the premise. The premise is as follows: Only a pure love of God devoid of all self-seeking can truly please God. Any love tainted by the desire for one's own good falls short of such pure love.[24] But we humans regularly act out of selfish interests; we regularly sin. Luther appears to have agreed with Aristotle's opinion that human action is in practice based upon the desire to seek happiness. Given his premise above, Luther drew the conclusion: All human action is therefore sinful.[25] Every human person is a self-seeking sinner, unable to please God for his own sake. For this reason, disciples of Luther, most notably Nygren, castigated Aristotle and Plato for their opinions that eros or the desire for happiness is fundamental to human flourishing. Catholic doctors, indebted to the Greek valuation of eros, claimed that charity is the love by which human persons desire to see God and the love by which they merit the reward of that desire. This claim provides evidence for the Lutheran objection: The Catholic doctrine of *caritas* promotes the basically self-oriented love of sinful man, eros. All persons by "nature" desire happiness; therefore, all are by "nature" sinful, if nature is understood in the theological sense as sin. The Lutheran sees only one way out of this dilemma: Faith as simple trust in God's agapic love by which he promises life to the ungodly. Peura confidently locates the heart of Luther's concern here: "Luther's entire theological work can be viewed as an attempt to solve the problem of self-serving love."[26] Echoing this perspective, General Secretary Rev. Ishmael Noko stated in praise of the JD, "When we know that in Christ we are unconditionally accepted by God at the outset, we are set free to love one another unconditionally."[27] Luther showed the way to this selfless love: faith in God.[28]

More must be said about the existential dynamic here. Selfless love does not come from human effort. The sober sinner recognizes these self-seeking tendencies at the core of his being. He acknowledges that by no work can he unstain his soul. Hence, he writhes: "Out, damn'd spot!" The Law foments his fear, with its demands and accusations. The sinner, recognizing God for his enemy, hates his righteous judge, the one who is to meet out punishment. He is angry with God. Considering such a bind, one cannot conceive of this sinner genuinely loving God. Any "love" of God would be merely self-seeking love, such as the attempt to justify oneself by eliciting an act of love towards God in order to assuage his wrath.[29] Such love would obviously be disingenuous, tangled in the subtle snares of Pharisaic narcissism. Such "caritas" would be but a ladder by which the sinner presumptiously aspires to ascend to God: It would be the ancient tower once smote in Babel. In fact, the proud scale its lofty pretensions, but sinners cower beneath its shadow, fearing to bring their deeds before the dread wrath of God's holiness. Such sinners cannot possibly love God.

Only when God pronounces him righteous can the sinner begin to love God. God pronounces the sinner forgiven: "Though you are sinful, I forgive you." Forgiveness is not awarded to a righteous person but rests simply with the merciful condescension of God, which sets the sinner in a radically new situation—liberty! God withholds wrath from the one who deserves punishment and thus quickens the sinner's heart by the promise of mercy. Sin is no longer a loathsome burden to be borne by man, the ass of law. Christ has borne and destroyed the murderous weight of law, winning sinners the freedom in which to live. The accusations of law expended themselves in vain against the Son of God made man. The weight of sin and of the punishment due to sin has been borne in toto. In exchange, the sinner is given the promise: "God does not accuse those buried with Christ; instead, he grants the very righteousness of Christ." By grace, the sinner can accept this promise in faith, acknowledging his own sin and the fact that nothing in him deserves forgiveness. God thereby proves his righteous love, loving the unlovable (Rom 5:8). Accepting the promise through faith, the sinner henceforth wishes to receive everything from God and to achieve nothing by human power alone. The saved sinner no longer fears God as an angry judge; he in turn is no longer angry with God but trusts him as a merciful savior. The sinner's anxiety about salvation dies a death, since God has promised mercy. Together with the promise of mercy, the gift of agapic love is given. The sinner receives the divine mercy and the divine, selfless love.[30]

Once the sinner accepts God's mercy through faith, he can begin to love God and neighbor. Because the sinner's eternal life is assured through mercy and not through works, all of his subsequent love of God and neighbor cannot (at least in essence) be motivated by eros. The love that follows justification is thus not the stain of "charity" by which one supposedly merits eternal life. Rather, this love of God and neighbor is totally selfless; it is a participation in the selfless love of God. Faith brought the sinner outside of himself, raising him to Christ; now, agapic love enables the believer to descend from this height in order to love neighbor.[31] Love of neighbor is no longer yoked to the burden of meriting salvation, since the sinner has been freed from the anxious need to merit acquittal. Salvation is a gift that excludes merit. Salvation and justification form an indissolubly identical gift. The believer does not, therefore, seek to merit anything, since the love of reward is sinful. Pure love of neighbor is, in contrast, simply gratuitous, since it is offered out of thankfulness for the abundant mercy of God. Without such love, true faith could not exist. However, such love does not enter into the constitution of justifying faith, because faith is acceptance of what is offered freely. Justification never becomes a reward, even a reward for works done in faithful love.

Analysis. It should be clear from the forgoing that the fundamental presupposition of this line of thought is the sinfulness of the desire for happiness, under the shadow of which falls the desire for reward. Because humans are so enmeshed in the desire for happiness, they are ever attacked by sin. In fact, the very desire for happiness can be described as the essence of the concupiscence that Lutherans call sin. Agapic love cannot flourish in the stifling atmosphere of this erotic drive for happiness. Faith alone opens up the salvific space within which one can once again breathe tranquilly. Through faith, true love of God can grow until it is consummated in heaven.[32]

Many readers may be pleased with the above line of reasoning. It is dressed in biblical garb and invites the Romantic with its aesthetic appeal. Who, in our day, would subscribe to a self-righteous doctrine? Who would presume to have merited eternal life? Notwithstanding this appeal, the argumentation betrays a deadly ambiguity in the Lutheran doctrine. The current of promise is yet buried. The danger of the doctrine lies within.

Recall that faith enters the stage to quiet the sinner's fear and anger. The sinner is angry at God because of a fear of punishment. The sinner ceases to be angry upon hearing that his sins have been forgiven through faith, although they remain. Faith, therefore, provides the security within which the sinner can rest assured. Faith bears aloft the heavy burden of law—which the believer cannot bear and beneath which he would be crushed—so that he no longer stands condemned by its still valid accusations. Faith consoles the believer through the promise that his ultimate end, eternal life and the remission of the punishment due to sin, is unconditionally guaranteed. The *sinner's* ultimate end, however, is still in place. The sinner still longs ultimately for eternal life: namely, for the remission of punishment. Faith *serves* that end, certain warrant of its attainment. Faith is the means, the only means, by which this end is secured.

But the reader must remember: According to the Lutheran perspective, the desire for the remission of punishment and for the acquisition of eternal happiness is sinful. So, if faith is enlisted in the service of such sinful love, what of faith's own character? Without faith, Lutherans insist, the sinner's terror of and fury against God would mount to the heavens. Without faith, no supposedly "gratuitous" love of God would be possible. But gratuitous love is only "inchoately" established in the believer during this life. Such love can be described as a luxury, a luxury afforded by the stay of condemnation offered through the promise of forgiveness. Faith itself keeps this promise alive for the believer. Faith the ass secures the believer's actual end, eternal salvation, the desire for which is concupiscence. But man can have only one end, as our Lord teaches: "No one can serve two masters; for either he will hate the one and love the other, or he will be devoted to the one and despise the other. You cannot serve both God and mammon" (Mt 6:24). Therefore, faith serves man's sinful end. Turning the table on Nygren, then, one can ask whether by a structural, though unintended, logic what Lutherans call "faith" is but part and parcel of what they call "concupiscence," which in its nature is damnable. Has the sinner then been liberated from selfishness through faith, or has he been all the more enmeshed therein?

One might retort that Lutherans do not understand the motivation "to believe" as rooted in a desire for salvation.[33] "To believe," one could say, is a gift given to the believer, worked in him through the Holy Spirit. It must be said, in response, that Lutheran literature abounds in expressions that link faith with what humans desperately seek, an end to the bite of the law's accusations and certainty of deliverance from eternal punishment. More on this in a moment. In the Catholic world, on the contrary, the "terrified conscience" is not a premise for an entire theology; it is the occasion for sacramental grace, for sound counsel, and for spiritual growth. Moreover, if faith is to be a human act and not merely an act of a man, it must somehow be coordinated in its roots with human love and desire. Insofar as Lutherans stress the sole efficacy of the divine will and conceive of human cooperation in faith as merely passive, they risk eclipsing human action from the ambit of faith. But if faith is a human action, it must be undertaken with regard to an end, even though the power of that act is supplied by God's gratuitous will. If that end is remission from punishment, then, according to the Lutheran perspective, that end must be sin. If the end is sin, the act of faith undertaken with a view to that end must be sin.

It would appear that only this analysis of Lutheran thought can explain the breathtaking charge that Catholic "charity" is but a subtle form of Pharisaic narcissism. Lutherans do not shy from portraying those immured in Catholic practice as contending against God in the final judgment: "You owe me eternal life! Just look at this robe of charity!" Other Christians have felt similarly.[34] But this Lutheran critique is leveled against Catholicism from outside of the perspective of love. If charity is the love by which one loves God as ultimate friend, it is unthinkable that a person with charity would wield *charity* as a weapon to be interposed between himself and God. Charity is a power for relationship, not a weapon: "But to all who received him, who believed in his name, he gave power to become children of God" (Jn 1:12). Charity unites the soul to God; it is not thrust between God and man. Only if one were situated within a self-seeking desire merely for a remission of eternal punishment could one charge that Catholic "charity" is something to be used, or that could be used, as evidence *against* God's righteous judgment. The Lutheran evaluation of Catholic thought proceeds from a religious framework that systematically upholds the primacy of an end that is unwittingly concupiscent. Approaching Catholic thought from this concupiscent framework, Lutherans perceive in Catholicism a systematic defense of egoism, disguised as charity. Disgusted, they cling to faith as the way, the only way, to salvation. Grace is so highly praised within this framework.

Lutherans may argue, to the contrary, that faith itself is not concupiscence, that faith is truly love to God, that faith is the real love and trust that God seeks, that which Catholics call charity. For one, American Lutheran theologian Bruce Marshall describes faith as a life-giving power: "Through this very faith we come to have a new heart; we are transformed in the depths of ourselves precisely by relying upon that which is outside ourselves, namely the righteousness of Christ which God imputes to us." Faith is, accordingly, the *medium* of a relationship with Christ. He continues, "God's favor makes...introspection unnecessary, not because his favor fails to transform us, but because it makes us new creatures *by* leading us to look away from ourselves to Christ outside ourselves." To set one's heart on Christ is faith, and this faith is the holiness without which no one will see God: "When we set our hearts on him all that we need for salvation is ours, including that holiness without which no one will see him in the end."[35] It is not that Marshall perceives faith as a human work based upon natural powers; rather, faith is the work of the Holy Spirit, leading sinful man away from his painful solipsism.[36]

Faith is, to draw out the implication, a saving relationship with God through Jesus Christ. It is the relationship that God desired from the beginning. Similarly, Peura conveys this idea in summing up Luther's understanding of the First Commandment: "Luther counts fundamental trust as deciding who or what constitutes our god.... The requirement to believe in God, to trust in God, and to look for our refuge in him alone is basically the same as the commandment to love God purely."[37] The primal sin of Adam and Eve was to spurn this faith and to strive to achieve a righteousness of their own. In other words, the relationship of faith to God is that which God's righteous will demands; to violate this faith is to sin. Infidelity is that which God forbids. But God's righteous will is expressed in the commandments of the law, considered not merely in their legal and outward sense but according to their deeper, covenantal sense. To fulfill the law, then, is to love God purely above all things. Faith, as Marshall and Peura imply, is this love that honors God, the loyal clinging to God as God. Is it possible, then, that faith necessarily includes what *Catholics* wish to mean by charity, the divine love of God for his own sake? Is it possible that faith is *not* concupiscence but rather the fulfillment of authentic love, not a self-seeking love but a truly ecstatic, agapic, love? Insofar as affirmative answers to these questions are forthcoming, Lutheran thought on faith may dovetail with Catholic thought on the theological virtues. But we must also countenance a problem.

Would not a Lutheran who argues thus—that sin consists in unbelief precisely because faith is what God desires—enfold love within faith's justifying power, mingling the leaven of the Pharisees with the pure Gospel (Mt 16:6)? Did not Melanchthon condemn the idea?

> [Our opponents] do not attribute justification to faith except on account of love.... Where does this end but with the abolition of the promise again and a return to the law? If faith receives the forgiveness of sin on account of love, the forgiveness of sins will always be unsure, for we never love as much as we should. In fact, we do not love at all unless our hearts are sure that the forgiveness of sins has been granted to us.... For the forgiveness of sins is received by faith alone—and we mean faith in the [strict] sense of the word—since the promise can be received only by faith.[38]

Do not Peura's and Marshall's suggestions that faith justifies, not as a concupiscent trust in Christ for the remission of the wrath to come, but as an attitude that God most seeks from his creatures, relegate faith to the law, even an expansive notion of law that encompasses the covenantal responsibility incumbent upon the recipients of divine love? Since confessional Lutheran teaching resists even this expansive reading of law, faith must be distinguished from the love required in the law, the pure love untainted by self-seeking desire.[39] Since the law is impossible to obey, all stand condemned. Only by faith can sinners avoid the terrors of the sentence of condemnation. Faith secures salvation from the punishments of hell and the gift of heavenly life, which gifts have been defined as the end of the old Adam.

In confessional Lutheran teaching, then, we find that faith, in virtue of its distinction from the charity by which one can love God as required in the law (in its deeper sense), subserves the desires of the old man. Marshall, Peura, Pannenberg, Root, and many other Lutherans, wish to avoid this implication. Their very efforts to avoid this implication promise, in my opinion, the soundest basis upon which to dialogue. They ascribe to faith that other-centered, no, that God-centered and Christ-centered, ecstatic character which Catholics perceive as constitutive of charity. If Lutherans could admit that what they mean by justifying faith, precisely as justifying, is what Catholics refer to as faith, hope, and charity, then together we could surmount many obstacles to a common confession. The consequences for an agreement on this point would be manifold, and acknowledgment of these consequences would further confirm the genuine compatibility between the Lutheran concept "justifying faith" and the Catholic triad "faith, hope, and charity." These consequences would include the following: Denial of the character of remnant sin as worthy of damnation, the real ontological character of divine filiation, admission of the possibility for satisfactory obedience to the commandments, an increase in justifying grace through cooperation with God, the loss of this grace through every mortal sin, and the capacity to merit eternal life. Whether such consequences would be palatable for Marshall, the Finns, Pannenberg, Root, and others, is by no means clear. The promising current of thought struggles against an opposing force.

Marshall, for example, wishes to situate himself within a genuinely Lutheran understanding of justification. Perhaps for this reason, traces of the problematic logic, critiqued above, can be found even in his work, which otherwise tends in large part towards a description of faith that corresponds to what Catholics want to see as "faith formed by charity."[40] Marshall's own expressions chafe against his intent to locate in faith the basis for a right relationship with God, in which the human person becomes "other-centered." Marshall suggests that "to console terrified consciences"[41] was one of Luther's two "motives" for going beyond Paul's term "reckoned" (Rom 4) to the purely forensic term "imputed." Marshall explains this motive: "In this context the central question about salvation was one of trust or assurance. Upon what can I rely for salvation?"[42] Here, Marshall unwittingly discloses the sinner's eternal welfare as the final end of faith, an end that Luther in his commentary on Romans was at pains to denigrate as selfish and contemptible. Raunio, similarly, suggests that God enables selfless love by giving in advance more than greedy man would ever have wished for, slaking his thirst for God's "good gifts," so that, thus sated, he is unhindered in his capacity for gratuitous love: "Only when the Christian possesses such a God who continually gives him good things and whom he considers always the font of everything good, can he love the neighbor without searching for anything from him as reward."[43] Even Marshall and the Finns, who come quite close to the Catholic perspective, show tendencies, inimical to their core concerns, of making faith subserve the end of the old Adam.

If this is the case in the best of the Lutheran world, is not my critique valid *a fortiori* for Lutheran thought in general? Does not the following practical syllogism determine the lives of many Protestant Christians: "What will guarantee my salvation?; not works, not infused gifts, but faith alone; therefore, I believe."[44] Is it not the case, then, that what was understood to liberate in fact entraps? Does not Lutheran thought collapse beneath the weight of its initial premise and the faltering support of faith, which was meant to bear aloft the burden of that premise: Only pure love of God is pleasing? Why else, but that faith subserves a selfish love?

Luther himself fell prey to this logic. I will let him speak for himself out of the very document so prized in the recent dialogue, the *Antilatomus*. In distinguishing gift and grace, faith and favor, Luther labeled the former an inward good and the latter an outward good. This pair of goods wars against a pair of evils: Faith wars against the inward evil of sin and grace wars against the outward evil of wrath, the threatened punishment. Luther's evaluation of these four realities unveils the self-defeating character of his doctrine:

> We would perhaps have disregarded corruption [the inward evil] and been pleased with our evil unless this other evil, which is wrath [the outward evil], had refused to indulge our foolishness and had resisted it with terror and the danger of hell and death, so that we have but little peace in our wickedness. Plainly wrath is a greater evil for us than corruption, for we hate punishment more than guilt.[45]

Luther diagnoses man's greatest evil as eternal punishment (*poena damni*), not as the sin which incurs this punishment as its due. The attentive reader will note that Luther offered this evaluation not merely through the eyes of pre-regenerate man. Later in the same text, he thunders his praise of grace in light of this diagnosis of man's greatest evil,

> Just as wrath is a greater evil than the corruption of sin, so grace is a greater good than that health of righteousness which we have said comes from faith. Everyone would prefer—if that were possible—to be without the health of righteousness rather than the grace of God, for peace and the remission of sins are properly attributed to the grace of God, while healing from corruption is ascribed to faith.[46]

Praise of grace is yoked to fear of hell. This evaluation of sin and punishment can even be detected as early as Luther's *Commentary on Romans*: "For (if I may use an example) who does the good and omits the evil with that will whereby, even if there were no commandment or prohibition, he still would do it or omit it?"[47] He answers, "I believe that if we rightly examine our heart, no one will find himself to be that kind of person except one who is absolutely perfect, but rather, if he had the freedom, he would omit many good works and do many evil works." He then declares his assessment: "This is what it means to be in your sins before God."[48]

Because all desire their own fulfillment in everything they do, no one fulfills the law of love. This sin is not the greatest evil; the greatest evil is the punishment due to this sin. What stays the divine wrath is acquitting grace, which is grasped through faith alone, the only means by which one can escape judgment. In this way, faith is ecstatic: It is a means to a means outside oneself, the favor of God through Jesus Christ. Faith grasps another and is thus ecstatic; all other means grasp for something within and are thus solipsistic. Yet, that which faith grasps for is the way to freedom from judgment, not the way to freedom from sin. Faith itself is the beast that bears the sinner's end, an end already defined as sinful. The believer is still in his sins, abiding in Egypt while the Lord passes over. Is this the way to agapic love?[49] Does Luther hymn God as "rich in mercy" (Eph 2:4), or does he give us the justified man as *Dives in misera corde* (Lk 16:19–31)? How can Luther's fear of wrath compare with Thérèse's love of holiness in the face of wrath.[50] And yet St. John tells us, "There is no fear in love, but perfect love casts out fear. For fear has to do with punishment, and he who fears is not perfected in love" (1 Jn 4:18).

If the forgoing critique is valid, can one not ask whether *Christianity* can be redeemed? Has Nietzsche not called the bluff on us all, tracing back every human whim and endeavor to the Will to Power, that cruel desire for life, that which has manifested itself throughout history in Cain's pathetic jealousy, in the anger of prophets' killers, and in the cloister's bile? Are not all "fallen short" of the glory of Jesus' vision of love (Rom 3:23)? To what desolate island has the warmth of agapic love fled, only to mend its wounds?

These questions touch upon a certain set of traditions within Christianity; moreover, they have of late become burdensome questions for many, especially in light of Nietzsche's unmasking pen. In my opinion, though, these questions are based upon malformed presuppositions. They ought not, as such, be cause of anxious concern for Catholic and Orthodox Christians. Catholics and Orthodox rooted in their traditions do not consider the desire for happiness to be sinful; they believe it to be the God-given impetus to undertake a search for Truth, for Goodness, and for Beauty. By this desire, one comes to Jesus asking, "Teacher, what good deed must I do, to have eternal life?" (Mt 19:16). By this desire, one begs, "Sir, give me this water, that I may not thirst, nor come here to draw" (Jn 4:15). The desire for happiness draws men towards Life. Jesus accepts this desire; he ratifies it; and he guides it to its true fulfillment.[51]

Granted, in certain circles of contemporary Catholics, a form of piety leads to near revulsion against any form of self-love, relegates such love to the realm of nature, and severs from this "erotic" love a putatively "dis-interested" agape. I believe this recrudescence of spiritualism obscures principles central to monotheistic faith. François Fénelon, among other Catholics, gave classic expression to the "pure love" theory, praising charity as so utterly disinterested that the true lover ought to annihilate in his free will any desire for eternal salvation that is not strictly a command given by God extrinsically (i.e., not through nature). Through the Magisterium, Catholics have been consistently guided away from such theoretical scrupulosity.[52] Pope Innocent XIII, for instance, condemned a number of propositions on pure love taken nearly verbatim from Fénelon.[53] These sorts of condemnations were nothing new.

Theologically, such spiritualism is opposed to the most promising movements in contemporary Catholic moral thought.[54] Indeed, it has been increasingly observed that a merely "casuistic" approach to the moral life reduces Christian behavior to obedience to commandments that are not seen as intrinsically relevant to human flourishing. The merely casuistic approach emphasizes obedience, nearly blind obedience, and eschews any teleological conception of the commandments given by God. This casuistic approach is, more remotely, rooted in the decadent nominalism that so emphasized God's "freedom," if it can be called that, that it portrayed God as able to command anything he wills. Indeed, God does whatever he wills! Yet it is the conviction of Orthodox and Catholic doctors that God wills wisely. He does not lord his majesty over the frailty of man. Nor does he threaten that he could do so. Rather, he commands things that are wise: e.g., "Be fruitful and multiply" (Gen 1:28). The nominalist effort to downplay God's wisdom led to a conception of the moral life divorced from the human desire for beatitude.[55] Thus was born an undesirable moralism. Within the categories of this moralism, well-intentioned Christians zealous for holiness attempted to express their love for God for his own sake. The result was the hypothesis of disinterested love.[56] The objective falsity of this hypothesis was rightly unmasked by Nietzsche. Eros, conceived as the desire for human flourishing, is fundamental to Christian life and to psychic health. If man is to be involved in religion, touched by God's condescension, so too must his eros.

The venerable tradition of the Orthodox Churches does not counsel the Christian to eschew the desire for happiness as egocentric. The great Romanian Orthodox theologian of the 20th century, Dumitru Staniloae, would agree to the substance of the Catholic magisterial concern on this point. He stressed the importance of the human thirst for happiness, for the divine. Because grace is constitutive of the human person, although not to the exclusion of a distinction between "image" and "likeness," man "continues to aspire in some way after God and so remains in some relationship with him" even after the fall.[57] Staniloae described the blessing of communion with God as a quality in which the human person, made in the image of God, can grow, as the image tends towards its archetype and in this way grows in the likeness.[58] Because man's relationship with God is described most accurately as a *dialogue*, implying reciprocity, his growth in grace requires (as task, *Aufgabe*) his virtuous activity. For my present purposes, I wish simply to draw attention to Staniloae's sound insight that Christ came to heal, not to replace, sinful man. Therefore, Christ ratifies and leads to its logical consummation the natural desire of the human heart. Despite sin, the image still yearns for communion with God: "Hence, Christ is said to have reestablished the image or to have found the image that was lost, but it is not said that he created it again."[59] It is precisely because of this that Staniloae could prudently counsel pastors that sinful man is to be affirmed in his desire for communion (union) with things, even though that desire be unfruitfully, i.e., sinfully, directed through choice towards lesser goods. From this desire as from a starting point, the good pastor leads the wandering person back to the fountain of life wherein that desire can be fulfilled. Staniloae's words shock the "piety" of Western ears: "It is easy for the human being to be brought back to a positive response."[60] More recently, Valerie Karras has said the same: "Our natural freewill is oriented toward God precisely because humanity is created *by* God, in *his* image. A special act of God's grace (i.e., prevenient grace) is not required for us to orient ourselves toward him; orientation toward God is at the heart of our human nature."[61] The point is both theistic: God remains the author of nature, and the first act of created existence (the will's natural orientation, preceding choice, *voluntas ut natura*) cannot be distorted, unless God has become wicked. This point is also fundamental to Christology: Christ had *two wills*, divine and human. Since he was to take on our nature without being sin itself, then our nature is not sin itself.[62] These insights are at the heart of the Catholic position as well.[63] For Staniloae, God designed man to strive after communion with himself and "does wish to satisfy that thirst for life and for more abundant life."[64] Like de Lubac, Staniloae located the condition for the possibility of hell precisely in this desire, which, if thwarted, frustrates and alienates.[65]

The proper evaluation of the desire for happiness is fundamental to situating the dispute between Lutherans and Catholics. Because Lutherans so radically deny the goodness of this desire, they find themselves washed upon the shores of despair. The only way out appears to be Luther's *sola fide*, which as *Luther* describes it is not only noxious in its fruits but poisonous at its root.[66] It ought to come as no surprise that the lucid Catholic philosopher Josef Pieper chastized Nygren for uprooting agape from the human realm entirely, since in the end the sinner can serve only as the empty vessel for God's love. In agape, God loves God; man has no part in it.[67] Any continuity between human longing and agape, Nygren opined, would stain the latter. Thus, the plea "Out, damn'd spot" ushered the very petitioner away, and none but the beneficiary was left! Creation and redemption were sundered from one another. Nygren's presuppositions led him away from the Jewish roots of Christianity and allied him with the heretic Marcion as "one of the first advocates of the idea of agape."[68] Luther's journey paved the way: From the praise of agape to the condemnation of nature, making some in the world writhe in agony: "O Hamlet, speak no more: Thou turns't mine eyes into my very soul; And there I see such black and grained spots As will not leave their tinct."[69]

Catholics and Orthodox, together with their elder Jewish siblings, affirm the human thirst for the divine, even after the tragic incident in the garden.[70] Nevertheless, there is no doubt that, because of the sinful condition in which we find ourselves, fulfillment of this good desire must come by way of renunciation, suffering, and death.[71] Jesus draws those who are impelled towards him by this desire for happiness towards deeper waters. Jesus directs them to the demands of the fulfillment of this desire, which demands amount to entrance into his life. Thus, he tells the fishermen: "Put out into the deep [*duc in altum*]" (Lk 5:4)! Heading into the deep demands an offering of one's life: "If any man would come after me, let him deny himself and take up his cross and follow me" (Mk 8:34). Thus, the passage to life is by way of death. But this is not a dialectical knot; it is sharing in the Life that is towards the Father (*pros ton patera*, 1 Jn 1:2), the Life that is the Way (Jn 14:6), so that the *via* of the pilgrim is not a means to a foreign end but the progressive assimilation to that Way that is the End (Rom 10:4). The passage to life, to eternal life in the Spirit, is the way of faith, hope, and charity, by which God brings the human person to surrender all attachment to every obstacle to the beatific fruition.[72] If we are made new in Christ, we become the Passover of Christ: As Israel passed over from Egypt to the Promised Land, so we pass over from the world, through Christ, in the Spirit, to the Father. By faith, hope, and love, the human person cleaves to Christ so as to become one with him. By these, he is engrafted into Christ, through whom alone he finds the path to eternal union with the triune God, in whom alone that human thirst is fulfilled.[73]

What is the Seed of this Beatitude?

I would now like to return to a consideration of the relationship between eternal life and justification. In the first major section of this chapter, I argued from the ground up, from justification to eternal life: If justification is of such and such a nature, then eternal life must be of such and such a nature. I now wish to reverse my approach, beginning from a Catholic appreciation of the mystery of eternal life and inquiring into its implications for justification.

In beatitude, the saints see, adore, and love their Divine Bridegroom. As spotless brides, they are capable of receiving their Lord in their very being through their spiritual powers. Now, how could an "alien" righteousness formally equip someone for this beatific friendship? It could, perhaps, account for the absence of punishment and the presence of pleasing "objects" since even unregenerate sinners could appreciate these. But delightful objects and the absence of pain cannot of themselves constitute divine intimacy. Friendship requires reciprocity. Divine friendship consists in mutual presence within a reciprocal commitment. Jason Ripley, New Testament scholar and member of the United Methodist Church, perceives the scriptural sense of "righteousness" in a way that is in accord with the spirit of Catholic thought: "At the core, righteousness in the Hebrew Bible is inherently relational, involving the fulfillment of the demands of a relationship, both those among humans and those between humans and God."[74] The following question arises: What are the constituents of a right relationship with God, specifically those on the side of the human creature? Catholics name at least the following: created grace and the theological virtues, an upright will, and concrete, satisfactory obedience to the commandments which are articulations of a proper relationship to God and neighbor.

Upholding the reality of the created aspect of divine friendship does not imply that a sinner "contributes" something to God which is not itself a gift. The category "created grace" helps one acknowledge the reality of creaturely being and of the conditions necessary for a creature's fulfillment. It is a question of the human person having the mind and heart to enjoy God who already enjoys himself and says, "Enter into the joy of your master" (Mt 25:21). To the blind, the splendor of the Grand Canyon is inaccessible. To the person who in no way loves and knows God, divine Beauty cannot be attractive. The object of heavenly happiness is God himself, yet happiness formally is one's loving knowledge of God, not God himself, who is the object of happiness. Unless the human person actually enjoys the God who is all Good, he cannot be beatifically happy. This is the reason that, when the sun of justice appears, he shall save those who love him and burn those who spurn him, unto condemnation for mortal sinners and unto healing consolation for venial sinners: "For you who fear my name the sun of righteousness shall rise, with healing in its wings" (Mal 4:2).

If God declares a miserable wretch happy, the latter cannot be happy by that decree itself. The divine "decree" makes one happy precisely by bringing about genuine happiness. The sacred scriptures liken this happiness to the purifying espousal of the soul-bride. To be capable of treasuring nuptial intimacy with God, the human bride must love him with all her mind and strength, for where the heart is, there is its treasure (Lk 12:34). This is the truest desire of the human heart: to be united with God. This is no foul desire; it is not a self-enclosed love but the God-given impulse for union with the Holy Trinity: "Scarcely had I passed them, when I found him whom my soul loves. I held him, and would not let him go until I had brought him into my mother's house, and into the chamber of her that conceived me" (Song of Songs 3:4). Lovers long for the real presence of their beloved, and spiritual creatures contact each other by means of spiritual faculties. Union with God entails something real in the creature. Therefore, there must be something real in the creature in order for this creature to be happy. The creaturely condition for happiness provides the necessary *ratio* for the Catholic tradition's esteem for created grace, since the creature longs not merely for an acquittal from punishment but for eternal life and is fitted for such life by being turned towards and attuned to God. Since this attunement is a change and since it ought to be a stable change, allowing for the requisite spontaneity of a child of God, Catholic tradition appeals to grace as a created, sanctifying quality. Ripley deftly expresses the sentiment behind the overall Catholic outlook:

> Relational ontology can also speak powerfully to the felt needs of current culture, in ways impossible for the forensic model. Simply put, we do not yearn merely to avoid punishment, to be let off the hook for our rebellion and merely proclaimed "righteous," while we are left in the fractured abyss of our isolation and misery. Rather, we seek wholeness, *shalom*, an intimate reconciliation to fulfill our created need for a relationship with God.[75]

The person who opposes God cannot *be* in a divine friendship. The sinner cannot truly be at peace with God. But since God does not change (or does he?), the sinner must be changed within the depths of his being. As the seed of eternal life, sanctifying grace constitutes the basis of this change in the creature, admitting and equipping a man for beatitude by establishing him in a real friendship with God. Sanctifying grace is not the agent of this change but the establishment of this change, wrought by God; through sanctifying grace, God brings his bride back to himself and *thus* finds her pleasing: "You have ravished my heart, my sister, my bride, you have ravished my heart with a glance of your eyes, with one jewel of your necklace. How sweet is your love, my sister, my bride!" (Song of Songs 4:9–10). This beauty of the bride, bestowed by the Divine Bridegroom, is no obstacle to intimacy. The bride sees this beauty, if at all, as but the working of the Groom who draws her up with one hand through his grace and caresses her with the other hand. She cries out, "O that his left hand were under my head, and that his right hand embraced me!" (Song of Songs 8:3). More, the very beauty of the bride is filial. Just as the only begotten God (Jn 1:18), true God from true God, exists forever *pros ton patera*, so the human person, tumbling out from God's regenerating love, is situated within the eternal "Abba!" of the Son, progressively and dynamically conformed to this cry of "Abba" by the Spirit (Rom 8:15, 29). Filial holiness is not a cause of pride; it is directly proportionate to humility.[76]

On earth, intimacy with God is veiled, for "now we see in a mirror dimly"; earthly intimacy is enjoyed through faith but not through faith alone, for without charity no one can love God as Friend: "Faith, hope, love abide, these three; but the greatest of these is love" (1 Cor. 13:12–13). This very seed of spiritual life planted in justification is nourished and grows through sanctification according to God's will and human cooperation: "But once sanctifying grace is received, if good use is made of it, it merits its own increase in the present life."[77] Through this purification and God's nuptial advance, the seed blossoms into that by which the Christian happily attains God (Jn 4:14). Though it *is* possible for God to change a damnable sinner instantaneously at death, he desires to draw all to himself while they live, sweetly disposing all things. The Master of love, St. Francis de Sales, hymns a praise to God for his provident wisdom:

> Let no one think that thou draggest me after thee like a forced slave, or a lifeless
> wagon. Ah! No, thou drawest me by the odour of thy ointments; thou enticest me; thy
> drawing is mighty, but not violent, since its whole force lies in its sweetness.[78]

So much for the eschatological argument.

Two-Languages for the Faith

Sketch of the Proposal

There has long been the complaint against many Lutherans and Catholics that their dispute is primarily due to differences in words, emphases, and intellectual approaches. A contemporary version of this complaint runs as follows. The mystery of justification transcends both approaches, each approximating to it in different but compatible ways. These two ways constitute irreducibly distinct approaches to the question of justification. Since the approaches are irreducible, the categories of one cannot be readily and easily compared with the categories of the other. Great care must be taken to discern whether or not a dynamic equivalence or contradiction exists.

Recent interpretative endeavors along these lines can trace their proximate origin to the work of Otto H. Pesch, O.P.[79] In light of Pesch's accomplishments, some maintain that Lutheran teaching typically affirms in an experiential and existential manner what Trent affirms in a philosophical and sapiential manner. The properly Catholic and properly Lutheran teachings are in fact "two complementary languages" for the faith, each of which is valid according to its own perspective. We have seen that each of the ecumenical dialogues discussed above appeals to this complementarity. The dialogues note that Catholics emphasize transformation without excluding favor and that Lutherans emphasize gracious favor without excluding transformation. The "two-language" theory, while noting this complementary difference in emphasis and terminology, attempts to discover the ultimate reason why there are different emphases. It represents one of the better efforts to find a single thematic explanation for the (apparently) vast difference between Lutheran and Catholic thought, the so-called *Grunddifferenz*.[80]

There is a divergence, it is said, in the very approaches of the predominant theological schools of each communion. Catholics, taking the lead from St. Thomas, tend to conceive of things from a "neutral" or rather non-confessional point of view. By "non-confessional" I do not mean non-denominational; rather

I mean not from the stance of the believing sinner. According to this reading, the typical Catholic theologian situates himself outside of the existential stance of the believer and rationally deduces conclusions from the principles of faith. He thinks of God and of the sinner as though he himself were in the distance, describing objectively what does and does not obtain in the actual state of affairs. In order for the sinner to be justified, he argues, God must infuse that which purges sin, namely, sanctifying grace. The scholastic account of sin and reconciliation is not so much the narration of experience, the confession of guilt, and reception of mercy; it is rather a third party description of what sin and righteousness must be, given the nature of man as a rational creature. This approach is legitimate, but it is not experiential.

Luther and those who follow his approach, in contrast, do not abstract from the confessional dynamism of faith. Rather, as we have seen, they find themselves within the perspective of the sinner trusting in God alone for mercy. They dare not assert in God's presence that they are totally cleansed from their sins interiorly, for such an assertion would amount to a declaration that they no longer needed Christ. Instead, as believers, they ever acknowledge their guilt and simply fix their gaze on the Merciful Savior. Thus, the fact that Luther denied that the believer is now righteous in reality (*in re*) and held that righteousness is an object of hope (*in spe*) did *not* mean that he denied the Christian's present righteousness. He simply meant that sinners do not now experience the reality of the righteousness they really have through faith. They will experience this only in the future, when it is disclosed.[81] Some contemporary Catholic theologians believe there to be support for this very existential approach in various Catholic spiritualities represented by saints who emphasize their sinfulness and helplessness, such as Augustine, Bernard of Clairvaux, Teresa of Avila, Francis de Sales, and Thérèse, not to mention the Apostle Paul. These theologians also invoke liturgical expressions, such as the daily recitation of the "Our Father," which includes a plea for mercy, "Forgive us our trespasses," that is not to be understood as a "pious lie." Again, there is the exclamation at Mass, "Oh Lord, I am not worthy to receive you, but only say the word, and I shall be healed." Rather than favoring one approach at the expense of the other, the "two-language" approach wishes to keep both in tension, since the mysterious and ineffable nature of justification cannot be comprehended by any particular thought or framework.

Assessment

The ecumenical suggestion of "two complementary languages" offers an a priori valid exploratory avenue by which a legitimate diversity of expression

Engrafted into Christ

and emphasis might be accommodated, entirely faithful to Catholic teaching and satisfactory to Lutheran concerns. The difference in unity between the Orthodox view of deification and the Catholic view of justification-sanctification is a case in point. Moreover, theological developments are possible and desirable. Members of the Catholic Church can deepen their understanding of the deposit of faith by culling not only from their own heritage but also from other Christian communions and from contemporary culture. There is no question that Catholics can learn from Lutherans in countless ways, since the genuine piety of many Lutherans resonates with that of many Catholic saints and since evidence of their sanctity and wisdom not infrequently surpasses evidence of the holiness of Catholics. I question not the a priori possibility of a legitimate diversity in this regard. Indeed, the possibility of coming to agreement on new expressions *of the same faith* offers hope for ecumenical efforts as well as for theological progress. Yet all such new expressions must neither dilute nor distort the truth as taught in the original formulas, according to the "same sense and the same meaning."

Despite the a priori possibility of a genuine "unity in legitimate difference" and the consequent possibility of a genuine, albeit differentiated, consensus, it seems to me that the Reformation era teachings of the Lutheran communions cannot be seen as compatible with traditional Catholic expressions, even from a supposedly higher point of view. It seems to me not possible to see the original, official condemnations as no longer church-dividing. It has been the burden of this book to demonstrate a substantial conflict that is not reducible merely to differences in expression and approach. It is not necessary to repeat the demonstrations already put forth. I wish only to sketch five summary reasons that the "two-language" theory does not as yet offer a satisfactory solution to the ecumenical impasse.

First, can the differences between the two theories sincerely be reduced to pastoral or theological "concerns" or "approaches"? Are the theories presented simply in different modes that are essentially, albeit not rhetorically, open to one another in reciprocal fashion? Two illustrations tell against this.

Lutheran theology is not commonly limited to experiential statements within a confessional frame of reference. Nor is it restricted to words of consolation, e.g., "Sinner, be consoled: God loves you. Believe, and express your gratitude through good deeds. You may still feel worthy of damnation, but take heart and trust in God, your only Savior."[82] Can any one gainsay such consolation? Still, Lutherans do not stop at descriptive words such as these. Instead, they venture beyond experiential and pastoral realms to propound explanatory statements about the way things are. This is evident when Luther and his followers carry on an extensive debate with the Catholic "approach" precisely because they believe the latter to be fundamentally misguided. Luther took Catholic thought to task because he recognized therein something antithetical to his own point of view. Bellarmine, too, took his stand against Lutheran teaching, precisely because he knew that Lutherans were not speaking merely of their "experience." If Seripando assented to the doctrines of Trent and yet retained all the while a personal preference to express his abiding need for God's *mercy*, Luther's followers codified more and more explicitly their insistence that Trent erred about the truth, not merely of experience, but of reality. Luther conceived of justification as the attribution of righteousness to which is affixed the gift of sanctification that can coexist with damnable sin. These are not conceptions of a pious simpleton. They are cleverly wrought propositions, not void of ontological import—not alien to a sapiential frame of reference. If this doctrine was forged in the fires of the terrified conscience, the claims were wrought with determination. In sympathy with this assessment, Joseph Cardinal Ratzinger wrote, "Simply to trace all these differences back to misunderstandings is in my eyes a presumptuousness that has its roots in the Enlightenment and that cannot do justice either to that person's passionate struggle or to the weight of the realities at issue."[83] He continues, "Hence love, which for Catholics forms the inward aspect of faith, is completely excluded from the concept of faith to the point of the polemical formulation of the great commentary on Galatians, *Maledicta sit caritas*."[84]

If Lutheran assertions about consolation were not in some genuine way oriented towards a sapiential frame of reference, what would be the need to deny the "inhering" nature of justifying grace? What would be the need to describe remnant sin as *"truly"* sin, as though the character of one's *experience* were in question? If it were merely an admission of still-present sinful tendencies of the heart, why add the elaborate formulations of non-imputation?[85] One can also bring this situation to bear in Catholic pastoral practice. Would not a Catholic who confessed sinful inclinations and temptations, as though they were damnable, be counseled to look upon his anxiety as scrupulosity? A confessor would rightly advise that such inclinations are not even venially sinful. The confessor might even judge that this person, so overwhelmed by sins, either suffers from a lack of existential knowledge of God's merciful love or is undergoing temporary, purifying trials of conscience. Luther himself chided all who fail to experience this misery as being proud pharisees, but he totally ignored the experience of many Christians who, trusting in God alone for mercy, dwell in the experience of forgiveness without having to turn to the law's accusation as indirect fuel for their comfort. There are genuine Christians who experience not constant anxiety about sin but the joy of a grace-filled life. A good confessor draws from the whole truth, objectively believed, in order prudently to apply mercy to those who judge themselves too harshly and in order to rebuke the self-satisfied. The good confessor does not rebuke those who are at peace with God, clinging to him ever more closely, and not aware of any sin. The good confessor does not invent sin in order to humble, so that fiducial faith might be awoken. St. Bernard warns about exaggerated confessions: They are the ninth step of pride.[86] Paradoxically, false confessions lead to the neglect of the sin that lies close at hand. If everything is sin, then what is actually sin is but a small swelling atop a tidal wave upon which one rides without any control. Little can one grieve for committing actual sin. Pastorally, the divergent application of the objective truth to those in various circumstances is not an endeavor to cover up Christ's role as judge against the truth of the Gospel; rather, it is an effort to lead all, who grope at times for light to see, to that one Truth which dispenses grace to those who accept him and wrath to those who reject him.[87]

I would like to offer another illustration that tells against the idea of a merely experiential approach in Lutheranism. Luther clung to the perfectly sound principle, "Works follow upon being [*operare sequitur esse*]." With this principle, he waged battle against "works righteousness," which he perceived to be the dominant Catholic theology of his day.[88] Luther maintained, in contrast, that works *follow* upon the righteous being of the believer. Catholics confess the same. However, for Luther, the human being becomes righteous through faith alone, which, at times, he did not hesitate to place in the graced *intellect* while its concomitant, hope, he situated in the will.[89] For Luther, faith provides the new being of the Christian, from which righteous works can and must follow. We should observe that the distinction he drew rests upon an ontological foundation: Works follow being. Luther's thought cannot thus be contained and explained simply by the hypothesis of a structural approach that distinguishes two "fundamental attitudes" in dialectical tension with one another, faith and self-righteousness.[90] His thought traversed more than a mere juxtaposition of the simultaneity of sin as self-trust and righteousness as genuine faith and the corresponding confluence of two juridical situations of the believing sinner, wrath and acquittal. To assert, "*operare sequitur esse*" with intelligence requires the insight that action is always predicated of an agent. It is this insight, in turn, that undergirds the Catholic predilection for the model of the transformation of a subject, which model alone sufficiently accounts for the *de facto* mystery of justification. I will turn to a consideration of the importance of this category in the next section. The point I have made with these two examples is that Luther's thought cannot be exhaustively described as "existential" for it in fact repeatedly draws upon the categories of ontology, purports to explain the things of faith, and is not simply a description of faith's experience.

Second, the two-language theory fails to countenance the fact that Lutheran doctrine does not reflect the totality of Catholic liturgical expressions and the writings of Catholic saints. Frequently, Lutheran doctrine chafes against these expressions. The Catholic liturgy does not assert that anyone is at once totally sinner and totally just. The multifarious liturgical expressions address the total ecclesial experience of various degrees of sin and holiness so that every person can meaningfully participate in the liturgy.[91] The fact that Catholics are catechized not to approach the altar when conscious of mortal sin ought to clarify the meaning of the liturgical statements adduced in favor of the "two-language" theory.

Moreover, the liturgy hymns not merely human sinfulness but also, and with greater exuberance, the sanctifying power of God's mighty arm. At the Easter Vigil, most privileged of all solemnities, the Deacon announces God's saving work through Christ: "This is the night when Christians everywhere, washed clean of sin and freed from all defilement, are restored to grace and grow together in holiness."[92] On this same night, Catholics hear the Psalmist chant, "The law of the Lord is perfect, it revives the soul," in affirmation of a reading from Baruch: "This is the book of the commandments of God, the Law that stands for ever; those who keep her live, those who desert her die."[93] This Old Testament proclamation (part of the Catholic canon) stands forever. Even St. Paul, in union with this proclamation, admits, "It is not the hearers of the law who are righteous before God, but the doers of the law who will be justified" (Rom 2:13). Yet, though the Old Testament proclamation stands forever, the Old Covenant was not ignorant of sin's endemic character; must less is the New Covenant ignorant of sin's universality. Paul teaches Christians that by the works of the law no one will be justified, since all have fallen short of God's glory (Rom 3:20–28). As Baruch is proclaimed, in the darkness, Christian confidence may well shudder, yet it does not falter. The Easter Vigil encourages hope in the night of darkness. Moments before the Easter lights are lit and the bells are rung, Christians hear a consoling promise from the prophet Ezekiel. God promises,

> I shall pour clean water over you and you will be cleansed; I shall cleanse you of all your defilements and all your idols. I shall give you a new heart, and put a new spirit in you; I shall remove the heart of stone from your bodies and give you a heart of flesh instead. I shall put my spirit in you, and make you keep my laws and sincerely respect my observances.[94]

This promise anticipates the baptismal waters, soon to be poured over the candidates. The good news then rings out as St. Paul's hymn on baptism is proclaimed: We have been buried into Christ's death and we shall rise with him in his resurrection (Rom 6:3–4). Christians nourish a double hope from this baptism. First, in the liturgy they receive or re-appropriate spiritual life with God. Second, they confidently await the glorification of their bodies, which have been handed over to suffering and death as a just punishment and pedagogical way (*via*) back to God. This glorification will be gained only if they follow the lamb wherever he goes (Revelation 14:4), walking in their baptismal call to "die with Christ." So, the Catholic liturgy is far from affirming the categorical pleas of Luther on the presence of damnable sin in the justified. The eschatological tension present in the Catholic liturgy is not that of a "still damnable sinner" awaiting the bestowal of satisfactory righteousness while enjoying merely the inchoate beginning of God's gift. The eschatological tension is worked out genuinely within the marriage of veiled union, for heaven comes down to earth, and God and man are joined together in this feast. The eschatological tension, the waiting for the *hope*, not the bestowal, of righteousness (Gal 5:5), is the groaning we suffer "as we wait for adoption as sons, the redemption of our bodies" (Rom 8:23). This groaning is chiefly that of the lover made on spirit with Christ. As the Catholic popes have repeatedly taught, the difference between the indwelling of the Trinity enjoyed through grace and the eschatological vision of God is one of degree only, not one of quality.[95] The Lutheran "simul iustus et peccator" is thus irreconcilable with the Catholic liturgical celebration of God's in-breaking triumph over sin.

Turning to the saints, one can see that they do not deny the "one formal cause" of justification. Granted, few address the matter directly. At times, they employ hyperbole and ought to be understood as doing so. For instance, in saying, "I am she who is not," Catherine of Siena was not denying her very existence. She was, in unison with Paul and Augustine, not to mention Thomas, exclaiming the utter gratuity of God's creating and redeeming love. It was the source of all gifts that she extolled (Jas 1:17), not the existence of her person and her gifts that she denied. The very saints to whom the two-language theory makes appeal boldly assert things antithetical to Lutheran doctrine. Those of theological bent identify infused charity or grace with the formal cause of justification.[96] As of one harmonious though polyphonous choir, these saints proclaim: "All generations will call me blessed" (Lk 1:48); "If I have all faith so as to remove mountains, but have not love, I am nothing" (1 Cor 13:2); and, "He who created you without your help will not justify you without it."[97] St. Francis de Sales wrote, "[God] will fortify the soul, and conduct her through various movements of faith, hope and penitence, even till he restore her to true spiritual life, which is no other thing than charity."[98] St. Bernard wrote, "Certainly [the beauty of the bride] is made up of charity and justice and patience. And what of voluntary poverty? What of humility? Does not the one merit an eternal kingdom and the other external exaltation?"[99] These statements are not qualified by negations of the one formal cause. Nevertheless, were there a conflict between a saint's writings and the Church's teaching (as has been said about Augustine on predestination), the former, not the latter, would be in need of qualification.

Third, the saints also give witness to a fuller scope for spiritual life than simply a relationship to a "Mediator [*Mittel*]" by whom sins are forgiven. The three stages of spiritual life are the common patrimony of the saints. Prior to being forgiven, a sinner can be roused towards God's grace by the preaching of the law and Gospel. In this stage, fear of the punishments associated with sin is the uppermost concern. For this reason, the sinner cannot cooperate with God to merit justification, for his freely willed end is not the end God wills. Therefore, God justifies the ungodly by remitting the sins of the sinner. The forgiveness of sins leads to the purgative life, in which because of God's operating grace, the believer's ultimate end is to love God. Still, in the purgative life, concern over one's sinfulness predominates in one's thoughts. This concern for one's sins is rooted both in love of God and in love for one's own welfare. The purgative life matures into the illuminative life, in which concern for God and his will begins to predominate. Finally, the Christian life reaches its earthly perfection in the unitive life, in which concern for God and his will totally absorbs the living saint. Christians who are blessed to walk in the illuminative and unitive ways do indeed still reach out for Christ as their mediator; however, their very reaching is motivated simply by the desire not to commit infidelity against the Lord of the covenant. They thus no longer fall into the logic of the Law-Gospel dichotomy. Even ordinary, justified Christians, called to that same perfection yet walking merely in the purgative way, ought not to cling to Christ merely as the mediator by whom divine wrath is averted. They are not mercenaries. The question is, does Lutheran piety have the theological space for anything like this? Does not the intense concentration on the Law-Gospel dichotomy hinder such a progressive shift of perspective? It seems as though the Law-Gospel dichotomy is the machinery through which Lutheran logic processes all Christian truth. The divergence between Catholic and Lutheran thought thus appears to be constituted not merely by an isolated doctrine, nor merely by a set of correlated doctrines, but rather by the very relational patterns of existence objectively called for by these diverse frameworks of thought. This observation would seem to call for considerable attention in the ecumenical dialogue.

Fourth, would not too facile an employment of the two-language theory open pandora's box? If Lutheranism and certain portions of the JD were acceptable on "experiential" grounds, what would prevent some form of Pelagius's doctrine from being acceptable? Pelagianism certainly resonates with the contemporary cultural desire that God be just and that humans be responsible. It might even serve as a timely corrective for the "easy grace, no Cross" Christianity of the contemporary West. Could we not dig until we found some common denominator between semi-Pelagians and Lutherans, and then strike an agreement? But this would be patently loathsome. Catholics and Lutherans would agree that none of these concerns can justifiably reconcile Pelagius's teachings to Christian faith.[100]

Fifth, the mysterious nature of justification does not give license to just any theory. No account comprehends the totality of the mystery, but that is not to say that every one of them errs. Some, however, do err. To be complementary with Catholic faith, any account must uphold the truth the Church has taught in all its rigor and vigor. It is not sufficient merely not to negate any portion of Catholic teaching; the whole truth must be held. To take a parallel example, it is not sufficient merely to affirm the divinity of the Son of God. One must also affirm his humanity. In the present case, the Church has defined particular aspects of the doctrine of justification, among which is the formal cause. Those aspects that have been defined cannot be denied, either in part or in whole.

Christology and Soteriology: Differing Structures of Thought

Introduction

Daphne Hampson has attempted to find the *Grunddifferenz* between Catholicism and Lutheranism.[101] She locates it in a divergence of thought structures. In each tradition, there predominates one thought structure, quite alien to that of the other. Catholics view everything to do with justification through their Augustinian lens: the subject that must change, the sinner that must be transformed into a righteous person. There is one subject, the sinner, and there are two predicates, sin and righteousness, the one contradicting the other. Sin and righteousness, according to this perspective, are by necessity inversely proportionate. Imbued with this perspective, Catholics cannot comprehend the Lutheran *simul iustus et peccator*, for they find it to be self-contradictory. The Lutheran teaching issues from a fundamentally different thought structure. For this reason, Hampson entitles the third chapter of her work, "Catholic Incomprehension."[102] While certainly not all Lutherans accept Hampson's thesis, it offers a powerful explanation as to a fundamental cause for communicative failure between the two communions.

Given Hampson's thesis, attempts to reconcile Lutheran and Catholic thought by appeal to Augustine do not help. The reason is that Augustine provided the very lens through which Catholics marshal the data of faith. Augustine and the Catholic tradition disagreed with Pelagians just as much as Lutherans did. Good Lutheran scholars admit as much. Although both Lutherans and Catholics would dispute Pelagius both about the character of our supernatural calling and about the agent that justifies, it is the latter dispute that is more pertinent for this investigation. Augustine rejected Pelagius's understanding of the agent of justification, but both considered justification to involve the transformation of a single subject. So, the two shared the same structure of thought: They conceived of a self-identical subject as being brought from a state of enmity to a state of friendship with God. They bitterly disputed the identity of the agent of this transformation. Pelagius believed that the human person by himself is responsible for this transformation, whereas Augustine believed that God operates on the sinner to bring about this transformation. Both, however, submitted to the following logic: Insofar as one is sinful, one is not righteous; insofar as one is righteous, one is not sinful.

The Lutheran structure of thought, in contrast, diverged from the Augustinian model of transformation. This is true even in the many different theological schools among Lutherans. According to Lutheran thought, God slays the old Adam and brings into being a new Adam.[103] Lutheran thought does not pivot about a single subject but dwells upon a dialectical judgment that reveals both sinfulness and righteousness simultaneously. The sinner hears the law's accusation. In faith, he both acknowledges the legitimacy of this accusation and also clings to the promise of mercy in Christ. The "word of promise" calls sinners to die to themselves and to live to Christ. Instead of dwelling within their own attempts at self-justification and self-contemplation, believers leave themselves behind and enter into relationship with Christ outside themselves.[104]

This exodus occurs through the death of the old Adam and the divine creation of a new Adam through faith. "The justifying judgement," Jüngel writes, "is effectual in two senses: it kills the old nature, which is crucified and buried with Christ, in order immediately to bring into being a new person."[105] Continuity of subject is downplayed if not completely forgone. Lindbeck also describes a new subject, as though there were two subjects in justification:

> Lutherans affirm this authentic renewal of the justified while avoiding the language of inherent righteousness. They do not talk of the transformation of the old self by the infusion of grace, but are more likely to speak in terms of the gift, birth, or creation of a new self. The redeemed self is discontinuous with the old. It is constituted by the new relation to God in which it stands, not by an alteration of its prior and continuously existing identity.[106]

Forde asserts that there are two "persons" in the divine act of justification, the sinner and the righteous believer.[107] Yet, these two are one. One is sinner insofar as one looks to oneself and attempts to justify oneself before God. One is righteous insofar as one goes out from oneself and clings to Christ, who alone saves. While the Catholic model of transformation presupposes that sin leaves something "good" behind which can be transformed,[108] Lutherans insist, that nothing good is left in the sinner. For this reason the sinner must undergo not merely a transformation but a death. Just as Jesus died to sin, so must the sinner die to himself, sin, to be created anew.

This brief sketch of the two fundamentally divergent structures of thought raises the question: Are these structures of thought utterly incommensurable, or can one be shown to be more adequate to the data of Christian faith? In what follows, I will attempt the beginnings of an evaluation of these structures of thought in light of Christological soteriology. This section, most of all, should be taken as a sketch intended to foster discussion on the interrelation between soteriology and Christology.

Catholic Christology and Soteriology

Contemporary theologians are basically agreed that Christology is rooted in soteriology. The soteriological underpinnings of Christology cannot be removed except at the expense of orthodox faith in Christ. Soteriologies are numerous, for Christ's work cannot be exhaustively told or comprehended. Among the central soteriological themes are four basic lines of thought: Jesus Christ paid the price of human salvation; Jesus Christ conquered the powers of evil, thus freeing humans from the *tyranny* of fear and temptation; Jesus Christ divinized the human race; and Jesus Christ taught the human race the truth about God. The first can be described as a juridical model of soteriology; the second, as a combative model; the third as an ontological model; and the fourth as a revelatory model. In many broad Christian writers, we see all four of these models: One can think of Irenaeus and Athanasius. In some, we see a focus on one or another of these models: Consider St. Anselm's focus on the juridical model. These are only four basic soteriological themes. Undoubtedly others could be added, some under these titles and others coordinated with them. I wish to investigate those soteriologies that supply reasonably sufficient grounds for articulating an orthodox Christology—by appeal to the analogy of faith, which is the harmony and inner unity of the doctrines of the faith. The combative model is, of course, necessary to retain, since humans could not sustain the devil's might unless by God's mercy his envious malice were contained. Still, Lutherans and Catholics would agree that the defeat of the devil alone would not suffice for the justification of sinful man. Furthermore, despite the noteworthy work of 20th century theologians on the revelatory model, I would suggest that the two models that have enjoyed most favor among Lutherans and Catholics are the juridical and the ontological models. Lutherans favor the juridical model of soteriology—though, of course, not without distancing themselves from Anselm—as the chief anchor for Christology. Catholics have held both the juridical and the ontological models in esteem. In agreement with Valerie Karras, I would argue for a priority of the ontological model, a priority that can be traced back to the early Fathers.[109] Before discussing the ontological approach, I would like to note an often overlooked aspect of Anselm's theory of vicarious satisfaction, according to which Jesus, God and man, offered his life out of obedient love and thus paid the price for our salvation.

Anselm's Juridical Model. Anselm's theory of vicarious satisfaction rested upon the presupposition of Christ's fundamental solidarity with the human race. Jesus was of our race. Conversely, Anselm's theory presupposed that the human person who would benefit from this satisfaction must be in solidarity with Jesus. American theologian Joan Nuth writes,

> Anselm's stress upon the humanity of Christ is a deliberate way of saying how important it is that human beings be enabled by God to cooperate in their own salvation. And this idea is dependent upon a profound sense of the solidarity of the human race, of all people with one another and with Christ, the new Adam.[110]

Nuth identifies the primary reason for God to seek human cooperation: to make his children happy. "It is out of the desire that humanity be happy, out of faithfulness to who humans are meant to be, that God demands that they participate in the work of redemption."[111] Incorporation into the mystical body of Jesus Christ (even in ways known only to God) provides the grounds upon which Jesus actually gains victory over one's own sins through his one death. Therefore, "Christ makes satisfaction for guilty human beings in their stead, but as their representative, not their substitute."[112] Anselm's teaching on the Eucharist as the way in which Christians "reenact" and appropriate the sacrificial death of Christ corresponds to this keen awareness that unless the sinner becomes happy by following in the way of Christ, he has not truly been redeemed.[113]

From this perspective, it should be clear that Anselm's theory cannot rightly be described as "penal substitution." According to the theory of penal substitution, Christ took the place of guilty sinners by taking on sin itself. Thus, Christ became as guilty as the worst of sinners, though he committed no sin, and bore the entirety of the punishment due to sin. Those who grasp this salvific work through faith are justified: They receive the benefits Christ won. Anselm's theory is not tantamount to that of penal substitution. Ensuring a proper reading of Anselm, Thomas Aquinas asserted that Christ's solidarity with the human sinner, which is consummated through the gift of charity, is necessary to account for the universal merit of Christ's work.[114] Christ's death is satisfaction "for me" precisely insofar as I am incorporated into him, not through faith alone, but through baptismal regeneration. Hence, my own mortifications, with Christ and under Christ, contribute to the satisfaction owed for post-baptismal sins.

Anselm's articulation of the juridical aspect of Christ's work, especially as refined by Aquinas, does greater justice to the overall scope of Paul's thought. Fernand Prat has shown the delicate balance of Pauline soteriology and its firm basis in the principle of solidarity. I close this reflection on the "juridical" kinds of soteriology with a citation of Prat's well known work on Paul:

> The theory of ransom is right, for sin really made us debtors to God, and we were unable to pay our debt; but it is not a stranger who pays it for us; it is the human race itself which discharges it through its representative, Jesus Christ. The theory of substitution is right, for Christ has endured for us a punishment which he did not deserve; but the substitution is incomplete, since he who expiates our faults is the Head of our family, and thus we expiate them in him and by him. The theory of satisfaction is right, but only if it is not based exclusively upon a substitution of persons, for an offence is really washed away only if the offender takes part in the reparation as he took part in the offence. Thus, whichever road is taken, unless indeed we halt on the way, we always end by coming to the principle of solidarity....
>
> The theory of penal substitution would force us to conclude: If one died for all, then all have no more to die. St. Paul teaches the very opposite conclusion: "If one died for all, then all died" ideally and mystically in him and with him. This is because he starts from the principle of solidarity which makes the death of Christ our death and the life of Christ our life. Instead of writing "One died *in the place* (*anti*) of all," he writes, perhaps intentionally: "One died in favor and to the profit (*huper*) of all."[115]

If even the juridical model of soteriology does not admit, in Catholic theology, of the forensic imputation that underlay Luther's theory of atonement, much less does the patristic appreciation of "deification." Having alluded to the scriptural foundations for this theory throughout this book, I wish now to investigate the patristic expression of Christ's deifying work. I will begin with one of its earliest proponents, Irenaeus.

Ontological Model. Irenaeus, so seminal a theologian, ranged over a vast swath of territory, speculatively anticipating the development of the revelatory, juridical-combative, and ontological models of Christology. One observes that even his statements allusive of the juridical model are notably lacking in what has come to be a predominant western interpretation of Pauline soteriology. In discussing Irenaeus, I include two models together, the juridical and the combative, because this more accurately reflects Irenaeus's thought. He wrote of Christ's victory over sin and his "legitimate" and "just" defeat of the devil. God sent Christ into the world in order to deliver the world "justly" from the power of Satan. Though superficially akin to the juridical model of soteriology, Irenaeus's understanding of "justice" differs from both Luther and Anselm. The incarnation was God's "legitimate" way of overthrowing the tyranny of

Satan.[116] Thus, Christ conquered the territory once stolen from him, not by using his omnipotence but by depriving the usurper of any legitimacy whatsoever. This analysis lead Irenaeus directly to a discussion of free will. Since the devil had conquered the human race through deception, winning their free wills for his purposes, God undercuts him by leading humans to salvation through the attractive power of his love. God appeals to their free will. He "persuades" them to come out of their imprisonment, and he turns them towards himself by a gentle and loving example.[117] This is not to say, of course, that for Irenaeus God is not the author *ex nihilo* of all things and, by implication, the primary author of all motion towards himself. One might perceive a tension between Irenaeus's insistence on the free will of believers and Augustine's anti-Pelagian writings. It would be wrong, however, to label Irenaeus a proto-Pelagian since he, in contrast to the Gnostics, clung tenaciously to the unicity of God and to his universal sovereignty. His battle against the Gnostics helped him articulate yet another reason for the "justness" of Christ's saving act: God redeems his own creation by means of what is his own, assuming flesh from a virgin descendant of Adam.[118] Irenaeus even links the virgin's free obedience to God to Christ's free obedience in suffering. He thus follows out the Pauline logic, according to which the disobedience of one man, Adam, is overturned by the obedience of the new man, Christ (1 Cor 15:21 and Rom 5:18). Mary thus became a cause of salvation for the entire human race.[119] In its appeal to human freedom, Irenaeus's linking of Christ's just victory over sin and over Satan dovetails with his appreciation of the deifying effect of the incarnation.

For Irenaeus, sinners stand in need of transformation. The driving force of Irenaeus's concern was that humans, who can be happy only in loving communion with God,[120] are to be made participants in the divine life and friends of God.[121] For Irenaeus, the Son of God quickens all of human nature by uniting himself to one man so as to become that one man: The Son of God became man so that man could become the Son of God.[122] For this reason also, the Son of God experienced all the stages of human development, tasting each stage so that each stage might be recapitulated in God.[123] Let us recall that Irenaeus's main opponents were the Gnostics. With respect to Jesus, Gnostics were divided. Some of them bifurcated Jesus into two beings, one divine and one human (i.e., proto-Nestorians), and others of them denied the human nature altogether (i.e., proto-Eutychians).[124] The former can be called dualists and the latter, docetists.[125] The docetists simply could not attribute any saving efficacy to Christ's humanity; the dualists simply would not. Both sets of Gnostics disparaged creation, ascribing it to the work of a fallen god or gods and portraying it as captive to an evil Demiurge, the executor of the law. According to the Gnostics, salvation does not involve the total human person but only part of the human person; not the body but the spirit alone is saved. The spirit was not the work of the fallen gods but that of a misguided deity from the spiritual realm. Thus, Gnostics reduced the human person to a dualism, the product of two (or more) gods. The division in the human person is mirrored by a division in the human race: Some can be saved and some *can*not. Gnostics held that the first Adam was not saved; he was cut off from the race of the redeemable. Irenaeus contended, against this, that the very same Adam who fell is eventually to be saved, not only in spirit but also in body. Irenaeus went to lengths defending the salvation of Adam, staking the salvation of the whole human race on this point.[126] Why? It seems to me that Irenaeus's fundamental insight was that precisely the old Adam must be saved, not simply the first Adam but the whole being, ontologically speaking, of each human person. Whereas Gnostics despaired of Adam, Christian faith acknowledges God's will to save his own handiwork. Similarly, whereas Gnostics either denied Christ's humanity or divorced the saving Christ from the man born of Mary, Christians identify the one born of Mary as the Son of God. Christians insist that Jesus' flesh came from the same race as Adam, since God intended not to displace the human race, but to restore it to its original greatness, and more! Borrowing from St. Paul and developing the theology of Justin Martyr, Irenaeus declared that in Jesus God summed up everything, things in heaven and things on earth (Eph 1:10), so that the human race could once again realize the purpose for which God created it: adoptive sonship. To undertake this task, Jesus became truly human, taken from a daughter of Adam; Jesus' accomplishment of this task implies that he was divine, begotten of the Father.[127] In sum, to repeat, the Son of God was made man so that man might be made the son of God.

Athanasius picked up and adapted this line of reasoning, making it the foundation of his argument against Arian tendencies. Athanasius also offered a more pronouncedly juridical reading of Christ's work, for even in his early work, *On the Incarnation*, he spoke of the law's condemnation of all and of Christ's death as exhausting the law's claim on sinners. Notably, however, Athanasius subordinated the juridical aspect of soteriology to the ontological in the order of finality. Even after the fall, he argued, God desired the good outcome of his creation, for creation's going to ruin would not reveal his goodness. God's chief aim for humans was their coming to incorruption. What stood in the way of this aim was the sentence of the law: The sinner must die. This sentence had to be upheld if God was not to be a liar. Thus, God was caught in a bind, as it were: Either his creation would go to ruin, or he would renege on his word. He had to remain true to his word and yet he wanted to restore creation. The Word made flesh met both aims of the divine love: He restored men to the divine communion, and he atoned for the sins of all. For Athanasius, what was primary was not that Christ paid the price for sin—although that was a condition *sine qua non* of sinners being rescued—but that, by assuming human nature, he restored it to its original likeness and thus enabled all to participate in eternal fellowship with the triune God.[128] Athanasius based much of his theological reasoning, in addition to his scriptural arguments, on this premise: God became man so that man could become God.[129] On this basis, he defended the divinity of Christ against the Arians and the sundry groups of semi-Arians.

Whereas Athanasius's chief battle was against the Arians, Gregory of Nazianzus's chief dispute was against the Apollinarians, who denied the full humanity of Christ. Gregory adopted Athanasius's reasoning to his own purposes. This time, the focus was on the human nature of Christ. The Apollinarians claimed that Christ had a human body and soul but no human spirit or mind. It is here that we encounter Gregory's famous dictum, "What God has not assumed, he has not healed."[130] Gregory contended that Word made flesh came to heal all of man; therefore, the Word took on all of human nature. Gregory of Nazianzus thus completes the logic of Athanasius from another point of view. Gregory of Nyssa, following the fecund Irenaeus's application of this principle to life's stages, applied his peer's dictum to the life of Christ, emphasizing not simply the "ontological" assumption of manhood but also the "dynamic-experiential" assumption of the stages of life.[131] Jesus had to be fully man, the Cappadocian argued, in order to heal the whole man.

The forgoing patristic arguments rest upon the soteriological claim that Jesus came to heal the human race. Fundamental to the patristic argumentation for the identity of Jesus Christ, then, is the soteriological insistence that it is the sinner himself who is to be made new so as to become a child of God. The patristics insisted on the continuity of the person who is a sinner but is to be brought into fellowship with Christ. Jesus assumed all of human nature precisely to heal all of human nature. Roman Catholic patristic scholar Brian Daley sums up the soteriology of Gregory of Nyssa along these lines:

> For each of us, in Gregory's view, salvation from the corrupting, deadly disease of sin can only come about through a transformation of our human nature similar to that which we see in Christ, which draws its healing energy from him: a transformation that begins in our growth in virtue, a created reflection of the divine light which is the true human glory, and which reaches its perfection, as far as the material side of our nature is concerned, in the resurrection of the body.[132]

By his incarnation, Jesus healed human nature and opened up the way to salvation. The anthropological presupposition of this soteriological basis for Christology is as follows: Sin does not destroy human nature but wounds it. Sin is not the essence of man but changes him for the worse. This change for the worse does not preclude a contrary change for the better, at least not if one calls to mind the power of God. Indeed, change for the better is necessary if *the sinner* is to be saved, if the *ungodly* are to be justified. But human salvation is the *purpose* of the incarnation; therefore, the sinner's change for the better is, concretely, a presupposition (*causa finalis*) of the incarnation. Daley, referring to the work of Rowan Greer, writes, "Gregory sees the changeability of creatures not only as morally neutral in itself, but as the ontological foundation for that endless progress towards the Good which is his definition of created perfection."[133] Karras shares this outlook: Man remains in the "image of God" despite sin.[134]

Let me sum up the above argumentation. The ontological model of soteriology maintains that Jesus assumed human nature from the line of Adam in order to heal and to deify every aspect of human existence: human nature and all stages of human life. In order for Jesus to become like sinners in all things except sin, human nature had to remain in its fundamental principles despite man's fall from grace. Two objections appear to stand in the way of these claims. First, one must heed the fact that no human being, with the exceptions of Jesus and Mary, is perfectly righteous. All fall short daily. Therefore, it would appear that there is an eschatological delay in our healing. Protestants accentuate this delay, without denying the fact that the sinners on earth are already being transformed and are to be made saints in heaven. Second, sin touches all of man; it does not leave any pristine realm untouched. I will address these in order.

Granted, the total healing of the human person awaits eschatological completion. Baptismal healing, then, is the commencement of this sojourn of convalescence and progressive divinization. Yet we must not allow the distinction between commencement and perfect arrival to obscure the *greatness* of the Christian beginning. Baptismal grace establishes the conditions for this sojourn to be a truly human, hence free, undertaking. Whereas what was lost precisely by the act of the fall was the love of God and the grace of his fellowship, what is recovered through baptism are precisely these: grace and charity. What is not recovered are the concomitant blessings of paradise. Not all of the punishments meted out as punishment for the fall are obliterated by the waters of new birth. Suffering, death, and concupiscence remain. These punishments are left as vehicles for the purification of the proper seat of sin, the human person acting through intellect and will. The eschatological delay of the healing of this "body of death" (Rom 7:24) does not entail, contrary to Gnostic belief, a fundamental duality in the human person. Rather, this delay makes possible the genuine purgation of the distinctively rational aspect of man, for it is in fighting sin that man achieves through the grace of God a greater participation in divine attributes and in divine filiation. Now, if the waters of baptism did put an end to physical defects, suffering, and death, then one's motivation for being baptized could easily be limited to a narrow horizon.

Many supposed "converts" would easily set their sights too low: They would desire only an extension of goods available in this world and the avoidance of evils opposed to these goods. Therefore, the point of baptism would easily be lost on them: They would be "hostile to God," unable to "submit to God's law" (Rom 8:7). The eschatological delay of the body's healing and glorification fittingly underscores the primary importance of filial obedience to God. Baptism recovers for the human sinner the grace and virtue by which he can rightly come towards his heavenly Father as a child, renewed by the Spirit according to the image of the true Son (Rom 8:14–30). The human journey to life, through suffering and death, existentially links justified persons with Jesus Christ, who assumed human nature in its entirety in order to lead it from captivity to freedom. So, as Jesus divinized human nature and yet endured the humility of the Cross, the baptized are inducted into the divine life so that they might bear the punishment of sin with charity and advance in fellowship with God (Rom 8:17). Truly, the curse of death is thoroughly undone in this process. Yet the Protestant will insist on a great discontinuity between the old man stuck in sin and the new man divinely created through faith. This leads me to respond to the second objection.

If there were no "good remainder" left in man, if there were nothing good that could be salvaged and transformed, then what could the Son of God have assumed? If we are simply sin, and if Jesus assumed our nature except for sin, then what did he assume? The Epistle to the Hebrews states:

> Since therefore the children share in flesh and blood, he himself likewise partook of the same nature, that through death he might destroy him who has the power of death, that is, the devil, and deliver all those who through fear of death were subject to lifelong bondage. For surely it is not with angels that he is concerned but with the descendants of Abraham. Therefore he had to be made like his brethren in every respect (Heb 2:14–17).

The sinner must still be human, capable of being transformed by God's grace into the new Adam that will live forever. This ontological continuity of the sinner with the righteous person is a necessary condition for the Word's incarnation from the stock of Adam. So, it may fairly be asked: If Jesus does not heal, did he really become human? If God does not save precisely the old Adam, but simply brings into being a new Adam, then in what way can Jesus be fully human, a descendant of Adam?

Catholics cling to the "Augustinian" model of transformation—I should say Catholics and Orthodox cling to Irenaeus's model of transformation—precisely because they cling to the fundamentally Christian insight that God does not repent of his act of creation. God does not do away with what he has made. Illustrating this, the Catholic Easter Vigil likens the Christian journey to the

Jewish exodus from Egypt towards the Promised Land.[135] The congregation listens to this great event in which the children of Abraham are themselves led through the desert (Ex 14:15–15:1). Underlying this epoch journey is the following theological datum: God does not bring into being a new race but liberates the slaves. He has not once introduced a new race. He brings back home what was lost; he woos his bride Israel, the unfaithful harlot, back to himself: "Therefore, behold, I will allure her, and bring her into the wilderness, and speak tenderly to her.... And I will betroth you to me forever; I will betroth you to me in righteousness and in justice, in steadfast love, and in mercy" (Hosea 2:14, 19). The bride is not abandoned; she is not slain in the wilderness. God does not go in search of a new Israel or cast off the wife of his youth (Is 54:5–14).[136] Or was Marcion right? Intolerable. Even if Israel does not now accept the present season of grace, she is to be brought back in due time, since God does not repent of his works (Rom 11:24–36). Scholastics put it this way: Grace does not destroy nature. Grace neither replaces nor displaces nature but heals and elevates it.

This fundamental insight is at the heart of Catholic and Orthodox thought on the incarnation, on justification, and on the sacraments. Catholics perceive continuity in the process of transformation. Jesus assumed human nature from a woman (Gal 4:4) but assumed it so as to heal it. Out of the abundance of his mercy, God the Father justifies those who are sinners, making them to be righteous. The Holy Spirit now receives the gifts of bread and wine but receives them so as to transform them into the Body and Blood of Jesus Christ.

It would be fruitful to reflect for a moment on Catholic Eucharistic doctrine. Perhaps it appears a bit contrary for Catholics to say, on the one hand, that the sinner is cleansed of all sins at baptism, and, on the other hand, that in the conversion of the Eucharistic elements, the "accidents" of bread remain. The oddity is only apparent. The fact that accidents remain in the Eucharistic feast is obvious to all who have eyes. That accidents remain is a testimony to God's fidelity to his creation. God does not destroy the bread only to bring forth the presence of his Son. God does not carve out a portion of the bread in order to make room for Jesus Christ. God does not uncreate and recreate. Rather, God transforms the very substance of bread into the very substance of Christ. Now, for Jesus' body to be really present, his bodily substance must be present. But if the substance of Jesus is present, the substance of bread cannot remain, since substance is not portioned spatially.[137] Rather, substance is the very "what it is" of the bread before the consecratory prayer and the very "what it is" of the Eucharist after the prayer. The accidents that remain show that it is precisely the substance of bread that becomes the substance of the body of Christ. In the case of baptism, God wishes to rescue the sinner from his sins. Therefore, God does away with sins but does not do away with the sinner.

Rather, in doing away with sins, God liberates the human person to be that which he was meant to be. The essence of the person remains the same. The old Adam does not undergo a change in species. Rather, the old Adam dies to sin so that precisely he, the old Adam, can be raised to life in the recreating act of God (Eph 2:1–2). Short of this change, there is no salvation. If the old Adam were destroyed, he would no longer exist that he might be saved. Again, if the old Adam were not transformed, he would not be liberated from his bondage. But no, the old Adam is not destroyed, yet he does not remain the same. The Catholic teaching rests upon these twin premises: the continuity and transformation of the old Man. Fernand Prat sums up the Pauline witness in terms of this sanctifying transformation:

> Thus in the present order of things justification is not merely a remission of sins; it is a reconciliation with God, who restores to us the divine friendship, and with it the privileges lost in Adam. Hence it is represented as a transformation of our entire being, a metamorphosis, which makes of every Christian "a new creature."[138]

Inherent in the Catholic-Orthodox structure of thought is a pivot about one axis: the human heart. The human heart must turn from sin and cling to God, to his saving mercy, and to his glorious grace. This radical conversion is the response to Jesus' first words, attested as authentic by nearly all scholars, "Repent, and believe in the gospel" (Mk 1:15). "*Metanóeī*": turn around! It is the same subject that must turn around. The question at stake is the human person's ultimate master, the object of his ultimate desire. If that desire is sin or the love of some creature to the contempt of God, then the old Adam remains, fighting against hope. But if that person receives from God the grace of a heart that desires him above all things, then the old Adam has become new, inserted into Jesus Christ. Drawing life from his savior, this new man is endowed with blessings from on high by which he participates in the very righteousness of Christ himself, as a branch draws life from the vine.

Reality of Creaturely Being. What is implicitly at stake in all the issues discussed in this book—the formal cause of justification, forgiveness of sins, obedience to the law, sanctification of the human person, and the meriting of eternal life—is the reality of creaturely being. God's fullness of being does not prevent creatures from enjoying a dependent yet distinct existence. Rather, God brings them into existence from his own plenitude of being. So too God's sovereign causality is so great that he enables some of his creatures to enjoy a real, albeit secondary, causality. This causality utterly depends upon God, both in the realm of nature and in the realm of grace. Yet human freedom cannot be denied, except at the price of human *being*.

The entire Catholic and Orthodox outlook on human life and on God is impregnated by the distinction and communion between God's being and human being. The world is not God, but the world exists. The world somehow participates in being, not standing autonomously over against God, but drawing sustenance from God. So too in the order of grace, the human person is justified precisely by receiving a share in Christ's grace, by being engrafted into this living vine. The old Adam is transformed into the new Adam. The human race is enkindled with life. What rises is precisely that which fell. What passes over into the promised land is that which was enslaved in the land of bondage. What continues unto eternity is exactly that which once was fit for damnation. Christ assumed everything that man is, except sin, and sin is man's fall towards nothingness. Christ divinized what he touched. And in heaven this day, Jesus is not simply divine but also truly human. What he did not assume, he does not heal. Conversely, what he does not heal, he did not assume. There can be no Mediator between God and man if the Son of God did not become man. But more: Christ is not only the *Mittel* standing between wrath and sin; he is the Light that enlightens the world, suffusing it with Life so that the dead who hear already rise (Jn 5:24 and 14:26). Through his incarnation, he gives the grace of the Holy Spirit to the human race.

Christology and the Communication of Idioms. As we have seen, the Chalcedonian teaching on the ontological constitution of Christ is not opposed to a dynamic approach to Christ. Irenaeus's and Nyssa's application of the ontological principle—God became man so that man could become God—to the events and stages of human life shows the compatibility, better, the inseparability, of the two. Christ could not recapitulate the human race unless he did so freely, as a human being. The compatibility of ontological and dynamic Christologies surfaced also at the sixth council of the era of undivided Christianity, Constantinople III. At this council, the Church proclaimed the integral operation of the human intellect and will of Christ our God. Each nature was preserved in its integrity, neither diminishing the other; but through the ineffable union of the two, the humanity of Christ was ineffably divinized. Now, through his fulness, we all receive grace upon grace (Jn 1:16). The council stated,

> For as his most holy and immaculate animated flesh was not destroyed because it was deified but continued in its own state and nature, so also his human will, although deified, was not suppressed, but was rather preserved according to the saying of Gregory Theologus: "His will [i.e., the Saviour's] is not contrary to God but altogether deified."[139]

The council preserved both the intimate union of the two natures, already defined at Ephesus and again at Constantinople II, and the full integrity of

Jesus' humanity, already defined at Constantinople and reaffirmed at Chalcedon. Even though his humanity does not subsist on its own but only in the Word of God, even though this ineffable union according to hypostasis entitles Jesus in his human nature to a rightful share (something owed) in divine grace, still, the human nature participates in grace but is not itself the uncreated grace: "For we will not admit one natural operation in God and in the creature, as we will not exalt into the divine essence what is created, nor will we bring down the glory of the divine nature to the place suited to the creature."[140] The deification of the human nature of Jesus is his share in the grace proper to God. As Athanasius believed, his human nature is a rightful recipient of grace, "For He received it as far as His man's nature was exalted; which exaltation was its being deified. But such an exaltation the Word Himself always had according to the Father's Godhead and perfection, which was His."[141] But however ineffable the divinizing grace of Christ's human nature is, his share in the divine grace is not absolutely infinite. That which is something "by virtue or grace" is so not in substance but by virtue or modification.[142] As such, therefore, all who are divinized by grace, considered as such (and prescinding from a union according to hypostasis), differ chiefly in degree one from another. As Athanasius said, "For the more or less does not indicate a different nature; but attaches to each according to the practice of virtue."[143] Athanasius navigated the path between continuity of substance and transformation of character: Man the creature partakes in the divine, and Jesus in his humanity shares in the Spirit. From Jesus' share in the Holy Spirit, the sinner becomes holy. Athanasius firmly defended, all the while, the absolute supremacy of the gift of the Holy Spirit as the divinizing agent in souls, including the soul of Jesus Christ, who divinizes his own soul through the Holy Spirit, which remains his Spirit eternally. But by the participation of the Holy Spirit "We do not lose our own proper substance," just as the Lord did not lose his divinity; rather, as the Lord was humbled in his flesh, we are divinized in our being.[144]

The delicate Christological balance constitutive of orthodox Christology is reflected in the doctrine of the communication of idioms (or *idiomata*), which concerns the legitimate ways in which attributes of the two natures of Christ can be predicated. This is not merely a game of logic; it bespeaks the ontology of Christ. At least three basic principles developed in the first seven centuries; these principles underlie the patristic practicing of articulating the communication of idioms. First, predicates of one nature cannot be said of the other nature in the abstract. Cyril showed fealty to this rule when he thwarted Nestorius's objections to calling Mary "Mother of God": Cyril frankly avowed that the divinity cannot suffer. The second rule is the classic expression and centerpiece of the doctrine, central to Cyril's argument that Mary is "Mother of God": Whatever can be said of either nature of Jesus Christ can be said of the one divine Person. For instance, since "suffering" can be said of the humanity of Christ, "suffering" can be said of the Word of God, in whom the human nature subsists. Again, since "was born of Mary" can be said of the human nature of Christ, it can be said of the Second Person of the Trinity; therefore, Mary is truly the "Mother of God." Third, this second rule can be pushed further without violating the first rule: Predicates of one nature can be said *concretely* of the other nature in virtue of the hypostatic unity. For instance, one can say, "This man created the universe." Properly speaking, this third rule does not entail that the natures themselves actually share the predicates *qua* natures. Rather, they share the predicates qua subsistent in the one divine person. Moreover, as John Damascene adds, the two natures are unconfusedly united in a perichoretic dance which highlights at once their unity and distinction.[145] For this reason, a predication that "redoubles" the reference to the nature said to enjoy the predicate of another nature violates the first rule. For example, "This man as man created the universe" is in violation of the first rule and therefore does not follow the spirit of the third rule. The redoubling phrase "as man" cancels the reference to the concrete subsistence of the nature "this man" and thus brackets the hypostatic union that serves as the conveyor of predicates in the concrete manner.

These governing rules are evident in the teaching of Constantinople III, which reiterated that the hypostatic union between and perichoretic dance of the two natures does not abolish the distinction. Therefore, the predicates cannot be exchanged without reference to the union according to hypostasis. Before turning to Luther's Christology, I would like to reflect briefly upon both Athanasius's and Cyril's understandings of the communication of idioms.

Athanasius tied the communication of the predicates to the soteriological work of Christ. He maintained that on account of the incarnation (what Cyril would come to label the union according to hypostasis), "The properties of the flesh are said to be His [i.e., those of the Word], since He was in it, such as to hunger, to thirst, to suffer, to weary, and the like, of which the flesh is capable." Again, "While on the other hand the works proper to the Word Himself, such as to raise the dead, to restore sight to the blind, and to cure the woman with an issue of blood, He did through His own body."[146] Athanasius saw the communication of idioms as manifesting a marvelous exchange of properties: Jesus bore human sin and bestowed a share in his divine nature. Hence, Athanasius cited the song of the suffering servant. The Word bore human infirmities not in appearance, but "in truth."[147] This realism does not contradict the fact that these sufferings "did not touch Him according to His Godhead."[148] The realism does not obscure the distinction of natures; rather, it emphasizes the union and, consequently, the soteriological effects of that union: the eradication of sinful passions and the deification of nature. "Now the Word having become man and having appropriated what pertains to the flesh, no longer do these things touch the body, because of the Word who has come in it." Instead, "They are destroyed by Him, and henceforth men no longer remain sinners and dead according to their proper affections but having risen according to the Word's power, they abide ever immortal and incorruptible."[149] Sins are *truly* done away with. Thus, the marvelous exchange, for Athanasius, means that the sinful *properties* of the flesh are borne by the Word made flesh so as to be destroyed. The fruit of this atoning act is the eradication of sin and the recovery of that grace of incorruption—divinization—in which and for which human nature was made. It is in this context that Athanasius warns his readers with the statement cited at the beginning of Part Four: "For if you object to my being rid of that corruption which is by nature, see that you object not to God's Word having taken my form of servitude; for as the Lord, putting on the body, became man, so we men are deified by the Word as being taken to Him through His flesh, and henceforward inherit life everlasting."[150]

I would now like to turn to the theology of Cyril of Alexandria, Cyril of the city impugned for its "monophysitism." Monophysitism is the heresy that denies the distinction of natures in Christ, almost invariably at the expense of the human nature. Cyril was confronted with the opposing heresy emanating from Nestorius, who appeared to risk divorcing the natures one from the other by his refusal to allow the second rule of the communication of idioms. In the midst of this controversy, Cyril did not omit to recognize the boundaries of orthodoxy behind him, as he charged into battle with Nestorius: "On this account we say that [the Word of God] suffered and rose again; not as if God the Word suffered in his own nature stripes, or the piercing of the nails, or any other wounds, for the Divine nature is incapable of suffering."[151] Cyril succeeded, but some of his "disciples" failed to apprehend him, wrongly (fundamentalistically) reading his expressions "Christ has one nature" as implying the obliteration or absorption of the human nature. These "disciples" failed to follow the trajectory of his genuine theological insight; namely, they failed to adopt the distinction between nature and hypostasis with reference to Christology, a distinction Cyril himself recognized as being in organic harmony with the Council of Ephesus (431) which defined that Mary is the Mother of God. It was left to Pope Leo to quell the quarrels of Cyril's putative disciples. Leo defended the distinct integrity of the natures in his letter to Flavian, in response to the errors of Eutyches, whose doctrine militated against the integrity of the human nature:

> To hunger, to thirst, to be weary, and to sleep, is evidently human. But to satisfy five thousand men with five loaves...is unquestionably Divine. It does not belong to the same nature...to hang on the wood, and to make all the elements tremble.... For although in the Lord Jesus Christ there is one Person of God and man, yet that whereby

contumely attaches to both is one thing, and that whereby glory attaches to both is another.[152]

The fine lines of orthodoxy were drawn again and again with respect to the implications inherent in the basic data of Christian faith. Constantinople II defended the faith against the Nestorian "disciples" of Chalcedon who wrongly considered themselves exonerated and thus permitted to cling to Nestorius's teaching. Against an illegitimate Nestorian caution, Constantinople II did not hesitate to proclaim that one of the Holy Trinity died. But against a theological compromise denying the human will of Christ, a compromise rooted in imperial interests, Constantinople III and Maximus the Confessor clung to the content and implications of Leo's tome: Christ has an integral human nature, an integral human will, and an action proper to that will.

This fine Christological balance also informs the heart of Vatican II's teaching. In an article that has come to form the centerpiece of John Paul II's pontificate, *Gaudium et spes* recalls the Christian truth that Jesus Christ reveals man to himself (art. 22). In the same article, the council finds a simple and ancient way of articulating technical Christological doctrine: "Human nature, by the very fact that it was assumed, not absorbed, in him, has been raised in us also to a dignity beyond compare. For, by his incarnation, he, the son of God, has in a certain way united himself with each man."[153] At long last it is time to turn to Martin Luther's Christological soteriology.

Luther's Christological Soteriology

Luther's reflections on Christology depart from the patristic witness. Granted, his explicit statements on the being of Christ are frequently sound and orthodox.[154] He indeed intended to maintain the orthodox (scriptural) doctrine on Christ. Moreover, his followers explicitly adhered to the Chalcedonian reading of scripture.[155] It is not Luther's explicit adherence to that which was taught by the early Church which is in question.[156] Notwithstanding this, one observes that when Luther worked out his Christology from his soteriology, certain defects resulted. Peter Manns remarks that Luther's "*ad hoc*" Christology, a product of his thought on justification (soteriology), is often in conflict with his more traditional statements on Chalcedon.[157]

Christ's Divinity and Humanity in the Redemption. As with traditional Christology, Luther's Christology is indebted to his soteriology. Since human nature *is* sin, the "assumption" of human nature must be the assumption of defect, of sinful hostility towards God.[158] Christ must assume this sin in order to destroy it. For Luther, Christ addresses human sinners as follows: "'I shall assume your clothing and mask; and in this I shall walk about and suffer death, in order to set you free from death.'"[159] The assumption of a mask of humanity! This has a Nestorian ring. In this mask, Christ—the divinity?—was captured, tortured, and killed. But death could not hold him, for he was divine; so he rose. I would ask the following question: What is the identity of the *resurrected* Christ? Is the resurrected Christ still constituted by what he assumed? Luther writes, "Now He lives eternally; nor can sin, death, and our mask be found in Him any longer; but there is sheer righteousness, life, and eternal blessing."[160] The mask of sin has been destroyed in the encounter with righteousness. Do we find here some form of Nestorianism with respect to Christ on earth and some form of monophysitism with respect to Christ in heaven?

Manns, who attempts to defend Luther, admits that Luther at times excluded the humanity of Christ from the divine act of redemption, apparently denying the humanity any redemptive role. Luther drew the following analogy between his soteriology—his theory of justification—and his understanding of Christology: Faith alone justifying is to the divinity of Christ as faith formed by love is to the divinity become incarnate. On this analogy, Christ's redemptive act is located simply in the divinity; the humanity is tasked only with expressing this act.[161] Here, we do not have a denial of the human nature but rather a denial that the human nature contributes effectively to the redemption. A trace of Nestorianism appears: One nature operates without the other nature. Because of such depictions, Manns recognizes a problem in Luther's explicit statements but explains that Luther was concerned to deny any independent activity to the humanity of Christ.[162] Manns would have the reader follow out the positive lines of thought in Luther, those in which he emphasizes that faith does work, and that therefore the divinity does become human. Yet, following Manns's exegesis is not an easy task. At the height of his career, Luther wrote, in a passage partially cited by Manns:

> The kingly authority of the divinity is given to Christ the man, not because of His humanity but because of His divinity. For the divinity alone created all things, without the cooperation of the humanity. Nor did the humanity conquer sin and death; but the hook that was concealed under the worm, at which the devil struck, conquered and devoured the devil, who was attempting to devour the worm. Therefore the humanity would not have accomplished anything by itself; but the divinity joined with the humanity did it alone, and the humanity did it on account of the divinity. So here faith alone justifies and does everything; nevertheless, it is attributed to works on account of faith.[163]

This passage must be seen in light of Luther's teaching on justification through faith alone. As we have seen, faith *alone* justifies, although faith is never alone. So too, the divinity of Christ alone redeems, but the divinity is never without the humanity after its kenotic condescension.

Yves Congar, whom Manns himself called "the greatest ecumenist," was for a time considerably apprehensive about this monergism in Luther's Christology. Congar was most wary of a certain Nestorianism, but he was also wary of an incipient monophysitism.[164] Congar focused on the former problem, indicated by Luther's monergistic reading of the redemption. Luther's soteriology involved but a transposition of situations, not a divine-human (theandric) work:

> In virtue of this "admirable exchange" of which Luther was never tired of talking, the economy which brings us a future salvation primarily vested in Jesus Christ, was not a mutual co-operation between God and man but a transposition of situation; God substituting for man. Here we are recalled once more to our central problem, the part which the human nature, even the human nature of Christ, plays or does not play in the work of salvation.
>
> For if salvation is wholly an *opus Dei*, the *sole* act of God, what becomes of the part played by Christ's humanity itself, since our own part, and the parts of our Lady and the Church are held to have no place. God, according to Luther, does our works in us. Faith, the one thing that should respond in us to God's action is, in his view, itself the work of God.[165]

There is little if any redemptive role for the humanity of Christ. Rather, God in an instance of human nature conquered sin.[166] Hence, there is the Nestorian implication of two opposed natures tightly bound: eternal righteousness and infinite sin. Congar concluded, "We should say that in spite of his fidelity to the conciliar definition he was in fact something of a Nestorian in his Christology." But this does not prevent Congar from observing also that Luther was "at the same time something of a Monophysite."[167] Congar attributed the latter tag to Luther in light of his restriction of redemptive activity to the divinity.[168] He explains:

> [Luther] tended to Nestorianism, as Protestant theology tends to it, because of the wide distance he marks out between the two natures, and the vacuum set up between the *opus Dei*, the Divinity in action on the one hand, and human nature on the other. But by this very fact, because he attributes everything to the divinity he empties of its value the part played by the human nature of the Word made flesh. He sees God at work in the Incarnation cloaked in the self-abasement of humanity, and, with only that part of the economy of salvation in view which answers to his personal interest, he ends in a kind of Monophysitism, or rather Monoenergism, because he has eyes only for divine activity using human nature as no more than a kind of garment.[169]

It remains puzzling that Luther would exhibit both Nestorian and monophysitic tendencies in his Christological soteriology. This apparent discord may be resolved if one heeds the dynamic of Luther's soteriology.

The Joyous Exchange, or "Penal Substitution." Luther's theory of soteriology rests in large part upon his understanding of what he called, borrowing from tradition, the "joyous exchange [*fröhlicher Wechsel*]." As he understood it, the following exchange takes place between Christ and sinners: Christ gives sinners his divine righteousness and takes from sinners their sin.[170] In contrast to Athanasius, though, Luther's realism in this "exchange" applies chiefly to Christ becoming sin. It does not apply to the eradication of our sin. Christ redeemed us by *becoming* the sin of sinners. Spotless divinity assumed cursed humanity:

> With gratitude and with a sure confidence, therefore, let us accept this doctrine, so sweet and so filled with comfort, which teaches that Christ became a curse for us, that is, a sinner worthy of the wrath of God; that He clothed himself in our person, laid our sins upon His own shoulders, and said: "I have committed the sins that all men have committed."[171]

Christ became the greatest sinner and thus owed the Father the punishment that sinners owed. He truly stood guilty before the Father. It was therefore necessary that he bear the wrath of God.[172] It is not that he truly eradicated the stain of sin; rather, he bore away the punishment due to be inflicted upon sinners. He stood in the breach. Here, we encounter the doctrine of penal substitution, summarily described above.[173]

Luther's theory of the juridical model thus differs from those of Athanasius and Anselm.[174] Athanasius wrote of the eradication of sins, an eradication which he understood as mediated through sacramental life. Luther spoke of the non-imputation of sins. The theories are in manifest tension with one another.

Luther rightly rejected the excessively juridical character of Anselm's theory, even if Anselm, a saint and doctor, would not have us read him as merely upholding some feudal idea. Luther's criticism of the received understanding of Anselm and his attention to the scriptural message of the "righteousness of God" are well taken. Still, Luther's reading of the "righteousness of God" is problematic, for it is premised upon the theory of *substitution.* He implicitly rejected the principle underlying the Catholic reading of atonement, according to which Christ's obedient charity satisfies for the justice of God opposed to the offense of sin. The Catholic reading of atonement presupposes Christ's solidarity with the human race: Christ pays not simply as a substitute but as head of the race of debtors. Moreover, the Catholic reading totally rejects the notion that Christ was punished by the Father, as is the case in the theory of *penal* substitution. This is not merely unthinkable; it is blasphemous. It would seem that by portraying Christ as becoming a guilty *sinner*, Luther emphasized Christ's solidarity with sinners all the more. Yet, this is not the case. Luther's realism did not include the real eradication of sins.

Rather, the realism was aimed at the punishment due to sins, which Christ bore away. On this basis, he concluded that faith serves to realize for the sinner the redemptive work of Christ. To those who have faith, God imputes no sin. To attribute satisfying power to any act other than Christ's was, for Luther, to blaspheme him. Yet, precisely here it becomes evident that Luther's theory of substitution neglects rather than upholds Christ's solidarity with the race of human debtors. His focus on the punishment due to sin obscured from sight the foci of Christ's mission: the eradication of sin itself and the divinization of fallen human nature. This neglect of the principle of solidarity may be a chief reason why Luther failed to see anything valid in the Catholic idea of good works as satisfying for sin. He complained that members of the Church pursue and undertake *other* sacrifices, in *lieu* of Christ's single sacrifice. For Luther, one has to choose only Christ as the only sacrificial victim. To think that one's own mortifications could contribute towards satisfaction is to displace Christ.[175]

Let me return to faith as the means of the "joyful exchange" being realized. The Word became incarnate and died for one purpose: the salvation of the human race. Today, sinners come into contact with Christ's action through faith. By faith *alone* the sinner grasps the benefit of Christ's redemptive victory over sin.[176] It is noteworthy that precisely in this context, one can detect Luther's dis-interested examination of Christology. He is *not* interested in the ontology of Christ, except insofar as it leads him to the salvation for which he grasps. To repeat, the sinner must grasp Christ because sin threatens to damn him at every moment. Once a believer, the sinner is "given" the attributes of Christ's divinity. The sinner thus enjoys a dual identity: He is sinner and righteous person. The sinner's dual identity mirrors the dual identity of Christ: divinity *in* the mask of sin. This dual identity will be resolved in the eschaton: Christ "wants us to believe that just as in His Person there is no longer the mask of the sinner or any vestige of death, so this is no longer in our person, since He has done everything to us."[177] The following question arises: If the incarnation involved the divine Son becoming a curse, and if in his passion-death-resurrection he destroyed the curse so that all might be freed from the curse, then in what way is the divine Son *still* incarnate? Luther's "apostolic" interpretation of the work of the Word incarnate tends to obscure from sight the ontology of the incarnation. Does his Christological soteriology imply the eschatological identity of Christ as simply eternal righteousness? Is this eternal righteousness strictly divine or divine and human? In short, does Luther's eschatological soteriology imply a monism with respect to Christ's heavenly identity? If so, then the apparent discord between the Nestorian and monophysitical elements in his thought may achieve resolution in eternity.[178]

In any case, on the basis of the patristic witness to the privileged soteriological foundation for an orthodox Christology, one can legitimately ask whether Luther's thought on justification—that damnable sin remains within the justified but is not imputed to them unto punishment—logically hinders him from accurately articulating the ontology of Christ, at least by way of this privileged foundation. The appeal of recent Lutherans to the difference between the Augustinian approach and Luther's dialectical approach, an appeal with which Hampson's observations resonate, issues in the divorce between the sinner and the saved. This divorce correlates with Luther's reading of redemption as the divinity in Christ winning our salvation in his humanity. Perhaps, then, the apparent discord between Luther's Nestorian and monophysitical tendencies correspond to his reading of the goal of redemption, given the definition of human nature as sin. In any case, Luther's tendency towards monophysitism comes to the fore in his reading of the communication of idioms.

Communication of Idioms. Luther did not follow in the footsteps of the balanced patristic approach to the communication of idioms. His disciples recognize that he radicalized the doctrine.[179] His thought on this topic manifests distinct traces of monophysitism. He was not content even with John Damascene's carefully-articulated understanding of the "perichoretic dance" of the two natures.[180] He applied the proper attributes of one nature to the other nature, and vice-versa: "But since the two natures dwell in the one undivided Person of Christ, one also ascribes to the divine nature what properly pertains to the human nature."[181]

It is significant that Luther's radicalization of the communication of idioms took place later in his career. At first, he borrowed largely from the tradition. In 1515, he wrote:

> Just as the one and the same Person of Christ is both dead and alive, at the same time suffering and in a state of bliss, both working and at rest, etc., because of the communication of His attributes, although neither of the natures possesses the properties of the other, but are absolutely different, as we all know.[182]

Similarly, in his dispute with Latomus in 1521, he wrote:

> He who wishes to discuss sin and grace, law and gospel, Christ and man, in a Christian way, necessarily discourses for the most part on nothing else than God and man in Christ; and in doing this one must pay the most careful attention to predicating both natures, with all their properties, of the whole Person, and yet take heed not to attribute to this what belongs exclusively to God or exclusively to man.[183]

It appears that Luther maintained this traditional position fairly consistently until his controversy with Zwingli over the Eucharist.[184] On the occasion of this controversy, Luther claimed that the divinity itself suffers.[185] Throughout the

1530's he emphasized the communication of the properties of each nature to such an extent that he attributed divine "omnipresence" to the humanity and human "suffering" to the divinity.[186] Some would claim that Luther took shelter in the third rule, focused as he was on the one reality of Christ. Yet in fact he bent this rule to the point of violating the first rule: He predicated attributes of one nature properly to the other. This more radical sense of the communication of idioms he paired with an analogy of the union of natures to the union of body and soul in man: the two natures form one reality. While Cyril also appealed to the analogy of the union of body and soul, we ought not confuse Cyril and Luther, for Cyril could sit down with John of Antioch and make the proper distinctions when pressed.[187] The same analogy, when coupled with Luther's radical sense of the communication of idioms, obscured the distinct and unconfused integrity of the natures. Although Luther at times articulated the communication of idioms in accordance with the second rule, ascribing the attributes of both natures to the one Person, his expressions at other times explicitly affirm an exchange of properties themselves, so that, e.g., "to be born" is ascribed to the divine nature.[188] On the basis of this radical sense of communication, he condemned *both* Eutyches and Nestorius, while contending that the bishops and councils of the past failed to understand Eutyches and Nestorius as well as he. In rebuking Nestorius, he wrote,

> From this one can see that he was a very peculiar saint and an injudicious man, for after he concedes that God and man are united and fused into one person, he can in no way deny that the *idiomata* of the two natures should also be united and fused. Otherwise, what could God and man united in one person be?[189]

Here, one observes imprecise expressions tending toward monophysitism.

This imprecision is manifest even in the midst of his more traditional articulations of the communication of idioms. At times, when attributing the predicates of either nature to the one person, he interpreted the "two natures" as "two persons." For instance, he suggested that Nestorius "declined to ascribe the idiomata of the natures to the same person of Christ," a charge with which few would disagree even though many today wish to exonerate Nestorius in light of his reasons for declining to communicate both properties to "one *hypostasis*." Luther's subsequent remarks are surprising: "We Christians must ascribe all the *idiomata* of the two natures of Christ, both persons, equally to him."[190] How should we read this? Is he identifying person and nature? Should we, on the one hand, read the "two persons" as an exaggeration, interpreting it in accordance with Luther's emphasis on the "unity" of the person of the Incarnate Word? That is, should we excuse this as ambiguity? Or should we, on the other hand, interpret his more accurate articulations of the communication of idioms in accord with his apparent identification of two natures with two persons? If we were to interpret Luther in the latter way, the apparently traditional articulation of the communication would, in fact, approach his assertion that the natures themselves exchange properties. That is, if he did not clearly distinguish the meaning of "person" and "nature," then what did he mean in applying the attributes of both natures to one "person"? To what was he referring? Is the "one person" the fusion of the two natures?[191]

Although indeed his thought was not consistent, and hence not consistently reducible to the one or the other of these possibilities, yet a not insignificant current of his thought can be read in the second manner, which harmonizes with his repudiation of Zwingli. Perhaps alluding to his controversy with Zwingly, Luther came to say: "I too have been confronted by Nestorians who fought me very stubbornly, saying the divinity of Christ could not suffer."[192]

It is clear that Congar's observations on problems in Luther's Christology find confirmation in Luther's theory of the communication of idioms. In contrast to Congar, Manns prefers not to take Luther at face value, except when he appears to be Catholic. One wonders whether Manns would have pleased or offended Luther by his patient exegesis. More forthrightly, Marc Lienhard admits Luther's tendency towards monophysitism. He claims that Luther misinterpreted Eutyches's Christological error *because* he tended toward that error:

> [Luther] reproaches Eutyches for something for which he could only with difficulty be blamed. He reproaches him for failing to bind sufficiently strongly the humanity and the divinity, since, according to Luther, he refused to apply the attributes of the divinity to the humanity. In reality, Eutyches had so strongly bound them together that humanity disappeared! This is a point that Luther did not see. We might add that he could not see it because he was above all attached to the idea of the unity of Christ.[193]

Lienhard defends Luther's emphasis on the unity by appealing to the Alexandrian emphasis on the communication of the natures. He contrasts the Alexandrian notion of the communication to the Antiochene conception. He identifies what I have called the classical rule—the second rule, allowing attributes of both natures to be attributed to the one person—with the Antiochene position. In point of fact, however, Cyril expressed this second rule in his second letter to Nestorius.[194] Lienhard contends that the Alexandrians *did* allow communication of attributes between the natures themselves. They stopped short, he maintains, only by limiting this communication to a movement from the divinity "down" to the humanity. They confessed that Jesus' humanity was divinized, but they would not grant the converse of this, that his divinity was humanized.[195] Lienhard argues that Luther pressed the Alexandrian logic to its conclusion: The divinity must, contrary to Nestorius, share in the human attributes. Lienhard's reading of the Alexandrian tradition is inaccurate.[196] Despite this significant inaccuracy, he justly remarks: "One might well ask whether [Luther] does not tend toward a certain Monophysitism, that is toward a certain confusion of the natures. The communication is so emphasized that certain expressions lead us to believe that his thought is tending in this direction."[197]

In light of the soteriological roots of Christology, one can discern that the Lutheran theory of justification chafes against the most privileged soteriological basis for an orthodox Christology. Paradoxically, the radical nature of Luther's communication of idioms in Christ was coupled with an underemphasis on the transformative effects of the grace of Christ upon the human person. Insofar as one attributes righteousness to an individual, Luther maintained, one withholds righteousness from Christ. The grace of Christ and the righteousness of the human person he placed on a scale, to be weighed against one another. He considered them to be related by inverse proportion. To appeal to Luther's thought as expressive and existential at this point would only concede the point: Luther's soteriology cannot without qualification support an orthodox ontology of Christ. To draw the requisite qualifications only leads one to surrender the attributes "truly" and "damnable" to the remnant sin. But this is to concede the entire case.

One might object, however, that for Luther the human person is said to *participate* in the attributes of Christ. I would maintain that, for Luther, participation includes *both* an identification of Christ's own divine attributes with the human person's righteousness and also an identification of the human person's own attributes with sin. Hence, the joyous exchange is a union between Christ and the soul as an exchange between *sin* and divinity, an exchange *of* sin for divinity.[198] In other words, the human person has "being" only in Christ and is in this way identical with Christ, since "Christ himself is our righteousness." In himself, the human person is bereft of being or rather is an active opposition to God. On account of this, Congar rightly observed in both Luther and Barth a collapsing of the dialogue between man and God: "God is not simply he who speaks to us, but also he who hears in us."[199] I have shown in chapter 4 that Mannermaa, for all his promise, tends towards the same reductionism. This collapsing of the dialogue reduces the doctrine of participation to meaninglessness.

Similarly, Luther's doctrine of consubstantiation falls prey to the same logic of temporary juxtaposition.[200] Luther eschewed the doctrine of transubstantiation. In place of this doctrine, he held Christ to be present *along side* the bread and wine. Christ's presence, moreover, is not something *effected* through the sacramental act. Christ is always already present *in his humanity* everywhere. This is the doctrine of the so-called "ubiquity" of Christ's humanity, an "omnipresence" attributable to his humanity in virtue of the communication of idioms. At the preaching of the Word, this presence becomes manifest to the congregation. The bread and wine are *not* transformed; they remain what they are. Along side of them Christ's presence is made manifest. The juxtaposition of bread and Christ resembles the juxtaposition of sin and righteousness, which in turn resembles the juxtaposition of Christ's humanity and divinity. Luther's reluctance to attribute any active role in salvation to Christ in his humanity is in line with the analogy of these pairs.

This lack of appreciation for Christ's humanity is further illustrated, Congar contends, in his treatment of Mariology. In his Mariology, Luther depicts an inverse proportion between the causality of God and man, between Christ and the redeemed. He opined in a reflection on John that the greater a theologian is, the less time he spends on Mary: "For the greater the men of God and the larger the measure of the Spirit in them, the greater the diligence and attention they devote to the Son rather than to the mother."[201] Did Luther find devotion to Mary or theological reflection upon her share in the communication of idioms to be an obstacle to Christ? As Steiger relates, Luther vividly portrayed the way in which a believer should imagine the event of the incarnation: "The believer should face [Mary] impertinently and sassily and remind her of the fact that her child is not her property but belongs to all who have the desire to make him their own in faith."[202] The sinner has only one task, to grasp Christ: "It is not enough to look at and worship the new-born God."[203] The lack of a contemplative dimension, rooted in the *metanoia* of Christian discipleship, is evident in his lack of interest in Christology itself.

The conclusion cannot be avoided: The fundamental principles underlying Luther's views on Mary, the sacraments, soteriology, and Christology stand opposed to the very heart of Catholic and Orthodox sensibilities. Nor are these sensibilities antiquated. The Second Vatican Council defended the irreplaceable role of Mary and insisted that "Mary's function as mother of men in no way obscures or diminishes this unique mediation of Christ, but rather shows its power."[204] Mariology and anthropology go hand in hand. As at the Council of Trent the Church upheld the depths of the transformative effects of God's love, insisting that this shows forth God's glory and power, so too at the Second Vatican Council, the Church upheld Mary's rightful role in the history of salvation and also insisted that this unique role does not displace that of the one Mediator. The logic also works in reverse: The unique role of the Mediator does not exclude participation in his mediation. The council fathers proclaim:

> No creature could ever be counted along with the Incarnate Word and Redeemer; but just as the priesthood of Christ is shared in various ways both by his ministers and the faithful, and as the one goodness of God is radiated in different ways among his creatures, so also the unique mediation of the Redeemer does not exclude but rather gives rise to a manifold cooperation which is but a sharing in this one source.[205]

The problematic elements of the Lutheran theory of justification appear, ultimately, to be based upon a distorted view of the world's relation to God. Luther weighed Christ against man, faith against works, the Creator against the created. It is as though, while stammering to find God utterly great and alone glorious, he brought God down from heaven to make him compete with his creation, stamping out the latter to elevate once again the former. But does it have to be this way? Must God be "so great" that he is but the greatest among others? Must he be so measured against the smallness of the world that he is but one among many and yet, as alone good, therefore, alone? Is his glory so exclusively his that no creature can participate it?

Can anyone gainsay Karl Barth's assertion that should a Protestant fall ever so slightly to the other side of the fine blade of the "analogy of being," he should find no theological excuse for ceasing to be Catholic?[206] But even the most carefully crafted Protestant outlook viscerally eschews the *analogia entis* as well as any continuity between nature and grace, ruling out every last trace of potency, even obediential potency.[207] According to the analogy of being, all things "exist" in different ways. Rocks, plants, animals, and humans exist, yet each in different ways. Plants add life to the elements; animals add sensitivity to plants; and humans add spiritual powers to animals, powers open to the Good, the True, and the Beautiful. Ultimately, God exists beyond all things that exist, even though he is not "beyond" as we conceive "beyond." From him out of nothing, everything that is comes into being (Jn 1:3; Heb 11:3), so that, in consequence, "In him we live and move and have our being" (Acts 17:28). The heart of a Catholic appreciation of the analogy of being consists in the following insight: God exists and man exists, but there is no competition between the two. The true glory of man redounds to the eternal glory of God, for the glory of God is man fully alive.[208] The end or goal (*telos*) of all earthly progress in the grace of God is eternal participation in the very glory of God. The second epistle of St. Peter is the *locus classicus* for this catholic truth:

> His divine power has granted to us all things that pertain to life and godliness, through the foreknowledge of him who called us to his own glory and excellence, by which he has granted to us his precious and very great promises, that through these you may escape from the corruption that is in the world because of passion, and become partakers of the divine nature (2 Pet 1:3–4).

This is the goal of all creation: eternal, intuitive (non-mediated) participation in the triune life. The great drama in the world theater is drawn forward by the nearly insatiable desire for that happiness, implanted by the Father of lights (Jas 1:17), which is found only in the ineffable marriage between the human bride and her Spouse, with whom she becomes one spirit. And this consummation of grace, which is eternal life (Rom 6:23), is not an uncreated act. Caught in the land of shadows, born without the light and grace by which to undertake this exodus out of the world to the Father, we sinners must be incorporated into Christ by the power of the Spirit. So incorporated, we can undertake this exodus in solidarity with our Savior who merited our redemption, who is the very way, not merely out of darkness (redemption from the curse) but into the light, *pros ton patera.*

NOTES

1   For this point, I am indebted to Prof. Giuseppe Butera of Providence College.
2   See LW 27: 4.
3   See CCC, art. 1035.
4   Augustine of Hippo, *Confessions*, trans. R.S. Pine-Coffin (New York: Penguin Classics, 1961), I, chap. 1, p. 21.
5   Henri Cardinal de Lubac, *The Mystery of the Supernatural*, trans. Rosemary Sheed (New York: Crossroad Herder, 1998), pp. 57 and 54, respectively.
6   St. Augustine, *Confessions*, I, chap. 3, p. 22.
7   St. Bonaventure, *The Breviloquium*, V, 1. Again, the translation is faithful to the Latin: "Nullus omnino ad illud summum bonum dignus est pervenire, cum sit omnino supra omnes limites naturae, nisi, Deo condescendente sibi, elevetur ipse supra se. Deus autem non condescendit per sui essentiam incommutabilem, sed per influentiam ab ipso manantem; nec spiritus elevatur supra se per situm localem, sed per habitum deiformem" (Bonaventure, *Tria opuscula*, p. 101).
8   See St. Augustine, *The City of God*, XII, 6.
9   The Church's teachings on indulgences may help illustrate the notion of an extrinsic remission of sensible punishment. An indulgence is the gratuitous remission of temporal punishment in those who are properly disposed and who undertake certain actions prescribed by the Church. The disposition of the recipient involves a willing submission to God and renunciation of evil. In such a person, the disorder of sin is removed by inhering grace, love for God, and his hatred for sin. Though well-disposed, this person may still deserve temporal punishment for past sins. That such punishment can remain in the well-disposed person would appear to be the only reason for a self-application of a plenary indulgence (i.e., full remission of all temporal punishment), which of its nature requires perfect detachment from all sins whatsoever. If perfectly detached, the person seeking an indulgence is free from even venial sin in the moment of his act of love. How, then, could purgatorial punishments involve *only* purification? Does not the condition for gaining a plenary indulgence imply no need of purgation from sin? So, if purgatory consisted solely in purification, the person who gained a plenary indulgence would not need it. Thus, it would be irrational for anyone to attempt to obtain a plenary indulgence. As it is, however, the Church's practice implies that it is reasonable to apply a plenary indulgence to oneself. But self-application of plenary indulgences can be reasonable only if purgatorial punishment involves not simply purification but also the payment of a debt due to past sins. To restore this debt, either the culprit or someone else must make atonement. An indulgence supplies satisfaction for justice from the merits of the saints, whose good works in union with Christ won such merit. Temporal punishment is thus something additional to the evil will and consequent spiritual misery that are the primary punishments of sin and hell. Few

Catholics today can stomach this implication of Catholic piety. But is there any other explanation? Thankfully, Catholic theologians and pastors these days emphasize the purifying aspect of purgatory, for this is truly the most significant aspect of it and this is the aspect acceptable to the Orthodox and, increasingly, among Protestants. Now, in light of this correct present-day emphasis, the following question must be asked: How can one emphasize the "healing" side of purgatory and subsequently overlook the formal cause of justification? How can Catholic theologians both identify purgatory with purification and also accept formulations of justification that imply that forgiveness does not per se involve the eradication of sins (purification of the sinner of all damnable sins)? Is this not to strain the gnat and swallow the camel? See canon 30, DE, 681: 12–16. Cf. *Apology*, XII: 174–76.

10　See Scheeben, *Mysteries*, pp. 616–48.

11　See Thomas Aquinas, ST, IaIIae, q. 113, art. 1, ad 1.

12　See Scheeben, *Mysteries*, p. 619, and Thomas Aquinas, ST, IaIIae, q. 87, art. 6; q. 109, art. 7; q. 113, arts. 1, 2 and 8; 3, q. 86, arts. 2, 3, and 4; and *De Veritate*, q. 28, arts. 1, 2, 6, and 7. Thomas Aquinas distinguished between forgiveness of sins and the infusion of grace, though he acknowledged that the two are intrinsically connected in the same motion (change) of the sinner becoming a child of God. Thomas did not distinguish between a "declaration" and an "effect." His distinction accounted for the fact that an infusion of grace into a sinner differs from that into a "purely natural" person. The latter is simply elevated, the former is both elevated and healed. Far from being declarative and extrinsic, the forgiveness of sins involves—in addition to infused grace—the penitent's act of hatred for past sins, enabled and caused by that grace and God's special help. Both the infusion of grace and the hatred of sin are "in the penitent" as effects of the one act of God, the justification of the ungodly. See also Johann Adam Möhler, *Symbolism*, pp. 82–86.

13　Lutheranism generally sees justification and salvation as one and the same for all believers, though "Afterwards works merit other bodily and spiritual rewards because they please God through faith. There will be distinctions in the glory of the saints" (*Apology*, IV: 355). Here, it is affirmed that one can merit an "accidental reward" (to use scholastic terminology). But, if justification itself can be increased, so too can the primary reward: the saint's enjoyment of God.

14　See Annex, 2–E; *The Large Catechism*, II: 57–59, in *The Book of Concord*; and LW 32: 29–32.

15　See William of Ockham, *Quodlibet* VI, 4.1: 26–33.

16　See DS 1304–06 and 1970.

17　See Peura, "Die Teilhabe," pp. 158–60. For an excellent presentation of Luther's thought on becoming nothing in oneself, faithful to the Finnish reading, see Karkkäinen, "'Evil, Love and the Left Hand of God': The Contribution of Luther's Theology of the Cross to an Evangelical Theology of Evil," *Evangelical Quarterly* 74 (2002): 215–234.

18　Peura, "What God Gives," p. 83.

19　Peura, "What God Gives," p. 84.

20　LW 27: 8.

21　See Peura, "What God Gives," pp. 84–85.

22　See Root, "Aquinas," p. 16.

23　Newman, *Lectures*, p. 336. Marshall also cites this (Marshall, "Justification as Declaration and Deification," p. 18).

24　See LW 25: 293–95.

25　See LW 25: 222; LW 27: 63–65.

26 Peura, "What God Gives," p. 78.

27 *Origins* 24 (June 24, 1999): 91.

28 Manns agrees in this respect with Nygren (see Manns, "Absolute and Incarnate," p. 146).

29 For a nuanced, but somewhat problematic, article presenting such concerns about the possible interpretations of tridentine teaching (e.g., the Baltimore Catechism), see David Yeago, "Lutheran-Roman Catholic Consensus on Justification: The Theological Achievement of the Joint Declaration," *Pro Ecclesia* 7 (1998): 449–59. For yet another presentation of this concern, see Johannes Schwanke, "Luther on Creation," *Lutheran Quarterly* 16 (2002): 1–20, translated by John Betz (see esp. pp. 11–14).

30 "When true faith lets God be the Giver in life, it also receives pure love as God's gracious gift" (Peura, "What God Gives," p. 84).

31 See Manns, "Absolute and Incarnate," pp. 137–43.

32 See LW 25: 344–64.

33 Manns writes, "The true goal of faith is consummation in love" (Manns, "Absolute and Incarnate," p. 145). Still, when it comes to specifying the role of *faith*, which is not the role of charity towards neighbor, Manns suggests that faith's object is one's "own divinization" (ibid., p. 141). This is correct, and it tells against Manns's generous thesis.

34 See C.F. Alllison, *The Rise of Moralism: The Proclamation of the Gospel from Hooker to Baxter* (New York: The Seabury Press, 1966), passim.

35 Marshall, "Justification as Declaration and Deification," p. 20.

36 For a similar presentation, see Wenz, "Damnamus," pp. 110–19.

37 Peura, "What God Gives," pp. 80–81.

38 *Apology* IV: 109–10 and 112. Tappert has "true sense of the word," and Kolb has "strict sense of the word" (Kolb, octavo edition, p. 139).

39 See Raunio, "Natural Law," pp. 102–10.

40 By contrast, see Pfnür, "Condemnations," pp. 136–38.

41 Marshall, "Justification as Declaration and Deification," p. 13.

42 Marshall, "Justification as Declaration and Deification," p. 14.

43 Raunio, "Natural Law," p. 114.

44 For an illuminating essay on the practical syllogism as determinative of behavior (the conclusion is not reached except if the action is actually willed to be done), see Fulvio di Blasi, "Practical Syllogism, *Proairesis*, and the Virtues: Toward a Reconciliation of Virtue Ethics and Natural Law Ethics," *Nova et Vetera* 2 (2004): 21–42.

45 LW 32: 224. Moreover, the attentive reader of Pannenberg's article, "Luther's Contribution," will discern therein grounds for a similar judgment. Luther's excessive zeal for utterly disinterested love, no doubt inflamed by the misguided advice of his confessor Staupitz early in his monastic life, led him to that "*resignatio ad infernum*," also condemned by the Church (DS 2356–62), that was subsequently redirected into the anxious search for a gracious God. Pannenberg is right to notice that Luther's "later doctrine on law and gospel continued to be indebted to his early penitential struggles as a monk; and he often identified salvation almost completely with the forgiveness of sins" (Pannenberg, "Luther's Contribution," p. 285). This points to the troubling possibility that the overarching truth of God, for Luther, was wrath, and that shelter from that wrath constituted the motive for faith; instead of an utterly disinterested love of God, Luther wedded himself to penal substitution (see ibid., p. 286).

46 LW 32: 227.

47 LW 25: 221.

48 LW 25: 221.

49　See LW 25: 293.

50　I disagree with Root's reading of Luther. Although Root's own understanding of faith has much in common with Thérèse, does this reading do justice to the driving force behind Luther (see Root, "Aquinas," pp. 16–17)?

51　There is not space to undertake this point in greater depth, although that would be desirable. Hopefully, a sketch will suffice in this context. Luther placed faith at the basis of human life, much as Maslow might place physical survival at the bottom of his pyramid. Maslow's pyramid assumes both that the lower level is a *sine qua non* condition of all higher levels and also that each higher level is superior in ultimate value to the lower levels. For Luther, without faith, no further level can be reached. "Faith alone justifies," Luther insisted, though this is not the faith that depends upon charity for its justifying character. Luther located this doctrine chiefly in Paul's Epistle to the Romans. When Paul maintained, in First Corinthians, that love is the "greatest" of the theological virtues (1 Cor 13:13), he was not, Luther claimed, speaking of justification. Rather, he was speaking of the height of Christian life. That height depends upon the foundation, justification through faith alone. At the top of the pyramid is charity. Luther did not hesitate to say that growth in charity is the goal of Christian living. Hence, he placed charity at the apex of the pyramid. The difficulty I have with his thought is that he portrays *faith* as subserving an end he has defined as selfish. Faith and charity have different ultimate ends and are, therefore, at war with one another. For these to be situated within one pyramid, therefore, is problematic. Catholicism, in contrast, does not consider the desire for salvation to be sinful. It does not consider that those who desire God's gifts are sinning by their desire for these things. However, Catholics would agree with Luther that, short of a love for God above all things, no human person can be truly pleasing to God. Many Catholics would agree with Luther that the initial Christian impulse towards love of God is rooted in a desire for life, for something good for the human person. In the order of generation, then, motives for one's salvation and freedom from hell are conducive to a Christian conversion. Once certain that God alone can be one's true happiness, the sinner is encouraged to convert, empowered by God's grace. From this conversion, love of God as ultimate end and friend can arise. However, the dependence of the love of God as friend upon the security of one's own welfare does not obscure the supremacy of the former. Charity is "dependent" upon a natural eros—one that precedes choice, that is, the natural desire for happiness—in the order of generation. This is so as follows: one seeks one's own good by nature because God instills this desire in each that each might seek him. Once the new birth has taken place, however, the scope of Christian desire is transformed: it is now a desire chiefly to please God. In fact, although the occasion for this divine desire was consideration of one's own welfare, this desire, once in place, maintains itself as supreme and brings everything else in line with itself. For this reason, even the loss of one's own welfare could be endured for the sake of the love of God (Rom 9:3). For Catholics, therefore, Maslow's pyramid would be ill-equipped to express the mystery of justification. The inferior levels of the pyramid do not reign as conditions *sine qua non* of the higher levels. To apply Maslow's scheme of analysis to Catholic thought on justification would be to blend the order of generation with that of finality. Perhaps Maslow's scheme cannot be applied to Luther's thought either. And yet there may be some application to Luther. The sinner is ever sinful, and the righteous person is only under construction. Falteringly undergoing the divine motion, the sinner never truly becomes the righteous person; the sinner is always only in process and is not the child of God (cf. 1 Jn 3:2). Or perhaps we must assume the existence of two persons, the old man and the new man, and construct two pyramids. If the *believer* is the one who is to love God, however, then we must use one pyramid. If so, we stumble upon our question: Does Luther not insist that the foundational level always operates as a *sine qua non* condition of higher levels?

52   See the definitive condemnation of Eckhart's propositions on radically "selfless" love, a love that does not even seek sanctity, and on conformity with the divine will unto sin (see DS 958, 964, and 965; see also related errors, such as opinions that the fear of hell and of the loss of heaven is in itself sinful, DS, 1456, 1489, 1576, 1581, 2207, 2216, 2310, 2314, 2315, 2351–73, 2460, 2462, and 2625). Augustine and the other great doctors of the early Church, east and west, were not engrossed in a convoluted self-analysis about the "selfish" nature of loving God so as to want to be with him. Augustine defined charity by *"frui,"* contending that to want to enjoy God for his own sake is the most healthy of human desires. Although he did condemn the mere use (*uti*) of God, he was far from describing authentic *"frui"* as selfless and disinterested. A search of his *Confessions* yields an abundance of evidence that he, like the Psalmist, he would chant, "My soul thirsts for God, for the living God. When shall I come and behold the face of God?" (Psalm 42:2). Augustine could not rest until he rested in God; he was seeking God as the greatest good, the source of all good. See also his remarks on Jesus' saying in Jn 6:44: "No one can come to me unless the Father *attracts* him to me" (Augustine, *In Iohannis evangelium*, tractatus XXVI, in *Corpus Christianorum*, La, vol. 36, pp. 261–62). Nyssa and others maintained the same perspective: God made all things for himself and all things have an innate inclination ultimately to the heavenly Father.

53   See the excellent article on the subject by Robert Merrihew Adams, "Pure Love," *Journal of Religious Ethics* 8 (1980): 83–99. Adams shows the dangers of piety gone to an extreme. Prudent and balanced, Francis de Sales managed not to let zeal for the purity of love sour his thought.

54   I am thinking, particularly, of the work of Servais Pinckaers (see Servais Pinckaers, *The Sources of Christian Ethics*, trans. Sr. Mary Thomas Noble [Washington, D.C.: The Catholic University of America Press, 1995]).

55   See Augustine DiNoia, "Imago Dei—Imago Christi: The Theological Foundations of Christian Humanism," *Nova et Vetera* 2 (2004): 267–78.

56   The spiritualists interpreted Augustine's *"frui"* to be a disinterested love for God. This interpretation was, in fact, alien to the intention of Augustine, whose passion for union with God and whose charity towards him—*frui*—were one and the same.

57   See Dumitru Staniloae, *The World: Creation and Deification*, vol. 2, *The Experience of God: Orthodox Dogmatic Theology*, trans. Ioan Ionita and Robert Barringer (Brookline, MA: Holy Cross Orthodox Press, 2000), p. 84.

58   See Ibid., pp. 85–86.

59   Ibid., p. 90.

60   Ibid., p. 91.

61   Karras, "Beyond Justification," p. 110.

62   See Ibid., p. 109.

63   Bernard Lonergan astutely notes, "What moves the sinner is not an appeal to his pure love of God, for he does not love God. To touch his heart, the appeal must be directed to his self-love. To hold in check his appetites, considerations must be adduced that offer deterrents to egoism. Of course his heart always can be touched, for he has not the fixity in evil of the demons; deterrents can always be found, for what is against God is ultimately also against himself" (Bernard Lonergan, *Grace and Freedom: Operative Grace in the Thought of St. Thomas Aquinas*, vol. 1, *Collected Works of Bernard Lonergan* [Toronto: University of Toronto Press, 2000], p. 53). See also Bernard

Lonergan, *Method in Theology* (Toronto: University of Toronto Press, 1996), pp. 105–07.

64   Staniloae, *The World*, p. 154. See also p. 103.

65   See ibid., p. 155.

66   There can be no question that all are called to a life of gratuitous love, for Christ freely gives life and all are charged to share it freely with others. Nevertheless, the gratuitous and unconditional nature of love ought not be misunderstood as something that can be pitted against the desire for happiness. Such misunderstandings appear especially when infused justice is not identified as the formal cause of justification. The denial of such identity implicitly ruptures the intrinsic connection between the life of love and the desire (and capacity) for beatitude. Within this rupture, the desire for reward can appear selfishly sinful. But this rupture and its implications involve misconceptions. First, the chief reward sought by charity is God himself. To love is to seek God and, thus, to seek reward, the Beloved himself. Nothing is so proper to friends as to dwell together (see Thomas Aquinas, ST, IIaIIae, q. 23, art. 1, obj. 1, citing Aristotle's *Nichomachean Ethics*, VIII, chap. 5). Second, the rupture entails an uncanny twist. Many of those who so eloquently speak of "disinterested" love are steeped in some form of *duplex iustitia*, seeking to attribute all glory to God. Unwittingly, they often ascribe to man the kind of love *only* God can have, for God alone loves others without thereby perfecting himself. Third, if loving others does not perfect the human creature, an unfitting alternative arises. Either (a) because everyone by nature seeks perfection, no one can desire to love others. Or (b) God creates beings whose highest acts are not perfective of them. Two strains of thought emerge from this unfitting alternative: (a) that which cannot uphold the weight of the moral law and (b) that which praises agape and condemns eros. The latter dries up in moralism. The former—a once-enchanted Dionysius—ends in quiet desperation. Although I have put this matter in terms of the individual and his relationship with God, the same analysis would bear troubling results for an application to political theory. For a society to flourish, it must recognize the centrality of the common good as the mediating principle of humans freely acting. Early Christians stressed the upright character of Christians in the political arena, a character to be desired both because of civil judges and because of an all-seeing heavenly judge. This much is minimal; the drive of the divinized man makes character a thing to be desired for itself, as God himself is to be desired. The Orthodox, faithful to this tradition, continue to find a basis for responsible civic activity in the integral union between *theosis* and culture.

67   See Josef Pieper, *About Love*, trans. Richard and Clara Winston (Franciscan Herald Press, 1974), pp. 64–65.

68   Pieper, *About Love*, p. 67. Nygren perceived Marcion as peerless between Paul and Augustine in his appreciation for agape (see Anders Nygren, *Agape and Eros*, trans. Philip Watson [Chicago: University of Chicago Press, 1953], p. 317). Marcion's appreciation of the newness of Christianity was intimately linked with his sundering the God of creation from the God of Jesus Christ (see ibid., p. 318), thus reviving the Pauline teaching in Rom 5:8 that had been obscured (see ibid., p. 319). Marcion's separation of law and Gospel was on the mark though his total abolition of law consequently led to a devaluation of agape. Against what could agape any longer be compared (see ibid., p. 332)? So, Nygren was critical of Marcion not for sundering law and Gospel but for failing to retain the dialectical function of law, against which agape's true colors are manifest. It almost seems as though, for Nygren, evil is a necessary backdrop for the good. In any case, Nygren lamented the Church's victory over Marcion, for the overreaction eclipsed agape from ecclesiastical radar (see ibid.,

p. 333).

69 William Shakespeare, *Hamlet: Prince of Denmark*, 3.4, in *The Complete Works of William Shakespeare* (New York: Avenel Books, 1975).

70 American Jewish scholar Jon Levenson offers a marvelous vision of the Exodus, counterbalancing the prevailing one-sided Marxist readings of this great event. The movement in Exodus was not merely *away* from Egypt; it was, much more, a movement *toward* the Lord. Slavery was not abolished; rather, the Lord freed his people so that they might serve him. This service is true liberation (Jon D. Levenson, *The Hebrew Bible, the Old Testament, and Historical Criticism: Jews and Christians in Biblical Studies* [Louisville, KY: Westminster, John Knox Press, 1993], pp. 140–151).

71 For an excellent article on this topic, defending Thomas Aquinas's thought against *Catholic* critiques that tend to divorce nature and person (man and grace), see Michael Waldstein, "Dietrich von Hildebrand and St. Thomas Aquinas on Goodness and Happiness," *Nova et Vetera*, 1 (2003): 403–63.

72 Basil of Caesarea, chap. 15, par. 35, pp. 21–22.

73 See St. Gregory of Nazianzus, *The Second Theological Oration*, chap. 17.

74 Jason Ripley, "Covenantal Concepts of Justice and Righteousness, and Catholic-Protestant Reconciliation: Theological Implications and Explorations," *Journal of Ecumenical Studies* 38 (2001): 98. I would only add two remarks, which are in harmony with the basic thrust of Ripley's thesis. First, I would add that a true relationship with God—i.e., being rightly ordered to God—necessarily entails the life of charity and obedience to the moral laws that God has inscribed in human nature (see ibid., p. 106). Second, I would suggest that Catholics stress the "proleptic realization" of the definitive righteousness to which men are called in Christ. That is, although this righteousness will be purified and magnified in heaven, it is sufficiently "realized" that one endowed with this righteousness is no longer damnable.

75 Ripley, "Covenantal Concepts," p. 108.

76 See Meis, "El problema," p. 117. Meis follows Balthasar in holding that the Christian is impelled ever more to enter into solidarity with sinners, as Jesus Christ himself did through his vicarious suffering for all mankind. By being incorporated into Christ, holy persons have solidarity with him and thus, with those he loves (see ibid., pp. 118–19).

77 Bonaventure, *Breviloquium*, V, 2, p. 187.

78 St. Francis de Sales, *Treatise on the Love of God*, trans. Dom Henry Benedict Mackey, O.S.B. (Rockford, IL: Tan Books, 1997), p. 101.

79 His relevant works include, among others, the following: "Existential and Sapiential Theology–the Theological Confrontation between Luther and Thomas Aquinas," chap. in *Catholic Scholars Dialogue with Luther*, pp. 61–81, ed. Jared Wicks, S.J. (Chicago: Loyola University Press, 1970); and Pesch and A. Peters, *Einführung in die Lehre von Gnade und Rechtfertigung* (1981).

80 See Root, "Aquinas," p. 7 and p. 19, note 18.

81 See Manns, "Absolute and Incarnate," pp. 132–34.

82 For such consolation, in itself valuable, see LW 27: 6.

83 Joseph Cardinal Ratzinger, *Church, Ecumenism and Politics*, trans. Robert Nowell (New York: Crossroad, 1988), p. 104

84 Ibid., p. 111.

85 Manns is a fine example of well-intentioned efforts to read thinkers of another tradition in as positive a light as possible. He reads Luther's great anxiety as the sensitivity of a lover who knows that he does not love with the joy and spontaneity requisite for the relationship (see Manns, "Absolute and Incarnate," p. 150). Luther experienced this

anxiety, he holds, as a sign that he had violated the whole law (see ibid., p. 148). These imperfections of the lover Luther labeled "sin." In light of this background, Manns concludes: "In functional conjunction with the powers of the new life, with Christ and with the Holy Spirit, this 'sin' experiences a change in meaning, making it necessary to distinguish it strictly from sin as such" (ibid., p. 151). As I have established in my argument, this domestication of Luther is foreign to his fire.

86   See St. Bernard, *The Steps of Humility and Pride*, art. 18.

87   We can contrast this to Luther's effort to control Christ's role as judge as though he were his own spiritual director (LW 27: 33–35 and 226). One might even conjecture that Luther plants the seeds of diagnosis of his own position right here: "For the devil is a highly skilled persuader; he knows how to inflate a minute and almost ridiculous peccadillo until the one who has been tempted supposes it to be the most heinous offense, worthy of eternal punishment" (LW 27:33). This line of reasoning represents a distinct current of thought in Luther which might be fruitful for consideration in another forum. Such reflection would have to confront the Reformer with the question, "*Where* do you stand? Is it or is it not truly damnable sin?"

88   By "works righteousness," Luther meant the notion that by doing good deeds, for example, eliciting an act of charity, one supposedly "earns" God's favor. Certain nominalists tended towards this position in their reading of the popular saying, "If you do what is within your ability, God will not deny His grace (*facienti quod in se est, Deus non denegat gratiam*)." Though the nominalist whom he studied, Gabriel Biel, held this position, the mature Thomas Aquinas did not hold it (Bernard Lonergan, *Grace and Freedom*, esp. pp. 21–43, 119–42, and 229–51). Bonaventure also did not hold this position. Moreover, it is contrary to the Catholic teaching articulated at Orange (A.D. 529), at Trent, and later in the condemnations of Baius.

89   Luther's *1535 Lectures on Galatians* manifests an emphasis on the cognitive nature of faith (see esp., LW 27: 22–23, and LW 26: 284–85).

90   See Hampson, *Contradictions*, passim.

91   On venial sins, see chap. 11, DE, 675: 23–24. See also *The City of God*, XXI, 27. Lauren Pristas provides a cogent antidote to a certain reductionism in the contemporary liturgical reforms. Reforms of some ancient prayers were undertaken in order that the liturgy might be made more "adequate" to contemporary sensibilities. Taking issue with this approach, Pristas contends, "The relevance of a particular oration for the Church universal is not something that can always be judged by persons of any one time or place" (Lauren Pristas, "Theological Principles that Guided the Redaction of the Roman Missal [1970]," *The Thomist*, 67 [2003]: 165). The thrust of her argument is that the liturgy is food for all Christians throughout the vicissitudes of time, culture, and life experience. Because the liturgy casts such a wide net, no single affirmation ought to be taken out of the context of the whole. If the saying *lex orandi, lex credendi* is to be held genuinely, the liturgist should discern that the *lex credendi* of Trent issued also from the *lex orandi* of the preceding centuries.

92   James Socias, ed., *Daily Roman Missal: Weekday and Sunday Masses* (Princeton, NJ: Scepter Publishers, 1993), p. 367.

93   Ibid., pp. 378–79.

94   Ibid., p. 380.

95   See, e.g., Pope Leo XIII, *Divinum illud munus*, art. 9.

96   See St. Bonaventure, *Breviloquium* V, 1 and I *Sent*. 17.

97   St. Augustine, *Sermo* CLXIX, chap. 11, par. 13 (PL 38: 923).

98   St. Francis De Sales, *Treatise on the Love of God*, p. 134.

99   St. Bernard of Clairvaux, *On the Canticle of Canticles*, chap. 17, in *On the Love of God*

and Other Selected Writings, ed. and trans. Charles J. Dollen (New York: Alba House, 1996), p. 61.

100   To convey the striking audacity of this method in its concrete application, perhaps a satire would be more to the point. See the humorous observations in Manfred Hauke, "Die Antwort," pp. 103–04.

101   Again, see Root, "Aquinas," p. 7 and p. 19, note 18.

102   See Hampson, *Christian Contradictions*, pp. 97–142.

103   One finds the same approach in Reformed thought (see Mark Seifrid, *Christ our Righteousness: Paul's Theology of Justification* [Downers Grove, IL: Inter Varsity Press, 2000], esp. p. 185).

104   See Jüngel, *Justification*, esp. pp. 211–24.

105   Jüngel, *Justification*, p. 214.

106   Lindbeck, "Compatibility," p. 237.

107   See Forde, "Forensic Justification," passsim.

108   See Peura, "Die Teilhabe," pp. 128–29.

109   Greek theology attests to the superiority of ontological or "existential" soteriology (Karras does not mean "existential" the way Pesch does!). Accordingly, Karras says, Greeks hardly touch the juridical model. Notwithstanding the fact that Athanasius does in fact touch this model in his *On the Incarnation*, still, I concur with her point: the ontological model is greater than the juridical (see Karras, "Beyond Justification," pp. 100, 105, 111, and 118).

110   Joan Nuth, "Two Medieval Soteriologies: Anselm of Canterbury and Julian of Norwich," *Theological Studies* 53 (1992): 623.

111   Nuth, "Two Medieval Soteriologies," p. 624.

112   Nuth, "Two Medieval Soteriologies," p. 624. See the rich discussion on solidarity that follows.

113   See Nuth, "Two Medieval Soteriologies," p. 626 and note 48 for more literature on the topic of Eucharistic appropriation of Christ's sacrifice.

114   Thomas Aquinas, ST IIIa, q. 48, arts. 1–2 and SCG, III, chap. 158 and IV, chap. 55.

115   Prat, *Theology of St. Paul*, II, pp. 201–02.

116   See Irenaeus, *Against the Heresies*, III, chaps. 18 and 23, pp. 445–48 and 455–58.

117   See Irenaeus, *Against the Heresies*, V, chap. 1, pp. 526–27.

118   See Irenaeus, *Against the Heresies*, V, chap. 18, pp. 546–47.

119   See Irenaeus, *Against the Heresies*, III, chap. 22, p. 455.

120   See Irenaeus, *Against the Heresies*, IV, chaps. 20 and 39, pp. 487–92 and 522–23.

121   See Irenaeus, *Against the Heresies*, IV, chaps. 14–39, pp. 478–523.

122   See Irenaeus, *Against the Heresies*, III, chap. 19, pp. 448–49. For a recent study of Irenaeus, see Eric Osborn, *Irenaeus of Lyons* (New York: Cambridge University Press, 2001).

123   See Irenaeus, *Against the Heresies*, III, chap. 18, pp. 445–48.

124   Eutyches was a fifth century monk who, in the wake of the Council of Ephesus, stressed the unity of Christ to the point of eclipsing the human nature altogether. He compared the union of the two natures to honey being swallowed up by the ocean.

125   Docetists held that Jesus merely appeared to be human but was not actually human. The name came from the Greek word *dokein*, "to appear."

126   See Irenaeus, *Against the Heresies*, III, chap. 23, pp. 455–58.

127   See Irenaeus, *Against the Heresies*, III, chap. 16, pp. 440–44. It would be quite anachronistic to impute an Arian theology to Irenaeus.

128   See, chiefly, St. Athanasius's youthful work, *On the Incarnation*, chaps. 1–8 and 54.

129   The historical context made it necessary for Athanasius to use the term "God" rather

than the term "Son of God" because what was at stake was the "truth" of his divinity. However, now that this *Sitz im Leben* no longer dominates—or does it?—we can, with Khaled Anatolios, return to Irenaeus's more Trinitarian formula in order to draw out an even richer anthropological truth: the human person is brought into the Godward God. Now, if we were to follow out this line of thought, not only would we be able to come to grips (better) with Schleiermacher's Sabellian objections but we would also be able to do justice to Rahner's critique of the excessively "mono-" theistic Trinitarian theology of the schools (see Khaled Anatolios, "The Immediately Triune God: A Patristic Response to Schleiermacher," *Pro Ecclesia* 10 [2001]: 159–78).

130   Gregory of Nazianzus, "Letters on the Apollinarian Controversy," in *Christology of the Later Fathers*, ed. Edward Rochie Hardy and Cyril C. Richardson (Philadelphia: The Westminster Press, 1954), p. 218.

131   See Gregory of Nyssa, *Address on Religious Instruction*, art. 32.

132   Brian Daley, S.J., "'Heavenly Man' and 'Eternal Christ': Apollinarius and Gregory of Nyssa on the Personal Identity of the Savior," *Journal of Early Christian Studies* 10 (2002): 484.

133   Daley, "'Heavenly Man,'" p. 485.

134   See Karras, "Beyond Justification," pp. 106–07 and 110.

135   See *Daily Roman Missal*, p. 374.

136   See *Daily Roman Missal*, p. 376.

137   For Aquinas, the notion of consubstantiation is, in fact, an excessively *phsysical* description of the transformation.

138   Fernand Prat, *Theology of St. Paul*, II, p. 253.

139   "Definition of the Faith by III Constantinople," in *The Seven Ecumenical Councils of the Undivided Church: Their Canons and Dogmatic Decrees*, ed. Henry R. Percival, vol. 14, *Nicene and Post-Nicene Fathers*, second series, ed. Philip Schaff and Henry Wace (Charles Scribner's Sons, 1900; reprint, Peabody, MA: Hendrickson Publishers, Inc., 1999), p. 335.

140   "Definition of the Faith by III Constantinople," p. 335.

141   Athanasius of Alexandria, *Four Discourses*, I, par. 45, p. 333.

142   See Athanasius of Alexandria, *Four Discourses*, I, par. 37, p. 328.

143   Athanasius of Alexandria, *Defence of the Nicene Definition*, chap. III, par. 10, in *Athanasius: Select Works and Letters*, p. 156.

144   Athanasius of Alexandria, *Defence*, chap. III, par. 14, p. 159.

145   See John Damascene, *On the Orthodox Faith*, trans. S. D. F. Salmond, in *Hilary of Poitiers, John of Damascus*, vol. 9, *Nicene and Post-Nicene Fathers, Second Series*, ed. Philip Schaff and Henry Wace (Peabody, MA: Hendrickson Publishers, Inc., 1999) Book III, chap. 4.

146   Athanasius of Alexandria, *Four Discourses*, III, par. 31, pp. 410–11.

147   Ibid., par. 32, p. 411.

148   Ibid, p. 411.

149   Ibid., par. 33, pp. 411–12.

150   Athanasius of Alexandria, *Four Discourses*, III, par. 34, pp. 412–13.

151   Cyril of Alexandria, "Epistle to Nestorius," in *The Seven Ecumenical Councils*, p. 198.

152   Pope Leo, "The Tome of St. Leo," in *The Seven Ecumenical Councils*, p. 256.

153   *Gaudium et spes*, art. 22. The council highlights Rom 8 in this very article, for it is Catholic belief that only in ontological and (consequently) spiritual-moral fellowship with Christ, animated by charity, that one partakes of the benefits of Christ's meritorious death.

154   See, e.g., Martin Luther, *Sermons on the Gospel of St. John: Chapters 1–4*, trans.

Martin H. Bertram, vol. 32, *Luther's Works*, ed. Jaroslav Pelikan (St. Louis: Concordia Publishing House, 1957), pp. 102–03 (LW 22: 102–03). This work was written in 1537.

155 I am thinking of the *Formula* and the *Apology*.

156 This is true, even if he at times reviled the term "homoousion" as being unscriptural (see LW 32: 243–44).

157 See Manns, "Absolute and Incarnate," p. 128.

158 Of course, one will object that for Luther nature is understood theologically as a state before God (*coram Deo*). I do not deny this. I simply wish to show that, on the basis of this anti-ontological approach, the data of Christian faith do not receive an adequate accounting.

159 LW 26: 284.

160 LW 26: 284.

161 See LW 26: 272–73, and Manns, "Absolute and Incarnate," pp. 129–31.

162 See Manns, "Absolute and Incarnate," p. 129.

163 LW 25: 267.

164 See Yves Congar, *Christ, Our Lady and the Church: A Study in Eirenic Theology*, trans. Henry St. John (New York: Longmans, Green and Co, 1957), pp. 21–30. Congar later modified his views (see Yves Congar, *Martin Luther, sa foi, sa réforme: études de théologie historique* [1983]).

165 Congar, *Christ*, p. 27.

166 See Congar, *Christ*, pp. 28–29.

167 Congar, *Christ*, p. 30.

168 See LW 26: 266–67.

169 Congar, *Christ*, p. 30.

170 See Johann Anselm Steiger, "The *communicatio idiomatum* as the Axle and Motor of Luther's Theology," *Lutheran Quarterly* 14 (2000):128–33, trans. Carolyn Schneider.

171 LW 26: 283–84.

172 See Steiger, "Axle," pp. 129–30.

173 See LW 27: 241 (his 1519 *Commentary on Galatians*).

174 In contrast, Eckardt apparently sees no substantive divergence between Luther's "happy exchange," which is said to occur by extrinsic imputation, and Anselm's vicarious substitution. He writes, "[Luther's] manner of discourse certainly differs from that of St. Anselm, a fact which has thrown some researchers off the trail while abetting the preconceptions of others, but the substance of his thought is as bound to the theme of substitution as is that of [Anselm]" (Eckardt, "Luther and Anselm," p. 59).

175 See Jan D. Kingston Siggins, *Martin Luther's Doctrine of Christ* (New Haven: Yale University Press, 1970), pp. 131–33.

176 See Steiger, "Axle," p. 130.

177 LW 26: 284.

178 Perhaps, then, the ultimate end envisioned by Luther in his soteriology would be the best locus in which to perceive his tendency towards monophysitism. The reason would be this: If humans are by nature a curse—and Luther would not be moved from this conclusion, for he considered precise distinctions not to be apostolic—then redemption from the curse frees humans from their nature. Human destiny is to be divine, not to be divinized, for only when love is perfect, that is, eternal and divine, can one "satisfy" the divine requirement (see LW 27: 64–65). In sum, Luther exhibited Nestorian tendencies in his articulation of the redemptive activity of Christ, but he concluded eschatologically to a kind of corporate monophysitism.

179 See Steiger, "Axle," p. 125.

180   See Steiger, "Axle," p. 126. Steiger, of course, does not consider Luther a monophysite; rather, he argues that Luther took Chalcedon to its logical conclusion.

181   LW 22: 327. Steiger writes, "All things that apply to the human nature of Christ are also attributed to his divine nature" (Steiger, "Axle," p. 127).

182   LW 25: 332.

183   LW 32: 257.

184   See Marc Lienhard, *Luther: Witness to Jesus Christ*, trans. Edwin H. Robertson (Minneapolis: Augsburg Publishing House, 1982), pp. 170–76 and 195–220.

185   See Lienhard, *Luther*, pp. 214–15.

186   See Steiger, "Axle," pp. 137–44. If we think of one of the subbtler rules of the communication of idioms—that the properties of one nature may be said of the other nature in the concrete, not in the abstract—would we find a way of accepting Luther's Christology? I am disinclined to think we would, for this subtle rule still requires the intellectual reduction (*reductio*, or leading back) of the communicability to the hypostatic union; that is, the theologian must recognize that the reason predicates of one nature may be said of the other concretely is that the two natures are unconfusedly united in one hypostasis. So, analytic theology, incapable of the symbolic power of Melito of Sardis, yet recognizes that *what* Melito affirms *cannot* be that the divinity itself suffers.

187   Cyril could agree to distinguish nature and hypostasis; he could agree to John's brilliant addition to Christology: Christ is consubstantial with us as to his humanity.

188   See LW 22: 328.

189   Martin Luther, *On the Councils and the Church*, trans. Charles M. Jacobs and Eric W. Gritsch, in *Church and Ministry III*, vol. 41, *Luther's Works*, ed. Eric W. Gritsch (Philadelphia: Fortress Press, 1966), p. 101 (LW 41:101).

190   LW 41: 103.

191   For a brief discussion of this apparent ambiguity, see Lienhard, *Luther*, pp. 230–35. According to Lienhard, the sense of person as *hypostasis* is not alien to Luther, especially in his Latin writings; nor, however, is the sense of person as the concrete union of the two natures, the single acting subject, foreign to Luther. Still, the exchange of predicates serves as the hermeneutical testing ground for Luther's deepest Christological intent.

192   LW 41: 105. See also pp. 109 and 117.

193   Lienhard, *Luther*, p. 317.

194   See Lienhard, *Luther*, pp. 335–39.

195   See Lienhard, *Luther*, p. 341.

196   I would contend that Cyril refused to exchange the proper characteristics of the natures (see, e.g., Letter 17 in Cyril of Alexandria, *St. Cyril of Alexandria: Letters 1–50*, trans. John McEnerney [Washington: The Catholic University of America Press, 1987], p. 83). Cyril's use of "*physis*" was supple, and fidelity to his thought demands an appreciation of that dexterity; without such an appreciation, one cannot make sense of his integrity in assenting to the Formula of Reunion proposed by John of Antioch. Nor was Cyril alone. Since there was lingering confusion due to an aging and poorly-trained theologian, Leo in Rome and the bishops at Chalcedon entered the stage to establish greater clarity. Subsequently, Constantinople II was followed by Constantinople III. I would submit that the Alexandrian fathers did not attribute properly divine qualities to the humanity of Jesus without qualification. The "vehicle" for the attribution was the key concept "participation." The humanity of Jesus participates in the divine uncreated grace in a manner so ineffable that it is truly life-giving: it is the humanity of the Word. Still, the humanity is not swallowed up by the divinity; it remains integrally human. For

this reason, Jesus in his earthly humanity enjoyed a vision of God but was not, in his humanity, that very vision. The perichoretic dance of the natures illustrates this intimate participation and enhypostatized humanity, but not in any way to the detriment of the integrity of the natures. There is no alteration of the substance of his human nature as such, just as the perichoretic dance of the divine persons in no way obscures the distinction of Trinitarian persons. It seems to me that failure to perceive the notion of *participation* in the Christology of the East blinds one from accurately understanding the "divinization" of the humanity of Christ. While the East refused to allow the divinity to suffer, it was also unwilling to allow the "divinization" of the humanity to be taken in a sense other than participation, all the while enfolding this divinization within the union according to hypostasis, so that the ineffable character of this divinization is retained and so that this divinization cannot be misunderstood *either* as rendering Jesus a God-bearer *or* as making him "two" sons.

197 Lienhard, *Luther*, p. 344.

198 Even Peura, with so much promise for Catholic and Orthodox dialogue, does not come clean on this (see Peura, "Die Teilhabe," pp. 148–50).

199 Congar, pp. 27–28.

200 See Steiger, "Axle," pp. 137–44.

201 LW 22:109.

202 Steiger, "Axle," p. 131.

203 Steiger, "Axle," p. 130.

204 *Lumen gentium*, art. 60 (Catholic Church, *Vatican Council II: The Conciliar and Post Conciliar Documents*, ed. Austin Flannery [Northport, NY: Costello Publishing Company, 1992]).

205 *Lumen gentium*, art. 62. For the most recent work touching upon the problematic aspects of Luther's Christology, see Christian Washburne, "St. Roberto Bellarmino's Defense of Catholic Christology against the Lutheran Doctrine of Ubiquity." Ph.D. diss., The Catholic University of America, 2004.

206 Karl Barth, *The Doctrine of the Word of God*, vol. 1, part. 1, *Church Dogmatics*, ed. G.W. Bromiley and T.F. Torrance, trans. G.W. Bromiley (Edinburgh: T&T Clark, 1975), pp. 238–39.

207 How could any Catholic walk here with Barth: "In this sense, as a possibility which is proper to man *qua* creature, the image of God is not just, as it is said, destroyed apart from a few relics; it is totally annihilated. What remains of the image of God even in sinful man is a *recta natura*, to which as such a *rectitudo* cannot be ascribed even *potentialiter*" (ibid., p. 238)? See Molnar, "The Theology," p. 238.

208 See Irenaeus, *Against the Heresies*, IV, chap. 20, no. 7, pp. 489–90.

CONCLUSION

THIS BOOK has accomplished three things. First, through historical investigation, it identifies from a Catholic perspective some necessary elements of an adequate point of departure for dialogue. Demonstrating an original, substantive divide between the communions, the argument entails that the Lutheran-Catholic dialogue, if it is to reach fruition, must include doctrinal emendation of previous doctrine. The JD's claim to present a substantial agreement that implies emendation of neither Lutheran nor Catholic doctrine is not sustainable; it is the JD's most notable flaw. Second, through a systematic approach, this book offers a sustained critical reflection on the fruits of the contemporary dialogue. It illuminates issues on which the dialogue, especially the JD, either deficiently represents or differs in substance from authentic Catholic doctrine. It traces the organic interconnection of these deficiencies, showing that they roughly form a fabric into which certain distinctively Catholic expressions, though present, are not integrated. A genuinely Catholic interpretation of the JD would stretch even this rough fabric beyond recognition and might well disillusion Lutherans of goodwill who have consented to its signing. Third, this book closes with a nexus of theological investigations on the relevance of justification for other elements of faith, for pastoral practice, and for the existential significance of earthly life.

Given the largely critical task of this work, I find it necessary to close by tracing out several lines of hope for ongoing dialogue, well-known though they may be.

First, neither grace nor the virtue of charity is a "work." Grace is a *principle* of charity, which is a *principle* of charitable acts. Good works do not establish a relationship with God. They do, however, express this relationship (action follows being). They are necessary for its sustenance (Jn 15:2); they are a cause for its maturation; and by them God's children can gain an eternal inheritance. Insofar as Lutherans view faith both as a divine gift and as something truly human, is not a parallel view of sanctifying grace possible?

Second, justifying grace "inheres" in the human person but never becomes a proper accident of human nature. It is infused by God not just at the moment of justification but continually. The continual influx and any increase of sanctifying grace are caused by God. For this reason, grace is not man's possession of God but God's possession of man. This Bonaventurian principle seems to resonate well with Lutheran doctrinal concerns.

Third, sanctifying grace is not a reason for self-trust. Rather, it imbues faith and hope with a filial character. Moreover, grace is a participation in the righteousness of Jesus Christ, the font of the supernatural justice created in human hearts (Ps 51:10). From his pierced side flows forth the grace by which all are being saved. When he expired for our salvation, he breathed forth the Spirit. This Holy Spirit seeks the unholy and the godless in order to hallow them. Through the grace of the exhaled Spirit, human sinners are forgiven; enemies are adopted; those who once mounted their own Babel, or who scoffed at the Publican, or who took up an angry dagger, or who regretted sin unto death (2 Cor 7:10), now chant "Abba!" in filial simplicity. They have been engrafted into the living Vine so as to bear fruit that will last. Grace as an inhering qualification of the human person *per se* leads no one to chase after the morning star in lieu of the sun. *Per se* it enables the faithful to love God unto death. To this love the lives of the saints bear witness. Contemporary Lutheran reflections on the gift of faith emphasizes its relational, participatory, and ecstatic character. If these lines of thought could be followed out to their best conclusion, and not pitted against a "charity" conceived as self-glorification, then Lutherans and Catholics could have even firmer ground upon which to dialogue. Might not the following words of Luther serve as a fitting eulogy of St. Thérèse: "Indeed, one who loved God truly and perfectly would not be able to live very long but would soon be devoured by his love"?[1] Thérèse taught us both to trust in Christ alone and to desire that he move us in all we do. Moreover, Thérèse made transparent the fact that beatitude consists not in self-contemplation but rather in an ecstatic rapture of the lover—made lover by the Love that first loved (1 Jn 1:11)—towards her Beloved.

These second and third loci for ecumenical progress offer us sinners two reasons to cling to Jesus. With one arm, we cling to him without whose love and merits we would forever gnash our teeth. With the other, we embrace him. Let us only note that those made lovers of God through the love of God shed abroad (whether this is a subjective *or* objective genitive) do not approach their mediator chiefly out of servile fear but rather in filial fear.

Fourth, the distinction between formal and efficient causality is crucial. New analogies can be drawn, or perhaps forgotten ones recovered, to make the truth more accessible. Attention to the distinction between efficient and formal causality highlights the important distinction that should be made: that between the gratuity and the inhering reality of grace. To draw a metaphor, no flower can "exact its due" from the sun and rain and soil, yet the sun and rain and soil are not the very life of the flower.[2] The sinner pines for God's loving gaze. As an unregenerate sinner, he does not merit this gaze, and his pining is not filial. Yet the very pining is the natural root (*voluntas ut natura*) from which, by grace, filial love may blossom forth. Spiritual awakening, then, is not God's love itself but the transformation wrought by that love. As God's regenerate child, the Christian cannot fail to be loved by his Father and to "draw" his Father's gaze. All this, because by the Spirit he is a member of Christ.

Fifth, although Catholics confess that baptism erases all that is truly sin, perhaps this belief can be rethought in light of itself and in light of Luther's polyvalent distinction between reality and experience. Although baptism removes sin and makes the human person a child of God, all can admit that most baptized persons do not have much to show for themselves. They are not necessarily great persons. Perhaps we can say, then, not only that sin is indeed removed from the seat of the baptized person's free and intelligent activity but also that the reach of the neophyte's activity is not very wide. Neophytes are typically "small" persons. They come together with much that is unlikable. Because of a lack of integration, they are not held accountable—*cannot* be held accountable—for everything in them that is contrary to God. A distinct current in Luther's work, from his *Commentary on Romans* through his 1535 *Commentary on Galatians*, is compatible with such a suggestion. Observe that this is not to take refuge in the "non-imputation" of sins; rather, it is to recognize another factor in the evaluation of one's status before God: maturity and immaturity. Immaturity itself may at times dovetail with sins not truly damnable, but it cannot be confused with damnable sins. Some aspects of immaturity can simply be imperfections. Now, failure to struggle towards maturity could indeed be sin, even damnable sin, for all are called to perfection (Mt 5:48). Those who become more integrated, enjoy a wider scope of personal action. They can dedicate themselves more and more radically to God, ruling their fleshly passions more and more. They thus recover themselves by their dedication to God. Somewhat paradoxically, persons who have entered into the divine covenant more intimately have the "capacity" to offend the holiness of God more seriously, for such persons wrestle more directly with pride and envy than do those struggling with sins of sensuality. This hypothesis therefore helps to account for the phenomenon of radical holiness. Though we ordinary Christians cannot hold ourselves to the exalted standards of the saints, many saints have considered even a look or a word to be an infidelity. Perhaps the reason they see matters thus is their greater integrity and capacity for personal action. Through Christ, they truly do rule their flesh, fulfilling the polyvalent prophecy the Lord spoke to the serpent (Gen 3:15). This hypothesis is not an effort to excuse the inexcusable; it is a suggestion that we advert to the dynamically changing conditions for the possibility of what needs forgiving, and thus acknowledge the phenomenon, which Luther rightly acknowledged, without conceiving of forgiveness as forensic non-imputation of debts.

Finally, the doctrine of justification needs to be situated within a comprehensive framework that includes creation, sin, Christological insertion into the body of Christ, eschatology, and Trinitarian relations. Attention to eschatological issues shows concretely the existential importance of one's conception of the beginning of the journey towards the promised land.

May we traverse the rough terrain of our pilgrimage towards doctrinal reconciliation in truth and in love. We can abandon neither but only look upon the Crucified who is Truth and Love:

> Steadfast love and faithfulness will meet;
> Righteousness and peace will kiss each other. (Ps 84:11)

NOTES

1   LW 27: 65.
2   Perhaps we can recover Peter Lombard's image of the seed, the rain, the soil, and the fruit (see Peter Lombard, *Sententiae*, Book II, dist. 27, chap. 2.3, p. 482).

BIBLIOGRAPHY

Primary Sources

Anderson, H. George, T. Austin Murphy, and Joseph A. Burgess, eds. *Justification by Faith.* Vol. 7, *Lutherans and Catholics in Dialogue.* Minneapolis: Augsburg Publishing House, 1985. "Annex." *Origins* 29:6 (1999): 87–88.

Athanasius of Alexandria. *Athanasius: Select Works and Letters.* Translated by John Henry Newman. Vol. 4, *Nicene and Post-Nicene Fathers.* Second series. Edited by Philip Schaff and Henry Wace. Christian Literature Publishing Company, 1894. Reprint, Peabody, MA: Hendrickson Publishers, Inc., 1999.

Augustine of Hippo. *Confessions.* Translated by R.S. Pine-Coffin. New York: Penguin Classics, 1961.

———. *Expositions on the Book of Psalms.* Edited and translated by A. Cleveland Coxe. Vol. 8, *Nicene and Post-Nicene Fathers.* First series. Edited by Philip Schaff. Peabody, MA: Hendrickson Publishers, Inc, 1994.

Basil of Caesarea. *On the Spirit.* In *Letters and Select Works.* Translated by Blomfield Jackson. Vol. 8, *Nicene and Post-Nicene Fathers.* Second series. Edited by Philip Schaff and Henry Wace. Christian Literature Publishing Company, 1895. Reprint, Peabody, MA: Hendrickson Publishers, Inc., 1999.

Bellarmine, Robert. *De justificatione impii.* Vol. 6, *Opera omnia.* Paris: Minerva, 1873.

Bernard of Clairvaux. *On the Canticle of Canticles.* In *On the Love of God and Other Selected Writings.* Edited and translated by Msgr. Charles J. Dollen. New York: Alba House, 1996.

Bonaventure. *The Breviloquium.* Translated by José de Vinck. Paterson, N.J.: St. Anthony Guild Press, 1963.

———. *Tria opuscula.* Vol. 5, *Opera theologica selecta.* Edited by Augustini Sépinski. Florence: Quaracchi, 1964.

Cajetan, Thomas de Vio. *De fide et operibus.* In *Opuscula omnia.* Lyon: Ex officina iuntarum: 1587. Reprint: New York: Georg Olms Verlag, 1995.

———. *Commentary on the Summa theologiae.* In Thomas Aquinas, *Summa theologiae.* Vol. 7, *Sancti Thomae Aquinatis doctor angelici Opera omnia iussu Leonis XIII. P.M. edita.* Rome: Ex Typographia Polyglatta, 1882.

———. *Peccatorum summula,* Novissime Recognita. Ex Typographia Baltazaris Belleri, 1613.

Catechism of the Catholic Church. Translated by the United States Catholic Conference. Vatican City: Libreria Editrice Vaticana., 1994.

Catechism of the Council of Trent. Translated by John A. McHugh and Charles J. Callan. Rockford, IL: Tan, 1982.

Cervini, Marcello. "Briefe und Traktate aus den Carte Cerviniane." Appendix to *Briefwechsel Johannes Gropper*, pp. 127–28. Arranged by Reinhard Braunisch. Vol. 32, Corpus Catholicorum. Münster: Aschendorff, 1977.

Chemnitz, Martin. *Examination of the Council of Trent, Part I.* Translated by Fred Kramer. St. Louis: Concordia Publishing House, 1971.

"A Common Statement of the Australian Lutheran-Roman Catholic Dialogue." [Online; accessed June 19, 2002]. Available at http://www.home.gil.com.au/~stillerk/justification.html.

Concilii Tridentini actorum: Pars altera. Edited by Stephen Ehses. Vol. 5, *Concilium*

Tridentinum: Diariorum, actorum, epistularum, tractatuum. Societas Goerresiana. Freiburg: B. Herder, 1911.

Daily Roman Missal: Weekday and Sunday Masses. Edited by James Socias. Princeton, NJ: Scepter Publishers, 1993.

Dominic de Soto. *De natura et gratia.* Paris: John Foucher, 1549.

Evangelical Lutheran Church in America. "Response to *Justification by Faith.*" *One in Christ* 29 (1993): 342–49.

Francis de Sales. *Treatise on the Love of God.* Translated by Dom Henry Benedict Mackey, O.S.B. Rockford, IL: Tan Books, 1997.

———. *Troisième Série—Controverse.* Vol. 23.2, *Œvres de Saint François de Sales.* Annecy: Monastery of the Visitation, 1928.

Gregory of Nazianzus. "Letters on the Apollinarian Controversy." In *Christology of the Later Fathers.* Edited by Edward Rochie Hardy and Cyril C. Richardson. Philadelphia: The Westminster Press, 1954.

———. "The Oration on Holy Baptism." Translated by Charles Gordon Browne and James Edward Swallow. In *Cyril of Jerusalem, Gregory Nazianzen.* Vol. 7, *Nicene and Post-Nicene Fathers.* Second Series. Edited by Philip Schaff and Henry Wace. Christian Literature Publishing Company, 1894. Reprint, Peabody, MA: Hendrickson Publishers, Inc., 1999.

Irenaeus of Lyons. *Against Heresies.* In *The Apostolic Fathers with Justin Martyr and Irenaeus.* Vol. 1, *Ante-Nicene Fathers.* Edited by Alexander Roberts and James Donaldson. Christian Literature Publishing Company, 1894. Reprint, Peabody, MA: Hendrickson Publishers, Inc., 1999.

John Chrysostom. *Homilies on Galatians.* Translate by Gross Alexander. In volume 13, *Nicene and Post-Nicene Fathers.* First series. Edited by Philip Schaff. Christian Literature Publishing Company, 1894. Reprint, Peabody, MA: Hendrickson Publishers, Inc., 1999.

John Damascene. *On the Orthodox Faith.* Translated by S. D. F. Salmond. In *Hilary of Poitiers, John of Damascus.* Vol. 9, *Nicene and Post-Nicene Fathers, Second Series.* Edited by Philip Schaff and Henry Wace. Christian Literature Publishing Company, 1894. Reprint, Peabody, MA: Hendrickson Publishers, Inc., 1999.

John Paul II, Pope. *Dominum et Vivificantem.* Washington, D.C.: USCC, 1986.

———. *Ut unum sint.* Vatican Translation. Boston: St. Paul Books & Media, 1995.

———. *Veritatis splendor.* Vatican Translation. Boston, St. Paul Books & Media, 1993.

"Joint Declaration on the Doctrine of Justification." *Origins* 28:8 (1998): 120–27. In German, "Gemeinsame Erklärung zur Rechtfertigungslehre." [Online; accessed July 16, 2004]. Available at www.theology.de/rechtfertigungslehre.html.

Kolb, Robert and Timothy Wengert. *The Book of Concord: The Confessions of the Evangelical Lutheran Church.* Translated by Charles Arand, Eric Gritsch, Robert Kolb, William Russell, James Schaaf, Jane Strohl, and Timothy Wengert. Minneapolis: Fortress Press, 2000.

Lehmann, Karl and Wolfhart Pannenberg, eds. *The Condemnations of the Reformation Era: Do They Still Divide?* Translated by Margaret Kohl. Minneapolis: Fortress Press, 1990. In German, *Lehrverurteilungen—Kirchentrennend?* Band 4, *Dialog der Kirchen.* Freiburg: Herder, 1986.

Leo XIII, Pope. *On Jesus Christ our Redeemer.* Boston: St. Paul Editions, 1978.

Lumen gentium. Translated by Colman O'Neill. In *Vatican II: The Conciliar and Post Conciliar Documents,* pp. 350–426. Edited by Austin Flannery. Northport, NY: Costello Publishing Company, 1992.

Luther, Martin. *Against Latomus.* Translated by George Lindbeck. In *Career of the Reformer II.* Edited by George W. Forell, pp. 137–264. Vol. 32, *Luther's Works.* Edited by Helmut T. Lehmann. Philadelphia: Fortress Press, 1958.

————. *On the Councils and the Church.* Translated by Charles M. Jacobs and Eric W. Gritsch. In *Church and Ministry III.* Vol. 41, *Luther's Works.* Edited by Eric W. Gritsch. Philadelphia: Fortress Press, 1966.

————. *Lectures on Galatians (1519).* Translated by Richard Jungkuntz. Vol. 27, *Luther's Works.* Edited by Jaroslav Pelikan, pp. 151–410. St. Louis: Concordia Publishing House, 1963.

————. *Lectures on Galatians (1535): Chapters 1–4.* Translated by Jaroslav Pelikan. Vol. 27, *Luther's Works.* Edited by Jaroslav Pelikan. St. Louis: Concordia Publishing House, 1963.

————.*Lectures on Galatians (1535): Chapters 5–6.* Translated by Jaroslav Pelikan. Vol. 27, *Luther's Works.* Edited by Jaroslav Pelikan, pp. 1–149. St. Louis: Concordia Publishing House, 1963.

————. *Lectures on Romans* (Chapters 3–16). Translated by Jacob A. O. Preus. Vol. 25, *Luther's Works.* Edited by Hilton C. Oswald, pp. 25–524. St. Louis: Concordia Publishing House, 1972.

————. *Sermons on the Gospel of St. John: Chapters 1–4.* Translated by Martin H. Bertram. Vol. 32, *Luther's Works.* Edited by Jaroslav Pelikan. St. Louis: Concordia Publishing House, 1957.

Lutheran World Federation. "Implications of Justification in the World's Contexts." Statement of October 31, 1998. [Online; accessed July 16, 2004]. Available at www.ecumenism.net/archive/justification-today.htm.

————. "'Justification Today,' Document 75—Assembly and Final Versions." *Lutheran World* 12, 1, Supplement (1965): 1–11.

Melanchthon, Philip. *Loci praecipui theologici von 1559 (2. Teil) und Definitiones.* Edited by Hans Engelland. Vol. 2, *Melanchthons Werke in Auswahl.* Edited by Robert Stupperich. Gütersloh: C. Bertelsmann Verlag, 1953.

————. *Römerbrief - Kommentar 1532.* Edited by Rolf Schäfer. Vol. 5, *Melanchthon's Werke in Auswahl.* Edited by Robert Stupperich. Gütersloh: Gütersloher Verlagshaus Gerd Mohn, 1965.

Miranda, Bartolomé Carranza de. *Comentarios sobre el Catechismo Christiano; edición crítica y estudio histórico,* vol. 2. Edited by José Ignacio Tellechea Idígoras (Madrid: Biblioteca de Autores Cristianos, 1972.

Möhler, Johann Adam. *Symbolism or Exposition of the Doctrinal Differences between Catholics and Protestants as Evidenced by their Symbolical Writings.* Translated by James Burton Robertson. 5th ed. New York: Benzinger Brothers, 1906. In German, *Symbolik oder Darstellung der dogmatischen Gegensätze der Katholiken und Protestanten nach ihren öffentlichen Bekenntnisschriften.* Cologne: Jakob Hegner, 1958.

National Conference of Catholic Bishops. "An Evaluation of the Lutheran-Catholic Statement *Justification by Faith.*" *One in Christ* 29 (1993): 335–42.

Newman, John Henry Cardinal. *Lectures on Justification.* New York: Longmans, Green, and Co, 1900.

"Official Common Statement." *Origins* 29:6 (1999): 85–87.

"Official Vatican Response." *Origins* 28:8 (1998): 130–32.

Origen of Alexandria. *On First Principles.* Translated by G. W. Butterworth. Gloucester, MA: Peter Smith, 1973.

Percival, Henry R., ed. *The Seven Ecumenical Councils of the Undivided Church: Their Canons and Dogmatic Decrees.* Vol. 14, *Nicene and Post-Nicene Fathers.* Second series. Edited by Philip Schaff and Henry Wace. Charles Scribner's Sons, 1900. Reprint, Peabody, MA: Hendrickson Publishers, Inc., 1999.

Scheeben, Matthias Joseph. *Handbuch der Katholischen Dogmatik,* vol. 3. Edited by Wilhelm Breuning and Franz Lakner. Freiburg: Herder, 1961.

————. *The Mysteries of Christianity*. Translated by Cyril Vollert, S .J. St. Louis: B. Herder Book Co., 1947. In German, *Die Mysterien des Christenthums*. 2nd ed. Freiburg im Breisgau: Herder, 1898.

Scotus, John Duns. *In Lib. I. Sententiarum*. Vol. 2, *Opera omnia*. Hildesheim: Georg Olms Verlagsbuchhandlung, 1968.

Tanner, Norman P., ed. *Trent to Vatican II*. Vol. 2, *Decrees of the Ecumenical Councils*. Washington: Georgetown University Press, 1990.

Tapper, Ruard. *Opera omnia*. Tom. 2. Cologne, 1582.

Tappert, Theodore G. *The Book of Concord: The Confessions of the Evangelical Lutheran Church*. Philadelphia: Fortress Press, 1959. In German, *Die Bekenntnisschriften der evangelisch-lutherischen Kirche*. Göttingen: Vandenhoeck & Ruprecht, 1955.

Thérèse of Lisieux. *Story of a Soul*. Translated by John Clarke, O.C.D. Washington, D.C.: ICS Publications, 1996.

Thomas Aquinas. *Summa theologiae*. Vol. 7, *Sancti Thomae Aquinatis doctor angelici Opera omnia iussu Leonis XIII. P.M. edita*. Rome: Ex Typographia Polyglatta, 1882.

United Evangelical Lutheran Church. "Comment." *Lutheran Quarterly* 9 (1995): 359–64.

Vega, Andreas de. *De Iustificatione*. Vol. 1, *Opera omnia*. Cologne: 1572.

William of Ockham. Vol. 3, *Opera theologica*. St. Bonaventure, N.Y.: Editiones franciscani, 1977.

————. Vol. 9, *Opera theologica*. St. Bonaventure, N.Y.: Editiones franciscani, 1980.

Secondary Sources

Adam, Karl. *One and Holy*. New York: Greenwood Press Publishers, 1951.

Althaus, Paul. *The Theology of Martin Luther*. Translated by Robert Schultz. Philadelphia: Fortress Press, 1966.

Anderson, Herbert. "The Agreed Statement on Justification: A Lutheran Perspective." *Ecumenical Trends* 28, no. 5 (1999): 1–6.

Augros, Robert and George Stanciu. *The New Biology: Discovering the Wisdom in Nature*. Boston: Shambhala, 1988.

Balás, David. *METOYΣIA ΘEOY: Man's Participation in God's Perfections according to Saint Gregory of Nyssa*. Studia Anselmiana, no. 55. Rome, Libreria Herder, 1966.

Balthasar, Hans Urs von. *The Dramatis Personae: Man in God*. Vol. 2, *Theo-Drama: Theological Dramatic Theory*. Translated by Graham Harrison. San Francisco: Ignatius Press, 1990.

————. "Thérèse of Lisieux." Translated by Donald Nichols and Anne England Nash. In *Two Sisters in the Spirit: Thérèse of Lisieux and Elizabeth of the Trinity*, pp. 13–362. San Francisco: Ignatius Press, 1992.

Becker, Karl Josef. *Die Rechtfertigungslehre nach Domingo de Soto: Das Denken eines Konzilsteilnehmers vor, in und nach Trient*. Vol. 156, Analecta Gregoriana, Series Facultatis Theologicae. Rome: Verlagsbuchhandlung, 1967.

Beisser, Friedrich. "The Doctrine of Justification in the Formula of Concord: How Far Do Its Condemnations Apply to the Roman Catholic Church?" In *Justification by Faith: Do the Sixteenth-Century Condemnations Still Apply?* Translated by Michael Root and William G. Rusch, pp. 149–60. New York: The Continuum Publishing Company, 1997.

Birmelé, André. *La communion ecclésiale: Progrès œcuméniques et enjeux méthodologiques*. Paris: Les éditions du cerf, 2000.

————, Theodor Dieter, Michael Root, and Risto Saarinen, eds. *Joint Declaration on the*

Doctrine of Justification: A Commentary by the Institute for Ecumenical Research. Translated by staff team. Hong Kong: Clear-Cut Publishing & Printing Co., 1997.

Brandt, Reinhard. "Gemeinsame Erklärung—kritische Fragen: Die 'Gemeinsame Erklärung zur Rechtfertigungslehre' und Fragen zu ihrer Rezeption in den deutschen lutherischen Kirchen." *Zeitschrift für Theologie und Kirche* 95 (1998): 63–102.

Brown, Raymond. *The Epistles of John.* Vol. 30, *The Anchor Bible.* New York: Doubleday, 1982.

Burgess, Joseph A. "Rewards, But in a Very Different Sense." In *Justification by Faith.* Vol. 7, *Lutherans and Catholics in Dialogue.* Edited by H. George Anderson, T. Austin Murphy, and Joseph A. Burgess, pp. 94–110. Minneapolis: Augsburg Publishing House, 1985.

Braaten, Carl. E. "Response to Simo Peura, 'Christ as Favor and Gift.'" In *Union with Christ: The New Finnish Interpretation of Luther.* Edited and translated by Carl E. Braaten and Robert W. Jenson, pp. 70–75. Grand Rapids: Eerdman's, 1998.

——— and Robert W. Jenson, eds. *Union with Christ: The New Finnish Interpretation of Luther.* Translated by Carl E. Braaten and Robert W. Jenson. Grand Rapids: Eerdman's, 1998.

Burghardt, Walter. *The Image of God in Man According to Cyril of Alexandria.* No. 14, Studies in Christian Antiquity. Edited by Johannes Quasten. Woodstock, MA: Woodstock College Press, 1957.

Cavanaugh, William T. "A Joint Declaration?: Justification as Theosis in Aquinas and Luther." *The Heythrop Journal* 41 (2000): 265–80.

Clifford, Catherine. "The Joint Declaration, Method, and The Hermeneutics of Ecumenical Consensus." *Journal of Ecumenical Studies* 38 (2001): 79–91.

Congar, Yves. *Christ, Our Lady and the Church: A Study in Eirenic Theology.* Translated by Henry St. John. New York: Longmans, Green & Co., 1957.

"The Critical Response of German Theological Professors to the *Joint Declaration on the Doctrine of Justification.*" In *Dialogue* 38 (1999): 71–72.

Cross, Richard. *Duns Scotus.* In *Great Medieval Thinkers.* Edited by Brian Davies. New York: Oxford University Press, 1999.

Daley, Brian. "'Heavenly Man' and 'Eternal Christ': Apollinarius and Gregory of Nyssa on the Personal Identity of the Savior." *Journal of Early Christian Studies* 10 (2002): 469–88.

Dulles, Avery Cardinal. *The Craft of Theology: From Symbol to System.* New York: Crossroad, 1992.

———. "Justification: The Joint Declaration." *Josephinum Journal of Theology* 9 (2002). [Online; accessed July 16, 2004]. Available at www.pcj.edu/journal/Dulles9-1.htm.

———. "Justification in Contemporary Catholic Theology." In *Justification by Faith.* Vol. 7, *Lutherans and Catholics in Dialogue.* Edited by H. George Anderson, T. Austin Murphy, and Joseph A. Burgess, 256–77. Minneapolis: Augsburg Publishing House, 1985.

———. "Two Languages of Salvation: The Lutheran-Catholic Joint Declaration." *First Things* 98 (1999): 25–30.

Dunn, James D.G. *Jesus, Paul and the Law: Studies in Mark and Galatians.* Louisville, KY: Westminster/John Knox Press, 1991.

Eckardt Jr., Burnell. "Luther and Anselm: Same Atonement, Different Approach." In *Ad Fontes Lutheri: Toward the Recovery of the Real Luther: Essays in Honor of Kenneth Hagen's Sixty-fifth Birthday.* Edited by Kenneth Hagen, Franz Posset, and Joan Skocir, pp. 54–66. Marquette Studies in Theology, no. 28. Milwaukee: Marquette University Press, 2001.

Ehses, Stephan. "Johannes Groppers Rechtfertigungslehre auf dem Konzil von Trient." *Römische Quartalschrift für christliche Altertumskunde und für Kirchengeschichte* 20 (1906): 175–88.

Fédou, Michel. "L'accord luthéro-catholique sur la justification." *Nouvelle revue théologique* 122 (2000): 37–50.

Fenlon, Dermot. *Heresy and Obedience in Tridentine Italy: Cardinal Pole and the Counter Reformation.* Cambridge: Cambridge University Press, 1972.

Fitzmeyer, Joseph. *Romans: A New Translation with Introduction and Commentary*. New York, Doubleday, 1993.

Forde, Gerhard. "Forensic Justification and Law in Lutheran Theology." In *Justification by Faith*. Vol. 7, *Lutherans and Catholics in Dialogue*. Edited by H. George Anderson, T. Austin Murphy, and Joseph A. Burgess, pp. 278–303. Minneapolis: Augsburg Publishing House, 1985.

Garrigues, Jean-Miguel. "La doctrine de la grâce habituelle dans ses sources scripturaires et patristiques." *Revue Thomiste* 103 (2003): 179–202.

Gerrish, B. A. *Grace and Reason: A Study in the Theology of Luther*. Oxford: Clarendon Press, 1962.

Gleason, Elizabeth G. *Gasparo Contarini: Venice, Rome, and Reform*. Berkeley: University of California Press, 1993.

Göttingen Theological Faculty. "An Opinion on *The Condemnations of the Reformation Era*. Part One: Justification." *Lutheran Quarterly* 5 (1991): 1–62.

Gros, Br. Jeffrey. "Toward Full Communion: Faith and Order and Catholic Ecumenism." *Theological Studies* 65 (2004): 23–43.

Haight, Roger. *The Experience and Language of Grace*. New York: Paulist Press, 1979.

Hampson, Daphne. *Christian Contradictions: The Structures of Lutheran and Catholic Thought*. New York: Cambridge University Press, 2001.

Hauke, Manfred. "Die Antwort des Konzil von Trient auf die Reformatoren." In *Der Mensch zwischen Sünde und Gnade: Theologische Sommerakademie Dießen 2000*. Edited by Anton Ziegenaus, pp. 75–109. Buttenwiesen: Stella-Maris-Verl., 2000.

Hefner, Josef. *Die Entstehungsgeschichte des Trienter Rechtfertigungsdekretes: Ein Beitrag zur Dogmengeschichte des Reformationszeitalters*. Paderborn, 1909.

Hoffmann, Norbert. *Natur und Gnade: Die Theologie der Gotteschau als volendeter Vergöttlichung des Geistgeschöpfes bei M. J. Scheeben*. Analecta Gregoriana, no. 160. Rome: Gregorian University Press, 1967.

Holc, Paweł. *Un ampio consenso sulla dottrina della giustificazione: Studio sul dialogo teologico cattolico-luterano*. Rome: Editrice Pontificia Università, Gregoriana, 1999.

Iserloh, Erwin. "Luther and the Council of Trent: The Treatment of Reformation Teaching by the Council." In *Justification by Faith: Do the Sixteenth-Century Condemnations Still Apply?* Translated by Michael Root and William G. Rusch, pp. 161–73. New York: The Continuum Publishing Company, 1997.

Jedin, Hubert. *The First Sessions at Trent (1545–47)*. Vol. 2, *A History of the Council of Trent*. Translated by Ernest Graf. St. Louis: B. Herder Book Co., 1961. In German, *Die erste Trienter Tagungsperiode (1545–47)*. Bd. 2, *Geschichte des Konzils von Trient*. Freiburg: Herder, 1957.

Johnson, John F. "Justification According to the Apology of the Augsburg Confession and the Formula of Concord." In *Justification by Faith*. Vol. 7, *Lutherans and Catholics in Dialogue*. Edited by H. George Anderson, T. Austin Murphy, and Joseph A. Burgess, pp. 185–99. Minneapolis: Augsburg Publishing House, 1985.

Jüngel, Eberhard. *Justification: The Heart of the Christian Faith*. Translated by Jeffrey Cayzer. New York: T&T Clark.

Juntunen, Sammeli. "Luther and Metaphysics: What is the Structure of Being According to Luther?" In *Union with Christ: The New Finnish Interpretation of Luther*. Edited and translated by Carl E. Braaten and Robert W. Jenson, pp. 129–60. Grand Rapids: Eerdman's, 1998.

Kärkkäinen, Veli-Matti. "Justification as Forgiveness of Sins and Making Righteous: The Ecumenical Promise of a New Interpretation of Luther." *One in Christ*, 37 (2002): 32–45.

Karras, Valerie. "Beyond Justification: An Orthodox Perspective." In *Justification and the Future of the Ecumenical Movement: The Joint Declaration on the Doctrine of Justification.* Edited by William Rusch, pp. 99–131. Collegeville: Liturgical Press, 2003.

Kasper, Walter. "The *Joint Declaration on the Doctrine of Justification*: A Roman Catholic Perspective." In *Justification and the Future of the Ecumenical Movement: The Joint Declaration on the Doctrine of Justification.* Edited by William G. Rusch, pp. 14–22. Collegeville: The Liturgical Press, 2003.

Kolb, Robert. "Melanchthonian Method as a Guide to Reading Confessions of Faith: The Index of the Book of Concord and Late Reformation Learning." *Church History* 72 (2003): 504–24.

Küng, Hans. *Justification: the Doctrine of Karl Barth and a Catholic Reflection.* Translated by Thomas Collins, Edmund E. Tolk, and David Granskou. New York: Thomas Nelson & Sons, 1964. In German, *Rechtfertigung: Die Lehre Karl Barths und eine Katholische Besinnung.* Einsiedeln: Johannes Verlag, 1957.

Ladaria, Luis F. *Antropologia teologica.* Number 24, Analecta Gregoriana. Rome: Univerità Gregoriana Editrice, 1983.

Lane, Anthony. *Justification by Faith in Catholic-Protestant Dialogue: An Evangelical Assessment.* New York: T&T Clark, 2002.

———. "Twofold Righteousness: A Key to the Doctrine of Justification?" In *Justification: What's at Stake in the Current Debates.* Edited by Mark Husbands and Daniel Treier, pp. 205–24. Downers Grove, IL: InterVarsity Press, 2004.

Lang, Albert. "Der Bedeutungswandel der Begriffe 'fides' und 'haeresis' und die dogmatische Wertung der Konzilsentscheidungen von Vienne und Trient." *Müncher Theologische Zeitschrift* 4 (1953): 133–46.

Legrand, H. "Le consensus différencié sur la doctrine de la Justification (Augsbourg 1999): Quelques remarques sur la nouveauté d'une méthode." *Nouvelle revue théologique* 124 (2002): 30–56.

Lehmann, Karl. "Is the 'Step Backward' Ecumenical Progress?: Introduction to the Method and Hermeneutics of the Study." In *Justification by Faith: Do the Sixteenth-Century Condemnations Still Apply?* Edited by Karl Lehmann. Translated by Michael Root and William G. Rusch, pp. 45–68. New York: The Continuum Publishing Company, 1997.

———, ed. *Justification by Faith: Do the Sixteenth-Century Condemnations Still Apply?* Translated by Michael Root and William G. Rusch. New York: The Continuum Publishing Company, 1997.

Lienhard, Marc. *Luther: Witness to Jesus Christ.* Translated by Edwin H. Robertson. Minneapolis, Augsburg Publishing House, 1982.

Lindbeck, George. *The Nature of Doctrine: Religion and Theology in a Postliberal Age.* Louisville: Westminster John Knox Press, 1984.

———. "Response to Gabriel Fackre on the Joint Declaration." Section in *Story Lines: Chapters on Thought, Word, and Deed (For Gabriel Fackre).* Edited by Skye Fackre Gibson, pp. 22–27. Grand Rapids: Eerdmans Publishing Company, 2002.

Lonergan, Bernard. *Grace and Freedom: Operative Grace in the Thought of St. Thomas Aquinas.* Vol. 1, *Collected Works of Bernard Lonergan.* Toronto: University of Toronto Press, 2000.

———. *Insight.* Vol. 3, *Collected Works of Bernard Lonergan.* Buffalo: University of Toronto Press, 1992.

———. *Method in Theology.* Toronto: University of Toronto Press, 1996.

Löser, Werner. "'Jetzt aber seid ihr Gottes Volk' (1 Petr 2,10): Rechtfertigung und sakramentale Kirche." *Theologie und Philosophie* 73 (1998): 321–33.

Lubac, Henri de. *A Brief Catechesis on Nature and Grace.* Translated by Richard Arnandez. San Francisco: Ignatius Press, 1984.

———. *The Mystery of the Supernatural.* Translated by Rosemary Sheed. New York: Crossroad

Herder, 1998.

McGrath, Alister E. *Iustitia Dei: A History of the Christian Doctrine of Justification.* 2nd ed. Cambridge: Cambridge University Press, 1998.

Mannermaa, Tuomo. "Justification and *Theosis* in Lutheran-Orthodox Perspective." In *Union with Christ: The New Finnish Interpretation of Luther.* Edited and translated by Carl E. Braaten and Robert W. Jenson, pp. 25–41. Grand Rapids: Eerdman's, 1998.

———. "Theosis as a Subject of Finnish Luther Research." Translated by Norman M. Watt. *Pro Ecclesia* 4 (1995): 37–48.

———. "Why is Luther so Fascinating?" In *Union with Christ: The New Finnish Interpretation of Luther.* Edited and translated by Carl E. Braaten and Robert W. Jenson, pp. 1–20. Grand Rapids: Eerdman's, 1998.

Manns, Peter. "Absolute and Incarnate Faith—Luther on Justification in the Galatian's Commentary of 1531–1535." In *Catholic Scholars Dialogue with Luther.* Edited by Jared Wicks, pp. 121–56. Chicago: Loyola University Press, 1970.

Marshall, Bruce. "Justification as Declaration and Deification." *International Journal of Systematic Theology* 4 (2002): 2–28.

Maxcey, Carl E. "Double Justice, Diego Laynez, and the Council of Trent." *Church History* 48 (1979): 269–78.

Mayer, Thomas F. *Reginald Pole: Prince & Prophet.* Cambridge: Cambridge University Press, 2000.

Meis, Anneliese. "El problema de la salvación y sus mediaciones, en el contexto de la *Declaración Conjunta* católico-luterana sobre la doctrina de la justificación." *Teología y Vida* 42 (2001): 89–121.

Meßner, Reinhard. "Rechtfertigung und Vergöttlichung – und die Kirche: Zur ökumenischen Bedeutung neuerer Tendenzen in der Lutherforschung." *Zeitschrift für Katholische Theologie* 118 (1996): 23–35.

Meyer, Harding. "Ecumenical Consensus: Our Quest for and the Emerging Structures of Consensus." *Gregorianum* 77 (1996): 213–25.

———. "La 'Déclaration Commune sur la Doctrine de la Justification' du 31 Octobre 1999." section in *Agapè: Études en l'honneur de Mgr Pierre Duprey M. Afr., Évêque Tit. De Thibar.* Edited by Jean-Marie Roger Tillard, pp. 185–209. Geneva: Centre Orthodoxe du Patriarcat Œcuménique, 2000.

———. "The Text 'The Justification of the Sinner' in the Context of Previous Ecumenical Dialogues on Justification." In *Justification by Faith: Do the Sixteenth-Century Condemnations Still Apply?* Translated by Michael Root and William G. Rusch, pp. 69–97. New York: The Continuum Publishing Company, 1997.

Molnar, Paul. "The Theology of Justification in Dogmatic Context." In *Justification: What's at Stake in the Current Debates.* Edited by Mark Husbands and Daniel Treier, pp. 225–48. Downers Grove, IL: InterVarsity Press, 2004.

Nichols, Aidan. "The Lutheran-Catholic Agreement on Justification: Botch or Breakthrough?" *New Blackfriars* 82 (2001): 375–86.

Nørgaard-Højen, Peder. "A Point of No Return? The Joint Declaration and the Future of Lutheran-Catholic Dialogue." *The Ecumenical Review* 52 (2000): 211–22.

Nuth, Joan. "Two Medieval Soteriologies: Anselm of Canterbury and Julian of Norwich." *Theological Studies* 53 (1992): 611–45.

Nygren, Anders. *Agape and Eros.* Translated by Philip Watson. Chicago: University of Chicago Press, 1953.

O'Callaghan, Paul. *Fides Christi: The Justification Debate.* Portland, OR: Four Courts Press, 1997.

Pannenberg, Wolfhart. "Can the Mutual Condemnations between Rome and the Reformation

Churches be Lifted?" In *Justification by Faith: Do the Sixteenth-Century Condemnations Still Apply?* Translated by Michael Root and William G. Rusch, pp. 31–43. New York: The Continuum Publishing Company, 1997.

———. "Luther's Contribution to Christian Spirituality." *Dialog: A Journal of Theology* 40 (2001): 284–89.

———. *Systematic Theology.* Vol. 3. Translated by Geoffrey W. Bromiley. Grand Rapids, MI: Eerdmans, 1998. In German, *Systematische Theologie.* Band III. Göttingen: Vandenhoeck & Ruprecht, 1993.

———. "Theses to the 'Joint Declaration' about Justification." *Pro Ecclesia* 7 (1998): 135–37.

Pas, Paul. "La doctrine de la double justice au Concile de Trente." *Ephemerides theologicae Lovaniensis* 30 (1954): 5–53.

Pelikan, Jaroslav. *Reformation of Church and Dogma* (1300–1700). Vol. 4, *The Christian Tradition: A History of the Development of Doctrine.* Chicago: The University of Chicago Press, 1984.

Perry, John F. "Newman's Treatment of Luther in the *Lectures on Justification.*" *Journal of Ecumenical Studies* 36 (1999): 303–17.

Pesch, Otto Hermann. "The Canons of the Tridentine Decree on Justification: To Whom did they apply? To Whom do they apply today?" In *Justification by Faith: Do the Sixteenth-Century Condemnations Still Apply?* Translated by Michael Root and William G. Rusch, pp. 175–216. New York: The Continuum Publishing Company, 1997.

———. *Thomas von Aquin: Grenze und Größe mittelalterlicher Theologie.* Maiz: Matthias-Grünwald-Verlag, 1988.

Peter, Carl J. "The Decree of Justification in the Council of Trent." In *Justification by Faith.* Vol. 7, *Lutherans and Catholics in Dialogue.* Edited by H. George Anderson, T. Austin Murphy, and Joseph A. Burgess. Minneapolis: Augsburg Publishing House, 1985.

Peura, Simo. "Christ as Favor and Gift: The Challenge of Luther's Understanding of Justification." In *Union with Christ: The New Finnish Interpretation of Luther.* Edited and translated by Carl E. Braaten and Robert W. Jenson, pp. 42–69. Grand Rapids: Eerdman's, 1998.

———. "Die Teilhabe an Christus bei Luther." In *Luther und Theosis: Vergöttlichung als Thema der abendländischen Theologie.* Edited by Simo Peura and Antti Raunio, pp. 121–61. Helsinki, Finland: Luther-Agricola-Gesselschaft, 1990.

———. "What God Gives Man Receives: Luther on Salvation." In *Union with Christ: The New Finnish Interpretation of Luther.* Edited and translated by Carl E. Braaten and Robert W. Jenson, pp. 76–95. Grand Rapids: Eerdman's, 1998.

———. and Antti Raunio, eds. *Luther und Theosis: Vergöttlichung als Thema der abendländischen Theologie.* Helsinki, Finland: Luther-Agricola-Gesselschaft, 1990.

Pfnür, Vinzenz. "The Condemnations on Justification in the Confessio Augustana, the Apology, and the Smalcald Articles." In *Justification by Faith: Do the Sixteenth-Century Condemnations Still Apply?* Translated by Michael Root and William G. Rusch, pp. 129–47. New York: The Continuum Publishing Company, 1997.

———. *Einig in der Rechtfertigungslehre?: Die Rechtfertigungslehre der Confessio Augustana und die Stellungnahme der katholischen Kontroverstheologie zwischen 1530 und 1535.* Abteilung abendländische Religionsgeschichte, ed. Joseph Lortz, no. 60. Wiesbaden: Franz Steiner Verlag, 1970.

Philips, Gérard. *L'Union personnelle avec le Dieu vivant: Essai sur l'origine et le sens de la grâce créée.* Leuven: Leuven University Press, 1989.

Prat, Fernand. *The Theology of St. Paul.* 2 volumes. Translated by John Stoddard. Westminster, MD: Newman Bookshop, 1956.

Pristas, Lauren. "Theological Principles that Guided the Redaction of the Roman Missal (1970)."

The Thomist. Vol. 67 (2003): 157–95.

Prumbs, Anton. *Die Stellung des Trienter Konzils zu der Frage nach dem Wesen der heiligmachenden Gnade: Eine dogmengeschichtliche Abhandlung."* Paderborn: Druck und Verlag von Ferdinand Schöningh, 1909.

Rahner, Karl. "Nature and Grace." In *More Recent Writings*. Vol. 4, *Theological Investigations*. Translated by Kevin Smyth, pp. 165–88. Baltimore: Helicon, 1966.

————. "Questions of Controversial Theology on Justification." In *More Recent Writings*. Vol. 4, *Theological Investigations*. Translated by Kevin Smyth, pp. 189–218. Baltimore: Helicon, 1966.

————. "Some Implications of the Scholastic Concept of Uncreated Grace." In *God, Christ, Mary, and Grace*. Vol. 1, *Theological Investigations*. Translated by Cornelius Ernst, pp. 319–46. Baltimore: Helicon Press, 1961.

Raitt, Jill. "From Augsburg to Trent." In *Justification by Faith*. Vol. 7, *Lutherans and Catholics in Dialogue*. Edited by H. George Anderson, T. Austin Murphy, and Joseph A. Burgess, pp. 200–17. Minneapolis: Augsburg Publishing House, 1985.

Ratzinger, Joseph Cardinal. *Church, Ecumenism and Politics*. Translated by Robert Nowell. New York: Crossroad, 1988.

Raunio, Antti. "Natural Law and Faith: The Forgotten Foundations of Ethics in Luther's Theology." In *Union with Christ: The New Finnish Interpretation of Luther*. Edited and translated by Carl E. Braaten and Robert W. Jenson, pp. 96–124. Grand Rapids: Eerdman's, 1998.

Ripley, Jason. "Covenantal Concepts of Justice and Righteousness, and Catholic-Protestant Reconciliation: Theological Implications and Explorations." *Journal of Ecumenical Studies* 38 (2001): 95–108.

Root, Michael. "Aquinas, Merit, and Reformation Theology after the *Joint Declaration on the Doctrine of Justification*." *Modern Theology* 20 (2004): 5–21.

————. "The Implications of the *Joint Declaration on Justification* and Its Wider Impact for Lutheran Participation in the Ecumenical Movement." In *Justification and the Future of the Ecumenical Movement: The Joint Declaration on the Doctrine of Justification*. Edited by William Rusch, pp. 47–60. Collegeville: Liturgical Press, 2003.

Rosemann, Philipp. "*Fraterna dilectio est Deus*: Peter Lombard's Thesis on Charity as the Holy Spirit." In *Amor amicitiae = On the Love that is Friendship: Essays in Medieval Thought and Beyond in Honor of the Rev. Professor James McEvoy*. Edited by Thomas A. F. Kelly and Philipp W. Rosemann, pp. 409–36. Vol. 6, Recherches de Théologie et Philosophie médiévales. Dudley, MA: Peeters, 2004.

Rusch, William. "The History and Methodology of the *Joint Declaration on Justification*: A Case Study in Ecumenical Reception." Section in *Agapè: Études en l'honneur de Mgr Pierre Duprey M. Afr., Évêque Tit. De Thibar*. Edited by Jean-Marie Roger Tillard, pp. 169–84. Geneva: Centre Orthodoxe du Patriarcat Œcuménique, 2000.

Scheffczyk, Leo Cardinal. "'Differenzierter Konsens' und 'Einheit in der Wahrheit': Aum Ersten Jahrestag der Unterzeichnung der Gemeinsamen Offiziellen Festellung zur Rechtfertigungslehre." *Theologisches: Katolische Monatsschrift* 30 (2000): 437–46.

————. "Die Gemeinsame Erklärung zur Rechtfertigungslehre" und die Norm des Glaubens (Teil I)." *Theologisches Katholische Monatsschrift* 28 (1998): 61–68.

————. "Die 'Gemeinsame Erklärung zur Rechtfertigungslehre' und die Norm des Glaubens (Teil II)" *Theologisches Katholische Monatsschrift* 28 (1998): 125–32.

————. "'Ungeschaffene' und 'geschaffene' Gnade." *Forum Katholische Theologie* 15 (1999): 81–97.

Schmaus, Michael. *Justification and the Last Things*, vol. 6, *Dogma*. Westminster, MD: Christian Classics, 1984.

Sheridan, Thomas L. "Newman and Luther on Justification." *Journal of Ecumenical Studies* 38 (2001): 217–45.

Siggins, Jan D. Kingston. *Martin Luther's Doctrine of Christ*. New Haven: Yale University Press, 1970.

Staniloae, Dumitru. *The World: Creation and Deification*. Vol. 2, *The Experience of God: Orthodox Dogmatic Theology*. Translated by Ioan Ionita and Robert Barringer. Brookline, MA: Holy Cross Orthodox Press, 2000.

Steiger, Johann Anselm. "The *communicatio idiomatum* as the Axle and Motor of Luther's Theology." *Lutheran Quarterly* 14 (2000):125–58. Translated by Carolyn Schneider.

Stubenrauch, Bertram. "Consensus without Unity?" *Theology Digest* 47 (2000): 47–53.

Tavard, George. *Justification: An Ecumenical Study*. New York: Paulist Press, 1983.

Turcescu, Lucian. "Soteriological Issues in the 1999 Lutheran-Catholic Joint Declaration on Justification: An Orthodox Perspective." *Journal of Ecumenical Studies* 38 (2001): 64–72.

Vandervelde, George. "Justification and Deification—Problematic Synthesis: A Response to Lucian Turcescu." *Journal of Ecumenical Studies* 38 (2001): 73–78.

Vercruysse, Jos E. "Luthers Reformation und ihre Bedeutung für die katholische Kirche." *Zeitschrift für Katholische Theologie* 121 (1999): 25–44.

Villar, José R. "La Declaración común Luterano-Católica sobre la doctrina de la justificación." *Scripta theologica* 32 (2000): 101–29.

Wainwright, Geoffrey. "The Lutheran-Roman Catholic Agreement on Justification: Its Ecumenical Significance and Scope from a Methodist Point of View." *Journal of Ecumenical Studies* 38 (2001): 20–42.

Wendebourg, Dorothea. "Zur Entstehungsgeschichte der 'Gemeinsamen Erklärung.'" *Zeitschrift für Theologie und Kirche*. Beiheft 10, *Zur Rechtfertigungslehre*, ed. Eberhard Jüngel, pp. 140–206. Mohr Siebeck, 1999.

Wenz, Gunther. "Damnamus?: The Condemnations in the Confessions of the Lutheran Church as a Problem in the Ecumenical Dialogue between the Lutheran and Roman Catholic Churches." In *Justification by Faith: Do the Sixteenth-Century Condemnations Still Apply?* Translated by Michael Root and William G. Rusch, pp. 99–128. New York: The Continuum Publishing Company, 1997.

White, Richard. "Justification in Ecumenical Dialogue: An Assessment of the Catholic Contribution." Ph.D. diss., Marquette University, 1995.

Willig, Irene. *Geschaffene und Ungeschaffene Gnade: Bibeltheologische Fundierung und Systematische Erörterung*. Münster Westfallen: Aschendorffsche Verlagsbuchhandlung, 1964.

Wood, Susan. "Observations on *Official Catholic Response to Joint Declaration*." *Pro Ecclesia* 7 (1998): 419–26.

———."Lutherans and Roman Catholics: Two Perspectives on Faith." *One in Christ* 37 (2002): 46–60.

Yeago, David S. "Interpreting the Roman Response to the *Joint Declaration on Justification*." *Pro Ecclesia* 7 (1998): 404–14.

INDEX

accident, grace as: Finnish critique of, 148–52, 154–57; Pannenberg's critique of, 172, 176–77, 180; tradition and, 91–101; Trent and, 88–91. *See also* inhering grace

Adam, Karl, 40, 56n. 72

agape, Lutheran thought on, 35–38, 324–28

Annex, purpose of, 2

Apology of the Augsburg Confession: authority of; 7; Finnish critique of, 145–47, 154; Pannenberg's critique of, 169, 171–72, 175–76

Athanasius, 96–99, 315, 354–55, 361–63

Augsburg Confession, the document: 6–7

Augustine of Hippo: justice of God and, 25–27; model of transformation and, 37, 159, 189, 195–200, 208–09, 211–12, 246, 250, 348–50, 353–59

Balás, David, 96, 98

Balthasar, Hans Urs von, 101, 161, 187

baptism: Catholic teaching on, 30–32, 63–64, 73–74, 215, 233, 272, 345, 391; confessional Lutheran teachings on, 41, 43, 215; Joint Declaration on, 233–34, 272, 275–77, 288–89; Pannenberg on, 178–82, 186–90; Thomas Aquinas on, 71

Basil of Caesarea, 96–97

Beisser, Friedrich, 305

Bellarmine, Robert, 91

Birmelé, André, 227, 230–31, 240, 286

Bonaventure, 87, 99, 101, 157, 306, 319–20

Burgess, Joseph A., 300

Cajetan, Thomas de Vio, 71, 109–10nn. 87–89

Catechism of the Catholic Church on justification, 31, 55n. 46

Cervini, Marcello, 65, 69, 71, 82–83, 85, 89

Chemnitz, Martin, 105–06n. 28, 79, 206, 228–29, 291

Christ's righteousness as formal cause of justification: through ecstatic fellowship, 172–79, 185–87, 318, 325, 331, 333, 390; through extrinsic imputation, 38–42, 86–88, 212–15, 235–37 (*see also* forensic forgiveness); through divine indwelling, 146–52, 154–57, 235–37 (*see also* indwelling); Joint Declaration on, 222–27, 229–34, 235–37, 251–57, 267–72

Christology. *See* communication of idioms; soteriological roots of Christology

communication of idioms: classical view of, 360–64; Luther's view of, 369–73

concupiscence: Catholic teaching on, 155, 280, 321, 356–57; Joint Declaration on, 272, 276–80; Luther on, 248–49; Lutheran thought on, 328–30; Pannenberg on, 180–81, 186–87; Seripando on, 63–67. *See also* remnant sin

Congar, Yves, 366, 371–73

created grace: Augustine and, 25–27; background dialogues and, 196, 201, 215; Finnish school and, 158–60; John Paul II and, 100–01; Joint Declaration and, 231–33, 239–40, 270, 271; Küng and, 126, 130, 132; liturgy and scripture and, 344–47; Pannenberg and, 176; rationale for, 317–23, 337–40; Trent and, 25–31, 34, 52n. 31, 75–77, 93–94. *See also* accident; increase of grace; McGrath, Alister; Philips, Gérard

desire for happiness, divergent evaluations of, 323–37

doctrine: authority of, 6–7, 77–78; historical conditioning of, 201–03; scripture and, 205–06

Dominic de Soto, 92

double justice: origins, 60–63; Seripando's theory of, 66–69; Tridentine condemnation of, 74–84; Tridentine discussion of, 69–74

Dulles, Avery, 5, 220, 257, 290, 297

Eckardt, Burnell, 157

efficient cause: Catholic teaching on efficient cause of grace, 20, 24–25, 32; concept of efficient causality, 20–21; confessional